THE CAMBRIDGE HANDBOOK OF THE SUSTAINABLE DEVELOPMENT GOALS AND INTERNATIONAL LAW

In 2015, the United Nations established seventeen Sustainable Development Goals (SDG) that aimed 'to achieve a better and more sustainable future for all' by 2030. The chapters within this collection address each of these SDGs, considering how they relate to one another and international law, and what institutions could aid their implementation. Development has been a contentious topic since the decolonization period after World War II, and issues surrounding sustainable development are necessarily impacted by the multifaceted relationship between the Global South and Global North. Confronting the context and challenge of sustainable development, this collection outlines how the international economic system problematizes the attainment of the SDGs. Introducing a novel, cosmopolitan approach, this book offers new ways of understanding sustainable development and suggests potential solutions so that we might finally achieve it.

JONAS EBBESSON is Professor of Environmental Law, former Dean of Faculty of Law (2012–17), and Director of Stockholm Environmental Law and Policy Centre, at Stockholm University. He was member of the Aarhus Convention Compliance Committee 2005–2021, and its Chair 2011–21. He is a member of the Swedish Academy of Letters, History and Antiquities.

ELLEN HEY is Professor of Public International Law at Erasmus School of Law of Erasmus University Rotterdam, the Netherlands, Adjunct Professor at the Norwegian Center for the Law of the Sea (NCLOS) at UiT – The Arctic University of Norway and Advisor to the Centre for Environmental Law and Policy (CELP), Columbo University. She was a member of the Aarhus Convention Compliance Committee (2008–2014) and a legal advisor to the government of the Netherlands (1986–1990). Her research interests include international environmental law, law of the sea and international institutional law.

The Cambridge Handbook of the Sustainable Development Goals and International Law

Edited by

JONAS EBBESSON

Stockholm University

ELLEN HEY

Erasmus University Rotterdam

CAMBRIDGE
UNIVERSITY PRESS

CAMBRIDGE
UNIVERSITY PRESS

University Printing House, Cambridge CB2 8BS, United Kingdom

One Liberty Plaza, 20th Floor, New York, NY 10006, USA

477 Williamstown Road, Port Melbourne, VIC 3207, Australia

314–321, 3rd Floor, Plot 3, Splendor Forum, Jasola District Centre, New Delhi – 110025, India

103 Penang Road, #05-06/07, Visioncrest Commercial, Singapore 238467

Cambridge University Press is part of the University of Cambridge.

It furthers the University's mission by disseminating knowledge in the pursuit of education, learning, and research at the highest international levels of excellence.

www.cambridge.org
Information on this title: www.cambridge.org/9781108477338
DOI: 10.1017/9781108769631

First published 2022

A catalogue record for this publication is available from the British Library.

Library of Congress Cataloging-in-Publication Data
NAMES: Ebbesson, Jonas, editor. | Hey, Ellen, editor.
TITLE: The Cambridge handbook on the sustainable development goals and international law / edited by Jonas Ebbesson, Stockholms Universitet; Ellen Hey, Erasmus Universiteit Rotterdam.
DESCRIPTION: Cambridge, United Kingdom ; New York, NY : Cambridge University Press, 2022. | SERIES: Hbk Cambridge law handbooks | Includes bibliographical references and index.
IDENTIFIERS: LCCN 2022007405 (print) | LCCN 2022007406 (ebook) | ISBN 9781108477338 (hardback) | ISBN 9781108769631 (epub)
SUBJECTS: LCSH: Sustainable development–Law and legislation. | Law and economic development–International cooperation. | International law–Economic aspects. | International law–Environmental aspects. | Environmental law, International. | BISAC: LAW / International
CLASSIFICATION: LCC K3585.5 .C369 2022 (print) | LCC K3585.5 (ebook) | DDC 344.04/6–dc23/eng/20220531
LC record available at https://lccn.loc.gov/2022007405
LC ebook record available at https://lccn.loc.gov/2022007406

ISBN 978-1-108-47733-8 Hardback

Contents

Contributors

Alessandra Arcuri is Professor of Inclusive Global Law and Governance in the Erasmus School of Law, and in the Erasmus Initiative "Dynamics of Inclusive Prosperity," at Erasmus University Rotterdam, the Netherlands.

Daniel Bodansky is Regents' Professor in the Sandra Day O'Connor College of Law at Arizona State University in Phoenix, United States.

Hilmer Bosch is working on his PhD dissertation on property rights in water in the Amsterdam Institute of Social Science Research at the University of Amsterdam, the Netherlands.

Stuart Bruce is Director of Climate Risk and Decarbonisation Strategy at KPMG in London, United Kingdom; expert reviewer of the Intergovernmental Panel on Climate Change's Sixth Assessment Report (Working Group III); and Vice-Chair of the International Chamber of Commerce United Kingdom Energy & Environment Committee.

Fons Coomans holds the UNESCO Chair in Human Rights and Peace in the Department of International and European Law in the Faculty of Law at Maastricht University, the Netherlands. He is Director of the Maastricht Centre for Human Rights and a member of the Netherlands Network for Human Rights Research. He is Advisor to the Right to Education Initiative.

Philippe Cullet is Professor of International and Environmental Law at SOAS University in London, United Kingdom, and Senior Visiting Fellow at the Centre for Policy Research in New Delhi, India.

Stéphanie Dagron is Professor of International Law, specializing in international health and social security law, in the Faculty of Law and the Faculty of Medicine at the University of Geneva, Switzerland. She is also attached to the Global Studies Institute and the Institute of Global Health.

Jonas Ebbesson is Professor of Environmental Law and Director of the Stockholm Environmental Law and Policy Centre at Stockholm University, Sweden.

Duncan French is Pro Vice Chancellor of the College of Social Science and Professor of International Law at the University of Lincoln, United Kingdom.

Carmen G. Gonzalez is Morris I. Leibman Professor of Law in the Loyola University Chicago School of Law, United States.

Joyeeta Gupta is Professor of Environment and Development in the Global South in the Amsterdam Institute of Social Science Research at the University of Amsterdam and at the IHE Institute for Water Education in Delft, the Netherlands. She was Co-chair of the UN Environment's Global Environmental Outlook-6 and is presently Co-chair of the Earth Commission.

Ellen Hey is Professor of Public International Law in the Erasmus School of Law at Erasmus University Rotterdam, the Netherlands; Adjunct Professor in the Norwegian Centre for the Law of the Sea in the School of Law at UiT-The Arctic University of Norway in Trømso, Norway; and Advisor to the Center for Environmental Law and Policy at the University of Colombo, Sri Lanka.

Nkatha Kabira is Senior Lecturer in the School of Law at the University of Nairobi, Kenya. She is also Iso Lomso ("Eye of Tomorrow") Fellow at the Institute for Advanced Studies in Stellenbosch, South Africa; a fellow at the Institute of Advanced Studies in Berlin, Germany; and a fellow at the Ife Institute for Advanced Studies in Ife, Nigeria.

Patricia Kameri-Mbote is Director of the Law Division at the United Nations Environment Programme and a member of the Governing Board of the International Council on Environmental Law. She has served as Professor of Law and Dean in the Faculty of Law at the University of Nairobi, Kenya; a founding research director and Programme Director for Africa in the International Environmental Law Research Centre; and Chair of the Association of Environmental Law Lecturers in African Universities.

Louis J. Kotzé is Research Professor of Law at North-West University in Potchefstroom, South Africa, and Senior Professorial Fellow in Earth System Law at the University of Lincoln, United Kingdom.

Elisa Morgera is Professor of Global Environmental Law in the Strathclyde Centre for Environmental Law and Governance at Strathclyde University Law School, United Kingdom, and Director of the One Ocean Hub, a global interdisciplinary research program on transformative ocean governance, which is funded by UK Research and Innovation.

Andria Naudé Fourie is Research Fellow in the Erasmus School of Law and Visiting Scholar in the Erasmus Initiative "Dynamics of Inclusive Prosperity" at Erasmus University Rotterdam, the Netherlands.

Tonia Novitz is Professor of Labour Law at the University of Bristol, United Kingdom.

Enrico Partiti is Assistant Professor in Transnational Regulation and Governance at Tilburg University and Associate Researcher at the Asser Institute in The Hague, the Netherlands.

Anél du Plessis is Professor of Law and the South African Research Chair in Cities, Law and Environmental Sustainability at the North-West University in Potchefstroom, South Africa.

Karen N. Scott is Professor of Law at the University of Canterbury, New Zealand; Editor-in-Chief of *Ocean Development and International Law*; and President of the Australian and New Zealand Society of International Law (2019–23).

Dire Tladi is Professor of International Law in the Department of Public Law and the Institute for International and Comparative Law in Africa at the University of Pretoria, South Africa. He is South African Research Chair in international constitutional law and a member of the International Law Commission, as well as its special rapporteur on jus cogens. He is also an associate member of the Institut de Droit International.

Jorge E. Viñuales Harold Samuel Professor of Law and Environmental Policy and founding Director for the Cambridge Centre for Environment, Energy and Natural Resource Governance at the University of Cambridge, United Kingdom. He is also a Research Professor of International Law at LUISS, Rome, Italy.

Pål Wrange is Professor and Head of Subject for Public International Law at Stockholm University and Director of the Stockholm Centre of International Law and Justice, Sweden.

Preface

The Cambridge Handbook of the Sustainable Development Goals and International Law was sparked by our curiosity about how a remarkable set of global policy goals for a wide range of areas – the Sustainable Development Goals (SDGs) adopted by the UN General Assembly in 2015 – might relate to and influence international law. We also asked ourselves how the relevant areas of international law could promote or hamper the achievement of the SDGs and the overarching aim of attaining sustainable development. To explore this further, we engaged colleagues who were willing to join us on this exciting journey, and we thank them for their most insightful contributions to this volume.

The chapters in this handbook highlight the multifaceted relationship between the SDGs and international law as well as how international law might need to change in order to support the achievement of the SDGs and the realization of sustainable development. Our journey toward this result turned out to be bumpier than expected, given the COVID-19 pandemic. Most of us needed to turn to online teaching, some faced other setbacks, and the three-day workshop, originally planned for June 2020 in Stockholm, was canceled. What had been planned as an authors' retreat to exchange ideas and further develop first drafts of the chapters – at Stockholm University and at the Swedish Academy of Letters, History and Antiquities (Vitterhetsakademien) – had to be turned into an online workshop. While regretting that we could not meet in person, we found the two-day online workshop to be a vibrant occasion for exchanging ideas and active collaboration. All the authors engaged enthusiastically and with creativity and humor. Taking into account the almost twenty hours of time difference between participants as well as the drawbacks of an online environment, the workshop was remarkably fun and fruitful and achieved more than we could have wished for. We have now completed this exciting journey, including a couple of "intellectual roller coaster" moments, and we are delighted with the result.

We thank the Swedish Academy of Letters, History and Antiquities for having agreed to fund the originally planned workshop in Stockholm. We also thank the Cassel Foundation (Justitierådet Edvard Cassels stiftelse) for its generous financial support, Stacy Belden for excellent copyediting, and, last but not least, Finola O'Sullivan and Marianne Nield at Cambridge University Press for wonderful support throughout the project.

Abbreviations

AB	Appellate Body
ABNJ	areas beyond national jurisdiction
AoA	Agreement on Agriculture
ASEAN	Association of Southeast Asian Nations
AU	African Union
BBNJ	biodiversity beyond national jurisdiction
BIT	bilateral investment treaty
BRI	Belt and Road Initiative
CAO	compliance advisor/ombudsman
CBD	Convention on Biological Diversity
CBDR	common but differentiated responsibilities
CCAMLR	Commission for the Conservation of Antarctic Marine Living Resources
CDE	Convention on Discrimination in Education
CDM	Clean Development Mechanism
CEDAW	Convention on the Elimination of All Forms of Discrimination against Women
CESCR	Committee on Economic, Social and Cultural Rights
CITES	Convention on International Trade in Endangered Species of Wild Fauna and Flora
COMESA	Common Market for Eastern and Southern Africa
COP	Conference of the Parties
CRC	Committee on the Rights of the Child
CRPD	Convention on the Rights of Persons with Disabilities
CSD	Commission on Sustainable Development
CSO	civil society organization

DFI	development finance institution
DSB	Dispute Settlement Body
DSM	dispute settlement mechanism
EAC	East African Court
ECHR	European Convention on Human Rights and Fundamental Freedoms
ECOWAS	Economic Community of West Africa
EEZ	exclusive economic zone
EGA	Environmental Goods Agreement
ESG	environmental, social, and governance
EU	European Union
FAO	Food and Agriculture Organization
FDI	foreign direct investment
FENSA	Framework of Engagement with Non-State Actors
FET	fair and equitable treatment
FGM	female genital mutilation
FTA	free trade agreement
G7	Group of Seven
G8	Group of Eight
G20	Group of Twenty
GAP	Global Action Plan for Healthy Lives and Well-Being for All
GATS	General Agreement on Trade in Services
GATT	General Agreement on Tariffs and Trade
GDP	gross domestic product
GEF	Global Environment Facility
GFF	Global Financing Facility for Women, Children and Adolescents
GHG	greenhouse gas
GNI	gross national income
GPBHR	Guiding Principles on Business and Human Rights
H5N1	avian influenza A
HFC	hydrofluorocarbon
HIV/AIDS	human immunodeficiency virus/acquired immunodeficiency syndrome
HLPF	High-Level Political Forum
HLPFSD	UN High-Level Political Forum on Sustainable Development
IACtHR	Inter-American Court of Human Rights
IAM	independent accountability mechanism

IBRD	International Bank for Reconstruction and Development
ICAO	International Civil Aviation Organization
ICCPR	International Covenant on Civil and Political Rights
ICESCR	International Covenant on Economic, Social and Cultural Rights
ICJ	International Court of Justice
ICLEI	International Council for Local Environmental Initiatives
ICZM	integrated coastal zone management
IEC	International Electrotechnical Commission
IFC	International Finance Corporation
IFI	international financial institution
IHR	International Health Regulations
IIA	international investment agreement
ILC	International Law Commission
ILF	international legal feminism
ILO	International Labour Organization
IMF	International Monetary Fund
IMO	International Maritime Organization
IPBES	Intergovernmental Science-Policy Platform on Biodiversity and Ecosystem Services
IPCC	Intergovernmental Panel on Climate Change
IPP	intellectual property protection
IPRs	intellectual property rights and protections
IRENA	International Renewable Energy Agency
ISA	International Seabed Authority
ISDS	investor-state dispute settlement
ITLOS	International Tribunal for the Law of the Sea
ITPGRFA	International Treaty on Plant Genetic Resources for Food and Agriculture
ITU	International Telecommunication Union
IUCN	International Union for Conservation of Nature
IUU	illegal, unreported, and unregulated
MAPS	Mainstreaming, Acceleration and Policy Support
MDB	multilateral development bank
MDG	Millennium Development Goal
MEA	multinational environmental agreement
MIA	multilateral investment agreement
MIGA	Multilateral Investment Guarantee Agency
MNE	multinational enterprise

MPA	marine protected area
MSP	marine spatial planning
NAP	national adaptation plan
NBSAPs	national biodiversity strategies and action plans
NCD	noncommunicable disease
NCP	national contact point
NDC	nationally determined contribution
NGO	nongovernmental organization
NHRI	national human rights institution
NIEO	New International Economic Order
NSA	nonstate actor
ODA	official development aid
ODS	ozone-depleting substances
OECD	Organisation for Economic Co-operation and Development
OIE	World Organization for Animal Health
OWG	Open Working Group
PPP	public–private partnership
PSSA	particularly sensitive seas area
R&D	research and development
RFMO	regional fisheries management organization
RTA	regional trade agreement
SCM	Subsidies and Countervailing Measures
SCP	sustainable consumption and production
SDG	Sustainable Development Goal
SDH Commission	Commission on the Social Determinants of Health
SEforALL	Sustainable Energy for All
TRIPS Agreement	Agreement on Trade-Related Aspects of Intellectual Property Rights
TSD	trade and sustainable development
TST	Technical Support Team
TT	technology transfer
UDHR	Universal Declaration of Human Rights
UHC	universal health coverage
UN-Habitat	UN Human Settlements Programme
UNAIDS	Joint UN Programme on HIV/AIDS
UNCCD	UN Convention to Combat Desertification in Countries Experiencing Serious Drought and/or Desertification, Particularly in Africa
UNCITRAL	UN Commission on International Trade Law
UNCLOS	UN Convention on the Law of the Sea

UNCRC	UN Convention on the Rights of the Child
UNCSD	UN Conference on Sustainable Development
UNCTAD	UN Conference on Trade and Development
UNDP	UN Development Program
UNECE	UN Economic Commission of Europe
UNEP	UN Environment Programme
UNESCO	UN Educational, Scientific and Cultural Organization
UNFCCC	UN Framework Convention on Climate Change
UNFPA	UN Population Fund
UNGA	UN General Assembly
UNHCR	UN High Commissioner for Refugees
UNICEF	UN International Children's Emergency Fund
UNMD	UN Millennium Declaration
VCLT	Vienna Convention on the Law of Treaties
VGGT	Voluntary Guidelines on the Responsible Governance of Tenure of Land, Fisheries, and Forests in the Context of National Food Security
WASH	Water, Sanitation and Hygiene
WB	World Bank
WFP	World Food Programme
WHA	World Health Assembly
WHO	World Health Organization
WSSD	World Summit on Sustainable Development
WTO	World Trade Organization
WWC	World Water Council
WWF	World Water Forum

Introduction: The Sustainable Development Goals, Agenda 2030, and International Law

Jonas Ebbesson and Ellen Hey

ABSTRACT

The Sustainable Development Goals (SDGs), Agenda 2030, and international law interact in multifaceted and complex ways. On the one hand, neither Agenda 2030 nor the SDGs fundamentally question the role of the international economic system, which is entrenched in international law and supportive of activities that do not necessarily further sustainable development. On the other hand, Agenda 2030 aims to transform our world, by evoking a bold cosmopolitan understanding of sustainable development, so that no one is left behind. This cosmopolitan understanding of sustainable development should inspire the application and development of international law, if indeed no one is to be left behind. International law offers ample opportunities for implementing such an approach to sustainable development.

KEYWORDS

SDGs, Agenda 2030, sustainable development, cosmopolitan approaches, justice, equity, international economic law, human rights law, international environmental law

I.1 LEAVING NO ONE BEHIND: IMPLICATIONS FOR SUSTAINABLE DEVELOPMENT AND INTERNATIONAL LAW

The Sustainable Development Goals (SDGs) provide ambitious political commitments and define international policy-making in an exceptionally broad manner, covering almost all policy areas relating to human well-being. They are intended to inform international politics and policy-making during the second decade and a half of the twenty-first century, but they will most likely affect international politics and policy-making for a significantly longer period. The achievement of the SDGs will also require new approaches to, thinking about, and shifts of focus in international law. The contributions to the *Cambridge Handbook of the Sustainable Development Goals and International Law* provide ample and inspirational food for thought on this account.

The overarching aim of the seventeen SDGs can be summarized as "transforming our world" so that "no one will be left behind." The former quotation is the title of the UN General Assembly (UNGA) resolution, also known as Agenda 2030, by way of which the SDGs were adopted on 25 September 2015;[1] the latter is the pledge that government leaders make in the Preamble and reiterate in the Declaration that, in addition to the SDGs, are part of Agenda 2030.[2] The Agenda is to be achieved in 2030 through the implementation of the seventeen SDGs, accompanied by 169 targets, with indicators added later to enhance the measurability of progress.[3] Agenda 2030 and the SDGs are set out to be "integrated and indivisible and balance the three dimensions of sustainable development: the economic, social and environmental."[4]

Agenda 2030 is presented as a "comprehensive, far-reaching and *people-centred* set of *universal* and transformative Goals and targets."[5] We suggest that this people-centered approach, aiming at transforming our world so that no one will be left behind, normatively expresses an innovative and bold cosmopolitan understanding of sustainable development. This approach suggests that Agenda 2030, and the SDGs, focus on each and every one of the close to 8 billion inhabitants of the planet. It signals that the benchmark for determining the success of a policy initiative or legal regime is the individual. In other words, states and other relevant actors are to act in the interest of all individuals. Accordingly, an individual left behind signals that a policy or legal regime intended to attain an SDG has failed. Concomitantly, the pledge in Agenda 2030 that no one be left behind comes with an audacious call for solidarity:

> The scale and ambition of the new Agenda requires a revitalized Global Partnership to ensure its implementation. We fully commit to this. This Partnership will work in a spirit of global solidarity, in particular solidarity with the poorest and with people in vulnerable situations. It will facilitate an intensive

1 *Transforming Our World: The 2030 Agenda for Sustainable Development*, UN Doc. A/Res/70/1, 25 September 2015.

2 *Id.*, Preamble, para. 2; Declaration, para. 4. Agenda 2030 consists of a preamble, a declaration, the SDGs and their targets, and a section entitled "Means of Implementation and the Global Partnership."

3 *Work of the Statistical Commission Pertaining to the 2030 Agenda for Sustainable Development*, UN Doc. A/Res/71/313, 6 July 2017. For all goals, targets and indicators, see "The 17 Goals," sdgs.un.org/goals.

4 *Transforming Our World*, n. 1, Preamble, para. 3.

5 *Id.*, Declaration, para. 2 (emphasis added).

global engagement in support of implementation of all the Goals and targets, bringing together Governments, the private sector, civil society, the United Nations system and other actors and mobilizing all available resources.[6]

While Agenda 2030 sets a high level of ambition to be achieved by multiple stakeholders in a spirit of global solidarity, there is a discrepancy between the purported ambitions of the SDGs and their targets and indicators. Pål Wrange, in this volume with respect to SDG 16, *Peace, Justice, and Strong Institutions*, for instance, notes that "[i]t was surely no coincidence that ambition not only declined 'significantly' from the goals to the targets, but also dropped from the targets to the indicators."[7] Dire Tladi, also in this volume, provides an illustrative example with respect to SDG 1, *No Poverty*. He first remarks that "[t]he language of SDG 1 itself reveals the strong ambition to '[e]nd poverty in *all its forms everywhere*,'" but then he notes that "[p]ointing out the low ambition reflected in the targets of SDG 1 is not a criticism but a statement of fact and a recognition by the drafters that the ultimate objective of poverty eradication will likely not be met by 2030 and that, by any standard, there will remain people living in poverty in 2030."[8]

The contributions to this *Handbook* show that international law is a decisive factor in achieving the SDGs; it may either support or compromise the stipulated ambitions. In particular, the chapters illustrate how the international economic system, and, thus, the associated legal and institutional frameworks, is especially problematic for achieving the SDGs and implementing Agenda 2030. It is therefore striking that neither Agenda 2030 nor the SDGs in any meaningful way question the nature of the international economic system and its impact on sustainable development. Long-standing demands of developing states are reiterated in the Declaration, including permanent sovereignty over wealth, natural resources, and economic activity;[9] the importance of international public finance, including official development aid (ODA);[10] and an equitable multilateral trade and investment system.[11] Yet these aims cannot be achieved without addressing, for example, land grabbing, the duties of transnational corporations, the voluntary nature of ODA, the vague commitments on technology transfer, and the manner in which intellectual property rights are protected. In other words, if no one is to be left behind, the nature of the international economic system, which is entrenched in international law,[12] needs to be addressed. It is this situation that prompts Alessandra Arcuri and Enrico Partiti, in this volume, in relation to SDG 12, *Responsible Consumption*

6 *Id.*, Declaration, para. 39.
7 See Pål Wrange, "SDG 16," in this volume (footnote omitted).
8 Dire Tladi, "SDG 1," in this volume (footnotes omitted; emphasis in original).
9 *Transforming Our World*, n. 1, Declaration, para. 18.
10 *Id.*, para. 43.
11 *Id.*, para. 68.
12 Quinn Slobodian, *Globalist, The End of Empire and the Birth of Neoliberalism* (Harvard University Press, 2018).

and Production, to refer to international economic law as "the elephant in the room." They conclude that the approach reflected in the SDGs "does not reverse the dichotomy between economic and non-economic systems that is well grounded within international law, and this factor has almost structurally constrained public regulatory intervention. At a more fundamental level, this dichotomy prevents us from imagining a more humanized economy."[13]

This dichotomy undermines the ambition expressed in Agenda 2030 and is likely to hamper the attainment of sustainable development for all. It also marks the history of the role of international law in attaining development and, subsequently, sustainable development. Below, we show how this tension has manifested itself by tracing how the role of the international economic system has been perceived over time. In addition, we illustrate how in international economic law the call for sustainable development often is sidelined to the realm of "soft" international instruments and commitments, instead of duties, on the part of developed states.

We then enquire what we refer to as a cosmopolitan understanding of sustainable development, reflected in Agenda 2030 and the SDGs, implies for international law. The contributions to this *Handbook* reveal significant shortcomings in the SDGs. However, Agenda 2030 also provides a normative vision that has the potential of ensuring that no one is left behind. This vision is reflected in the cosmopolitan understanding of sustainable development and has a bearing on justice and equity. It requires an equitable distribution of benefits and burdens among individuals, rather than states or generations, within the boundaries of what the earth system can sustain. We suggest that this understanding of sustainable development needs to be incorporated into both the application and development of international law if sustainable development is to be attained for all. In other words, a cosmopolitan approach to sustainable development should inform all areas of international law relevant for attaining sustainable development, including those that impact poverty, health, labor, the environment, the status of women and girls, and, not least, those that pertain to economic matters.

In highlighting the cosmopolitan and people-centered approach to sustainable development, we concede that Agenda 2030, as did its precursors, adopts an anthropocentric approach to sustainable development. Given the extensive evidence that humans are significantly impacting the earth system, as reflected, for instance, in planetary boundaries research[14] and the signs that we are living in the

[13] Alessandra Arcuri & Enrico Partiti, "SDG 12," in this volume (footnotes omitted).

[14] Johan Rockström et al., "Planetary Boundaries: Exploring the Safe Operating Space for Humanity" (2009) 14 *Ecology and Society* 32; Johan Rockström et al., "A Safe Operating Space for Humanity" (2009) 461 *Nature* 472; Will Steffen et al., "Planetary Boundaries: Guiding Human Development on a Changing Planet" (2015) 347 *Science* 1259855; Steven J. Lade et al., "Human Impacts on Planetary Boundaries Amplified Earth System Interactions" (2020) 3 *Nature Sustainability* 119.

Anthropocene,[15] one would have expected Agenda 2030 to address the implications of these findings.[16] While there are references to "protect[ing] the planet from degradation," living "in harmony with nature" and "Mother Earth" in Agenda 2030,[17] there is no attempt to contextualize sustainable development in terms of the limits of what the earth system can sustain.[18] We consider this to be a missed opportunity and a serious flaw in Agenda 2030.[19]

Before engaging with the manner in which the role of the international economic system has been conceptualized over time and the cosmopolitan understanding of sustainable development reflected in Agenda 2030, we present the contours of this *Handbook*.

I.2 THE *HANDBOOK* IN A NUTSHELL

International law is both a means for achieving the SDGs and a body of law that may be impacted by the SDGs. In other words, the SDGs and international law mutually interact. How that interaction might take place prompted the topic of this *Handbook*: the SDGs and international law. Each chapter reflects on how a particular SDG relates to the substance of international law and to the international institutional setting for its implementation. As the chapters illustrate, the interaction between the SDGs and international law is multifaceted and complex, with the aims of the SDGs and international law and its institutions not necessarily being mutually

[15] Paul J. Crutzen & Eugene F. Stoermer, "The 'Anthropocene'" (2000) 41 *Global Change Newsletter* 17; Will Steffen et al., "The Anthropocene: Conceptual and Historical Perspectives" (2011) 369 *Philosophical Transactions of the Royal Society* 842; Colin N. Waters et al., "The Anthropocene Is Functionally and Stratigraphically Distinct from the Holocene" (2016) 351 *Science* 2622.

[16] See, e.g., Duncan French & Louis J. Kotzé (eds.), *Research Handbook on Law, Governance and Planetary Boundaries* (EE, 2021); Louis J. Kotzé & Rakhyun E. Kim, "Earth System Law: The Juridical Dimensions of Earth System" (2019) 1 *Earth System Governance* 100003; Jonas Ebbesson, "Planetary Boundaries and the Matching of International Treaty Regimes" (2014) 59 *Scandinavian Studies in Law* 259; Jonas Ebbesson, "Social-ecological Security and International Law in the Anthropocene", in Jonas Ebbesson et al. (eds.), *International Law and Changing Perceptions of Security: liber amicorum Said Mahmoudi* (Brill Nijhoff, 2014), 71; Ellen Hey, "International Law, Planetary Boundaries and Teleconnections," in French & Kotzé, *id.*, 167; Ellen Hey, "International Law and the Anthropocene" (2016) 5(10) *ESIL Reflections*, esil-sedi.eu/esil-reflection-international-law-and-the-anthropocene-2/; Ellen Hey, "The Anthropocene, Five Discourses and Frontier Space", Richard Barnes & Ronán Long (eds.), *Frontiers in International Environmental Law: Oceans and Climate Change Challenges: Essays in Honour of David Freestone* (Brill Nijhoff, 2021), 515.

[17] See, e.g., *Transforming Our World*, n. 1, Preamble, paras. 6, 7; Declaration, paras. 9, 59; target 12.8.

[18] This is all the more astonishing since the idea of environmental limits has been part of the concept of, and discourse on, sustainable development since the late 1980s. See World Commission on Environment and Development, *Our Common Future*, 1987, 43–46.

[19] For critique of Agenda 2030 in this regard, see, e.g., Sam Adelman, "The Sustainable Development Goals, Anthropocentrism and Neoliberalism," in Duncan French & Louis J. Kotzé (eds.), *Sustainable Development Goals: Law, Theory and Implementation* (EE, 2018), 15.

supportive. This conclusion perhaps is not surprising, given that the SDGs address a heavily contested – possibly, the most contested – topic in international relations: how to attain sustainable development.[20] Addressing sustainable development goes to the heart of the relationship between the global South and the global North and has been a contentious topic ever since the decolonization period after the Second World War, even if the term "sustainable development" had not been coined at the time.

From a normative point of view, the SDGs define goals, rather than rights, with the implied normative difference that the SDGs do not determine entitlements. Although neither Agenda 2030 as a whole nor the specific SDGs are legally binding, the SDGs can underpin or detract from international law. Then again, international law can either facilitate or hamper the implementation of Agenda 2030 and the achievement of the SDGs.

Here, we draw out two points from the many insights developed in the chapters on the specific SDGs and international law. First, the references to international legal instruments in Agenda 2030 are asymmetrical, to say the least. While Agenda 2030, including the SDGs, is to be "grounded in the Universal Declaration of Human Rights [and] international human rights treaties," human rights instruments are only referred to in the Declaration, and not in the SDGs or their targets. However, as the chapters in this *Handbook* illustrate, most, if not all, of the SDGs indeed relate to, and depend upon, international human rights law for their realization.[21] As Elisa Morgera points out in this volume when connecting the achievement of SDG 15, *Life on Land*, to the other SDGs, "[s]everal of these connections can be best explored through the lens of the interdependency of biodiversity and international human rights."[22] In the same vein, Daniel Bodansky highlights in this volume the relevance of human rights law for SDG 13, *Climate Action*: "Global warming has been called 'the greatest threat to human rights in the twenty-first century,' potentially undermining the rights to health, food, and housing, among others. Responses to climate change can also raise human rights concerns, as the Paris Agreement acknowledges."[23]

Excluding references to legal instruments from the SDGs clearly was not a matter of principle, given that several targets refer to treaties. Relevant examples include SDG 13, which in its target 13.b refers to the 1992 UN Framework Convention on

[20] Oran R. Young, "Conceptualization: Goal Setting as Strategy for Earth System Governance" and Peter M. Haas & Casey Stevens, "Ideas, Beliefs, and Policy Linkages: Lessons from Food, Water, and Energy Policies," both in Norichika Kanie & Frank Biermann (eds.), *Governing through Goals: Sustainable Development Goals as Governance Innovation* (MIT Press, 2017), 31, 137.

[21] See also Lynda M. Collins, "The Sustainable Development Goals and Human Rights: Challenges and Opportunities," in French & Kotzé, n. 19, 66.

[22] Elisa Morgera, "SDG 15," in this volume.

[23] Dan Bodansky, "SDG 13," in this volume (footnotes omitted).

Climate Change (UNFCCC) and SDG 14, *Life below Water*, which in target 14.b refers to the 1982 UN Convention on the Law of the Sea.[24] In these cases, the treaty instruments are referred to as, respectively, "the primary international intergovernmental forum" and "the legal framework" for realizing the SDG in question. Human rights instruments clearly did not receive similar treatment.

Second, as most of the chapters illustrate, while international economic law and its institutions may form a barrier for the implementation of the SDGs, the normative content of other areas of international law – in particular, human rights law and international environmental law – go well beyond what some of the SDGs aim for. This finding points to the substantive disconnect between international economic law and other bodies of international law and to the relative weakness of the institutional framework of those other bodies of law. As mentioned above, neither the Declaration nor the SDGs fundamentally question the nature of the international economic system or international economic law. Had the international economic system and international economic law been subjected to fundamental questioning in the Declaration or the SDGs, a different situation would prevail. In that situation, at least the problem posed by international economic law would have been acknowledged, as is the case with subsidies for fisheries addressed in SDG 14.[25]

For details on how the above-mentioned rough characterization of the relationship between the SDGs and international law plays out, we direct the reader to the individual chapters of this *Handbook*. Each of the seventeen chapters focuses on a particular SDG and is similarly structured, facilitating comparisons across the chapters and the SDGs. Every chapter, in its introduction, sets out the contours of the challenges that a given SDG aims to address. Thereafter follows a section that sets out the content of the SDG and how it relates to the other SDGs. Subsequently, each chapter examines the relationship between the SDG in question and the substantive content of international law and the relevant institutional setting for achieving the SDG in question. Within these different sections, the contributors focus on themes that best illustrate how a given SDG relates to international law and its institutions. In this introduction, we include some of the many salient points that the contributors make in their chapters so that the reader gets a flavor of the overall content of the *Handbook*. We point the reader who wishes to get an overview of the wealth of analysis in the individual chapters to the abstracts accompanying each chapter and, of course, to the entire chapters in order to fully appreciate the wealth of analysis.

[24] Other targets that refer to treaties include target 3.a, which refers to the 2003 Framework Convention on Tabaco, and target 3.b, which refers to the 1995 Agreement on Trade-Related Aspects of Intellectual Property Rights (TRIPS Agreement).

[25] Target 14.6.

I.3 THE LACK OF SUSTAINABLE DEVELOPMENT IN INTERNATIONAL ECONOMIC LAW

I.3.1 *"Hard" and "Soft" Law in the Struggle for Equitable Distribution*

As the chapters in this *Handbook* illustrate, the international economic system, which in different ways hampers the achievement of the SDGs, is protected and maintained by "hard" law instruments and strong institutions, such as the World Trade Organization (WTO), the International Bank for Reconstruction and Development (IBRD or the World Bank), the International Monetary Fund (IMF), and arbitral tribunals that settle investor-state disputes based on bilateral investment treaties (BITs). This situation persists, even if developing states since the decolonization period after the Second World War have striven for an international economic system in which burdens and benefits, including access to natural resources, would be distributed more equitably. To date, these efforts have had limited results, with "hard" law instruments reflecting conditioned burdens, and, thus, commitments rather than duties, on the part of developed states and "soft" law instruments reflecting the concerns of developing states. Agenda 2030, despite its message of solidarity, reflects this situation, given that it does not fundamentally question the building blocks of the international economic system.

Below, we first discuss the origins of the international economic system and its institutions in light of the call for sustainable development. Thereafter, we trace the shifts in thinking about the role of the international economic system over time by focusing on relevant UNGA resolutions. Finally, we end this section by discussing two examples that illustrate how concerns for sustainable development are reflected in "soft," but not "hard," law instruments. We focus on the transfer of funds, technology, and medicine from developed to developing states and on the regulation of the private sector.

I.3.2 *The Origins of the Contemporary International Economic System and Its Institutions*

At the time when developing states in Asia and Africa attained independence, starting in the second half of the 1940s, the contours of the contemporary international legal system and its institutions were mostly in place. Think of the composition of the UN Security Council, with only China, as a then developing state, attaining a permanent seat on the Council.[26] Imbalances are also reflected in international law and institutions governing economic relations. This system and its institutions have their origin in the establishment of the IMF and the World Bank

[26] 1945 Charter of the United Nations, art. 13.

in 1944 and the operationalization of the General Agreement on Tariffs and Trade (GATT) in 1947.[27] Moreover, BITs have gained currency since 1959, when Germany concluded the first BIT with Pakistan.[28] In October 2021, 2,270 BITs and 324 treaties with investment provisions were in force.[29] Most of these treaties offer foreign direct investors significant protection, especially by way of their stabilization and dispute settlement clauses.[30]

Illustrative are also the 1966 International Covenant on Civil and Political Rights (ICCPR) and the 1966 International Covenant on Economic Social and Cultural Rights (ICESCR). By 1955, the first articles on the right to political and economic self-determination of the covenants had been negotiated.[31] In their second paragraph, these articles qualify the right of all peoples to freely dispose of their natural resources and wealth: "All peoples may, for their own ends, freely dispose of their natural wealth and resources without prejudice to any obligations arising out of international economic cooperation, based upon the principle of mutual benefit, and international law. In no case may a people be deprived of its own means of subsistence."[32] When increasing numbers of newly developed states joined the negotiations, they argued for a renegotiation of this provision.[33] This attempt failed and, instead, a provision was added to each of the covenants: "Nothing in the present Covenant shall be interpreted as impairing the inherent right of all peoples to enjoy and utilize fully and freely their natural wealth and resources."[34] Together, these two provisions in the covenants illustrate the contestation between developed and developing states about the nature of economic self-determination. Developing states feared that, given the power of transnational corporations within their territories and over their resources, they would not be able to realize the right to self-determination and to develop economically and socially. Developed states, on their part, sought to protect the property owned by their nationals in developing states – in

[27] For the history and establishment of the IMF, the IBRD, and the GATT, see respectively www.imf.org/external/about/histcoop.htm; www.worldbank.org/en/about/history; www.wto.org/english/thewto_e/whatis_e/tif_e/fact4_e.htm.

[28] UNCTAD, *The Entry into Force of Bilateral Investment Treaties (BITs)*, Doc. UNCTAD/WEB/ITE/IIA/2006/9, unctad.org/system/files/official-document/webiteiia20069_en.pdf.

[29] See "Investment Policy," investmentpolicy.unctad.org/international-investment-agreements.

[30] Alessandra Arcuri, "The Great Asymmetry and the Rule of Law in International Investment Arbitration," in Lisa Sachs, Lise Johnson & Jesse Coleman (eds.), *Yearbook on International Investment Law and Policy 2018* (Oxford University Press, 2020), 394.

[31] Ben Saul, David Kinley & Jacqueline Mowbray, "Article 1: The Right of Peoples of Self-Determination, Article 25: The Right to Freely Utilize Natural Resources," in Ben Saul, David Kinley & Jaqueline Mowbray (eds.), *The International Covenant on Economic, Social and Cultural Rights: Commentary, Cases, and Materials* (Oxford University Press, 2014), 12, 18, 110–13; see also Manfred Nowak, *UN Covenant on Civil and Political Rights: CPPR Commentary*, rev. ed. (N.P. Engel, 2005), 6–26, 800–1.

[32] ICCPR, art. 1(2); ICESCR, art. 1(2).

[33] Saul, Kinley & Mowbray, n. 31, 110–13.

[34] ICCPR, art. 47; ICESCR, art. 25.

particular, the assets of transnational companies – from nationalization without, in their eyes, sufficient compensation.[35] Contestation did not end here, but it has continued to date and can be traced, in particular, through successive resolutions adopted by the UNGA, which at different times has conceptualized the role of the international economic system in different ways in relation to development and, subsequently, sustainable development.

I.3.3 *Shifts in Thinking about the Role of the International Economic System*

From the early 1950s, the concerns of developing states about the international economic system were articulated in UNGA resolutions.[36] In addition, the leaders of the then newly independent states in Asia and Africa as well as China adopted the 1955 Bandung Declaration.[37] Three broad themes stand out in the Bandung Declaration and in subsequent UNGA resolutions: permanent sovereignty/effective control over natural resources, the nature of the international economic system, and the right to development. Relevant early UNGA resolutions include the 1962 resolution on permanent sovereignty over natural resources,[38] the 1974 resolutions on the New International Economic Order (NIEO),[39] and the 1986 resolution on the right to development.[40] Significantly, the 1974 Declaration on the Establishment of the NIEO concluded that "[i]t has proved impossible to achieve an even and balanced development of the international community under the existing international economic order. The gap between the developed and the developing countries continues to widen in a system which was established at a time when most of the developing countries did not even exist as independent States and which perpetuates inequality."[41] Moreover, it pointed to the need for "[r]egulation and

35 Saul, Kinley & Mowbray, n. 31, 110–13.

36 Among the first relevant UNGA resolutions were *Integrated Economic Development and Commercial Agreements*, UN Doc. A/Res/532/VI, 12 January 1952; *Rights to Exploit Freely Natural Wealth and Resources*, UN Doc. A/Res/626/VII, 21 December 1952.

37 *Final Communiqué of the Asian-African Conference of Bandung*, 24 April 1955, www.cvce.eu/en/obj/final_communique_of_the_asian_african_conference_of_bandung_24_april_1955-en-676237bd-72f7-471f-949a-88b6ae513585.html#:~:text=Twitter-,Final%20Communiqu%C3%A9%20of%20the%20Asian%2DAfrican,of%20Bandung%20(24%20April%201955)&text=On%2024%20April%201955%2C%20the,principles%20adopted%20at%20the%20Conference. The meeting took place in Bandung, Indonesia, was attended by twenty-nine states, and was the first meeting attended by only developing states. It also planted the seed for the establishment of the Non-Aligned Movement in 1961 and the Group of Seventy-Seven in 1964, organizations that also include states from Latin America. For further information, see Amitav Acharya, "Studying the Bandung Conference from a Global IR Perspective" (2016) 70(4) *Australian Journal of International Affairs* 343.

38 *Permanent Sovereignty over Natural Resources*, UN Doc. A/Res/1803/XVII, 14 December 1962.

39 *Declaration on the Establishment of a New International Economic Order*, UN Doc. A/3201/S-VI, 1 May 1974 (*NIEO Declaration*); *Programme of Action on the Establishment of a New International Economic Order*, UN Doc. A/Res/3202/SVI, 1 May 1974.

40 *Declaration on the Right to Development*, UN Doc. A/Res/41/128, 4 December 1986.

41 *NIEO Declaration*, n. 39, para. 1.

supervision of the activities of transnational corporations by taking measures in the interest of the national economies of the countries where such transnational corporations operate on the basis of the full sovereignty of those countries."[42] In other words, the international economic order and the activities of transnational corporations were perceived as hampering development.

This perception also informed the context in which the 1972 Stockholm Declaration on the Human Environment (Stockholm Declaration) was adopted. Developing states threatened to withdraw from the preparatory negotiations for the conference due to the initially one-sided focus of the negotiations on environmental degradations as a result of unsustainable industrial activities.[43] Due to their insistence, the Stockholm Declaration includes references to the environmental consequences of underdevelopment,[44] the need for price stability and adequate earning for primary products and raw materials,[45] the need for the environmental policies of all states not to hamper development and better conditions for all,[46] the need to make available financial resources to cover the costs that developing states may make if they incorporate environmental consideration into their development policies,[47] the need for additional technical and financial assistance,[48] and permanent sovereignty over natural resources.[49] The concerns expressed by developing states, however, did not enter into "hard" law, and the international economic system remained in place and eventually would be strengthened by the adoption of the 1994 Agreement Establishing the World Trade Organization (WTO Agreement).[50]

Interestingly, the 1992 Rio Declaration on Environment and Development (Rio Declaration)[51] shows a moment of remarkable agreement among states on how to address sustainable development. It reiterates the principle of permanent sovereignty over natural resources,[52] calls for states to "cooperate in a spirit of global partnership

[42] *Id.*, para. 4(g).

[43] To see the way in which the concerns of developing states were incorporated into the preparations for the conference, see the *Founex Report on Development and Environment*, 1971, earthsummit2012.stakeholderforum.org/index.php/about-us/historical-documents/ngo-papers/96-the-founex-report. For further information, see Alden Lowell Doud, "International Environmental Developments: Perceptions of Developing and Developed Countries" (1972) 12 (4) *Natural Resources Journal* 520.

[44] Stockholm Declaration, para. 9.

[45] *Id.*, para. 10.

[46] *Id.*, para. 11.

[47] *Id.*, para. 12.

[48] *Id.*, para. 12.

[49] *Id.*, para. 21.

[50] On the negotiation and establishment of the WTO, see Thomas J. Dillon Jr., "The World Trade Organization: A New Legal Order for World Trade?" (1995) 16(2) *Michigan Journal of International Law* 349.

[51] *Report of the United Nations Conference on Environment and Development*, UN Doc. A/CONF.151/26, vol. 1, 3–14 June 1992.

[52] Rio Declaration, principle 2.

to conserve, protect and restore the health and the integrity of the Earth's ecosystem," and introduces the principle of common but differentiated responsibilities (CBDR) into international environmental law.[53] The principle of CBDR reflects an element of equity at the interstate level, with developed states acknowledging the particular responsibility they bear in the pursuit of sustainable development.[54] However, principle 12 of the same declaration, referring directly to the international economic system, emphasizes economic growth as means to achieve sustainable development:

> States should cooperate to promote a supportive and open international economic system that would lead to economic growth and sustainable development in all countries, to better address the problems of environmental degradation. Trade policy measures for environmental purposes should not constitute a means of arbitrary or unjustifiable discrimination or a disguised restriction on international trade. Unilateral actions to deal with environmental challenges outside the jurisdiction of the importing country should be avoided. Environmental measures addressing transboundary or global environmental problems should, as far as possible, be based on an international consensus.

The Rio Declaration can be seen as part of the international consensus that emerged after the fall of the Berlin Wall in 1989 and the end of the Cold War.[55] At this time, matters that were previously perceived as essentially national became of international concern. It can also be seen as the beginning of a period in which dominant actors, including international economic institutions, perceived economic growth as key to achieving sustainable development, which would become known as the Washington Consensus.[56]

Roughly two and a half decades after the adoption of the NIEO resolutions, the perception of the role of the international economic system and transnational corporations in development had clearly changed. The 1997 UNGA resolution entitled Agenda for Development reflected this change:

> One such increasingly important change affecting all countries is the process of market-driven globalization, including as a result of rapid progress in information exchange and telecommunications. Globalization encompasses the varying degrees of increasing integration of world markets of goods, services, capital, technology, and labour. This has generated greater openness and freer movement of factors of

[53] *Id.*, principle 7.

[54] *Id.*

[55] For an insightful account of the end of the Cold War, see Jeremi Suri, "Expaining the End of the Cold War: A New Historical Consensus?" (2002) 4(4) *Journal of Cold War Studies* 60.

[56] See John Williamson, "A Short History of the Washington Consensus," Initiative for Policy Dialogue Working Paper Series, 2007, policydialogue.org/files/publications/papers/Ch_2.pdf; see also J.E. Stiglitz, "The Post Washington Consensus Consensus," *Initiative for Policy Dialogue*, 2004, policydialogue.org/files/events/Stiglitz_Post_Washington_Consensus_Paper.pdf.

production and has created greater opportunities for international cooperation. Greatly increased trade and capital flows and technological developments open new opportunities for growth of the world economy, particularly in developing countries.[57]

The agenda notably treated economic globalization, driven by the international economic institutions such as the IMF, the World Bank, and the WTO, which were all created by international law, as a given, and private sector actors as part of the solution, instead of focusing on the need to revise the former and regulate the latter, as the NIEO resolutions had done earlier.[58] It also continued to closely link sustainable development with economic growth.[59] While the Agenda for Development recognized that many developing states are not able to participate in the globalization process,[60] it failed to note that market-driven economic globalization leaves many behind. Another noteworthy shift in policy – from the Bandung Declaration and the NIEO resolutions – is that the focus was no longer only on interstate relations. Instead, besides the private sector, other stakeholders were identified as relevant actors that are to contribute to the development process.[61] Moreover, conditions inside a state, such as poverty, food insecurity, gender inequality, and lack of access to education were identified as problematic.[62] However, the resolution failed to identify the international economic system as part of the problem in maintaining these unsustainable conditions within states.

Cooperation with the private sector was also central in the 2002 World Summit on Sustainable Development (WSSD), which is remembered especially for its focus on the importance of public-private partnerships in addressing sustainable development.[63] Turning globalization into a positive process also for developing states was a leitmotif of the 2000 UN Millennium Declaration (UNMD),[64] the UNGA resolution by way of which the Millennium Development Goals (MDGs) were adopted. It provided as follows:

> We believe that the central challenge we face today is to ensure that globalization becomes a positive force for all the world's people. For while globalization offers great opportunities, at present its benefits are very unevenly shared, while its costs are unevenly distributed. We recognize that developing countries and countries

57 *Agenda for Development*, UN Doc. A/RES/51/240, 20 June 1997, para. 6, para. 7.
58 See n. 41 and n. 42 and accompanying text.
59 See, e.g., *Agenda for Development*, n. 57, paras. 21, 44.
60 *Id.*, para. 15.
61 *Id.*, para. 7.
62 *Id.*, para. 1.
63 Philipp Pattberg et al. (eds.), *Public–Private Partnerships for Sustainable Development* (EE, 2013).
64 Ellen Hey, "The MDGs, Archeology, Institutional Fragmentation and International Law: Human Rights, International Environmental and Sustainable (Development) Law," in Hélène Ruiz Fabri, Rüdiger Wolfrum & Jana Gogolin (eds.), *Selected Proceedings of the European Society of International Law*, vol. 2 (Hart, 2010), 488.

> with economies in transition face special difficulties in responding to this central challenge. Thus, only through broad and sustained efforts to create a shared future, based upon our common humanity in all its diversity, can globalization be made fully inclusive and equitable. These efforts must include policies and measures, at the global level, which correspond to the needs of developing countries and economies in transition and are formulated and implemented with their effective participation.[65]

The MDGs, which were the precursors of the SDGs, in turn reflected the outcomes of earlier multilateral conferences and the International Development Goals, presented by the Organisation for Economic Co-operation and Development (OECD) in 1996.[66] Seven of the eight MDGs provide substantive goals that were to be reached by 2015 or earlier in developing states. Thus, MDGs 1–7 concern, respectively, the reduction of poverty and food insecurity, achieving universal primary education, the promotion of gender equality, the reduction of child mortality, and the need to improve mental health, combat diseases, and ensure environmental sustainability. MDG 8 focuses on developing a global partnership for development and is noteworthy for both what it includes and excludes. MDG 8 refers to the need to develop "an open, rules-based, predictable, non-discriminatory trading and financial system," to "address the special needs of least developing countries, land-locked states and small island developing states," to "deal comprehensively with the debt problems of developing countries," to "develop and implement strategies for decent and productive work," and, together with the private sector, to "provide access to affordable, essential drugs in developing countries" and "make available the benefits of new technologies, especially information and communications." Notably, MDG 8, which might be characterized as being about making available resources for development, does not include quantifiable targets or deadlines, even if the targets under other MDGs contain either or both. The MDGs then continued to deliver a message that the international economic system is the solution to the problem of underdevelopment amidst calls for solidarity with developing states.

In 2015, when the UN Secretary-General issued his last report on the implementation of the MDGs, the report found the following:

> As we reach the end of the MDG period, the world community has reason to celebrate. Thanks to concerted global, regional, national and local efforts, the MDGs have saved the lives of millions and improved conditions for many more. ... Although significant achievements have been made on many of the MDG targets worldwide, progress has been uneven across regions and countries, leaving significant gaps. Millions of people are being left behind, especially the poorest and those disadvantaged because of their sex, age, disability, ethnicity

65 UNMD, para. 5.

66 John W. McArthur, "The Origin of the Millennium Development Goals" (2014) 34(2) *SAIS Review of International Affairs* 5.

> or geographic location. Targeted efforts will be needed to reach the most vulnerable people.[67]

The latter finding, by way of its reference to "[m]illions of people ... being left behind," foreshadowed the adoption of the SDGs in 2015. The process for the adoption of the SDGs was set in motion by the 2012 UN Conference on Sustainable Development (UNCSD), which also did not suggest major changes to the international economic system.[68]

This rather cursory overview of how the perception of the international economic system has changed over time illustrates at least two points. First, it points to the fact that the international economic system has not been subject to meaningful challenges, even if developing states continue to press for change. The 2018 UNGA resolution entitled Towards a New International Economic Order provides an example of the persistence of these calls for change.[69] Second, it shows that, increasingly, the situation in states and of individuals in those states has become a concern of international policy regarding sustainable development. As we suggest below, Agenda 2030 significantly develops this concern by introducing a cosmopolitan approach to sustainable development.

I.3.4 *International Economic Law Relegating the Position of Developing States to "Soft" Law Instruments and Exceptions*

I.3.4.1 "Soft" Law Commitments and "Hard" Law Exceptions

As mentioned, the SDGs present a comprehensive set of goals that seek to achieve sustainable development and, contrary to the MDGs, address the situation in both developed and developing states. Agenda 2030 reiterates references to permanent sovereignty over wealth, natural resources, and economic activity,[70] the importance of international public finance, including ODA,[71] and an equitable multilateral trade system.[72] It also alludes to the inequities in the international economic system by providing that

> national development efforts need to be supported by an enabling international economic environment, including coherent and mutually supporting world trade, monetary and financial systems, and strengthened and enhanced global economic

[67] *The Millennium Development Goals Report 2015* (United Nations, 2015), 4. 8.

[68] *The Future We Want*, UN Doc. A/Res/66/288, 27 July 2012, paras. 245–51.

[69] *Towards a New International Economic Order*, UN Doc. A/Res/73/240, 20 December 2018. The resolution was adopted with 133 votes in favour by developing states, forty-eight against by developed states, and five abstentions. *Record of the UNGA 62nd Plenary Meeting*, UN Doc. A/73/PV.62, 20 December 2018, 23–24.

[70] *Transforming Our World*, n. 1, para. 18.

[71] *Id.*, para. 43.

[72] *Id.*, para. 68

> governance. Processes to develop and facilitate the availability of appropriate knowledge and technologies globally, as well as capacity-building, are also critical. We commit to pursuing policy coherence and an enabling environment for sustainable development at all levels and by all actors, and to reinvigorating the Global Partnership for Sustainable Development.[73]

However, as its predecessors, neither Agenda 2030 nor the SDGs fundamentally question the role of the international economic system,[74] which most chapters in this *Handbook* suggest is crucial if sustainable development is to be attained. But how has the relationship between developed and developing states faired so far in international economic law? We illustrate, as do the chapters in this *Handbook*, that in international economic law the concerns of developing states are present in "soft" law instruments or commitments, instead of in duties on the part of developed states and in "hard" law instruments by way of exceptions. As mentioned, in this section, we highlight the transfer of funds, technology, and medicine from developed to developing states and the regulation of the private sector.

I.3.4.2 The Transfer of Funds, Technology, and Medicine from Developed to Developing States

While international trade and investments are protected by "hard" law regimes, the transfer of funds, technology, and medicine from developed to developing states is either provided for in "soft" law instruments or expressed in terms of conditioned duties on the part of developed states. The regulation of the transfer of funds from developed to developing states is an example of the former, while the regulation of the transfer of technology and medicine from developed to developing states is an example of the latter. Duncan French and Louis Kotzé, in this volume, situate SDG 17, *Partnerships for the Goals*, in this very context: "In relation to SDG 17, one can – and must – make mention of the 'hard' regimes of trade and investment, the politico-normative dominance of the international financial institutions, as well as the 'softer' regimes of development aid, and the inchoate rules on technology transfer."[75]

The ODA to be transferred to developing states by developed states – 0.7 percent of gross domestic product / gross national income (GDP/GNI),[76] which was adopted

[73] *Id.*, para. 63.

[74] Instead, the role of the WTO is acknowledged, and international trade is presented as "an engine for inclusive economic growth and poverty reduction, and contributes to the promotion of sustainable development." *Id.*, para. 68.

[75] Duncan French & Louis J. Kotzé, "SDG 17," in this volume (footnote omitted).

[76] The percentage was initially expressed as a percentage of GDP; since 1993, it has been expressed as a percentage of GNI. See OECD, www.oecd.org/development/financing-sustainable-development/development-finance-standards/the07odagnitarget-ahistory.htm.

in 1970 in a "soft" instrument[77] – was to have been attained by the mid-1970s.[78] Preliminary figures for 2020 show that this commitment was met by only six developed states.[79] In the SDGs, the commitment is repeated in target 17.2, together with the commitment that developed states devote 0.15 to 0.20 percent of GDP/GNI to least developed states. The latter commitment was first adopted in 1981.[80] In 2020, the UN Conference on Trade and Development (UNCTAD) reported that this goal also had not been met.[81]

Furthermore, where developed states have obligations to contribute financially, such as to the IMF and the organizations making up the World Bank Group, it is developed states, historically and continuing to date, that have a major voice in determining the conditions on which the finances are made available to developing states. While voting arrangements in the World Bank Group have been adjusted, developed states continue to control around 60 percent of the vote.[82] Moreover, while changes in distribution of votes in the IMF have taken place,[83] the United States continues to hold 16.51 percent of the vote,[84] which, in practice, amounts to a right of veto.[85] One of the very few exceptions to this type of decision-making in global financial institutions is noted by Philippe Cullet in this volume, in relation to SDG 10, *Reduced Inequalities*. Cullet observes that "[t]he GEF [Global Environment Facility] was established specifically to address North-South inequality through the provision of environment-specific financial aid. Further, a specific attempt was made to ensure that the decision-making structure for disbursing funds would not replicate that of the World Bank. The attempt to better reflect donor and recipient countries in decision-making is thus noteworthy."[86]

77 *International Development Strategy for the Second United Nations Development Decade*, UN Doc. A/Res/2626/XXV, 24 October 1970, para. 43.

78 *Id.*

79 See OECD, *COVID-19 Spending Helped to Lift Foreign Aid to an All-time High in 2020*, 13 April 2021, www.oecd.org/dac/financing-sustainable-development/development-finance-data/ODA-2020-detailed-summary.pdf.

80 The commitment to devote 0.15 percent originated in the first UN Conference on the Least Developed Countries in 1981. For the report, see *Report of the United Nations Conference on the Least Developed Countries*, Doc. A/CONF.104/22/Rev.1, 28 March 1982, para. 63. Thomas G. Weiss, "The United Nations Conference on the Least Developed Countries: The Relevance of Conference Diplomacy in Paris International Negotiations" (1983) 59(4) *International Affairs* 649.The 0.2 percent was added in 1990 at the second UN Conference on the Least Developed Countries. For the report, see *Report of the Second United Nations Conference on the Least Developed Countries*, Doc. A/CONF.147/18, 1991 para. 23(c).

81 UNCTAD, *The Least Developed Countries Report 2020* (United Nations, 2020), 12, 141.

82 Jakob Vestergaard, *The World Bank and the Emerging World Order Adjusting to Multipolarity at the Second Decimal Point* (Danish Institute for International Studies, 2011).

83 Saliha Metinsoy, *Unending Reform Attempts at the IMF: Organised Hypocrisy or Bricolage?* 19 March 2019, www.e-ir.info/2019/03/19/unending-reform-attempts-at-the-imf-organised-hypocrisy-or-bricolage/.

84 See *International Monetary Fund*, www.imf.org/en/About/executive-board/members-quotas.

85 "US Blocks IMF Voting Rights Redistribution," *Bretton Woods Observer*, Winter 2019, 11.

86 Phillipe Cullet, "SDG 10," in this volume (footnotes omitted).

With respect to the transfer to technology, developed states have generally not agreed to an unconditioned duty to transfer technology in hard law instruments. Instead, as Andria Naudé Fourie points out in this volume in relation to SDG 9, *Industry, Innovation, and Infrastructure*, partly quoting a 2003 UNCTAD report, "[m]ost treaties with TT [technology transfer] provisions 'contain only "best efforts" commitments, rather than mandatory rules'. And where they are phrased more clearly as 'mandatory rules', state parties are allowed considerable flexibility in determining the means of implementation."[87] Such flexibility is attained, for example, by subjecting the transfer of technology to mutual agreement[88] or to the mutual advantage of technology holders and users.[89] As Naudé Fourie shows, the lack of duties on the part of developed states to transfer technology is related to the regime of the 1994 Agreement on Trade-Related Aspects of Intellectual Property Rights (TRIPS Agreement), which, in practice, has proven to offer holders of intellectual property rights strong protections, even if it addresses the transfer of technology and recognizes the special position of the least developed states by offering them exemptions.[90]

Particularly noteworthy is the effect of the TRIPS Agreement on the accessibility of medicine to developing states, a situation that has become most urgent during the COVID-19 pandemic. In this volume, Stéphanie Dagron provides in relation to SDG 3, *Good Health and Well-Being*, that "the UN High Level Panel on Access to Medicines, … found that difficulties in interpreting and implementing the TRIPS Agreement meant that access to medicines had been made very difficult for the poorest states. During the COVID-19 pandemic, the TRIPS Agreement's rules and exceptions were criticized for hampering states to effectively respond to the pandemic."[91] As Dagron illustrates, the way out of this situation will be to rely on waivers of parts of the TRIPS Agreement. In other words, in order to address public health imperatives, we need to rely on exceptions to "hard" rules of international law gaining acceptance within the WTO, which operates in principle on the basis of consensus.

The strong regime for the protection of intellectual property rights (IPRs) also has affected the transfer of technology in international environmental law. The 1992 Convention on Biological Diversity (CBD), for example, provides that

> [a]ccess to and transfer of technology referred to in paragraph 1 above to developing countries shall be provided and/or facilitated under fair and most favourable terms, including on concessional and preferential terms *where mutually agreed*, and,

87 Andria Naudé Fourie, "SDG 9," in this volume (footnotes omitted).
88 See, e.g., CBD, art. 16(2).
89 See, e.g., TRIPS Agreement, art. 7.
90 Carlos M. Correa, "Innovation and Technology Transfer of Environmentally Sound Technologies: The Need to Engage in a Substantive Debate" (2013) 22(1) *Review of European, Comparative and International Environmental Law* 54.
91 Stéphanie Dagron, "SDG 3," in this volume (footnotes omitted).

> where necessary, in accordance with the financial mechanism established by Articles 20 and 21. In the case of technology subject to patents and other intellectual property rights, such access and transfer shall be provided on terms which recognize and are consistent with the adequate and effective protection of intellectual property rights.[92]

The CBD thereby foregrounds mutual agreement and the protection of IPRs. Furthermore, in relation to the climate change regime, Stuart Bruce and Jorge Viñuales, in this volume in the context of SDG 7, *Affordable and Clean Energy*, attribute the unsuccessful realization of "the 2009 agreement in Copenhagen to provide a minimum of $100 billion annually for projects in developing countries by 2020 . . . in part to concerns by developed states and their companies over IPRs and sharing patented technology with developing states without reward or incentive."[93]

Lastly, this Janus-faced approach to the transfer of technology and medicine has also entered the text of some of the targets of the SDGs – namely, SDG 14 and SDG 17. Target 14.a refers to the "transfer of marine technology taking into account the Intergovernmental Oceanographic Commission Criteria and Guidelines on the Transfer of Marine Technology." These criteria and guidelines in turn subject the transfer of technology, among other things, to the rights and duties of those who hold the technology.[94] Also relevant in this context is the fact that the indicator for target 14.a refers to the "[p]roportion of total research budget allocated to research in the field of marine technology" – that is, not to a criterion that could be used to measure the transfer of marine technology. Target 17.7 refers, among other things, to the transfer of environmentally sound technologies, "including on concessional and preferential terms, as mutually agreed," thus also conditioning the transfer of technology.

The transfer of finances from developed to developing states, in terms of ODA, has been included since the 1970s in legally non-binding commitments that have not been met by the vast majority of developed states. The importance of the transfer of technology and medicines from developed to developing states is alluded to in both "soft" and "hard" law instruments. However, these transfers are impaired by the conditions to which they are subjected – in particular, the IPRs of the holders, which are protected by, among other instruments, the TRIPS Agreement. In other words, the concerns of developing states regarding a more equitable sharing of burdens and benefits, which is essential for the achievement of the SDGs, are not reflected in the applicable "hard" law instruments, and Agenda 2030 does little to address this situation.

92 CBD, art. 16(2) (emphasis added).

93 Stuart Bruce & Jorge E. Viñuales, "SDG 7," in this volume (footnote omitted).

94 The Intergovernmental Oceanographic Commission's Criteria and Guidelines are available at unesdoc.unesco.org/ark:/48223/pf0000139193.locale=en. See, in particular, para. B(c)(ii).

I.3.4.3 Regulating the Private Sector

The private sector increasingly has come to be seen as part of the solution and a relevant actor in attaining sustainable development. Agenda 2030 is no exception. While announcing the revitalization of the global partnership for sustainable development, it does not set out how these partnerships are to be achieved and what the role of the private sector is to be in those partnerships and in furthering sustainable development. Instead, the relevant paragraph outlining what is expected of the private sectors in terms of implementation reiterates well-known clichés. After stating that "[p]rivate business activity, investment and innovation are major drivers of productivity, inclusive economic growth and job creation," Agenda 2030 "call[s] upon businesses to apply their creativity and innovation to solving development challenges."[95] That is all. French and Kotzé observe in this volume that "SDG 17 is Janus-faced when it comes to partnerships. It makes mention of the need for breadth and diversity in such relationships [that is, partnerships], but it focuses in detail almost exclusively on the state level, with limited focus given to the role of civil society and only partial recognition of the role of business and the private sector."[96]

Even if they make their point specifically in relation to SDG 17, we suggest that their conclusion is equally valid for the implementation of Agenda 2030 and the attainment of all the other SDGs. Most of the implementing measures, defined either in the targets or in the section of Agenda 2030 about implementation and global partnership,[97] refer to states. In this respect, Agenda 2030 follows the approach in previous policy outcomes, where, despite calls for global partnerships, the specific measures are to be taken by states. In other words, when it comes to the regulation of the private sector, neither Agenda 2030 nor the SDGs provide much that is new. Yet, as many chapters in this *Handbook* illustrate, international trade and investment law, instead of regulating the private sector, provide significant protection to transnational private sector actors that are not conducive to attaining sustainable development.

Thus, Carmen Gonzalez points out in this volume, in relation to SDG 2, *Zero Hunger*, that "international investment law strengthens the property rights of foreign investors on agricultural land at the expense of the host state and of food insecure rural communities. It limits the ability of states to respect, protect, and fulfill the human right to food and to redirect land use toward more equitable and sustainable food production for the local market instead of industrialized agro-export production."[98]

[95] *Transforming Our World*, n. 1, para. 67.
[96] French & Kotzé, n. 75.
[97] *Transforming Our World*, n. 1, paras. 60–71.
[98] Carmen Gonzalez, "SDG 2," in this volume.

Tonia Novitz likewise provides in this volume, with respect to SDG 8, *Decent Work and Economic Growth*, that "[t]here is a danger that economic concerns regarding trade may in this context outweigh the priority for social justice advocated in ILO instruments" and that "[i]nvestors have notoriously relied on the terms of these agreements [referring to BITs and multilateral investment agreements] to make claims (in investment arbitration) that seek to restrict state regulation of labour markets."[99]

Similarly, Fons Coomans concludes in this volume, in relation to SDG 4, *Quality Education*, "that there is a need to regulate the role of the private sector in providing for-profit educational services with a view to avoiding a societal divide between the haves and the have-nots when it comes to accessibility of education."[100] In other words, the right to education and the achievement of SDG 4 may be compromised by unregulated private actors – a problem that, as Coomans highlights, would be exacerbated if WTO member states were to further the liberalization of education under the 1994 General Agreement in Trade in Services.

In the same vein, while also pointing to the opportunities that these bodies of law may offer, Morgera states in this volume that "[i]t has been widely documented that international trade and foreign investment can increase pressures on biodiversity, as well as lead to violations of biodiversity-dependent human rights. International trade law, international investment law and intellectual property law can also place limitations on the capacity of states to conserve or ensure the sustainable use of biodiversity."[101]

Finally, Karen Scott remarks in this volume, in relation to SDG 14, that the WTO "made a commitment to address fishing subsidies in 2001, although negotiations that were due to end in 2019 were still ongoing" at the time of writing. As she points out, "[e]ffective regulation of fishing … is also clearly supported by ending fishing subsidies that contribute to overcapacity and to IUU [illegal, unreported and unregulated] fishing."[102] In other words, reducing subsidies to fishing activities that contribute to IUU fishing, especially subsidies for larger-scale industrial fishing activities, is crucial for sustainably regulating the fishing industry.

What the chapters referred to above, as well as many others in this volume, illustrate is that there is a need to regulate the private sector – in particular, the transnational private sector – if sustainable development and the SDGs are to be attained. Not doing so also comes with the substantial risk of the continued violation of human rights. Implementation of the SDGs and attaining sustainable development, then, require a fundamental reconsideration of international trade and investment law. As many chapters in this volume illustrate, instruments that suggest the

99 Tonia Novitz, "SDG 8," in this volume.
100 Fons Coomans, "SDG 4," in this volume.
101 Morgera, n. 22.
102 Karen N. Scott, "SDG 14," in this volume (footnotes omitted).

way forward are available; however, they tend to be of a "soft" law character, a point that we come back to in Section 5. Perhaps the best example of such an instrument is the Guiding Principles on Business and Human Rights (GPBHR).[103] By emphasizing that host and home states as well as the private sector hold responsibilities to protect the rights of individuals and groups in society, the GPBHR would unequivocally further the attainment of sustainable development.

While the manner in which the economic system has been perceived has changed over time from being part of the problem to being part of the solution, "hard" law instruments – in particular, international trade and investment law – continue to protect the interests of powerful economic actors, including the transnational private sector. In other words, neither the concerns raised by developing states nor the ambitions of the SDGs – and certainly not the message of solidarity incorporated in the cosmopolitan understanding of sustainable development evoked by Agenda 2030 – are reflected in international trade and investment law. Nevertheless, if international trade and investment law are to be part of "solving the sustainable development challenges"[104] or "the promotion of sustainable development,"[105] these bodies of law must engage with and incorporate a cosmopolitan understanding of sustainable development.

In the following section, we explore how such an understanding of sustainable development might impact international law, including international economic law.

I.4 A COSMOPOLITAN UNDERSTANDING OF SUSTAINABLE DEVELOPMENT

I.4.1 *Why Cosmopolitan?*

As set out in the introduction to this chapter, we suggest that Agenda 2030 and the SDGs evoke a cosmopolitan understanding of sustainable development by accentuating the situation of each individual rather than the broad categories of generations or states. This "people-centered" approach makes the individual the benchmark for determining the success of measures, initiatives, institutions, and legal regimes. Moreover, these measures, initiatives, institutions, and legal regimes pertain not only to states but also to other actors, including the private sector, who influence the well-being of individuals. Agenda 2030 thus offers a constructive way forward for identifying adequate implementing instruments to achieve the SDGs and for

[103] Endorsed by the Human Rights Council, *Human Rights and Transnational Corporations and Other Business Enterprises*, UN Doc. A/HRC/RES/17/4, 16 June 2011. For further information, see *OHCHR and Business and Human Rights*, www.ohchr.org/en/issues/business/pages/businessindex.aspx.

[104] *Transforming Our World*, n. 1, para. 67.

[105] *Id.*, para. 68.

developing a means to review these instruments – a way forward that, we suggest, should impact international law and the governance of sustainable development.

While there are different strands of cosmopolitan thinking, we will not explore these here.[106] Instead, we use the term "cosmopolitan" to denote a way of thinking that ties in with theories about cosmopolitan justice and equity in international law. Key to this thinking is the notion that "everyone has an equal moral status in the world ... and should enjoy, in principle, equal consideration of their interests."[107] Individuals, then, are the subjects to which principles of justice and equity apply.[108] Justice and equity, in turn, refer not only to the distribution of burdens and benefits but also to fairness and procedural opportunities, to remedies and correction (including restoration, reparation, and compensation),[109] and to minimum social and economic rights, including protection against poverty and hunger.[110] Sustainable development has always engaged all these concerns.[111] However, as we will show, Agenda 2030 marks a move away from translating these concerns at the international level primarily into interstate relations. In addition, it moves away from translating these concerns only into the responsibility and interest of the state where the individual resides. In other words, Agenda 2030 broadens the range of actors that ought to be concerned with attaining justice and equity for each individual.

[106] For different cosmopolitan theories, see Simon Caney, "Cosmopolitanism and the Environment," in Teena Gabrielson et al. (eds.) *Oxford Handbook of Environmental Political Theory* (2016), 238. We addressed cosmopolitan aspects of justice in environmental contexts in Jonas Ebbesson, "Introduction: Dimensions of Justice in Environmental Law"; Jonas Ebbesson, "Piercing the State Veil in Pursuit of Environmental Justice"; and Ellen Hey, "Distributive Justice and Procedural Fairness in Global Water Law," all in Jonas Ebbesson & Phoebe Okowa (eds.), *Environmental Law and Justice in Context* (Cambridge University Press, 2009), 1, 270, 351.

[107] David Held, "Law of States, Law of Peoples" (2002) 8 *Legal Theory* 1, 24–25.

[108] This accords with the principles for cosmopolitan justice set out by Held. *Id.* Without referring to "cosmopolitan justice," Thomas W. Pogge applies John Rawls's theory and conception of justice, including the "original position," directly to the international arena in focusing on the worst-off participants and least advantaged groups rather than states. Thomas W. Pogge, *Realizing Rawls* (Cornell University Press, 1989). John Rawls himself distances himself from the cosmopolitan view of justice. John Rawls, *The Law of Peoples* (Harvard University Press, 1999), 82–83, 119–20,

[109] For a brief comparison on different conceptions of justice in transboundary contexts, see Ebbesson, "Introduction," n. 106; Ebbesson, "Piercing the State Veil, n. 106.

[110] See, e.g., Held, n. 107, 29, on the "amelioration of urgent needs" and referring to "intermediate needs," such as "drinking water, nutritional food, appropriate housing, health care, adequate education, and economic security," without which people cannot fully participate in the socio-political processes that structure their opportunities. See also Caney, n. 106, 243–46, on cosmopolitan approaches that appeal to human rights.

[111] In addition, Edith Brown Weiss includes the element of the conservation (of options, quality and access) in relation to recourses as elements of fairness, justice and equity. Edith Brown Weiss, *In Fairness to Future Generations: International Law, Common Patrimony, and Intergenerational Equity* (Transnational Publishers, 1989); Alan Boyle and David Freestone also identity distributive and procedural "elements" in sustainable development. Alan Boyle & David Freestone, "Introduction," in Alan Boyle & David Freestone (eds.), *International Law and Sustainable Development* (Oxford University Press, 1999), 8.

While states have been the traditional subjects as well as units for attaining justice in international law,[112] David Held, when advocating "cosmopolitan sovereignty," refers to the processes and forces of globalization "that increasingly enmesh us in overlapping communities of fate" and to the rapidly growing degrees of mutual connectedness and vulnerability as "new [in 2002] circumstances of cosmopolitanism" in the international context.[113] He reminds us of basic values enshrined in international law, such as human rights law "that no agent, whether a representative of a government, state or civil association, should be able to cross"[114] and of political regulation and lawmaking that transcend the claims of "nation-states." Cosmopolitan thinking is "not, thus, made up of political ideals for another age but embedded in rule systems and institutions that have already transformed state sovereignty in many ways."[115] As we point out below, this understanding is reflected in Agenda 2030 and in the individual SDGs.

Making each individual the benchmark for sustainable development also has implications for deliberations about justice and equity. Typically, such deliberations in relation to sustainable development have focused on generations and states rather than on individuals (or nonhuman species). Writing in the late 1980s, when the concept of sustainable development was coined, Edith Brown Weiss summarized this understanding of sustainable development accordingly:

> In the intragenerational context, intergenerational equity requires wealthier countries and communities, which will benefit from protecting the general planetary environment for future generations, to contribute to the costs incurred by poor countries and communities in protecting these resources, to help them gain access to the economic benefits from them, and to help protect them from suffering degraded environmental quality.[116]

Rather than considering the situation of generations (or countries), a cosmopolitan approach to sustainable development highlights the distribution of burdens and benefits (social, economic, and environmental), fairness and procedural opportunities, and remedies and means of correction from the perspective of each individual. To this notion, two points should be added on how we perceive the cosmopolitan elements in Agenda 2030. The first point concerns responsibilities. Traditionally, sustainable development discourse has focused on the duties that states owe toward those individuals within their jurisdiction and toward each other as states. This approach is still dominant today. A cosmopolitan understanding of sustainable development, however, also gives rise to states' transnational or "diagonal"

[112] See, e.g., Hilary Charlesworth, "International Law and International Justice," in Chris Brown & Robyn Eckersley (eds.), *The Oxford Handbook of International Political Theory* (Oxford University Press, 2018), 143.

[113] Held, n. 107, 23.

[114] *Id.*, 23

[115] *Id.*, 23–24.

[116] Brown Weiss, n. 111, 27ff.

duties – that is, the extent to which states owe extraterritorial duties to individuals in other states.[117] In addition, it highlights the responsibility and accountability of other actors exercising power in the public sphere, including transnational corporations. In other words, it raises questions as to how these actors are to act in achieving the SDGs[118] and what the consequences of their actions or inactions might be.[119] The second point concerns the relationship between a cosmopolitan order and human rights law.[120] While not suggesting that human rights law as such implies a cosmopolitan order, the "people-centered" element is strongly reflected in human rights law, where individuals are at the core and the subjects to which principles of justice apply. However, as we point out in Section 5.2.1 of this chapter, human rights law, like most of international law, is not generally understood to encompass diagonal rights in relation to states or rights in relation to transnational private actors.

In the next subsection, we consider how Agenda 2030 and the individual SDGs reflect a cosmopolitan understanding of sustainable development, in the sense described above, and how it differs from earlier policy frameworks.

I.4.2 *The Cosmopolitan Understanding of Sustainable Development in Agenda 2030 and the SDGs*

There is no globally agreed formal definition of sustainable development. Yet, in framing what might qualify as the generally accepted understanding of sustainable development before the adoption of Agenda 2030, the Rio Declaration provided four key components: intra- and intergeneration equity[121] the need to integrate

[117] We draw here on what John Knox describes as "diagonal rights" from the perspective of the right-holder. John Knox, "Diagonal Environmental Rights," in Mark Giney & Sigrum Skogly (eds.), *Universal Human Rights and Extraterritorial Obligations* (University of Pennsylvania Press, 2010), 82.

[118] Focusing on regulation in transnational contexts, Robert Wai suggests that "[t]he institutional form to achieve cosmopolitan justice in the global economy will therefore be a blend of traditional and novel, of individual, state, and international sources, but all attentive to both facilitation and regulation of cosmopolitan connections." Robert Wai, "The Cosmopolitanism of Transnational Economic Law," in Cecilia M. Baillet & Katja Franko (eds.), *Cosmopolitan Justice and Its Discontents* (Routledge, 2012), 153, 174.

[119] *Cf.* Held, n. 107, 31: "Personal responsibility means in this context that actors and agents have to be aware of, and accountable for, the consequences of their actions, direct and indirect, intended or unintended, that may restrict and delimit the choices of others."

[120] On the relation between cosmopolitanism and human rights, see, e.g., Jürgen Habermas, "The Postnational Constellation and the Future of Democracy" and "Remarks on Legitimation through Human Rights," both in Jürgen Habermas, *The Postnational Constellation: Political Essays (Studies in Contemporary German Social) Thought* (MIT Press, 2001); Sam Adelman, "Cosmopolitan Sovereignty," in Baillet & Franko, n. 118, 11; Sarah Sorial, "Law, Cosmopolitan Law and the Protection of Human Rights" (2008) 4 *Journal of International Political Theory* 241; Anthony Woodiwiss, "Human Rights and the Challenge of Cosmopolitanism" (2002) 19 *Theory, Culture and Society* 139.

[121] Rio Declaration, principle 3.

environment protection in development processes rather than considering it in isolation;[122] common but differentiated responsibilities of states in pursuit of sustainable development;[123] and the broad consensus that attaining sustainable development requires the balancing of economic, social, and environmental matters.[124] These components essentially sum up how sustainable development is generally understood in global policy contexts. It is striking that, despite these generally agreed components, the concept has remained notoriously vague as to what it means and implies normatively in specific situations.

Agenda 2030 and the SDGs change this approach in particular by focusing on each and every individual and by including references – even if they do so weakly – to new constellations of duties for states and private sector actors to achieve sustainable development. While we consider this an essentially new approach to sustainable development, traits of a cosmopolitan understanding can be observed in earlier policy documents. For example, the Stockholm Declaration provided that "[t]he environmental policies of all States should enhance and not adversely affect the present or future development potential of developing countries, nor should they hamper the attainment of better living conditions *for all*."[125] The reference to the living conditions "for all" reflects the notion that the distributive effects of environmental policies and other measures – beneficial or harmful – should not be limited to considering generations or countries as broad categories but, rather, take into account the situation of each and every one.[126] The Stockholm Declaration also contained explicit references to human rights in the context of environmental protection and development.[127] Moreover, in the context of international law, nothing prevents us from reading diagonal responsibilities of states into the quoted paragraph.

This approach was reversed by the Rio Declaration, which neither referred to human rights nor to the situation of each and every one. The UNMD once again linked its ambitions in different social and environmental areas to human rights, democracy, and good governance[128] and, several times, addressed concerns for all.[129] On one interesting point, the UNMD also went beyond interstate relations and called for cosmopolitan justice in proclaiming that "[g]lobal challenges must be managed in a way that distributes the costs and burdens fairly in accordance with

[122] *Id.*, principle 4.
[123] *Id.*, principle 7.
[124] *Id.*, principle 4; see also *Report of the World Summit on Sustainable Development*, UN Doc. A/CONF.199/20, 4 September 2002 (*WSSD Report*); *Future We Want*, n. 68.
[125] Stockholm Declaration, principle 11 (emphasis added); *Report of the United Nations Conference on the Human Environment*, UN Doc. A/CONF.48/14/rev.1, 16 June 1972.
[126] The Stockholm Declaration, principle 15, also refers to the maximum social, economic, and environmental benefits "for all."
[127] Stockholm Declaration, preamble and principle 1.
[128] UNMD, paras. 4, 24, 25, in particular.
[129] *Id.*, paras. 5, 25, 29.

basic principles of equity and social justice. Those who suffer or who benefit least deserve help from those who benefit most."[130] The WSSD and the UNCSD also acknowledged the close connection between sustainability and human rights.[131]

Nevertheless, Agenda 2030 and the SDGs take a radically different approach to sustainable development than previous policy frameworks. Its cosmopolitan approach is manifested in several ways. To start with, the entire resolution reflects the overlapping communities of fate and the mutual connectedness, described above, and transcends the realm of states. Agenda 2030 and the SDGs are "here and now and not in some remote utopia";[132] they address matters that are common and connected across state borders and provide normative expectations for each and every one. As mentioned, Agenda 2030 is set out to be "a comprehensive, far-reaching and *people-centred* set of *universal* and transformative Goals and targets," thus linking the full set of the SDGs and the concept of sustainable development to the situation of everyone.[133] We suggest that these expectations engage commitments owed by states and other actors to individuals located anywhere on the earth who are affected by activities of states, international organizations, and transnational actors.

This understanding of sustainable development is strongly reflected in the pledge that no one will be left behind, which is pertinently described by Wrange in this volume as the "leitmotif" of Agenda 2030.[134] As observed by Frank Biermann and colleagues, the very notion of leaving no one behind "represents the importance of equitable governance in the overall context of the Agenda 2030 for Sustainable Development."[135] Moreover, the integrated and indivisible nature of the SDGs[136] underscores the message that the focus of all SDGs is to leave no one behind. Conceptualizing sustainable development in this manner means that everyone should be on board, with the implied message of justice and equity.

The language and details of most of the SDGs also support a cosmopolitan reading of sustainable development. Thus, rather than broadly referring to intergenerational and intragenerational equity, they relate to human well-being, and some explicitly set out that their aim is to be achieved for each and every one. This approach is evident in SDG 1 and SDG 2, which provide that poverty and hunger are to be *ended*. While, on the one hand, the targets take away from these goals,[137] on the other hand, poverty and hunger can only be ended if no individual endures poverty or hunger. Furthermore, SDGs 3–8 on, respectively, healthy lives,

130 *Id.*, para. 6.
131 See *WSSD Report*, n. 124; *Future We Want*, n. 68.
132 *Cf.* Held, n. 107, 23.
133 *Transforming Our World*, n. 1, para. 2 (emphasis added).
134 Wrange, n. 7.
135 Frank Biermann et al., "Global Goal Setting for Improving National Governance and Policy," in Kanie & Biermann, n. 20, 77, 87.
136 *Transforming Our World*, n. 1, preamble and paras 5, 17, 18, 55, 74(b), 75, 85.
137 See n. 7 and n. 8 and accompanying text.

education, gender equality, availability of water and sanitation, access to energy, and decent work are each to be achieved for *all*. For some of these SDGs, references to "all" are also included in the targets. Relevant examples include to "*end all* forms of malnutrition" (target 2.2; emphasis added) and to "*[e]nd all* forms of discrimination against *all* women and girls *everywhere*" (target 5.1; emphasis added).

While the remaining SDGs do not, as such, explicitly refer to the situation of all, some of the related targets are nevertheless drafted to apply to each and every one. This is the case, for instance, where reference is to the social, economic, and political inclusion of *all* (target 10.2), to *equal* opportunities in order to reduce inequality (target 10.3), to access to adequate, safe, and affordable housing and basic service and to safe, affordable, accessible, and sustainable transport systems for *all* (targets 11.1 and 11.2), and to *universal* access to safe, inclusive, and accessible green and public spaces (target 11.7). Importantly, this is also the case for SDG 16, with respect to access to justice, as target 16.3 aims to "[p]romote the rule of law at the national and international levels and ensure equal access to justice for *all*" (emphasis added).

Based on this overview, Agenda 2030 and the SDGs reflect a level of inclusiveness that has not been part of earlier policy frameworks or international law pertaining to sustainable development. On inclusiveness, Anél du Plessis makes the point in this volume, in relation to SDG 11, *Sustainable Cities and Communities*, that "[i]nclusiveness in cities refers to matters of social justice, cohesion, and inclusionary participation in urban governance" and, quoting Luis Eslava, that "[i]nclusiveness might call for a maximization of participation opportunities of all individuals present in a given city, regardless of their citizenship and formal voting rights at the national level. Also, security concerns can lead to a dissolution of informal settlements whose inhabitants are then pushed further out towards the margins of a given city, or even beyond."[138] We suggest that, while du Plessis makes these points in relation to SDG 11, her assertion has broader relevance for the achievement of the SDGs as a whole and also finds reflection, even if in rather general terms, in target 16.7, which provides for "responsive, inclusive, participatory and representative decision-making at all levels." We agree with Novitz in this volume that target 16.7 should be read broadly to include, for example, "the workplace as well as different levels of governance, locally, nationally, regionally, internationally, and transnationally."[139]

Finally, the people-centered approach is supported by the explicit link to international human rights law in the preamble and declaration of Agenda 2030.[140]

[138] Anél du Plessis, "SDG 11," in this volume; Luis Eslava, *Local Space, Global Life: The Everyday Operation of International Law and Development* (Cambridge University Press, 2015), 190ff.

[139] Novitz, n. 99.

[140] In the same vein, Collins concludes that "the SDGs explicitly endorse a human rights approach and would certainly achieve a huge step in the realization of human rights, particularly economic, environmental and social rights, if they are fully realized." Collins, n. 21, 89.

While we are critical of human rights instruments only being mentioned in the preamble and declaration, and not in the SDGs themselves,[141] their inclusion in Agenda 2030 clearly cannot be without significance. The fact that the "new Agenda … is grounded in the Universal Declaration of Human Rights [and] international human rights treaties," and "informed by other instruments such as the Declaration of the Right to Development"[142] and explicitly reaffirms "the importance of the Universal Declaration of Human Rights, as well as other international instruments relating to human rights and international law,"[143] matters for the understanding of sustainable development evoked by Agenda 2030. This assertion is underscored by Agenda 2030 itself, where it provides that "[t]he achievement of full human potential and of *sustainable development* is not possible if one half of humanity continues to be denied its full *human rights* and opportunities."[144]

New commitments, also "diagonal," are further suggested by the "Global Partnership for Sustainable Development, based on a spirit of strengthened global solidarity, focused in particular on the needs of the poorest and most vulnerable and with the participation of all countries, all stakeholders and all people."[145] This suggestion is supported by the assertion that the follow-up and review processes of the implementation of Agenda 2030 shall be "people-centred, gender-sensitive, respect human rights and have a particular focus on the poorest, most vulnerable and those furthest behind."[146] Agenda 2030, including the SDGs, then, can be characterized as marking a shift in thinking about sustainable development. It goes beyond conceptualizing equity between states, as in the principle of CBDR, and beyond intra- and intergenerational equity. As a result, the successful implementation of Agenda 2030 hinges on the equitable distribution of burdens and benefits among individuals. On this point, Joyeeta Gupta and Hilmer Bosch observe in this volume, in relation to SDG 6, *Clean Water and Sanitation*, that

> SDG 6 addresses the inequality question by only prioritizing 'access' issues, but it does not deal with 'allocation' issues. In other words, it focuses on meeting minimum needs but does not address the bigger issues of whether unfair allocation through the allocation of property rights and permits/concessions, or through the impacts of climate change may be the cause of access challenges.[147]

As argued by Gupta and Bosch, in order to attain an equitable distribution of burdens and benefits, it is insufficient to focus only on providing access to satisfy minimum human needs – that is, just above the level of what living a life in dignity

141 See n. 21 and accompanying text.
142 *Transforming Our World*, n. 1, para. 10.
143 *Id.*, para. 19.
144 *Id.*, para. 18 (emphasis added).
145 *Id.*, preamble.
146 *Id.*, para. 74
147 Joyeeta Gupta & Hilmer Bosch, "SDG 6," in this volume.

would entail. Instead, equitable distribution of burdens and benefits requires that allocation issues be addressed.

Moreover, as du Plessis suggests, "the implementation of the SDGs requires inclusionary governance, including meaningful participation in decision-making and access to justice for all individuals."[148] In examining opportunities for participation and gender equality, Patricia Kameri-Mbote and Nkatha Kabira distinguish in this volume, in relation to SDG 5, *Gender Equality*, between formal and substantive equality and argue that "SDG 5 adopts a formal equality matrix," where

> equality relates to the dignity and worth of men and women and equality in their rights and opportunities to participate in political, social, economic, and cultural development and to benefit from the results. Equity and substantive equality, on the other hand, relate to fairness in the treatment of different subjects of law. It adverts to the possibility of inequality, which necessitates the application of differential treatment to get rid of inequality.[149]

In examining how inequalities play out in different contexts and at different levels, Cullet observes in this volume that "SDG 10 breaks some new ground insofar as it recognizes the need to tackle inequality domestically and takes a step forward in calling for a reduction in inequalities of outcome. This development could be the starting point for considering inequality as a common concern of humankind, which would then be addressed through cooperative action at the international level."[150] As mentioned above, Agenda 2030 extends this commitment to cooperate, so as to leave no one behind, to states, also diagonally, and to other actors, including the transnational private sector. While the role of the private sector is only addressed in Agenda 2030 to a limited extent,[151] its role is perceived as key in the attainment of the SDGs and in the mobilization of financial resources for attaining sustainable development.[152] The private sector, moreover, is to play a significant role in the various forms of partnerships intended to "work in a spirit of global solidarity, in particular solidarity with the poorest and with people in vulnerable situations"[153] and in the follow-up and review processes.[154] Agenda 2030 thereby suggests that relevant stakeholders, including transnational private actors, should not just be entitled to rely on their creativity[155] but should also be held accountable when it comes to implementing the SDGs, and, importantly, their performance should be reviewed. Thus, the cosmopolitan approach to sustainable development reflected in Agenda

[148] Du Plessis, n. 138.
[149] Patricia Kameri-Mbote & Nkatha Kabira, "SDG 5," in this volume.
[150] Cullet, n. 86 (footnote omitted).
[151] See Section 3.4.3.
[152] *Transforming Our World*, n. 1, paras. 41, 41, 67.
[153] *Id.*, para 39.
[154] *Id.*, paras. 79, 84.
[155] See n. 95 and accompanying text.

2030 evokes "diagonal" duties for states in respect of individuals located in other states and duties for transnational private actors.

In the next section, we consider where international law already reflects traits of this cosmopolitan understanding of sustainable development and where it could be furthered.

1.5 A COSMOPOLITANISM UNDERSTANDING OF SUSTAINABLE DEVELOPMENT AND INTERNATIONAL LAW

As the contributions to this volume show, all of the SDGs relate to international law, and the attainment of the SDGs crucially depends on whether international law supports or hampers their implementation. Although neither Agenda 2030 nor the SDGs are themselves legally binding, we suggest that the cosmopolitan understanding of sustainable development evoked in Agenda 2030 should impact international law and institutions, including international economic law and the institutions related thereto. Below, we highlight how international law can provide a basis for the implementation of this cosmopolitan approach to sustainable development. We start by discussing examples to illustrate how international law has changed under the influence of what were initially not legally binding concepts or principles. Thereafter, we consider human rights law, international environmental law, and international economic law to identify cosmopolitan traits in international law and how these might be further developed in these bodies of law.

1.5.1 *From Governance Concepts to Legal Development*

It is well documented that legal development is often preceded by the emergence and evolution of concepts in the context of governance.[156] In this subsection, we focus on how the evolution of the concept of sustainable development has impacted the rulings of international courts and tribunals and on the remarkable impact that principle 10 of the Rio Declaration on public participation in environmental matters has had on international law.

1.5.1.1 The Concept of Sustainable Development in Courts and Tribunals

Sustainable development has been a recognized concept of international law since the early 1990s.[157] Yet the concept has not been defined in any specific way in

[156] Alan Boyle, "Soft Law in International Law-Making," in Malcolm Evans (eds.), *International Law*, 5th ed. (Oxford University Press, 2018), 119.

[157] For comprehensive overviews, see, e.g., Nico J. Schrijver, "The Evolution of Sustainable Development in International Law: Inception, Meaning and Status," in *Collected Courses of the Hague Academy of International Law* (Martinus Nijhoff, 2008); Christina Voigt, *Sustainable Development as a Principle of International Law: Resolving Conflicts between Climate Measures and WTO Law* (Martinus Nijhoff, 2009); Alan Boyle & David Freestone

international law. Instead, international law has relied on the evolution of the concept in the context of international governance. Thus, if the understanding of sustainable development changes over time in international governance contexts, this understanding, unless clear legal indications are provided to the contrary, will influence how sustainable development is construed in international law, including by courts and tribunals. Development in the case law of the International Court of Justice (ICJ) is illustrative. In 1997, in *Gabčíkovo-Nagymaros Project*, the ICJ referred to "the concept of sustainable development" and linked it to "risks for mankind – for present and future generations."[158] Then, in 2010, in its ruling in the *Case Concerning Pulp Mills on the River Uruguay*, it found that the notification and consultation requirement contained in a 1975 treaty concluded between the two parties to the case and applicable to the River Uruguay "reflects not only the need to reconcile the varied interests of riparian States in a transboundary context and in particular in the use of a shared natural resource, but also the need to strike a balance between the use of the waters and the protection of the river consistent with the objective of sustainable development."[159] The ICJ thereby attributed a shared responsibility – "the need to strike a balance between" the use and protection of the river – to the two states involved in the case and thus attached legal significance to "the objective of sustainable development." In other words, international law evolves also as a result of developments in policy, even if perhaps too slowly.

Arcuri and Partiti also show in this volume how international trade law has evolved based on the principle of sustainable development, which is one of the objectives of the WTO, expressed in the preamble of the WTO Agreement. They point to the Appellate Body having emphasized that the term "exhaustible natural resources" in article XX(g) of the GATT was to be interpreted to include living resources in view of the following:[160]

> Given the recent acknowledgement by the international community of the importance of concerted bilateral or multilateral action to protect living natural resources, and recalling the explicit recognition by WTO Members of the objective of

(eds.), *International Law and Sustainable Development: Past Achievements and Future Challenges* (Oxford University Press, 1999).

158 *Gabčíkovo-Nagymaros Project (Hungary v Slovakia)*, ICJ Reports (1997), 7, para. 140. For a more elaborated treatment of sustainable development, see the separate opinion by the then vice-president of the ICJ, Christopher Gregory Weeramantry, in the aforementioned case. We note that the ICJ also referred to future generations and principle 25 of the Rio Declaration, which refers "[w]arfare [being] inherently destructive of sustainable development," in its advisory opinion in *Legality of the Threat or Use of Nuclear Weapons*, Advisory Opinion, ICJ Reports (1996), 226, paras. 29, 30, 36, 36.

159 *Case Concerning Pulp Mills on the River Uruguay (Argentina v Uruguay)*, Judgment, ICJ Reports (2010), 14, para. 177. See Jutta Brunnée & Ellen Hey, "Judicial Contributions to the Development of International Environmental Law: Refining the Duty to Cooperate in Environmental Harm Prevention" (2019) 30 *Yearbook of International Environmental Law* 45.

160 Arcuri & Partiti, n. 13 (footnote omitted).

> sustainable development in the preamble of the *WTO Agreement*, we believe it is too late in the day to suppose that Article XX(g) of the GATT 1994 may be read as referring only to the conservation of exhaustible mineral or other non-living natural resources.[161]

Arcuri and Partiti, even if expressing doubts as to whether this will materialize, proceed to point out that "SDG 12 is arguably part of that normative material that can be mobilized in interpreting WTO provisions. SDG 12 could inform the interpretation of the boundaries of the justificatory grounds in Article XX of the GATT."[162] Similarly, Scott points in this volume to how the ICJ, the International Tribunal for the Law of the Sea (ITLOS), and an arbitral tribunal have developed the responsibilities of states to protect the marine environment, based on the concept of due diligence. Scott, referring to ITLOS, points out that

> [d]ue diligence is a 'variable concept' that may change over time in response to scientific or technological knowledge and in relation to the risks involved in the activity. Arguably, however, the targets developed by, or in association with, SDG 14 may be relevant in determining whether a state has met its due diligence obligation in respect of areas such as ocean acidification, area-based protection, or ecosystem conservation, for example.[163]

We suggest that the cosmopolitan understanding of sustainable development forwarded by Agenda 2030 could and should play a similar role in future when international law is being interpreted and applied by courts and quasi-courts.

I.5.1.2 Public Participation in Environmental Matters

The other example of the remarkable impact of an initially "soft" provision in international law is principle 10 of the Rio Declaration on public participation, which means access to information, participation in decision-making, and access to justice in environmental matters.[164] Not only was principle 10 the key basis for the elaboration of the 2010 UN Environment Programme's (UNEP) Guidelines for the Development of National Legislation on Access to Information, Public Participation

[161] WTO, *United States – Import Prohibitions on Certain Shrimp and Shrimp Products*, WTO Doc. WT/DS58/AB/R, 12 October 1998, para. 131 (footnote omitted; emphasis in original).

[162] Arcuri & Partiti, n. 13 (footnotes omitted).

[163] Scott, n. 102 (footnotes omitted).

[164] Principle 10 of the Rio Declaration provides: "Environmental issues are best handled with the participation of all concerned citizens, at the relevant level. At the national level, each individual shall have appropriate access to information concerning the environment that is held by public authorities, including information on hazardous materials and activities in their communities, and the opportunity to participate in decision-making processes. States shall facilitate and encourage public awareness and participation by making information widely available. Effective access to judicial and administrative proceedings, including redress and remedy, shall be provided."

and Access to Justice in Environmental Matters,[165] but it has also significantly impacted treaty law. Where essentially no environmental treaty of global application agreed before 1992, when the Rio Declaration was adopted, provides for public participation, just about all global treaty regimes on environmental matters adopted since then contain provisions in support of public participation, even if at times these provisions are vague.[166]

Participatory rights have found even stronger resonance at the regional level – in Europe, the Caucasus region, and Central Asia[167] Latin America and the Caribbean[168] and Africa.[169] In each of these regions, treaties have been adopted that clearly define obligations resting on their parties to "ensure" or "guarantee" participatory rights for members of the public – that is, for individuals, environmental associations, and human rights defenders in environmental matters. The 1998 Convention on Access to Information, Public participation in Decision-making and Access to Justice in Environmental Matters (Aarhus Convention) and the 2018 Regional Agreement on Access to Information, Public Participation and Justice in Environmental Matters in Latin America and the Caribbean (Escazú Agreement) also provide for the establishment of international bodies that are mandated to examine compliance by the parties.[170] Moreover, it is salient how human rights courts and tribunals have interpreted established human rights to life, respect for private and family life, a fair trial, and property, so as to provide for participatory rights in environmental cases.[171] In this context, when applying relevant

[165] Governing Council of the United Nations Environment Programme, *UNEP Guidelines for the Development of National Legislation on Access to Information, Public Participation and Access to Justice in Environmental Matters*, Decision SS.XI/5, part A, 26 February 2010, wedocs.unep .org (also referred to as the Bali Guidelines).

[166] On the legal impact of Principle 10, see Jonas Ebbesson, "Principle 10: Public Participation," in Jorge Viñuales (ed.), *The Rio Declaration on Environment and Development: A Commentary* (Oxford University Press, 2015), 287.

[167] Aarhus Convention.

[168] Escazú Agreement.

[169] The revised 2003 Revised African Convention on the Conservation of Nature and Natural Resources, art. 16, without setting any details obliges the parties to adopt legislation on access to information public participation in decision-making and access to justice in environmental matters.

[170] So far, the only body that has been established is the Aarhus Convention Compliance Committee (ACCC). See Jonas Ebbesson, "Public Participation," in Lavanya Rajamani & Jacqueline Peel (eds.), *The Oxford Handbook of International Environmental Law*, 2nd ed. (Oxford University Press, 2021), 351; Ellen Hey, "Compliance Procedure: Aarhus Convention," in Hélène Ruiz Fabri (ed.), *Max Planck Encyclopedia of International Procedural Law* (2018), opil.ouplaw.com/view/10.1093/law-mpeipro/e2454.013.2454/law-mpeipro-e2454?prd=MPIL.

[171] See Ben Boer (ed.), *Environmental Law Dimensions of Human Rights* (Oxford University Press, 2015); Alan Boyle, "Human Rights and the Environment: Where Next?" (2012) 23(3) *European Journal of International Law* 613; Ebbesson, n. 170; Ellen Hey, "The Interaction between Human Rights and the Environment in the European 'Aarhus Space'", in Anna Grear & Louis J. Kotzé, *Research Handbook on Human Rights and the Environment* (EE, 2015), 353.

human rights, courts and tribunals have referred both to the Rio Declaration and the Aarhus Convention.[172]

Participatory rights in environmental matters illustrate how international law can develop on the basis of initially "soft" principles and notions from outside the legal realm – in this case, on the basis of Principle 10 of the Rio Declaration. As discussed below, they also add cosmopolitan elements to international law.[173] The two examples discussed above show how concepts stemming from extralegal settings – sustainable development and public participation – can enter into the realm of international law by informing both judicial decision-making and treaty making. We suggest that the cosmopolitan approach to sustainable development in Agenda 2030 and the SDGs should likewise influence the application and development of international law.

I.5.2 *Cosmopolitan Elements in International Law*

International law harbors traits of cosmopolitanism and thus offers opportunities for implementing a cosmopolitan understanding of sustainable development, especially where it recognizes the rights of individuals and of groups, such as Indigenous peoples, and the duties of transnational actors. Here, we highlight a number of examples in human rights law, international environmental law, and international economic law.

I.5.2.1 International Human Rights Law

Human rights law conceptually shares with the SDGs the trait that it is focused on the individual. A salient case is article 28 of the 1948 Universal Declaration of Human Rights (UDHR), which provides that "*[e]veryone* is entitled to a social and international order in which the rights and freedoms set forth in this Declaration can be fully realized."[174] The provision makes the link between each and every individual and the nature of the international order, which is to secure the realization of human rights. A cosmopolitan understanding of sustainable development clearly would promote such an international order. Concomitantly, the implementation of human rights would significantly promote the achievement of the SDGs.

[172] See, e.g., ECtHR, *Taskin et al. v Turkey*, Application no. 46117/99, 10 November 2004; IACtHR, *State Obligations in Relation to the Environment in Relation in the Context of the Protection and Guarantee of the Rights to Life and to Personal Integrity: Interpretation and Scope of Articles 1(1) and 2 of the American Convention on Human Rights*, Advisory Opinion OC-23/17, 15 November 2017.

[173] See Section 5.2.2.1.

[174] Emphasis added.

As illustrated by the chapters in this *Handbook*, human rights law and institutions are fundamental to that end.[175]

The content of Agenda 2030, including the SDGs, then, can and should impact the interpretation of established human rights. When human rights courts, treaty bodies, or UN special rapporteurs determine what, for example, the rights to life, to respect for private and family life, to nondiscrimination, to property, or to a satisfactory environment entail, they should consider how, for instance, ending poverty and hunger for all impact those rights. This argument can be extended to all matters addressed in the SDGs and to all human rights. As also quoted above, Agenda 2030 itself provides that "[t]he achievement of full human potential and of *sustainable development* is not possible if one half of humanity continues to be denied its full, *human rights* and opportunities."[176]

Despite some indications to the contrary,[177] under the current dominant approach in human rights law, states are not held to account for human rights violations in which they are implicated but for which the consequences materialize beyond their territory. This situation is likely to impact the achievement of the SDGs. As Tladi points out in this volume,

> the solidarity that is central to the brave new, communitarian-based international law is not reflected in the architecture of human rights law. States are responsible only for populations in their own territories – the 'me for mine and you for yours' philosophy. Without solidarity, implying the joint responsibility of states to address poverty everywhere, neither the targets nor the overall objective of SDG 1 can be met for developing states.[178]

Tladi's reference to "communitarian-based international law" resounds with our point about Agenda 2030's cosmopolitan understanding of sustainable development evoking "diagonal" duties on the part of states for individuals located in other states.

Similarly to Tladi, Gonzalez points in this volume to the need for diagonal human rights. Thus, "a human rights-based approach to SDG 2 should seek to hold accountable the Northern states whose trade, investment, and lending practices have contributed to right to food violations in the global South."[179] These "human rights are rights held by individuals against foreign governments for the transboundary consequences of their aid, trade, finance, and investment policies, including the power they wield in international financial institutions."[180] Gonzalez also points out

[175] In the same vein, Collins, n. 21, 89, concludes that "the SDGs explicitly endorse a human rights approach and would certainly achieve a huge step in the realization of human rights, particularly economic, environmental and social rights, if they are fully realized."

[176] *Transforming Our World*, n. 1, para. 20 (emphasis added).

[177] See, e.g., *State Obligations*, n. 172, where the court confirmed that "States must ensure access to justice, without discrimination, to persons affected by environmental damage originating in their territory, even when such persons live or ae outside this territory."

[178] Tladi, n. 8.

[179] Gonzalez, n. 98.

[180] *Id.*

that obligations to cooperate in the realization of human rights, such as in article 56 of the Charter of the United Nations and in human rights treaties, arguably also imply duties in transnational contexts.

Important starting points for developing a more cosmopolitan understanding of human rights are found in the GPBHR and the related Principles for Responsible Contracts.[181] The aim of the GPBHR is to attain respect for individual human rights by attributing responsibilities not only to host states but also to home states and private sector actors, including those that operate transnationally. Recognition of the responsibility of home states entails that the GPBHR include diagonal responsibilities for states. The GPBHR, then, seek to enhance corporate social responsibility by expanding the actors that hold duties under human rights law to home states and to private sector actors. Traits of a cosmopolitan understanding of sustainable development are also found in the work of UN special rapporteurs,[182] human rights treaty bodies, and the Human Rights Council. A relevant example is the 2015 statement on the SDGs by the chairpersons of the treaty-based bodies, in which they underscore the interdependence of the SDGs and human rights and assert that,

> [b]earing in mind the many gains which are to be drawn from harnessing the energy and resources of the private sector to ensure the successful implementation of the SDGs, accountability mechanisms should also include accountability of the private sector. We underline the relevance of the work of the human rights treaty bodies in the area of corporate sector accountability and call upon Member States to endorse the call for the full application of the United Nations' Guiding Principles on Business and Human Rights, as referred to in the Secretary-General's Synthesis report.[183]

Concomitantly, the Committee on Economic, Social and Cultural Rights, in its statement on the links between the SDGs and the ICESCR, provides that

> [s]tates parties are also required to analyse and take measures to protect all persons against violations of Covenant rights by private parties such as corporations over which they can exercise jurisdiction, whether such actors operate within their territory or beyond. Relevant protective measures include regulatory legislation,

[181] *Principles for Responsible Contracts*, Doc. HR/PUB/15/1, 2015, www.ohchr.org/EN/Issues/Business/Pages/InternationalStandards.aspx.

[182] See the work of UN special rapporteurs on human rights and the environment, e.g., *Report of the Special Rapporteur on the Issue of Human Rights Obligations Relating to the Enjoyment of a Safe, Clean, Healthy and Sustainable Environment*, UN Doc. A/73/188, 19 July 2018, www.ohchr.org/EN/Issues/Environment/SREnvironment/Pages/SRenvironmentIndex.aspx.

[183] *Joint Statement of the Chairpersons of the United Nations Human Rights Treaty Bodies on the Post-2015 Development Agenda*, 18 January 2015, www.ohchr.org/EN/NewsEvents/Pages/DisplayNews.aspx?NewsID=15505&LangID=E.

administrative, budgetary, educational and other measures, including providing access to effective legal remedies for victims.[184]

Furthermore, the Committee on Economic, Social and Cultural Rights is in the process of adopting General Comment 26, on land and economic, social, and cultural rights, which clearly reflects both duties for transnational private actors and diagonal duties for home states.[185] In the same vein, the Committee on the Elimination of Discrimination against Women importantly is in the process of extending this approach to the trafficking of women and girls in the context of global migration. The draft for a general recommendation on the topic links into Agenda 2030 and provides as follows:

> States parties' obligation of due diligence to suppress all forms of trafficking in women and girls extends to the acts or omissions of all perpetrators, including private persons, intimate or extended family members and intimate partners, as well as organizations or enterprises. This includes the regulation of the activities of national corporations operating extraterritorially as affirmed in general recommendations No. 28 (2010) and No. 37 (2018) and reinforced in the United Nations Guiding Principles on Business and Human Rights.
>
> States parties are responsible for all their actions affecting human rights, regardless of whether the affected persons are in their territory. This includes obligations towards States parties' nationals who are trafficked abroad. The obligations of States parties under the Convention apply without discrimination both to citizens and non-citizens, including refugees, asylum-seekers, migrant workers, migrants with irregular status and stateless persons, within their territory or effective control, even if not situated within the territory.[186]

These examples demonstrate how human rights bodies are integrating the SDGs, concomitantly with the GPBHR, into their work and highlighting the critical role of home states and private sector actors, including transnational ones. They are thereby developing diagonal responsibilities for states as well as responsibilities for private sector actors. As a result, they are recognizing states, beyond the state of residence, and private sector actors as duty bearers for the achievement of the SDGs and for leaving no one behind.[187] What this development illustrates is that a cosmopolitan

[184] *The Pledge to "Leave No One Behind": The International Covenant on Economic, Social and Cultural Rights and the 2030 Agenda for Sustainable Development*, UN Doc. E/C.12/2019/1, 8 March 2019, para. 12(d).

[185] *Draft General Comment 26 on Land and Economic, Social and Cultural Rights*, UN Doc. E/C.12/69/R.2, 3 May 2021, paras. 31, 33, 38.

[186] *Draft General Recommendation on Trafficking in Women and Girls in the Context of Global Migration*, n.d., paras. 16, 17, www.ohchr.org/EN/HRBodies/CEDAW/Pages/CallTraffickingGlobalMigration.aspx (footnotes omitted). For the link to Agenda 2030, see paras. 1, 98.

[187] See also, e.g., human rights treaty bodies contribution to the 2016 High Level Political Forum, May 2016, www.ohchr.org/Documents/Issues/MDGs/Post2015/HRTB_Contribution_26May2016.pdf, which also notes that "treaty bodies have also observed that multinational

understanding of sustainable development has already significantly impacted human rights law, influenced by the GPBHR and the SDGs, even if so far in "soft" instruments.

I.5.2.2 International Environmental Law

While much of international environmental law provides for interstate obligations, it also harbors cosmopolitan traits. First and importantly, international environmental law links to the legal situation of individuals and other non-state actors by providing for public participation and participatory rights – that is, the right to access to information, the right to participation in decision-making, and the right to access to justice in environmental matters.[188] Second, by way of example, we illustrate that the biodiversity and climate change regimes also harbor cosmopolitan traits.

PUBLIC PARTICIPATION AND PARTICIPATORY RIGHTS. The cosmopolitan element of participatory rights is apparent in the rights for "the public,"[189] which involve natural and legal persons, to have access to information, to participate in decision-making, and to have access to justice in environmental matters. These rights make individuals – alone or in associations – the benchmark for justice, fairness, and equity. Importantly, this is not limited to participatory rights for members of the public within the territory of each state. Rather, in these contexts, international law also provides for diagonal rights in two ways. First, it makes this provision through the principle of nondiscrimination.[190] This principle means that the state, where an activity takes place that may cause harm in another state, is obliged to provide individuals and groups located in that other state with the same rights to information, participation, and access to justice as it provides to individuals and groups in its own territory.[191] Second, as in the Aarhus Convention and the Escazú

enterprises, particularly the extractive industry, can have particularly negative effects on the livelihoods of indigenous and local communities and on the environment" (8). The Human Rights Council is also in the process of developing a "Legally Binding Instrument to Regulate, in International Human Rights Law, the Activities of Transnational Corporations and Other Business Enterprises," which recognizes the responsibility of transnational business actors as well as home states. See Open-ended Intergovernmental Working Group on Transnational Corporations and Other Business Enterprises with Respect to Human Rights, www.ohchr.org/en/hrbodies/hrc/wgtranscorp/pages/igwgontnc.aspx.

188 See also Section 5.1.2 in this chapter.

189 Aarhus Convention, art. 2(4); Escazú Agreement, art. 2(d).

190 Ebbesson, n. 170.

191 In addition to the Aarhus Convention and the 1991 Convention on Environmental Impact Assessment in Transboundary Context, both of regional scope, the principle of nondiscrimination is provided for by the 1977 OECD Recommendations on the Implementation of a Regime of Equal Access and Non-discrimination in Relation to Transfrontier Pollution, and by the International Law Commission's (ILC) 2001 Articles on Prevention of Transboundary Harm from Hazardous Activities.

Agreement, it provides minimum standards for access to information, participation in decision-making, and access to courts.[192] Importantly in terms of cosmopolitan traits, the right to access to justice can also be used to hold private sector actors to account for acts contravening laws relating to the environment. Moreover, as discussed above, the Aarhus Convention's minimum standards for access to information, public participation, and access to justice apply equally to the public concerned that is located in another state.[193]

Under the Aarhus Convention, then, the participatory rights for members of the public amount to diagonal rights, thus entailing corresponding diagonal duties for states. Hence, in situations where an activity subject to its jurisdiction may have effects in another state, a state party must also inform members of the public concerned that are located in that other state about the activity and ensure their right to participate in the decision-making process and to access to justice, based on the standards set by the convention. In addition, subject to certain restrictions, public authorities must make environmental information available to the public in response to a request, regardless of where the requester resides and without them having to state an interest.

The principle of nondiscrimination and minimum standards for participatory rights highlight procedural fairness and access to justice in international contexts, with the aim of attaining substantive justice – that is, with the aim of attaining an equitable sharing of burdens and benefits. They also illustrate how international law and institutions can be used to contribute to the implementation of different SDGs, whether in domestic cases or when diagonal obligations of states are triggered with respect to individuals located in other states. Thus, access to information, public participation in environmental decision-making, and access to courts may engage, for instance, SDG 3 on good health and well-being (target 3.9); SDG 6 on clean water (target 6.3); SDG 7 on clean energy (target 7.2); SDG 8 on decent work and economic growth (target 8.4); SDG 9 on industry innovation (target 9.4); SDG 11 on sustainable cities and communities (target 11.6); SDG 12 on responsible production

[192] Aarhus Convention, arts. 2–9; Escazú Agreement, arts. 2–9.

[193] An illustrative example of such diagonal duties/rights are the findings by the ACCC in a case concerning the United Kingdom, where a German citizen alleged that the United Kingdom did not comply with the convention because it did not provide the German public with opportunities to participate in a transboundary environmental impact assessment procedure concerning the proposed construction of two nuclear reactors in the United Kingdom. The committee found that the United Kingdom failed to comply with the convention by "not ensuring that the public concerned in Germany had a reasonable chance to learn about the proposed activity and the opportunities for the public to participate in the respective decision-making" and by not providing for notification outside its territory in its legislation. See *Findings and Recommendations with Regard to Communication ACCC/C/2013/91 Concerning Compliance by the United Kingdom of Great Britain and Northern Ireland*, UN Doc. ECE/MP.PP/C.1/2017/14, 24 July 2017.

(target 12.4); SDG 13 on climate action (target 13.2); SDG 14 on life below water (target 14.1–3); SDG 15 on life on land (target 15.1); and SDG 16 on access to justice (target 16.3, 16.10, and 16.a).

OTHER MULTILATERAL ENVIRONMENTAL AGREEMENTS. Multilateral environmental agreements (MEAs) of global scope also harbor traits of cosmopolitanism that could be built on, and further developed, to implement Agenda 2030. The biodiversity regime and the climate regimes provide examples. The CBD, in its preamble, characterizes the conservation of biodiversity as "the common concern of humankind"[194] and refers to "traditional dependence of many indigenous and local communities" on biological resources,[195] the importance of the "full participation of women at all levels of policy-making and implementation for biological diversity conservation,"[196] and the importance of "the non-governmental sector for the conservation of biological diversity and the sustainable use of its components."[197] Significantly, it also provides that "conservation and sustainable use of biological diversity is of critical importance for meeting the food, health and other needs of the growing world population, for which purpose access to and sharing of both genetic resources and technologies are essential."[198]

The preamble of the CBD, then, expresses both a people-centered aim and an awareness of the role of the private sector in conserving biodiversity. As indicated above, the CBD, adopted in 1992, also provides for increased public awareness and public participation,[199] and it highlights the approval and involvement of holders of traditional knowledge, innovations, and practices in the promotion of their wider application.[200] The 2010 Nagoya Protocol on Access to Genetic Resources and the Fair and Equitable Sharing of Benefits Arising from Their Utilization (Nagoya Protocol) further develops the position of Indigenous and local communities. It does so, in particular, by requiring the prior informed consent or approval of Indigenous or local communities when accessing genetic resources,[201] benefit sharing,[202] and participatory rights,[203] including in the compliance mechanism for

194 CBD, preamble, para. 3.
195 *Id.*, para. 12.
196 *Id.*, para. 13.
197 *Id.*, para. 14.
198 *Id.*, para. 20.
199 *Id.*, arts. 13(b), 14(1a).
200 *Id.*, art. 8(j).
201 Nagoya Protocol, arts. 6(3)(e)–(f), 7, 16. For a commentary on the Nagoya Protocol, see Elisa Morgera, Elsa Tsioumani & Matthias Buck, *Unraveling the Nagoya Protocol: A Commentary on the Nagoya Protocol on Access and Benefit-sharing to the Convention on Biological Diversity* (Brill Nijhoff, 2014).
202 Nagoya Protocol, arts. 5(2), 16.
203 *Id.*, art. 12(2).

the protocol.[204] In this respect, the CBD and the Nagoya Protocol may also bridge environmental and human rights dimensions of corporate accountability.[205] These people-centered traits in the CBD, we suggest, can be built upon in order to incorporate the cosmopolitan understanding of sustainable development evoked by Agenda 2030.

The 2015 Paris Agreement on climate change even more clearly reflects cosmopolitan traits, also beyond its preamble.[206] The preamble of the agreement reiterates what is in the preamble of the UNFCCC – namely, that climate change is "a concern of humankind."[207] In the same paragraph, it also provides that, "Parties should, when taking action to address climate change, respect, promote and consider their respective obligations on human rights, the right to health, the rights of indigenous peoples, local communities, migrants, children, persons with disabilities and people in vulnerable situations and the right to development, as well as gender equality, empowerment of women and intergenerational equity."[208] Moreover, the preamble refers to "the importance of education, training, public awareness, public participation, public access to information and cooperation at all levels on the matters addressed in this Agreement"[209] and "that sustainable lifestyles and sustainable patterns of consumption and production, with developed country Parties taking the lead, play an important role in addressing climate change."[210] The preamble of the Paris Agreement thereby importantly links human rights and climate change and emphasizes the position of vulnerable groups. Vulnerability is further addressed in the context of adaptation in the body of the agreement both in terms of particularly vulnerable states and vulnerable sectors of society. It provides that

> [p]arties recognize that adaptation is a global challenge faced by all with local, subnational, national, regional and international dimensions, and that it is a key component of and makes a contribution to the long-term global response to climate change to protect people, livelihoods and ecosystems, taking into account the urgent and immediate needs of those developing country Parties that are particularly vulnerable to the adverse effects of climate change.[211]

This provision, we suggest, resounds with both a people-centered approach and diagonal state obligations that are part of a cosmopolitan understanding of

[204] *Cooperative Procedures And Institutional Mechanisms to Promote Compliance with the Nagoya Protocol and to Address Cases of Non-Compliance*, Doc. UNEP/CBD/NP/COP-MOP/DEC/1/4, 20 October 2014, 2, para. B.

[205] Elisa Morgera, "Benefit-Sharing as a Bridge between the Environmental and Human Rights Accountability of Multinational Corporations," in Boer, n. 171, 37.

[206] See also Ellen Hey & Federica Violi, "The Hard Work of Regime Interaction: Climate Change and Human Rights," in Royal Netherlands Society for International Law (ed.), *Climate Change Options and Duties under International Law* (Asser Press, 2018), 1.

[207] Paris Agreement, preamble, para. 11; UNFCCC, preamble, para. 1.

[208] Paris Agreement, preamble, para. 11.

[209] *Id.*, para. 14.

[210] *Id.*, para. 16.

[211] *Id.*, art. 7(2).

sustainable development. The people-centered approach is further developed in other provisions of the Paris Agreement,[212] where interstate obligations are characterized in terms of "support" and "cooperation."[213] Moreover, like the CBD and the UNFCCC, the text of the Paris Agreement provides for the promotion and facilitation of public awareness and participation to enhance climate change policies, including in the implementation of the nationally determined contributions (NDCs).[214] We submit that Agenda 2030 and the SDGs should be taken into account when applying these provisions as well as the key provision that "[the Paris] Agreement will be implemented to reflect equity and the principle of common but differentiated responsibilities and respective capabilities, in light of different national circumstances."[215] Thus, the Paris Agreement offers a context in which a cosmopolitan understanding of sustainable development is already reflected, at least to some extent, and in which the SDGs clearly resound. The Paris Agreement also provides a proper basis for furthering this understanding of sustainable development and for promoting different SDGs. The parties should account for how their NDCs, for instance, ensure gender equality (SDG 5) and the availability of water and sanitation (SDG 6) and how these aims will be achieved for all.

A cosmopolitan understanding of sustainable development should also impact decision-making by treaty bodies and institutions associated with the Paris Agreement. While the principle of CBDR is essential to address inequality under the UNFCCC and the Paris Agreement, a cosmopolitan understanding of sustainable development also requires that the parties reduce inequalities at the level of individuals, as clearly reflected in SDG 10. The reduction of inequalities at the level of individuals involves duties on the part of the states (and the European Union [EU]) with respect to both individuals subject to their jurisdiction and individuals that may be impacted by activities that a state itself, or one of its transnational private actors, engages in in another state. This includes activities in other states to further the implementation of the Paris Agreement[216] – for example, based on the cooperative mechanisms that the agreement facilitates – and also projects that international financial institutions may engage in to mitigate climate change or further adaptation. In each of these types of situations, a party to the Paris Agreement should ensure that measures taken to reduce emissions of greenhouse gases do not have disproportionate adverse effects, for instance, on hunger or health or on certain groups or individuals. Given the integrated nature and indivisibility of the SDGs, these considerations also apply when projects are engaged in what might impact, for

212 *Id.*, art. 7(5).
213 *Id.*, art. 7(6).
214 UNFCCC, art. 6; Paris Agreement, arts. 6(8b), 12.
215 Paris Agreement, art. 2(2).
216 *Cf.* Paris Agreement, art. 6(b).

example, terrestrial ecosystems (SDG 15), either at home or abroad. As with respect for the promotion of public participation in domestic and transnational contexts, implementing the Paris Agreement in line with Agenda 2030 and the SDGs should serve all of the SDGs, not only SDG 13.

Older MEAs may not so clearly resound with Agenda 2030 and the SDGs. Yet we suggest that, as international courts and tribunals have done and as the parties to the Paris Agreement should do, the parties to these agreements, the treaty bodies of these agreements, and the international institutions linked to these agreements should incorporate the evolved understandings of sustainable development into their actions and decision-making.

I.5.2.3 International Economic Law

Admittedly, there are only a few cosmopolitan traits in international economic law. International investment law harbors such a trait, although it has not necessarily furthered sustainable development. This element is grounded in the rights that BITs and investment chapters in multilateral free trade agreements offer foreign investors, whether corporations or individuals. The rights granted to the investor pertain to, in particular, the protection of the value of the investment (stability clauses) and the right to claim this protection against the host state in arbitral procedures. These rights may have a "chilling effect" on host states, meaning that they may refrain from adopting new legislation that may entail costs for the investor. Host states pursue this route because investors regularly have recourse to investor-state arbitration procedures to obtain compensation for the costs incurred. As a result, international investment law sidelines other interests, such as those concerning the protection of safety at work, reasonable wages, the protection of the environment, and other matters addressed by the SDGs.

International investment law, then, does not adequately balance the rights provided to the investor with the responsibility of that investor for violations, for example, of human rights or harm to the environment. We suggest that the diagonal duties for home states and duties for private sector actors, including foreign investors, should be included in international investment law if the SDGs are to be achieved and no one is to be left behind. Doing so would result in international investment law reflecting a more balanced cosmopolitan approach to sustainable development, instead of this body of law lopsidedly protecting investors. Arcuri and Partiti offer some cautious hope in this volume:

> Recent treaty reforms partly address this issue. New (model) treaties, particularly from developing countries, include various provisions establishing investors' obligations and home state liability for investors that cause "significant damage," personal injury, and loss of life in the host state. Overall, these agreements represent an important step towards making investment law more compatible with the goal of

sustainability. However, none of these treaties has yet entered into force, and most of the provisions on investors' obligations lack enforcement mechanisms.[217]

In addition, Morgera points, in this volume, to the case

> *David Aven v Costa Rica*, [in which] the tribunal found that Costa Rica's actions to protect wetlands in an investment area was in line with the 1971 Convention on Wetlands of International Importance Especially as Waterfowl Habitat (Ramsar Convention) and the CBD and therefore did not breach the relevant investment agreement and the international obligations to ensure fair and equitable treatment.[218]

In other words, MEAs may be emerging as standards for assessing the conduct of states vis-à-vis investors. We suggest that human rights law and Agenda 2030, including, in particular, its cosmopolitan approach to sustainable development, could and should play a similar role.

The link between international economic law in general and a cosmopolitan reading of the SDGs and human rights is clearly articulated in this volume by Gonzalez. She argues that duties to cooperate, as set out in article 56 of the UN Charter and in human rights treaties, imply diagonal obligations for states in international economic law if human rights are to be realized and SDG 2 is to be attained:

> Northern states should respect the right to food in the global South by negotiating, interpreting, and applying trade and investment agreements in ways that provide Southern countries with sufficient flexibility to regulate in the public interest and to deploy subsidies, tariffs, and other import barriers to enhance the livelihoods of small farmers and other food-insecure populations. Northern states should protect the right to food by ensuring that third parties subject to their jurisdiction and control, such as transnational corporations, do not violate the right to food in other countries. States that are members of the IMF, the World Bank, and regional development banks should take affirmative steps to guarantee that the policies and practices of these institutions are consistent with their right-to-food obligations. Finally, Northern countries should fulfil the right to food by providing food aid in ways that enhance, rather than undermine, the livelihoods of small farmers in the global South by, for example, purchasing such food from Southern farmers rather than using food aid as a pretext for Northern export dumping.[219]

These illustrative examples, which are related to SDG 2 and the right to food, are equally applicable to the relationship between international economic law and the other SDGs and other human rights. If the SDGs are to be realized, it is imperative that the cosmopolitan approach to sustainable development that is reflected in Agenda 2030 and resounds in human rights law also be reflected in international

[217] Arcuri & Partiti, n. 13 (footnotes omitted).
[218] Morgera, n. 22 (footnote omitted).
[219] Gonzalez, n. 98.

economic law. Below, we consider a few examples that illustrate possible ways forward.

A pertinent example is offered by the GPBHR, which have started to impact international economic law, even if cautiously and mostly by way of "soft" law instruments that address corporate due diligence and liability.[220] In 2011, the GPBHR found resonance in the OECD's Guidelines for Multinational Enterprises (OECD Guidelines), by way of the human rights chapter included in the guidelines at the time.[221] The OECD Guidelines require the so-called adhering states to implement the guidelines as home states and address private sector actors, including transnational ones.

Similarly, with respect to multilateral development banks (MDBs), Naudé Fourie shows in this volume that MDBs have started to commit their "private sector clients" to human rights standards as contained in the law of the host state of a project and reflected in the GPBHR.[222] Moreover, as Coomans points out in this volume,

> On the basis of the GPBHR, edu-businesses have a responsibility to avoid infringing on the right to education, to address negative impacts of their activities on the enjoyment of the right to education, and to operate with due diligence – for example, by establishing a human rights impact assessment trajectory prior to carrying out their business activities, such as setting up a fee-based school for primary or secondary education.[223]

Arcuri and Partiti also point in this volume to the GPBHR increasingly being implemented in national and EU law.[224] Furthermore, home state duties and corporate due diligence and liability in transboundary contexts have been addressed by the International Law Commission in its work on environment protection in relation to armed conflicts.[225]

[220] See also Jonas Ebbesson, "Transboundary Corporate Responsibility in Environmental Matters: Fragments and Foundations for a Future Framework," in Gerd Winter (ed.), *Multilevel Governance of Global Environmental Change* (Cambridge University Press, 2006), 200.

[221] The OECD Guidelines are available at mneguidelines.oecd.org/mneguidelines/. For their relationship to the GPBHR, see foreword, 3. The OECD Guidelines are part of a wider OECD framework for promoting Due Diligence Guidance for Responsible Business Conduct. See *Responsible Business Conduct*, mneguidelines.oecd.org/duediligence/. See Peter Muchlinski, "Implementing the New UN Corporate Human Rights Framework: Implications for Corporate Law, Governance and Regulation" (2012) 22(1) *Business Ethics Quarterly* 145; Stephan W. Schill, "The OECD Guidelines for Multinational Enterprises and International Investment Agreements: Converging Universes," in Nicola Bonucci & Catherine Kessedjian (eds.), *Quarante ans des lignes directrices de l'OCDE pour les entreprises mulinationales/Forty Years of the OECD Guidelines for Multinational Enterprises* (Pedone, 2018).

[222] Naudé Fourie, n. 87.

[223] Coomans, n. 100.

[224] Arcuri & Partiti, n. 13.

[225] See ILC, *Protection of the Environment in Relation to Armed Conflicts, Text and Titles of the Draft Principles Provisionally Adopted by the Drafting Committee on First Reading*, UN Doc. A/CN.4/L.937, 9 August 2019, draft principles 10 and 11.

Finally, we briefly turn our attention to WTO law. Based on the chapters in this *Handbook*, we conclude that the cosmopolitan understanding of sustainable development reflected in Agenda 2030 should influence international trade law in general, including the interpretation of WTO law by the dispute settlement bodies, for instance, when interpreting the boundaries of the justificatory grounds in article XX of the GATT. It should also influence the TRIPS Agreement with the aim of facilitating the transfer of technology. As illustrated in Section 3.4.2, the TRIPS Agreement, as well as other regimes for the transfer of technology, has been linked to hampering the transfer of medicine during the COVID-19 pandemic,[226] the transfer of technology to mitigate climate change,[227] and, more generally, the transfer of technology in support of achieving sustainable development.[228]

The examples discussed in this section show that cosmopolitan elements are present in international law – in particular, in human rights law and international environmental law – and in "soft" instruments that address the due diligence of transnational private actors as well as the responsibilities of home states. These examples also highlight where international law – not least, economic law – needs to develop and change in order to achieve the SDGs.[229] Yet there are no legal barriers to the incorporation of a cosmopolitan understanding of sustainable development into international law in accordance with Agenda 2030. On the contrary, there are good reasons to do so if no one is to be left behind.

1.6 CONCLUSIONS

As with any policy document, it is difficult to foresee how Agenda 2030 will fare in the future. In 1948, it would have been impossible to predict that the UDHR would have had such an immense influence on the development of international law and that it would still be highly relevant more than seventy years after its adoption.[230] Likewise, in 1972 or in 1992, no one would have known, respectively, that the Stockholm Declaration and the Rio Declaration would have a lasting influence on international law – even if in all three cases their impact on international economic law has not been as pronounced as we might have wished. Whether the cosmopolitan understanding of sustainable development, reflected in Agenda 2030 and the SDGs, will be able to overcome the barriers that international economic law, in particular, poses to attaining the SDGs, of course, remains to be seen.

[226] See Dagron, n. 91.

[227] See Bruce & Viñuales, n. 93.

[228] See Naudé Fourie, n. 87.

[229] International economic law stands out in this respect, but it does not stand on its own. Dagron in this volume, for example, reminds us that the fragmented nature of health law also is highly problematic. Dagron, n. 91.

[230] Ellen Hey, "The Universal Declaration of Human Rights in 'The Anthropocene'," *AJIL Unbound*, 10 December 2018, www.cambridge.org/core/journals/american-journal-of-international-law/article/universal-declaration-of-human-rights-in-the-anthropocene/BDF72CE1821F4B3C12A2BB695788B813.

Overcoming these barriers may be difficult, given how the international economic system is entrenched in international law both historically and extant. However, as the earlier understanding of sustainable development has impacted the interpretation of WTO law and is cautiously impacting new investment treaties, new understandings of sustainable development can and should impact these areas of international law.

So what might the impact of Agenda 2030 and the SDGs be on international law and governance? Again, while this is impossible to predict, we do venture that the manner in which the Paris Agreement links human rights and environmental concerns and highlights vulnerability provides a starting point, even if it does not address private sector duties or home state duties when a private sector actor operates abroad. Similar links may be found in other MEAs. The manner in which the GPBHR are influencing human rights law also provides room for further development, even if the adoption of a "hard" law instrument has not materialized. In this sense, the impact of principle 10 of the Rio Declaration on the evolution of participatory rights, including in transnational contexts, in "hard" law instruments is inspirational.

Perhaps one of the biggest challenges facing international governance and law is how to integrate the cosmopolitan understanding of sustainable development with the fact that the earth system is significantly affected by human activities. If we do not take the latter idea on board, no understanding of sustainable development will be realized, let alone a cosmopolitan understanding of sustainable development. Leaving no one behind then requires a shift in thinking both in terms of how humans should relate to each other and how humans relate to nature. A cosmopolitan understanding of sustainable development addresses the former relationship but not the latter. We revert to article 28 of the UDHR. By providing that "*[e]veryone* is entitled to a social and international order in which the rights and freedoms set forth in this Declaration can be fully realized," it offers a starting point for drawing conclusions for international law and governance in the Anthropocene.[231] Of course, neither human rights nor the SDGs can be realized unless the limits of the earth system are heeded. The link between each and every individual and the nature of the international order made by the UDHR can be strengthened by implementing the cosmopolitan understanding of sustainable development reflected in Agenda 2030, provided due account is taken of the limits of the earth system.

We note that Agenda 2030 and the SDGs also illustrate what human imagination is able to deliver in a deeply divided world. From this point of view, the cosmopolitan understanding of sustainable development reflected in Agenda 2030, including the SDGs, offers hope also for positive change in international law. The analyses and conclusions drawn in the chapters in this *Handbook* regarding the interplay

[231] Emphasis added.

between the different SDGs and international law offer a wealth of information and insights on how to consider international law in relation to the SDGs and their implementation processes. Perhaps, most significantly, the chapters point to the need to adopt an integrated approach to international law in order to realize equitable governance and sustainable development.

1

SDG 1: End Poverty in All Its Forms Everywhere

Dire Tladi

ABSTRACT

Poverty is a scourge affecting billions of people throughout the world. It is unsurprising that the international community has declared a fight against poverty. Sustainable Development Goal (SDG) 1, No Poverty, provides the clearest reflection of that declaration against poverty. This chapter assesses the contribution that SDG 1 can make to international law in pursuit of a world free of poverty. The assessment is made through the prism of ambition and solidarity – that is, whether the SDGs' commitment to the fight against poverty reflects a sufficient level of ambition and solidarity. The chapter's point of departure is that international law has paid lip service to the notion of solidarity. Through a survey of the areas of international law that are most relevant to poverty eradication – international human rights law and international economic law – this chapter assesses international law's potential to be a vehicle for the fight against poverty in line with the aspirations of SDG 1.

KEYWORDS

SDG 1, poverty, solidarity, cooperation, international human rights law, international economic law, World Bank, World Trade Organization, Human Rights Council

1.1 INTRODUCTION

Sustainable Development Goal (SDG) 1, No Poverty, aims to end poverty in our world.[1] Given that the global levels of poverty and inequality are quite simply staggering, this is

[1] See *Transforming Our World: The 2030 Agenda for Sustainable Development*, UN Doc. A/Res/70/1, 25 September 2015, para. 3.

an important goal in the overall architecture of the SDGs. According to a recent World Bank report, in 2015 the levels of "extreme poverty," defined as persons living below US $1.90 a day, stood at 736 million.[2] Statistically, this might be seen as an improvement compared to the nearly 2 billion people living in extreme poverty in 1990.[3] Yet, these statistics do not reveal all. First, the threshold of US $1.90 excludes many persons living in poverty.[4] The picture looks bleaker when considering higher thresholds.[5] Indeed, the World Bank's more complex measure of poverty, which goes beyond consumption levels, shows that "the number of people who are poor stood at 2.1 billion as of 2015," a figure that is three times that of persons living on below US $1.90 a day.[6] Second, whatever the decrease in the rate of extreme poverty, if we accept the slogan "Leave no one behind," then, by these numbers, the international community is failing at least 736 million times over. Third, the World Bank report indicates that the rate of reduction in levels of extreme poverty has been on the decline in recent years.[7] Fourth, while extreme poverty has decreased globally, it has increased in sub-Saharan Africa, making extreme poverty "a sub-Saharan African problem."[8]

This picture of poverty is one that ought to trouble the "international community," if such a community exists. This international community should be concerned that the number of hungry people is increasing while there is enough food to feed everyone in the world.[9] From an ethical standpoint, the international

2 World Bank Group, *Piecing Together the Poverty Puzzle: Poverty and Shared Prosperity* (World Bank, 2018), 1.

3 *Id.* The report states that "[d]espite the more sluggish global growth of recent years, the total count of people in extreme poverty declined by more than 68 million people between 2013 and 2015 – a number roughly equivalent to the population of Thailand or the United Kingdom."

4 *Id.* In this connection, the report itself notes that the measure of US $1.90 does not cover the many people who "can be defined as poor relative to their societies even at a consumption levels well above the US $1.90 level." In truth, there are many who can be described as poor in absolute terms, and not only "relative to their societies," since the threshold of US $1.90 is for "extreme poverty." The CESCR has defined poverty more broadly as "a human condition characterized by sustained or chronic deprivation of resources, capabilities, choices, security and power necessary for the enjoyment of an adequate standard of living and other civil, cultural, economic, political and social rights." See CESCR, *Substantive Issues Arising in the Implementation of the International Covenant of Economic, Social and Cultural Rights: Poverty and the ICESCR*, Doc. E/C.12/2001/10, 10 May 2001, para. 8.

5 World Bank Group, n. 2, 7. In addition to the US $1.90 threshold, the World Bank also reports on the higher thresholds of US $3.20 and US $5.50. According to its most recent statistics, "nearly half of the world (46 per cent) lives on less than US $5.50." For criticism of the low threshold of the SDGs, see Liu Qian-Qian, Yu Man, & Wang Xiao-Lin, "Poverty Reduction within the Framework of the SDGs and Post-2015 Development Agenda" (2015) 6 *Advances in Climate Change Research* 67, 70.

6 World Bank Group, n. 2, 8.

7 *Id.*, 15.

8 *Id.*, 2.

9 William P. Quigley, "Revolutionary Lawyering: Addressing the Root Causes of Poverty and Wealth" (2006) 20 *Journal of Law and Policy* 101, 110.

community should be concerned that, while a few have plenty, the vast majority are impoverished and live in squalor.[10] International law is a vehicle through which the concerns of the international community are expressed. Yet, there is no obligation under international law to act to eradicate poverty, nor do the SDGs set out legally binding obligations to eradicate poverty by 2030.

Yet, while SDG 1 does not constitute a rule of international law, it affects, and is affected by, international law in several ways. First, with the apparent shift of international law from a state-centric system anchored on bilateralism to one that is concerned with the human condition and based on community interests,[11] there seems to be much scope for international law's engagement with poverty and the pursuit of its eradication. After all, the levels of poverty undermine international law's purported pursuit of a better world. Second, many areas of international law address topics that relate to poverty eradication, including international human rights law, environmental law, and trade and investment law. Third, the search for international law's role in addressing poverty predates the SDGs.[12]

This chapter reviews the opportunities for, and the hurdles standing in the way of, international law playing a role in efforts to eradicate poverty through the lens of solidarity and ambition. First, like many of the SDGs, perhaps even more so, the achievement of SDG 1 is dependent on cooperation and solidarity.[13] Second, given the high levels of poverty described above, the achievement of SDG 1 will require a high degree of ambition. While other areas of international law, such as the law related to environmental protection, labor rights, and the suppression of corruption, are also relevant to poverty eradication, the focus of this chapter is on areas of international law that are most directly relevant to the eradication of poverty: human rights law and aspects of economic law – in particular, international trade law and the law relating to international financial institutions.

[10] Writing in 2005, Jeffrey Sachs expressed the optimism that "extreme poverty can be ended not in the time of our grandchildren, but in *our* time." He explained his cause for optimism as follows: "The wealth of the rich world, the power of today's vast storehouses of knowledge, and the declining fraction of the world that needs help to escape from poverty all make the end of poverty a realistic possibility by the year 2025." Jeffrey Sachs, *The End of Poverty: Economic Possibilities for Our Time* (Penguin Press, 2005), 3 (emphasis in original).

[11] See, e.g., Bruno Simma, "From Bilateralism to Community Interests in International Law" (1994) 250 *Collected Courses of the Hague Academy* 229. See also Emmanuelle Jouannet, espressing a related sentiment in "Universalism and Imperialism: The True–False Paradox of International Law?" (2007) 18 *European Journal of International Law* 379.

[12] See, e.g., Christine Chinkin, "The United Nations Decade for the Elimination of Poverty: What Role for International Law?" (2001) 54 *Current Legal Problems* 553; see also John Dugard, "The Future of International Law: A Human Rights Perspective – with Some Comments on the Leiden School of International Law" (2007) 20 *Leiden Journal of International Law* 729.

[13] Abdul Koroma, "Solidarity: Evidence of an Emerging International Legal Principle," in Holga Hestermeyer et al. (eds.), *Co-existence, Cooperation and Solidarity: Liber Amicorum Rüdiger Wolfrum* (Martinus Nijhoff, 2012), 103.

1.2 THE CONTENT OF SDG 1 IN THE CONTEXT OF THE OTHER SDGS

1.2.1 *The Content of SDG 1*

The language of SDG 1 itself reveals a strong ambition. It is to "[e]nd poverty in *all its forms everywhere.*"[14] The absolutist ambition of the goal extends to both the type of poverty to be eradicated (in all its forms) and the geographical scope (everywhere). Achieving the geographic element of this goal – "everywhere" – will require solidarity. Well-resourced developed states may be able to address, unilaterally and without external assistance, the poverty of their own populations. However, without the cooperative assistance inherent in the concept of solidarity, poorer states will not be able to pull their populations out of poverty.

This lofty and ambitious goal is to be measured against a set of five targets to be achieved by 2030. These targets do not exhibit the same absolute pretense of the overall objective of SDG 1. Target 1.1 provides an example. It aims to "eradicate extreme poverty for all people everywhere" by 2030. In some respects, there is an absolutism about the ambition: it targets "poverty for all people" and "everywhere." Moreover, the target is not to reduce poverty but, rather, to eradicate it, which is another indication of an absolutist ambition. Yet, the target lacks the absolutist pretense of SDG 1, since it is only "*extreme* poverty" and not all poverty that is targeted. Moreover, the benchmark for what constitutes "extreme poverty" is US $1.25 a day, which is even less ambitious than the US $1.90 used by the World Bank to indicate extreme poverty. Target 1.2 also reveals an absolutist ambition in that it is directed at "poverty in *all its dimensions*," not only extreme poverty. Yet this apparently absolutist ambition is relative, since it is to be determined "according to national definitions" and only requires that the proportion of those living in poverty be reduced by at least half.

Pointing out the low ambition reflected in the targets of SDG 1 is not a criticism but, rather, a statement of fact and a recognition by the drafters that the ultimate objective of poverty eradication will likely not be met by 2030 and that, by any standard, there will remain people living in poverty in 2030. Other targets of SDG 1 seek to address the relatively low ambitions in targets 1.1 and 1.2 by addressing the living conditions of those who, in 2030, will remain in poverty – those left behind. Target 1.3, for example, requires that there should be "social protection systems and measures for all" and that, by 2030, states should have achieved "substantial coverage of the poor and the vulnerable." This target, which is intended to cover those left behind, itself lacks an absolutist ambition, leaving the determination of the appropriate levels of social protection and coverage up to national standards. Targets 1.4 and 1.5 are similarly geared toward enhancing the lives of those who may have

[14] Emphasis added.

been left behind due to the low levels of ambition of poverty reduction in targets 1.1 and 1.2.

Developed states may well be able to meet the targets under SDG 1 for their own populations. They may even be able to meet the overall, absolutist, objective of SDG 1. This situation, however, creates the risk that the poor in developing states, particularly in the least developing states, are going to be left behind. To ensure that developing states are not left behind requires shared responsibility in uplifting the poor. Targets 1.a and 1.b are directed at this need for solidarity. Target 1.a recognizes the need to "[e]nsure significant mobilization of resources," and the need for "enhanced development cooperation" in order to ensure that the poor in developing countries are not left behind. Similarly, the recognition of the need for action and "sound policy frameworks" not only at the national level but also at "regional and international levels" is indicative of a pursuit for solidarity. This need for collective action, to some extent, is also reflected in SDG 17, Partnerships for the Goals, on the means of implementation. SDG 17 is peppered with references to collective action to finance the achievement of the SDGs, including SDG 1. Nonetheless, SDG 17, and its individual targets, is still crafted in a way that falls short of solidarity: The poor in developing countries are the responsibility of developing states, and developed states will assist to the extent that they choose to. Section 1.3 of this chapter illustrates that this philosophy is largely consistent with the general framework of international law.

1.2.2 *SDG 1 in the Context of Other SDGs*

While SDG 1 specifically addresses poverty eradication, this theme also runs throughout the SDGs. It may even be said that the SDGs are about poverty eradication. The SDGs are, after all, a continuation of the 2000 Millennium Development Goals (MDGs),[15] which were more explicitly centered on poverty alleviation and securing a life of dignity for the most disadvantaged in our society.[16] Then, Secretary-General Ban Ki-Moon's opening words in the foreword to the 2015 *Millennium Development Goal Report* are reflective of the centrality of poverty eradication to the MDGs. He characterized the MDGs as "the most successful *anti-poverty* movement in history," reflecting world leaders' commitment to "spare

[15] The relationship between the MDGs and the SDGs has been reflected in different ways in the literature. For a more positive outlook, see Nina Weitz, Måns Nilsson & Marion Davis, "A Nexus Approach to the Post-2015 Agenda: Formulating Integrated Water, Energy and Food SDGs" (2014) 34 *School of Advanced International Studies Review of International Affairs* 37, 37; see also Liu et al., n. 5, 70. For a more somber perspective, see Stephen McCloskey, "From MDGs to SDGs: We Need a Critical Awakening to Succeed" (2015) 12 *Policy and Practice: A Development Education Review* 186, 186.

[16] See *UN Millennium Declaration*, UN Doc. A/Res/55/2, 8 September 2000, para. 11.

no effort to free our fellow men, women and children from the abject and dehumanizing conditions of extreme poverty."[17]

The MDGs were developed as part of the evolution of sustainable development, and it is no surprise that the eradication of poverty, which is at the center of sustainable development,[18] was interwoven into the fabric of the MDGs.[19] This theme is carried forward in the 2030 Agenda for Sustainable Development, which was presented as "a plan of action for people, planet and prosperity."[20] The goals underlying Agenda 2030 are said to be "integrated and indivisible" and "balance the three dimensions of sustainable development: the economic, social and environmental."[21] The fact that sustainable development underpins Agenda 2030, and therefore the SDGs, is testament to the idea that poverty eradication constitutes the leitmotif for the SDGs.[22] According to Agenda 2030, the goals are "people-centred" and "transformative."[23]

Of course, the SDGs address more than poverty eradication. More so than the MDGs, the SDGs are rooted explicitly in the law and policy of sustainable development, which is concerned with more than poverty eradication. Yet, poverty eradication is a "core philosophy" of sustainable development.[24] Describing the importance of poverty eradication under the SDGs, Liu Qian-Qian, Yu Man, and Wang Xiao-Lin express the view that "[e]nding extreme poverty and achieving sustainable development by 2030 is the summary of the SDGs, reflecting the significance of poverty reduction in the issue of development."[25]

That the eradication of poverty is the leitmotif that permeates the SDGs can be seen in individual goals. SDG 2, Zero Hunger, for example, concerns ending hunger, ensuring food security, and promoting improved nutrition. There is an inextricable connection between hunger and poverty, given that it is the poor that

[17] See *Millennium Development Goals Report*, 2015, 3 (emphasis added).

[18] World Commission on Environment and Development, *Our Common Future* (World Commission on Environment and Development, 1987), 43, in which the Brundtland Commission's report described the definition of sustainable development as containing two elements, the first being that the essential needs of the world's poor must be given priority.

[19] Dire Tladi, *Sustainable Development in International Law: An Analysis of Key-Enviro Economic Instruments* (Pretoria University Law Press [PULP], 2007), 31.

[20] *Transforming Our World*, n. 1, preamble.

[21] *Id.*

[22] For example, the first recital of the preamble states "that eradicating poverty in all its forms and dimensions, including extreme poverty, is the greatest global challenge and an indispensable requirement for sustainable development." In the second recital, world leaders committed to "free[ing] the human race from the tyranny of poverty."

[23] *Id.*, para. 2.

[24] Liu et al., n. 5, 68; see also the 2002 Johannesburg Declaration on Sustainable Development, para. 11, in which poverty eradication is described as both an objective and an essential requirement for sustainable development. See also Tladi, n. 19.

[25] Liu et al., n. 5, 69.

suffer from hunger, lack of food security, and malnutrition.[26] Therefore, addressing poverty will contribute to addressing hunger, food security, and malnutrition. Similarly, the eradication of poverty will contribute to healthy lives and the promotion of the well-being of people, which is the subject of SDG 3, Good Health and Well-Being. Moreover, education, addressed in SDG 4, Quality Education, is an important factor for addressing poverty. The cause-and-effect relationship between education and poverty is generally well recognized.[27] There is an almost obvious connection between SDG 1 and other SDGs – for example, SDG 6, Clean Water and Sanitation; SDG 7, Affordable and Clean Energy; SDG 8, Decent Work and Economic Growth; SDG 9, Industry, Innovation and Infrastructure; and SDG 10, Reduced Inequalities.

Even those SDGs whose connection with poverty eradication may not be so obvious connect to the aim of SDG 1. For example, SDG 14, Life below Water, has as its primary objective conservation. Yet, the pursuit of "sustainable use" also concerns "access for small-scale artisanal fishers to marine resources and markets," which impacts poverty.[28] Given the centrality of poverty eradication for sustainable development, the permeation of the goal of eradicating poverty through the SDGs is understandable.

1.3 POSITIONING SDG 1 IN INTERNATIONAL LAW

1.3.1 *Is International Law Geared toward Achieving SDG 1?*

Whether the nature of international law is geared toward achieving SDG 1 depends in large part on whether it can exhibit a sufficient degree of solidarity to ensure that those in the poorest states are not left behind in the drive to eradicate poverty. While international law traditionally was seen as a system driven by the national interests of states, and shaped by their bargaining power,[29] there is a growing consensus that this traditional international law is giving way to a more value-based, community-oriented system of law, and the debate, if there is one, concerns the rate of the shift

[26] See generally Ngcimezile Mbano-Mweso, "Poverty, Women and the Human Right to Water for Growing Food," in Ebenezer Durojaye and Gladys Mirugi-Mukundi (eds.), *Exploring the Link between Poverty and Human Rights in Africa* (PULP, 2020).

[27] Ebenezer Durojaye and Gladys Mirugi-Mukundi, "General Introduction to Poverty and Human Rights," in Durojaye and Mirugi-Mukundi, n. 26, 3.

[28] See target 14.b; see also generally Henrik Österblom, Colette Wabnitz and Dire Tladi, *Blue Paper 13: Towards Ocean Equity – A Paper Commissioned by the High-Level Panel on Ocean Economy*, 2019, 5ff.

[29] See Simma, n. 11, 229–33; Philip Allot, *Eunomia: New Order for a New World* (Oxford University Press, 1990), 324; David Held, "The Changing Structure of International Law: Sovereignty Transformed?," in David Held & Anthony McGrew (eds.), *The Global Transformations Reader: An Introduction to the Globalization Debate*, 2nd ed. (Polity, 2003), 162; Antonio Augusto Cançado Trindade, "International Law for Humankind: Towards a New Jus Gentium" (2005) 316 *Recueil des Cours de l'Académie d Droit International de la Haye* 21.

rather than the fact of the change. Bruno Simma has observed that international law is "overcoming the legal and moral deficiencies of" the bilateralist international legal system and "maturing into a much more socially conscious legal order."[30] John Dugard has described this emerging international law as being premised on "a brave new world" in which "state sovereignty is no longer a factor ... in which the community of personkind is governed by the rule of law ... in which peace and human rights are secure and in which the energy of personkind is addressed toward resolving poverty and inequality."[31] This brave new world, described by Dugard, suggests a system of international law based on solidarity. Solidarity in international law, according to Abdul Koroma, "represents more than a general notion of 'neighbourliness' but in fact an emerging structural principle which in many cases creates negative obligations on States not to engage in certain activities, and in an increasing number of contexts establishes concrete duties on States to carry out certain measures for the common good."[32]

While there is some consensus in scholarly writings about this new, emerging international law, it is not apparent that the enthusiasm of scholars is matched by the practice of states and the actual state of international law.[33] The discussion of the areas of international law relevant to poverty eradication illustrates this state of affairs.

1.3.2 *Areas of International Law Relevant to Poverty Eradication*

In this subsection, the areas of international law most relevant for poverty eradication – namely, human rights law and economic law – are addressed. For both these areas of international law, this chapter will assess the extent to which they are geared to contribute to the achievement of SDG 1, from the perspectives of both ambition and solidarity.

1.3.2.1 Human Rights Law

The area of international law that is most relevant to the eradication of poverty is human rights law, given that, at its core, it is about the human condition.[34] Poverty is also about the human condition. The question that flows from this is which human

[30] Simma, n. 11, 234.

[31] See Dugard, n. 12.

[32] Koroma, n. 13, 103.

[33] I have recently suggested that the rhetoric and enthusiasm in the academic literature have not been matched by the practice of states. See Dire Tladi, "Populism's Attack on Multilateralism and International Law: Much Ado about Nothing" (2020) 19 *Chinese Journal of International Law* 369.

[34] For a discussion, see Jack Donnelly, *Universal Human Rights in Theory and Practice* (Cornell University Press, 2003), 13ff.

rights are relevant for the eradication of poverty.[35] While the argument can be made that many – possibly all – human rights have some relevance to poverty,[36] socioeconomic rights are most closely associated with the fight against poverty.[37] Socioeconomic rights are established precisely to ensure the protection of "the poor and otherwise marginalised" in society.[38] The purpose of socioeconomic rights is to ensure that basic needs are met, and it is the poor whose basic needs are often not met.[39] Onyeka Osuji and Ugochukwu Obibuaku have noted that socioeconomic rights "can serve as a powerful tool for reducing and eliminating poverty."[40]

A survey of the catalog of rights in the 1966 International Covenant on Economic, Social and Cultural Rights (ICESCR) reveals that they directly concern the fight against poverty and are of eminent relevance for the attainment of other SDGs. While the ICESCR and other relevant instruments, as such, do not provide a right to be free of poverty or an obligation to alleviate poverty, the fulfillment of socioeconomic rights together will ensure the eradication of poverty.[41] The universal achievement of the rights to work, just and equitable conditions of work, social security, an adequate standard of living, the highest attainable standard of health, and education would enhance the prospects of achieving SDG 1.[42] For example, unemployment, which is addressed by the work-related rights, is one of the major causes of poverty; high health standards are often unattainable for the poor; and education is one of the key tools for addressing poverty.

The recognition of socioeconomic rights in international law, then, has the potential to play an important role in poverty eradication. However, that potential is limited by several factors. First, treaties, including those providing socioeconomic

35 See Chinkin, n. 12, 556; see also Jumoke Oduwole, "Global Poverty and the Right to Development: An African Perspective on Maklem's *The Sovereignty of Human Rights*" (2017) 15 *Jerusalem Review of Legal Studies* 98, 99 ("Thus, international human rights are envisioned as moral instruments that protect universal features of what it means to be a human being"); John C. Mubangizi & Betty Mubangizi, "Poverty, Human Rights Law and Socio-economic Realities in South Africa" (2005) 22 *Development Southern Africa* 277, 282; see generally David Bilchitz, *Fundamental Rights: Justification and Enforcement of Socio-economic Rights* (Oxford University Press, 2007), 1.

36 See Durojaye & Mirugi-Mukundi, n. 26.

37 See generally Sibonile Khoza, "Promoting Economic, Social and Cultural Rights in Africa: The African Commission Holds a Seminar in Pretoria" (2004) 4 *African Human Rights Law Journal* 334.

38 See Danie Brand, "Introduction to the Socio-economic Rights in the South Africa," in Danie Brand & Christof Heyns (eds.), *Socio-economic Rights in South Africa* (PULP, 2005), 2.

39 Onyeka K. Osuji & Ugochukwu L. Obibuaku, "Rights and Corporate Social Responsibility: Competing or Complementary Approaches to Poverty Reduction and Socioeconomic Rights?" (2016) 126 *Journal of Business Ethics* 329, 331.

40 *Id.*, 333.

41 Chinkin, n. 12, 559. Other relevant instruments include 1989 Convention on the Rights of the Child and the 1981 African Charter on Human and Peoples' Rights.

42 ICESCR, respectively arts. 6, 9, 11, 12, 13.

rights, apply only to state parties.[43] Second, treaty provisions on socioeconomic rights are generally couched not as immediately and absolutely enforceable rights but, rather, as obligations that a state is to progressively realize and subject to resource constraints of each individual state.[44] There is a third, and potentially more crippling constraint to the potential of socioeconomic rights to impact poverty. Socioeconomic rights are couched as rights owed by a state to the population in its territory.[45] While there has been some movement toward the extraterritorial application of human rights, this has largely been limited to those instances where the state in question exercises some control or jurisdiction over the activities or actors in another state.[46]

Indeed, with respect to socioeconomic rights, the International Court of Justice determined that the ICESCR "guarantees rights which are essentially territorial," noting that it may also apply to a state in respect of territories "over which that state exercises territorial jurisdiction."[47] The problem with this general construction is that it places the burden of dealing with the most serious cases of poverty – those in developing states – on precisely those states that, due to their economic situation and developmental state, are not in a position to allocate the necessary resources to effectively addressing poverty. It undermines the idea of solidarity implied by the transition of international law from bilateralism to a system based on community interests.[48] To truly enable socioeconomic rights to play a meaningful role in the eradication of poverty, relevant human rights instruments should be interpreted to establish the idea that the international community as a whole is responsible for ensuring that such rights are enjoyed by all.

While socioeconomic rights potentially provide the most direct avenue for addressing poverty, other human rights are also relevant. Poverty, for example, affects the dignity of people, meaning that for those living in poverty the right to dignity cannot be realized. Similarly, a broad interpretation of the right to life would

43 While it may be argued that socioeconomic rights, or some of them, are customary international law, this is not a generally accepted proposition. *Cf.* Chinkin, n. 12, 558, who states that these are rights established under the UN Charter and which, therefore, states cannot disown even if not provided for in a particular treaty.

44 ICESCR, art. 2(1); see, e.g. Lilian Chenwi, "Unpacking 'Progressive Realisation', Its Relation to Resources, Minimum Core and Reasonableness, and Some Methodological Considerations for Assessing Compliance" (2013) 46 *De Jure* 742.

45 See Elif Askin, "Economic and Social Rights, Extraterritorial Application," in *Max Planck Encyclopedia of Public International Law* (Oxford University Press, 2019).

46 *Id.* In regard to civil and political rights, see *Legal Consequences of the Construction of a Wall in the Occupied Palestinian Territory*, Advisory Opinion, ICJ Reports (2004) 136, para. 109; see also IACtHR, *State Obligations in Relation to the Environment in Relation in the Context of the Protection and Guarantee of the Rights to Life and to Personal Integrity: Interpretation and Scope of Articles 1(1) and 2 of the American Convention on Human Rights*, Advisory Opinion OC-23/17, November 2017, paras. 73ff.

47 *Legal Consequences of a Wall*, n. 46, para. 112.

48 See n. 31 and accompanying text, quoting Dugard's reference to "the brave new world of international law."

establish a link between the protection of life and the "chronic and yet pervasive threats to life" flowing from poverty.[49] Moreover, as Christine Chinkin points out, the attainment of socioeconomic rights provides the basis for the enjoyment of all civil and political rights.[50] She notes that the denial of civil and political rights is a daily occurrence for the poor.[51] Chinkin's approach, arguing against the "categorisation of rights" and calling for "mutually reinforcing interpretation of both sets of rights directed toward poverty reduction," is consistent with the view that considers the right to development to be the unifier between socioeconomic and civil and political rights. Consistent with the broad definition of poverty adopted by the Committee on Economic, Social and Cultural Rights,[52] it affirms the idea of the indivisibility of human rights.[53] In this context, the right to development has been characterized as "a composite right of all universal rights."[54] In essence, it is a right concerned with improving the human condition and the overall well-being of humans, which is the very purpose of the pursuit of the eradication of poverty.[55]

The ability of human rights law to contribute to poverty eradication thus is limited by a number of factors. First, the ambition of human rights law is especially low in relation to those rights most closely associated with the alleviation of poverty – that is, socioeconomic rights. These rights are subject to several qualifiers that reduce their overall effectiveness. Second, and perhaps more importantly, the solidarity that is central to the brave new communitarian-based international law is not reflected in the architecture of human rights law. States are responsible only for populations in their own territories – the "me for mine and you for yours" philosophy. Without solidarity, which implies the joint responsibility of states to address poverty everywhere, neither the targets nor the overall objective of SDG 1 can be met for developing states. Given the low ambition and lack of solidarity evidenced in socioeconomic rights, SDG 1, together with its targets, reflects a higher level of ambition. Yet the SDGs, being mere policy objectives, do not establish legal obligations and cannot, on their own, enhance the content of international law. The relatively higher level of ambition, together with some commitment to solidarity reflected in SDG 1, could be used to interpret socioeconomic rights, both to enhance their ambition in terms of content and to promote broader extraterritoriality in order to enhance solidarity.

49 See African Commission on Human and Peoples' Rights, *General Comment 3 on the African Charter on Human and Peoples: The Right to Life (Article 4)*, 2015, para. 42.

50 Chinkin, n. 12, 560.

51 *Id.*

52 See CESCR, n. 4, para. 8.

53 Lanse Minkler & Shawna Sweeney, "On the Indivisibility and Interdependence of Basic Rights in Developing Countries" (2011) 33 *Human Rights Quarterly* 351.

54 See Arjun Sengupta, "On Theory and Practice of the Right to Development" (2002) 24 *Human Rights Quarterly* 837, 870.

55 Tladi, n. 19, 68, noting that there are as many definitions of international economic law "as there are authors on the subject."

1.3.2.2 International Economic Law

International economic law, another area of international law with potential relevance for the eradication of poverty, includes trade law, investment law, the law relating to financial institutions, and intellectual property law.[56] In general, international economic law is geared toward wealth creation, which can impact poverty.[57] There is therefore an obvious relationship, at least potentially, between international economic law and poverty alleviation. This subsection addresses trade law and the law related to international financial institutions.

The pursuit of free trade – the basic objective of international trade law – has often been characterized as an important tool for poverty alleviation and eradication.[58] The preamble of the 1994 Agreement Establishing the World Trade Organization (WTO Agreement) sets objectives that are closely related to poverty alleviation. It determines that activities under the World Trade Organization (WTO) should be "conducted with a view to raising standards of living" and "ensuring full employment." The idea is that, through income generation, free trade improves and enhances the livelihood of persons.[59] Fernando Tesón and Jonathan Klick make a rather strong claim concerning the relationship between poverty alleviation and free trade. First, they state, perhaps optimistically, that "virtually everyone agrees" that alleviating poverty "should be a priority of international law."[60] Second, based on the virtues of trade as a tool for economic growth,

[56] See Makane Moïse Mbengue & Apollin Koagne Zouapet, "Ending the Splendid Isolation … *Jus Cogens* and International Economic Law," in Dire Tladi (ed.), *Peremptory Norms of General International Law: Disquisitions and Disputations* (Brill, 2021). On intellectual property law, see, in particular, chapters 3, 7, 9, 10 in this volume.

[57] WTO, *Background Paper: The WTO's 2 Year Strategy Comes to Fruition*, January 2002, www.wto.org/english/news_e/news01_e/wto2year_strategy_17dec01.doc ("complete liberalisation of merchandise trade and elimination of subsidies could add US $1.5 trillion to developing country incomes. And reshaping the world's trading system and reducing barriers to trade in goods could reduce the number of poor in developing countries by 300 million by 2015 and boost the global income by as much as $2.8 trillion over the next ten years").

[58] See, e.g., generally, World Bank Group and WTO, *The Role of Trade in Ending Poverty*, 2015. More cautiously, see Chios Carmody, Frank Garcia & John Linarelli, "Introduction," in Chios Carmody, Frank Garcia & John Linarelli (eds.), *Global Justice and International Economic Law: Opportunities and Prospects* (Cambridge University Press, 2014); Caroline Dommen, "Safeguarding the Legitimacy of the Multilateral Trading System: The Role of Human Rights Law," in Frederick M. Abott, Christine Breining-Kaufmann, & Thomas Cottier (eds.), *International Trade and Human Rights: Foundations and Conceptual Issues* (University of Michigan Press, 2006), 122–23.

[59] World Bank Group and WTO, n. 58, 7; see also Michael Moore, "The Multilateral Trading System in Support of Africa-led and Africa-owned Development" (Paper presented at UN Economic and Social Council, High Level Policy Dialogue, United Nations, 16 July 2001), www.wto.org/english/news_e/spmm_e/spmm07_e.htm.

[60] Fernando Tesón & Jonathan Klick, "Global Justice and Trade," in Carmody, Garcia, & Linarelli, n. 58, 217, 217.

they claim that "free trade is *required*" for this purpose.[61] One commentator has remarked that the "view that free trade is good for the poor is so widely accepted that it is hard to get a word in edge-wise."[62]

It is not possible here to test empirically the claims that trade liberalization contributes to poverty eradication. The claim that free trade alleviates poverty, however, is contested and has been the subject of severe criticism.[63] Marjorie Cohn, for example, has noted that the "WTO's *raison d'être* is the elevation of property interests above the protection of human rights."[64] She disputes the idea that wealth created through globalization has trickled down and asserts that the "gap between rich and poor has widened geometrically *because of* the global trading system."[65] In a report to the Human Rights Commission – the predecessor to the Human Rights Council – Joseph Oloka-Onyango and Deepika Udagama described the WTO rules as "grossly unfair and even prejudiced" and a "veritable nightmare" for "certain sectors of humanity" – in particular, those from developing countries.[66] Equally scathing is Barbara Stark, who notes that, due to neoliberal economic policies, including free trade rules, the "chasm between the rich and the poor has become unfathomable."[67] Indeed, even some who take a somewhat more sympathetic view of free trade note that there are "good reasons to be sceptical of the claim that free trade is always the best way to reduce poverty."[68]

The activities of international financial institutions also have been identified as being central to economic growth and, following the logic that economic growth leads to poverty reduction, as contributing to the eradication of poverty. These institutions, even more so than trade institutions, are regarded as the most powerful agents of economic development.[69] Loans provided by development banks, such as the International Bank for Reconstruction and Development and the International

61 *Id.* (emphasis in original).

62 Nicole Hassoun, "Free Trade, Poverty and the Environment" (2008) 22 *Public Affairs Quarterly* 353, 353.

63 In general terms, the current author has argued that tools designed to enhance economic growth do not necessarily lead to poverty reduction. See Tladi, n. 19, 81–82.

64 Marjorie Cohn, "The World Trade Organisation: Elevating Property Interests above Human Rights" (2001) 29 *Georgia Journal of International and Comparative Law* 427, 427; see also Nii Lante Wallace-Bruce, "Global Free Trade and Sustainable Development: Two Steps Forward in the WTO?" (2002) 35 *Comparative and International Law Journal of Southern Africa* 236, 237.

65 Cohn, n. 64, 428.

66 Joseph Oloka-Onyango & Deepika Udagama, *The Realisation of Economic, Social and Cultural Rights: Globalisation and Its Impact on the Full Enjoyment of Human Rights*, preliminary report to the Commission on Human Rights, Doc. E/CN.4/Sub.2/2000/13, 15 June 2000, paras. 13–15.

67 Barbara Stark, "Jam Tomorrow: A Critique of International Economic Law," in Carmody, Garcia & Linarelli, n. 58, 262.

68 Hassoun, n. 62, 369.

69 Thomas Stubbs & Alexander Kentikelenis, "International Financial Institutions and Human Rights: Implications for Public Health" (2017) 38 *Public Health Reviews* 27, 28.

Finance Corporation (both part of the World Bank Group), for infrastructure development, and the International Monetary Fund's (IMF) stabilization lending are designed to promote economic growth. These loans, in turn, can have a positive impact on human rights.[70] International financial institutions, at least on paper, are geared toward the achievement of SDG 1.[71] The World Bank has adopted what it has referred to as the twin objectives – namely, ending extreme poverty and boosting prosperity.[72] Moreover, the World Bank's 1945 Articles of Agreement, for example, seek to encourage investment, inter alia, to assist "in raising productivity, the standard of living and conditions of labour" in member states.[73] Similarly, while earlier the IMF characterized itself as a financier and monetary agency and not as a development agency, today it embraces its role in addressing poverty.[74]

While international financial institutions have as a stated objective poverty eradication, the activities of these institutions have often been criticized as harming and not helping the poor.[75] For example, it has been argued that international financial institutions work to the benefit not of the poor countries that are their clients but, rather, of the rich countries, which are their major shareholders.[76] The independent expert on the promotion of a democratic and equitable order has noted that some of the policies of international financial institutions "have resulted in the erosion of the enabling human rights environment in some countries," including by promoting "policies that weaken the public sector and hinder states in the fulfilment of their

70 Adam Macbeth, "A Right by Any Other Name: The Evasive Engagement of International Financial Institutions with Human Rights" (2008–9) 40 *George Washington International Law Review* 1101.

71 See World Bank Group, *A Measured Approach to Ending Poverty and Boosting Shared Prosperity: Concepts, Data and the Twin Goals* (World Bank, 2015), 6–12.

72 *Id.*

73 See, e.g., 1945 Articles of Agreement of the International Bank for Reconstruction and Development, as amended, art. 1.

74 François Gianviti, "Economic, Social, and Cultural Human Rights and the International Monetary Fund," in Philip Alston (ed.), *Non-State Actors and Human Rights* (Oxford University Press, 2005), 131, 135.

75 See generally Paul Clements, "Multilateral Development Banks and the International Monetary Fund," in Carmody, Garcia & Linaralli, n. 58; Bruce Rich, *Mortgaging the Earth: The World Bank, Environmental Impoverishment and the Crisis of Development* (Routledge, 1994); Michel Chossudovsky, *The Globalisation of Poverty: The Impacts of IMF and World Bank Reforms* (Zed Books, 1997); Korinna Horta, "Boundaries in the Field of Human Rights: Rhetoric and Reality: Human Rights and the World Bank" (2002) 15 *Harvard Human Rights Journal* 227; Christiana Ochoa, "Advancing the Language of Human Rights in a Global Economic Order: An Analysis of Discourse" (2003) 23 *Boston College Third World Law Journal* 57.

76 See generally Anthony Anghie, "International Financial Institutions," in Christian Reus-Smit (ed.), *The Politics of International Law* (Cambridge University Press, 2004), 14. See the current author's criticism of the two main international financial institutions. Dire Tladi, "International Law for Sustainable Development: Sombre Reflections on World Bank Efforts" (2004) 29 *South African Yearbook of International Law* 165; Dire Tladi, "IMF Conditionality, Debt and Poverty: Towards a 'Strong' Anthropocentric Model of Sustainable Development" (2004) 16 *South African Mercantile Law Journal* 31.

human rights obligations" – in particular, socioeconomic rights.[77] Speaking more broadly about international financial institutions, Thomas Stubbs and Alexander Kentikelenis express the view that these institutions often have the effect of "reducing national policy and undermining national development agendas" and "have implications for the enjoyment of human rights" – in particular, socioeconomic rights.[78] Much of the criticism against the international financial institutions have been directed at the conditionalities imposed on developing countries when accessing loans.[79] These conditionalities aim at economic austerity, require reduction in social spending, and target those social services that are most essential for the poor. An empirical review of conditionalities imposed by international financial institutions concluded that they have been a dismal failure.[80]

Since the 2000s and in response to scathing criticism, international financial institutions such as the World Bank and the IMF have explicitly adopted poverty reduction as an objective. Yet it has been suggested that this has been a little more than a façade.[81] For example, the IMF's Poverty Reduction and Growth Facility, which was a response to the criticism of structural adjustment programs, has been described "as the new name for structural adjustment loans."[82] Thus, notwithstanding the declared turn in official posture, international financial institutions continue to be criticized for policies that, instead of contributing to eradicating poverty, are harming the poor.[83] Indeed, while international financial institutions have embraced, on paper, poverty reduction as a key objective, they continue to reject the idea that international human rights – in particular, those human rights contained in the ICESCR – could apply to them. Philip Alston, then special rapporteur

77 *Report of the Independent Expert on the Promotion of a Democratic and Equitable International Order (Alfred de Zayas)*, Doc. A/HRC/36/40, 20 July 2017, para. 3; see also Diane Desierto, "Lingering Asymmetries in SDGs and Human Rights: How Accountable Are International Financial Institutions in the International Accountability Network," *EJIL: Talk!*, 2 February 2019.

78 Stubbs & Kentikelenis, n. 69, 28; see also Michel Chossudovsky, *The Globalisation of Poverty and the New World Order* (Global Research, 2003).

79 See, e.g., Axel Drehel, "A Public Choice of IMF and World Bank Lending and Conditionality" (2004) 119 *Public Choice* 445; see also B.S. Chimni, "Critical Theory and International Economic Law: A Third World Approach to International Law (TWAIL) Perspective," in John Linarelli (ed.), *Research Handbook on Global Justice and International Economic Law* (EE, 2013), 261.

80 Walden Bello, Shea Cunningham & Bill Rau, *Dark Victory: The United States and Global Poverty*, 2nd ed. (Pluto Press, 1999), 3.

81 See *Report of the Special Rapporteur on Extreme Poverty and Human Rights (Philip Alston)*, Doc. A/HRC/38/33, 8 May 2018, para. 7. The report refers to a study that assesses IMF practice both in the era of the Washington Consensus and in the post-reform era. Alexander E. Kentikelenis, Thomas Stubbs & Lawrence King, "IMF Conditionality and Development Policy Space, 1985– 2014" (2016) 23 *Review of International Political Economy* 543.

82 William Easterly, *The White Man's Burden: Why the West's Efforts to Aid the Rest Have Done So Much Ill and So Little Good* (Penguin Press, 2006), 191; see also Tladi, "IMF Conditionality," n. 76.

83 See, e.g., Clements, n. 75, 121.

on extreme poverty, after interacting with officials of the IMF, summarized the fund's position:

> [T]he International Covenant on Economic, Social and Cultural Rights is not applicable to IMF; its provisions have not attained customary international law status that would make them applicable independently of the Covenant; IMF promotes economic and social rights indirectly by contributing to conducive economic conditions; and IMF cannot promote human rights directly without contravening the Articles of Agreement. The Deputy General Counsel of IMF informed the Special Rapporteur that this position remained unchanged. He reiterated that it was not bound by human rights norms, "except perhaps in cases of genocide."[84]

The conscious integration of human rights, especially socioeconomic rights, into international economic law would make it possible for international economic law to contribute to the objectives of SDG 1. The exceptions to free trade – for example, in article XX of the 1947 General Agreement on Tariffs and Trade – could be interpreted liberally to permit trade restrictions in order to give effect to the rights in the ICESCR. This would be consistent with the customary international law rules of interpretation.[85] Both the object and purpose of the treaty ("raising standards of living" in the preamble of the WTO Agreement) and the principle of systemic integration in article 31(3)(c) of the 1969 Vienna Convention on the Law of Treaties (VCLT): could be used to integrate socio-economic rights into the law of the WTO. The same argument applies to international financial institutions. SDG 1, in its own right and as a means for an enhanced interpretation of human rights instruments, as suggested in Section 1.3.2.1, should be considered as a pathway for international economic law to contribute meaningfully to poverty eradication.

1.4 POSITIONING SDG 1 IN THE INTERNATIONAL INSTITUTIONAL CONTEXT

1.4.1 *Human Rights Institutions*

This subsection addresses the role of institutional settings in achieving SDG 1. The increase in the number and growth in influence of international organizations under international law justifies thinking about institutional frameworks in relation to the SDGs.[86] Nonetheless, the role of institutional rules should not be overstated. Institutional settings and frameworks, no matter how well conceived and applied, cannot lead to eradicating or reducing poverty without an appropriate set of

84 *Report on Extreme Poverty*, n. 81, para. 16.

85 VCLT, art. 31.

86 See, e.g., Chittharanjan Felix Amerasinghe, *Principles of the Institutional Law of International Organizations*, 2nd ed. (Cambridge University Press, 2005), 4, 6; see also David Zaring, "International Institutional Performance in Crisis" (2010) 10 *Chicago Journal of International Law* 475, 476.

substantive rules and normative framework. One of the most common criticisms of international financial institutions is their lack of accountability mechanisms.[87] Yet the usefulness of any accountability mechanism remains dependent on the normative framework against which the institutions are to be held accountable. At best, the institutional settings can facilitate the effective implementation and application of the rules designed to eradicate poverty where these rules themselves are effective. In other words, institutions are only as useful as the norms they are charged with giving effect to. It is in this context that the institutions charged with developing the rules discussed in Section 1.3 are considered.

The first area of international law identified as being relevant for the eradication of poverty is human rights law. The Human Rights Council, a subsidiary organ of the UN General Assembly, has overall responsibility for "promoting universal respect for the protection of all human rights and fundamental freedoms."[88] Under its constitutive resolution, the council is responsible for addressing "situations of violations of human rights" and making "recommendations thereon,"[89] and it is charged with playing a coordinating role within the UN system.[90] It is serviced by the Office of the High Commissioner for Human Rights, which has a broad mandate for the promotion and protection of human rights.[91] The Human Rights Council performs its functions through a number of subsidiary organs, some of which are engaged in processes that may contribute to the achievement of SDG 1. The Working Group on the Right to Development is a prime example. As described in Section 1.3.2.1, the right to development is the composite right of all universal rights and concerned with improving the overall well-being of humans, which is the very essence of SDG 1. The working group itself was established in 1998 with the mandate to promote the right to development. In 2018, the Human Rights Council decided that the Working Group on the Right to Development should "commence the discussion to elaborate a draft legally binding instrument on the right to development."[92] Of course, whether the instrument to be negotiated will have an impact depends on its content – in particular, the levels of ambitions and solidarity exhibited and whether it will be widely ratified.[93]

Special procedures refer to independent human rights experts who report on specific human rights issues and advise the Human Rights Council. Some special

[87] See, e.g., Smita Narula, "The Right to Food: Holding Global Actors Accountable" (2006) 44 *Columbia Journal of Transnational Law* 691.

[88] See UNGA Resolution A/RES/60/251, 15 March 2006, para. 2, which established the Human Rights Council.

[89] *Id.*, para. 3.

[90] *Id.*

[91] See UNGA Resolution A/RES/48/141, 7 January 1994.

[92] See Human Rights Council Resolution 39/9, 25 September 2018. This resolution was adopted by a vote of thirty to twelve, with five abstentions.

[93] See Chimni, n. 79, 260, suggesting that there have been attempts within the Human Rights Council to limit the scope of the right to development.

procedures that are relevant to SDG 1 include the special rapporteurs on the right to development[94] and on the right to food,[95] the independent expert on the effects of foreign debt on the full enjoyment of all human rights, particularly economic, social, and cultural rights,[96] and, most relevant, the special rapporteur on extreme poverty and human rights.[97] Special procedures provide an interesting institutional avenue for normative development because, unlike most other institutions, the experts are constrained by neither political dynamics nor legal instruments. They survey the landscape of law and policy within their mandate. Their reports, and the recommendations contained therein, need not be constrained by the strictures of law, which, as suggested above, are not sufficiently robust for the attainment of SDG 1. Successive special rapporteurs with various mandates have made recommendations, which are not strictly required by law, on how institutions of international economic law can better contribute to the achievement of SDG 1.[98] These special procedures thus provide pathways for increased ambition and innovative approaches that make it possible to advance solidarity.

However, the same flexibility that provides special procedure mandate holders with the freedom to make recommendations that are unconstrained by the strictures of legal rules and the methodology of international law affects the status and value of their outputs. While they are independent, and not constrained, at least not as rigidly, by any particular instrument, their reports and recommendations lack legal status, even if they are used in academic discourse and debate to push the envelope. The recommendations may be taken up by the institutions to which they are directed, such as the WTO or international financial institutions, or they may influence states and either be incorporated into legal instruments or assume legal relevance as subsequent practice under article 31(3) of the VCLT. However, their transition into the legal system depends on the endorsement and action by states or international institutions.

Another subsidiary organ of the Human Rights Council that may contribute to the achievement of SDG 1 is the Intergovernmental Working Group on Transnational Corporations.[99] This working group was established "to elaborate an international legally binding instrument to regulate," in accordance with human

94 See UN Human Rights Council Resolution 33/14, 29 September 2016, para. 14.

95 See Commission for Human Rights Resolution E/CN.4/Res/2000/10, 17 April 2000, para. 10.

96 See Commission on Human Rights Resolution A/HRC/Res/2000/82, 27 April 2000.

97 See Commission on Human Rights Resolution E/CN.4/Res/1988/25, 29 February 1988.

98 See Oloka-Onyango & Udagama, n. 66, paras. 12ff (postulating that the WTO should be subject to international human rights law to make it more responsive to the needs of the poor); see also *Report on Extreme Poverty*, n. 81, especially paras. 65ff (recommending that the IMF adopt a more "ethical framework"); *Report of the Special Rapporteur (Philip Alston) on Extreme Poverty and Human Rights "Climate Change and Poverty,"* Doc. A/HRC/41/39, 17 July 2019, para. 68.

99 Human Rights Council Resolution on Elaboration of an International Legally Binding Instrument on Transnational Corporations and Other Business Enterprises with Respect to Human Rights, Doc. A/HRC/RES/26/9, 14 July 2014.

rights law, "the activities of transnational corporations and other business enterprises."[100] Transnational corporations have been accused of operating in resource-rich developing states, exploiting the resources for profit with little regard for the human rights of the population – particularly, their socioeconomic rights.[101] Establishing obligations for private entities to fulfill socioeconomic rights as they benefit from the resource-rich, but economically poor, states would be an important element in achieving SDG 1. Whether this materializes will depend on the ambition of the instrument and on whether it will be widely ratified, including by the home states of the entities being regulated.

Bodies charged with interpreting human rights instruments – both universal and regional – also have the potential to contribute to the achievement of SDG 1. These bodies include judicial bodies, such as the African Court on Human and Peoples' Rights, the European Court of Human Rights, and the Inter-American Court of Human Rights, and quasi-judicial human rights monitoring bodies, such as the UN Human Rights Committee and the UN Committee on Economic, Social and Cultural Rights (CESCR). They can contribute to the achievement of SDG 1 by interpreting the rights related to the eradication of poverty in an expansive manner, as discussed in Section 1.2. This applies both to the content of the rights, which impacts on ambition, and to their territorial scope, which affects solidarity. Yet their findings are governed and constrained by the rules of interpretation. Moreover, the interpretive authority of quasi-judicial bodies is dependent on the readiness of states to adopt their interpretation as subsequent practice under article 31(3)(b) of the VCLT.[102]

1.4.2 *International Economic Institutions*

International economic law too has institutions that could potentially contribute to the eradication of poverty. As a matter of rhetoric, international financial institutions have committed themselves to contributing toward meeting the SDGs and, in particular, SDG 1.[103] These institutions include the members of the World Bank Group, the IMF, and the WTO, and they have come under severe criticism for their

[100] *Id.*, para. 1.

[101] Beth Stephens, "The Amorality of Profit: Transnational Corporations and Human Rights" (2002) 20 *Berkeley Journal of International Law* 70; Alison Shinsato, "Increasing the Accountability of Transactional Corporations for Environmental Harms: The Petroleum Industry in Nigeria" (2005) 4 *Northwestern Journal of International Human Rights* 195; Sigrun Skogly, "Economic and Social Human Rights, Private Actors and International Obligations," in Michael Addo (ed.), *Human Rights Standards and the Responsibility of Transnational Corporations* (Kluwer, 1999), 239.

[102] See "Draft Conclusion 13 of the 2018 ILC Draft Conclusion on Subsequent Agreements and Subsequent Practice in the Interpretation of Treaties," Doc. A/73/10, in *Yearbook of the International Law Commission*, vol. 2, part 2 (International Law Commission, 2018).

[103] See Suresh Nanwani, "SDGs and the Role of International Financial Institutions," in Julia Walker, Alma Pekmezovic, & Gordon Walker (eds.), *Sustainable Development Goals:*

unwillingness to contribute positively toward poverty reduction.[104] While many of these criticisms are normative in nature,[105] there are also many institutional concerns about equity in decision-making in these bodies. These concerns relate to the applicable decision-making procedures in financial institutions where participation in decision-making is based on financial contribution and developing states are not afforded an equitable role.[106] It has also been observed that "wealthy countries ... have been able to coordinate their interests more easily through a variety of international economic legal and semi-legal entities" than poorer states.[107]

Institutions themselves tend to be restricted by the constituent instruments and the states that created them.[108] This militates against the possibility of innovative solutions to address poverty reduction. Action, whether in the form of litigation before courts or complaints before quasi-judicial bodies, might provide a pathway to developing international law in a way that makes it more responsive to poverty concerns. The Inspection Panel of the World Bank is an example of an internal forum, established by the World Bank, with the mandate to hear and make determinations on complaints by members of society affected by the activities of the World Bank.[109] However, the Inspection Panel is limited in its mandate to consider harm caused by the "failure of the Bank to follow its *operational policies and procedures*" in relation to bank-financed projects.[110] It is these operational policies and procedures, and not the broad objective of poverty eradication, that the panel applies in assessing the World Bank's performance.[111]

Harnessing Business to Achieve the SDGs through Finance, Technology, and Law Reform (Wiley, 2019), 37, 38.

104 See, e.g., Rich, n. 75; Chossudovsky, n. 75; Horta, n. 75; Ochoa, n. 75.

105 See Tladi, "Sombre Reflections," n. 76; Tladi, "IMF Conditionality," n. 76. See also Genoneva Hernandez Uriz, "To Lend or Not to Lend: Oil, Human Rights, and the World Bank's Internal Contradictions" (2001) 14 *Harvard Human Rights Journal* 197, 197.

106 See Anghie, n. 76; see also Armin von Bogdandy, Phillip Dann & Matthias Goldmann, "Developing the Publicness of Public International Law: Towards a Legal Framework for Global Governance Activities," in Armin von Bogdandy et al. (eds.), *The Exercise of Public Authority by International Institutions: Advancing International Law* (Springer, 2010), 3, 8.

107 David Zaring, "International Institutional Performance in Crisis" (2010) 10 *Chicago Journal of International Law* 475, 478. An example of the outcome of such institutional coordination is the Group of 20 (G-20). A forum of twenty states made up of mainly developed states with Argentina, Brazil, India, and Indonesia, the G-20 self-describes as "the premier forum for international cooperation" in which "leaders of the largest economies of the world ...discuss financial and socioeconomic issues." See G-20 website, g20.org/en/about/Pages/default.aspx.

108 Henry Schemers & Niels Blokker, *International Institutions Law: Unity within Diversity*, 5th ed. (Martinus Nijhoff, 2011), 15.

109 See para. 12 of the identical 1993 resolutions of the International Bank for Reconstruction and Development and the International Development Association (Resolution no. IBRD 93-10 and Resolution no. IDA 93-6).

110 *Id.* (emphasis added).

111 For a detailed discussion, see Tladi, "Sombre Reflections," n. 76, where both the operational policies and procedures, as well as the inspection panel's assessment of these in particular complaints are addressed.

However, there is room for greater synergy between instruments from different areas of international law and cross-fertilization, including through the principle of systemic integration. Both the World Bank and the panel could consider socio-economic rights instruments, in interpreting and applying the Articles of Agreement and the operational policies and procedures in a manner that contributes to the achievement of SDG 1. Relying on human rights – in particular, socioeconomic rights and the right to development – in the interpretation of the World Bank's instruments would be in line with the fact that the World Bank has adopted its twin objectives: ending extreme poverty and boosting prosperity.[112] This same reasoning can be applied by other institutions of international economic law, to the extent that their instruments permit. For example, as discussed above, the WTO Agreement proclaims in its preamble that raising the standard of living is an objective of the organization. This wording permits its institutions, including the panels and the Appellate Body, to integrate socioeconomic rights into their decision-making in order to contribute to the achievement of SDG 1.[113]

There is therefore significant room for the institutions of international economic law, in interpreting and applying the rules of their institutions, to reach into other areas of international law – in particular, human rights law – in order to enhance the ability of international economic law to contribute to the achievement of SDG 1 and, indeed, all SDGs. Doing so, however, would not obviate the need for states to be more ambitious and conscious of the need to advance solidarity when making and developing the substantive rules of international law.

1.5 CONCLUSIONS

The SDGs set out the policy objective of the United Nations to make our world a better place for all who live in it. The SDGs are not a set of rules of international law. SDG 1 does not set forth a rule to eradicate poverty. Indeed, such an obligation does not exist under international law. International law, as a system, is not geared toward the eradication of poverty.[114] This was illustrated through an overview of the areas most closely related to poverty eradication – namely, international human rights and economic law. The human rights most closely associated with the eradication of poverty– socioeconomic rights – are subject to a number of qualifiers. Moreover, reflective of the general posture of international law, these human rights, in a practical way, do not exhibit a shared responsibility or solidarity, which undermines international law's ability to fight poverty. Similarly, international

[112] VCLT, art. 31, includes the object and purpose of a treaty amongst the main elements of treaty interpretation.

[113] See, e.g., Dommen, n. 58, 121.

[114] It has been argued that international law is designed to perpetuate the existing patterns of inequality and, thus, poverty. See generally B.S. Chimni, "Third World Approaches to international Law: A Manifesto" (2006) 8 *International Community Law Review* 3, 3.

economic law has been at the receiving end of some harsh criticism for, at best, its failure to contribute to poverty eradication and, at worst, its contribution to the increase of poverty. If international law is to contribute toward poverty eradication, a major recalibration is required.

The question that this chapter has sought to address is whether SDG 1 could be the impetus for recalibrating international law in support of poverty eradication. To contribute to advancing the rules of international law on poverty eradication would depend on the ambition of SDG 1, in terms of content, and on the extent to which it promotes solidarity. While the overall objective of SDG 1 is highly ambitious and couched in absolutist terms, the individual targets for its achievement lack the same absolutist character. Yet, even though these targets do not show an absolutist ambition, they are still, as far as content goes, more ambitious than current rules of international law and could contribute to the improvement of international law if they are taken into account in the making, molding, and interpretation of international law.

2

SDG 2: End Hunger, Achieve Food Security and Improved Nutrition and Promote Sustainable Agriculture

Carmen G. Gonzalez

ABSTRACT

This chapter examines the relationship between Sustainable Development Goal (SDG) 2, Zero Hunger, and international law. It argues that SDG 2 is supported by international human rights law. However, international economic law (trade, investment, finance) impedes the achievement of SDG 2 by undermining the livelihoods of small farmers and restricting the ability of states to regulate in the public interest. When these bodies of law conflict, international economic law generally prevails as a consequence of the powerful mechanisms through which it is enforced, including the World Trade Organization's dispute settlement system, investor-state arbitration under international investment agreements, and the loan conditionalities imposed by the International Monetary Fund and the World Bank.

KEYWORDS

SDG 2, hunger, right to food, structural adjustment, trade liberalization, IMF, World Bank, World Trade Organization, international investment agreements, food security, sustainable agriculture

2.1 INTRODUCTION

Sustainable Development Goal (SDG) 2, Zero Hunger, seeks to address the problem of world hunger and to promote sustainable agriculture. Despite ample food production at the global level, the UN Food and Agriculture Organization (FAO) reports that over 2 billion people did not have regular access to safe, nutritious, and sufficient food in 2019.[1] In 2020, the COVID-19 pandemic aggravated food insecurity by disrupting food supply chains, driving more people into poverty, and curtailing the purchasing power of consumers.[2] The FAO also acknowledges that the world is not on track to meet the targets of SDG 2 on plant and animal diversity that are vital to sustainable agriculture.[3] The rapid expansion of industrial agriculture in the aftermath of the Second World War has produced a worldwide decline in both wild and cultivated animal and plant species.[4] In 2019, the Intergovernmental Science-Policy Platform on Biodiversity and Ecosystem Services concluded that the loss of local varieties and breeds of domesticated plants and animals, including genetic diversity, "poses a serious risk to global food security by undermining the resilience of many agricultural systems to threats such as pests, pathogens, and climate change."[5]

Food insecurity is a function of poverty rather than food scarcity.[6] Although the world's population is anticipated to reach 9.7 billion in 2050,[7] the global food system produces sufficient food to feed 12–14 billion people.[8] However, people who live in poverty, most of whom are small farmers in Asia, Africa, and Latin America (the global South), do not earn sufficient income or possess sufficient land to purchase or grow the food they need.[9] These small-scale farmers are also the custodians of the planet's diverse plant and animal species.[10] Consequently, protecting the livelihoods

1 FAO et al., *The State of Food Insecurity and Nutrition in the World 2020: Transforming Food Systems for Affordable, Healthy Diets* (FAO, 2020), viii.

2 See generally Global Network against Food Crises & Food Security Information Network, 2020 *Global Report on Food Crises*, 2020, docs.wfp.org/api/documents/WFP-0000114546/download/?_ga=2.245386820.1387951072.1590272575-1372614706.1590272575.

3 FAO, *Tracking Progress on Food and Agriculture-related SDGs Indicators*, 2019, 12–15, www.fao.org/fileadmin/templates/SDG-progress-report/2019-final/sdg-progress-report-print.pdf.

4 Christopher M. Piccone & David Van Tassel, "Agriculture and Biodiversity Loss: Industrial Agriculture," in Niles Eldredge (ed.), *Life on Earth: An Encyclopedia of Biodiversity, Ecology, and Evolution* (ABC-Clio, 2002), 100.

5 Intergovernmental Science-Policy Platform on Biodiversity and Ecosystem Services (IPBES), *Summary for Policymakers of the Global Assessment Report on Biodiversity and Ecosystem Services of IPBES*, 6 May 2019, 12, para. A.6, ipbes.net/sites/default/files/2020-02/ipbes_global_assessment_report_summary_for_policymakers_en.pdf.

6 See generally Amartya Sen, *Poverty and Famines: An Essay on Entitlement and Deprivation* (Oxford University Press, 1990); Olivier de Schutter, "International Trade in Agriculture and the Right to Food," Friedrich-Ebert-Stiftung Occasional Paper no. 64, 2009, 10.

7 UN Department of Social and Economic Affairs, *World Population Prospects 2019: Highlights*, 2019, www.un.org/development/desa/publications/world-population-prospects-2019-highlights.html.

8 UNCTAD, *Trade and Environment Review 2013, Wake Up before It's Too Late: Make Agriculture Truly Sustainable Now for Food Security in a Changing Climate*, 2013, 2, unctad.org/en/PublicationsLibrary/ditcted2012d3_en.pdf.

9 Carmen G. Gonzalez, "Institutionalizing Inequality: The WTO Agreement on Agriculture, Food Security, and Developing Countries" (2002) 27 *Columbia Journal of Environmental Law* 431, 444.

10 Miguel Altieri, "Linking Ecologists and Traditional Farmers in the Search for Sustainable Agriculture" (2004) 2 *Frontiers in Ecology and the Environment* 35, 35–36.

of small farmers is essential to the achievement of both the food security and agro-biodiversity objectives of SDG 2.

While many areas of international law are relevant to SDG 2, there is no coherent body of international law governing food and agriculture. This chapter will focus on international human rights law and international economic law because these have the greatest bearing on the realization of SDG 2. The chapter argues that SDG 2 is supported by international human rights law. However, international economic law (trade, investment, finance) impedes the achievement of SDG 2 by exacerbating poverty, facilitating the expulsion of farmers from their lands, and promoting chemical-intensive, greenhouse gas-emitting industrial agriculture. When these bodies of law conflict, international economic law generally prevails as a consequence of the powerful mechanisms through which it is enforced, including the World Trade Organization's (WTO) dispute settlement system and investor-state arbitration under international investment agreements (IIAs). This chapter does not discuss international environmental law, including climate and biodiversity law, because these are addressed elsewhere in this volume and because international environmental law's fragmented regulatory interventions have been eclipsed by the threats to sustainable agriculture posed by the international trade, finance, and investment regimes.[11]

2.2 THE CONTENT OF SDG 2 IN THE CONTEXT OF THE OTHER SDGS

The targets designed to achieve SDG 2 by 2030 seek to end hunger and ensure access to safe, nutritious, and sufficient food (target 2.1) and to double the agricultural productivity and incomes of small-scale farmers, including through secure and equal access to land and other productive resources and inputs (target 2.3). Target 2.4 requires states to promote sustainable food production systems that strengthen the capacity to adapt to climate change and enhance land and soil quality. Target 2.5 seeks to promote the genetic diversity of seeds, plants, and animals and their related wild species.

There are numerous synergies between SDG 2 and other SDGs. Because food insecurity is a function of poverty, the achievement of SDG 2 depends, in large measure, on progress toward SDG 1, No Poverty. Because food production requires a healthy environment, SDG 2 also depends on the protection of marine and terrestrial ecosystems (SDG 14, Life below Water, and SDG 15, Life on Land) and on action to combat climate change (SDG 13, Climate Action). SDG 5, Gender

[11] Carmen G. Gonzalez, "Global Justice in the Anthropocene," in Louis Kotzé (ed.), *Environmental Law and Governance for the Anthropocene* (Hart Publishing, 2017), 229; Saverio di Benedetto, "Agriculture and the Environment in International Law: Towards a New Legal Paradigm," in Massimo Monteduro et al. (eds.), *Law and Agroecology: A Transdisciplinary Dialogue* (Springer, 2015), 99, 113–18 (discussing the absence of a coherent body of environmental law related to agriculture).

Equality, is important to the achievement of SDG 2 because women produce 50 percent of the world's food and bear primary responsibility for its cooking and preparation.[12] Rural women, many of whom constitute the heads of households, are particularly vulnerable to food insecurity because they own only 2 percent of agricultural land and frequently face gender discrimination that limits their access to financing and technical assistance as well as their ability to participate in decision-making regarding land use.[13] Similarly, SDG 10, Reduced Inequalities, is essential to the attainment of SDG 2 because food insecurity is concentrated in poverty-stricken agriculture-dependent countries, especially among women, small-scale farmers, and Indigenous peoples.[14] Without attaining SDG 2, it is difficult to imagine the fulfillment of SDG 16, Peace, Justice, and Strong Institutions, because food shortages have frequently triggered violent upheaval.[15] Finally, SDG 17, Partnerships for the Goals, is indispensable to the fulfillment of SDG 2 because food insecurity is a global problem that cannot be resolved without international cooperation.

However, there are also tensions and inconsistencies within and among the SDGs. The SDGs, including SDG 2, "fail to reconcile the contradiction between growth and sustainability at the core of sustainable development."[16] For example, SDG 8, Decent Work and Economic Growth, and SDG 10 are premised on a physical impossibility: unlimited economic growth on a finite planet.[17] Target 8.1 calls for "at least 7 percent gross domestic product growth per annum in the least developed countries." Target 10.1 seeks to "progressively achieve and sustain income growth of the bottom 40 percent of the population at a higher rate than the national average." However, the SDGs do not address the logical corollary – the need to reduce economic growth in affluent countries (the global North) in order to avoid exceeding ecological limits. On the contrary, target 8.2 calls for higher levels of economic productivity everywhere, and target 8.4 merely encourages states to decouple economic growth from environmental degradation. Studies using historical data and modeling projections to assess the feasibility of decoupling the growth of gross domestic production from environmental impact have concluded that it is

[12] UN General Assembly (UNGA), *Interim Report of the Special Rapporteur on the Right to Food*, UN Doc. A/70/287, 5 August 2015, para. 35.

[13] *Id.*, paras. 35–36.

[14] UNGA, n. 12, paras. 29–40.

[15] Robin McKie & Heather Stewart, "Hunger. Strikes. Riots. The Food Crisis Bites," *The Guardian*, 12 April 2008.

[16] Sam Adelman, "The Sustainable Development Goals, Anthropocentrism and Neoliberalism," in Duncan French & Louis Kotzé (eds.), *Global Goals: Law, Theory and Implementation* (EE, 2018), 15, 34.

[17] Ruth Gordon, "Unsustainable Development," in Shawkat Alam et al. (eds.), *International Environmental Law and the Global South* (Cambridge University Press, 2015), 50, 68; Haydn Washington, *Demystifying Sustainability: Towards Real Solutions* (Routledge, 2015), 36.

"misleading to develop growth-oriented policy around the expectation that decoupling is possible."[18]

This growth-based approach to poverty and inequality is also evident in SDG 2. SDG 2 seeks to end hunger, achieve food security, and promote sustainable agriculture by doubling the agricultural productivity and income of small-scale food producers (target 2.3) and by increasing agricultural productivity and production everywhere (target 2.4). This emphasis on increasing production threatens to entrench environmentally destructive industrial agriculture and appears to erroneously attribute food insecurity to food scarcity rather than lack of access to land, remunerative employment, and social safety nets.

As explained more fully in the next section, an approach to food security grounded in international human rights law would protect vulnerable groups (such as small farmers) by challenging the laws and institutions that have deprived them of income, land, and food instead of single-mindedly seeking to increase food production. To the extent that the SDGs call for the intensification of the same laws and policies that have disenfranchised rural communities, they may exacerbate rather than eliminate food insecurity.

2.3 POSITIONING SDG 2 IN INTERNATIONAL LAW

2.3.1 *The Historic Roots of Hunger and Unsustainable Agriculture*

An analysis of the underlying causes of hunger and ecologically unsustainable farming practices must necessarily begin with colonialism. From the colonial period until the Second World War, European states achieved a standard of living far beyond the limits of their natural resource base by plundering the natural wealth of their colonies.[19] European colonizers shifted vast tracts of land in Africa, Asia, and the Americas from food production to cash crop production and constructed roads and railways to transport these commodities from the interior to the coast instead of facilitating regional trade.[20] After achieving political independence, Southern states were integrated into the global economy on disadvantageous terms as producers of primary products and consumers of Euro-American manufactured goods.[21] This agro-export specialization subjected them to the volatility of agricultural commodity prices (including boom-and-bust cycles) and balance of payments difficulties caused

[18] James D. Ward et al., "Is Decoupling GDP Growth from Environmental Impact Possible?" (2016) 11(10) *PLoS One* 10, 14.

[19] Liz Young, *World Hunger* (Routledge, 1997), 41–42.

[20] Peter Robbins, *Stolen Fruit: The Tropical Commodities Disaster* (Zed Books, 2003), 25–26.

[21] Young, n. 19, 41–42.

by low prices for exported agricultural products and high prices for imported manufactured goods.[22]

In the decades following the Second World War, the United States and Western European states provided generous subsidies to their agricultural producers to ensure an adequate supply of food and imposed both tariff and nontariff import barriers to protect them from foreign competition.[23] These practices were permitted under the 1947 General Agreement on Tariffs and Trade (GATT), which largely exempted agriculture from its trade liberalization requirements.[24] When these agricultural subsidies resulted in overproduction, the United States and Western Europe exported their surplus food to the global South free of charge as food aid or sold it at reduced prices.[25] The export of surplus food enabled Northern grain traders to establish a foothold in the global South, but it also depressed food prices in Southern countries and undermined the livelihoods of small farmers.[26] Many small farmers lost their lands, swelling the ranks of landless rural workers and causing wages for agricultural labor to decline.[27] Prime agricultural lands became concentrated in the hands of affluent farmers, who produced coffee, cocoa, beef, vegetables, bananas, and feed grains for export rather than for domestic consumption.[28] Food production stagnated, and countries that were once net food exporters gradually became dependent on imported food.[29]

In the 1960s and 1970s, during the height of the Cold War, the United States sought to alleviate chronic malnourishment in the global South and prevent communist revolutions by exporting not just food but also the industrial agricultural model, including new high-yielding seeds, fossil fuel–based pesticides and fertilizers, and machinery.[30] Known as the Green Revolution, this industrial agricultural model increased global food production but displaced ecologically sustainable agricultural practices and fostered dependence on agricultural inputs manufactured by Western transnational corporations.[31] While the Green Revolution enabled food

22 *Id.*; Clive Ponting, *A New Green History of the World: The Environment and the Collapse of Great Civilizations* (Penguin Books, 2007), 186–88; Carmen G. Gonzalez, "Trade Liberalization, Food Security, and the Environment: The Neoliberal Threat to Sustainable Rural Development" (2004) 14 *Transnational Law and Contemporary Problems* 419, 434–35.

23 Terence P. Stewart (ed.), *The GATT Uruguay Round: A Negotiating History (1986–1992)* (Kluwer Law, 1993), 125, 141, 155–56; M. Ataman Aksoy, "Global Agricultural Trade Policies," in M. A. Aksoy & John C. Beghin (eds.), *Global Agricultural Trade and Developing Countries* (World Bank, 2005), 37.

24 Gonzalez, n. 9, 438.

25 Jennifer Clapp, *Food* (Polity Press, 2012), 26–33.

26 James Wessel, *Trading the Future: Farm Exports and the Concentration of Economic Power in Our Food System* (Institute for Food and Development Policy, 1983), 153–55, 168.

27 *Id.*, 166–68.

28 *Id.*, 167.

29 *Id.*, 166.

30 Clapp, n. 25, 33.

31 Cary Fowler & Pat Mooney, *Shattering: Food, Politics, and the Loss of Genetic Diversity* (University of Arizona Press, 1990), 54–79.

production to outpace population growth, it also increased rural inequality by benefiting the large farmers who could afford the agricultural machinery, irrigation systems, and other expensive inputs.[32] When rising food production caused prices to plummet, many small farmers were rendered destitute and landless.[33] An influential study analyzing over three hundred published reports on the Green Revolution concluded that the Green Revolution generally exacerbated rural inequality.[34] The primary beneficiaries of food aid and of the rapid industrialization of agriculture in the global South were the US and European industrial farmers, grain traders, and input manufacturers who received generous government subsidies, access to new consumer markets in Southern countries, and the opportunity to supply these markets with machinery, pesticides, fertilizers, and seeds.[35]

The transition to industrial agriculture also generated a variety of negative environmental consequences that currently threaten food production, including a dramatic worldwide decline in crop genetic diversity, dependence on fossil fuel–based inputs, massive soil erosion, the depletion of aquifers, and rising greenhouse gas emissions.[36] Approximately 75 percent of the planet's food crop diversity was lost in the twentieth century as farmers ceased to cultivate an assortment of local crops in favor of the genetically uniform, high-yielding varieties of corn, wheat, rice, and potato introduced by the Green Revolution.[37] This loss of genetic diversity increased the vulnerability of the global food system to drought, floods, pests, and other external shocks, including those associated with climate change.[38] Thus, the achievement of SDG 2, including food security and sustainable agriculture, will require enhancing the livelihoods of small farmers in the global South and promoting environmentally friendly cultivation practices. The following subsections examine the role of international law in achieving these goals.

2.3.2 *Human Rights Law and the Right to Food*

The SDGs are grounded, at least implicitly, in human rights law. The UN General Assembly Resolution adopting the Sustainable Development Agenda calls for

32 Clapp, n. 25, 38–41; Vandana Shiva, *The Violence of the Green Revolution* (Zed Books, 1991), 176–77.

33 Shiva, n. 32, 177; Keith Griffin, *The Political Economy of Agrarian Change: An Essay on the Green Revolution* (Harvard University Press, 1974), 73.

34 Douglas K. Freebairn, "Did the Green Revolution Concentrate Incomes? A Qualitative Study of Research Reports" (1995) 23 *World Development* 265, 277.

35 Clapp, n. 25, 32–33; Harriet Friedmann, "From Colonialism to Green Capitalism: Social Movements and Emergence of Food Regimes" (2005) 22 *Research in Rural Sociology* 227, 243.

36 Jules N. Pretty, *Regenerating Agriculture: Policies and Practices for Sustainability and Self-Reliance* (Joseph Henry Books, 1995), 58–80; Fredercik Kirschenmann, "Do Increased Energy Costs Offer Opportunities for a New Agriculture," in Fred Magdoff & Brian Tokar (eds.), *Agriculture and Food in Crisis* (Monthly Review Press, 2010), 227.

37 Pretty, n. 36, 93.

38 Fowler & Mooney, n. 31, 42–46.

"a world of universal respect for human rights and human dignity . . . in which the needs of the most vulnerable are met."[39] The right to food is recognized in article 25 of the 1948 Universal Declaration of Human Rights and is addressed in a more comprehensive manner in article 11 of the 1966 International Covenant on Economic, Social and Cultural Rights (ICESCR), which requires states to take measures individually and through international cooperation to ensure the realization of the right to adequate food and freedom from hunger. The right to food is also protected through article 6(1) of the 1966 International Covenant on Civil and Political Rights, which guarantees the right to life and has been interpreted to require the implementation of affirmative measures to eliminate chronic undernourishment.[40] Additional human rights instruments affirm the right to food of specific groups, including women,[41] children,[42] persons with disabilities,[43] and peasants and rural workers.[44] Finally, the 1989 International Labour Organization's Convention no. 169 Concerning Indigenous and Tribal Peoples in Independent Countries and the 2018 UN Declaration on the Rights of Indigenous Peoples indirectly protect the right to food of Indigenous peoples by recognizing their rights to lands, natural resources, and the conservation and protection of the environment.[45] The 2018 UN Declaration on the Rights of Peasants and Other People Working in Rural Areas, which explicitly recognizes the right to food, also protects the lands, natural resources, and environment of small-scale agricultural producers.[46]

In order to provide authoritative guidance on the right to food under the ICESCR, the UN Committee on Economic Social and Cultural Rights published General Comment 12, which clarifies the obligations of states to respect, protect, and fulfill this right. First, states must respect the right to food by "not taking any measures that result in preventing such access."[47] In other words, states must consider the impact of legislation, regulations, and treaties on the right to food and must refrain from actions that interfere with the ability of communities and

39 *Transforming Our World: The 2030 Agenda for Sustainable Development*, UN Doc. A/Res/70/1, 15 September 2015, preamble, para. 8.

40 Office of the High Commissioner for Human Rights, *General Comment 6: The Right to Life*, UN Doc. HRI/GEN/REV.8, 8 May 2006, 166, para. 5

41 1997 Convention on the Elimination of All Forms of Discrimination against Women, arts. 12, 14.2.

42 1989 Convention on the Rights of the Child, art. 24.

43 2006 Convention on the Rights of Persons with Disabilities, art. 28.

44 2018 UN Declaration on the Rights of Peasants and Other People Working in Rural Areas, art. 15.

45 Arts 13, 19; see also 2007 UN Declaration on the Rights of Indigenous Peoples, arts. 26–29.

46 Arts 5, 17, 18.

47 Committee on Economic Social and Cultural Rights (CESCR), *General Comment 12: The Right to Adequate Food*, UN Doc. E/C.12/1999/5, 12 May 1999, para. 15.

individuals to feed themselves.[48] Second, General Comment 12 requires states to protect the right to food by implementing measures "to ensure that enterprises or individuals do not deprive individuals of their access to adequate food."[49] In other words, states should prevent third parties (such as local elites and foreign corporations) from depriving vulnerable populations of access to land, water, and other inputs necessary to grow food and should prevent the degradation of ecosystem services that support agricultural production.[50] Third, states must fulfill the right to food by providing food directly "whenever an individual or group is unable, for reasons beyond their control, to enjoy the right to adequate food by the means at their disposal."[51] States must also facilitate the right to food by enhancing the livelihoods of food-insecure populations through social safety nets and other assistance programs.[52]

Finally, states have a duty to cooperate to realize the right to food. Articles 1, 55, and 56 of the 1945 Charter of the United Nations (UN Charter) require states to take joint and separate action in cooperation with the United Nations to promote human rights and fundamental freedoms. Article 11 of the ICESCR specifically requires states to cooperate to achieve the right to adequate food and "to ensure an equitable distribution of world food supplies in relation to need."[53] While SDG 2 is generally congruent with international human rights law, there is a tension between human rights law and targets 2.3 and 2.4 that emphasize increasing agricultural production. As the former UN special rapporteur on the right to food observes,

> [a] human rights-based approach to food security is contrary to the conventional, economist view that is primarily preoccupied by food production. The conventional approach focuses on interventions and services to meet human needs and often regards beneficiaries as passive recipients of acts of generosity or charity. ... The right to food requires that states provide an enabling environment in which people can produce food for themselves or are able to purchase food for them[selves] and their families.[54]

In other words, a human rights–based approach seeks to empower food-insecure populations and to overcome the structural barriers that impede access to food, including the lack of secure land rights, employment, and social safety nets. A conventional economic or productivist approach operates on the false premise

[48] Nadia C.S. Lambek, "Respecting and Protecting the Right to Food: When States Must Get Out of the Kitchen," in Nadia C.S. Lambek et al. (eds.), *Rethinking Food Systems: Structural Challenges, New Strategies, and the Law* (Springer, 2014), 108.

[49] CESCR, n. 47, para. 15.

[50] Lambek, n. 48, 109–10.

[51] CESCR, n. 47, para. 15.

[52] Lambek, n. 48, 110.

[53] Art. 11(2)(b).

[54] Hilal Elver, "Human Rights Based Approach to Sustainable Agricultural Policies and Food Security," in Harald Ginsky et al. (eds.), *International Yearbook of Soil Law and Policy 2018* (Springer, 2019), 347, 363.

that there is insufficient food to feed the world's population and emphasizes the need to increase food production, often through ecologically unsustainable industrial means. In general, SDG 2 appears to embrace a human rights approach, but targets 2.3 and 2.4 suggest that the productivist approach has not been fully abandoned.

2.3.3 *International Economic Law and the Right to Food*

International economic law stands as an obstacle to the realization of the right to food and SDG 2: "[T]he routine operation of international economic life, organized around global value chains, free trade, and open markets, produces a system of compulsion such that food is exported to foreign lands, while the people who grow it are undernourished."[55] This subsection examines the ways in which international economic law has undermined the livelihoods of small farmers, promoted industrial agriculture, and frustrated the right to food.

2.3.3.1 International Finance and Trade Law

An account of contemporary economic law must necessarily begin with the two Bretton Woods institutions that established the legal architecture for contemporary globalization. Created by treaty when most of the world's population was still under colonial domination, the World Bank and the International Monetary Fund (IMF) were designed to coordinate international monetary and financial matters.[56] Both institutions are governed by articles of agreement that give greater decision-making authority to affluent nations by providing for weighted voting based on the financial contributions of their members.[57] Both institutions have provided loans to the global South subject to various "conditionalities" that required debtor states to adopt a variety of free market reforms.[58] As noted previously, an additional post–Second World War legal agreement – the 1947 GATT – inaugurated a new economic order committed (at least rhetorically) to free trade but generally exempted agriculture from its trade liberalization commitments due to postwar concerns about ensuring an adequate food supply.[59]

[55] Anne Orford, "Food Security, Free Trade, and the Battle for the State" (2015) 11 *Journal of International Law and International Relations* 1, 16.

[56] Antony Anghie, *Imperialism, Sovereignty and the Making of International Law* (Cambridge University Press, 2004), 258.

[57] World Bank Articles of Agreement, 2012, art. V, s. 3; IMF Articles of Agreement, 2020, art. XII, s. 5.

[58] Anghie, n. 56, 258–59.

[59] Orford, n. 55, 51–53. For a detailed discussion of the provisions of the 1947 General Agreement on Tariffs and Trade and country-specific waivers that exempted agriculture from the agreement's trade liberalization commitments, see Gonzalez, n. 9, 441–45; Joseph A. McMahon & Melaku Geboye Desta (eds.), *Research Handbook on the WTO Agriculture Agreement*

The US and European agricultural subsidies authorized by the 1947 GATT devastated peasant and small-scale farming in the global South by producing food surpluses that were exported to Southern states as food aid or dumped on global markets at low prices.[60] In the 1960s and 1970s, Southern governments could protect rural livelihoods by imposing both tariff and nontariff import barriers on these imported food products.[61] This policy space was eroded in the 1980s as a consequence of the loan conditionalities imposed by the IMF and the World Bank in response to the sovereign debt crisis. To secure loan repayment assistance from the IMF and the World Bank, countries in the global South acceded to loan agreements that required them to adopt a standard package of neoliberal economic reforms, known as structural adjustment[62] The power of the IMF to impose conditions on borrowing states is derived from its Articles of Agreement, which authorize lending by the IMF to member states "under adequate safeguards, thus providing them with opportunity to correct maladjustments in their balance of payments without resorting to measures destructive of national or international prosperity."[63] The World Bank's Articles of Agreement likewise authorize loans "on suitable conditions."[64] The resulting loan agreements, once approved by the debtor country under its laws, are regarded as binding international agreements.[65]

The structural adjustment programs (SAPs) mandated by the IMF and the World Bank created double standards that afflict international agricultural trade to this day: protectionism in wealthy countries and relatively open markets in poor countries.[66] These SAPs required Southern countries to lower tariffs, eliminate nontariff import barriers, devalue their currencies to make exports more competitive, and slash government subsidies to the agricultural sector.[67] US and European agricultural

(EE, 2012), 1; Joseph A. McMahom, *The WTO Agreement on Agriculture: A Commentary* (Oxford University Press, 2006), 2–5.

60 Clapp, n. 25, 26–33.

61 Carmen G. Gonzalez, "World Poverty and Food Insecurity" (2015) 3 *Pennsylvania State Journal of Law and International Affairs* 56, 61.

62 Richard Peet, *Unholy Trinity: The IMF, World Bank and WTO*, 2nd ed. (Zed Books, 2010) 84–99, 141–45.

63 IMF Articles of Agreement, art I(v); Sundhya Pahuja, "Technologies of Empire: IMF Conditionality and the Reinscription of the North/South Divide" (2000) 13 *Leiden Journal of International Law* 749, 758. For an explanation of how the legal instruments through which these safeguards (known as IMF conditionality) are imposed, see IMF, *Fact Sheet, IMF Conditionality*, 22 February 2021, www.imf.org/en/About/Factsheets/Sheets/2016/08/02/21/28/IMF-Conditionality.

64 World Bank Articles of Agreement, art. I(ii).

65 Nicholas Kremmydas, "The Cross-Conditionality Phenomenon: Some Legal Aspects" (1989) 23 *International Lawyer* 651, 665–66.

66 Carmen G. Gonzalez, "Markets, Monoculture, and Malnutrition: Agricultural Trade Policy through an Environmental Justice Lens" (2006) 14 *Michigan State Journal of International Law* 345, 362–68.

67 Michael Chossudovsky, *The Globalisation of Poverty: Impacts of the IMF and World Bank Reforms* (Zed Books, 1997), 62–63; John Madeley, *Hungry for Trade: How the Poor Pay for Free Trade* (St. Martin's Press, 2000), 77.

producers, however, continued to receive generous agricultural subsidies from their governments and benefited from the opening of additional export markets in the global South.[68]

The reduction of government assistance to small farmers in the global South, coupled with the elimination of import barriers, devastated rural livelihoods and increased food insecurity by putting resource-poor small-scale farmers in direct competition with highly subsidized agricultural producers from Europe and the United States.[69] As cheap food imports flooded Southern markets, waves of small farmers abandoned agricultural production and migrated to urban slums.[70] In order to comply with IMF loan conditionalities that mandated increases in exports to service the foreign debt, land that was once used to cultivate food for the domestic market was diverted to the chemical-intensive cultivation of cash crops, increasing dependence on imported food and intensifying the environmental damage caused by industrial agriculture, including the loss of agro-biodiversity and runoff of pesticides and fertilizers into lakes and rivers.[71]

Another legal instrument, the 1994 WTO Agreement on Agriculture (AoA), which entered into force in 1995, purported to mitigate the double standards in global agricultural trade by requiring WTO members to reduce trade-distorting agricultural subsidies (including both domestic subsidies and export subsidies), convert all import barriers to tariffs (a process known as "tariffication"), and reduce these tariffs over time.[72] The AoA permitted countries that used domestic subsidies and export subsidies to continue to do so (subject to reduction over time), while prohibiting the introduction of new subsidies.[73] The AoA entrenched the double standards in international agricultural trade by failing to curb Northern domestic and export subsidies. Northern countries evaded the obligation to reduce domestic subsidies by making use of the AoA's generous exemptions, including de minimis exemptions and exemptions for allegedly non-trade-distorting subsidies.[74]

68 Carmen G. Gonzalez, "The Global Food Crisis: Law, Policy, and the Elusive Quest for Justice" (2010) 13 *Yale Human Rights and Development Law Journal* 462, 469.

69 *Id.*

70 *Id.*, 469–70.

71 Friedmann, n. 35, 251; Anuradha Mittal, "UNCTAD, The 2008 Food Price Crisis: Rethinking Food Security Policies," G-24 Discussion Paper no. 29, June 2009, 13–15; Structural Adjustment Participatory Review International Network (SAPRIN), *The Policy Roots of Economic Crisis and Poverty: A Multi-Country Participatory Assessment of Structural Adjustment* (SAPRIN, 2002), 124–26.

72 Art. 4 (market access), arts. 6, 7 (domestic support), arts. 9, 10 (export subsidies); Gonzalez, n. 9, 450–56.

73 Arts 3.2, 3.3, 10.1; Melaku Geboye Desta, *The Law of International Trade in Agricultural Products* (Kluwer Law International, 2002), 253–59, 394; Gonzalez, n. 9, 456.

74 The AoA, art. 6.4(a) permits developed countries to subsidize up to 5 percent of the total value of agricultural goods per year (the so-called de minimis exception). Developing countries are authorized to subsidize up to 10 percent of the total value of agricultural production (art. 6.4 (b)). As a practical matter, few developing countries can afford to reach this threshold, while all

While Northern countries reduced export subsidies in accordance with the AoA, they also deployed other export promotion tools not prohibited by the AoA (such as government loans on concessional terms) until the WTO member states reached an agreement in 2015 eliminating all forms of export subsidies.[75] Agricultural subsidies in the United States and the European Union actually increased in the aftermath of the AoA.[76] As a consequence of these Northern agricultural subsidies, cheap food imports from the global North continued to threaten rural livelihoods in the global South. Prior to structural adjustment, governments could simply raise tariffs to make imported food more expensive. After structural adjustment, Southern governments were prohibited by loan conditionalities (and later by bilateral and regional free trade agreements that reduced tariffs with trading partners to zero) from defensively raising tariffs.[77] In general, Southern states did not challenge these Northern subsidies under the AoA or under other WTO agreements (such as the 1994 Agreement on Subsidies and Countervailing Measures) due to the complexity of the applicable WTO rules, the resources required to mount a WTO challenge, and the geopolitical consequences of bringing such a challenge.[78]

The international trade regime also neglected to regulate transnational corporations that dominate international agricultural trade.[79] As one source reveals, "[e]ven before the recent wave of mergers – Bayer-Monsanto, ChemChina-Syngenta, and Dow-Dupont – three seed companies controlled 50 percent of the commercial market."[80] A handful of companies dominate the markets for agrochemicals, and four companies control 90 percent of the global grain trade.[81] These companies use their monopsony power and their global supply chains to drive down the prices paid to agricultural producers while charging high prices for fertilizers, pesticides, machinery, and seeds.[82]

Target 2.b, which seeks to eliminate trade restrictions and distortions in world agricultural markets, is only a partial solution to the problem of food insecurity.

developed countries can. Sarah Joseph, *Blame It on the WTO? A Human Rights Critique* (Oxford University Press, 2011), 186. In addition, the AoA completely exempts supposedly non-trade-distorting subsidies from the AoA's subsidy-reduction obligations, including income safety nets for farmers not linked to volumes of production, crop insurance, subsidies to discourage overproduction, and government-funded agricultural research, pest control, marketing, and infrastructure (arts 6.4, 6.5, Annex 2). The exemptions for non-trade-distorting subsidies have been controversial, "as it is argued that these subsidies in fact have significant protectionist effects." Joseph, *id.*

75 Gonzalez, n. 9, 463–65; WTO, *Nairobi Ministerial Declaration*, Doc. WT/MIN(15)/DEC, 2015 (eliminating export subsidies).

76 Gonzalez, n. 66, 366.

77 Joseph, n. 74, 188.

78 *Id.*, 188–90.

79 Gonzalez, n. 22, 490–91.

80 Timothy A. Wise, *Eating Tomorrow: Agribusiness, Family Farmers, and the Battle for the Future of Food* (New Press, 2019), 277.

81 *Id.*, 277–78.

82 Gonzalez, n. 22, 490–92; Joseph, n. 74, 198.

While phasing out Northern agricultural subsidies is indeed necessary to protect the livelihoods of small farmers in the global South, it is also essential to combat market concentration in the agricultural sector through various means, including the aggressive deployment of competition law, and to modify the trade agreements and loan conditionalities that restrict the ability of Southern states to use tariffs, subsidies, and other forms of government intervention to support small-scale sustainable agriculture. Furthermore, studies show that Southern states have paid $4.2 trillion in interest to large commercial banks since 1980 instead of using this money to combat poverty and promote food security.[83] This suggests that debt cancellation needs to be a central part of the Sustainable Development Agenda and not simply the "debt financing, debt relief, and debt restructuring" called for by target 17.4.

SDG 2 will not be achieved if the Sustainable Development Agenda uncritically embraces trade liberalization instead of recognizing the need to reduce Northern agricultural subsidies while also ensuring ample policy space for Southern states to deploy subsidies and tariffs to protect the right to food and to promote cultivation methods that preserve biodiversity, minimize pollution, manage water wisely, and maintain healthy soils. Even if Northern subsidies were eliminated, small-scale farmers do not have the ability to compete in global markets with mechanized, chemical-intensive industrial agriculture.[84] Markets will always favor low-cost agricultural producers in the global North at the expense of small-scale farmers in the global South. They will inevitably divert finite arable lands to produce meat and other luxury commodities for wealthy consumers instead of cheaper food staples for the poor.[85]

2.3.3.2 International Investment Law and Land Grabbing

International investment law also poses significant challenges to the achievement of SDG 2. One of the major threats to the livelihoods of farmers in the global South is the proliferation of large-scale leases or purchases of agricultural lands on terms that may deprive current users of resources needed for food production and may expand the frontiers of industrial agriculture.[86] According to a 2012 report by the

[83] Jason Hickel, "Aid in Reverse: How Poor Countries Develop Rich Countries," *The Guardian*, 14 January 2017.

[84] Joseph, n. 74, 192–93.

[85] *Id.*, 194.

[86] GRAIN, *The Global Farmland Grab in 2016: How Big, How Bad?*, grain.org/e/5492; Ward Answeeuw et al., *Land Rights and the Rush for Land: Findings of the Global Commercial Pressure on Land Research Project* (IL Coalition, 2012); Lorenzo Cotula et al., *Land Grab or Development Opportunity? Agricultural Investment and International Land Deals in Africa* (FAO/IIED/IFAD, 2009); Alexandra Spieldoch & Sophia Murphy, "Agricultural Land Acquisitions: Implications for Food Security and Poverty Alleviation," in Michael Kugelman & Susan L. Levenstein (eds.), *Land Grab? The Race for the World's Farmland* (Woodrow Wilson International Center for Scholars, 2009). GRAIN, an international non-profit supporting small farmers and biodiversity-based food systems, provides regular updates on large-scale

International Land Coalition, a global alliance of civil society organizations, an area eight times the size of the United Kingdom or nearly the size of Western Europe was transferred between January 2000 and November 2011.[87] While the International Land Coalition has since revised this figure to nearly 76 million hectares transferred or under negotiation, the size of the global land rush remains significant.[88] These "land grabs" have been driven by transnational corporations eager to exploit the growing demand for biofuels; by foreign investors (including Northern hedge funds, investment banks, and pension funds) speculating on arable land; and by middle-income Southern countries (such as Saudi Arabia, Qatar, China, India, and South Korea) seeking to engage in the offshore production of food to mitigate food price volatility on international markets and domestic shortages of arable land and irrigation water.[89]

These transactions pose serious risks to small farmers in the targeted Southern countries, including eviction from their lands, depletion or pollution of water resources, and loss of access to forests, fisheries, and other natural resources.[90] For example, small farmers and herders whose ownership or usufruct rights are not recognized by government officials may be dispossessed by foreign investors or by local elites eager to sell or lease these lands to foreign investors.[91] The conversion of labor-intensive subsistence farms to highly mechanized export-oriented industrial agriculture may reduce local food availability, intensify poverty by shrinking rural employment, contaminate the local water supply with pesticide and fertilizer runoff, degrade the land through intensive cultivation, increase greenhouse gas emissions, and deplete water resources needed by local communities.[92]

These land acquisitions are accelerating the South's transition from peasant cultivation to large-scale industrial agriculture at the precise moment when scientists and policy-makers are advocating a shift to small-scale sustainable agriculture in food-insecure countries. In 2013, the UN Conference on Trade and Development

land transactions all over the world. See *Farm Land Grab: The Global Rush for Farmland and People's Struggles against It*, www.farmlandgrab.org/.

87 Answeeuw et al., n. 86, 19.

88 Land Matrix, *Global Observatory*, landmatrix.org/global/.

89 Spieldoch & Murphy n. 86, 41–42; Answeeuw et al., n. 86, 21; Clapp, n. 25, 150–51; Chidi Oguanaman, "Bioenergy and Land Grabs," in Shawkat Alam et al. (ed.), *International Environmental Law and the Global South* (Cambridge University Press, 2015), 237, 255.

90 Spieldoch & Murphy, n. 86, 43–48; Kaitlin Cordes, Lise Johnson & Sam Szoke-Burke, *Grievances, Human Rights, and Investor Protections* (Columbia Center on Sustainable Investment, 2016) (proving multiple examples of local community grievances arising from land-based investments).

91 Raul Q. Montemayor, "Overseas Farmland Investments: Boon or Bane for Farmers in Asia?," in Kugelman & Levenstein, n. 86, 1–102; Olivier de Schutter, "The Green Rush: The Global Race for Farmland and the Rights of Land Users" (2011) 52(2) *Harvard International Law Journal* 501, 537.

92 Ruth Meinzen-Dick & Helen Markelova, "Nuance: Toward a Code of Conduct in Foreign Land Deals," in Kugelman & Levenstein, n. 86, 74; Montemayor, n. 91, 102–5; Spieldoch & Murphy, n. 86, 46–47.

(UNCTAD) published a major report urging a paradigm shift in agriculture – away from industrial agriculture and toward sustainable, regenerative production systems that enhance the productivity of small-scale farmers.[93] In 2020, in the midst of the COVID-19 pandemic, a panel of experts convened by the Committee on World Food Security, under the FAO, called for comprehensive policy reforms to promote shorter agricultural supply chains (more local food production) and a shift toward more sustainable production methods.[94] It has been shown that sustainable agriculture can produce significant increases in agricultural yields in Asia, Africa, and Latin America while enhancing environmental quality, reducing dependence on external inputs, and protecting the traditional agro-ecological knowledge of small farmers and Indigenous communities.[95]

International investment law has facilitated land grabbing by enabling foreign investors to obtain more favorable treatment than rural communities.[96] Contracts between the foreign investor and the host state typically provide the foreign investor with rights and benefits not guaranteed to the local population, including secure land and water rights, tax incentives, the right to export the agricultural commodities produced, and the right to have disputes resolved by binding arbitration.[97] Many contracts also include "stabilization" clauses that require the host state to compensate the foreign investor for any economic losses attributable to the host state's modification of the regulatory framework applicable to the investment.[98] This provision essentially "freezes" the law applicable to the investment and may deter host states from taking legal action to protect human rights and the environment for fear of commercial arbitration claims. Thus, states may refrain from redistributing land or reallocating water rights to ensure that local communities can grow food,

93 See generally UNCTAD, n. 8.

94 Committee on World Food Security, High Level Panel of Experts on Food Security and Nutrition, *Food Security and Nutrition: Building a Global Narrative Toward 2030*, 2020, www.fao.org/3/ca9731en/ca9731en.pdf.

95 UNGA, *Report Submitted by the Special Rapporteur on the Right to Food*, UN Doc. A/HRC/16/49, 20 December 2010; UNCTAD & UN Environment Programme, *Organic Agriculture and Food Security in Africa*, UN Doc. UNCTAD/DITC/TED/2007/15, 2008; Catherine Badgley et al., "Organic Agriculture and the Global Food Supply" (2007) 22 *Renewable Agriculture and Food Systems* 86; Jules Pretty et al., "Resource Conserving Agriculture Increases Yields in Developing Countries" (2006) 40 *Environmental Science and Technology* 1114; Nicholas Parrott & Terry Marsden, *The New Green Revolution: Organic and Agroecological Farming in the South* (Greenpeace Environmental Trust, 2002); Jules N. Pretty, "Reducing Food Poverty by Increasing Sustainability in Developing Countries" (2003) 95 *Agricultural Ecosystems and the Environment* 217.

96 Carin Smaller & Howard Mann, *A Thirst for Distant Lands: Foreign Investment in Agricultural Land and Water* (International Institute for Sustainable Development, 2009), 14.

97 *Id.*, 14.

98 Lorenzo Cotula, *Regulatory Takings, Stabilization Clauses and Sustainable Development* (Organisation for Economic Co-operation and Development Global Forum on International Investment, 2008), 27–28.

restricting food exports at times of critical food shortages, and enhancing labor and environmental standards as the country's regulatory framework evolves.[99]

In addition to the investment contract, the foreign investor's rights are also protected by the IIA between the host state (the Southern state where the land is located) and the home state (the state of the investor). This IIA could be a bilateral investment treaty or the investment chapter of a free trade agreement.[100] IIAs are typically negotiated between countries with vast power and wealth differentials and therefore reflect the interests of the party with the greatest bargaining power.[101] IIAs typically incorporate certain core principles, including national treatment; most favored nation; the prohibition against expropriation without compensation; fair and equitable treatment (also known as international minimum standards of treatment); full protection and security of the investment; and the investor-state dispute settlement mechanism, which authorizes the foreign investor to commence arbitration against the host state in the event of a breach.[102]

The prohibition on expropriation encompasses both direct expropriation (seizure of property) and indirect expropriation (regulations that diminish the value of the property in a significant way).[103] The fair and equitable treatment provision requires the host state to honor the "legitimate expectations" of the investor arising from the contract or other government commitments.[104] These provisions may chill the willingness of states to strengthen the ability of small farmers to grow food, for example, by reallocating water rights because an arbitration tribunal might conclude that this action violated the investor's "legitimate expectations" of water for irrigation and triggered a duty to compensate the investor.[105] Similarly, the foreign investor may bring a claim for compensation if the host state imposes export restrictions on agricultural commodities to address domestic food shortages, even if these export restrictions are otherwise permissible under international trade law.[106]

In sum, international investment law strengthens the property rights of foreign investors on agricultural land at the expense of the host state and of food-insecure rural communities. It limits the ability of states to respect, protect, and fulfill the human right to food and to redirect land use toward more equitable and sustainable

[99] UN Department of Economic and Social Affairs (UNDESA), "Foreign Land Purchases for Agriculture: What Impact on Sustainable Development?," Sustainable Development Innovation Briefs, January 2020, 2.

[100] Anna Clare Bull, Jagit Pahe, & Lachlan Gregory, "International Investment Agreements and the Escalation of Private Power in the Global Agri-Food System" (2019) 170 *Journal of Business Ethics* 519, 520–21.

[101] Joseph E. Stiglitz, "Multinational Corporations: Balancing Rights and Responsibilities" (2007) 101 *Proceedings of the American Society of International Law* 3, 9.

[102] Smaller & Mann, n. 96, 11–13; Muthucumaraswamy Sornarajah, *The International Law on Foreign Investment*, 4th ed. (Oxford University Press, 2017), 238–42, 254–57.

[103] Smaller & Mann, n. 96, 11–13.

[104] *Id.*, 12.

[105] *Id.*, 16–17; UNDESA, n. 99, 3.

[106] UNDESA, n. 99, 4.

food production for the local market instead of industrialized agro-export production. In addition to circumscribing the policy space of states, it accelerates the commodification of land, including lands that were once used communally for hunting, gathering, and grazing livestock. In so doing, international investment law ensures that agricultural lands in the global South will be used in ways that favor those with the greatest purchasing power to the detriment of food-insecure communities and the environment.

SDG 2 does not address the threats posed to food security and agro-biodiversity by international investment law. On the contrary, target 10.b uncritically encourages greater development assistance and financial flows, including foreign direct investment, without recognizing that they have historically been part of the problem rather than part of the solution. SDG 2's ability to achieve food security and promote sustainable agriculture is compromised by its failure to confront the challenges posed by IIAs. Finally, some states have adopted new IIAs that seek to balance investor protection with the state's obligation to regulate in the public interest.[107] For example, some of these treaties adopt more narrowly formulated fair and equitable treatment standards or include annexes with criteria for determining what constitutes an indirect expropriation.[108] There is insufficient data to assess how arbitration tribunals will interpret these new IIAs.[109] In addition, the vast majority of IIAs currently in force predate the new models,[110] and many states have entered into IIAs that do not feature the revised provisions.[111]

2.4 POSITIONING SDG 2 IN THE INTERNATIONAL INSTITUTIONAL CONTEXT

The successful implementation of SDG 2 will turn on the ability of human rights institutions to promote compliance with the right to food despite the challenges posed by international economic law. Since 1945, the FAO has been one of the key institutions implementing the right to food. The FAO has promoted international cooperation through aid and technical assistance to eradicate hunger and has produced annual reports measuring progress toward this objective.[112] The FAO has developed soft law instruments to support state compliance with the right to food, including the 2005 Voluntary Guidelines to Support the Progressive Realization of the Right to Adequate Food in the Context of National Food Security (2005

[107] Muthucumaraswamy Sornarajah, *Resistance and Change in the International Law of Foreign Investment* (Cambridge University Press, 2015), 347–65.

[108] Lorenzo Cotula, "'Land Grabbing' and International Investment Law: Toward a Global Reconfiguration of Property," in Andrea K. Bjorklund (ed.), *Yearbook of International Investment Law 2014–2015* (Oxford University Press, 2016), 177, 203.

[109] *Id.*, 204.

[110] UNCTAD, *World Investment Report 2017*, 2017, xii.

[111] Cotula, n. 108, 204.

[112] Anna Chadwick, *Law and the Political Economy of Hunger* (Oxford University Press, 2019), 3–4.

Voluntary Guidelines)[113] and the 2012 Voluntary Guidelines on the Responsible Governance of Tenure of Land, Fisheries, and Forests in the Context of National Food Security (VGGT).[114] The 2005 Voluntary Guidelines provide general recommendations to governments on an array of policies to promote food security, including policies related to labor, land, economic development, and social safety nets. The VGGT provide more specific guidance on the recognition and protection of land tenure rights, including land redistribution to address significant rural poverty, land restitution to dispossessed communities, and land tenure reform to recognize customary, informal, unrecorded, and Indigenous land rights.[115] While these soft law instruments provide much-needed clarity on the right-to-food obligations of states, their major limitation is that they are not legally enforceable, even though they might be taken into account by tribunals interpreting the right to food under applicable treaties, such as the ICESCR.

The human right to food is also implemented by the United Nations and regional human rights institutions that issue decisions in response to individual complaints and provide authoritative interpretations of treaties through general comments.[116] Because the governance capacity of many Southern states has been diminished by IMF or World Bank loan conditionalities and by international trade and investment agreements, a human rights–based approach to SDG 2 should seek to hold accountable the Northern states whose trade, investment, and lending practices have contributed to right to food violations in the global South. This could be accomplished by recognizing and enforcing what John Knox, the former UN special rapporteur on human rights and the environment, calls diagonal human rights. Diagonal human rights are rights held by individuals against foreign governments for the transboundary consequences of their aid, trade, finance, and investment policies, including the power they wield in international financial institutions.[117]

Article 56 of the UN Charter arguably imposes diagonal or transboundary obligations on all states by requiring all UN members to "take joint and separate action in cooperation with the Organization" to ensure the realization of human rights. In addition, article 2(1) of the ICESCR obligates states parties to "take steps, individually and through international assistance and cooperation" to progressively realize the rights set forth in the treaty. General Comment 12 explains the transboundary aspects of the right to food as follows:

[113] FAO, *Voluntary Guidelines to Support the Progressive Realization of the Right to Adequate Food in the Context of National Food Security*, 2005.

[114] FAO, *Voluntary Guidelines on the Responsible Governance of Tenure of Land, Fisheries, and Forests in the Context of National Food Security*, 2012.

[115] Sections 7, 9, 10, 14, 15.

[116] Joseph, n. 74, 14–18.

[117] John Knox, "Diagonal Human Rights," in Mark Gibney & Sigrun Skogly (eds.), *Universal Human Rights and Extraterritorial Obligations* (University of Pennsylvania Press, 2010), 83.

> In the spirit of article 56 of the Charter of the United Nations, . . . States parties should take steps to respect the enjoyment of the right to food in other countries, to protect that right, to facilitate access to food, and to provide necessary aid when required. States parties should, in international agreements whenever relevant, ensure that the right to adequate food is given due attention and consider the development of further international legal instruments to that end.[118]

In order to comply with these obligations, Northern states should respect the right to food in the global South by negotiating, interpreting, and applying trade and investment agreements in ways that provide Southern countries with sufficient flexibility to regulate in the public interest and to deploy subsidies, tariffs, and other import barriers to enhance the livelihoods of small farmers and other food-insecure populations. Northern states should protect the right to food by ensuring that third parties subject to their jurisdiction and control, such as transnational corporations, do not violate the right to food in other countries. States that are members of the IMF, the World Bank, and regional development banks should take affirmative steps to guarantee that the policies and practices of these institutions are consistent with their right-to-food obligations. Finally, Northern countries should fulfill the right to food by providing food aid in ways that enhance, rather than undermine, the livelihoods of small farmers in the global South by, for example, purchasing such food from Southern farmers rather than using food aid as a pretext for Northern export dumping.

While there are currently no adjudicated cases recognizing the transboundary right-to-food obligations of states, such recognition is long overdue given the responsibility of Northern states for global poverty and inequality and the urgent need for international cooperation.[119] One important limitation of human rights institutions, however, is that compliance often relies on the naming and shaming of recalcitrant states, whereas international economic law imposes formidable economic sanctions.[120] A second limitation is the absence of enforceable human rights obligations on nonstate actors, including transnational corporations.[121] By contrast, international financial institutions such as the World Bank and the IMF exert great leverage over the domestic policies of Southern states through their ability to withhold loans from countries that fail or refuse to comply with loan conditionalities.[122] Northern states can induce Southern states to comply with their WTO obligations by using or threatening to use the WTO dispute settlement system, which permits the victorious WTO member to impose economic countermeasures on the recalcitrant nonprevailing party. However, low-income Southern states are less likely to bring a claim

[118] CESCR, n. 47, para. 36.
[119] Chadwick, n. 112, 179–80.
[120] Joseph, n. 74, 15–16
[121] See generally Smita Narula, "The Right to Food: Holding Global Actors Accountable Under International Law" (2006) 44 *Columbia Journal of Transnational Law* 691.
[122] Peet, n. 62.

against their Northern trading partners due to the expense, the likelihood of retaliation (such as the withdrawal of aid), and the inability to secure compliance by credibly threatening serious economic harm through economic countermeasures.[123] Finally, the investor-state dispute resolution clause in IIAs and land contracts promotes state compliance because arbitral decisions awarding compensation to foreign investors are enforceable in any country that is a party to either or both of the leading treaties on the enforcement of arbitral awards in foreign jurisdictions.[124]

International investment law's chilling effect on state compliance with SDG 2 is not simply hypothetical. According to the Columbia Center on Sustainable Investment, there has been an increase in arbitration cases initiated since 2003 challenging the food and agriculture policies of Southern states.[125] Many of these cases arise when states attempt to redistribute or return land to marginalized communities in order to comply with their right-to-food obligations in accordance with the FAO's VGGT recommendations.[126] For example, in *Bernardus Henricus Funnekotter and Others v Republic of Zimbabwe*, the arbitration tribunal held that the government of Zimbabwe breached the applicable IIA when it expropriated the investor's property for redistribution to local farmers pursuant to land reform legislation without paying the investor the full market value of the confiscated farms.[127] This case illustrates important differences between the jurisprudence of human rights tribunals and arbitration tribunals in matters related to state regulatory authority. In cases involving expropriation, human rights tribunals, especially in Europe, balance the private and public interests at stake and consider in the computation of damages the public purpose served by the expropriation and whether the expropriation is part of a larger systemic reform.[128]

By contrast, most arbitral decisions do not balance public and private interests and require full market value compensation "independently . . . of the number and aim of the expropriations done."[129] The procedural rules governing investor-state arbitration are also more favorable to foreign investors than the procedures

[123] Joseph, n. 74, 65–57.

[124] The 1958 UN Convention on the Recognition and Enforcement of Foreign Arbitral Awards and the 1965 Convention on the Settlement of Investment Disputes between States and Nationals of Other States. See Marc Bungenberg & August Reinisch, "From Bilateral Arbitral Tribunals and Investment Courts to a Multilateral Investment Court," in Marc Bungenberg et al., (eds.), *European Yearbook of International Economic Law 2019* (Springer, 2019).

[125] Jesse Coleman, Sarah Brewin & Thierry Berger, *Agricultural Investments under International Law* (Columbia Center on Sustainable Development, 2018), 4.

[126] Lorenzo Cotula, *Land Rights and Investment Treaties: Exploring the Interface* (International Institute for Environment and Development, 2015), 8–23.

[127] ICSID, *Bernardus Henricus Funnekotter and Others v Republic of Zimbabwe*, ICSID Case no. ARB/05/6, 2009, para. 130, www.italaw.com/sites/default/files/case-documents/ita0349.pdf.

[128] Lorenzo Cotula, "Land, Property and Sovereignty in International Law" (2017) 25 *Cardozo Journal of International and Comparative Law* 219, 255-256.

[129] *Funnekotter and Others*, n. 127, para. 24; Cotula, n. 128, 255–56.

in human rights cases. While human rights claimants must exhaust domestic remedies before bringing a case to an international human rights tribunal, IIAs permit foreign investors to bypass the domestic legal system, proceed directly to arbitration, and obtain judicial enforcement of the arbitration award.[130] The prospect of becoming embroiled in an expensive and time-consuming arbitration and the risk of having to compensate the foreign investor can deter states from complying with their human rights obligations, even when ordered to do so by an international human rights tribunal.

For example, in *Sawhoyamaxa v Paraguay*, the Inter-American Court of Human Rights (IACtHR) ordered the Paraguayan government to return ancestral lands to an Indigenous community.[131] When Paraguay resisted on the ground that the property was owned by a German investor and protected under an IIA,[132] the IACtHR, in its 2006 decision, emphasized the primacy of human rights obligations over commercial treaties and ordered restitution within three years.[133] However, Paraguay did not pass legislation expropriating the land and returning it to the community until 2014 – a full twenty-three years after the community first commenced restitution proceedings in national courts.[134] The foreign investors immediately challenged the constitutionality of the legislation. While their claims were ultimately rejected by the Paraguayan Supreme Court,[135] government officials cited the constitutional challenge and litigation regarding the amount of compensation for the expropriated lands to explain their delay in complying with the IACtHR's order.[136] In June 2015, the IACtHR found that Paraguay had not complied with its obligation to return the lands to the Sawhoyamaxa community.[137] In May 2019, the IACtHR found that the Sawhoyamaxa community had de facto use of their land, but the state had failed to transfer legal title.[138] While the implementation of the restitution law has not yet given rise to an investor-state arbitration claim, this case illustrates the tension between international human rights law and international economic law, especially in cases involving land redistribution. In sum, international human rights law

[130] Cotula, n. 128, 256.
[131] IACtHR, *Case of the Indigenous Community Sawhoyamxa v Paraguay*, Series C, No 146, 29 March 2006, paras. 144, 210, www.corteidh.or.cr/docs/casos/articulos/seriec_146_ing.pdf.
[132] *Id.*, paras. 115(b), 125.
[133] *Id.*, paras. 140, 215.
[134] Cotula, n. 126, 18.
[135] David Hill, "Paraguay's Supreme Court Issues 'Historic' Land Ruling," *The Guardian*, 7 October 2014.
[136] *Sawhoyamxa v Paraguay*, n. 131, Monitoring Compliance with Judgment, Resolution, 14 May 2019, paras. 16–21, www.corteidh.or.cr/docs/supervisiones/sawhoyamaxa_14_05_19.pdf.
[137] *Sawhoyamxa v Paraguay*, n. 131, Monitoring Compliance with Judgment, Order of the President of the Court, 24 June 2015, para. 27, www.corteidh.or.cr/docs/supervisiones/yakie_24_06_15.pdf.
[138] *Sawhoyamxa v Paraguay*, n. 131, Monitoring Compliance with Judgment, Resolution, 14 May 2019, paras. 13, 15, 22, 23, www.corteidh.or.cr/docs/supervisiones/sawhoyamaxa_14_05_19.pdf.

generally supports SDG 2, whereas international economic law does not. When these bodies of law conflict, states are more likely to comply with international economic law due to the stronger institutional mechanisms through which it is enforced.

2.5 CONCLUSIONS

SDG 2's grounding in international human rights law has the potential to achieve food security to the extent that it seeks to empower small farmers by promoting secure land rights, remunerative employment, adequate social safety nets, and sustainable and regenerative cultivation practices. In order to be successful, SDG 2 should also recognize the responsibilities of affluent states for global food insecurity and should seek to hold global actors accountable for their transnational right-to-food obligations.

However, SDG 2 suffers from several key limitations. First, its emphasis on increasing food production threatens to accelerate environmental degradation and appears to erroneously attribute food insecurity to food scarcity rather than to a lack of access to land, jobs, and social safety nets. Second, instead of questioning the underlying structural causes of poverty, inequality, and unsustainable production, the SDGs call for the intensification of the same growth-based economic model that caused the problems in the first place. Third, several SDG targets uncritically favor trade liberalization (target 2.b), greater development assistance and financial flows, including foreign direct investment (target 10.b), and limited debt relief without an adequate account of the ways in which these arrangements keep food flowing from the poor to the affluent. The right to food will not be achieved without a clear-headed analysis of the ways in which international economic law allows powerful actors to systematically deprive the planet's most vulnerable populations of food, land, and water. In addition to focusing on the needs of the poor and marginalized, international human rights scholars and institutions should focus on those who benefit from right-to-food violations and on the laws and institutions that maintain their power.

3

SDG 3: Ensure Healthy Lives and Promote Well-Being for All at All Ages

*Stéphanie Dagron**

ABSTRACT

The centrality of Sustainable Development Goal (SDG) 3, Good Health and Well-Being, for the realization of Agenda 2030 highlights the importance and weaknesses of international health law as an instrument to realize the SDG itself. An analysis of SDG 3 – its targets, indicators, and institutional structure – reveals that law, in general, has been sidelined and that certain institutions – and their expertise – have not been fully, or, indeed, sufficiently, involved in its implementation. Efforts should be made to facilitate the contribution of international health law in the realization of SDG 3, which implies addressing the material and institutional weaknesses of this fragmented branch of international law.

KEYWORDS

SDG 3, international health law, global health, well-being, universal health coverage, World Health Organization, human rights, right to health

3.1 INTRODUCTION

"What sort of world do we want? … Now more than ever, we need a healthier world. Now more than ever, we need a safer world. Now more than ever, we need a fairer world. Healthy, safe and fair."[1] It was with these words that the World Health

* With thanks to Angus E. M. Wallace and Dr. Jennifer Hasselgard-Rowe.

[1] WHO, *WHO Director-General's Opening Remarks at the World Health Assembly*, 18 May 2020, www.who.int/dg/speeches/detail/who-director-general-s-opening-remarks-at-the-world-health-assembly.

Organization's (WHO) director general summed up the central challenges posed by the biggest health crisis in a century, in his opening remarks at the World Health Assembly (WHA) on 18 May 2020. COVID-19, declared by the WHO first as a public health emergency of international concern on 30 January 2020[2] and then a pandemic on 11 March 2020,[3] has brutally confronted the international community in its entirety with its responsibility to realize health and well-being for all, while respecting the principles of social justice, equity, and human rights. These sentiments echo Agenda 2030's "supremely ambitious and transformational vision."[4]

In adopting health as one of the seventeen Sustainable Development Goals (SDGs) to be achieved by 2030, the United Nations General Assembly (UNGA) recognized the importance of health for development as well as for peace and security for the first time since the adoption of the 1945 Charter of the United Nations (UN Charter)[5] and the 1946 WHO Constitution.[6] It also recognized the broad definition of health, first formulated in the WHO Constitution[7] and later confirmed in declarations and other international instruments. For instance, in Alma-Ata in 1978, on the occasion of the International Conference on Primary Health Care, the WHO member states reaffirmed that

> health, which is a state of complete physical, mental and social wellbeing, and not merely the absence of disease or infirmity, is a fundamental human right and that the attainment of the highest possible level of health is a most important world-wide social goal whose realization requires the action of many other social and economic sectors in addition to the health sector.[8]

This broad definition of health has been generally adopted by the UN member states[9] as well as by other global and regional institutions, including courts.[10] The links established between healthy lives and well-being in Agenda 2030 further confirm this approach – the promotion of well-being implying the integration of

[2] *Id.*

[3] WHO, *Rolling Updates on Coronavirus Disease (COVID-19)*, www.who.int/emergencies/diseases/novel-coronavirus-2019/events-as-they-happen.

[4] *Transforming Our World: The 2030 Agenda for Sustainable Development*, Doc. A/Res/70/1, 25 September 2015, para. 7.

[5] UN Charter, art. 55.

[6] According to the preamble of the WHO Constitution, "the health of all peoples is fundamental to the attainment of peace and security and is dependent upon the fullest co-operation of individuals and States."

[7] *Id.*, preamble.

[8] WHO, *Declaration of Alma-Ata International Conference on Primary Health Care, Alma-Ata, USSR, 6–12 September 1978*, 1978, para. 1.

[9] See, e.g., for Switzerland: 2006 Geneva Canton Law on Public Health, art. 2.1.

[10] See, e.g., UN Committee on Economic, Social and Cultural Rights, *General Comment 14: The Right to the Highest Attainable Standard of Health (Art. 12)*, UN Doc. E/C.12/2000/4, 11 August 2000, para. 4; European Union (EU) Regulation 282/2014, 11 March 2014; CJEU, *United Kingdom of Great Britain and Northern Ireland v Council of the European Union*, Case C-84/94, 1996, para. 15.

mental and physical health as well as factors in the physical, social, economic, and work environment.[11] Moreover, this definition rejects the medical approach that connects health solely with diseases and calls only for medical strategies as a response to ill-health, and underlines the necessity of developing a multitude of interventions in order to address the impact of globalization on health in an increasingly interdependent world, with respect to economic, political, social, and environmental matters. Understanding health as a special issue that must be dealt with through cooperation at the international level is not new. Indeed, it was this understanding that triggered the establishment of international public health institutions at the beginning of the twentieth century. However, this understanding gained in relevance with the intensification of globalization at the end of the 1990s.[12]

Improving health is thus at the center of many soft and hard legal instruments of global and regional scope. At the regional level, some legal instruments directly concerning public health issues have been adopted, for instance, within the framework of the Council of Europe.[13] However, a larger number of instruments have been adopted at the global level.[14] These instruments either relate directly to public health issues, such as the ones adopted by the WHO, or address issues within the realms of other fields of international law, such as human rights law, humanitarian law, medical law, environmental law, trade law, and labor and social security law. Together, these norms make up the fragmented body of international health law.[15] As a distinct field of international law, international health law is essential for the realization of SDG 3, as discussed in Section 3.2 of this chapter. The corpus of international health law, itself incomplete and limited, is discussed in Section 3.3. This corpus of legal norms is to be implemented through an institutional structure, whose particularities are discussed in Section 3.4.

[11] On the definition of well-being, see Ed Diener & Martin E.P. Seligman, "Beyond Money: Towards an Economy of Well-being" (2004) 5 *Psychological Science in the Public Interest* 1.

[12] Derek Yach & Douglas Bettcher, "The Globalization of Public Health, I: Threats and Opportunities" (1998) 88(5) *American Journal of Public Health* 735.

[13] See the following Council of Europe public health instruments: 1997 Convention for the Protection of Human Rights and Dignity of the Human Being with Regard to the Application of Biology and Medicine and its additional protocols adopted in 1998, 2002, 2005, and 2008; 2011 Convention on the Counterfeiting of Medical Products and Similar Crimes Involving Threats to Public Health. The EU has harmonized regulations applicable to pharmaceutical products, increased the protection against tobacco products, regulated access to healthcare in all member states, authorized recognition of degrees for medical personnel, and so on. On pharmaceutical products, see, e.g., Stéphanie Dagron, "Regulating Pharmaceuticals in Europe: a Human Rights Approach," in André den Exter (ed.), *European Health Law* (Maklu, 2017), 133–54.

[14] See Section 3.3 in this article.

[15] The existence of international health law as its own field of international law is contested by certain scholars, but it is my contention that it does. See generally Stéphanie Dagron, "L'avenir du droit international de la santé" (2016) 2(1) *Revue de droit suisse* 5, 20–23.

3.2 THE CONTENT OF SDG 3 IN THE CONTEXT OF THE OTHER SDGS

SDG 3 and its targets confirm the broad understanding of global health issues that should be resolved for the realization of health for all. Within the list of targets, the implementation of universal health coverage (UHC) has been clearly identified as central for the achievement of SDG 3 and, as such, for the realization of the other SDGs, health being closely linked with the Agenda 2030's overall goal. These topics will be discussed in the following subsections.

3.2.1 *The Choice of Targets for SDG 3: A Large Catalog of Global Health Issues*

Since the middle of the twentieth century, the importance of health for development has not been completely ignored by the international community. In fact, three of the time-limited targets included by world leaders in the eight 2000 Millennium Development Goals (MDGs),[16] were directly connected to health issues: reducing child mortality (MDG 4), improving maternal health (MDG 5), and combating HIV/AIDS, malaria, and other (contagious) diseases (MDG 6).[17] The MDGs nevertheless reflected a restrictive medical approach to health, as confirmed by the choice of indicators to measure the progress realized.[18] They also reflected the more limited conceptualization of "international public health issues" that was dominant until the end of the twentieth century. This term groups issues that primarily concerned low- and middle-income countries and was limited to maternal and children's health and the prevention of contagious diseases, originating mostly in the global South.[19]

Since the end of the twentieth century and the intensification of globalization,[20] the international community's field of intervention has broadened as a result of the acceptance of two conclusions that have come to condition the definition of "global health issues." First, health is no longer considered to be a purely national issue. Instead, public health issues are today influenced and conditioned by elements that transcend national borders. Second, and by implication, it has become accepted

[16] UNGA, *United Nations Millennium Declaration*, Doc. A/Res/55/2, 18 September 2000.

[17] MDG target 8.E is also indirectly connected to health.

[18] E.g., "[b]y [2015], to have reduced maternal mortality by three quarters, and under-five child mortality by two thirds, of their current rates"; "[t]o have, by then, halted, and begun to reverse, the spread of HIV/AIDS, the scourge of malaria and other major diseases that afflict humanity." UNGA, n. 16, para. 19.

[19] See, e.g., UNGA, *International Development Strategy for the Second United Nations Development Decade*, Resolution 2626 (XXV), 24 October 1970. See Theodore M. Browne et al., "The WHO and the Transition from 'International' to 'Global' Public Health" (2006) 96 (1) *American Journal Public Health* 62; Dagron, n. 15, 23.

[20] Nicholas Crafts, *Globalization and Growth in the Twentieth Century*, International Monetary Fund Working Paper no. 44, IMF Doc. WP/00/44, 1 March 2000; see also Peter Vanham, "A Brief History of Globalization," *World Economic Forum*, 17 January 2019.

that global health issues cannot be dealt with by states individually but that they require interstate cooperation.[21] However, despite the consensus on the elements of this definition, the identification of global health issues by international organizations, states, and in the literature has been far from harmonious since the 1990s.[22] On the one side are proponents of a restrictive list of major issues concerning, for instance, emerging or reemerging infectious diseases; the use of chemical, radioactive, or biological weapons; and the circulation and selling of dangerous products.[23] On the other side are proponents of a broader approach, identifying global health issues that include mental health, infectious diseases, noncommunicable diseases, health systems, shortage of skilled personnel, funding of research and development, access to medicines, vaccines, water, and food, poverty and migration, and so on.[24]

The list of targets included in SDG 3 is in harmony with this latter, broader approach to health and confirms a change of paradigm with regard to the understanding of "global health issues."[25] Out of the thirteen targets of SDG 3, three address the traditional international health issues mentioned above: reducing maternal mortality (target 3.1); ending preventable deaths of newborns and children under five years of age (target 3.2); and ending the epidemics of HIV/AIDS, tuberculosis, malaria, and other communicable diseases (targets 3.3). Five targets focus on global health issues identified as major health challenges for the twenty-first century.[26] Targets 3.4–3.6 are concerned with the development of medical and nonmedical strategies to reduce premature mortality from noncommunicable diseases, substance abuse, and road traffic. Targets 3.9 and 3.a are concerned with health issues resulting from chemical hazards and pollution as well as from the consumption of tobacco. Finally, five targets address infrastructure and strategies more broadly, involved with the financing and functioning of national health systems. They include the development of, and access to, sexual and reproductive healthcare services (target 3.7) and indispensable social and economic structures enabling access to healthcare services for all (target 3.8); supporting research and development of vaccines and medicines for communicable and noncommunicable diseases (target 3.b); increasing health financing and support for the recruitment, training, and retention of a

[21] See US Board on International Health, Institute of Medicine, *America's Vital Interest in Global Health: Protecting Our People, Enhancing Our Economy, and Advancing Our International Interests* (National Academies Press, 1997).

[22] Dagron, n. 15, 84–85.

[23] US Board on International Health, n. 21.

[24] Yach & Bettcher, n. 12.

[25] This list of targets is considered, in any case, a practical starting point. See the Inter-Agency and Expert Group on SDGs, *Global Indicator Framework for the Sustainable Development Goals and Targets of the 2030 Agenda for Sustainable Development*, March 2017, contained in UNGA, *Work of the Statistical Commission Pertaining to the 2030 Agenda for Sustainable Development*, UN Doc. A/RES/71/313, 6 July 2017.

[26] WHO, *Urgent Health Challenges for the Next Decade*, 13 January 2020, www.who.int/newsroom.

health workforce (target 3.c); and the implementation of the medical and nonmedical capacities necessary for all countries to prevent and respond to global health risks, including early warning capacities (target 3.d).

3.2.2 *The Tight Links between SDG 3 and the Other SDGs as a Result of the Interdependency between Health and the Development and End of a Poverty Strategy*

SDG 3 is closely related to the other SDGs in two ways. First, health is essential for the realization of Agenda 2030 in its entirety, which was confirmed explicitly by the UNGA in its resolution on universal health coverage, in which it stated that health is "a precondition for and an outcome and indicator of the social, economic and environmental dimensions of sustainable development and the implementation of the 2030 Agenda."[27] Second, the development and end of the poverty strategy adopted in 2015, as a whole, should be considered central for the realization of SDG 3. This goal is confirmed by the numerous references to health being conditioned on the realization of social determinants.[28] The WHO's Commission on the Social Determinants of Health (SDH Commission)[29] concluded in 2008 that individual and public health are determined by the structural elements and conditions of daily life, which constitute "the social determinants of health and cause much of the health inequity between and within countries."[30] The distribution of healthcare is therefore equally important as the "structural conditions in which people are born, grow, live, work and age."[31] According to the SDH Commission, the improvement of daily living conditions implies the following actions, which are similar to several SDGs: access to safe, nutritious, and sufficient food (target 2.1); interventions and investments during the early years of life (SDG 4, Quality Education); promotion of gender equality and empowerment of women (SDG 5, Gender Equality); access to safe and affordable drinking water (SDG 6, Clean Water and Sanitation, and target 6.1); access to good quality housing and shelter (SDG 11, Sustainable Cities and Communities); fair employment and decent work (SDG 8, Decent Work and Economic Growth); social protection schemes throughout life (SDG 1, No Poverty; SDG 5; SDG 8; SDG 10, Reduced Inequalities); universal health coverage

27 UNGA, *Political Declaration of the High-level Meeting on Universal Health Coverage*, UN Doc. A/RES/74/2, 10 October 2019, introduction.

28 See the references in Michael Marmot & Richard Wilkinson, *Social Determinants of Health* (Oxford University Press, 2006).

29 WHO, *The Commission on Social Determinants of Health: What, Why and How?*, WHO Backgrounder, www.who.int/social_determinants/final_report/csdh_who_what_why_how_en.pdf?ua=1.

30 WHO Commission on Social Determinants of Health, *Closing the Gap in a Generation: Health Equity through Action on the Social Determinants of Health – Final Report of the Commission on Social Determinants of Health*, WHO Doc. WHO/IER/CSDH/08.1, 2008, 1.

31 *Id.*, 43.

(target 3.8); and the translation of policies into laws and regulations (SDG 16, Peace, Justice, and Strong Institutions).

In practice, the links between individual and public health and the social and economic environments have become increasingly evident in the twenty-first century. The negative impacts on health engendered by recent environmental catastrophes and climate change – such as Hurricane Dorian in the Bahamas in 2019 or the 2010 Haiti earthquake – illustrate this situation. Similarly, the austerity measures – characterized by the reduction of public expenditures, including social protection interventions – adopted by Western European countries after the 2008 financial and economic crisis negatively impacted individual and public health.[32] In 2020, the COVID-19 crisis also highlighted the links between poverty and health, disproportionately affecting more disadvantaged populations everywhere. In April 2020, the UN special rapporteur on extreme poverty made the following comment on the crisis: "This is a crisis that disproportionately affects poor people, who are more likely to have health complications, live in crowded housing, lack the resources to stay home for long periods, and work low-paid jobs that force them to choose between risking their health or losing their income."[33]

3.3 POSITIONING SDG 3 IN INTERNATIONAL LAW

International legal instruments can influence global health in a variety of ways: they can influence social relations and behavior; they can regulate and protect the possession and transfer of wealth and goods; they can create and preserve social structures; and they can recognize and protect individual rights that could be central to avoiding diseases and bad health.[34] Numerous international law instruments do, in fact, fulfill functions that, together, either directly or indirectly cover the thirteen targets of SDG 3. These instruments include the soft and hard law instruments adopted under the realm of the WHO or within other fields of international law, which, in their entirety, constitute the field of international health law. SDG 3 poses different challenges for international law: first, the choice of targets and indicators for SDG 3 greatly marginalizes law as a useful instrument in the field of health, and, second, it underlines the weaknesses of international law as an instrument for global health.

[32] See, e.g., Charalampos Economou et al., *The Impact of the Financial Crisis on the Health System and Health in Greece: Case Study* (WHO, 2014).

[33] Office of the UN High Commissioner for Human Rights (OHCHR), *Responses to COVID-19 Are Failing People in Poverty Worldwide: UN Human Rights Expert*, 22 April 2020, www.ohchr.org/EN/NewsEvents/Pages/DisplayNews.aspx?NewsID=25815.

[34] Scott Burris, "Law as a Structural Factor in the Spread of Communicable Disease" (1999) 36(5) *Houston Law Review* 1755.

3.3.1 *The Choice of Key Targets and Indicators as a Rejection of Law as a Key Instrument*

The analysis of the lists of targets and indicators[35] reveals a refusal both to rely on a human rights–based approach for the realization of SDG 3 and to integrate legal considerations into monitoring efforts. First, concerning the choice of targets, it is important to note that none of the SDG 3 targets have been formulated in human rights language.[36] In fact, with the exception of its Preamble and the Declaration, Agenda 2030 does not make much use of this language throughout its text. This choice can be explained by the complexity and sensitivity of the discussions concerning human rights protection at the international level.[37] Except in target 4.7 on education, human rights are not mentioned in any of the SDGs: it is the implementation of UHC that has been clearly chosen as the central target of SDG 3 at the expense of the right to health.[38]

One the one hand, this approach aligns with the extremely slow recognition by the international community of the role that human rights have to play for the improvement and realization of individual and public health.[39] On the other hand, this approach is surprising, given the efforts made by UN agencies since 2003 to encourage a human rights–based approach in the field of development[40] as well as the various critiques formulated in the literature concerning the absence of a human rights–based approach in the MDGs[41] and the multiple analyses of the importance

[35] UNGA, *Work of the Statistical Commission Pertaining to the 2030 Agenda for Sustainable Development*, Resolution 71/313, 6 July 2017, and revised regularly.

[36] Inga T. Winkler & Carmel Williams, "The Sustainable Development Goals and Human Rights: A Critical Early Review" (2017) 21(8) *International Journal of Human Rights* 1023.

[37] As an illustration, see WHO, *Helsinki Statement on Health in All Policies: 8th Global Conference on Health Promotion*, 2013.

[38] The UNGA in its declaration on the Agenda 2030 first mentions UHC in its list of the instruments for the promotion of physical and mental health and well-being. *Transforming Our World*, n. 4, para. 26.

[39] Jonathan Mann, "Medicine and Public Health, Ethics and Human Rights" (1997) 27 *Hasting Center Reports* 6. The importance of human rights for health has been strongly bound during decades with isolated and specific threats to public health such as HIV/AIDS. See Jonathan Mann & Daniel Tarantola, "Responding to HIV/AIDS: A Historical Perspective" (1998) 2 *Health and Human Rights* 5.

[40] UN Sustainable Development Group (UNSDG), Human Rights Working Group, *The Human Rights Based Approach to Development Cooperation Towards a Common Understanding Among UN Agencies* (UNSDG, 2003).

[41] See, e.g., Alicia E. Yamin & Vanessa M. Boulanger, "Why Global Goals and Indicators Matter: The Experience of Sexual and Reproductive Health and Rights in the Millennium Development Goals" (2014) 15(2–3) *Journal of Human Development and Capabilities* 218; Claire E. Brolan, Peter S. Hill, & Gorik Ooms, "'Everywhere but Not Specifically Somewhere': A Qualitative Study on Why the Right to Health Is Not Explicit in the Post-2015 Negotiations" (2015) 15 *BMC International Health and Human Rights* 22.

of a human rights–based approach to health.[42] However, the importance of the human rights–based approach for the implementation of Agenda 2030 has gradually been recognized since its adoption. This development might have been influenced by the accumulation of evidence showing the necessity of adopting a human rights–based approach for successful health strategies.[43] The UNGA, for instance, endorsed this approach in 2018 in connection with combating the global epidemics of tuberculosis (target 3.3)[44] and noncommunicable diseases (target 3.4)[45] and in its previously mentioned 2019 Resolution on UHC (target 3.8).[46] This trend may well endure and amplify. In fact, the COVID-19 crisis has triggered many reactions in this direction from the WHA,[47] the UN Secretary-General, the UN High Commissioner for Refugees (UNHCR), and other human rights institutions.[48] Human rights and, more particularly, the right to health now form the implicit basis for the realization of SDG 3.[49]

Second, concerning the choice of indicators, it seems that law has been ignored as an important instrument for the implementation of the targets of SDG 3. Not even the indicators chosen for monitoring targets 3.a, 3.b, and 3.d – targets that are explicitly connected with the implementation of legal instruments – refer explicitly to national legislation. The list contains traditional medical indicators, such as the ones used for monitoring the MDGs: mortality rates (indicators linked with targets 3.1, 3.2, 3.3, 3.4, 3.6, 3.9); disease prevalence (target 3.3); percentage of infection (indicator 3.d.2); statistics reflecting access to healthcare services and medicinal products (targets 3.5, 3.7, 3.8, 3.b); and the density of health workers (indicators 3. c.1, 3.1.2). The list also contains economic indicators, such as those chosen to measure country performance in implementing UHC (target 3.8). The relevant indicators are concerned solely with economic performance, measuring only the catastrophic incidence of health expenditures and the impoverishment due to

42 See, e.g., Audrey R. Chapman, "Evaluating the Health-related Targets in the Sustainable Development Goals from a Human Rights Perspective" (2017) 21(8) *International Journal of Human Rights* 1098.

43 Concerning this development, see Mann, n. 39.

44 UNGA, *Political Declaration on the High-level Meeting of the General Assembly on the Fight against Tuberculosis*, UN Doc. A/RES/73/3, 10 October 2018.

45 UNGA, *Political Declaration of the Third high-level Meeting of the General Assembly on the Prevention and Control of Non-communicable Diseases*, UN Doc. A/RES73/2, 10 October 2018.

46 UNGA, n. 27, para. 5.

47 See, e.g., WHA, *Strengthening WHO Preparedness for and Response to Health Emergencies*, Resolution 74/4, 31 May 2021.

48 See the references in Stéphanie Dagron, "Going beyond the Rhetoric: Taking Human Rights Seriously in the Post-COVID-19 New Paradigm," *Verfassungsblog*, 27 March 2021.

49 Lawrence O. Gostin & Benjamin M. Meier, *Foundations of Global Health and Human Rights* (Oxford University Press, 2020); Christine Chinkin, "Health and Human Rights" (2006) 120(1) *Public Health* 52; OHCHR, *The Right to Health: Fact Sheet no.* 31 (2008), www.ohchr.org/documents/publications/factsheet31.pdf.

out-of-pocket health payments.[50] While these indicators can give insights on the incidence of catastrophic health spending, they do not provide any incentives or guidance on the type of social health protection mechanisms that should be used in order to permit access to essential care services to vulnerable groups. Moreover, they ignore the question concerning the translation into national law of these mechanisms, and they sideline relevant international norms that have been adopted by the International Labour Organization (ILO).[51]

These choices have been discussed at the international level and criticized in the literature.[52] Indeed, the exclusion of legal indicators for the SDG 3 targets is both surprising and problematic. It is surprising, first, because of the enormous encouragement provided by UN agencies for states to develop their national legislation on health. Law, for instance, was presented as essential for the implementation of fair and equitable health strategies by the ILO in its 2017 report on social protection. The report states that "national legislation is the backbone of equitable access [and] should ensure fair financing methods, adequacy of benefits, gender equality and non-discrimination as well as social inclusion."[53] Law is also undoubtedly part of the accepted strategy for the implementation of the 2005 International Health Regulations (IHR), as confirmed by the WHO's guidance for the implementation of the IHR.[54] Second, the exclusion of legal indicators is problematic because law is an essential element for the realization of all health strategies, as argued by the more recent literature on the role of (international) law as a determinant of health.[55] Law has been described as a

[50] WHO & World Bank Group, *Tracking Universal Health Coverage, 2017 Global Monitoring Report* (WHO, 2017).

[51] The ILO has adopted numerous norms that are adapted to its definition of UHC. See ILO, *World Social Security Report 2010/11: Providing Coverage in Times of Crisis and Beyond* (ILO, 2010); ILO, *Universal Social Protection for Human Dignity, Social Justice and Sustainable Development* (ILO, 2019).

[52] See, e.g., the critic of the medical indicators in Elizabeth Eckermann, "SDG 3: A Missed Opportunity to Transform Understandings and Monitoring of Health, Well-being and Development?" (2018) 13 *Applied Research Quality Life* 261; see also the discussions concerning the choice of indicators for target 3.8. UN Statistical Commission, *Report of the Inter-Agency and Expert Group on Sustainable Development Goal Indicators*, UN Doc. E/CN.3/2016/2, 2016, Annex IV, 42.

[53] ILO, *World Social Report 2017–19: Universal Social Protection to Achieve the Sustainable Development Goals* (ILO, 2017), 103.

[54] See WHO, *IHR Core Capacity Monitoring Framework: Checklist and Indicators for Monitoring Progress in the Development of IHR Core Capacities in States Parties*, WHO Doc. WHO/HSE/GCR/2013.2, April 2013; see also WHO, *IHR (2005): Toolkit for Implementation in National Legislation*, WHO Doc. WHO/HSE/IHR/2009.3, 2009.

[55] Lawrence O. Gostin et al., "The Legal Determinants of Health: Harnessing the Power of Law for Global Health and Sustainable Development" (2019) 393(10183) *The Lancet* 1857; see also Scott Burris et al., "A Transdisciplinary Approach to Public Health Law: The Emerging Practice of Legal Epidemiology" (2016) 37(1) *Annual Review of Public Health* 135.

powerful instrument "for global health and sustainable development" and should be used in order to "help build strong health systems, ensure safe and nutritious foods, evaluate and approve safe and effective drugs and vaccines, create healthier and safer workplaces, and improve the built and natural environments."[56] In fact, law is one of the first tools used by governments to implement policy ideas and has a central role to play in public health considering its structuring impact on health-related institutions and societal processes relevant to tackling population health problems such as an epidemic.

3.3.2 *The Weaknesses of International Health Law as Revealed by Agenda 2030*

The field of international health law is highly fragmented. It consists of norms adopted by the WHO, which is the UN agency in charge of public health, as well as by other UN agencies and international organizations. The challenges that international health law faces are also reflected in SDG 3. The first challenge arises from the fact that there are too few norms that directly address health issues, let alone the global health targets that are key for the realization of SDG 3. Despite its broad normative competence, the WHO has made a limited contribution to the development of hard international health law.[57] Since its establishment, the WHO has adopted one convention and a few regulations.[58] A binding legal response has only been achieved when it comes to problems linked to infectious diseases and emergency situations (target 3.d) and to one dangerous product causing noncommunicable diseases (NCDs) (target 3.a): the 2005 International Health Regulations[59] and the 2003 Framework Convention on Tobacco Control respectively.

The WHO's adoption of a multitude of soft law instruments, applicable to a large number of issues, including issues identified in SDG 3, does not compensate for the absence of hard law instruments. These soft law instruments, some of which were developed in collaboration with other UN agencies,[60] take the form of

[56] Gostin et al., n. 55, 1857.

[57] WHO Constitution, n. 6, arts. 2(a), 2(b), 2(c), 2(d), 2(e), 2(h), 2(i), 2(j).

[58] In practice, the WHO did relinquish most of its competencies to intervene for the regulation of medicines. On this issue, see Stéphanie Dagron, "Global Harmonization through Public-private Partnership: The Case of Pharmaceuticals," IRPA Working Paper (2012), 2.

[59] WHO, *International Health Regulations (2005)*, 3rd ed. (WHO, 2016); initially adopted in WHA, *Revision of the International Health Regulations*, Resolution 58/3, WHO Doc. WHA58/2005/REC/1, 23 May 2005.

[60] See WHO & UNICEF, *International Code of Marketing of Breastmilk Substitutes*, WHO Doc. WHA34.22, 1981, Annex 1; FAO & WHO Codex Alimentarius Commission, *Codex Alimentarius: International Food Standards*, 1992, www.fao.org/fao-who-codexalimentarius.

recommendations,[61] technical standards,[62] guidelines,[63] strategies,[64] and declarations.[65] Codes of practice such as the 1981 International Code of Marketing of Breastmilk Substitutes and the 2010 Code on the International Recruitment of Health Personnel are also good examples of the WHO attempting to deal with specific issues without resorting to "hard law" instruments.[66] With regard to the issues addressed through these codes, which directly concern targets 3.2, 3.8, and 3.c, analysis has shown that their impact has been quite limited. Despite the continued efforts of the WHO to secure their implementation,[67] the reports and analyses of their national implementation show disappointing results – for instance, with respect to the unethical and inappropriate marketing of breast-milk substitutes[68] and the global shortage of healthcare personnel.[69]

The second challenge concerns the fragmented nature of international health law. This field of international law is not only composed of norms adopted under the realm of the WHO, but it is also composed of norms that have emerged from other types of policies with a direct or indirect bearing on global health issues. As mentioned above, one relevant body of law is international human rights law. A second relevant body of international law consists of international humanitarian norms pertaining to access to healthcare services in times of war. These norms are found in the 1949 Geneva Conventions and were elaborated within the framework of the International Committee of the Red Cross.[70] International medical norms

[61] See WHO, *Guidelines on Physical Activity and Sedentary Behaviour*, 2020.

[62] See WHO, *Compendium of WHO Guidelines and Associated Standards: Ensuring Optimum Delivery of the Cascade of Care for Patients with Tuberculosis*, 2nd ed (WHO, 2018).

[63] See, for example, the multiple guidelines concerning maternal health or pharmaceutical regulation. WHO, *Guidelines on Maternal, Reproductive and Women's Health*, www.who.int/reproductivehealth/publications/evidence/en/; WHO, *Good Manufacturing Practices for Pharmaceutical Products: Main Principles*, published as Annex 3 in the WHO Technical Report Series no. 961, 2011.

[64] See WHO, *WHO Model List of Essential Medicines*, WHO Doc. WHO/MVP/EMP/IAU/2019.06, 2019.

[65] WHO, n. 8.

[66] On the role of soft law, see Julia Richter, *Soft Law in International Health Law: The Case of the WHO's Global Code of Practice on the International Recruitment of Health Personnel* (Schulthess, 2018).

[67] See, e.g., WHA, Resolution 65.6, 2012, endorsing a Comprehensive Implementation Plan on Maternal, Infant and Young Child Nutrition with a series of actions to be achieved by member states by the year 2025.

[68] See WHO, UNICEF & International Baby Food Action Network, *Marketing of Breast-milk Substitutes: National Implementation of the International Code: Status Report of 2016; 2018; and 2020* (WHO, 2016, 2018, and 2020).

[69] WHO, *WHO Global Code of Practice on the International Recruitment of Health Personnel: Report of the WHO Expert Advisory Group on the Relevance and Effectiveness of the WHO Global Code of Practice on the International Recruitment of Health Personnel*, WHO Doc. A73/9, 8 May 2020, 5.

[70] See International Committee of the Red Cross (ICRC), *Respecting and Protecting Health Care in Armed Conflicts and in Situations Not Covered by International Humanitarian Law*, 2021, www.icrc.org/en/document/respecting-and-protecting-health-care-armed-conflicts-and-situ

concerning the guarantees and obligations pertaining to the medical profession form another relevant body of law. These norms have been codified by the World Medical Association and have normative value.[71] Similarly, environmental conventions cannot be discounted from the field of international health law. They have a huge impact on public health outcomes and have generally been developed in order to promote and protect population health.[72] The 2015 Paris Agreement on Climate Change, for instance, although it does not mention public health as one of its objectives, was presented in 2016 at the occasion of the WHA by Christiana Figueres, the then executive secretary of the 1992 UN Framework Convention on Climate Change (UNFCCC) as a "public health treaty."[73] Finally, two additional bodies of law are relevant because they often interact with health issues. The first one is international trade law and, in particular, the 1994 Agreement on Trade-Related Aspects of Intellectual Property Rights (TRIPS Agreement), which defines the international patent system for protecting innovations such as medicines or vaccines. The second one is the broad domain of international labor and social security law. Conventions and recommendations concerning universal social protection,[74] social protection of health,[75] and occupational health[76] are essential for the realization of health and well-being for all.

In practice, however, the existence of a multitude of legal instruments, adopted with different policy objectives under different regimes of international law, can be counterproductive. Two potential scenarios illustrate the difficulties. The first scenario is one where there is a legal vacuum, and reference is made to legal rules developed for a purpose other than the protection of health. This scenario can be illustrated by the Indonesian case regarding the sharing of influenza samples. In February 2007, Indonesia refused to share samples of avian influenza A (H5N1) with the WHO, denouncing the inequitable system that, while essential for pandemic influenza preparedness (target 3.d), had resulted in limiting developing countries' access to vaccines developed by pharmaceutical companies in industrialized countries, on the basis of information and virus samples provided by developing countries. At the time of the decision, no specific international health law existed on the

ations-not-covered; see also Eugène Borel, *L'Organisation Internationale de a Croix-Rouge* (Recueil des Cours de l'Académie de Droit International, 1923), 575; Gabor Rona, *Le Statut du CICR: dans une catégorie à part, ICRC: Mandat et mission du CICR*, 17 February 2004; Jean-Marie Crouzatier, *Droit International de la Santé* (Paris, 2009).

71 Crouzatier, n. 70, 65–76.

72 Dagron, n. 15.

73 Address by Christiana Figueres, Executive Secretary, UN Framework Convention on Climate Change, Sixty-ninth World Health Assembly, Geneva, 24 May 2016, unfccc.int/news/sixty-ninth-world-health-assembly.

74 1955 Convention no. 102 Concerning Minimum Standards of Social Security.

75 ILO, *Recommendation no. 69 Concerning Medical Care*, 12 May 1944; ILO, *Recommendation no. 202 Concerning National Floors of Social Protection*, 14 June 2012.

76 1983 ILO Convention no. 155 Concerning Occupational Safety and Health and the Working Environment.

matter, and Indonesia based its decision on rules protecting biological and genetic resources enshrined in the 1992 Convention on Biological Diversity.[77] Although this reasoning was criticized as being inappropriate, a general legal solution to the issue of the sharing of samples and pathogens has so far not been found – the soft law instrument adopted (the so-called 2011 Pandemic Influenza Preparedness Framework) being of very limited applicability.[78]

The second scenario involves "conflict of norms," which are understood by the International Law Commission as "a situation where two rules or principles suggest different ways of dealing with a problem."[79] This situation can result in barriers and obstacles to the realization of specific targets linked to SDG 3. For example, the rules on protecting intellectual property rights (mentioned in target 3.b), contained in the TRIPS Agreement, allow states some flexibility in order to guarantee access to certain medicines, which are essential for the health of their populations.[80] That said, however, the UN High-Level Panel on Access to Medicines, created to analyse the barriers to access to medicines, found that difficulties in interpreting and implementing the TRIPS Agreement meant that access to medicines had been made very difficult for the poorest states.[81] During the COVID-19 pandemic, the TRIPS Agreement's rules and exceptions were criticized for hindering states from effectively responding to the pandemic.[82] A proposal, initiated by India and South Africa and submitted to the World Trade Organization (WTO) in October 2020, suggests that certain provision of the TRIPS Agreement be waived. It focuses on provisions concerning the protection and enforcement of patents as well as other forms of intellectual property rights such as copyrights or the protection of trade secrets, given that they may present an obstacle to a rapid response to COVID-19. The proposal perfectly illustrates the conflict between trade rules and the public health imperatives expressed in SDG 3.[83]

77 For more information on the link between the 1992 Convention on Biological Diversity and health, see Convention on Biodiversity Secretariat, *Health and Biodiversity*, 2021, www.cbd.int/health/.

78 See David P. Fidler, "Influenza Virus Samples, International Law, and Global Health Diplomacy" (2008) 14(1) *Emerging Infectious Diseases* 88; Michelle Rourke et al., "Policy Opportunities to Enhance Sharing for Pandemic Research" (2020) 368(6492) *Science* 716.

79 International Law Commission, *Fragmentation of International Law: Difficulties Arising from the Diversification and Expansion of International Law: Report of the Study Group of the International Law Commission*, UN Doc. A/CN.4/L.682, 2006, 19.

80 See also WTO, *Doha Ministerial Declaration on the TRIPS Agreement and Public Health*, WTO Doc. WT/MIN(01)/DEC/W/2, 14 November 2001.

81 UN Secretary-General's High Level Panel on Access to Medicines, *Promoting Innovation and Access to Health Technologies*, 14 September 2016.

82 Hans M. Haugen, "Does TRIPS (Agreement on Trade-Related Aspects of Intellectual Property Rights) Prevent COVID-19 Vaccines as a Global Public Good?" (2021) 24(3–4) *Journal of World Intellectual Property* 195.

83 Communication from India and South Africa, *Waiver from Certain Provisions of the TRIPS Agreement for the Prevention and Containment and Treatment of COVID-19*, WTO Doc. IP/C/W/669, 2 October 2020.

3.4 POSITIONING SDG 3 IN THE INTERNATIONAL INSTITUTIONAL CONTEXT

The institutional architecture of global health has developed significantly over the past decades. It has developed from a simple structure involving primarily a unique UN specialized agency – the WHO, whose role it is "to act as the directing and coordinating authority on international health work"[84] – to a complex network of actors intervening in a host of ways, including standard setting, financing, and implementation. In 2019, the UNGA launched the Global Action Plan for Healthy Lives and Well-being for All (GAP), bringing together some of these actors in order to support countries in delivering on the health-related targets of SDG 3.[85] There are thirteen GAP signatory agencies that can be classified into three groups specialized in the activities of standard setting (UN specialized agencies), financing (UN funds and programmes), and implementation (public-private partnerships [PPPs]).

The choice of institutions and their organization within the GAP will be analyzed with regard to the main challenges for global health governance that have appeared since the end of the twentieth century. The designation of specific institutions to be part of the GAP puts the emphasis on specific challenges and concretizes specific approaches to the issues of leadership, fragmentation, and participation, which will be addressed in turn.

3.4.1 *The GAP for SDG 3: No Explicit Leadership for the WHO and No Predominance of Standard-Setting Agencies*

At first, only two UN specialized agencies, which are autonomous international standard-setting bodies, were members of the GAP: the WHO and the World Bank (WB). The ILO only joined the GAP in February 2021.[86] These agencies are without doubt central institutions in global health. The WHO is the central UN agency in the field of global health; its mandate being nothing less than "the attainment by all peoples of the highest possible level of health"[87] – a particularly ambitious objective given the broad definition of health in the WHO Constitution.[88] On the contrary, the WB does not have a direct mandate in the

84 WHO Constitution, n. 6, art. 2(a).

85 See WHO, *Stronger Collaboration, Better Health: Global Action Plan for Healthy Lives and Well-being for All. Strengthening Collaboration among Multilateral Organizations to Accelerate Country Progress on the Health-related Sustainable Development Goals* (WHO, 2019).

86 WHO, *ILO Joins the Global Action Plan for Healthy Lives and Well-being for All*, 10 February 2021, www.who.int/news/item/10-02-2021-ilo-joins-the-global-action-plan-for-healthy-lives-and-well-being-for-all.

87 WHO Constitution, n. 6, art. 1.

88 The preamble to the WHO Constitution, n. 6, defines health as "a state of complete physical, mental and social well-being and not merely the absence of disease or infirmity."

field of health. However, it has been extremely active and influential in this field since the 1980s in its capacity as a development bank. The WB has invested its efforts and financial capacities in family planning, healthcare services and infrastructure, nutrition, and health and education.[89] These activities – as well as the activities of the International Monetary Fund[90] and regional development banks – have been the subject of strong criticism, especially for their neoliberal approaches to healthcare.[91] The ILO, finally, has also received a large mandate in the health field. According to its Constitution, its normative and political competences are to achieve "adequate protection for the life and health of workers in all occupations"[92] as well as "the extension of social security measures to provide a basic income to all in need of such protection and comprehensive medical care."[93]

Interestingly, and despite the importance of these agencies' mandates and activities, none of them have been attributed a leadership role within the GAP by the UNGA. This manner of proceeding is both surprising and problematic. First, it is surprising given how other task forces established by the UN Secretary-General have been organized under the leadership of one specific central institution. For example, the UN Inter-Agency Task Force on the Prevention and Control of Non-communicable Diseases (UN Inter-Agency Task Force) is under the leadership of the WHO,[94] while the UN Interagency Coordination Group on Antimicrobial Resistance has attributed a special coordination role to the three UN agencies most concerned with the topic: the WHO, the Food and Agriculture Organization (FAO), and the World Organization for Animal Health (OIE).[95] Second, it is problematic because it seems to question not only the WHO's leadership position in global health – although, in practice, the WHO seems to have taken over the

[89] See, e.g., Jennifer P. Ruger, "The Changing Role of the World Bank in Global Health" (2005) 95(1) *American Journal of Public Health* 60; Lawrence O. Gostin, *Global Health Law* (Harvard University Press, 2014), 134–43.

[90] David Stuckler & Sanjay Basu, "The International Monetary Fund's Effects on Global Health: Before and after the 2008 Financial Crisis" (2009) 39(4) *International Journal of Health Services* 771; Thomas Stubbs et al., "The Impact of International Monetary Fund Conditionality on Government Health Expenditure: A Cross-National Analysis of 16 West African Nations" (2017) 174 *Social Science and Medicine* 220.

[91] See, e.g., Gostin, n. 89, 134–43

[92] 2019 Constitution of the International Labour Organization, part III(g).

[93] "Declaration of Philadelphia" (Twenty-sixth International Labour Conference, 1944), part III (f).

[94] UN Economic and Social Council, *United Nations Inter-Agency Task Force on the Prevention and Control of Non-communicable Diseases*, UN Doc. E/RES/2013/12, 22 July 2013; WHO, *Terms of Reference for the UN Interagency Task Force on the Prevention and Control of NCDs*, WHO Doc. E/2014/55, 2015.

[95] See UNGA, *Political Declaration of the High-level Meeting of the General Assembly on Antimicrobial Resistance*, UN Doc. A/RES/71/3, 5 October 2016; FAO, OIE & WHO, *Memorandum of Understanding Regarding Cooperation to Combat Health Risks at the Animal Human-Ecosystems Interface in the Context of the "One Health" Approach and Including Antimicrobial Resistance*, 30 May 2018.

organization of the GAP– but also because of the importance of standard-setting agencies in general. In the GAP, all thirteen agencies are apparently equal, the UNGA having refrained from giving priority to normative agencies over financing and implementation initiatives or programmes. The fact that the current institutional architecture for achieving SDG 3 does not include the many other multilateral agencies who play a role in developing international law also points to the idea that standard setting is not being prioritized. While some standard-setting bodies might be active in the GAP through their involvement in the governance structure of some of the participating UN funds and programmes – although their normative influence is weak when they act in this capacity – others are completely excluded from the GAP.

Normative agencies that are excluded from the GAP include most predominantly UN agencies concerned directly or indirectly with health issues such as the UN Educational, Scientific and Cultural Organization, the International Atomic Energy Agency, the FAO, as well as organizations whose role in public health has become evident since the COVID-19 pandemic: the OIE, the World Intellectual Property Organization, and the WTO. This last organization deserves a special mention. For many years, public health issues have been considered external to the WTO's mandate. However, WTO norms have attracted much attention since the turn of the century in connection with multiple public health issues such as equitable access to antiretroviral therapy for people affected by HIV,[96] the right of countries to implement public health measures concerning tobacco control,[97] and, more recently, the issue of equitable access to vaccines in the time of a pandemic.[98] It is evident that the WTO's rules affect public health policies and, more precisely, those policies linked with the SDG 3 targets such as tobacco control, environment, health services, infectious disease control, food safety, and access to medicines and vaccines (target 3.b).[99] It has also been underlined how essential effective health and trade policy coordination is at all levels – implying integration of all relevant institutions in cross-sectoral bodies such as the GAP – to advance the goal of sustainable development for all, rendering the absence of the WTO from the GAP all the more problematic.

Noteworthy is also the noninvolvement in the GAP of agencies that are central for the protection and promotion of human rights such as the Office of the UN High Commissioner for Human Rights, or the UNHCR, as well as institutions whose role

96 Holger Hestermeyer, *Human Rights and the WTO: The Case of Patents and Access to Medicines*, 2007.

97 Thamara Romero, "Public Health and Plain Packaging of Tobacco: an Intellectual Property Perspective," South Centre Research Paper no. 108, 30 April 2020.

98 Haugen, n. 82; see also WTO, *Developing and Delivering COVID-19 Vaccines around the World: An Information Note About Issues with Trade Impact*, December 2020.

99 See, e.g., WHO & WTO, *WHO and WTO on WTO Agreements and Public Health, A Joint Study*, 2002.

is central for the implementation of specific targets, such as the UN Office on Drugs and Crime (target 3.5) or the United Nations Environment Programme (target 3.9). All these institutions are part of other task forces such as the UN Inter-Agency Task Force.[100] Finally, it is also worth noting that, while the ILO's potential areas of cooperation and contribution in the field of global health are manifold, including "health financing, social protection, ... gender equality, and rights, standards and conditions for health workers,"[101] it seems that the ILO's participation in the GAP relates only to its work on occupational safety.[102]

3.4.2 *The GAP for SDG 3: A Collaborative Strategy against Fragmentation*

Since the end of the twentieth century, collaboration among the various international institutions involved in public health, development, and humanitarian activities has been strongly encouraged in order to improve work in the global health field through better coordination of international strategies, more precise and goal-oriented use of financial capacities, and the more coherent promotion of public health implementation activities. Reflecting on the WHO's role in global health governance in 2010, the then director general, Margaret Chan, underlined the difficulties resulting from fragmentation and the increase in political attention and financial resources for development and global health. She stated that "[the area of development] has attracted an increasingly crowded array of actors with little, if any, effective institutional architecture at the global level. As a result, countries frequently experience conflicting advice from different missions, duplication of efforts, fragmented channels of funding, high transaction costs, and burdensome reporting requirements."[103]

The GAP reflects an attempt to counter these difficulties and to encourage collaboration between the worlds of public health, humanitarian action, and development. Besides the three normative agencies, the GAP also includes a second category of organizations made up of six UN funds and programmes – that is, organizations that have been entrusted by the UN system with a specific and technical area of work or with a specific task – and two other "entities." The six UN funds and programmes include the UN Development Programme (UNDP), the UN International Children's Emergency Fund (UNICEF), the Joint UN Programme on HIV/AIDS (UNAIDS), UN Women, the UN Population Fund (UNFPA), and the World Food Programme (WFP).[104] The entities that are members of the GAP are the Global Financing Facility for Women, Children

[100] WHO, n. 94.
[101] WHO, n. 86.
[102] *Id.*
[103] WHO, *Report by the Director General: The Future of Financing for WHO*, WHO Doc. EB128/21, 15 December 2010, para. 19.
[104] See the complete list in WHO, n. 85, 7.

and Adolescents (GFF) and Unitaid. The emphasis on these funds, programmes, and entities (as opposed to normative agencies) entails that the UNGA provides a double answer to the negative consequences of fragmentation. First, UN funds, programmes, and entities are composed of multiple stakeholders active in the fields of public health, development, and humanitarian activities. Second, they bring multiple competencies since they are involved in addressing public health issues as well as humanitarian and development issues. Some of these institutions have a direct mandate in the health matters reflected in the targets of SDG 3. For example, UNICEF has a general mandate for child health and runs programmes promoting children's rights, educational development, development assistance, and children and maternal health (targets 3.1 and 3.2);[105] the UNFPA is active in the field of sexual and reproductive health (target 3.1);[106] and UNAIDS is a programme created to develop a coordinated response to the HIV epidemic, support national governments, and promote social mobilization.[107] The work of UNICEF, UNFPA, and Unitaid has been reinforced through funding by new UN humanitarian and development programmes and entities. For example, Unitaid was established to help accelerate access to high-quality drugs and diagnosis for AIDS, tuberculosis, and malaria patients (target 3.3),[108] and UN Women and the GFF both work for the acceleration of progress toward better protection of women and children.[109] The UN's traditional development programmes – the WFP and the UNDP – have reorientated their broader activities toward global health.

3.4.3 *The GAP for SDG 3: The Unquestioned Involvement of Nonstate Actors*

Since the 1990s, the global health institutional landscape has also been characterized by the strong involvement of nonstate actors (NSAs), including nongovernmental organizations (NGOs), philanthropic foundations, and private sector entities – in the implementation of global health strategies. Partnerships between NSAs, on the one hand, and the WHO, other UN agencies, and national governments, on the other hand, have multiplied since then through the creation of UN funds and programmes that involve private partners as well as, more importantly, the creation of PPPs outside

[105] UNGA, *Establishment of an International Children's Emergency Fund*, UN Doc. A/RES/1/57 (1), 11 December 1946.

[106] See UNFPA, *About Us*, www.unfpa.org/about-us.

[107] Economic and Social Council, *Joint and Co-sponsored United Nations Programme on Human Immunodeficiency Virus/acquired Immunodeficiency Syndrome (HIV/AIDS)*, Resolution 1994/24, UN Doc. E/RES/1994/24, 26 July 1994.

[108] 2011 Unitaid Constitution, www.unitaid.org/about-us/governance.

[109] UNGA, *System-wide Coherence*, UN Doc. A/RES/64/289*, 21 July 2010; World Bank Group, *Global Financing Facility Launched with Billions Already Mobilized to End Maternal and Child Mortality by 2030*, World Bank Press Release no. 2016/022/HNPGP, 13 July 2015.

the UN system.[110] These PPPs have taken different forms: initiatives dedicated to the promotion of access to medicines (for instance, the partnership between the WHO's Multi Drug Therapy Programme and Novartis for the delivery of free leprosy treatment for all patients worldwide); initiatives focusing on the bolstering of drug discovery and development (for example, the Medicine for Malaria Venture and the Drugs for Neglected Diseases Initiative) or on the strengthening of health systems (the African Comprehensive HIV/AIDS Partnership); and even the development of guidelines proposing, for instance, useful standards for the harmonization of medicines marketing procedures and conditions (the International Council for Harmonisation of Technical Requirements for Pharmaceuticals for Human Use).[111]

The GAP for health includes two PPPs in its third category of members: the Global Alliance for Vaccines and Immunization and the Global Fund to Fight AIDS, Tuberculosis and Malaria.[112] Since their creation in 2000 and 2002 respectively, these two PPPs have rapidly become the most important and influential global health institutions with regard to the large number and nature of the involved partners (philanthropic foundations, donor governments, representatives from developing countries, UN special agencies, international development and finance organizations, NGOs, and vaccine and medicine manufacturers) – their financial capacities as well as their significant impacts on issues have been identified by the WHO as the main global health issues to be solved,[113] including targets 3.2, 3.3, and 3.c. Their inclusion in the GAP is in line with the efforts made by the WHO to deepen its collaboration with stakeholders from the private and voluntary sectors[114] and also in line with the UN development strategy expressed, for instance, in the Addis-Ababa Action Agenda[115] and confirmed in target 17.17, encouraging effective public, public-private, and civil society partnerships.

However, the participation of PPPs in the GAP blurs the fragile lines between public and private actors in global health that the WHO has tried to draw since the turn of the century in order to restrict and control inappropriate and illegitimate interventions that might interfere with its normative activities. Multiple efforts toward the regulation of interactions have been made,[116] culminating in 2016 with the adoption by the WHA of the Framework of Engagement with Non-state Actors

[110] See, e.g., Theodore M. Brown, Marcos Cueto & Elizabeth Fee, *The World Health Organization: A History* (Cambridge University Press, 2019), chap. 10.

[111] See generally Dagron, n. 58.

[112] On both institutions, see, e.g., Gostin, n. 89, chap. 5.

[113] See the WHO list established in 2020, which includes communicable diseases. WHO, *Ten Global Health Issues to Track in 2021*, December 2020.

[114] See WHA, *Health Development in a Changing World: A Call for Action*, Resolution WHA46.17, 1993.

[115] UNGA, *Addis Ababa Action Agenda of the Third International Conference on Financing for Development (Addis Ababa Action Agenda)*, UN Doc. A/RES/69/313, 27 July 2015.

[116] See *Principles Governing Relations between the WHO and Nongovernmental Organizations*, WHO Doc. WHA40.25, 1987; *Guidelines on Interaction with Commercial Enterprises to Achieve Health Outcomes*, Doc. EB107/20, 2000, Annex; see also Kent Buse & Amalia

(FENSA).[117] This framework, which provides rules concerning conflicts of interests, risk evaluation, and transparency, is supposed to respond to the double challenge of broadening "engagement beyond governments to include other stakeholders," while ensuring that "the development of norms, standards, policies and strategies [is] protected from the influence of any form of categorical interest."[118] In other words, it must allow for the strengthening of the WHO's capacities and activities in global health through the participation of private actors, while not compromising the exercise of normative competences that are the central expression of its legitimacy and leadership.

However, so far, and despite the fact that the FENSA offers an interesting model for other institutional strategies for the implementation of Agenda 2030, it has not been positively received. The criticisms concern, for instance, the absence of distinctions between NGOs representing the public interest and private sector entities with commercial objectives and also the weak protection against undue influence over the global health agenda exercised by the private sector or large global philanthropic donors such as the Bill and Melinda Gates Foundation. Again, the absence of a hierarchy between institutional stakeholders participating within the GAP for health has to be questioned since it institutionalizes – and seems to legitimize – the participation of these actors as equals with UN organizations and member states that have so far been the central actors of the multilateral system.

3.5 CONCLUSIONS

Defining health for all as a specific SDG has had negative, as well as positive, impacts on the understanding of international law as a general instrument for the promotion and protection of human health. First, concerning the negative impacts, the analysis of the targets and indicators, as well as of the institutional structure designed to implement SDG 3, has revealed not only that law has been sidelined by states preferring to concentrate mainly on medical and/or economic strategies but also that specific institutions intervening in the field of global health law have been excluded from the list of the main actors. It should be noted that Agenda 2030 did not create the difficulties that have characterized international health law: the norms belonging to that branch of international law are fragmented, incomplete, and sometimes contradictory, and its institutional architecture presents a complexity that renders the exercise of clear leadership difficult. While it should be noted that SDG 3 does refer to some global health law instruments, the indicators themselves do not encourage states to properly implement their existing legal obligations that

Waxman, "Public-private Health Partnerships: A Strategy for WHO" (2001) 79 *Bulletin of the World Health Organization* 748.

[117] WHA, *Framework of Engagement with Non-state Actors*, WHO Doc. WHA69.10, 28 May 2016.

[118] WHO, *Report by the Director-General: WHO Reforms for a Healthy Future*, WHO Doc. EBSS/2/2, 15 October 2011, paras. 85, 87.

have an impact on global health or to develop new legal norms or resolve potential norm conflicts. As such, by asking states to concentrate at once on the fulfillment of specific medical or economic indicators accepted by all and for all, SDG 3 may have diverted the efforts and human and financial capacities of states away from already accepted legal engagements, such as those resulting from human rights treaties.

Second, and more positively, a global consensus on which specific objectives to push toward, as well as the political will to do so, is crucial for the development and implementation of international (health) law: just as law is essential for the implementation of public health strategies, a strong and coherent political will is essential for international (health) law to be improved and effective. Agenda 2030 affirmed a global consensus on objectives and identified health as a central element of the global development and end of poverty strategy – a consensus that has been reaffirmed by states as a consequence of the COVID-19 pandemic. Although the crisis might have negatively impacted many of the targets of SDG 3[119] – as has already been documented for target 3.3 on tuberculosis, for example[120] – it has also confirmed the necessity for states to address collectively, and as a solidary community, the global health issues identified by Agenda 2030: no population can be healthy until all populations are healthy. International law – as has been confirmed by the proposition to adopt a new international treaty on pandemic preparedness[121] – is from now on undoubtedly considered part of the solution.

[119] WHO, *Report by the Director-General: Implementation of the 2030 Agenda for Sustainable Development* WHO Doc. A74/11, 20 May 2021.

[120] WHO, *Global Tuberculosis Report 2020*, 2020.

[121] *Strengthening WHO Preparedness for and Response to Health Emergencies*, WHO Doc. WHA74.7, 31 May 2021.

4

SDG 4: Ensure Inclusive and Equitable Quality Education and Promote Lifelong Learning Opportunities for All

Fons Coomans

ABSTRACT

This chapter analyzes Sustainable Development Goal (SDG) 4, Quality Education, by comparing its content to the standards of international law – in particular, human rights law and trade law. It focuses on the added value of SDG 4 for the further development of the right to education in international law and in relation to international institutions. It analyzes three themes: the existence of an international body of law on education; education as a public good versus education as a commodity; and the need to regulate the conduct of private actors in education. SDG 4 and the Education 2030 Framework for Action politically reaffirm the legal obligations that states have under human rights treaties. International human rights law, in general, and the right to education, in particular, have paved the way for a strong implementation of SDG 4 at the domestic and international level through a human rights–informed approach.

KEYWORDS

SDG 4, right to education, human rights law, international trade law, Incheon Declaration and Education 2030 Framework for Action, public good, private actors, UNESCO

4.1 INTRODUCTION

Today, many people still do not have access to basic education, are illiterate, or do not possess educational qualifications to be able to find appropriate employment.[1]

[1] UNESCO, *Global Education Monitoring Report 2020: Inclusion and Education – All Means All*, 2020, en.unesco.org/gem-report/report/2020/inclusion.

Sustainable Development Goal (SDG) 4, Quality Education, aims to promote education opportunities for everyone worldwide. It has a universal ambition and reach, and it focuses, in particular, on those who do not have access to education and learning opportunities, especially vulnerable and marginalized groups in the North and the South. Inclusive education entails that no one should be left out of school because of gender, disability, socioeconomic status, ethnic background, or living in a conflict area. It links to lifelong learning pathways, irrespective of age, to be able to fully participate as a member of society and to be prepared for living and working in a society that is developing rapidly. SDG 4 also aims at improving quality education and learning outcomes through education systems that are responsive and resilient to changing situations and needs, such as economic crisis, conflicts, digital developments, natural disasters, and pandemics.[2]

Traditionally, education has been a topic regulated by domestic law, including by constitutional law. It has been, and still is, essentially a domestic issue, where states retain a significant degree of discretion, and few international standards prescribe what to teach. Education deals with national particularities in the sense that it reflects the history and cultural identity of a country. Education is treated as an issue subject to the sovereignty of each state, often codified as a basic right in the constitution. At the international level, education is primarily part of human rights law and included in treaties of global and regional scope. These treaties impose on states obligations to realize the individual human right to education. Respecting the typical features of domestic educational systems, as mentioned, international human rights law also grants states some discretion in implementing these obligations. Traditionally, education has been seen as a public good with the state as the main provider and funded through public, tax-generated resources. As a result of the liberalization of the world economy, as reflected in World Trade Organization (WTO) agreements, states have opened some sectors of education to the private sector. In these instances, education has become a tradeable service regulated by the WTO's 1994 General Agreement on Trade in Services (GATS) and, in these cases, education qualifies as a commodity, subject to the provisions of international trade law.[3]

The UN Educational, Scientific and Cultural Organization (UNESCO) acts as the key international organization responsible for coordinating the role of the

[2] 2015 Incheon Declaration for Education 2030, iite.unesco.org/publications/education-2030-incheon-declaration-framework-action-towards-inclusive-equitable-quality-education-lifelong-learning/; 2015 Education 2030 Framework for Action, section 1: Vision, Rationale and Principles, iite.unesco.org/publications/education-2030-incheon-declaration-framework-action-towards-inclusive-equitable-quality-education-lifelong-learning/.

[3] John Morijn, *Reframing Human Rights and Trade: Potential and Limits of a Human Rights Perspective of WTO Law on Cultural and Educational Goods and Services* (Intersentia, 2010).

international community to achieve SDG 4. It does so through partnerships, policy guidance, capacity development, and the monitoring of progress and advocacy.[4] The 2015 Incheon Declaration for Education 2030 and the 2015 Education 2030 Framework for Action have entrusted UNESCO with this role.[5] These two documents provide approaches, targets, strategies, and modalities for implementing SDG 4, and, together, they provide a vision for implementing SDG 4 to which all relevant stakeholders have agreed. Signatories of the two documents include UNESCO, the UN Development Programme, the UN Population Fund, the UN High Commissioner on Human Rights, the United Nations International Children's Emergency Fund (UNICEF), UN Women, the World Bank Group, and the International Labour Organization (ILO). Signatories also include representatives of governments, civil society organizations, the teaching profession, youth organizations, and the private sector. The Education 2030 Framework for Action lists a number of principles, drawn from international human rights instruments that should inform the implementation of the framework for action. These principles set out that education is a fundamental right and an enabling right; that education is a public good for which the state is the duty bearer; and that achieving gender equality is linked to the right to education for all.[6]

This chapter will also discuss the content of SDG 4 by comparing it to the standards of international law as developed in the framework of the UN human rights treaties, UNESCO standards, ILO standards, WTO law, and the Education 2030 Framework for Action. It examines existing and emerging legal standards (hard and soft) as elements of an international body of law on education. In addition, the chapter highlights several current issues that are relevant for giving effect to SDG 4 from a legal perspective, including the increasing role of private parties in offering education. The chapter will evaluate the added value, if any, of SDG 4 for the further development of (the right to) education in international law.

4.2 THE CONTENT OF SDG 4 IN THE CONTEXT OF THE OTHER SDGS

4.2.1 *The Content of SDG 4*

SDG 4 aims to ensure inclusive and equitable quality education and to promote lifelong learning opportunities for all. The focus is not only on the individual young

4 UNESCO, *Leading SDG 4: Education 2030*, en.unesco.org/themes/education2030-sdg4. One example of a monitoring tool is UNESCO's Observatory on the Right to Education, which provides for legal and policy frameworks at the country level related to education. See Observatory on the Right to Education, *Welcome to UNESCO Observatory on the Right to Education*, www.unesco.org/education/edurights/.

5 Incheon Declaration for Education 2030, n. 2; Education 2030 Framework for Action, n. 2.

6 Education 2030 Framework for Action, n. 2, 28.

pupil and student but also on adults who, at a later stage in life, may feel a need to develop their learning capacities. It refers to concepts such as inclusiveness, equity, quality education, and lifelong learning, the realization of which is imperative for attaining sustainable development. More precisely, SDG 4 focuses on two main issues: ensuring free, equitable, and quality primary and secondary education for all boys and girls (target 4.1) and ensuring equal access to all levels of education for the vulnerable (target 4.5). The importance of technical and vocational skills for employment is highlighted (targets 4.4 and 4.b). Target 4.6 aims to ensure that all youth and a substantial proportion of adults, both men and women, achieve literacy and numeracy. It should be noted that the concept of lifelong learning opportunities is not addressed explicitly in the targets. Special attention is given to tackling gender disparities in education, for example, when it comes to offering a safe and non-violent learning environment (target 4.a).[7]

New in an international document is the target on quality early childhood development, care, and pre-primary education (target 4.2). It reflects recent developments in pedagogics that emphasize the importance of early childhood development. A target that may be difficult to concretize and for which implementation may be hard to assess is target 4.7 on the need to have the knowledge and skills to promote different dimensions of sustainable development, such as lifestyles, human rights, a culture of peace and non-violence, global citizenship, and cultural diversity.

In comparison to the 2000 Millennium Development Goals (MDGs), the goal on education has expanded considerably. MDG 2 on education aimed to ensure that children everywhere – boys and girls alike – would be able to complete a full course of primary schooling and that boys and girls would have equal access to all levels of education.[8] This goal was limited to primary education, while target 4.1 covers both primary and secondary education. In addition, target 4.1 includes the requirements that education should be free of charge and meet certain quality standards. It is interesting that SDG 4 uses the proverbs 'equal' and 'equitable'. The term 'equal' refers to equality and is widely used in human rights law; it is about non-discrimination and equal treatment. The word 'equitable' refers to the idea of giving everyone a fair and equal opportunity, not necessarily the same treatment. The reference to free of charge education in SDG 4 is important; it was absent in MDG 2. Direct or indirect costs for primary and secondary education, such as school fees, expenses for books and electronic devices, school meals, school uniforms, or school transport, constitute key barriers for parents to send their children to school.

7 The indicator for target 4.a is the proportion of schools with access to: (1) electricity; (2) Internet for pedagogical purposes; (3) computers for pedagogical purposes; (4) adapted infrastructure and materials for students with disabilities; (5) basic drinking water; (6) single-sex basic sanitation facilities; and (7) basic handwashing facilities, the percentage of students experiencing bullying in the last twelve months, and the number of attacks on students, personnel, and institutions.

8 *UN Millennium Declaration*, UN Doc. A/Res/55/2, 8 September 2000, para. 19.

States have agreed to achieve twelve years of public and free primary and secondary education, of which nine years must be compulsory.[9]

SDG 4 is also interesting for what is not included, such as the mobility of students across borders; the importance of education for refugees, asylum seekers, and undocumented migrants; the digital divide between the global North and global South when it comes to access to teaching materials; the need to re-emphasize that education is a public good in light of the increasing role of private parties in education. Also excluded are well-known problems such as the tension between the need to attend education and the reality of child labour and education in conflict zones where schools have been closed or are under attack by warring parties. There is a brief reference to Indigenous groups as an example of vulnerable populations; however, it does not deal, for example, with the language of instruction or the trend in some countries to assimilate Indigenous peoples into mainstream education. These are important dimensions of inclusive education and the idea of leaving no one behind.

4.2.2 *The Relationship of SDG 4 with the Other SDGs*

SDG 4 is about the key role of education in achieving the economic and social development of a country: a well-educated citizenry contributes to the economic prosperity of society as a whole. It is also about the personal development of learners to move up the social ladder, which will also benefit the development of the family or the wider social unit, such as the community or the village. Education can be seen as a tool to empower people to achieve an adequate standard of living. In this sense, SDG 4 is related to other SDGs. For example, having enjoyed an education is an important asset for moving out of poverty (SDG 1, No Poverty). A well-educated citizen is in a much better position to find a job and participate in society (SDG 8, Decent Work and Economic Growth). Girls and women who have been educated are empowered and emancipated as full members of society and able to contribute to personal and social development. Education is an important means for girls and women to escape from poverty (SDG 1) and discrimination in society (SDG 5, Gender Equality). SDG 4 on education also has links with other basic needs such as food and health. For example, vocational training may help farmers to learn about how to apply new agricultural techniques and thus improve food production and income. A person who has had a basic education is more aware of health risks and better able to make informed choices about healthy ways of living, nutrition, and reproduction (SDG 2, Zero Hunger, and SDG 3, Good Health and Well-being).[10]

9 Education 2030 Framework for Action, n. 2, paras. 30, 34.

10 For an overview of links between SDG 4, Quality Education, and the other SDGs, see UNESCO & Right to Education Initiative, *Right to Education Handbook* (UNESCO, 2019), 161–62.

From the perspective of the promotion of decent work for all (SDG 8), education plays a key role as an alternative option for children with a view to eliminating child labour (target 8.7).

The paramount role of education in achieving the other SDGs can also be seen in the legal domain where the right to education has been recognized as a key right that unlocks the enjoyment of other rights.[11] Food, work, and health have been recognized as human rights in several international instruments, such as the 1966 International Covenant on Economic, Social and Cultural Rights (ICESCR).[12] For example, SDG 5 on gender equality and the empowerment of girls has its legal counterpart in the 1979 Convention on the Elimination of All Forms of Discrimination against Women (CEDAW). Article 10 of CEDAW extensively deals with the right to education for girls and women.

SDG 4 does not deal with the educational consequences of global health crises, an issue that became acute in 2020 as a result of the COVID-19 pandemic. It is clear that the consequences of COVID-19 put at serious risk the availability and equal accessibility of education, which are key elements of SDG 4.[13] Responses to the educational challenges posed by the consequences of the COVID-19 pandemic should be informed by the pledge of the 2030 Agenda for Sustainable Development 'that no one will be left behind'.[14]

4.3 POSITIONING SDG 4 IN INTERNATIONAL LAW

4.3.1 *The Added Value of SDG 4 for International Law*

It is submitted that SDG 4 does not give rise to major complexities or challenges for international law. SDG 4 is rather conservative, not really ambitious, and only touches upon a few issues that may trigger further developments in international (human rights) law. It largely reflects and builds upon existing standards of international human rights law. SDG 4 calls attention to a number of special issues that are relevant from the perspective of stronger policy implementation. The right to education has been recognized as a legal right in domestic (constitutional) law as well as regional and international human rights law. However, the meaning/value that is added by SDG 4 for the progressive development of international law is limited.

[11] CESCR, *General Comment 13 on the Right to Education*, UN Doc. E/C.12/1999/10, 1999, para. 1; Fons Coomans, '"Education and Work"', in Daniel Moeckli, Sangeeta Shah, & Sandesh Sivakumaran (eds.), *International Human Rights Law*, 3rd ed. (Cambridge University Press, 2018), 242.

[12] ICESCR, arts. 6, 11, 12.

[13] For a discussion, see *UN Special Rapporteur on the Right to Education*, UN Doc. A/HRC/44/39, 2020.

[14] *Transforming Our World: The 2030 Agenda for Sustainable Development*, UN Doc. A/Res/70/1, 25 September 2015, preamble, para. 4.

One notable exception is target 4.2 on pre-primary education, which is an important stage in the development of children as they prepare for primary education. Increasingly pre-primary or early childhood education is recognized as a key element of the care economy.[15] The right to pre-primary education is not included explicitly in international human rights law. The large majority of UN member states do not provide for a legal right to pre-primary education at the domestic level.[16] With a view to implementing target 4.2, states have agreed to introduce at least one year of free and compulsory quality pre-primary education,[17] and this decision may be indicative of the further development of the right to education as a human right. The UN Committee on the Rights of the Child interprets 'the right to education during early childhood as beginning at birth and closely linked to young children's right to maximum development'.[18]

Another exception relates to the emerging notion of lifelong learning.[19] SDG 4 mentions 'lifelong learning opportunities for all' as part of its heading; however, the term is not used in the targets. There is a reference to 'adults' in targets 4.4 and 4.6, but this is not explicitly linked to the concept of lifelong learning. The notion of lifelong learning has been defined by the UN special rapporteur on the right to education as 'covering learning activities for people of all ages in all life-wide contexts through a variety of modalities (formal, non-formal and informal) that together meet a wide range of learning needs and demands'.[20] The ILO's Human Resources Development Recommendation defines the term 'lifelong learning' as 'all learning activities undertaken throughout life for the development of competences and qualifications'.[21] There is a link with the right to vocational training.[22] It has been recognized that 'adult learning and education is a core component of lifelong learning'.[23] The Education 2030 Framework for Action states that the concept of lifelong learning will guide its implementation.[24] The right to lifelong learning as such does not yet exist in international human rights law. However,

[15] ILO, *Early Childhood Education*, www.ilo.org/global/topics/care-economy/early-childhood/lang--en/index.htm.

[16] UNESCO, *Majority of Countries Do Not Ensure the Right to Pre-primary Education, According to UNESCO Study*, 28 January 2021, en.unesco.org/news/majority-countries-do-not-ensure-right-pre-primary-education-according-new-unesco-study.

[17] Education 2030 Framework for Action, n. 2, paras. 35–37.

[18] UN Committee on the Rights of the Child, *General Comment 7 on Implementing Child Rights in Early Childhood*, UN Doc. CRC/C/GC/7/Rev.1, 2005, para. 28.

[19] See the UNESCO Institute on Lifelong Learning, *Lifelong Learning*, uil.unesco.org/lifelong-learning.

[20] UN Special Rapporteur on the Right to Education, *Report on the Right to Education*, UN Doc. A/71/358, 2016, para. 37.

[21] *Human Resources Development Recommendation*, ILO Recommendation no. 195, 2004, art. 2a.

[22] 1961 European Social Charter, art. 10; ICESCR, art. 13(2); 1975 ILO Convention no. 142 on Human Resources.

[23] UNESCO Recommendation on Adult Learning and Education, UN Doc. ED-2016/WS/29, 2015, s. I.1.

[24] Education 2030 Framework for Action, n. 2, 30, 33–34.

article 13(2)(d) of the ICESCR recognizes fundamental education as a component of the right to education 'for those persons who have not received or completed the whole period of their primary education'. The Committee on Economic, Social and Cultural Rights (CESCR) has stated that 'fundamental education . . . is an integral component of adult education and life-long learning'.[25] So far, there is no soft law or hard law norm that explicitly provides for the right to lifelong learning. SDG 4 may constitute a trigger for developing such a norm.

Target 4.7 deals with the type of knowledge and skill needed to promote sustainable development, which is an issue that has not been developed as of yet in international human rights law. This type of knowledge and skill refers, inter alia, to education for sustainable lifestyles, human rights, gender equality, promotion of a culture of peace and non-violence, global citizenship, and cultural diversity. It is submitted that, to some extent, a link can be established with the aims of education as codified in international human rights treaties. For example, article 29(1) of the 1989 UN Convention on the Rights of the Child (UNCRC) stipulates that the education of the child shall be directed, inter alia, towards respect for civilizations different from their own; human rights; peace, tolerance, and understanding; and the natural environment.[26] It is also submitted that target 4.7 expands on these goals by putting them in a broader sustainable and global perspective. The notions of education for sustainable development (ESD) and global citizenship education (GCE) have been defined in policy terms in several ways. First, ESD

> empowers learners to take informed decisions and responsible actions for environmental integrity, economic viability and a just society, for present and future generations, while respecting cultural diversity. It is about lifelong learning, and is an integral part of quality education. ESD is holistic and transformational education which addresses learning content and outcomes, pedagogy and the learning environment. It achieves its purpose by transforming society.[27]

Second, GCE

> aims to equip learners with the following core competencies: (a) a deep knowledge of global issues and universal values such as justice, equality, dignity and respect; (b) cognitive skills to think critically, systemically and creatively, including adopting a multi-perspective approach that recognizes different dimension, perspectives and angles of issues; (c) non-cognitive skills including social skills such as empathy and conflict resolution, and communicative skills and aptitudes for networking and interacting with people of different backgrounds, origins, cultures and perspectives;

[25] CESCR, n. 11, para. 24.

[26] UNCRC, art. 29(1) has been explained and interpreted by the UN Committee on the Rights of the Child in *General Comment 1 on the Aims of Education*, UN Doc. CRC/GC/2001/1, 2001. On the aims of education, see also ICESCR, art. 13(1); UDHR, art. 26(2).

[27] UNESCO, *Roadmap for Implementing the Global Action Programme on Education for Sustainable Development*, 2014, unesdoc.unesco.org/images/0023/002305/230514e.pdf.

and (d) behavioural capacities to act collaboratively and responsibly, and to strive for collective good.[28]

It is questionable whether the rather broad notions that are part of target 4.7 can be further developed in detail in international legal standards. Instead, these primary goals of education need to be transposed and implemented at the domestic level in laws and policies. States have a large degree of discretion in doing this, taking into account the particular features of their education systems and the latitude given to education stakeholders on the local level. However, some general state obligations to promote and facilitate education on climate change and biodiversity have been included in multilateral environmental agreements.[29]

4.3.2 *The Development of a Body of International Law on Education*

4.3.2.1 Relevant Instruments

Since the end of the Second World War, a body of international law on education has emerged. In that process, human rights law, both international and regional, has played a leading role. This body of law is of a mixed nature and diverse in terms of sources. Key UN human rights treaties, such as the ICESCR,[30] the UNCRC,[31] CEDAW,[32] and the 2006 Convention on the Rights of Persons with Disabilities (CRPD),[33] all contain extensive provisions on education as a human right. Also relevant is the 1960 Convention on Discrimination in Education (CDE), which is hosted by UNESCO. On the regional level, the right to education is included in the 1952 European Convention on Human Rights and Fundamental Freedoms (ECHR),[34] the 1988 Protocol of San Salvador to the 1969 American Convention on Human Rights,[35] the 1990 African Charter on the Rights and Welfare of the

[28] UNESCO, *Outcome Document of the Technical Consultation on Global Citizenship Education: Global Citizenship Education – An Emerging Perspective*, 2013, unesdoc.unesco.org/images/0022/002241/224115E.pdf.

[29] 1992 United Nations Framework Convention on Climate Change, art. 6; 2015 Paris Agreement on Climate Change, art. 12; 1992 Convention on Biological Diversity, art. 13.

[30] ICESCR, arts. 13, 14.

[31] UNCRC, arts. 28, 29.

[32] CEDAW, art. 10.

[33] CRPD, art. 24.

[34] 1952 Protocol no. 1 to the ECHR, art. 2. The European Court of Human Rights (ECtHR) has given a number of judgments that interpret the right to education laid down in art. 2 of Protocol no. 1 to the ECHR. The focus of its case law on art. 2 has been on interpreting the freedom dimension of the right to education – namely, the rights of parents and learners to choose the types of education that are in accordance with their convictions. The court has dealt in a very limited way with the duty of states to make education available and accessible to all as a positive obligation. For a detailed discussion, see Pieter van Dijk et al. (eds.), *Theory and Practice of the European Convention on Human Rights*, 5th ed. (Intersentia, 2018), 889–908.

[35] 1988 Protocol of San Salvador., art. 13.

Child,[36] and the 2004 Arab Charter on Human Rights.[37] Some of the provisions on the right to education in these regional treaties follow the structure and wording of the ICESCR and the UNCRC. Next to treaty law, there is a relatively small body of case law mainly by the European Court of Human Rights.

4.3.2.2 The Background to Addressing Education as a Human Right

The 1948 Universal Declaration of Human Rights and, in particular, the ICESCR depart from the idea that 'the ideal of free human beings enjoying freedom from fear and want can only be achieved if conditions are created whereby everyone may enjoy his economic, social and cultural rights as well as his civil and political rights'.[38] Economic, social, and cultural rights, such as the right to food, health, work, and education, are key rights to be able to live a life in dignity. After the Second World War, states agreed to lay down and respect a number of fundamental rights with a view to preventing tyranny and oppression. Education was to play a key role in promoting understanding, tolerance, and friendship among all nations as well as ethnic and religious groups. The 1945 UNESCO Constitution provides in its preamble that 'the education of humanity for justice and liberty and peace are indispensable to the dignity of man and constitute a sacred duty which all the nations must fulfil in a spirit of mutual assistance and concern'. The founders of UNESCO believed 'in full and equal opportunities for education for all'.[39] The UNESCO Constitution also provides for the need 'to advance the ideal of equality of educational opportunity without regard to race, sex or any distinctions economic or social'.[40] International agreements in the area of human rights are an appropriate way in which to achieve this goal. There is clearly a link with the notion of inclusive education of SDG 4. Education as a human right also has an instrumental function – namely, as a tool to achieve the full development of the human personality.[41] With a view to achieving this goal, eliminating the urgent problem of illiteracy through education has been strongly advocated by UNESCO since the late 1940s.[42]

36 1990 African Charter on the Rights and Welfare of the Child (1990 African Charter), art. 11.

37 2004 Arab Charter on Human Rights, art. 41.

38 ICESCR, preamble.

39 1945 UNESCO Constitution, preamble.

40 *Id.*, art. I(2)(b). During the drafting of the ICESCR, UNESCO played an active role in promoting detailed provisions on education in the treaty. Art. 13, as it was finally adopted, was very much inspired by, and based upon, UNESCO proposals. See Working Group on Economic, Social and Cultural Rights, *Compilation of Proposals Relating to Economic, Social and Cultural Rights*, UN Doc. E/CN.4/AC.14/2/Add.4, 1951.

41 ICESCR, art. 13(1).

42 *Intervention by Mr. Elvin (UNESCO) at a Session of the UN Commission on Human Rights*, UN Doc. E/CN.4/SR.226, 1951, 12–16.

4.3.2.3 Dimensions of the Right to Education

Human rights treaties do not explicitly deal with the notion of quality education as SDG 4 does. This notion seems to be implicit in the human rights provision on the right to education: once education is offered to learners, it must meet certain quality standards, some of them related to the aims of education. The right to education as a human right is composed of two dimensions. The first dimension is the right to receive an education. This dimension concerns the right of everyone to different types of education (primary, secondary, and higher) and the obligation of the state to realize this right progressively as stipulated in article 2(1) of the ICESCR. This right is part of articles 13 and 14 of the ICESCR and article 28 of the UNCRC. It requires the state to take measures (building schools, paying teachers, developing a curriculum, establishing an inspection system, and so on) and thus involves positive obligations for the state.

The right to receive education is contained in article 13 of the ICESCR and has been interpreted and explained by the CESCR and the UN special rapporteur on the right to education. As set out in General Comment 13, which was adopted by the CESCR in 1999, the right to education consists of four interrelated features (the Four A Scheme):

Availability: functioning educational institutions and programs have to be available in sufficient numbers, through a public educational system and allowing private parties to establish non-public schools.

Accessibility: educational institutions and programs have to be accessible to everyone, without discrimination on any ground, also implying physical and economic accessibility.

Acceptability: the form and substance of education, including curricula and teaching methods, have to be relevant, culturally appropriate, of good quality, and in accordance with the best interests of the child; this includes a safe and healthy school environment.

Adaptability: education has to be flexible, so that it can adapt to the needs of changing societies and communities and respond to the needs of students within their specific social and cultural context, including the evolving capacities of the child.[43]

Most UN treaty bodies follow the approach adopted by the CESCR. As a result, the Four A Scheme is now generally accepted as an authoritative framework for describing the key features of the right to education and for monitoring its implementation. In essence, the various targets of SDG 4 cover the different elements of the right to receive an education and the Four A Scheme.

[43] CESCR, n. 11; *Preliminary Report of the Special Rapporteur on the Right to Education*, UN Doc. E/CN.4/1999/49, 1999, part II.

The second dimension of the right to education provides for the freedom to choose an education. It involves the freedom of parents to decide which religious or philosophical education should be given to their children and the right to establish schools outside the system of public education (article 13(3) and (4) of the ICESCR). The freedom to choose an education entails a negative obligation on the part of the state. It entails that the state must abstain from interfering in the freedom of parents to choose.[44] While, in the European context, this right has been interpreted as an obligation for the state to ensure an objective and pluralist curriculum and a lack of indoctrination,[45] in the African context, it has been interpreted as a duty for the state to promote and protect African morals and traditional values recognized by the community.[46]

Implementation of the freedom to establish schools is subject to educational standards laid down in domestic law. This freedom has a solid basis in universal and regional human rights treaties and case law. According to international human rights law, there is no obligation for a state to provide financial support to private educational institutions. However, if it does, it should do so on a non-discriminatory basis.[47] The right to establish educational institutions outside of the public education system is particularly relevant for members of national, ethnic, or linguistic minorities, especially for teaching the minority language or practising their religion.[48] This right used to be a cornerstone of the minority protection system established under the auspices of the League of Nations during the Interbellum.[49] More recently, article 14 of the 2007 UN General Assembly (UNGA) Declaration on the Rights of Indigenous Peoples lays down the right of Indigenous groups to establish their own educational institutions, providing for education in their own language, in a manner that is appropriate to their cultural methods of teaching and learning. In other words, education that is adapted to them and acceptable for them in accordance with the characteristics of the group.[50] The freedom dimension of (the right to) education is absent from SDG 4 because it essentially entails a state obligation not to interfere, while SDG 4 is mainly about measures to actively ensure quality education.

44 The basis for ICESCR, arts. 13 and 14 is to be found in the UDHR, art. 26, which already provides for the right to receive an education and the right to choose an education.

45 ECtHR, *Case of Kjeldsen, Busk Madsen and Pedersen*, Application nos. 5095/71, 5920/72, 5926/72, 1976, 26, 27. This judgment provides an interpretation of Protocol no. 1 to the ECHR, art. 2.

46 1981 African Charter on Human and Peoples' Rights, art. 17(3); 1990 African Charter, art. 11(2)(c).

47 Views of the Human Rights Committee in the case of *Arieh Hollis Waldman v Canada*, UN Doc. CCPR/C/67/D/1996, 1999.

48 See CDE, art. 5(1)(c); 1966 International Covenant on Civil and Political Rights, art. 27; 1998 Council of Europe Framework Convention for the Protection of National Minorities, arts. 12–14; 1992 Declaration on the Rights of Persons Belonging to National or Ethnic, Religious and Linguistic Minorities, art. 4.

49 PCIJ, *Minority Schools in Albania*, Advisory Opinion, Series A/B, No. 64, 6 April 1935.

50 UN Doc. A/RES/61/295, 13 September 2007.

4.3.3 Non-Discrimination

A key principle underlying the realization of the right to education is non-discriminatory access to education and the enjoyment of this right. It means that no one shall be denied the right to education on discriminatory grounds. This idea has been the raison d'être for the adoption of the UNESCO's CDE. The purpose of the CDE is not only to eliminate and prevent discrimination in education but also to promote equality of opportunity in matters of education.[51] The latter is relevant when access to education is denied because of discrimination on the basis of sex, religion, birth, disability, language, nationality, or ethnicity. Such discrimination is often faced by members of minorities who seek access to schools for public education – for example, Roma children in Europe.[52] Similarly, pregnant girls may have been denied access to education. Importantly, in 2019, the Court of Justice of the Economic Community of West Africa (ECOWAS) held that a law in Sierra Leone banning pregnant girls from access to education was contrary to the right to education on a non-discriminatory basis.[53] The legal basis for the ruling was the 1990 African Charter on the Rights and Welfare of the Child.[54] In Latin America, the Inter-American Court for Human Rights ruled that the discriminatory treatment of an HIV-positive person in a school setting was a violation of the right to education, as provided for in article 13 of the 1988 Protocol of San Salvador to the 1969 American Convention on Human Rights.[55]

Non-discriminatory access to education and equality of opportunity constitute the cornerstone of article of 10 of the CEDAW, which aims to guarantee the same rights for girls as boys have in the matter of education. The CEDAW Committee has extensively interpreted this provision in its General Recommendation 36 by focusing on the right of access to education, rights within education, and rights through education.[56] In the view of the CEDAW Committee, the right of access to education involves actual participation in education. Rights within education are aimed at promoting substantive gender equality in education. Rights through education define the ways in which schooling shapes rights and gender equality in aspects of life outside the sphere of education.[57]

[51] See CDE, arts. 3, 4. The historical background of the CDE was the system of discrimination and segregation in education under apartheid in South Africa.

[52] ECtHR, *Case of D.H. and Others v Czech Republic*, Application no. 57325/00, 2007; ECtHR, *Case of Sampani & Others v Greece*, Application no. 59608/09, 2012.

[53] ECOWAS Court of Justice, *WAVES v Sierra Leone*, Case no. ECW/CCJ/JUD/37/19, 2019, www.escr-net.org/caselaw/2020/women-against-violence-and-exploitation-society-waves-v-republic-sierra-leone.

[54] 1990 African Charter, art. 11(6).

[55] IACtHR, *Case of Gonzales Lluy v Ecuador*, Series C, No 298, 2015.

[56] CEDAW Committee, *General Recommendation 36 (2017) on the Rights of Girls and Women to Education*, UN Doc. CEDAW/C/GC/36, 27 November 2017.

[57] *Id.*, paras. 15–17.

A similar key provision on eliminating discrimination in education and promoting real equality of opportunities is article 24 of the CRPD on inclusive education. This article stipulates that state parties shall ensure that persons with disabilities are not excluded from the general education system because of their disability.[58] In the view of the Committee on the Rights of Persons with Disabilities, inclusive education 'entails a transformation in culture, policy and practice in all formal and informal educational environments to accommodate the differing requirements and identities of individual students, together with a commitment to removing the barriers that impede that possibility'.[59] While the principle of non-discrimination is absent from SDG 4, it is implicit in the notion of equal access in targets 4.2, 4.3, and 4.5. Moreover, guaranteeing non-discriminatory treatment is referred to in the 2030 Agenda for Sustainable Development as a general human rights obligation.[60]

4.3.4 *Providing for Primary Education as a Core Obligation*

Some obligations have been characterized by the CESCR as minimum core obligations that must be implemented by states under all circumstances because they concern the essence of the right. A prominent example includes the obligations to provide compulsory primary education free of charge.[61] This key dimension of education is also paramount in target 4.1; however, the compulsory nature of primary education is not included. Primary education is so fundamental for a person's abilities that it can be qualified as minimum entitlement. No one can withhold a child from attending primary education.[62] Relevant in this context is article 22(1) of the 1951 Convention Relating to the Status of Refugees, which stipulates that states parties shall accord to refugees the same treatment as is accorded to nationals with respect to elementary (primary) education. Providing primary education as a core obligation means that states have an obligation to protect this right from encroachment by third persons such as parents or employers. This obligation is related to banning economic exploitation of children (article 32 of the UNCRC) and eliminating child labour as provided for in the 1999 ILO Convention no. 182 on the Worst Forms of Child Labour.[63] Primary education

58 CRPD, art. 24(2)(a).

59 Committee on the Rights of Persons with Disabilities, *General Comment 4 on the Right to Inclusive Education*, UN Doc. CRPD/C/GC/4, 2016, para. 9.

60 *Transforming Our World*, n. 14, para. 19.

61 CESCR, n. 11, paras. 10, 51, 57, 59; see also UNCRC, art. 28(1)(a); ICESCR, art. 14. For a discussion of the core content of the right to education, see Fons Coomans, 'In Search of the Core Content of the Right to Education', in Audrey Chapman & Sage Russell (eds.), *Core Obligations: Building a Framework for Economic, Social and Cultural Rights* (Intersentia, 2002), 217–46.

62 CESCR, *General Comment 11: Plans of Action for Primary Education*, UN Doc. E/1992/23, 1999, para. 6.

63 1999 ILO Convention no. 182 on the Worst Forms of Child Labour, art. 7(2)(a); see also 1973 ILO Convention no. 138 on Minimum Age.

has to be compulsory in domestic law,[64] and it has to be free, which means that no direct or indirect costs for parents may act as a constraint against parents being able to send their children to school.[65] Primary education must have priority in resource allocation because it deals with the fundamental basis for a person's development and the development of society as whole.[66] The Court of Justice of ECOWAS has ruled that the embezzlement of funds for public education has a negative effect on the enjoyment of the right to education because fewer financial resources will be available for the provision of public education.[67] States have an immediate duty to provide primary education for all.[68] For those states that have not yet realized compulsory and primary education, there is an 'unequivocal obligation' to adopt and implement a detailed plan of action as provided for in article 14 of the ICESCR.[69] Implementing this provision underscores the importance of primary education as a fundamental right.

4.4 POSITIONING SDG 4 IN THE INTERNATIONAL INSTITUTIONAL CONTEXT

4.4.1 *Institutional Aspects of Education as a Public Good and as a Commodity*

Relevant international institutions for implementing education at the domestic level traditionally include UNESCO and UNICEF.[70] UNICEF has adopted a human rights–based approach that informs its Education Strategy 2019–2030 for the implementation of SDG 4.[71] The World Bank is the largest funder of education projects in developing countries. In many projects, the focus is on promoting the education of girls. The International Finance Corporation (IFC), a member of the World Bank Group that funds private sector projects, is the largest investor in private education in developing countries. The WTO, and, in particular, the GATS, has become more important recently because of its role in regulating the activities of private providers of educational services. A core question for the implementation of

64 UNCRC, art. 28(1)(a); CDE, art. 4(a).
65 CESCR, n. 62, para. 7.
66 CESCR, n. 11, para. 51.
67 ECOWAS Court of Justice, *SERAP v Nigeria*, Case no. ECW/CCJ/JUD/07/10, 2010, para. 19.
68 CESCR, n. 11, para. 51.
69 CESCR, n. 62, para. 9.
70 This subsection is partly drawn from Fons Coomans, 'Commercialisation of Educational Services and Extraterritorial Human Rights Obligations', in Lilian Chenwi & Takele Soboka Bulto (eds.), *Extraterritorial Human Rights Obligations from an African Perspective* (Intersentia, 2018), 63–86.
71 UNICEF, *Every Child Learns: UNICEF Education Strategy 2019–2030*, 2019, www.unicef.org/media/59856/file/UNICEF-education-strategy-2019-2030.pdf. For a discussion of the implementation of UNICEF's programme and policies in education in India, see Joel Oestreich, *Development and Human Rights: Rhetoric and Reality in India* (Oxford University Press, 2017), 86–97.

SDG 4 in the context of international law and institutions is whether education is perceived as a public good or a commodity. This distinction is relevant for fulfilling the pledge of SDG 4 – namely, to ensure inclusive education for all.

Traditionally, education has been regarded as a public good or a public service. It means that the state is the duty bearer and takes responsibility for setting educational standards and rules.[72] A government cannot waive that responsibility by giving more room to the private sector or by stimulating public-private partnerships for financing the educational infrastructure.[73] It has to make sure that everyone has an equal opportunity to take part in a good quality education. It also means that the state has to make tax-generated financial and other resources available for its implementation. The state is the only actor that is capable of generating the financial resources required for organizing and maintaining a comprehensive system of schools.[74] Public education plays a key role in developing society as a whole. The state and society share a general interest in a highly educated population that may benefit not only individuals but also society at large. The idea of education as a public good is rather different from education as a commodity or private good, which is based on the idea that benefits from education can only be obtained if one is willing to pay for an educational service offered by a commercial provider. Private education, therefore, is not equally accessible to all but only to those who can afford it. Reliance on private education may have discriminatory effects and can lead to a societal divide between the rich and the poor segments of the population.

As a result of globalization and market liberalization, which have been promoted by the WTO and other international financial institutions, new players have entered the educational arena. They are offering educational services as a private good or commodity for which fees are levied. The rise of non-public education offered by commercial parties – 'edu-business', particularly in developing countries[75] – cannot be seen separately from the policies of the World Bank and the IFC to promote private investment in education.[76] In addition, the WTO's GATS has been instrumental in strengthening this trend. The GATS aims at liberalizing trade in services, including educational services. As mentioned, education can be approached from two perspectives: as a tradeable service on the basis of demand by consumers and

[72] Education 2030 Framework for Action, n. 2, 6, 28.

[73] With respect to right to education in the ECHR, the ECtHR has held that a state cannot absolve itself from this responsibility by delegating its obligations to private school bodies. ECtHR, *Case of Costello-Roberts v United Kingdom*, Application no. 13134/87, 25 March 1993, para. 27; see also GPBHR, UN Doc. A/HRC/17/31, 2011, annex, Principle 5 and commentary.

[74] CESCR, n. 11, para. 48.

[75] 'Low-cost Private Schools: Learning Unleashed', *The Economist*, 1 August 2015; UN Special Rapporteur on the Right to Education, *Protecting the Right to Education against Commercialization*, UN Doc. A/HRC/29/30, 10 June 2015, paras. 36–39.

[76] See the World Bank Project Education Markets for the Poor, which were started in 2013. See, for example, the IFC co-funded project to invest in higher education in Mexico. IFC, *IFC Announces US$ 9.8 Million Co-investment in Lottus Education with Alta Growth Capital*, 5 August 2021, pressroom.ifc.org/all/pages/PressDetail.aspx?ID=26558.

supply by commercial providers – that is, as a private good – or as a public service provided by the state, which is very much related to the idea that education is a public good. This double nature of education as a service has been recognized in the GATS. Article I(3) about definition and scope deals with services:

> (b) 'services' includes any service in any sector except services supplied in the exercise of governmental authority;
> (c) 'a service supplied in the exercise of governmental authority' means any service which is supplied neither on a commercial basis, nor in competition with one or more service suppliers.

From this provision, it can be derived that, when educational services in a country are provided by the state, only these shall be characterized as an exercise of governmental authority. Supplying education then is seen as the exercise of a state monopoly. However, many countries provide possibilities for private actors to establish educational institutions as a practical application of the freedom of education. The effect of the GATS is that it liberalizes the services sector by opening it up to foreign private suppliers.

With a view to liberalizing the services sector, each state party may submit commitments indicating the extent to which it has liberalized its economic system for each service.[77] Sectoral commitments concern market access for foreign parties and the application of the rule of non-discrimination and national treatment.[78] The presence of private actors in the education market would strengthen efficiency and further innovative approaches. It would also lead to higher tax revenues for the state, which is an important incentive for states to liberalize.[79] However, member states of the WTO are not required to open markets to foreign services suppliers. In principle, all levels of education may come within the scope of the GATS. So far, not many states have made commitments for education as a traded service under the GATS, which may have resulted because primary and secondary education in most countries are a public service in the sense of exercising governmental authority.[80] For WTO law and practice, primary and secondary education are treated as a public service, while higher education is considered a tradeable service.[81] States may also allow foreign actors access to the educational market without making official GATS commitments.

77 See GATS, art. XX.

78 Morijn, n. 3, 41.

79 *Id.*, 62, 77.

80 Schedules of specific commitments made by member states are available through the I-Tip Services Database of the WTO, i-tip.wto.org/services/default.aspx.

81 WTO, *Education Services: Background Note by the Secretariat*, Doc. S/C/W/49, 23 September 1998, para. 13; WTO, *Education Services: Background Note by the Secretariat*, Doc. S/C/W/313, 1 April 2010, s. IVA, para. 3; see also Katarina Tomasevski, 'Globalizing What: Education as a Human Right or Traded Service?' (2005) 12 *Indiana Journal of Global Legal Studies* 1.

Several risks are connected to this trend of commercializing educational services – for instance, the character of education as a public good may be undermined and, '[i]nstead of being oriented to the needs of society as a whole and the right of everyone to education … education may become increasingly oriented to the generation of profit'.[82] In this respect, it is important to emphasize that a distinction must be made between the liberalization of the education market, with commercial actors playing a key role, on the one hand, and private bodies establishing schools on the basis of religious or philosophical convictions or pedagogical views, on the other. The former may find a legal basis for their activities in international trade law, while the latter can derive rights from international human rights law. One can safely say that when the human rights treaties were drafted in the 1950s and 1960s, governments only had religious organizations and parents in mind as entities that could invoke the freedom to establish schools.[83] Companies as legal holders of the freedom to undertake profit-based educational activities were clearly not an issue. It is submitted that commercial providers of educational services cannot rely on the educational freedoms laid down in international human rights law because their goal is not to contribute to education as a public good but, rather, to promote educational services as a private commodity in a market that has been liberalized.

The liberalization of trade in services governed by the GATS rules is a process that will go on in the future, particularly as a result of digital developments in education. Education as a commodity that can be sold and purchased on the global market is clearly contrary to the traditional and well-established idea that education is a public good for which the state takes prime responsibility. From this perspective, there are disconnections between SDG 4 and its Education 2030 Framework for Action, the human rights–monitoring bodies, and the international community, on the one hand, and the actors that are involved in international trade in services, on the other hand. It can be concluded that there is a need to regulate the role of the private sector in providing for-profit educational services with a view to avoiding a societal divide between the haves and the have-nots when it comes to accessibility of education. Education must maintain its nature as a public good and a fundamental right.[84] The latter is to be understood as entailing a duty not to discriminate between pupils in terms of economic accessibility of education.

82 Susan Marks & Andrew Clapham, *International Human Rights Lexicon* (Oxford University Press, 2005), 146.

83 UNGA, *Annotations on the Text of the draft International Covenants on Human Rights*, UN Doc. A/2929, 1955, 112–13; UNGA, *Report of the Third Committee*, UN Doc. A/3764, 1957, 2–7, with respect to ICESCR, art. 13(3), (4); Pierre Juvigny, *The Fight against Discrimination, Equality in Education* (UNESCO, 1963), 32–36, with respect to CDE, art. 2.

84 See also UNESCO & ILO Committee of Experts on the Application of the Recommendations Concerning Teaching Personnel, *Education Is Not a Commodity: Declaration*, 2018, www.ilo.org/global/industries-and-sectors/education/WCMS_646338/lang--en/index.htm.

4.4.2 *Commercial Actors in Education*

While SDG 4 does not deal with the increasing role of private actors in education,[85] it is submitted that their institutional role and function, as well as the approach to education as a public or private good, matter for its implementation. The 2030 Agenda for Sustainable Development reaffirms the key role of the state and of public finance in providing essential services and public goods. However, it also acknowledges the role of the private sector in the process of its implementation.[86] As a result of processes of economic globalization and liberalization, commercial actors have entered the education systems of countries that have traditionally been characterized by the state as the main providers, funders, regulators, and enforcing actors. However, this traditional picture is changing rapidly. For example, there is no doubt that the role of big players such as Microsoft and Google in the education sector, as a result of the COVID-19 pandemic and the closure of schools and the need to switch to online teaching, has increased significantly. These corporations offer different programmes for online teaching as commercial goods for those schools and countries that can afford it. Their influence on teaching has increased,[87] which may further enlarge the digital divide between the global North and the global South.

The increasing involvement of private actors in primary education in African countries[88] has led to calls from non-governmental organizations (NGOs) and the UN special rapporteur on the right to education to set clear limits to this trend of commercialization. These schools offer fee-based educational services in situations and countries where the education budget has been cut, the quality of public education is poor, and rich parents can afford to send their children to private schools. This situation raises questions about the availability and equal accessibility of education. In the view of the UN special rapporteur, '[s]tates must expand educational opportunities, recognising the paramount importance of public investment in education as their essential obligation. Under no circumstances should a state provide financial support to private providers of education or allow private companies to operate multiple schools'.[89] The special rapporteur has observed that

85 SDG 17, Partnerships for the Goals, targets 17.16 and 17.17 only briefly refer to multi-stakeholder partnerships.

86 *Transforming Our World*, n. 14, para. 41.

87 See the annual BETT Fair in London, which has been characterized as 'the meeting place for the education technology community'. *Welcome to Bett: The Global Community for Education Technology*, www.bettshow.com.

88 For examples, see Coomans, n. 70, 71–78; UN Special Rapporteur on the Right to Education, *The Implementation of the Right to Education and Sustainable Development Goal 4 in the Context of the Growth of Private Actors in Education*, UN Doc. A/HRC/41/37, 2019, paras. 19–25.

89 UN Special Rapporteur on the Right to Education, n. 75, para. 122; see also Kishore Singh, 'Education Is a Basic Right: Which Is Why Private Schools Must Be Resisted', *The Guardian*, 23 April 2015.

'public-private partnerships in education that focus on involving private actors for service delivery have empirically largely failed, in particular in fragile countries'.[90] States therefore must prioritize free, quality, public education.[91] The IFC is the largest multilateral investor in private education in developing countries. These for-profit investments have been criticized by NGOs and civil society organizations for their negative impact on quality, accessibility, and affordability of education, especially for poor households.

The rise of private actors in providing educational services in other countries can also be analyzed by looking at the notion of extraterritorial human rights obligations. In the field of economic, social, and cultural rights, this notion has mainly been developed through expert opinions and soft law documents, including the Maastricht Principles.[92] According to CESCR's General Comment 24, 'the extraterritorial obligation to protect requires States Parties to take steps to prevent and redress infringements of Covenant rights that occur outside their territories due to the activities of business entities over which they can exercise control'.[93] States are also required to legally, or otherwise, regulate the activities of companies in other countries that are registered or domiciled in their territory.[94] The Guiding Principles on Business and Human Rights (GPBHR) call for regulation, adequate oversight and enforcement of laws by home and host states to ensure that corporations respect human rights.[95] In addition, on the basis of the GPBHR, edu-businesses have a responsibility to avoid infringing on the right to education, to address negative impacts of their activities on the enjoyment of the right to education, and to operate with due diligence – for example, by establishing a human rights impact assessment trajectory prior to carrying out their business activities, such as setting up a fee-based school for primary or secondary education.[96]

In several resolutions, the UN Human Rights Council has called for a strong framework to regulate the activities of (commercial) education providers, guided by international human rights obligations, that lays down minimum standards for the establishment and operation of educational services with a view to addressing any

90 UN Special Rapporteur on the Right to Education, n. 75, para. 91.

91 *Id.*

92 See 2011 Maastricht Principles on the Extraterritorial Obligations of States in the Area of Economic, Social and Cultural Rights; CESCR, *General Comment 24 on State Obligations under the ICESCR in the Context of Business Activities*, UN Doc. E/C.12/GC/24, 2017.

93 CESCR, n. 92, para. 30.

94 Maastricht Principles, 24, 25. According to the GPBHR, n. 73, Guiding Principle 2 and commentary, 'States are not generally required under international human rights law to regulate the extraterritorial activities of businesses domiciled in their territory and/or jurisdiction'.

95 GPBHR, n. 73, annex.

96 *Id.*, Principles 11, 13, 17, 18 and commentary. The Agenda 2030 for Sustainable Development also refers to the GPBHR as relevant international standards. *Transforming Our World*, n. 14, para. 67.

negative impacts of the commercialization of education.[97] One such normative and regulatory framework, developed bottom up as the outcome of an extensive participatory consultation and drafting process, are the so-called Abidjan Principles. Adopted by a group of experts, they deal with the human rights obligations of states to provide public education and to regulate private involvement in education.[98] The text is drafted as a quasi-legal document that should give rise to obligations for states.

The key provisions of the Abidjan Principles stipulate that, where private actors are involved in the provision of education, both host and home states must adopt and enforce effective regulatory measures to ensure the realization of the right to education.[99] In addition, states must prioritize the funding and provision of free, quality, public education and may only financially support private educational institutions in accordance with applicable human rights law and standards.[100] International assistance and cooperation must support free, quality, public education systems and refrain from supporting private educational institutions in a manner that is inconsistent with human rights.[101] States as members of international organizations shall not agree to loans or financial support for projects in developing countries that would undermine the realization of the right to education.[102]

SDG 4 is to be implemented from the perspective of leaving no one behind, which means that public education must be the primary focus of governments.[103] Private actors can play a complimentary role; however, their activities must be in accordance with applicable human rights law. The Abidjan Principles may guide

97 Human Rights Council, *Resolution on the Right to Education*, UN Doc. A/HRC/RES/32/22, 2016, para. 2(e); Human Rights Council, *Resolution on the Right to Education*, UN Doc. A/HRC/RES/38/9, 2018, para. 5.

98 See 2019 Abidjan Principles on the Right to Education, www.abidjanprinciples.org. This website also contains information about the process of developing the principles. The process was facilitated by a number of non-governmental organizations, including Amnesty International, the Global Initiative for Economic, Social and Cultural Rights, and the Right to Education Initiative.

99 *Id.*, Principles 4, 61. Principle 55 lays down a set of detailed minimum standards for regulating private providers, such as

> protection for learners against all forms of discrimination in the enjoyment of the right to education, to guarantee equality and inclusive education for all learners, including by ensuring that the conditions of enrolment, admission, and learning are not directly or indirectly discriminatory; and paying particular attention to their impacts on the rights to equality and non-discrimination of vulnerable, marginalised, or disadvantaged groups. Such protection must guarantee the existence of and re-entry into inclusive education for pregnant girls, young mothers, and married girls under 18 years of age, by enabling them to remain in or return to school without delay.

100 *Id.*, Principle 5.

101 *Id.*, Principle 6.

102 *Id.*, Principle 22; Maastricht Principles, Principle 15.

103 Incheon Declaration for Education 2030, n. 2, para. 12; Education 2030 Framework for Action, n. 2, para. 10.

states in this respect. Together with General Comment 24 and the Maastricht Principles, they contribute to a new emerging normative framework in an area not yet covered by hard law.

4.5 CONCLUSIONS

From the analysis presented in this chapter, it can be concluded that SDG 4 is quite similar to existing international human rights law in terms of its content on the right to education. SDG 4 is rather conservative in the sense that it does not add many new subjects that pose challenges for the further development of international law. Overall, SDG 4 does not touch new ground, with a few exceptions. The latter deal with the right to pre-primary education and the right to lifelong learning. These two components of the right to education should be further developed in standard-setting documents.

The Education 2030 Framework for Action politically reaffirms the legal obligations that states have under human rights treaties. However, SDG 4 is interesting for what is not included, such as the challenges that the increasing involvement of the private sector in education pose for its implementation and the right to education as a human right at the domestic level. The relationship between the right to education as a human right and SDG 4 and the links with other rights and SDGs will mutually strengthen their implementation.

When assessing this international consensus, one may come to the conclusion that there is synergy between the main international institutions involved in implementing SDG 4, at least on paper. In practice, however, there are differences between the key institutions. UNESCO, UNICEF, and the UN Human Rights Council have adopted in very clear terms a human rights–based approach, while the World Bank Group institutions have made very little progress in this direction. For the former institutions, education is a human right of the individual giving rise to obligations for duty bearers, while, for the latter, education is primarily a tool for achieving economic and social development. We have seen that so far the role of the private sector in providing educational services is limited. Efforts undertaken by private providers of primary education services in developing countries have been criticized. On the other hand, the liberalization of trade in services governed by the GATS rules under the WTO is a process that will go on in the future. From this perspective, there are disconnections between SDG 4 and its Framework for Action, the human rights–monitoring bodies, and the international community, on the one hand, and the different actors that are involved in international trade in services, on the other.

The role of private actors engaged in commercial educational services is increasingly informed by, and embedded in, a solid body of international law on education that provides for legal standards for a human rights–based approach aimed at the domestic implementation of SDG 4. The statement in the Incheon Declaration for

Education 2030 and the Education 2030 Framework for Action that education is a human right and a public good reaffirms this commitment. This political agreement should be understood as a signpost for the further development of trade law in the field of educational services as part of the WTO/GATS framework. To conclude, SDG 4 does not really pose serious challenges for international law. Rather, it is the other way around: international human rights law, in general, and the right to education, in particular, have paved the way for a strong and challenging implementation of SDG 4 at the domestic and international level through a human rights–informed approach.

5

SDG 5: Achieve Gender Equality and Empower All Women and Girls

Patricia Kameri-Mbote and Nkatha Kabira

ABSTRACT

Although Sustainable Development Goal (SDG) 5, Gender Equality, references many international law provisions and principles on gender equality and empowerment of women and girls, nevertheless, like their precursor, the 2000 Millennium Development Goals, the SDGs do not integrate gender as a cross-cutting issue across all the SDGs. The adoption of the gender mainstreaming approach endorsed by the 1995 Beijing Declaration and Platform for Action during the fourth World Conference on Women in Beijing in September 1995 compromises the implementation of SDG 5. This chapter argues that by adopting a formalist approach to equality, SDG 5 does not fully recognize the differences among women – differences of class, race, disabilities, ethnicities, nationalities, religion, and those brought about by colonialism – and thus falls victim to the classical criticism of international law's genderedness and essentialism.

KEYWORDS

SDG 5, gender equality, empowerment, women, girls, international law

5.1 INTRODUCTION

For years, feminist legal scholars have argued that the state is generally constructed as male and that it is a direct expression of patriarchal male interests and, as such, does not reflect women's role in structuring society.[1] As Hilary Charlesworth and

[1] Hilary Charlesworth & Christine Chinkin, *The Boundaries of International Law* (Manchester University Press, 2000).

other feminist legal scholars have argued, this situation is because the concreteness of international law is based on gendered abstractness and normativity that has for far too long been gendered. The norms fail to recognize and situate women's roles within them. In essence, feminist legal scholars have challenged international law for having a historically located man in mind. The man of international law, like the man of law, is John Locke's *'economic proprietor'*, Thomas Hobbes's *'entrepreneur'*, Jean-Jacques Rousseau's *'noble savage'*, and so on.[2] The person depicted in these theories is gendered and not universal, ageless, disembodied, sexless, and classless, as it is purported to be. Sustainable Development Goal (SDG) 5, Gender Equality, challenges this 'man' of international law by recognizing the importance of achieving and promoting gender equality and empowering women and girls at political, economic, and sociocultural levels.

From a theoretical perspective, SDG 5 adopts a formalist approach to rights and equality, neglecting substance that is critical for a holistic understanding. SDG 5 therefore fails to fully recognize the differences among women – differences of class, race, disabilities, ethnicities, nationalities, religion, and those brought about by colonialism – and thus falls victim to the classical criticism of international law's genderedness and essentialism. The plurality of laws at the international, national, and local levels complicates the application of the concepts of non-discrimination and equality, rendering them ambiguous.[3] Indeed, despite the stipulation in international and local laws that all men are equal, discrepancies exist, and inequalities inevitably creep in that are fuelled by power relations. Normative provisions of local and international legal instruments are not enough to ensure equality among men and women because they adopt a formalist approach. Formal equality assumes that measures put in place to achieve equality should be stopped when the playing field is levelled to ensure that the perceived advantaged group does not become disadvantaged. Substantive equality, on the other hand, suggests that because differences are structural, fair treatment requires sustained recognition of pluralities. Substantive equality or equity becomes the means of levelling the playing field, where formal equality fails to address historical injustices and structural distinctions.[4]

Two examples illustrate that gender neutral laws have failed to promote gender equality in an environment that is skewed against women.[5] First, the reservation in some countries of some professions, such as the military, for the male gender makes

2 Ngaire Naffine, *The Man of Law*, 6 December 2001; Ngaire Naffine, *Law and the Sexes: Explorations in Feminist Jurisprudence* (Allen & Unwin, 1990); Carole Pateman, *The Sexual Contract* (Stanford University Press, 1998); see also Nkatha Kabira & Patricia Kameri-Mbote, 'Woman of Law: Kenyan Women's Triumph in the Constitution of Kenya 2010', in Wanjiku Mukabi Kabira et al. (eds.), *Changing the Mainstream: Celebrating Women's Resilence* (African Women Studies Center, 2018), 27.

3 Patricia Kameri-Mbote, 'Fallacies of Equality and Inequality: Multiple Exclusions in Law and Legal Discourses' (Inaugural lecture delivered at the University of Nairobi, 24 January 2013).

4 Kameri-Mbote, n. 3.

5 *Id.*

equality a fallacy. Second, in some countries, patriarchal norms still apply that prevent women from owning land, thereby negating the principle of formal equality in the enjoyment of land rights enshrined in law. In applying this argument to SDG 5 and its implementation, this chapter reveals that there is a tension between equality and non-discrimination, inequality, and discrimination, on one side, and inclusion and exclusion, on the other side. The rhetoric associated with equality and non-discrimination results in inequality and discrimination in practice as the application of principles meant to include results in exclusion. The 'fallacies of equality and inequality' is one of the major hurdles that the implementation of SDG 5 must overcome to achieve gender equality for women and girls.

Although SDG 5 takes many international law provisions and principles on gender equality and empowerment of women and girls on board, nevertheless, like its precursor, the 2000 Millennium Development Goals (MDGs), the SDGs do not integrate gender as an issue cutting across all seventeen SDGs. This chapter argues that the adoption of the gender mainstreaming approach endorsed in the 1995 Beijing Declaration and Platform for Action during the fourth World Conference on Women compromises the implementation of SDG 5 because the vision of gender equality embedded in the Platform for Action reproduces a tension between "gender equality and the mainstream". The tension arises from attempts to 'add and stir' women to a pre-existing and established international law mainframe that is centred on a predominantly male world view. Gender mainstreaming in international law needs to go beyond 'adding and stirring women' and move towards 'integrationist approaches' that critically interrogate the man's place in international law and pursue substantive gender equality and the empowerment of women and girls.

5.2 THE CONTENT OF SDG 5 IN THE CONTEXT OF THE OTHER SDGS

The SDGs bring together several issues that for far too long have been addressed in silos. Even though SDG 5 in many ways reflects international law on women's rights, it nevertheless fails to recognize that SDG 5 cuts through all seventeen SDGs because the vision of equality and gender mainstreaming embedded in the SDGs is formal and, as such, does not consider pluralities and multiplicities in international, regional, and local legal orders. We begin by unpacking the content in SDG 5. SDG 5 has nine targets that focus on women's political, economic, and sociocultural empowerment. In essence, SDG 5's nine targets challenge the 'man' of international law in three main ways.

First, SDG 5 challenges the 'man' of international law through women's political empowerment. For years, the man of international legal systems prevented women from participating in politics through the right to vote, political representation, and elections, reflecting prevailing patriarchal norms. It was not until the enactment of the 1952 Convention on the Political Rights of Women that international law began to recognize women's place in politics. Building on various international legal instruments that have sought over the years to give voice to women's experiences and perspectives in international law, SDG 5 aims at 'women's full and effective participation and equal opportunities of leadership in decision making in political, economic and public life'.[6]

Second, SDG 5 challenges the 'man' of international law through women's economic empowerment. Like political rights, the 'economy' historically has been the place of men, and women's participation in it has been limited to reproductive roles. As a result, international law embodied norms that did not recognize women's rights of ownership and access to land and resources. Over the years, women have sought to disaggregate the 'man' of international law by ensuring that their rights to equal economic participation is chronicled and recognized in international law. As a result, SDG 5 aims to undertake reforms to give women equal rights to economic resources as well as access to ownership of, and control over, land and other forms of property, financial services, inheritance, and natural resources.[7] It also aims to enhance the use of enabling technology[8] and recognize and value unpaid care and domestic work through the provision of public services, infrastructure, and social protection policies and the promotion of shared responsibility within the household and the family.[9]

Third, SDG 5 challenges the 'man' of international law through women's sociocultural empowerment. Like political and economic rights, sociocultural norms in many societies around the world continue to reflect patriarchal norms such as child, early, and forced marriages. SDG 5 seeks to unmask the 'man' of international law by ensuring that international legal structures and norms promote the elimination of all forms of discrimination against all women and girls everywhere;[10] eliminate all forms of violence against all women and girls in the public and private spheres,[11] including trafficking and sexual and other types of exploitation; and eliminate all harmful practices, such as child, early, and forced marriage and female genital mutilation (FGM). It also seeks to ensure universal access to sexual and reproductive health rights as agreed to in the 1995 Beijing Declaration and Platform for Action and the outcome documents of their review conferences.[12]

SDG 5 further challenges the gendered nature of international law through its fourteen indicators aimed at adopting and strengthening sound policies and enforceable legislation for the promotion of gender equality and the empowerment of all women and girls at all levels. These indicators assume that an increase in laws,

6 Target 5.5.
7 Target 5.a.
8 Indicator 5.b.1.
9 Target 5.4.
10 Target 5.1.
11 Target 5.2.
12 Target 5.6.

women in representation, women who own mobile phones, and women in employment indicates an improvement in gender equality. These assumptions demonstrate that the adoption of the gender mainstreaming approach endorsed in the 1995 Beijing Declaration and Platform for Action compromises the implementation of SDG 5, which is because the vision of gender equality embedded in the declaration and platform for action reproduces a tension between "gender equality and the mainstream".[13] 'Adding and stirring' women to a pre-existing and established international law mainframe centred on a male world view is not enough.[14] Gender mainstreaming in international law needs to adopt 'integrationist approaches'[15] that critically interrogate the 'man' of international law, moving to substantive gender equality and the empowerment of women and girls.

These indicators also assume that availing basics such as food, water, and mobile phones will lead to the realization of gender equality. Sara Longwe's framework on gender equality and the empowerment of women, however, illustrates that empowerment is a means of overcoming gender inequalities at five levels: the zero level, the access level, the 'conscientization' level, the participation level, and the control level.[16] At the zero or welfare level, the material conditions required for survival, such as food and water, are met. At the access level, the means of obtaining basic needs, goods, and services are met. For example, ensuring access to factors of production such as land and credit, which is critical as such access can lead to the creation of circumstances in which women's basic needs for survival are met. The SDG indicators assume that women's ownership of land guarantees access and control. At the conscientization level, women are aware of the systemic nature of gender inequality. This consciousness enables them to understand why welfare and access needs are not met. At this level, lobbying is required. Like the MDGs, the SDG indicators assume that education and consciousness raising lead to desired outcomes such as ending FGM, early marriages, abortion, and marital rape. In fact, laws outlawing these cultural practices have remained for the most part in the statute books, while the practices continue unabated in the communities.

At the participation level, the active involvement of women in policy and leadership is expected to bring about change. The indicators assume that increasing the

[13] Wanjiku Mukabi Kabira, 'The Next Season of Harvest', in Mukabi Kabira et al., n. 2, 8; see also Sylvia Walby, 'Gender Mainstreaming: Productive Tensions in Theory and Practice' (2005) 12 (3) *Social Politics: International Studies in Gender, State and Society* 321, 322.

[14] Sandra Harding, 'Just Add Women and Stir', in Gender Working Group (ed.). *Missing Links: Gender Equity in Science and Technology for Development* (International Development Research Centre, 1995), 295.

[15] Walby, n. 13.

[16] Sara Hlupekile Longwe, 'Gender Awareness: The Missing Element in the Third World Development Project', in Tina Wallace & Candida March (eds.), *Changing Perceptions: Writings on Gender and Development* (Oxfam, 1991), referred to in Candida March, Ines A. Smyth, & Maitrayee Mukhopadhyay, *A Guide to Gender-Analysis Frameworks* (Oxfam, 1999), 93–95.

numbers of women in parliament and in leadership positions will necessarily result in gender equality. This assumption has proved not to be the case in many parts of Africa where, despite an increase in numbers, the changes have not served to change or influence the deeply patriarchal institutional forms.[17] Essentially, an 'add and stir' approach has been adopted to measure the extent to which gender equality has been realized. This approach, as Sandra Harding argues, does not address issues of 'gender relations, gendered structures and philosophy' of the development process, among other issues.[18] As Wanjiku Mukabi Kabira and her colleagues explain, we cannot assume that sociocultural institutions, in which we are 'adding women and stirring' are value free.[19] These institutions have a history and a tradition and are based on epistemology around which ideologies are created. Adding women and stirring them may increase the numbers in parliament, and in managerial positions as envisioned in the SDGs, but this increased presence does not result in the achievement of gender equality. Change in the books may be discernible, but, in practice, the institutional forms remain the same. This situation is particularly true for parliaments, judiciaries, and executives the world over. As Maria Nzomo argues, 'formal access and presence in governance institutions is neither an end in itself nor does it necessarily translate into influence and capacity for substantive representation'.[20] Indeed, increasing numbers alone does not translate into the realization of gender equality.

The next level of gender equality and empowerment relates to control. This level has to do with autonomy and ownership. At this stage, women are able to access and control resources and benefits. The SDG 5 indicators do not necessarily reveal the fact that most institutions, structures, and systems are gendered. Gender equality can only truly be achieved when women have institutional capacity to control resources and benefit from them. A good example is the two-thirds gender rule in the Kenyan Parliament. While the Constitution of Kenya provides for the enactment of legislation to ensure gender equality through affirmative action in parliament, the Parliament continues to operate outside the constitutional threshold for women representation, despite numerous attempts to challenge the unconstitutionality of its composition.[21] However, as the previous paragraph illustrates, equality of control on its own will not serve to attain gender equality in practice.

SDG 5 is based on five main assumptions. First, it assumes that women are heterogeneous the world over. Even though SDG 5 seeks to achieve gender equality

[17] Mukabi Kabira et al., n. 2, 49.

[18] Harding, n. 14; see also Mukabi Kabira et al., n. 2, 5.

[19] Referred to in Mukabi Kabira et al., n. 2, 6.

[20] Maria Nzomo, 'Gender and Governance in Kenya: Women's Journey Beyond Numbers', in Mukabi Kabira et al., n. 2, 49.

[21] 'Chief Justice's Advice to the President on the Dissolution of Parliament for Failure to Enact the Gender Rule', *Kenya Law*, 22 September 2020, www.kenyalaw.org/kenyalawblog/chief-justices-advice-to-the-president-on-dissolution-of-parliament/.

through political, economic, and sociocultural empowerment, it still has a man in mind in many ways. The 'man' of international law and gender blindness continue to play out in SDG 5. For instance, it assumes that the eradication of FGM is desirable for women around the world, and it takes a radical feminist approach to trafficking and violence against women. Radical feminists focus on the embedded structures of power that make men's characteristics the norm from which 'difference' is constructed.[22] Radical feminists like Simone de Beauvoir, and Shulamith Firestone have argued that women's oppression lies in childbearing and child-rearing roles.[23] For Firestone, the denial of the mother's sexual desire within the social organization of the family was the primary instrument of female control.[24] In addition, Catherine MacKinnon, a major proponent of radical feminism, has emphasized that pornography is a tool to subordinate and exploit women.[25] Radical feminists, like SDG 5 itself, thereby fail to take into account the differences among women.

Second, the fallacies of formal equality and inequality are embedded within SDG 5. The assertion that all people are equal and therefore need to be treated alike and not discriminated against is deceptive because people are affected differently by space and natural endowments that cause inequality, and, consequently, such inequality is not inherent in them but, rather, is due to their capacities.[26] Therefore, the proposition of equality and fairness does not fully pertain to states and individuals as 'no categories of like legal persons exist and this affects the principles of like treatment'.[27] According to Peter Westen, who considers the rights of race and sex to be included in equality clauses, they are independent rights without reference to equality or likeness.[28] However, race and sex are critical identifiers that are relevant in determining how people fare in terms of equality and likeness and, therefore, how people should be treated.

Third, SDG 5 fails to recognize the place of intersectionality in addressing gender equality concerns. Gender is a cross-cutting issue that directly contributes to the achievement of several SDGs. SDG 1, No Poverty, commits to ending poverty by 2030. But, according to a UN Women's report, 'that aspiration can only be achieved by ending the discrimination that traps women in poverty. Globally, one in five girls are in households living on less than US $1.90 a day, a sum that leaves them without

[22] Nancy M. Baraza, 'Legal Feminism and Traditional Legal Doctrine: Contrasting the Dominant Paradigm' (2015) *East African Law Journal* 245.
[23] Cited in Catherine MacKinnon, 'Marxism, Method, and the State: An Agenda for Theory' (1982) 7(3) *Signs* 515.
[24] Shulamith Firestone, *The Dialectic of Sex: The Case for Feminist Revolution* (Paladin, 1971).
[25] MacKinnon, n. 23.
[26] Kameri-Mbote, n. 3, 8.
[27] *Id.*, 15.
[28] Peter Westen, 'The Empty Idea of Equality' (1982) 95(3) *Harvard Law Review* 537.

enough food, housing, health care or education'.[29] This statement means that achieving gender equality is critical for the realization of the goal of poverty reduction. SDG 4, Quality Education, affects gender equality and women's empowerment in very direct ways. Education expands opportunities for girls and young women and raises their aspirations for work outside the home.[30] As women acquire more education, they increasingly expand their work opportunities.[31] Policies to ensure that women and girls can access services including health and education have contributed to significant advances in women's standards of living.[32] Women's empowerment through education and conscientization shapes attitudes of both girls and boys to gender equality, with greater education leading to more positive attitudes towards gender equality among both males and females.[33]

Similar intersections can be identified between SDG 5 and other SDGs. For example, SDG 3, Good Health and Well-being, is also closely connected to SDG 5 in that women's access to reproductive healthcare is directly linked to reductions in maternal mortality and in diseases such as HIV/AIDS. The immediate causes of health crises may manifest themselves in the form of life-threating conditions such as high blood pressure and diabetes, but the root causes of the issue may be poverty and the inability of women to participate and control resources, which then links back to SDG 1. Indeed, implementing other SDGs will contribute to the realization of SDG 5. For instance, ending all forms of discrimination against women might lead to poverty reduction (SDG 1), through, for instance, access to land. It might also leads to the realization of SDG 16, Peace, Justice, and Strong Institutions. In addition, promoting women's political empowerment may also lead to the realization of SDG 16. Women's participation and leadership also contributes to the achievement of improved water and sanitation governance (SDG 6, Clean Water and Sanitation), reduced inequalities (SDG 10, Reduced Inequalities), and women's participation in agriculture (SDG 2, Zero Hunger).

Moreover, promoting women's sociocultural empowerment through the elimination of violence and harmful practices such as FGM may also lead to the realization of peace, security, and human rights. Furthermore, promoting women's economic empowerment can contribute to poverty eradication (SDG 1) and the promotion of industrial development (SDG 9, Industry, Innovation, and Infrastructure),

29 UN Women, *SDG 1: End Poverty in All Its Forms Everywhere*, www.unwomen.org/en/news/in-focus/women-and-the-sdgs/sdg-1-no-poverty.

30 UN Population Fund (UNFPA), *State of World Population: Adolescents, Youth and the Transformation of the Future* (UNFPA, 2014); World Bank, *World Development Report 2007: Development and the Next Generation* (World Bank, 2006).

31 World Bank, n. 30.

32 UN Women, *Progress of the World's Women: In Pursuit of Justice* (UN Women, 2011).

33 UNFPA, *State of World Population: Adolescents, Youth and the Transformation of the Future* (UNFPA, 2014); UN Education, Scientific and Cultural Organization (UNESCO), *Education for All Global Monitoring Report: Teaching and Learning: Achieving Quality for All* (UNESCO Publishing, 2014).

among others. The realization of gender equality is predicated on the fact that gender is a cross-cutting issue and that the realization of each SDG is dependent on the realization of the other SDGs. Agenda setting and integrationist approaches to gender mainstreaming are crucial for transforming society.[34] According to Sylvia Walby, it involves transforming existing policy paradigms, changing the decision-making process, prioritizing gender equality objectives and rethinking policy ends.[35]

Fourth, SDG 5 adopts a formal equality matrix rather than a substantive equality matrix. International law considers equality as an assertion that human beings are equal and have equal rights.[36] Accordingly, equality relates to the dignity and worth of men and women and equality in their rights and opportunities to participate in political, social, economic, and cultural development and to benefit from the results. Equity and substantive equality, on the other hand, relate to fairness in the treatment of different subjects of law. It adverts to the possibility of inequality, which necessitates the application of differential treatment to get rid of inequality. However, there are several factors that hinder the societal quest for equality, equity, and equitable distribution of power and resources, including, among other things, plural legal systems, culture, and the inability to move the courts to apply formal equality provisions.

As noted above, SDG 5 seeks to ensure sociocultural empowerment through weeding out practices such as FGM. This approach, which mirrors the approach in the 1979 Convention on the Elimination of Discrimination against Women (CEDAW) and the 2003 Protocol on the Rights of Women in Africa (Maputo Protocol) to the 1981 African Charter on Human and Peoples Rights (Banjul Charter), adopts a formal equality matrix and ignores the deep entrenchment of culture and tradition, including in law. The various operative laws, including customary laws, ought to be reconfigured in a manner that ensures substantive equality and non-discrimination rather than covering up or wishing away these entrenchments. This situation raises the need to engage the positive aspects of customary law such as naming and marriage rituals, which can engender gender equality given the accessibility of customary law to most people at local levels. Such engagement will open opportunities to challenge and weed out negative customary law norms that perpetuate inequality.

Fifth, it is important to note that achieving SDG 5 assumes the centrality of the state in the realization of women's rights through the enactment of laws and policies. The centrality of the state in international law is problematic for international legal feminisms because women's interests and concerns are not defined exclusively, or, in many cases, even significantly, by state borders. They are shaped by gender,

[34] Mukabi Kabira et al., n. 2.
[35] Walby, n. 13.
[36] Kameri-Mbote, n. 3

sexuality, culture, and other factors. It is therefore important to locate SDG 5 in the broader context that encapsulates all other SDGs through an integrationist approach.

5.3 POSITIONING SDG 5 IN INTERNATIONAL LAW

5.3.1 *Women in International Law Generally*

Over the years, women all over the world have participated in the making of international law on gender equality and women's empowerment. From the 1953 Convention on the Political Rights of Women to the 1957 Convention on the Nationality of Married Women; from CEDAW to the 1999 Optional Protocol to CEDAW; from the 1985 Nairobi Forward-looking Strategies to the 1992 UN Declaration on Violence against Women; from the 1994 Plan of Action from the International Conference on Population and Development to the 1995 Beijing Declaration and Platform for Action; and from the MDGs to the SDGs, the United Nations and other international institutions have also played a significant role in promoting the rights of women and girls the world over. As a result, international law embodies women's human rights in all areas including rights of the child, slavery, anti-trafficking, environment, and natural resources, among other areas. Indeed, SDG 5 is the culmination of decades of women's struggle challenging international law's maleness.

Historically, feminist analysis of international law has had two roles. The first is the deconstruction of the explicit and implicit values of the international legal system, challenging its claim to objectivity and rationality because of the limited base on which it is built. The second and more difficult project is that of reconstruction of a truly humane system of international law. The objective and the aim of the literature on the sex of the state and the gender of jus cogens by scholars like Hilary Charlesworth, for instance, is an attempt to get contemporary international lawyers to change the conceptual foundations of international law.[37] The aim is to explore the ways in which gender can be made a fundamental category in the analysis of international law. This approach comprises a liberal theory of politics in the sense that it assumes that law emanates from legal subjects and, hence, it is necessary for these legal subjects to be identified and thus expose the sham by demonstrating that they are gendered. While challenging the gender of the state,

[37] Hilary Charlesworth, 'The Hidden Gender of International Law' (2002) 16 *Temple International and Comparative Law Journal* 93; Hilary Charlesworth, 'Feminists Critiques of International Law and Their Critics' (1995) 13 *Third World Legal Studies*, 1, scholar.valpo.edu/twls/vol13/iss1/1; Hilary Charlesworth, Christine Chinkin, & Shelly Wright, 'Feminist Approaches to International Law' (1991) 85 *American Journal of International Law* 613; Fernando Tesón, 'Feminism and International Law: A Reply' (1993) 33 *Virginia Journal of International Law* 647.

international feminisms presume the existence of legal subjects from whom law emanates. By accusing the state of being male and challenging international law's presumption of objectivity while it is essentially male, they argue that international law is too ineffective to be taken seriously in the construction of the world order. They argue that the maleness of international law is reflected in patriarchal legal norms that have prevented women from participating in economic, political, and social systems, thus negating the principle of equality.

In many ways, SDG 5 reflects the achievements of feminists in international law. More specifically, feminists have managed to challenge the maleness of the international legal system through the introduction of relevant principles and treaty regimes on gender equality in women's human rights international law instruments.[38] Broadly speaking, SDG 5 is positioned in the following areas: women's human rights,[39] human rights,[40] slavery and slavery-like practices,[41] torture, ill-treatment, and disappearance,[42] rights of the child,[43] employment and forced labour,[44] environment and natural resources,[45] education,[46] war crimes and crimes against humanity, genocide, and terrorism,[47] and disability,[48] among other areas.

[38] Nkatha Kabira, 'Constitutionalizing Traveling Feminisms' (2019) 52 *Cornell International Law Journal* 137.

[39] See, e.g., CEDAW, 13; 1999 Optional Protocol to CEDAW; UN General Assembly, *Implementation of the Nairobi Forward-looking Strategies for the Advancement of Women*, UN Doc. A/RES/40/108, 13 December 1985, www.refworld.org/docid/3b00f2255c.html; 1993 Declaration on the Elimination of Violence against Women; UNFPA, *Report of the International Conference on Population and Development*, 5–13 September 1994.

[40] See, e.g., ICESCR; ICCPR; MDGs.

[41] 1949 Convention for the Suppression of the Traffic in Persons and of the Exploitation of the Prostitution of Others.

[42] 1984 Convention against Torture and Other Cruel, Inhuman or Degrading Treatment or Punishment.

[43] See, e.g., 2000 Optional Protocol to the Convention on the Rights of the Child on the Sale of Children, Child Prostitution and Child Pornography.

[44] 1951 Equal Remuneration Convention; 1957 Abolition of Forced Labour Convention; 1958 Discrimination (Employment and Occupation) Convention; 1964 Employment Policy Convention; 1981 Convention Concerning Occupational Safety and Health and the Working Environment; 1990 Convention on the Protection of the Rights of All Migrant Workers and Members of Their Families.

[45] See, e.g., Commonwealth Secretariat, *Commonwealth Gender Equality Policy*, October 2019.

[46] 1960 Convention against Discrimination in Education; 1990 World Declaration on Education for All.

[47] 1948 Convention on the Prevention and Punishment of the Crime of Genocide; 1968 Convention on the Non-Applicability of Statutory Limitations to War Crimes and Crimes against Humanity; 1998 Rome Statute of the International Criminal Court; 1949 Geneva Convention IV Relating to the Protection of Civilian Persons in Time of War; 1977 Additional Protocol I Relating to the Protection of Victims of International Armed Conflicts; 1977 Additional Protocol II Relating to the Protection of Victims of Non-International Armed Conflicts.

[48] 2007 Convention on the Rights of Persons with Disabilities.

In each of these areas, gender equality remains a central goal of international law in women's political, economic, and sociocultural empowerment.

5.3.2 *Women's Political, Economic, and Sociocultural Empowerment*

With respect to women's political empowerment, several international treaties provide for gender equality through civil and political rights in international law. Broadly speaking, civil and political rights empower men and women to participate in governance through the right to liberty, the right to equality, the right to protection from discrimination, freedom of association, the right to vote, the right to access justice, citizenship rights, representation in decision-making bodies,[49] affirmative action provisions,[50] the right to participation in civil society and politics, equal access to public service,[51] and the right to equality before the law.[52] CEDAW entrenches women's human rights through the advancement of women's political empowerment. It affirms the 1948 Universal Declaration of Human Rights (UDHR), the 1966 International Covenant on Civil and Political Rights (ICCPR), and the 1966 International Covenant on Economic, Social and Cultural Rights (ICESCR) and notes that discrimination against women violates the principle of equality of rights and respect for human dignity embodied in the classical international human rights treaties. CEDAW further emphasizes the importance of promoting women's rights for full and complete development of a country, the welfare of the world, and the cause of peace, which require the maximum participation of women on equal terms with men in all fields.

With respect to women's economic empowerment, several international treaties provide for gender equality of women and girls through the protection of matrimonial property, the right to own property, the equal distribution of resources, the right to choose a trade, occupation, or profession,[53] the right to fair labour practices,[54] the

[49] 1995 Beijing Declaration and Platform for Action.

[50] CEDAW.

[51] UDHR, art. 21 provides that everyone has the right to equal access to public service in his country.

[52] UDHR, art. 7; CEDAW, art. 2 provides that all state parties are responsible for ensuring the legal protection of the rights of women on an equal basis with men and for ensuring through competent national tribunals and other public institutions the effective protection of women against any act of discrimination.

[53] UDHR, art. 23 provides that everyone has the right to work, to free choice of employment, to just and favourable conditions of work, and to protection against unemployment. It also provides at art. 2 that everyone, without any discrimination, has the right to equal pay for equal work.

[54] 1981 Workers with Family Responsibilities Convention, art. 3 provides that, with a view to creating effective equality of opportunity and treatment for men and women workers, each member shall make it an aim of national policy to enable persons with family responsibilities who are engaged, or wish to engage, in employment to exercise their right to do so without being subject to discrimination and, to the extent possible, without conflict between their employment and family responsibilities.

right to fair remuneration and reasonable working conditions,[55] the right to social security, and the right to health and consumer rights.

With respect to women's sociocultural empowerment, several international treaties and policies provide for gender equality for women and girls through the right to education, housing, food, water, sanitation,[56] a safe and healthy environment, family,[57] language and culture, and social protection.[58] Article 5 of CEDAW, for instance, provides that all state parties shall take appropriate measures:

> (a) To modify the social and cultural patterns of conduct of men and women, with a view to achieving the elimination of prejudices and customary and all other practices which are based on the idea of the inferiority or the superiority of either of the sexes or on stereotyped roles for men and women;
> (b) To ensure that family education includes a proper understanding of maternity as a social function and the recognition of the common responsibility of men and women in the upbringing and development of their children, it being understood that the interest of the children is the primordial consideration in all cases.

On education, article 10 of CEDAW provides:

> States Parties shall take all appropriate measures to eliminate discrimination against women in order to ensure to them equal rights with men in the field of education and ... to ensure, on a basis of equality of men and women: (a) The same conditions for career and vocational guidance, for access to studies and for the achievement of diplomas in educational establishments of all categories in rural as

[55] ICESCR, art. 7 provides the right of everyone to the enjoyment of just and favourable conditions of work should ensure, in particular:

> (a) remuneration that provides all workers, as a minimum, with: (i) Fair wages and equal remuneration for work of equal value without distinction of any kind, in particular women being guaranteed conditions of work not inferior to those enjoyed by men, with equal pay for equal work; (ii) A decent living for themselves and their families in accordance with the provisions of the present Covenant; (b) Safe and healthy working conditions; (c) Equal opportunity for everyone to be promoted in his employment to an appropriate higher level, subject to no considerations other than those of seniority and competence; (d) Rest, leisure and reasonable limitation of working hours and periodic holidays with pay, as well as remuneration for public holidays.

[56] UDHR, art. 25 provides that everyone has the right to a standard of living adequate for the health and well-being of himself and of his family, including food, clothing, housing, and medical care and necessary social services as well as the right to security in the event of unemployment, sickness, disability, widowhood, old age, or other lack of livelihood in circumstances beyond his control. It also provides at art. 2 that motherhood and childhood are entitled to special care and assistance. All children, whether born in or out of wedlock, shall enjoy the same social protection.

[57] ICCPR, art. 1 provides that the family is the natural and fundamental group unit of society and is entitled to protection by society and the state. Art. 2 further provides for the right of men and women of marriageable age to marry and to found a family.

[58] ICESCR, art. 9 provides the right of everyone to social security, including social insurance.

well as in urban areas; this equality shall be ensured in pre-school, general, technical, professional and higher technical education, as well as in all types of vocational training; (b) Access to the same curricula, the same examinations, teaching staff with qualifications of the same standard and school premises and equipment of the same quality; (c) The elimination of any stereotyped concept of the roles of men and women at all levels and in all forms of education by encouraging co-education and other types of education which will help to achieve this aim.

SDG 5 therefore mirrors CEDAW's approach to eliminating all forms of discrimination against women. However, the SDGs reduce the ambition that links the elimination of all forms of discrimination to education by addressing the provision of quality education in a different goal – SDG 4 – without reference to gender. Indeed, CEDAW, the Maputo Protocol, and the Banjul Charter reflect attempts to realize women's political, economic, and sociocultural empowerment in the form of women's human rights and thus integrate women's concerns across all areas, including access to food, shelter, water, clothing, education, and political participation, among others.

5.3.3 *Regional Laws, Policies, and Institutions*

At regional levels, various laws, policies, and institutions recognize and incorporate the need to realize gender equality. The 2000 Constitutive Act of the African Union (AU), for instance, underscores the AU's commitment to the principles of gender equality and to the effective participation of women in decision-making.[59] The Maputo Protocol and the 2004 Solemn Declaration on Gender Equality in Africa also reaffirm the continent's commitment to accelerate efforts to promote gender equality at all levels. The AU's 2009 Gender Policy guides the AU's process of gender mainstreaming and the promotion of women's empowerment. In addition, the African Women's Decade (2010–20) aimed at advancing gender equality by accelerating the implementation of the 2000 Dakar Framework for Action and the 1995 Beijing Platform for Action.[60] Other international regional instruments that underscore equality and non-discrimination provisions include the 1948 Charter of the Organization of American States,[61] the 1950 European Convention on Human Rights and Fundamental Freedoms, the 1994 Inter-American Convention on the Prevention, Punishment and Eradication of Violence against Women, and the 2011 Council of Europe's Convention on Preventing and Combating Violence against Women and Domestic Violence.

[59] 2000 Constitutive Act of the African Union, arts. 3 and 4.
[60] African Union, *The African Women's Decade: Grassroots Approach to Gender Equality and Women's Empowerment (GEWE)*, 2020, new-ndpc-static1.s3.amazonaws.com/pubication/AU+African+Women's+Decade+2010-2020.pdf.
[61] See 1948 Charter of the Organization of American States, art. 3(l).

Having recognized the successes of incorporating international feminist ideals into international law, it is important to note that the inclusion of gender equality and women's human rights in the international instruments discussed above does not overcome structural and foundational concerns inherent in international law. As noted earlier in this chapter, international legal feminists argue that international law is male and is based on the analogy between the individual in liberal society and the sovereign state.[62] Providing that women have a right to political participation in international law does not necessarily overcome the deeply entrenched patriarchal norms that, for example, prevent women from participating in active politics.

5.3.4 *SDG 5 and International Legal Feminism*

The SDGs, including SDG 5, rely on the state as a critical actor in the implementation of their ideals and goals. It is important to note here that state sovereignty is an ambivalent concept in both international law and the international legal imagination. This ambivalence nuances international legal feminists and their challenges to international law. International legal feminists adopt the state as a critical actor in the realization of women's rights, ignoring the fact that it is often a barrier to transparent global relations between individuals and groups. Women need to become conscious of their own assumptions about state sovereignty in order to understand its potential as a strategy of empowerment and to critically examine the ways in which state sovereignty sets the functional and allegorical parameters of international law. In critiquing international legal feminism (ILF), Charlesworth has noted that ILF is an epiphenomenon, the primary phenomenon being international law. As a result, ILF has conceptual difficulties because it embraces the liberal presumption that all values, ends, and purposes are based on individual self-interest. It is our view that SDG 5, like ILF, takes a pre-existing language of interpreting the world that must move within it to be heard and understood. The language of international lawyers precedes feminist thought in SDG 5's goal to achieve equality for women and girls. In this view, then, we do not say that international law emanates from legal subjects (women and girls), but, rather, we think so because that is what we say.[63]

While we agree with the ILF position that the social contract is gendered and that the resulting social order that arises in the form of a state is male, we also note that international feminisms mediate on a pre-theoretical world view and thus include the *problematique* within it. In addition, international law feminists are concerned with the constraints of meaning within the international legal order. In a sense, they are drawn into meanings that conceal, deceive, and distort concepts such as equality. Before attempting to reconstruct this international system, women must

[62] Charlesworth, 'Hidden Gender', n. 37.
[63] David Kennedy, *International Legal Structures* (Nomos Verlagsgesellschaft, 1987).

therefore appreciate the deep structure of meaning within the international order if they are to formulate strategies that overcome deeply entrenched patriarchal norms. In essence, SDG 5's quest for the realization of gender equality and non-discrimination embodies the tensions within liberal thought that homogenize the diverse experiences of women and men the world over. Adverting to the heterogeneity of men and women in SDG 5 would yield indicators that are informed by diverse experiences.

Further, beyond the conventional ILF approach, the context of a disaggregated colonial state must be critically interrogated to figure out how international lawyers have put law together. For instance, traditional international law suggests that, in order to qualify as a state, an entity must have a defined territory. Sovereignty over a specific territorial area is therefore an essential element of statehood. It is clear to us that international law's doctrines are not autonomous from one another, and they turn back on the state structure to be institutionalized. In essence, for all the international and regional instruments mentioned above to be institutionalized and implemented, the 'state' is key in ensuring that barriers to women's economic, political, and sociocultural empowerment are dismantled.

Within this context, two broad international law themes have an impact on SDG 5's positioning in international law: the liberal theory of politics and its reproduction in international law and the gendered nature of international law. First, liberalism is a tradition of political philosophy grounded in the social contract theories of Hobbes, Locke, and David Hume, which assume that society consists of autonomous individuals entertaining values that are based on subjective desires and the idea that society has common values and that these values can be accommodated through social, economic, political, and legal institutions. Liberalism thus accommodates these values and concepts rather than transforming them. ILF rejects this tradition based on the fact that the face of the person represented in the liberalist vision is gendered. However, ILF does not critique the idea that liberalism creates a false vision of human sociability.[64] ILF's view of society as rights-bearing citizens engenders a rights consciousness that isolates individuals and forces them to

[64] In contemporary jurisprudential thought, there are several versions of liberalism. For example, one version considers autonomy of law as being essential to democratic pluralism. Otto Kirchheimer & Franz Neumann, *Social Democracy and the Rule of Law* (Allen & Unwin, 1987), 222. Another version of liberalism maintains the primacy of freedom of citizens and their freely formed associations against the state (for instance, F.W. Maitland and J.N. Figgis; see David Nicholls, *The Pluralist State: The Political Ideas of J.N. Figgis and His Contemporaries* [Springer, 2016]). Another liberalism tradition propounds a legal order that its citizens accept as legitimate. H.L.A. Hart, *The Concept of Law*, 3rd ed. (Oxford University Press, 2012). Other traditions emphasize the need to recognize friendly enemy relations and the state of exception in the formulation of the rule of law. Liberal pluralism is premised on the idea that the freedom of citizens and their associations is of primary value, that public power itself must be governed by the rule of law, and that freedom exists because of the conflict of interests when regulated by law. William Galston, *Liberal Pluralism: The Implications of Value Pluralism for Political Theory and Practice* (Cambridge University Press, 2002).

juxtapose their existence with that of others. Further, ILF, like liberalism, envisions the world in dualities, such as, for example, individualism and selflessness, subjectivity and objectivity, freedom and necessity, among others. Like liberalism, ILF offers legitimacy to capitalism and masks exploitation with 'freedom' and 'individual rights'. As Charlesworth notes, the covering up of liberal ideals in the language of 'rights' and 'freedoms' misleads women into supporting and seeking to engender the same system that invisibilizes their experiences and perspectives. The assumption that liberal ideals in their classical form are desirable for all women is an assumption inherent in SDG 5's quest for gender equality, and it must be debunked as it embraces the fundamental contradiction of liberal theory – that the individual must be free to pursue their self-interest, whereas that pursuit requires a restraint of other individuals.[65]

We note that, like ILF, SDG 5 is erected upon contradictory assumptions. Therefore, its failure to produce a necessary outcome results from international law's indeterminacies produced by the contradictory nature of international law's assumptions. Both ILF and those liberals whose main goal is the formal equality of women claim that women must be treated the same way as men.[66] It is argued that women and men are rights-bearing, autonomous human beings. This classical ILF approach anchors its thoughts in the core concepts of liberal political theory (rationality, rights, equal opportunity) and argues that women are just as rational as men. Therefore, they should have an equal opportunity to make their own choices. It challenges the assumption of female inferiority and seeks to eliminate gender-based distinctions recognized in law by enabling women to compete equally in the market place. The critique of this approach, which we agree with, points out its fallacy in that it takes maleness to be the norm.[67] The defenders of this approach argue that it expands possibilities for female life experience, instead of reducing women to men. The approach works, it is argued, since it speaks the language that the legal system understands. They further argue that non-sex specific legal solutions are preferable to sex-specific laws. ILF views women as individual human beings rather than as a class (dominance), and it claims that these individuals have been dominated by men rather than by a class. Gender inequality should be viewed as a cause of systematic subordination, not a result of irrational discrimination. Gender should be a question of power, and they argue that ILF should not be satisfied by creating legal categories such as sovereignty, jurisdiction, and so on in order to accommodate the present reality.

According to this approach, which is championed by theorists such as Catherine MacKinnon, sex equality is accommodated based on a woman's difference from a man, not a mere accommodation of that difference.[68] Her identity of difference thus

[65] Charlesworth, 'Hidden Gender', n. 37.

[66] *Id.*

[67] *Id.*

[68] Catharine A. MacKinnon, 'Reflections on Sex Equality under Law' (1991) 100 *Yale Law Journal* 1, digitalcommons.law.yale.edu/ylj/vol100/iss5/6.

becomes central to normative debates about restructuring the world. However, as MacKinnon notes, differences among women must also be maintained because, otherwise, it might end up being essentialist.[69] We note that ILF argues for liberal equality and thus does not believe that there are socially constructed classes of women that differ from men. The issue of power therefore is not canvassed and thus results in changes in law that do not address inequality in power. Take, for instance, the example of the affirmative action provisions in SDG 5 that are geared towards increasing women's participation in politics. Increasing the number of women in parliament, the judiciary, and the executive does not necessarily address the structural biases that enhance the patriarchal norms. In essence, SDG 5 embodies liberal equality ideals that do not recognize the multiple ways in which law manifests itself.

5.4 POSITIONING SDG 5 IN THE INTERNATIONAL INSTITUTIONAL CONTEXT

In positioning SDG 5 in the international institutional context, it is important for us to reiterate that, traditionally, international law has assumed the centrality of the state. It assumes that the state system is the political unit that makes up the international community. However, today, the place of the state in the implementation of international law has been challenged as spaces have opened for other actors such as international institutions, civil society organizations, international non-governmental organizations (NGOs), corporations, judicial bodies, and quasi-judicial bodies. Indeed, all global actors are expected to participate in the implementation of SDG 5, and it is in so doing that a variety of approaches within the UN system towards mainstreaming SDG 5 into programmes and policies has been adopted. This approach, otherwise known as the Mainstreaming, Acceleration and Policy Support (MAPS) Approach, identifies applicable tools for the implementation of SDG 5.[70] Its main tools include raising public awareness and the use of multi-sectoral approaches; localizing the agenda; monitoring, reporting, and promoting accountability; assessing risks; and fostering adaptability.[71] According to MAPS, mainstreaming refers to the essential steps that are taken to ensure that the SDGs are achieved. The acceleration enables identifications of factors that allow for the achievement of the SDGs, while policy support addresses the need for a coordinated response within the UN network.[72] In essence, MAPS attempts to break down the traditional boundaries of international law by including a multiplicity of actors, sectors, and disciplines.

69 *Id.*
70 UN Women, *The Sustainable Development Goals (SDGs) and Africa's Agenda 2063* (UN Women, 2017), sustainabledevelopment.un.org/content/documents/2441UNWomenSDGReport.pdf.
71 *Id.*
72 *Id.*, 16.

Some notable international efforts towards the implementation of SDG 5 include initiatives geared towards financial inclusion,[73] the financing of sustainable development projects and programmes across various development sectors,[74] gender mainstreaming, abolishing forced marriage, ending violence against women,[75] the promotion of equal remuneration for women and men,[76] the promotion of diversity and equal opportunity, and access to sexual and reproductive healthcare services[77] In discussing some of the institutions working towards the implementation of SDG 5 in the remainder of this chapter, we highlight some of the successes and the challenges towards the realization of this goal.

First, all UN bodies are currently expected to work on the promotion and implementation of the 2030 Agenda for Sustainable Development and the SDGs.[78] The UN bodies most active in the implementation of SDG 5 include UN Women and the UN Population Fund, which focus on gender equality, FGM, child marriage, engaging men and boys, and gender-based violence. Moreover, other UN agencies such as the World Health Organization, the UN Office of the High Commissioner for Human Rights, the UN High Commissioner for Refugees, the UN Education, Scientific and Cultural Organization, the UN Department of Economic and Social Affairs, and the UN Environment Programme all have programmes geared towards the realization of SDG 5.[79] The United Nations has produced several reports that reveal gaps and opportunities for gender equality in the 2030 Agenda.[80] Among the programmes that UN Women has initiated to implement SDG 5 is the UN secretary-general's UNiTE by 2030 to End Violence against Women Campaign, which seeks to end violence against women and girls by bringing together governments and civil society organizations.[81] Despite these efforts, what SDG 5 terms 'harmful and prohibitive socio-cultural practices,' such

73 KfW Development Bank, *Kfw Promotes Gender Equality Worldwide*, www.Kfw-Entwicklungsbank.de/International-Financing/KfW-Development-Bank/Our-Topics/SDGs/SDG-5/.

74 International Institute for Sustainable Development, *World Bank Launches SDG 5 Bond*, 29 November 2019, sdg.iisd.org/news/world-bank-launches-sdg-5-bond/.

75 Zonta International, *Implementation of SDG5 A Report to the High-Level Political Forum from Zonta International, a Non-governmental Organization in General Consultative Status with* ECOSOC, 2017, sustainabledevelopment.un.org/content/documents/16909HLPF_Input_Zonta_International_SDG5.pdf.

76 GRI Global Impact, *SDG 5: Achieve Gender Equality and Empower All Women and Girls*, 2015, sdgcompass.org/sdgs/sdg-5/.

77 *Id.*

78 *Transforming Our World: The 2030 Agenda for Sustainable Development*, Doc. A/Res/70/1, 25 September 2015.

79 UN Economic and Social Council, *Progress towards the Sustainable Development Goals: Report of the Secretary-General*, UN Doc. E/2017/66, 2017.

80 UN Women, *Turning Promises into Action: Gender Equality in the 2030 Agenda for Sustainable Development*, 2018, www.unwomen.org/en/digital-library/sdg-report.

81 UN Women, *UNiTE to End Violence against Women*, www.unwomen.org/en/what-we-do/ending-violence-against-women/take-action/unite.

as FGM, continues to be practised in many parts of Africa. Although laws elaborately legislate against sexual and gender-based violence, it continues to be rampant. Moreover, persistent gender inequalities with regard to the access and control of resources and economic and political opportunities continue to be a major obstacle in the quest for the realization of SDG 5.[82]

Second, in addition to the traditional international institutions, collaborations and networks have emerged in the international space to implement SDG 5. For instance, the Every Woman Every Child Initiative, a multi-sector platform that was founded in 2010 and led by the UN secretary-general, aims at integrating women's, children's and adolescents' health in development.[83] This kind of international multi-sectoral engagement outside the traditional state in international law demonstrates a move in international law and policy towards implementation that engages different sectors and involves collaboration, inter-sectoral collaboration, and multidisciplinary and cross-disciplinary work towards the implementation of SDG 5. Other initiatives such as the Spotlight Initiative also play a role in implementing SDG 5. This initiative, which is a partnership between the European Union and the United Nations, seeks to achieve gender equality and women's empowerment and aims to respond to all forms of violence against women.[84]

Third, judicial and quasi-judicial bodies also play a role in the implementation of SDG 5. These institutions include national human rights institutions.[85] In addition, the role of regional bodies, such as the Common Market for Eastern and Southern Africa (COMESA),[86] in implementing SDG 5 has included projects such as the African Development Bank's Fifty Million African Women Speak project, which aims to create a networking platform dedicated to sub-Saharan African women entrepreneurs. There is also collaboration between the UN Conference on Trade and Development and COMESA in online training on trade and gender and in the young women and youth employment projects under COMESA's Youth Programme.[87] The East African Court (EAC) has also established national employment programmes, including vocational and technical training that targets girls and

[82] Ministry of Devolution and Planning, *Implementation of the Agenda 2030 for Sustainable Development in Kenya*, June 2017.

[83] World Health Organization & UN International Children's Emergency Fund, *Protect the Progress: Rise, Refocus and Recover – 2020 Progress Report on the Every Woman Every Child Global Strategy for Women's, Children's and Adolescents' Health (2016–30)*, Doc. CC BY-NC-SA 3.0 IGO, 2020, protect.everywomaneverychild.org/assets/img/2020-Progress-Report-on-the-EWEC-Global-Strategy-Final.pdf.

[84] Sustainable Development Goals Partnership Platform, *The Spotlights Initiative*, sustainable development.un.org/partnership/?p=23111.

[85] 2015 Mérida Declaration on the Role of National Human Rights Institutions in Implementing the 2030 Agenda for Sustainable Development.

[86] Mangasini Atanasi Katundu, 'Sustainable Development Goals and Their Implication on Economic Growth: An East African Perspective', in *Handbook of Research on Sustainable Development and Governance Strategies for Economic Growth in Africa* (IGI Global, 2018).

[87] UN Women, n. 70, 16.

women, gender mainstreaming training programmes for EAC staff, the implementation of regional projects aimed at improving the ability of women entrepreneurs to network and share information, and access to financial services.[88] In addition, other regional bodies such as the Association of Southeast Asian Nations (ASEAN) and the Inter-American Court on Human Rights have also highlighted the important role that regional bodies play in ensuring the implementation of the SDGs. In 2016, for instance, ASEAN adopted its own vision, which seeks to acknowledge the relationship between the 2030 Agenda and ASEAN's development.[89] ASEAN acknowledges that regional bodies can promote multi-sector collaboration to help drive the success of national efforts, to develop a system to track effectiveness, to promote knowledge sharing on best practices, and, finally, to provide an environment for peer evaluation of national efforts to implement the SDGs.[90]

Lastly, the implementation of SDG 5 depends on a multiplicity of actors including state and non-state actors, communities, individuals, and societies. Non-state actors include NGOs, community-based organizations, civil society organizations, and international NGOs. Zonta International, for instance, an international NGO works to implement SDG 5 through its global network of thirty thousand members in more than eleven hundred clubs in sixty-six countries.[91] As noted earlier, traditionally, international law has placed great reliance on the role of the state in ensuring compliance with international law. Despite the fact that the role of 'non-state' actors has become more and more prevalent in ensuring compliance with international law, the state continues to be the main actor in SDG reporting and thus continues to be a major hindrance to the implementation of SDG 5. In addition, even as the World Bank, the International Monetary Fund, and the institutions discussed above raise awareness and finance projects implementing SDG 5, their policies create deeper structural inequalities as they are unevenly designed.[92]

In fact, the Commission on the Status of Women in March 2020 observed that progress towards the implementation of SDG 5 has been painfully slow.[93] The commission further noted that twenty-five years after the fourth World Conference on Women, no country has fully achieved gender equality and the empowerment of

[88] *Id.*

[89] Government of ASEAN, *2015 ASEAN Community Vision 2025*, 21 November 2015.

[90] Temitayo O. Peters, *Four Ways Regional Bodies Can Help Deliver SDG Justice Commitments*, 13 June 2016, namati.org/news-stories/regional-bodies-sdgs/.

[91] Zonta International, *A Report to the High-Level Political Forum from Zonta International, a Non-governmental Organization in General Consultative Status with ECOSOC*, 2017, sdgs.un.org/sites/default/files/documents/16909HLPF_Input_Zonta_International_SDG5.pdf.

[92] Bretton Woods, *What Are the Main Criticisms of the World Bank and the IMF?* 4 June 2019, www.brettonwoodsproject.org/2019/06/what-are-the-main-criticisms-of-the-world-bank-and-the-imf/.

[93] Commission on the Status of Women, *Political Declaration on the Occasion of the Twenty-fifth Anniversary of the Fourth World Conference on Women*, 20 March 2020, au.int/sites/default/files/documents/38226-doc-csw64-politicaldeclaration.pdf.

women and girls.[94] The fact that women the world over continue to experience multiple and intersecting forms of discrimination is testament to the fact that international law and its institutions have failed to overcome structural patriarchal interests that perpetuate gender inequalities and thus hinder the socio-economic and political empowerment of women. Moreover, the inclusion of multiple actors transcending the traditional centre of international law – the state – has resulted in enhanced solidarity between different actors and the dispersal of power centres responsible for the implementation of SDG 5. Despite enhanced solidarity among actors, SDG 5 continues to be difficult to achieve due to the centrality of the state model in international law.

In fact, some feminist thinkers argue that, as happens between individuals, an ethic of care should apply to relations between states.[95] Using the same analogy to analyze the jurisdiction of international law, scholars such as Charlesworth demonstrate that, like the distinction between the public and private spheres in liberal thought, the international legal principle of non-intervention in the internal affairs of states leaves women vulnerable to discrimination and abuse.[96] Hence, the question of implementation is very critical when it comes to international women's human rights. If the personification of the state exposes international legal norms such as political, economic, and political rights as male, the acceptance of the sovereign state and the sovereign self denies the individual and collective identity of women within and across states. As Charlesworth argues, and we agree, in an international society peopled by states, women are analytically invisible because they belong to the state's sphere of personal autonomy.[97]

In essence, women's knowledge and experience are relegated to the private sphere where domestic reproductive roles of childbearing and home making are women's primary responsibility, while men's visibility is in economic and political leadership in the 'public' sphere. This mode of feminist analysis implicitly resurrects the old idea of international law as governing relations between states, leaving unexplored the modern voice that encompasses other participants, interactions, and trends. Despite the multiplicity of actors and institutions involved in the implementation of SDGs, the 'maleness' embedded in international law continues to pose a challenge in so far as the implementation of SDG 5 is concerned. Given ILF's critique that the state is generally constructed as male and is an expression of patriarchal male interests, institutions responsible for the implementation of international law have also not been immune to that critique and often fail to reflect women's role in structuring society. The fact that the state continues to be the main actor in SDG reporting continues to be a major hindrance to the implementation of SDG 5.

94 *Id.*
95 Charlesworth, 'Hidden Gender', n. 37.
96 *Id.*
97 *Id.*

5.5 CONCLUSIONS

For decades, feminist legal scholars have argued that the state is generally constructed as male and that the state is a direct expression of patriarchal male interests and, as such, does not reflect women's role in structuring society. In essence, they have argued that international law has had a historically located man in mind and, thus, women's voices and experiences have been excluded. This critique has contributed to major changes in the form and substance of international law as illustrated in the numerous treaties and conventions enacted to protect women's human rights in international law. Despite these major advancements in international law and ILF's attempts to engender international law, laws that discriminate against women remain a significant problem, and even when there are laws in place that guarantee gender equality, they are not yet being put into practice.[98] SDG 5 continues to face similar implementation challenges due to the lack of an integrationist approach towards it in relation to the other SDGs, discrepancies between international and local realities on gender equality, and a failure to accommodate international legal pluralist approaches in the quest for gender equality and women's economic empowerment. Furthermore, gender mainstreaming in international law needs to go beyond 'adding women and stirring' to 'integrationist approaches' to gender mainstreaming in order to disaggregate the 'man' of international law and achieve substantive gender equality.

[98] See UN Women, n. 32; UN High Commissioner for Human Rights, *Report on Good Practices in Efforts Aimed at Preventing Violence against Women*, Doc. A/ HRC/17/23, 2005.

6

SDG 6: Ensure Availability and Sustainable Management of Water and Sanitation for All

Joyeeta Gupta and Hilmer Bosch

ABSTRACT

This chapter reviews the role of Agenda 2030 in further developing water law. It concludes that Sustainable Development Goal (SDG) 6, Clean Water and Sanitation, is a step forward in recognizing the holistic nature of water but that it does not define water as a public good or common good/concern or heritage and also does not reflect on whether water limits require us to redefine growth. It goes beyond a sectoral approach to promote an urgent, coherent, systemic, and multi-level story rightly ignoring whether some of it is based on soft or hard (inter)national law. However, SDG 6 moves backward from limited sovereignty to emphasize full permanent sovereignty over natural resources, and while it emphasizes access to water and sanitation, it does not address the larger distributive issues on which, for example, the 1997 Convention on the Law of the Non-Navigational Uses of Transboundary Watercourses elaborates. Finally, the implementation of SDG 6 may undermine its lofty goals by engaging the profit-oriented private sector in service delivery to the poorest and by enabling the commodification and privatization of the water.

KEYWORDS

SDG 6, water law, international law, water, sanitation, equity, no harm, access and allocation, justice, sovereignty

6.1 INTRODUCTION

This chapter examines the role of Agenda 2030 in governing fresh water through Sustainable Development Goal (SDG) 6, Clean Water and Sanitation, and the way in which this SDG is embedded in Agenda 2030 and international water law. Freshwater is critical for life on Earth and for extraction, production, distribution, consumption, and disposal activities. Although freshwater is available as a renewable resource through the hydrological cycle, it is limited in quantity in time and is not evenly distributed worldwide.[1] Despite governance systems that can be traced back to more than four thousand years,[2] water governance has evolved in a fragmented manner with institutional responsibilities spread throughout the UN system and beyond.[3] At the national level, water governance is undertaken by multiple ministries, sectors, and actors simultaneously. It is therefore not surprising that Agenda 2030 adopted a comprehensive SDG on water with associated targets and indicators.[4]

Against this background, this chapter addresses the following questions: does SDG 6 deal with the inherent complexities of governing water by prioritizing key water-related issues? Does it challenge established concepts in international law? To what extent is it 'embedded' in international law and institutions, and to what extent does it implicitly require international water law to further develop? This chapter focuses primarily on international water law of a broader geographical application rather than on the hundreds of international basin-level agreements. It showcases the breadth of the relations with international law instead of targeting a specific relationship, as this is in line with the spirit of Agenda 2030, which aims at a systemic understanding.

In order to govern water effectively, SDG 6 needs to cover five issues. First, understanding the nature of water is critical. It is essential for life, is non-substitutable, is part of the hydrological cycle, flows downwards on land, upwards through capillary movement in plants, cycles through different physical states, is both within living organisms and can be passed through by living organisms; clearly, it is a complex system. Early Hindu law saw water rights as merely usufructuary rights,[5] and early Islamic law saw water as a gift of God: neither did encouraged property rights in water.[6] Indigenous systems of water law also saw water as a shared community resource. However, Roman law recognized different kinds of ownership

1 Paul Ekins, Joyeeta Gupta, & Pierre Boileau (eds.), *Global Environment Outlook: Healthy Planet Healthy People* (Cambridge University Press, 2019).

2 Joseph W. Dellapenna & Joyeeta Gupta (eds.), *The Evolution of the Law and Politics of Water* (Springer, 2009).

3 Claudia Pahl-Wostl, Joyeeta Gupta, & Daniel Petry, 'Governance and the Global Water System: A Theoretical Exploration' (2008) 14 *Global Governance: A Review of Multilateralism and International Organizations* 419; Charles J. Vörösmarty et al., 'What Scale for Water Governance' (2015) 349 *Science* 478.

4 *Transforming Our World: The 2030 Agenda for Sustainable Development*, UN Doc. A/Res/70/1, 25 September 2015.

5 Philippe Cullet & Joyeeta Gupta, 'India: Evolution of Water Law and Policy' in Dellapenna & Gupta, n. 2, 157.

6 Thomas Naff, 'Islamic Law and the Politics of Water' in Dellapenna & Gupta, n. 2, 37.

in water – public, private, and community[7] – and this understanding has pervaded till today. Water ownership is linked to land ownership (riparian rights) and is also increasingly marketed globally as part of the process of commodifying and privatizing water,[8] promoted, inter alia, by development agencies. Hence, a key question is whether water should be subject to property rights given its nature.[9] At the same time, differentiating between local, transboundary, and global water challenges and law is problematic given the shared hydrological cycle and how climate change, land use change, and trade influence this cycle.[10]

Second, water consists of blue water (consisting of surface and groundwater and water in ice/snow), green water (water in soils and trees), atmospheric water (water in the atmosphere in vapour and liquid), grey and black water (polluted water and sewage), each providing specific ecosystem services and challenges.[11] Although the earliest water governance systems developed in water scarce areas and addressed groundwater, today, most water law systems focus primarily on blue surface water, even though groundwater is 97 per cent blue fresh water.[12] Green and atmospheric water is underemphasized even though it makes up 50–60 per cent of all water.[13] International water law scarcely addresses green and atmospheric water.

Third, water problems are growing greatly,[14] encompassing issues of access, property rights, commodification, pollution, droughts, and floods. The United Nations Environment Programme's (UNEP) sixth Global Environment Outlook provides a state-of-the-art assessment of the current state of water problems and shows that about 1.4 million people die annually, and many more are unable to work, from water-related sicknesses. It also shows that a growing number of people are displaced

7 Joseph Dellapenna 'The Fundamental Concepts of Property in Water and the Role of Markets in Water Governance', in Joseph W. Dellapenna & Joyeeta Gupta (eds.), *Encyclopedia of Environmental Law, Water Law: The Expanding Boundaries* (EE, forthcoming).

8 Maude Barlow & Tony Clarke, *Blue Gold: The Fight to Stop the Corporate Theft of the World's Water* (New Press, 2002).

9 Dellapenna, n. 7; Joyeeta Gupta & Hilmer Bosch, 'Changing "Ownership" in Water Law: Comparative Experiences in the Developing World', in Dellapenna & Gupta, n. 7; Hilmer J. Bosch & Joyeeta Gupta, 'Access to and Ownership of Water in Anglophone Africa and a Case Study in South Africa' (2020) 13 *Water Alternatives* 205; Hilmer J. Bosch, Joyeeta Gupta, & Hebe Verrest, 'A Water Property Right Inventory of 60 Countries', *Review of European, Comparative and International Environmental Law (RECIEL)* (forthcoming).

10 Charles J. Vörösmarty & Dork Sahagian, 'Anthropogenic Disturbance of the Terrestrial Water Cycle' (2000) 15 *BioScience* 753.

11 Shakeel Hayat & Joyeeta Gupta, 'Kinds of Freshwater and Their Relation to Ecosystem Services and Human Well-being' (2016) 18 *Water Policy* 1229

12 Kirstin I. Conti & Joyeeta Gupta, 'Global Governance Principles for the Sustainable Development of Groundwater Resources' (2015) 16 *International Environmental Agreements (INEA)* 849.

13 Sofie te Wierik et al., 'The Need for Green and Atmospheric Water Governance' (2019) 7(2) *Wiley Water* 1.

14 Charles J Vörösmarty et al., 'Global Threats to Human Water Security and River Biodiversity' (2010) 467 *Nature* 555

by water-related droughts and floods.[15] These statistics reveal that international water law has been unable to address the health risks posed by water.

Fourth, in order to govern water, it is important to understand the causes (drivers and pressures) of water problems. The drivers of water problems are the pursuit of an increased gross domestic product (GDP); technology (which enables water control); climate change; and demographic factors such as population growth and urbanization. The pressures of water problems include demands from, and impacts of, agriculture, energy, industry, and households.[16] Underlying the drivers and pressures is global inequality, which implies that those who use/abuse water resources are often not those who are affected by the use/abuse.[17] Moreover, water is increasingly being used to provide goods and services elsewhere, which is referred to as virtual water trade.[18] International water law scarcely takes into account the global drivers of water use and the impacts of such water use on others.

Fifth, in dealing with justice issues, we use the access and allocation framework. Access refers to an individual's access to a minimum amount of water for human dignity. Allocation refers to (1) how water is allocated between different uses, users, villages/provinces/countries, and humans and nature; (2) how responsibilities with respect to water are allocated; and (3) how risks are allocated and addressed.[19] International water law has focused on some transboundary issues but has yet to account for a global understanding of the water law challenges. This chapter first discusses water and whether SDG 6 adequately addresses water challenges. It then explores how the content of SDG 6 as embedded within Agenda 2030 relates to the different bodies of international law and explores some of the implementation institutions and the challenges they raise before concluding.

6.2 THE CONTENT OF SDG 6 IN THE CONTEXT OF THE OTHER SDGS

6.2.1 *SDG 6 and Other SDGs*

We now assess how SDG 6 addresses the water issues mentioned earlier. SDG 6 aims to '[e]nsure availability and sustainable management of water and sanitation

15 Internal Displacement Monitoring Centre and Norwegian Refugee Council, *Global Report on Internal Displacement*, April 2020, www.internal-displacement.org/sites/default/files/publications/documents/2020-IDMC-GRID.pdf.

16 Ekins, Gupta & Boileau, n. 1.

17 Joyeeta Gupta et al., 'Re-imagining DPSIR from an Equity and Inclusive Development Perspective' (2020) 15 *Sustainability Science* 503

18 John A. Allan, *Virtual Water: Tackling the Threat to Our Planet's Most Precious Resource* (IB Tauris, 2011); John A. Allan, 'Water Use and Development in Arid Regions: Environment, Economic Development, and Water Resource Politics and Policy' (1996) 5 *RECIEL* 107.

19 Joyeeta Gupta & Louis Lebel (eds.), 'Special Issue: Access and Allocation in Earth System Governance' 20(2) *INEA* 197.

for all'. Unlike other more generally worded SDGs, such as SDG 1, No Poverty, and SDG 2, Zero Hunger, the goal of this SDG focuses on ensuring availability and sanitation for all as well as the sustainable management of water. The first issue prioritizes access and human health through two targets on drinking water and sanitation. The second prioritizes the health of the water system through four targets (that is, reduce pollution, enhance water-use efficiency, implement integrated water resource management, and protect water-based ecosystems). The transboundary context and related cooperation are hinted at in one target. This SDG does not emphasize the economic aspects of, or property rights in, water except in relation to affordability (target 6.1) and efficiency (target 6.4).

Moving to the relationship between SDG 6 and the other SDGs, we note that access to drinking water and sanitation services is critical for ensuring healthy lives (SDG 3, Good Health and Well-being), which may contribute to reducing poverty (SDG 1). Thus, synergy can exist between access to water (target 6.1), eradicating extreme poverty (target 1.1), and reducing half the proportion of people living in poverty (target 1.2). Since water and poverty are inextricably linked, poor access to water has an impact on the prospects for making a living.[20] Addressing poverty can allow people to access and/or purchase water. Given gender-specific water needs (for example, women have different hygiene needs than men) and water-related behaviour (for example, women in developing countries often have to collect the water), water systems need to take a gendered approach (SDG 5, Gender Equality).[21] Furthermore, ensuring that all men and women – in particular, the poor and the vulnerable – have equal rights to economic resources, including land ownership (target 1.4), can increase access to water (target 6.1). Access and allocation of water is critical for increased, inclusive, and sustainable economic growth (SDG 8, Decent Work and Economic Growth). A well-managed water system can enhance agricultural productivity (SDG 2) and implicitly contribute to reducing hunger. However, increased food production and economic growth can have a negative impact on water.

[20] Asian Development Bank, *Water and Poverty*, 2006, www.adb.org/sites/default/files/publication/28859/water-brief-water-and-poverty.pdf.

[21] Contribute across SDGs WASH underpins many of the SDGs. Within the 17 SDGs, UNICEF's priority cross-sectoral interventions to improve child health, welfare and development will include: WASH in education (SDG 4) and health care facilities (SDG 3), MHM and other interventions focusing on women and girls (SDG 5), targeted sanitation and hygiene interventions in support of programmes to reduce malnutrition (SDG 2) and to end child poverty (SDG 1), and sectoral interventions to protect children and women from violence and indignity (SDG 16). WASH inputs also contribute towards the achievement of other SDG goals and targets including sustainable cities (SDG 11), reduced inequalities between and within countries (SDG 10), environmental protection and climate change (SDG 13) and decent working conditions (SDG 8). UN International Children's Emergency Fund (UNICEF), Strategy for Water, Sanitation and Hygiene 2016–2030, 2016, www.unicef.org/documents/unicef-strategy-water-sanitation-and-hygiene-2016-2030

Water is essential for energy production, and accessing water often needs energy (SDG 7, Affordable and Clean Energy). Managing water must account for the impacts of climate change (SDG 13, Climate Action), water is essential for healthy ecosystems (SDG 15, Life on Land), and water is imperative for development and employment (SDG 8). Water management matters for the reduction of inequality within and among countries (SDG 10, Reduced Inequalities) and for ensuring sustainable consumption and production patterns (SDG 12, Responsible Consumption and Production). Understanding these interlinkages is crucial for 'integrated governance and policy coherence in implementing the SDGs'.[22] However, there is limited quantification of these interlinkages at the global or national level. We hypothesize that the achievement of SDG 6 is vital for the achievement of the other SDGs but that the achievement of the other SDGs may either enhance or reduce the potential for achieving SDG 6.

6.2.2 *Does SDG 6 in Relation to Other SDGs Address Water Issues?*

In assessing SDG 6 in relation to the five aspects of water mentioned in the introduction, we draw five conclusions. First, while Agenda 2030 recognizes the systemic nature of water, in that it requires that all goals are treated in an indivisible manner, it does not define water as a common concern, public good, and/or heritage. Also, it does not seem to commit to whether it can be commodified or not. However, it does seem to have responded to the national/international differentiation in international law by covering issues of domestic and transboundary relevance. Second, while SDG 6 covers all kinds of water, it covers green and atmospheric water to a limited extent and mostly implicitly. However, the links between SDG 6 and the other ecological goals implicitly implies that the entire water system is covered. Third, SDG 6 appears to cover all the negative impacts on the water system since it addresses high withdrawals of water and excess discharge of wastes, and its links to the other SDGs show that it also recognizes the impacts of climate change on water. Fourth, although SDG 6 and Agenda 2030 take a systemic approach to water, it is not self-evident that the document addresses the underlying drivers of water problems. Demographic and urbanization concerns are covered to some extent, but the document apparently sees growth and technology as unqualified solutions rather than also as a part of the problem. However, it does call for transformative change.

Finally, in terms of justice issues, SDG 6 covers issues of access to drinking water and sanitation services. Target 5.a recognizes the need for women to control and own land and thus implicitly covers access to water resources. SDG 6 deals with

[22] Xin Zhou & Mustafa Moinuddin (eds.), *Sustainable Development Goals Interlinkages and Network Analysis: A Practical Tool for SDG Integration and Policy Coherence*, Institute for Global Environmental Strategies (IGES) Research Report no. RR1602 (IGES, 2017).

pollution issues but does not require liability or compensation for harm caused. However, it does not deal with the way in which water resources are currently allocated through property rights, permits, purchases, contracts, or transboundary agreements. Nor does it deal with how water resources should be shared within nations or between nations except in terms of calling for transboundary cooperation. It also does not deal with the challenge of disaster risk management or how harm should be addressed. Thus, SDG 6 addresses the inequality question by only prioritizing 'access' issues, but it does not deal with 'allocation' issues. In other words, it focuses on meeting minimum needs but does not address the bigger issues of whether unfair allocation through the allocation of property rights and permits/ concessions, or through the impacts of climate change may be the cause of access challenges. Focusing on access without addressing allocation issues may ultimately undermine access and diverts attention away from the fundamental inequalities in the global system.[23] This issue is problematic as those with economic resources and technologies can access large quantities of water and exacerbate water injustices.[24] Finally, as indicated, SDG 6 does not address issues of responsibility and liability.

6.3 POSITIONING SDG 6 IN INTERNATIONAL LAW

6.3.1 *Introduction*

Having examined whether SDG 6 addresses key water-related issues, we now assess how SDG 6 and the related SDGs are embedded in international hard and soft law; whether and how SDG 6 goes beyond existing water, environmental, and developmental law; where SDG 6 falls behind the existing evolution of water law; and the missed opportunities. There are three water conventions of potential global application: (1) the 1971 Convention on Wetlands of International Importance Especially as Waterfowl Habitat (Ramsar Convention), which has been universally ratified; (2) the 1997 UN Convention on the Law of the Non-Navigable Uses of International Watercourses (Watercourses Convention), which has been ratified by less than one-quarter of the UN member states; and (3) the UN Economic Commission of Europe's (UNECE) 1992 Convention on the Protection and Use of Transboundary Watercourses and International Lakes (Water Convention) (and its protocols), which has been opened for global ratification but has also been ratified by less than one-quarter of the UN member states.

In addition, the two resolutions on the human right to water and sanitation adopted by the UN General Assembly and the UN Human Rights Council update

[23] *Id.*

[24] E.g., Rutgerd Boelens, Jeroen Vos, & Tom Perreault (eds.), *Water Justice* (Cambridge University Press, 2018).

the content of previous human rights declarations and laws in relation to water.[25] The UN General Assembly has also discussed the International Law Commission's (ILC) 2008 Draft Articles on the Law of Transboundary Aquifers (Draft Articles on Aquifers).[26] Moreover, as there are 263 transboundary rivers and 273 transboundary aquifers,[27] hundreds of water treaties between states form the backbone of international water law. Finally, several international court cases discuss critical issues with respect to water law.[28] The key issues that emerge from these documents include (1) the focus on blue transboundary water – surface and, to a limited extent, groundwater; (2) the treatment of sovereignty; (3) the need to meet minimum water needs; (4) the need for equitable sharing of water resources; (5) the need to reduce ecological damage and damage to other countries; and (6) instruments for implementing these agreements. These documents are relatively silent on the nature of water and on the issue of property rights in water.

6.3.2 *SDG 6, Other SDGs, and International Law*

Much of SDG 6 is embedded in the above-mentioned history of national and international water law. In examining SDG 6 and the other SDGs in relation to the existing body of water law and other related legal areas, we cluster the SDGs in terms of social, ecological, and economic goals. With respect to social issues, the targets on universal access to water and sanitation services can be seen as implementing the human right to water and sanitation, and they go beyond the 2000 Millennium Development Goals, which aimed merely at reducing by half the number of people without access to water and sanitation services.[29] These targets can be linked to rights included in the 1966 International Covenant on Economic, Social and Cultural Rights.[30] These links are obvious since, without water, achieving other rights such as the right to an adequate standard of living, to food, to housing, to health, and to development would not be possible.[31] This connection

[25] *The Human Right to Water and Sanitation*, UN Doc. A/Res/64/292, 3 August 2010; *Human Rights and Access to Safe Drinking Water and Sanitation*, UN Doc. A/HRC/Res/15/9, 6 October 2010.

[26] *Report of the International Law Commission on the Work of Its Sixtieth Session*, 63rd Session, Supplement no. 10, UN Doc. A/63/10, 2008, 19 (Draft Articles on Aquifers).

[27] College of Earth, Ocean, and Atmospheric Sciences, Oregon State University, *Transboundary Freshwater Dispute Database*, 2020, transboundarywaters.science.oregonstate.edu/content/transboundary-freshwater-dispute-database.

[28] Lilian del Castillo-Laborde, Joseph W. Dellapenna, & Joyeeta Gupta, 'Case Law on International Watercourses', in Dellapenna & Gupta, n. 2, 319.

[29] *UN Millennium Declaration*, UN Doc. A/Res/55/2, 8 September 2000.

[30] Pedi Obani & Joyeeta Gupta, 'The Evolution of the Right to Water and Sanitation: Differentiating the Implications' (2015) 24 *RECIEL* 27

[31] UNICEF, *Current Issues: The Right to Safe Water and to Sanitation* (UNICEF, 2014)

was also highlighted in General Comment 15.[32] Moreover, this right is included in the 1979 Convention on the Elimination of All Forms of Discrimination against Women and in the 1989 Convention on the Rights of the Child. In 2010, the Committee on Economic, Social and Cultural Rights produced the *Statement on the Right to Sanitation.*[33]

Although there is debate about whether the human right to water and sanitation is legally binding or not,[34] we believe that global and national governance is prioritizing this right in different parts of the world.[35] We also agree with the separate emphasis on drinking water and sanitation, since operationalizing and implementing each of these goals comes with very different challenges. Moreover, while target 6.1 mentions affordable drinking water, target 6.2 on sanitation does not. Does this mean that the sanitation goal must be achieved irrespective of affordability, and does the affordability clause for drinking water emphasize that people must pay? This ambiguity is problematic (see the discussion in Sections 6.3.3 and 6.3.4). We conclude that SDG 6 in itself and in its links to some other social goals is embedded within the human rights approach. However, human rights approaches have focused on the state-citizen relationship and have seldom given rise to transboundary obligations in law.

SDG 6 is also linked to environmental goals, such as those on climate change, biodiversity, and ecosystem protection, most of which are embedded in legally binding international treaties. Target 6.3 on reducing pollution into water bodies is supported by relevant articles in the Watercourses Convention and in the Water Convention. Of regional relevance, while not a part of international law, the 2000 European Union Water Framework Directive also has provisions on water pollution.[36] Other conventions focus on preventing specific types of pollution (for example, the 2013 Minamata Convention on Mercury, which addresses mercury pollution). SDG 6 goes beyond these conventions in emphasizing recycling and safe reuse of water. The 1989 Basel Convention on the Transboundary Movement of Hazardous Wastes requires states to reduce the movement of hazardous wastes. Addressing this problem is not as straightforward as it might seem, given that today (near) end-of-life wastes are sometimes sent to developing countries under the guise

[32] Office of the High Commissioner for Human Rights, *General Comment 15 (2002): The Right to Water (Arts. 11 and 12 of the International Covenant on Economic, Social and Cultural Rights)*, UN Doc. E/C.12/2002/11, 20 January 2003.

[33] Committee on Economic, Social and Cultural Rights, *Statement on the Right to Sanitation*, UN Doc. E/C.12/2010/1, 18 March 2011.

[34] Amanda Cahil, 'The Human Right to Water: A Right of Unique Status: The Legal Status and Normative Content of the Right to Water' (2006) 9 *International Journal of Human Rights* 389.

[35] Joyeeta Gupta, Rhodante Ahlers, & Lawal Ahmed, 'The Human Right to Water: Moving towards Consensus in a Fragmented World' (2010) 19 *RECIEL* 294.

[36] Council Directive 2000/60 Establishing a Framework for Community Action in the Field of Water Policy, [2000] OJ L327/1.

of enabling access to, for example, computers or plastic. Such transfer results in the responsibility of waste management being shifted to these countries.[37]

Target 6.4 on enhancing resource use efficiency is also reflected in the equity provisions of the Watercourses Convention and in the water efficiency articles of the Water Convention. Target 6.5 on water-related ecosystems – mountains, forests, wetlands, rivers, aquifers, and lakes – can be related to provisions in the Ramsar Convention, the 1992 Convention on Biological Diversity (CBD), and the 1994 Convention to Combat Desertification in Those Countries Experiencing Serious Drought and/or Desertification, Particularly in Africa. For example, indicator 6.5.2, on the proportion of transboundary basin areas with an operational arrangement for water cooperation, is supported by the Watercourses Convention, the Water Convention, and many river basin treaties. Regarding target 6.5, the definition and operationalization of integrated water resource management has been included in hard and soft law instruments.[38] Protection of transboundary groundwater is included in many river basin treaties, but the negotiations on the 2008 Draft Articles on Aquifers is stuck in the UN General Assembly. The impacts of climate change on water are being partially dealt with under the 1992 UN Framework Convention on Climate Change.

Since water is used for agriculture as well as for the extraction, production, and disposal of goods and energy, rules on trade, investment, and aid have become relevant. Agenda 2030 promotes free trade and emphasizes the need for aid for trade to ensure that least developed countries are also able to effectively participate. It also calls for increased investment to realize its implementation. Trade, investment, and international finance are firmly embedded in international law, and the goals of these systems (for example, competitive advantage, free trade, protection of contracts and investments, cost recovery) may not always be compatible with the socio-ecological narrative and the goals that the SDGs promote. In particular, investment law protects secretive contracts and enables confidential arbitration,[39] which affect the transparency of water-related contracts.[40] Worldwide, these traits of investment

[37] Benedetta Cotta, 'What Goes Around, Comes Around? Access and Allocation Problems in Global North–South Waste Trade' (2020) 20 *INEA* 255.

[38] E.g., the Water Convention's 2007 Protocol on Water and Health. Progress towards integrated water resource management (IWRM) is also included in indicator 6.5.1 for determining improved water management. Jan Hassing et al., *Integrated Water Resources Management (IWRM) in Action*, UN World Water Assessment Programme dialogue paper (United Nations Educational, Scientific and Cultural Organization, 2009).

[39] Emilie M. Hafner-Burton, Zachary C. Steinert-Threlkeld, & David G. Victor, 'Predictability versus Flexibility: Secrecy in International Investment Arbitration' (2016) 68 *World Politics* 413.

[40] Vincent Merme, Rhodante Ahlers, & Joyeeta Gupta, 'Private Equity, Public Affair: Hydropower Financing in the Mekong Basin' (2014) 24 *Global Environmental Change* 20; Amanda L. Norris & Katina E. Metzidakis, 'Public Protests, Private Contracts: Confidentiality in ICSID Arbitration and the Cochabamba Water War' (2010) 15 *Harvard Negotiation Law Review* 31.

law are facilitating large-scale international water acquisitions – 'water grabbing' – which may undermine any efforts at successfully managing water.[41]

6.3.3 *How SDG 6 Goes beyond International Water Law*

We suggest that SDG 6 goes beyond international water law in four respects. First, SDG 6 and Agenda 2030 go beyond international water law by setting very clear quantitative and qualitative goals for the global community.[42] Second, SDG 6 moves from a sectoral and fragmented approach towards a coherent approach by emphasizing the systemic nature of the socio-ecological and economic challenges before us: the SDGs 'are integrated and indivisible and balance the three dimensions of sustainable development: the economic, social and environmental'.[43] Third, SDG 6, in the context of Agenda 2030, emphasizes the need to consider all levels of governance simultaneously and thus goes beyond the normal emphasis of international law (barring human rights law) to address only interstate relationships. Fourth, SDG 6 also emphasizes that there is a short temporal window of fifteen years and calls on states and other actors to change their behaviour substantially in order to reduce socio-ecological damage.

6.3.4 *Where SDG 6 in the Context of Agenda 2030 Is a Step Backward in Relation to International Water Law*

SDG 6 is embedded within the broader narrative of Agenda 2030, and an analysis of its relationship leads to the identification of two key legal issues: the relationship with sovereignty and the no-harm principle and the relationship with equity and justice. First, although Agenda 2030 does not refer to the principles of water and environmental law, it does not necessarily contradict them either. The corpus of relevant international law principles includes the principles in the Watercourses Convention, the Water Convention, and the 1992 Rio Declaration on Environment and Development. However, one problem is the way in which sovereignty is dealt with in these agreements. Volumes of academic literature have been dedicated to the issue of sovereignty and how sovereignty needs to be curtailed to ensure that states do not cause harm to other states, following the *Trail Smelter* case in 1941.[44] In water law, sovereignty was initially dealt with under the heading of absolute territorial sovereignty – the Harmon doctrine – which gave states absolute control over the

[41] Maria C. Rulli, Antonio Saviori, & Paolo D'Odorico, 'Global Land and Water Grabbing' (2013) 110 *Proceedings of the National Academy of Sciences* 892.

[42] United Nations, *SDG Indicators: Global Indicator Framework for the Sustainable Development Goals and Targets of the 2030 Agenda for Sustainable Development*, 2020, https://unstats.un.org/sdgs/indicators/indicators-list/.

[43] *Transforming Our World*, n. 4, preamble.

[44] E.g., *Trail Smelter case (United States v Canada)*, 9 ILR 315, 317 (1941).

water that flowed in their territories. The alternative was absolute territorial integrity, which gave downstream countries the right to receive the same quality and quantity of water that they had always received. Because of the incompatibility of these two principles,[45] consensus was sought in the principles of equitable and reasonable utilization and no significant harm, which were then included in the Watercourses Convention.[46]

However, the 2008 Draft Articles on Aquifers moved back towards emphasizing sovereignty.[47] In relation to the no-harm principle, the Watercourses Convention explicitly calls on states not to harm others and, if harm is caused, to remedy such harm.[48] However, Agenda 2030 states: 'We reaffirm that every State has, and shall freely exercise, *full permanent sovereignty* over all its wealth, natural resources and economic activity.'[49] In doing so, it undermines the progress made on sovereignty and moves closer to the 2008 Draft Articles on Aquifers.[50] This development may reflect that the growing scarcity of water resources[51] (and other ecosystem services[52] or nature's contributions to humans,[53] reflected in the concept of ecospace) is leading states back to hegemonic approaches to international relations – that is, a decline in multilateralism[54] and a return to securitization – 'my country first' approaches.[55] The issue of harm is also not considered in Agenda 2030. Harm is implicitly seen as a side effect of development that has to be tolerated because it is caused by activities that are not forbidden by international law.[56]

International water law has made great strides in relation to water justice through the twin concepts of not causing harm to others and equitable and reasonable utilization of water. Moreover, two UN resolutions recognize the human right to

[45] Joseph W. Dellapenna, 'The Customary International Law of Transboundary Fresh Waters' (2001) 1 *International Journal of Global Environmental Issues* 264.

[46] Watercourses Convention, arts. 5–7.

[47] Draft Articles on Aquifers, n. 26, art. 3.

[48] *Id.*, art. 7. A special issue on the no-harm principle elaborates on the details of this concept within the water law world. See Susanne Schmeier & Joyeeta Gupta, 'The Principle of No Significant Harm in International Water Law', *INEA* (forthcoming).

[49] *Transforming Our World*, n. 4, para. 18 (emphasis added).

[50] Draft Articles on Aquifers, n. 26, art. 3

[51] Johan Rockström et al., 'A Safe Operating Space for Humanity' (2009) 461 *Nature* 472.

[52] Millennium Ecosystem Assessment, *Ecosystems and Human Well-being: Synthesis* (Island Press, 2005).

[53] Sandra Díaz et al., 'Assessing Nature's Contributions to People' (2018) 359 *Science* 270.

[54] Steven Bernstein, 'Rio+20: Sustainable Development in a Time of Multilateral Decline' (2013) 13 *Global Environmental Politics* 12; Paul Welfens, 'Trump's Trade Policy, BREXIT, Corona Dynamics, EU Crisis and Declining Multilateralism' (2020) 17 *International Economic Policy* 563.

[55] Joyeeta Gupta, 'Toward Sharing our Ecospace', in Simon Nicholson & Sikina Jinnah (eds.), *New Earth Politics Essays from the Anthropocene* (MIT Press, 2016).

[56] Alan E. Boyle, 'State Responsibility and International Liability for Injurious Consequences of Acts Not Prohibited by International Law: A Necessary Distinction?' (1990) 39(1) *International and Comparative Law Quarterly* 1.

water and sanitation.[57] If we then turn to how Agenda 2030 addresses justice, it states: 'We envisage a world of universal respect for human rights and human dignity, the rule of law, justice, equality and non-discrimination; of respect for race, ethnicity and cultural diversity; and of equal opportunity permitting the full realization of human potential and contributing to shared prosperity.'[58] It also aims to '[p]romote the rule of law at the national and international levels and ensure equal access to justice for all' in SDG 16, Peace, Justice and Strong Institutions. Agenda 2030 calls for '[a] just, equitable, tolerant, open and socially inclusive world in which the needs of the most vulnerable are met'.[59] Targets 6.1 and 6.2 also mention equitable access to water and sanitation services, but equitable sharing of water resources is not considered. We conclude that Agenda 2030 emphasizes access issues but does not address sharing issues or issues related to the allocation of resources in general and water in particular.[60]

6.3.5 *Missing Issues in SDG 6*

We suggest that SDG 6 and Agenda 2030 could have pursued some issues more effectively. First, the extractive industries are major polluters of water and are only partly regulated by the 2013 Minamata Convention, the CBD, and human rights law. However the bulk of mining law falls under soft law instruments such as the 2002 Berlin II Guidelines for Mining and Sustainable Development,[61] the 2008 UN Framework on Business and Human Rights 'Protect, Respect and Remedy', and their 2011 Guidelines for Implementation,[62] the 2017 Organisation for Economic Co-operation and Development's (OECD) Due Diligence Guidance for Meaningful Stakeholder Engagement in the Extractive Sector,[63] and the 2011 OECD Guidelines for Multinational Enterprises.[64] In addition, there are corporate social responsibility guidelines, principles from the International Council of Minerals and Metals, the Responsible Jewellery Council and its Chain of Custody Certification and Code of Practices in 2012,[65] the Fairmined Standard, and so on. But these are mostly

57 See n. 25.

58 *Transforming Our World*, n. 4, para. 8.

59 *Id.*

60 Gupta & Lebel, n. 19.

61 United Nations, *Berlin II: Guidelines for Mining and Sustainable Development*, 2002, www.yumpu.com/en/document/read/30850232/berlin-ii-guidelines-for-mining-and-sustainable-commdev.

62 UNGA, *Report of the Special Representative of the Secretary-General on the Issue of Human Rights and Transnational Corporations and Other Business Enterprises, John Ruggie: Guiding Principles on Business and Human Rights: Implementing the United Nations 'Protect, Respect and Remedy' Framework*, UN Doc. 17/31, 2011.

63 OECD, *OECD Due Diligence Guidance for Meaningful Stakeholder Engagement in the Extractive Sector* (OECD Publishing, 2017).

64 OECD, *OECD Guidelines for Multinational Enterprises*, 2011 ed. (OECD Publishing, 2011).

65 Mirja Schoderer, Jampel Dell'Angelo, & Dave Huitema, 'Water and Mining', in Dellapenna & Gupta, n. 7.

voluntary and have not been very effective. It would have been timely for SDG 6 to have included the role of water and the extractive industry.

Second, with respect to water disasters, SDG 6 focuses on 'reducing the number of people suffering from water scarcity' and, thus, on drought.[66] Target 11.5 includes water disasters in urban contexts; and target 11.b addresses disasters and refers to the UN General Assembly's 2015 Sendai Framework for Disaster Risk Reduction 2015–2030 and calls for holistic disaster risk management at all levels.[67] The question is whether water disasters are limited to urban contexts. However, there are enough references in Agenda 2030 to disasters to imply that, if SDG 6 is read in the context of Agenda 2030, it also calls for addressing the broader risks of water-related disasters. Is this enough to mainstream activities to reduce disasters and thereby reduce security risks?

Third, while neither international law nor SDG 6 recognize the river itself as an entity to be protected for its own sake, there is an emerging trend to promote the right of the river. National law and/or court cases are recognizing the right of the river in Colombia, Ecuador, New Zealand, and India.[68] This development is important to ensure that we do not take a very limited anthropocentric view of locally available water but, rather, recognize that water has an important intrinsic value and role to play in supporting a rich biodiversity.

Fourth, the role of market mechanisms with respect to water is left hanging in the air (see Sections 6.4.3–6.4.4). Because international organizations emphasize privatizing water, selling water to ensure cost recovery, and trading water both nationally and internationally, there are a number of challenges. Privatizing water makes it more difficult for the state to regulate this flowing system. Selling water to ensure cost recovery makes water and sanitation services quite unaffordable for the poorest billion people on Earth. Trading water encourages water speculation and hoarding in times of shortage and creates other kinds of challenges. These considerations raise questions regarding the conditions under which such commodification and trade in water can or should be allowed.

Fifth, although the SDGs are 'integrated and indivisible, global in nature and universally applicable',[69] there is no guidance on how to operationalize this vision.[70] Finally, water is critical for development and economic growth. Existing water law does not question development strategies, being content to limit direct harm and

66 Target 6.4.

67 UN Doc. A/69/283, 3 June 2015; also see *International Strategy for Disaster Reduction*, UN Doc. A/60/195, 22 December 2005.

68 Julia Talbot-Jones, 'Advancing Water Law through Rights in Nature', in Dellapenna & Gupta, n. 7.

69 *Transforming Our World*, n. 4, para. 55.

70 Working Group on Interlinkages of SDG Statistics to Allow for Integrated Analyses in the Monitoring, *Terms of Reference*, n.d., unstats.un.org/sdgs/files/Working-Group-ToR–Interlinkages.pdf.

promote equitable sharing. However, Agenda 2030 aims at a transformative narrative on development. It emphasizes inclusiveness fifty-five times and growth sixteen times. The references reflect a struggle between those who wanted inclusive development and those who wanted GDP growth. The critical literature argues that, given limited resources, unlimited GDP growth is not possible.[71] Absolute delinking of resource use and pollution from GDP growth is not possible; energy dissipates; food systems are difficult to close; and there are limits to recycling material systems. While the SDGs focus on enhancing water use efficiency and reducing pollutants, they do not show what kind of development is compatible with a safe and just world.

6.3.6 *Does SDG 6 Promote the Further Development of International Law?*

We conclude, first, that some parts of SDG 6 are embedded in hard law. While the water conventions of broader geographical application have been ratified by less than 25 per cent of UN member states, many of the provisions are included in hundreds of regional water treaties. Some parts of SDG 6 are embedded in human rights law and in environmental treaties. SDG 6 is linked to environmental goals that are mostly embedded in hard law, social goals that are embedded primarily in soft law, and economic goals that are indirectly embedded in hard trade, investment, and contract law. The result may be trade-offs in favour of economic issues and possibly environmental issues as opposed to social issues.

Second, Agenda 2030 goes beyond existing water law by (1) stating clear quantitative and qualitative goals, targets, and indicators for the global water system and (2) bringing together elements from different treaties, declarations, and resolutions regarding national and international issues and by emphasizing the need for a systemic approach to water governance. It does not involve the binary approach as to whether the underlying existing rules are legally binding or not. It thus advances international law and water law by uniting human rights approaches, hard and soft law, and by conceptualizing water as a unified whole and promoting coherence between different water law bodies. In addition, (3) Agenda 2030 goes beyond interstate water law by recognizing that water issues play out at multiple levels of governance, and (4) it emphasizes the urgency of the problem through the short time period within which Agenda 2030 aims to change our behaviour.

Third, however, SDG 6 and Agenda 2030 in some ways reverse the direction of water law. Since Agenda 2030 does not specify principles, one can only assume that the principles of water and environmental law will apply to the implementation of this SDG. However, it reincarnates the full permanent sovereignty principle and does not refer to the no-significant-harm principle or liability and compensation for harm caused. Although it emphasizes access to minimum rights such as rights to

[71] Robert Fletcher & Crelis Rammelt, 'Decoupling: A Key Fantasy of the Post-2015 Sustainable Development Agenda' (2017) 14 *Globalizations* 450.

drinking water and sanitation services, it does not look at broader justice issues, such as water allocation. Finally, SDG 6 and Agenda 2030 have missed a few critical opportunities, such as the opportunity to push for targets and indicators with respect to (1) the extractive industry; (2) disaster risk management; (3) rights of the river; (4) the role of markets; (5) methods for avoiding trade-offs; and (6) the need to develop within fresh water limits.

6.4 POSITIONING SDG 6 IN THE INTERNATIONAL INSTITUTIONAL CONTEXT

6.4.1 *SDG 6 Implementation through Multiple Governance Actors: Towards Coherent and Systemic Water Governance?*

SDG 6 needs to be implemented in relation to the other SDGs, which might mean that the fragmented nature of global water governance bodies may be an advantage as these bodies are spread through the UN system and beyond.[72] Almost all UN agencies are in some way working on water-related issues. Many non-governmental organizations and businesses are also engaged in water governance. UN Water was established in 2003 to promote coordination between different UN agencies and non-state actors; however, with limited resources, mandate, and power, it has an uphill battle ahead.[73] Institutions like the World Bank issue loans to developing countries that also address water management. The special rapporteurs on human rights have worked on how the human right to water and sanitation should be implemented, but the public and private sectors have paid inadequate attention to the affordability and ecological dimension of water management.

At the national level, water governance may be controlled to some extent by a ministry of water and/or a ministry of the environment, but governance on water-related issues is also spread through other ministries, such as those on land, energy, and agriculture. Moreover, there are river basin organizations established at the local level: (community-based organizations), catchment-based organizations, river basin organizations, and transboundary river-based organizations. These bodies have long histories and have developed complex governance structures over the years.[74] Furthermore, cities worldwide have water service organizations that can be state centred (for example, municipalities), private (for example, private operators), community based, and a hybrid version of all of these entities. Implementation mechanisms include setting minimum service standards and checking whether service

[72] Claudia Pahl-Wostl, Joyeeta Gupta, & Daniel Petry, 'Governance and the Global Water System: A Theoretical Exploration' (2008) 14 *Global Governance* 419.

[73] Thomas Baumgartner & Claudia Pahl-Wostl, 'UN–Water and Its Role in Global Water Governance' (2008) 18 *Ecology and Society* 3.

[74] Dave Huitema et al., 'Adaptive Water Governance: Assessing the Institutional Prescriptions of Adaptive (Co-)Management from a Governance Perspective and Defining a Research Agenda' (2009) 14(1) *Ecology and Society* 26.

providers meet these standards[75] and improving services where they contravene them;[76] addressing consumer complaints;[77] and ensuring that people understand their rights.[78]

In order to operationalize the SDGs, while building on existing work undertaken by the United Nations and avoiding duplication or working at cross purposes, the United Nations has appointed custodian institutions (UN agencies or other international bodies) to prepare common standards and to compile comparable data about how the SDGs are to be achieved. While most custodian institutions were established with a mandate defined by the United Nations, a few institutions were established as an outcome of international law. For example, the Secretariat of the CBD was established to support the goals of the convention.[79] The work of the Secretariat feeds into target 6.6 on protecting and restoring water-related ecosystems. A decision at the eighth Conference of the Parties aimed to ensure that work under the Ramsar Convention is aligned and not duplicative of work within the CBD to protect wetlands.[80] In theory, this implies that the implementation of SDG 6 could guide all actors engaged in multi-level water governance. SDG 6 and its targets may be able to create coherence in policy implementation and promote synergies in the implementation of other SDGs. This is the optimistic scenario. It could also lead the various actors to assume that another institution is responsible for implementing SDG 6 and reduce the commitment to implement it. Additionally, hard law goals and instruments, whether at the national or international level, might overshadow the soft law goals embodied in Agenda 2030, implying that countries may choose to prioritize hard law commitments over soft law commitments.

6.4.2 *Loans, Cost Recovery, Markets: Privatizing a Public or Merit Good?*

As argued above, SDG 6 does not clearly determine the legal nature of water: is it a public good/heritage or a commodity? However, when reviewing the implementation process, we note that, in trying to operationalize and implement the targets on access to water and sanitation, different UN bodies have adopted programmes focusing on water. The programmes include Water, Sanitation and Hygiene

75 South Africa, Water Services Act, Act 108, 1997, amended 2004, ss. 62, 63.

76 Namibia, Water Resources Management Act, Act no. 24, 2004, 26.

77 Kenya, Water Act 2002, Act no. 8, 2002, art. 47(c); Ghana, Public Utilities (Complaints Procedure) Regulation, 1999.

78 See Brazil, Law on Basic Sanitation, 2007, arts. 26, 27, 53; Colombia, Law 142 Establishing the Regime for Public Household Services, 11 July 1994, art. 9 (unofficial translation).

79 1992 Convention on Biological Diversity, art. 24.

80 Conference of the Parties to the Convention on Biological Diversity, *Decision Adopted by the Conference of the Parties to the Biological Diversity of Inland Water Ecosystems: Reporting Processes, Improving the Review of Implementation and Addressing Threats on Biological Diversity at Its Eighth Meeting VIII/20. Biological Diversity of Inland Water Ecosystems: Reporting Processes, Improving the Review of Implementation and Addressing Threats*, Doc. UNEP/CBD/COP/DEC/VIII/20, 2006.

(WASH), including the UN International Children's Emergency Fund (UNICEF) (Advancing WASH in Schools), the UN Development Programme (GoAL WaSH), the UN High Commissioner for Refugees (WASH), the UNECE (1999 Protocol on Water and Health), and the World Health Organization (WASH in Health Care Facilities).[81] Each programme tries to adopt an integrated approach. While operationalizing the target for water, water is pushed at the same time into a 'proprietary frame' that is based on the property rights regime. For example, UNICEF aims to leverage sustainable financial resources in collaboration with the World Bank and other international financial institutions,[82] the private sector, and other partners in mobilizing new innovative financing mechanisms. While this is an example of integration between different institutions – from global to local – we are convinced that this focus on market mechanisms and treating water as an economic good is problematic. The World Bank is both an advocate of treating water as an economic good and a supporter of private sector participation in water service provision.[83] However, the private sector needs to make profits, and it is difficult to make profits from a sector aimed at providing sanitation services to the poorest. Cost recovery may come at the cost of implementing the human right to water and sanitation. Who will be excluded, and to what extent does this exacerbate poverty (SDG 1)? Will the privately funded water and sanitation services be affordable for the 734 million people that live on less than US$1.90 a day or even to the 50 per cent of the world's population that lives on less than US$5.50 per day? UNICEF states that it will continue to support 'sustainable markets for water, sanitation and hygiene goods and services that balance demand and supply' and continue to place communities at the centre of their programmes.[84] However, there is clear evidence that even in the Western world, many cities are re-municipalizing water services. The private sector has been raising the price to enable profit maximization but is unwilling to invest in infrastructure maintenance in order to adequately clean waste water and increase water supply coverage.[85] We believe that meeting the water and sanitation needs of the poorest under SDG 6 is only possible through a well-developed and accountable publicly subsidized system that enables the poor to come out of the poverty trap. We thus question the way in which international development agencies are promoting

[81] UN Water, *Water, Sanitation and Hygiene*, n.d., www.unwater.org/water-facts/water-sanitation-and-hygiene/.

[82] The new innovative financing mechanisms include 'blended financing (involving bilateral grants, loans and other funding sources), south-south financing, microfinance models, trust funds, the use of cash transfers for WASH (in both emergency and development contexts), emergency revolving funds and other approaches'. UNICEF, n. 21, 17.

[83] World Bank, *World Bank Group Support to Public-Private Partnerships: Lessons from Experience in Client Countries* (World Bank, 2015); World Bank, *Working for a Water-Secure World* (World Bank, 2019).

[84] UNICEF, n. 21, 18.

[85] Water Remunicipalisation Tracker, *Water Remunicipalisation Tracker*, 2020, remunicipalisation .org/front/page/home.

market mechanisms and the private sector's increasing engagement in the provision of water services.

6.4.3 *The Private Sector: Protected by Trade, Contract, and Investment Law and the Risk to Achieving Normative Socio-Ecological Goals*

The use of sustainable water markets, cost recovery from water services, and the emphasis on loans from banks inevitably brings us to a discussion of the private sector. In our view, SDG 6, like many of the social goals, focuses on the poorest and most vulnerable people in society with limited ability to afford paid water and sanitation services. We know that 70 per cent of the poorest people depend on nature for their lives and livelihoods. Furthermore, protecting ecosystems, climate stability, and the integrity of the hydrological cycle are not 'profitable' activities under the current system of calculating GDP and profits. The question then is how SDG 6 can be achieved by engaging private sector investment. In our view, SDG 6 can only be achieved by setting limits on private sector exploitation of nature and society. However, an examination of the role of private sector actors in water shows (1) their growing engagement in the bottled water industry and in virtual water trade;[86] (2) their growing direct and indirect (permits/licences/concessions) acquisition of land and water elsewhere in the world for activities that are most profitable for them as opposed to meeting the water and food needs of the people living there (water grabbing);[87] (3) the use of technologies ranging from irrigation facilities, dams, desalination, cloud seeding, and now air-to-water technology that hands over control of water resources to the private sector; (4) the growing externalization of water and ecological impacts by such companies, although they increasingly talk about impact investing; and (5), increasingly, the growing replacement of labour in the water sector by machinery and artificial intelligence. Protests against, for example, land and water grabbing were clear at the 2015 World Social Forum and were recorded in the 2015 Declaration of the Global Convergence of Land and Water Struggles,[88] which called on states to use the SDGs, inter alia, to prevent water grabbing.

[86] Daniel Jaffee & Soren Newman, 'A More Perfect Commodity: Bottled Water, Global Accumulation, and Local Contestation' (2013) 78(1) *Rural Sociology* 1; Jeroen Vos & Leonith Hinojosa, 'Virtual Water Trade and the Contestation of Hydrosocial Territories' (2016) 41 *Water International* 37.

[87] Jennifer Franco, Lyla Mehta, & Gert Jan Veldwisch, 'The Global Politics of Water Grabbing' (2013) 34 *Third World Quarterly* 1651; Maria Cristina Rulli, Antonio Saviori, & Paolo D'Odorico, 'Global Land and Water Grabbing' (2013) 110 *Proceedings of the National Academy of Sciences* 892; Lyla Mehta, Gert Jan Veldwisch, & Jennifer Franco, 'Introduction to the Special Issue: Water Grabbing? Focus on the (Re)Appropriation of Finite Water Resources' (2012) 5 *Water Alternatives* 193.

[88] International Steering Committee, *Rights to Water and Land, a Common Struggle Dakar to Tunis: Declaration of the Global Convergence of Land and Water Struggles*, 28 March 2015,

Finally, at a time when banks in the Western world are finding it difficult to invest in profitable enterprises and interest rates are low, more money is being promised to developing countries. We are afraid that discussions about large loans to developing countries to increase infrastructure, including water infrastructure, at high market interest rates (as the higher the political risk, the greater the interest rate) might lead developing countries into a new period of high debt.[89] And we are also concerned that the commodification and privatization of land and water may undermine water justice, which might lead to a repetition of the great debt crises of the 1980s and undermine the success of SDG 6.

6.4.4 *Do the Implementation Process, Actors, and Tools Undermine the Normative Goals of SDG 6*

We argue above that while in theory Agenda 2030 and SDG 6 could benefit from the large number of actors engaged in water governance at the global and national levels by mainstreaming SDG 6, it is also possible that each body will interpret the water goal in its own manner and may relegate lower importance to it since it emerges from a soft law instrument. While many institutions have been established to monitor the individual SDGs and targets, there is less clarity regarding who is monitoring the trade-offs and synergies between the SDGs and their targets and, hence, who is winning at whose cost? The emphasis on loans, cost recovery, markets, and private sector participation is challenging since providing water and sanitation services to the poor increases their well-being, but it does not necessarily translate into cost recovery and profits. Improving water ecosystems enhances the health of the water system, but it too does not translate into profits. The question is whether this approach will lead to the gradual commodification and privatization of water.

Finally, given the growing engagement of the private sector in water – from extraction to disposal – and given that such engagement is protected by trade, contract, and investment law, de-privatizing water will be a very expensive process. There are examples from Spain[90] and South Africa[91] that show that regaining control over water resources from private ownership is very difficult and expensive. The increasing privatization of water in a globalized world implies growing private sector control of water through contracts that fall under international contracts and

www.waterhumanrighttreaty.org/wp-content/uploads/2015/04/Dakar-to-Tunis-Declaration_EN_finalfinal1.pdf.

[89] Joseph Onjala, 'China's Development Loans and the Threat of Debt Crisis in Kenya' (2018) 36 *Development Policy Review* 710.

[90] Jorge Molinero et al., 'Groundwater in Spain: Legal Framework and Management Issues', in Angelos Findikakis & Kuniaki Sato (eds.), *Groundwater Management Practices* (CRC Press, 2011), 1.

[91] Bosch & Gupta, 'Access', n. 9.

investment law. We are afraid that such trends will make it difficult for states to manage the water under public trust principles and undermine the achievement of the water goal. Trade and investment may pursue the narrative of 'growth' first and, with that goal, continue to externalize the environmental consequences of increased use and pollution of water. This outcome may affect the ability of actors to implement SDG 6.

6.5 CONCLUSIONS

This chapter has set out to understand whether SDG 6 and the way it is embedded within Agenda 2030 is a step forward in international law. It first analyzed whether SDG 6 and Agenda 2030 have accounted for the various dimensions of the water problem, then the extent to which they go beyond the existing law, and finally considered some aspects with respect to implementation. We conclude, first, that SDG 6 recognizes the holistic nature of water but that it stops short of describing it as a public good or common heritage; it implicitly addresses all the 'colours' of water and explicitly addresses most of the problems associated with water, but it does not address the underlying drivers of water problems; and, finally, while it addresses issues of access, it does not adequately address issues of distribution (allocation).

Second, in assessing the contribution of SDG 6 to international water law, we argue that, despite the fact that different aspects of SDG 6 are embedded in soft and/or hard law, the system of the seventeen SDGs is used to create coherence to address the systemic problem that links water issues to other social, ecological, and economic issues. Moreover, SDG 6 goes beyond transboundary water law and human rights law to address water law at multiple levels of governance and clearly emphasizes the urgency of achieving the seventeen SDGs. However, in the context of international water law, SDG 6 is a step backward in that it emphasizes full permanent sovereignty over natural resources and does not mention the no-harm principle. Furthermore, although it emphasizes the human right to water and sanitation by incorporating it into quantitative targets, thereby emphasizing minimum access, it does not address the larger distributive issues, which, for example, the Watercourses Convention elaborates on in detail in Article 6 on the equitable and optimal utilization of a watercourse. With respect to issues inadequately developed, SDG 6 does not cover the impacts of the extractive industry, water-related disasters, the integrity of the river system through the rights of nature/rivers, how trade-offs should be addressed, and, finally, whether and how development and related issues need to fit within a water budget(s).

Moving to implementation and actors, we note that the lofty ambition of ensuring coherence and synergies might be affected by the way in which different organizations implement SDG 6. Since many focus on achieving targets, they may ignore the synergies and trade-offs. Since there is emphasis on engaging the profit-oriented private sector in service delivery to the poorest, this might affect the achievement of the goal. Thus, in our view, SDG 6 appears to have taken two steps forward in terms of a rhetorical commitment (integration, access to water and sanitation) and two steps backward (sovereignty, equity, and the no-harm principle) with respect to water law. If fresh water resources are limited temporally, if some basins are 'closed' (implying that there is no more water to distribute), and if some cities are reaching day zero (when there is no water at all) – which might affect access to water at the local level – then the big fears are whether countries will ignore the fresh water limits in an effort to promote water-dependent GDP growth; whether countries will securitize water and retreat behind sovereignty; and whether water will become increasingly privatized and companies and other actors will engage in 'water grabbing' and hoarding water. Furthermore, if fresh water problems are exacerbated by extreme weather events, then who will be held responsible and how will these problems be handled? These are the issues that SDG 6 does not address.

7

SDG 7: Ensure Access to Affordable, Reliable, Sustainable and Modern Energy for All

Stuart Bruce and Jorge E. Viñuales

ABSTRACT

The global strategic priorities articulated in Sustainable Development Goal (SDG) 7, Affordable and Clean Energy, underscore a narrative of two 'economies' and the conscious evolution of political prioritization in economic structuring. SDG 7 represents an aspiration to move away from the 'old', entrenched, 'brown' economic activities that developed out of the Industrial Revolution, built upon conventional fossil fuels and exhaustible natural resources, and towards 'new', low-, or zero-carbon-based 'green' economic activities that are built upon clean energy, electrification, and the decarbonization of all aspects of modern life. This narrative gives rise to numerous legal complexities and challenges for international law, derived from its structure, content, and functions related to energy activities. This chapter first explores the content of SDG 7. It then surveys the international rules and processes that may assist and/or hinder the progressive realization of SDG 7. The chapter closes by considering the role and influence of selected international institutions and non-state actors in advancing and implementing SDG 7.

KEYWORDS

SDG 7, sustainable energy, energy poverty, human rights, climate change, trade and investment, global governance, international institutions, non-state actors

7.1 INTRODUCTION

The global strategic priorities articulated in Sustainable Development Goal (SDG) 7, Affordable and Clean Energy, underscore a narrative of two 'economies' and the conscious evolution of political prioritization in economic structuring.

SDG 7 represents an aspiration to move away from the 'old', entrenched, 'brown' economic activities that developed out of the Industrial Revolution, built upon conventional fossil fuels and exhaustible natural resources, and towards 'new', low, or zero-carbon-based 'green' economic activities that are built upon clean energy, electrification, and the decarbonization of all aspects of modern life. This narrative gives rise to numerous legal complexities and challenges for international law, which are explored in this chapter. To set the scene for that exploration, three preliminary remarks are in order.

First, while energy is central to the advancement of most, if not all, of the SDGs, the transition to a low-carbon or 'sustainable' energy matrix is only now starting to find clear expression in international law. Until relatively recently, little public international law existed that was specifically related to energy access, renewable energy, and energy efficiency.[1] This lack of specificity is partly due to clean technology choices and measures historically being considered as national or local issues, and partly to the absence of transboundary effects from these technologies.[2] Even beyond sustainable energy, as a general matter, no identifiable 'international energy law' has emerged in the system of public international law.[3] As a result, it is not possible to establish a simple and direct link between SDG 7 and an identifiable group of treaties. Instead, the entire corpus of public international law has to be read from the perspective of 'energy' and, more specifically, of the transition to low-carbon energy. It would therefore be more appropriate to speak of an 'international law of energy'.[4]

Second, by corollary, the relationship between international law and sustainable energy is, by definition, unstructured, evolving, and complex. Whereas international law can serve as a means to pursue SDG 7, it may also be an obstacle. In fact, the very same rules can have this dual effect. For example, an investment agreement can serve to protect a fossil fuel company from measures requiring the internalization of its negative externalities or, conversely, a renewable energy company from measures interfering with its supply of clean electricity. One consequence of this point is that

[1] For overviews, see Peter Cameron, Xiaoyi Mu, & Volker Roeben (eds.), *The Global Energy Transition: Law, Policy and Economics for Energy in the Twenty-first Century* (Hart, 2020); Mohammad Ershadul Karim et al., 'Energy Revolution for Our Common Future: An Evaluation of the Emerging International Renewable Energy Law' (2018) 11(7) *Energies* 1769; Jorge E. Viñuales, *The International Law of Energy* (Cambridge University Press, 2022), chaps. 1, 8; Stuart Bruce, 'International Law and Renewable Energy: Facilitating Sustainable Energy for All?' (2013) 14(1) *Melbourne Journal of International Law* 19.

[2] Catherine Redgwell, 'International Legal Responses to the Challenges of a Lower Carbon Future: Energy Law for the Twenty-first Century', in Stephan Farrall, Tawhida Ahmed, & Duncan French (eds.), *Criminological and Legal Consequences of Climate Change* (Hart, 2012), 36, 38.

[3] See Stuart Bruce, 'International Energy Law', in *Max Planck Encyclopedia of Public International Law* (Oxford University Press, 2015).

[4] See Viñuales, n. 1, chap. 1.

the transition to a sustainable energy matrix is being induced and organized through a wide range of 'policy' or 'soft law' instruments, which are superimposed on a bedrock of binding rules that either are non-energy specific or focus on conventional energy sources. It is principally through the evolution of soft law since the early 1980s that the energy transition has gained normative force on the international plane, culminating in the United Nations' Sustainable Energy for All (SEforALL) initiative in 2011[5] and SDG 7 in 2015. The targets established by SDG 7 are an extension of this process.

Third, as a consequence, while the targets of SDG 7 may be universal, their mode and scale of realization cannot be so. In practice, much of SDG 7 and the global energy transition will be implemented through regional and national laws, regulations, policies, incentives, and actions, according to domestic capabilities and circumstances. The implementation of those choices may be supported (or thwarted) by myriad international law rules, principles, and norms and by varying degrees of international diplomatic and institutional action.

Against this background, this chapter is structured as follows. Section 7.2 explores the content of SDG 7 and its interactions with other SDGs. Section 7.3 surveys the international rules and processes that are most relevant for the progressive realization of SDG 7, focusing on human rights law, climate change law, trade law, investment law, and intellectual property law. Section 7.4 considers the role and influence of selected international institutions and non-state actors in advancing and implementing SDG 7. Section 7.5 concludes by considering the challenges that SDG 7 poses for international law.

7.2 THE CONTENT OF SDG 7 IN THE CONTEXT OF THE OTHER SDGS

SDG 7 establishes three essentially quantitative, outcome-based targets, covering universal access to energy (target 7.1), growth in the proportion of renewable energy in the global energy mix (target 7.2), and energy intensity as a function of gross domestic product (GDP) (target 7.3). It also establishes two enabling targets related to international public finance to promote 'access to clean energy technology and investment' (target 7.a)[6] and clean energy infrastructure development, especially for vulnerable states (target 7.b).[7] SDG 7 is designed to coordinate global action around high-level targets that are founded on years of intergovernmental policy development,[8]

5 *International Year of Sustainable Energy for All*, UN Doc. A/RES/65/151, 16 February 2011.

6 International Energy Agency (IEA) et al., *Tracking SDG 7: The Energy Progress Report* (World Bank, 2020), 3.

7 Targets 7.a and 7.b are phrased in an overly complex manner and are not further deconstructed in this section, though the international law relevant to them is considered in Section 7.3.

8 See Bruce, n. 1, 27–34; Thoko Kaime & Robert Glicksman, 'An International Legal Framework for SE4ALL: Human Rights and Sustainable Development Imperatives' (2015) 38(5) *Fordham International Law Journal* 1409.

but it is silent in regard to states' domestic policy choices for its implementation. Each target is explored below.

Target 7.1 concerns intrinsic values related to human life and dignity. This much is reflected in its indicators, which emphasize the proportion of the population (1) with access to electricity and (2) that relies on clean fuels and technologies. The terms 'clean fuels and technologies',[9] 'modern energy', and 'modern energy services' are not defined in the SDG's text or in international law, nor are they used uniformly among international organizations, although some guidance can be derived from the latter. For instance, the International Energy Agency defines 'access to modern energy services' for tracking target 7.1 as 'a household having reliable and affordable access to both clean cooking facilities and to electricity', initially for basic services and then rising to regional average levels of supply.[10]

Targets 7.2 and 7.3 contain ambiguous terms in at least three contexts: the definition of 'renewable energy', what constitutes a 'substantial' increase in its share globally, and the meaning of 'rate of improvement' in energy efficiency globally. Targets 7.2 and 7.3 essentially replicate the renewable energy and energy efficiency goals in SEforALL, which sought to double the global renewable energy share from 15 to 30 per cent and to double energy efficiency from 1.2 to 2.4 per cent by 2030.[11] One significant difference – and step backwards – is that target 7.2 has replaced 'double' from SEforALL with 'substantially increase' renewable energy in the global energy supply. Although this phrasing does not impose an upper aspirational limit, challenges may arise in coordinating focused global collective action and in measuring progress without a quantitative target.[12] Nonetheless, because target 7.2 originated in international policy and SEforALL, it would be reasonable to use 30 per cent as a benchmark for the minimum growth in renewables globally.[13] The reporting on target 7.3 indicates a similar quantitative goal (1.3–2.6 per cent) to that which is included in SEforALL, despite its absence from the formal text.[14]

While neither the text nor the indicators of target 7.2 specify the types of renewable energy it covers, official reports track at least six categories: 'solar photovoltaic',

[9] The SDG 7 tracking report monitors clean heating and cooking, measures that formed the basis for the same goal in the Sustainable Energy for All (SEforALL). See Advisory Group on Energy and Climate Change, *Energy for a Sustainable Future: Report and Recommendations* (UN Secretary-General, 2010), 9–10.

[10] IEA, *Defining Energy Access: 2019 Methodology*, 2019, www.iea.org/articles/defining-energy-access-2019-methodology.

[11] High-level Group on Sustainable Energy for All, *Sustainable Energy for All: A Framework for Action* (UN Secretary-General, 2012), 9.

[12] IEA et al., n. 6, 71.

[13] In addition to SE for ALL, the origins of targets 7.2 and 7.3 are informed by the *Johannesburg Plan of Implementation of the World Summit of Sustainable Development*, UN Doc. A/CONF.199/20, 2002, Res. 2, Annex, chap. III, paras. 20(e), (h), (p). See *Compendium of Existing Goals and Targets under the 19 Focus Areas Being Considered by the Open Working Group*, March–April 2014, sustainabledevelopment.un.org/owg10.html.

[14] IEA et al., n. 6, 3, 93.

'wind', 'traditional biomass', 'modern bioenergy', 'hydropower', and 'other renewables' (which include 'solar thermal', 'geothermal', and 'tidal' power).[15] The extent to which 'modern' forms of renewables, such as solar power, should be preferred over 'older' forms such as hydroelectricity, is not addressed by SDG 7, although the technical potential of solar and wind to exceed energy demand has long been known.[16] Energy efficiency also lacks a definition, but 'primary energy intensity' (that is, the energy used per GDP) is tracked in official reports.[17] Overall, SDG 7 focuses on selective goals of the energy transition: energy access, decarbonization, and efficiency. Other, wider policy and commercial goals, which, in practice, have been the overriding catalyst for the energy transition – namely, cost of energy and energy security – are not clearly captured in SDG 7's targets or indicators. These goals, however, are implicit in the reference to 'affordable' and 'reliable' energy for all and are the practical reasons why the global transition is able to accelerate.[18]

In terms of implementation, SDG 7 progress has been patchy and is not on track for full realization by 2030. Over the last decade,

- Global electrification increased from 83 to 90 per cent (leaving over 750 million people without electricity);[19]
- Lack of access to clean cooking remained constant at around 3 billion people;[20]
- Global renewables in power consumption only increased by 1 per cent – from 16.3 to 17.3 per cent; renewable energy use in heating and transport grew minimally;[21]
- Energy efficiency improved by only 2.1 per cent, requiring a hefty 3 per cent average increase to meet the 2030 target;[22] and
- International public finance flows doubled to US $21.4 billion, but less than 12 per cent of those funds went to vulnerable countries.[23]

Based on those trends, hundreds of millions of people will still be without electricity in 2040,[24] and global decarbonization rates will need to 'triple to reach the 2°C target and quintuple to reach the 1.5°C target' in article 2(1)(a) of the

[15] *Id.*, 72.
[16] See Ottmar Edenhofer et al. (eds.), *Renewable Energy Sources and Climate Change Mitigation: Special Report of the Intergovernmental Panel on Climate Change* (Cambridge University Press, 2012) 3, 10, 12, 206–7.
[17] IEA et al., n. 6, 95.
[18] See generally REN21, *Renewables 2020: Global Status Report*, 2020.
[19] IEA et al., n. 6, 4, 15.
[20] *Id.*, 1, 4.
[21] *Id.*, 1, 8; see also REN21, n. 18.
[22] IEA et al., n. 6, 93.
[23] *Id.*, 2, 3, 120.
[24] See Independent Group of Scientists appointed by the UN Secretary-General, *Global Sustainable Development Report 2019: The Future Is Now – Science for Achieving Sustainable Development* (United Nations, 2019), xxvii.

2015 Paris Agreement on Climate Change so as to supply 75–85 per cent of electricity by 2050.[25]

Patchy implementation of SDG 7 has wider implications. Targets 7.1, 7.2, and 7.3 are indeed a means to advance numerous socially desirable ends articulated in other SDGs. For instance, increased use and adoption of renewable energy and energy efficiency technologies, particularly in developing countries, can contribute to

- Reducing poverty by providing off-grid access to clean electricity (SDG 1, No Poverty);
- Powering schools and medical facilities to improve education, health, and well-being (SDG 3, Good Health and Well-being, and SDG 4, Quality Education);
- Electrifying households to empower women to pursue other activities (SDG 5, Gender Equality);
- Creating jobs and industrial growth from installation and maintenance (SDG 8, Decent Work and Economic Growth, and SDG 9, Industry, Innovation and Infrastructure);
- Avoiding fossil fuel power generation that contributes to global warming (SDG 13, Climate Action); and
- Avoiding mining and use of finite natural resources (SDG 12, Responsible Consumption and Production, and SDG 15, Life on Land).[26]

Yet neither SDG 7 nor the SDGs as a whole provide any guidance on how these objectives are to be prioritized and integrated.

Impediments to progressing SDG 7 and the energy transition more broadly include a number of structural, technological, and market factors: lobbying efforts to maintain the status quo, insufficient electrical storage capability, unproven scalable emissions capture and negative emissions technologies, lack of reliable alternatives to fossil fuel for transport, over-reliance on biomass, and skewed economic incentives from fossil fuel subsidies.[27] Resolving these issues will largely depend on domestic action, coordinated through international diplomacy, but international law can also play a role, as discussed in the next section.

[25] *Id.*, 76; see also United Nations Environment Programme (UNEP), *Emissions Gap Report 2019*, 2019.

[26] Christian Kroll, Anne Warchold, & Prajal Pradhan, 'Sustainable Development Goals: Are We Successful in Turing Trade-offs into Synergies?' (2019) 5 *Palgrave Communications* 1; Kaime & Glicksman, n. 8, 1423–40; IEA, *World Energy Outlook Special Report: Energy Access Outlook 2017*, 2017.

[27] Independent Group of Scientists, n. 24, 78; see also Anna-Alexandra Marhold, 'Subsidy Regulation in WTO Law: Some Implications for Fossil Fuels and Renewable Energy', Tilburg Law School Legal Studies Research Paper Series no. 20/2016, 2016.

7.3 POSITIONING SDG 7 IN INTERNATIONAL LAW

As a general matter, international law defines the broad rules of the game within which the energy transition envisioned in SDG 7 may unfold. The relevant aspects of international law involve an interplay of binding treaty law, non-binding 'soft' law, foundational principles of international law, and, crucially, international actors and institutions. In the following subsections, we first review the nature of the legal 'patchwork' relevant to sustainable energy and then analyze the relevance of five domains of international law – human rights law, climate change law, trade law, investment law, and intellectual property law – for SDG 7.

7.3.1 *The 'International Law of Energy'*

Competence to regulate energy and natural resources under international or domestic law is largely derived from territorial jurisdiction. As a foundational tenet of international law, states possess entitlements over both the 'conventional' sources of energy (that is, fossil, hydro, and nuclear fuels) and 'new' sources of energy (that is, solar, wind, and geothermal) subject to their sovereignty or sovereign powers, and they are at liberty to determine how those resources are exploited, managed, and used, unless constrained by international law.[28] The broad range of potentially applicable 'constraints' serve multiple purposes, operate at different stages of the energy cycle, and hold varying degrees of influence depending on their legal source and geographic scope of application. In general, the influence of international law on energy activities (from exploration and exploitation to refining, storage, transport, consumption, waste management, and decommissioning) increases in relation to the degree of 'internationalization' of those activities. Factors relevant to ascertaining the role, scope, and function of potential constraints include the following:

(1) Resource location and practical need to cooperate with other states (exclusive, shared, onshore, offshore, common area resources);[29]
(2) Risk of significant harm arising from energy activities (transit of hazardous waste, ship design standards, civil liability for collisions and disasters);
(3) Conservation, protection, and management requirements associated with energy activities (access, emissions reductions, biodiversity, habitat, landscapes and species protection, and so on);
(4) Cross-border transportation, financing, and commerce associated with energy activities (navigation and shipping rights, trade obligations and

[28] Redgwell, n. 2, 29.

[29] See Catherine Redgwell, 'The Practice of Shared Responsibility in Relation to Energy', in André Nollkaemper & Ilias Plakokefalos (eds.), *The Practice of Shared Responsibility in International Law* (Cambridge University Press, 2017), 1071.

standards, intellectual property rights, in-bound investment protections); and

(5) Mandates of international organizations and bodies relevant to energy activities.[30]

When these factors are applied to conventional and new sources of energy, both commonalities and marked differences in regulatory approach are revealed.

First, operations and activities associated with the conventional sources of energy, such as oil and gas, tend to have a high degree of internationalization and are thus susceptible to multiple domains of regulation across the energy cycle under international law, industry practice, and national standardization.[31] Although the international rules related to the exploitation of straddling deposits are not fully settled,[32] a significant proportion of fossil fuels are extracted offshore, and transported and traded internationally, thereby implicating a swathe of binding and non-binding international laws relevant to subpoints (1)–(5), mentioned earlier.

Second, in contrast, the generation and consumption of newer sources of energy, such as solar and wind power, tend to be highly localized within states' onshore and offshore territory[33] and their installation and operation produce few significant transboundary effects.[34] Fewer international laws are thus implicated, and they tend to relate to aspects of subpoints (3)–(5), principally in conjunction with siting, habitat preservation, investment protection, and financial and technical assistance to other states for similar activities. Instead, states have pragmatically agreed to adopt global policy goals to guide their actions (for example, SDG 7) and have preserved their competence over how these goals are reached within the parameters set by international law. SDG 7 follows the trend of using non-binding instruments as a new form of regulation for energy (and other matters).[35] An indication of its relevance is provided by the fact that, as of 2019, over 170 states had adopted renewable energy targets or policies.[36]

Third, most international law relevant to subpoint (3) applies to domestic activities irrespective of the source of energy but can have particular normative force in

[30] For other conceptualizations, see Catherine Redgwell & Lavanya Rajamani, 'Energy Underground: What's Law Got to Do with It?', in Donald Zillman et al. (eds.), *The Law of Energy Underground* (Oxford University Press, 2014), 101.

[31] Peter Cameron & Michael Stanley, *Oil, Gas and Mining: A Sourcebook for Understanding the Extractives Industries* (World Bank, 2017).

[32] See Viñuales, n. 1, chap. 4.

[33] Offshore wind projects shared between states would likely be subject to an agreement, such as the North Sea Countries Offshore Grid Initiative.

[34] Redgwell, n. 2, 36.

[35] Riccardo Pavoni & Dario Piselli, 'The Sustainable Development Goals and International Environmental Law: Normative Value and Challenges for Implementation' (2016) 13(26) *Veredas Do Direito* 24.

[36] REN21, n. 18, 35.

encouraging sustainable energy generation.[37] For instance, most of the five hundred or more multilateral environmental agreements in which states have voluntarily entered,[38] including the 1992 UN Framework Convention on Climate Change (UNFCCC) and the 2015 Paris Agreement as well as the core rules and principles of international environmental law,[39] do not specifically address energy activities, but they do set legal parameters to guide and evaluate the action of states and other actors.[40] The following subsection considers selected aspects of the international legal order related to subpoints (3)–(4) that support or hinder the realization of SDG 7.

7.3.2 *Access to Energy: International Human Rights Law*

The goal of enhanced access to energy as encapsulated in target 7.1 and the related goal of energy security are expressions of diplomatic and political agreement. Thus, target 7.1 suffers from a disconnect between policy aspirations and their specific translation into international legal rules. In practical terms, global development goals, including poverty reduction and the improvement of physical and mental health, cannot be achieved without access to modern energy services, reliable electricity, and clean fuels.[41] Yet these goals are not expressly underwritten by an independent, substantive human 'right to energy', 'right to clean energy', or 'right to access' any form of energy (clean, affordable, and reliable or otherwise) in international human rights law or treaties. Therefore, creative approaches have been advanced by human rights bodies and courts in an attempt to integrate and manifest contemporary goals and aspirations through the existing international legal infrastructure.

First, the SDGs and 2030 Agenda for Sustainable Development incorporate, by reference, the major pillars of the human rights law framework to support the realization of the SDGs.[42] The SDGs express that they are 'grounded' in the 1948 Universal Declaration of Human Rights and 'international human rights treaties', the core of which include the 1966 International Covenant on Civil and Political Rights, the 1966 International Covenant on Economic, Social and Cultural Rights, and the 1989 Convention on the Rights of the Child.[43] As a corollary, rights

37 See Redgwell & Rajamani, n. 30, chap. 5.

38 See Ivar Baste et al. (eds.), 'Global Responses', in *Global Environment Outlook 6: Environment for the Future We Want* (UNEP, 2012), 457, 464.

39 See generally Leslie-Anne Duvic-Paoli & Jorge E. Viñuales, 'Prevention of Significant Environmental Harm', in Jorge E. Viñuales (ed.), *The UN Friendly Relations Declaration at 50: An Assessment of the Fundamental Principles of International Law* (Cambridge University Press, 2020), 283.

40 Raphael Heffron et al., 'A Treatise for Energy Law' (2018) 11 *Journal of World Energy Law and Business* 34; Catherine Redgwell, 'International Regulation of Energy Activities', in Martha Roggenkamp et al. (eds.), *Energy Law in Europe*, 3rd ed. (Oxford University Press, 2016), 2.195–2.223.

41 Kaime & Glicksman, n. 8, 1423–24.

42 See discussion in *id.*, 1434–43.

43 *Transforming Our World: The 2030 Agenda for Sustainable Development*, UN Doc. A/Res/70/1, 25 September 2015, Declaration, para. 10.

and obligations related to the SDGs cannot be interpreted as detracting from, but only as advancing, these and other instruments.

Second, despite the absence of a specific provision in those instruments expressly recognizing a right to energy, human rights bodies have elaborated on the primary rights in order to address, with various degrees of specificity, the link between energy and human rights, including in connection with a right to an environment of a certain quality.[44] Some observers have argued that certain human rights (for example, the rights to life, property, private and family life, housing, standard of living, health) either imply in law,[45] or, at minimum, necessitate in fact, access to energy. This claim is supported by reference to the interpretive practice of some human rights bodies. As early as 1991, the Committee on Economic, Social and Cultural Rights (CESCR) stated that the concept of 'adequate housing' implicates access to energy for cooking, heating and lighting[46] and that contracting states should ensure that personal or household financial costs (such as energy costs) are not so high as to inhibit the attainment of other basic rights.[47] By 2017, the CECSR had gone much further, specifically recommending that Australia take 'immediate measures aimed at reversing the current trend of increasing absolute emissions of greenhouse gases and pursue alternative and renewable energy production'.[48]

In recent years, international human rights treaty bodies have linked the promotion of, and access to, renewable energy with climate change mitigation and adaptation as a means to protect and fulfil primary rights to life, health, and a clean environment.[49] In 2019, the Human Rights Committee observed that

[44] *Social and Economic Rights Action Center/Center for Economic and Social Rights v Nigeria*, Decision Regarding Communication 155/96, Case no. ACHPR/COMM/A044/1, 27 May 2002; *Government of the Republic of South Africa and Others v Grootboom and Others*, 4 October 2000, (2000) 11 BCLR 1169.

[45] See Adrian Bradbrook & Judith Gardam, 'Placing Access to Energy Services within a Human Rights Framework' (2006) 28 *Human Rights Quarterly* 389, 405; Adrian Bradbrook, Judith Gardam, & Monique Cormier, 'A Human Dimension to the Energy Debate: Access to Modern Energy Services' (2008) 26(4) *Journal of Energy and Natural Resources Law* 526; Stephen Tully, 'The Contribution of Human Rights to Universal Energy Access' (2006) 4 *Northwestern Journal of International Human Rights* 518.

[46] CESCR, *General Comment 4: The Right to Adequate Housing*, UN Doc. E/1992/23, 1992, para. 8(b).

[47] *Id.*, para. 8(C). A similar statement is found in the 1979 Convention on the Elimination of All Forms of Discrimination against Women, which expressly requires that, in the context of rural development, women have the right to 'enjoy adequate living conditions, particularly in relation to housing, sanitation, electricity and water supply' (art. 14(2)(h)).

[48] CESCR, *Concluding Observations on the Fifth Periodic Report of Australia*, UN Doc. E/C.12/AUS/CO/5, 11 July 2017, para. 12.

[49] For a discussion of potential human rights obligations and aspirations within the global climate change regime, see Jorge E. Viñuales, 'The Paris Agreement on Climate Change: Less Is More' (2017) 59 *German Yearbook of International Law* 11; Daniel Klein et al. (eds.), *The Paris Agreement on Climate Change: Analysis and Commentary* (Oxford University Press, 2017); see also an earlier statement by the Human Rights Council, *Human Rights and Climate Change*, Resolution 7/23, UN Doc. A/HRC/7/23, 28 March 2008.

'[e]nvironmental degradation, climate change and unsustainable development constitute some of the most pressing and serious threats to the ability of present and future generations to enjoy the right to life, and in particular life with dignity', requiring states to take measures to address those issues caused by 'public and private actors'.[50] The CESCR has issued a similar statement, adding that states should 'dedicate the maximum available resources' to mitigate and adapt to climate change, including by 'accelerating the shift to renewable sources of energy' and 'improving the insulation of buildings'.[51] The Committee on the Rights of the Child (CRC) has further endorsed phasing out fossil fuels globally to protect children's right to health[52] and expressly encouraged Japan and Australia to accelerate their transition to renewable energy.[53] The Committee on the Elimination of Discrimination against Women (CEDAW) has made similar statements to Nigeria and Guyana in the context of development, empowerment, and equality through investment in clean energy jobs and infrastructure, noting the link to SDG 7.[54]

The growing body of precedent culminated in September 2019 in a landmark joint statement on human rights and climate change by the CESCR, CEDAW, CRC, the Committee on the Protection of the Rights of All Migrant Workers and Members of their Families, and the Committee on the Rights of Persons with Disabilities. The statement expressly links human rights, clean energy, and climate change, particularly in the context of the most vulnerable people and places:

> [I]n order for States to comply with their human rights obligations, and to realize the objectives of the Paris Agreement, they must adopt and implement policies aimed at reducing emissions ... [including] phasing out fossils fuels, promoting renewable energy and addressing emission from the land sector ... and ensure that public and private investments are consistent with a pathway towards low carbon emissions and climate resilient development.[55]

50 Human Rights Committee, *General Comment 36 on Article 6 and the Right to Life*, Doc. CCPR/C/GC/36, 3 September 2019, para. 62. The implications of this statement have been explored in multiple decisions. See, e.g., International Covenant on Civil and Political Rights Committee, *Concluding Observations on the Initial Report of Cabo Verde*, Doc. CCPR/C/CPV/CO/1/Add.1, 3 December 2019, para. 18.

51 CESCR, *Statement on Climate Change and the International Covenant on Economic, Social and Cultural Rights*, Doc. E/C.12/2018/1, 31 October 2018, para. 9.

52 CRC, *Concluding Observations on the Combined Fifth and Sixth Periodic Reports of Spain*, Doc. CRC/C/ESP/CO/5-6, 5 March 2018, para. 36.

53 CRC, *Concluding Observations on the Combined Fourth and Fifth Periodic Reports of Japan*, Doc. CRC/C/JPN/CO/4-5, 5 March 2019, para. 37(e); CRC, *Concluding Observations on the Combined Fifth and Sixth Periodic Reports of Australia*, Doc. CRC/C/AUS/CO/5-6, 1 November 2019, para. 41(b).

54 CEDAW, *Concluding Observations on the Combined Seventh and Eighth Periodic Reports of Nigeria*, 14 July 2017, para. 40(b); CEDAW, *Concluding Observations on the Combined Seventh and Eighth Periodic Reports of Guyana*, 12 July 2019, para. 42.

55 *Joint Statement on 'Human Rights and Climate Change'*, 16 September 2019, paras. 11–12, www.ohchr.org/EN/NewsEvents/Pages/DisplayNews.aspx?NewsID=24998.

While the statement does not expressly recognize independent energy rights, it emphasizes the role of emissions reductions and renewable energy to respect, protect, and fulfil a broad array of internationally protected human rights. Improving access to and use of clean, affordable energy as per target 7.1 is one practical approach to advance protected rights.[56]

Third, similar developments are unfolding in regional contexts. An implied human right to energy may exist to help secure the 'best attainable physical and mental health' standards protected by the 1981 African Charter on Human and Peoples' Rights and the 1988 Additional Protocol to the American Convention on Human Rights in the Area of Economic, Social and Cultural Rights. Two decisions from the Inter-American Court of Human Rights affirm that approach. One ordered that states party to the 1969 American Convention on Human Rights provide access to electricity to vulnerable people so as to fulfil primary human rights protected by the convention.[57] The other, in the form of an advisory opinion, stated that adequate protection of the environment is essential for human well-being as well as for the enjoyment of multiple human rights – in particular, the rights to life, personal integrity, health, and a healthy environment.[58] Those rights can be advanced through energy access and clean technology.

7.3.3 *Decarbonizing Energy: The International Law of Climate Change*

Measures relating to sustainable energy, such as those in target 7.2 (and target 7.3), are not central, textual features of the international climate change regime, despite patterns in energy generation and consumption being central elements to both the cause of anthropogenic climate change and the solution to realizing the regime's core objectives: to stabilize greenhouse gas emissions so as to avert catastrophic consequences of climate change,[59] to achieve mandated emissions reductions for

[56] Consultations continue on proposals for a new international human right to a 'safe, clean, healthy and sustainable environment', as articulated in the *Framework Principles on Human Rights and the Environment*, UN Doc. A/HRC/37/59, April 2018, which, in practice, would implicate newer sources of renewables, such as sun and wind, and energy efficiency technologies. While few jurisdictions have created enforceable rights to access energy, over 155 states have recognized the right to a healthy environment through treaties, constitutions, legislation, and judicial determination. *Report of the Special Rapporteur on Issue of Human Rights Obligations Relating to the Enjoyment of a Safe, Clean, Healthy and Sustainable Environment*, Doc. A/HRC/40/55, 8 January 2019, para. 16.

[57] Inter-American Court of Human Rights (IACtHR), *Case of the Río Negro Massacres v Guatemala*, Judgment (Preliminary Objection, Merits, Reparations, and Costs), 4 September 2012, para. 284.

[58] IACtHR, *State Obligations in Relation to the Environment in Relation in the Context of the Protection and Guarantee of the Rights to Life and to Personal Integrity: Interpretation and Scope of Articles 1(1) and 2 of the American Convention on Human Rights*, Advisory Opinion OC-23/17, November 2017, paras. 47–69.

[59] UN Framework Convention on Climate Change (UNFCCC), art. 2.

member states,[60] and to limit global temperature increases to well below 2 degrees Celsius and towards 1.5 degrees Celsius.[61]

The text of the UNFCCC does not expressly refer to renewable energy, and energy efficiency is noted only in the preamble as a measure to reduce growing energy consumption.[62] The 1997 Kyoto Protocol, which created market mechanisms to incentivize emissions reduction from renewables and energy efficiency projects,[63] refers to renewable energy as one among several other policy choices that states may adopt domestically, at their discretion, when implementing measures to reduce emissions.[64] The decision adopting the Paris Agreement implicitly supports targets 7.1 and 7.2 by acknowledging 'the need to promote universal access to sustainable energy in developing countries, in particular in Africa, through the enhanced deployment of renewable energy'.[65] However, the primary texts do not contain further express references to renewable energy.

As a system of law and governance that aspires to reduce global emissions, the climate change regime largely devolves to its member states the responsibility for, and approach to, decarbonization. But such discretion is not unfettered. It has to be exercised within legal parameters, not the least the good faith discharge of member states obligations. Member states are required to adopt nationally determined contributions (NDCs) that meaningfully address climate change mitigation and adaptation and to implement domestic laws and policies to achieve these goals. Sustainable energy laws, policies, and projects will be central to the attainment of NDCs and the decarbonization objectives. But to date, member states are not on track to meet their international obligations to avert the worst effects of climate change.[66]

The Paris Agreement, however, does provide strong signals to debt and capital markets that 'financial flows' (that is, private investment and public finance) should be directed towards 'low greenhouse gas emissions and climate-resilient development', thereby directing future funds into sustainable energy projects relevant to SDG 7 and especially targets 7.a and 7.b.[67] It also provides for the creation

[60] 1997 Kyoto Protocol to the UNFCCC, Annex B.

[61] 2015 Paris Agreement on Climate Change, art. 2(a).

[62] UNFCCC, preamble, para. 22.

[63] The Kyoto Protocol has generated over US$300 billion in climate and sustainable development investments and reduced global greenhouse gas emissions by almost 2 billion tonnes. UNFCCC, *Achievements of the Clean Development Mechanism 2001–2018*, 2019, 2–3.

[64] Kyoto Protocol, art. 2(1)(a) provides a non-exhaustive list of eight non-binding policy options, including 'enhancement of energy efficiency in relevant sectors of the national economy' and 'promotion, development and increased use of, new and renewable forms of energy'.

[65] *Adoption of the Paris Agreement*, Draft Decision -/CP.21, Doc. FCCC/CP/2015/L.P/Rev.1, 12 December 2015, preamble, para. 14.

[66] UNEP, n. 25, xx; Intergovernmental Panel on Climate Change, *Special Report on the Impacts of Global Warming of 1.5 degrees Celsius*, 2018; *Chile Madrid Time for Action*, Decision 1/CP.25, December 2019, paras. 6, 8.

[67] Paris Agreement, art. 2(1)(c).

of a global emissions trading regime, through the Sustainable Development Mechanism,[68] akin to a combined version of the Clean Development Mechanism (Article 12) and Joint Implementation (Article 6) of the Kyoto Protocol, which is anticipated to incentivize investments in sustainable energy projects and technologies.

Even though the climate change regime relies on target 7.2 (and target 7.3) to achieve its aims, it does not directly advance SDG 7 through mandated technology or policy choices. Its legal and practical relevance is indirect – first, by creating frameworks that seek to incentivize and encourage public and private activities that are consistent with SDG 7 and, second, by obliging member states to cooperate, share, and transfer low-carbon energy technologies and knowledge to developing country member states as well as to provide financial support.[69] The second objective has been underwritten by the creation of new international technology and finance mechanisms that indirectly advance SDG 7, which, in practice, have produced mixed results.[70]

7.3.4 *Reducing Energy Intensity: International Trade Law*

The 2030 Agenda for Sustainable Development considers international trade to be the 'engine for inclusive economic growth and poverty alleviation'.[71] The realization of this goal will involve trade in energy goods and services, including energy efficiency technologies related to target 7.3. The development, creation, and use of these goods and services are typically regulated by domestic law, often with reference to international standards.[72] But the movement of these goods and services across national borders is regulated by international law[73] – namely, by bilateral, regional, and global trade rules, disciplines, and obligations, including those contained in the 1947/1994 General Agreement on Tariffs and Trade (GATT), the 1994 General Agreement on Trade in Services, the 1994 Agreement on Subsidies

68 *Id.*, art. 6.

69 UNFCCC, arts. 4(1)(c), 4(1)(g), 4(1)(i), 4(3)–(5), 6(b), 11(1); Kyoto Protocol, arts. 10(c)–(e), 11(2).

70 See Section 8.3.5.

71 *Transforming Our World*, n. 43, para. 68; see also Matthias Helble & Ben Shepherd (eds.), *Win-Win: How International Trade Can Help Meet the Sustainable Development Goals* (Asia Development Bank Institute, 2017).

72 Domestic producers may adhere to the standards for certain products from the International Organization for Standardization or the International Electrotechnical Commission. A number of voluntary international initiatives created by the Group of Seven or Group of Twenty, noted in Section 8.4.2, focus on accelerating policy cooperation for particular domestic energy efficiency products and technologies.

73 See generally Stuart Bruce, 'Climate Change Mitigation through Energy Efficiency Laws: From International Obligations to Domestic Regulation' (2013) 31(3) *Journal of Energy and Natural Resources Law* 313.

and Countervailing Measures, the 1994 Trade-Related Investment Measures, and the 1994 Agreement on Technical Barriers to Trade (TBT Agreement).[74]

The World Trade Organization's (WTO) rules exemplify the difficulty of integrating national and international priorities and economic, social, and environmental objectives: no sector, including energy, is differentiated under trade law. The structure and content of the trade rules also brings to bear the inherent differences in the interests of producers, importers, and exporters of sustainable energy technologies. On the one hand, the trade rules seek to promote a level playing field in international trade relations (through common tariff and non-tariff barriers) in relation to energy goods and services. On the other hand, those rules seek to balance states' prerogative to provide fiscal support policies (that is, feed-in tariffs), subsidies, and incentives (including energy efficiency rebates and domestic content requirements) to grow local sustainable energy industries.[75]

One mechanism by which the trade rules seek to minimize such priority conflicts, as well as conflicts between trade and other international (environmental) obligations, is through the provision of derogations and exceptions that justify noncompliance with trade obligations.[76] For example, under articles III(8)(a), XX and XXI of the GATT, the derogations and exceptions most relevant to energy activities include public procurement and bona fide measures taken for national security purposes, for the protection of human, animal, or plant life or health, or for the conservation of exhaustible natural resources.[77] Yet, in practice, these provisions have failed to shield the renewable energy promotion schemes of Canada and India.[78]

Diplomatic efforts since 2001 to 'green' the WTO regime have all but failed. The mandate of the 2001 Doha Development Agenda to strengthen legislative and

[74] The TBT Agreement and its committee encourage progressive harmonization of technical product regulations and standards, including those related to energy efficiency, to avoid discriminatory treatment and trade inefficiencies. The TBT Agreement last considered energy efficiency in 2016 during an experience sharing exercise. Moderators to the TBT Committee, *Thematic Session on Regulatory Cooperation between Members: Energy Efficiency* (WTO Committee on Technical Barriers to Trade, 2016); see also Martijn Wilder & Leslie Parker, 'International Law, the Renewable Energy Sector and the Development of a Green Economy,' in Kevin R. Gray, Richard Tarasofsky, & Cinnamon Carlane (eds.), *The Oxford Handbook of International Climate Change Law* (Oxford University Press, 2016).

[75] Ilaria Espa & Gracia Marin Durán, 'Renewable Energy Subsidies and WTO Law: Time to Rethink the Case for Reform beyond Canada – Renewable Energy/FIT Program' (2018) 21 *Journal of International Economic Law (JIEL)* 621.

[76] WTO, *The Environment: A Specific Concern*, www.wto.org/english/thewto_e/whatis_e/tif_e/bey2_e.htm.

[77] GATT, arts. XXI, XX(b), XX(g); TBT Agreement, art. 2.2. Similar exceptions exist in other trade rules.

[78] WTO, *India – Certain Measures Relating to Solar Cells and Solar Modules*, Appellate Body Report, WTO Doc. WT/DS456/AB/R, 14 October 2016; WTO, *Canada – Certain Measures Affecting the Renewable Energy Generation Sector*, Appellate Body Report, WTO Docs. WT/DS412/AB/R, WT/DS426/AB/R, 24 May 2013.

executive coordination between WTO and multilateral environmental rules and secretariats, and to eliminate tariffs and non-tariff barriers on environmental goods and services,[79] has not been fulfilled. More promise was held for the plurilateral 2014 Environmental Goods Agreement (EGA), which sought to reduce or eliminate tariff and non-tariff barriers on a range of environmentally beneficial goods and services that could advance SDG 7, including those related to clean energy.[80] EGA negotiations frayed in 2016 and were largely held among developed Western nations, without participation from South America, Africa, the Middle East, and most of Asia,[81] raising doubts about the legitimacy of any purported level playing field in trade and environment. Greater traction has been made in a similar Asia-Pacific Economic Cooperation process, potentially highlighting the amenability of regional collaborations over global approaches.[82]

To sidestep the impasse in trade negotiations, numerous alternatives have been proposed to reconcile trade and non-trade interests, including carbon border adjustment taxes, carbon clubs, climate waivers, sustainable energy trade agreements, reforms to fossil fuel subsidies, and the creation of sustainable energy subsidies.[83] These proposals could offer pragmatic approaches to increase the global harmonization of regulations and standards related to energy efficiency, which would provide the dual benefits of non-discrimination among trade relations and greater deployment of technologies that benefit SDG 7 and other SDGs.

Modern bilateral and regional free trade agreements have also demonstrated greater, albeit incremental, success in accommodating energy efficiency and climate change priorities. For example, the text of the 'Environment' chapter of the 2018 Comprehensive and Progressive Agreement for Trans-Pacific Partnership expressly acknowledges that 'transition to a low emissions economy requires collective action' based on domestic circumstances and capabilities and encourages the parties to cooperate in relation to 'energy efficiency', 'low emissions technologies', and 'renewable energy sources', including through capacity building.[84] Similarly, the 'Climate Change' section of the 'Trade and Sustainable Development' part of the 2019 EU-Vietnam Free Trade Agreement commits the parties to 'consult and share information and experiences of priority or of mutual interest', including in

[79] WTO, *Doha WTO Ministerial 2001: Ministerial Declaration*, Doc. WT/MIN(01)/Dec/1, 14 November 2001, paras. 6, 31(iii).

[80] WTO, *Environmental Goods Agreement*, www.wto.org/english/tratop_e/envir_e/ega_e.htm.

[81] WTO, *Map of EGA Participants*, www.wto.org/english/tratop_e/envir_e/ega_map_e.htm.

[82] See Asia-Pacific Economic Cooperation, *2012 Leaders Declaration: Annex C – List of Environmental Goods*, www.apec.org/Meeting-Papers/Leaders-Declarations/2012/2012_aelm/2012_aelm_annexC.aspx.

[83] WTO, *Mainstreaming Trade to Attain the Sustainable Development Goals*, 2018; James Bacchus, *Triggering the Trade Transition: The G20's Role in Reconciling Rules for Trade and Climate Change*, white paper (International Centre for Trade and Sustainable Development, 2018); Richard Barron & Justine Garrett, *Trade and Environment Interactions: Governance Issues* (Organisation for Economic Co-operation and Development [OECD], 2017).

[84] Art. 20.15.

relation to 'the promotion of energy efficiency, low-emission technology and renewable energy'.[85] While such developments are welcome, they principally foster cooperation rather than ambitious action, which has led to calls from the World Economic Forum, among other bodies, for a comprehensive Low-Carbon Trade Agreement to directly and purposefully accelerate global decarbonization.[86]

7.3.5 *Cooperation and Infrastructure Development: International Investment Law and Intellectual Property Law*

To achieve SDG 7 by 2030, annual global investments amounting to US$680 billion in renewable energy, US$625 billion in energy efficiency, and US$45 billion in energy access will be required.[87] Overall, annual investments of US$5–7 trillion will be required to realize all of the SDGs, with over half of those amounts being directed to developing countries.[88] Yet, between 2010 and 2017, finance flows into developing countries in support of renewable energy and clean energy projects only doubled to a relatively modest US$21.4 billion, with less than 12 per cent of that amount directed to least developed countries. Half of those amounts funded 'older' renewable energy technologies – namely, hydropower – while 19 per cent funded solar power and 7 per cent funded wind power.[89] These figures reveal that less than 1.6 per cent of the needed annual investment in sustainable energy infrastructure and technologies is being directed to those most in need of that investment – developing countries. They also highlight the disparity between word (the abundant international treaty and political commitments for development finance, technology transfer, and cooperation)[90] and deed that would materially advance targets 7.a and 7.b. Multiple drivers fuel this disconnect. Two substantial obstacles ingrained in international law include the friction between international investment (and trade) law and the energy transition and the reluctance of states and private actors to cooperate beyond the strictures of international intellectual property rights and protections (IPRs).

85 Art. 13.6(2)(c).

86 Richard Samans, *It's Time to Bring Together Global Trade and Climate Action and Let Them Help Each Other*, www.weforum.org/agenda/2019/09/climate-low-carbon-trade-agreements/ (World Economic Forum, 2019).

87 IEA et al., n. 6, 120.

88 Jorge E. Viñuales, *International Investment Agreements and Sustainable Development: Safeguarding Policy Space and Mobilising Investment for a Green Economy* (UNEP, 2018), 1; UN Conference on Trade and Development (UNCTAD), *World Investment Report 2014: Investing in the SDGs*, 2014, xi; see also OECD, *Investing in Climate, Investing in Growth* (OECD Publishing, 2017), 28 (executive summary).

89 *Progress towards the Sustainable Development Goals*, Doc. E/2020/57, 28 April 2020, para. 72.

90 See, e.g., *Addis Ababa Action Agenda of the Third International Conference on Financing for Development*, UNGA Res. 69/313, UN Doc. A/RES/69/313, 17 August 2015, para. 49.

Regarding the first obstacle, a persistent criticism among states and scholars relates to the tendency of international investment agreements (IIAs)[91] to asymmetrically focus on economic goals and investor rights over public concerns and issues (such as social development and environmental protection). These concerns are typically more evident in the almost three thousand or more 'older generation' IIAs, which tend to be short and contain broad, general language.[92] That design is intended to provide certainty and rule-of-law-like benefits,[93] including protections against excessive and arbitrary governmental interference. But it is also linked to many challenges, ranging from extreme claims for protection and compensation to discouraging states from adopting or changing regulations that facilitate the clean energy transition in line with SDG 7.[94]

Numerous bilateral and multilateral projects have been undertaken to reform and modernize the IIA network so as to encourage greater allocation of capital into clean technology projects while also clarifying the scope of states' conduct in making decisions in law or practice that impact those investments without incurring responsibility,[95] thus benefiting targets 7.a and 7.b. 'Next generation' IIAs and new free trade agreements have a propensity to increasingly seek to 'rebalance' obligations and imperatives and to place environmental considerations within a tribunal's frame of reference.[96] For example, the preambular text of the 2009 Free Trade and Economic Partnership between Japan and the Swiss Confederation commits to 'protect the environment, to promote the optimal use of natural resources in accordance with the objective of sustainable development and to adequately address the challenges of climate change'.[97] Similarly, the preamble to the revised Dutch model IIA expressly commits to 'sustainable development' and to international trade

[91] Consisting of bilateral and multilateral investment treaties and investment chapters in free trade agreements.

[92] UNCTAD, *UNCTAD's Reform Package for the International Investment Regime* (UNCTAD, 2017); Kathryn Gordon, Joachim Pohl, & Marie Bouchard, *Investment Treaty Law, Sustainable Development and Responsible Business Conduct: A Fact Finding Survey* (OECD, 2014); Kathryn Gordon & Joachim Pohl, *Environmental Concerns in International Investment Agreements: A Survey* (OECD, 2011). See generally Jorge E. Viñuales, *Foreign Investment and the Environment in International Law* (Cambridge University Press, 2012).

[93] August Reinisch, 'The Rule of Law in International Investment Arbitration', in Photini Pazartzis et al. (eds.), *Reconceptualising the Rule of Law in Global Governance, Resources, Investment and Trade* (Hart, 2016), chap. 20.

[94] See generally Mavluda Sattorova, *The Impact of Investment Treaty Law on Host States: Enabling Good Governance?* (Hart, 2018); Michael Waibel et al. (eds.), *The Backlash against Investment Arbitration* (Wolters Kluwer, 2010).

[95] See Pierre-Marie Dupuy & Jorge E. Viñuales, *Harnessing Foreign Investment to Promote Environmental Protection: Incentives and Safeguards* (Oxford University Press, 2013).

[96] See Catherine Titi, *The Evolution of Substantive Investment Protections in Recent Trade and Investment Treaties*, RTA Exchange Think Piece (International Centre for Trade and Sustainable Development/Inter-American Development Bank, 2018); Manjiao Chi, *Integrating Sustainable Development Goals in International Investment Law* (Routledge, 2018).

[97] Preamble.

and investment to advance that goal, without compromising the Netherlands's right to regulate through measures that advance 'public health, safety, environment, public morals, labor rights, animal welfare, social or consumer protection or prudential financial' objectives.[98] It will be for tribunals in subsequent disputes to assess the content of each of these goals and to balance the various interests, rights, and obligations, but, on their face, these goals hold potential to encourage greater levels of investment in clean energy infrastructure projects.

With respect to the reluctance of states and private actors to cooperate beyond the strictures of their IPRs, one enduring challenge to international cooperation and technology transfer to developing states has been the risk of private entities creating undesirable market competition.[99] Since its inception, the global climate change regime has had difficulty in realizing the obligations of its developed country member states to provide both technology and financial assistance to developing country member states.[100] Pointedly, the 2009 understanding reached in Copenhagen to provide a minimum of US$100 billion annually for projects in developing countries by 2020 has not been achieved once and has been extended to 2025 to realize that goal.[101]

This inertia is due in part to concerns by developed states and their companies over IPRs and sharing patented technology with developing states without reward or incentive. SDG 7 does not create any additional concrete, tangible reasons to improve on that front. Moreover, when agreeing on the means of implementation for the 2030 Agenda for Sustainable Development, states supported the 'transfer of environmentally sound technologies to developing countries on favourable terms, including on concessional and preferential terms, as mutually agreed'.[102] There is a real risk that such an approach to transfers may not be consistent with international trade and IPR obligations,[103] including those under the 1994 Agreement on Subsidies and Countervailing Measures and the 1994 Agreement on Anti-Dumping, adding further complexity to the relationship between the SDGs and international law.[104]

98 2018 Draft Dutch Model International Investment Agreement, preamble.

99 See, e.g., Anthi Koskina et al., 'Trade in Clean Energy Technologies: Sliding from Protection to Protectionism through Obligations for Technology Transfer in Climate Change Law or Vice Versa?' (2020) 13(2) *Journal of World Energy Law and Business* 114.

100 UNFCCC, arts. 4(1)(c), 4(1)(g), 4(1)(i), 4(3)–(5), 6(b), 11(1); Kyoto Protocol, arts. 10(c)–(e), 11(2).

101 See also Chapter 13 in this volume.

102 *Transforming Our World*, n. 43, para. 41. Note that the UNGA also indicates that trade should be in accordance with its established rules and obligations. *Id.*, para. 68; see also SDG 17, Partnerships for the Goals, target 10.

103 See Matthew Rimmer, 'The Road to Paris: Intellectual Property, Human Rights, and Climate Justice', in Matthew Rimmer (ed.), *Intellectual Property and Clean Energy: The Paris Agreement and Climate Justice* (Springer, 2018), 1.

104 See Henok Birhanu Asmelash, 'Energy Subsidies and WTO Dispute Settlement: Why Only Renewable Energy Subsidies Are Challenged' (2015) 18(2) *JIEL* 261.

7.4 POSITIONING SDG 7 IN THE INTERNATIONAL INSTITUTIONAL CONTEXT

In contrast to states' resistance to adopting binding sustainable energy obligations under international law, states have demonstrated a willingness for international actors to exert considerable influence on the development and deployment of resources towards the low-carbon transition. But the resulting influence over SDG 7 through international organizations is not the result of a planned, coordinated, and deliberate intergovernmental or private process. Instead, organizations are advancing SDG 7 based on their particular (and overlapping) mandates regarding energy (for example, global/regional; broad/narrow; single/multiple issue), membership rules, legal powers, degrees of formality,[105] thematic approach (for example, environment, development, industrialization, capital markets), and technical expertise (for example, advocacy, data analysis, capacity building, technical assistance, political risk funding, adjudication). As a result, the international context that is relevant for the implementation of SDG 7 is much like the relevant international legal framework: a growing patchwork of bodies with various mandates and interests that directly or indirectly influence, shape, and implement SDG 7[106] – the legitimacy and effectiveness of which has been doubted.[107] The patchwork includes many international institutions and political forums, private actors, and civil society.

7.4.1 *International Institutions and Political Forums*

Beyond state organs, the broad array of international institutions and platforms that impact the implementation of SDG 7 include over forty UN agencies and programmes; general and specific political forums and conferences; international organizations; and international financial institutions (IFIs).[108] Each body's degree of influence and particular role in relation to SDG 7 is determined by its competence and mandate. At one end of the spectrum, the role of formal international organizations, such as the International Renewable Energy Agency (IRENA), is prescribed by their express and implied powers and subsequent practice. Established in 2011, IRENA's mandate is to 'promote the widespread and increased adoption and

[105] Stuart Bruce, 'Global Energy Governance and International Institutions', in Walter Leal Filho et al. (eds.), *Encyclopedia of the UN Sustainable Development Goals: Affordable and Clean Energy* (Springer, 2019), 6.

[106] See *id.*, 6–13; Stuart Bruce, 'The Sustainable Energy Transition through International and EU Law', in Stephen Minas & Vassilis Ntousas (eds.), *EU Climate Diplomacy: Politics, Technology and Networks* (EE, 2018), 74–76.

[107] Achim Steiner et al., 'International Institutional Arrangements in Support of Renewable Energy', in Dirk Assmann, Ulrich Laumanns, & Dieter Uh (eds.), *Renewable Energy: A Global Review of Technologies, Policies, and Markets* (Earthscan, 2016), 152.

[108] Vanora Bennett, *EBRD Puts Decarbonisation at Centre of New Energy Sector Strategy* (European Bank for Reconstruction and Development, December 2018).

the sustainable use of all forms of renewable energy'.[109] As a 'centre of excellence', it is to provide an essential role in enabling the transfer of renewable energy knowledge and technology, capacity building and concessional finance and in coalescing states, organizations, and private actors around renewable energy use and deployment.[110] By agreement among its founding states, its mandate does not extend to establishing global standards or targets related to renewable energy. But with membership now at 161 states,[111] IRENA holds considerable legitimacy as an influencer in international law related to target 7.2.

The role of 'subsequent practice' in shaping the mandate of formal international organizations in relation to SDG 7 is particularly evident in relation to IFIs. At the time of writing, many multilateral development banks have reoriented their structure, operations, and lending policies to align with the Paris Agreement and SDG 7's objectives and expressly reduced funding for fossil fuel-based projects,[112] despite those topics not appearing in their founding articles of association. For instance, in October 2019, the International Monetary Fund announced that it will include climate risk in its country assessments, which will ultimately influence investment flows towards low-carbon projects. Many other IFIs are redoubling their attention to the low-carbon transition as a response to COVID-19. While IFIs typically assist with de-risking private investments in developing states, bodies such as the Global Environment Facility and Green Climate Fund leverage blended public-private finance to fund in-country projects that help realize the Paris Agreement and SDG 7. Overall, the 2030 Agenda for Sustainable Development considers this category of actors as central to the implementation of the SDGs.[113]

At the other end of the spectrum, informal platforms, such as the SEforALL initiative or the Group of Seven (G7)/Group of Eight (G8)/Group of Twenty (G20) meetings, have greater latitude to consider interlinking global issues such as climate change, energy security, and economic development away from centralized bureaucracies.[114] These platforms have launched numerous international programmes to accelerate decarbonization and reduce energy intensity, such as the Energy Efficiency Action Plan and Climate and Energy Action Plan for Growth.[115] Since 2009, the Clean Energy ministerial political platform has enabled energy ministers and energy diplomats to share best practices and promote sustainable energy

[109] 2009 Statute of the International Renewable Energy Agency, art. 3.
[110] *Id.*, art. 4.
[111] International Renewable Energy Agency, *IRENA Membership*, www.irena.org/irenamembership.
[112] See, e.g., World Bank, *The 2030 Sustainable Development Agenda and the World Bank Group: Closing the SDGs Finance Gap*, 2019.
[113] *Transforming Our World*, n. 43, para. 44.
[114] See generally John Kirton & Brittaney Warren, 'G20 Climate Change Governance: Performance, Prospects, Proposals' (Conference paper presented to the pre-G20 Summit, Soka University, Japan, 10 December 2018).
[115] Bruce, n. 106, 10.

programmes and policies in more detail than the G7/G8/G20 processes. While the potential norm-shaping influence of these multilateral platforms is high, discussions related to climate change are subject to the vagaries of the political process, potentially diluting their effectiveness at materially addressing SDG 7.[116] New state collaborations to accelerate clean energy innovation, such as Mission Innovation, may provide more practical avenues to advance SDG 7-related goals.[117]

7.4.2 *Private Actors and Civil Society*

The high level of visibility and awareness of sustainable energy access and uptake is largely due to a handful of factors. One factor is civil society's decades-long advocacy for the development of international sustainable energy policy, the dissemination of technical information, the monitoring of impact, and the promotion of clean energy projects in emerging economies (for example, the World Resources Institute, the World Wide Fund for Nature, the International Union for Conservation of Nature, the International Institute for Sustainable Development, the International Institute for Environment and Development, the Renewable Energy and Energy Efficiency Partnership, the Renewable Energy Policy Network for the 21st Century, and the International Partnership for Energy Efficiency Cooperation). In general, the actions of many actors in this category have been considered credible and legitimate given their motivations and UN-observer status and have helped to keep sustainable energy on the international political agenda.

Another factor is the burgeoning enthusiasm from national and transnational private actors for political and legal certainty related to decarbonization incentives and trajectories (We Mean Business Coalition, RE100%, ClimateAction100+, Institutional Investors Group on Climate Change, and so on). With the global direction of travel in relation to emissions management set by the Paris Agreement, and climate change, degradation of the natural environment, environmental catastrophes, and risks to ecosystem collapse among the top ten corporate concerns globally,[118] private actors are increasingly seeking options to reduce regulatory and asset-stranding risk exposure in their investments, operations, and projects. Investments that advance targets 7.2 and 7.3, in particular – including enhanced energy efficiency in buildings, appliances, and industrial activities and greater deployment of large-scale and off-grid, distributed renewable energy generation and energy storage – fit that bill. While these private actors are (usually)

116 See generally Ann Florini & Benjamin Savocool, 'Who Governs Energy: The Challenges Facing Global Energy Governance' (2009) 37(12) *Energy Policy* 5239.

117 Mission Innovation, www.mission-innovation.net/.

118 World Economic Forum, *The Global Risks Report*, 2020, 2–3, Figures 1, 2. See Eduardo Brondizio et al., *Global Assessment Report on Biodiversity and Ecosystem Services* (Intergovernmental Science-Policy Platform on Biodiversity and Ecosystem Services, 2019); see also Partha Dasgupta, *The Economics of Biodiversity* (Her Majesty's Treasury, 2021).

independent from states, the intention of state-related initiatives such as the Financial Stability Board's Task Force on Climate-Related Financial Disclosures and the Network of Central Banks and Supervisors for Greening the Financial System is to create circumstances that leverage the incredible financial and organizational power of those private actors to advance and implement SDG 7 and the Paris Agreement.[119]

7.5 CONCLUSIONS

The progressive attainment of SDG 7 holds considerable promise for humankind and for reducing despoliation of the natural world. With three global, 'top-down' targets having been set in SDG 7 – universal access to energy and significant increases in renewable energy and energy efficiency – the intended, and agreed, direction of travel is clear. But the speed of travel towards the attainment of these goals, which is largely determined by 'bottom-up' national action (with international support), while increasing, is insufficient. States are widely off track to achieve the targets of SDG 7 (and SDG 13). To decarbonize the global economy within the time frames established by scientific evidence, greater coordination and collaboration between states, private actors, and civil society will be needed and quickly.

The extent to which international law may assist in that endeavour varies – it can both support and hinder progress. While energy is central to the advancement of most, if not all, of the SDGs, the transition to a low-carbon or 'sustainable' energy matrix is not clearly reflected in international law. By incidence of its historical structure, role, and function, no identifiable 'international energy law' has emerged in public international law. Instead, the entire corpus of public international law needs to be examined through the lens of 'energy', and the transition to low-carbon energy, in order to assess its relevance and utility to advance SDG 7.

The implementation of SDG 7 through the various bodies of international law thus results in an evolving and complex system, including, but not limited to, human rights law, climate change law, trade law, investment law, and intellectual property law. There is an urgent need to improve the integration of non-economic objectives in the major disciplines of international economic law. Doing so will help to promote and remove barriers to innovation, commerce, and financial flows for clean energy projects and the electrification and decarbonization of all aspects of modern life. Such developments would improve the prospects of realizing SDG 7.

[119] See generally Joyeeta Gupta, Arthur Rempel, & Hebe Verrest, 'Access and Allocation: The Role of Large Shareholders and Investors in Leaving Fossil Fuels Underground' (2020) 20 *International Environmental Agreements: Politics, Law and Economics* 303; Mark Carney, *A New Horizon* (Bank of England, 21 March 2019); Mariana Mazzucato & Gregor Semieniuk, 'Financing Renewable Energy: Who Is Financing What and Why It Matters' (2018) 127 *Technological Forecasting and Social Change* 8.

8

SDG 8: Promote Sustained, Inclusive and Sustainable Economic Growth, Full and Productive Employment and Decent Work for All

Tonia Novitz

ABSTRACT

This chapter examines the multifaceted content of Sustainable Development Goal (SDG) 8, Decent Work and Economic Growth, and its relationship with the other SDGs. It argues that, if the aim of SDG 8 is to end exploitative employment practices, then its stress on 'decent work for all' should inform the interpretation of all relevant targets and indicators. This is achievable insofar as SDG 8 offers inclusive protection of migrant and other precarious workers, attending to discrimination in the labour market. Also vital is the recognition of collective voice for all those at work, as advocated by International Labour Organization (ILO) and UN reports. While ILO and UN human rights instruments and institutions inform and promote this approach to SDG 8, international economic and investment law as well as financial institutions have the capacity to limit its potential. There are, however, positive shifts on the horizon, which include transnational collective bargaining and policy initiatives encompassing state and non-state actors.

KEYWORDS

SDG 8, decent work, labour standards, precarious work, migrant workers, freedom of association, collective bargaining, trade unions, economic growth, employment, International Labour Organization (ILO)

8.1 INTRODUCTION

This chapter reflects on the attempt made in Sustainable Development Goal (SDG) 8, Decent Work and Economic Growth, to reconcile 'economic' ambitions for growth with the 'promotion of employment' and 'decent work for all' as a 'social' facet of sustainable development. The way in which the adjectives 'sustained, inclusive and sustainable' are coined indicate an expectation of potential reconciliation. The reference to 'decent work' is also evocative of a long-standing agenda launched by the International Labour Organization (ILO), suggesting deference to internationally crafted and agreed labour standards that are now widely accepted.[1] However, by placing protection of those at work in a context where the SDGs are to be regarded as 'integrated and indivisible', new challenges regarding 'trade-offs' are likely to arise.[2]

Arguably, SDG 8 illustrates synergies and tensions between the economic, social, and environmental 'pillars' of sustainable development,[3] which might seem to operate as 'fragmented' systems in international law.[4] The achievement of the objectives set out in SDG 8 will require greater deference to be given by international economic and financial institutions to the findings and recommendations of the ILO and the UN human rights institutions. Moreover, there may need to be more active promotion of the representation of workers' voices at all levels to make effective change possible.

Given the dual (and seemingly divided) purposes of SDG 8, it could be claimed that there is no single problem that this goal seeks to address. Nevertheless, it is notable that the 2030 Agenda for Sustainable Development was adopted not long after the shocking Rana Plaza disaster of 2013. In Dhaka, Bangladesh, at least 1,132 people were killed and more than 2,500 were injured when an eight-storey commercial building containing five garment factories collapsed. Just five months previously, at least 112 workers had died when they were trapped in a factory fire, located on the outskirts of Dhaka.[5] These events highlighted the precarious conditions (indeed, the complete disregard for health and safety and failure to provide compensation for injury at work) experienced by workers subcontracted within global supply chains for the ready-made garment sector servicing higher income

1 See the 2008 Declaration on Social Justice; see also *Report of the Director-General: Decent Work* (ILO, 1999); *Report of the Director-General: Reducing the Decent Work Deficit* (ILO, 2001).

2 See preamble to the *Transforming Our World: The 2030 Agenda for Sustainable Development*, UN Doc. A/Res/70/1, 25 September 2015, sustainabledevelopment.un.org/post2015/transformin gourworld/publication.

3 Ben Purvis, Yong Mao, & Darren Robinson, 'Three Pillars of Sustainability: In Search of Conceptual Origins' (2019) 44(3) *Sustainability Science* 681.

4 See International Law Commission Study Group & Martti Koskenniemi, *Fragmentation of International Law: Difficulties Arising from the Diversification and Expansion of International Law*, 2006, legal.un.org/ilc/documentation/english/a_cn4_l682.pdf. Also raised in the context of international labour standards by Kerry Rittich, 'The ILO: Challenges in Times of Crisis' (2015) 154(1) *International Labour Review (ILR)* 85.

5 ILO, *The Rana Plaza Accident and Its Aftermath*, www.ilo.org/global/topics/geip/WCMS_614394/lang–en/index.htm.

countries in the global North.[6] These events further underscored the manifestation of persistent income inequalities between (so-called) 'developed' and 'developing countries'.[7] It was evident that the latter group of low-income states in what had become labelled the 'global South' had to be given access to economic growth in international markets, so as to change the current dynamics that left them vulnerable and subservient to the demands of foreign investors.

One would expect that these concerns motivated the adoption of SDG 8, but what is less clear is whether these problems can readily be remedied through SDG 8 as it is drafted. The next section of this chapter begins by examining the text of SDG 8, alongside connections between the targets in SDG 8 and the other SDGs. It is argued that the aims of 'economic growth' and 'employment promotion' should be read in light of the objectives concerning distributive equity, social justice at work, and environmental inter- and intra-generational justice. The International Labour Office – the ILO's Secretariat – has also observed the synergies between the notion of 'decent work for all' instantiated in SDG 8 and other SDGs.[8] The extent to which combining SDG 8 and other objectives could lead to the enhancement or compromise of internationally recognized standards may depend on how complementarity and conflict are navigated under international law and, more significantly, by international institutions.[9]

The third section of this chapter considers how SDG 8 may be interpreted in light of international law related to employment and labour and the mechanisms established for their protection. In this regard, the chapter not only focuses on ILO sources but also examines UN human rights instruments, which may further extend the ILO's conception of decent work. The relevance of international instruments relating to trade, investment, and finance for SDG 8 will also be considered, alongside acknowledgement of their significance in SDG 10, Reduced Inequalities, SDG 16, Peace, Justice and Strong Institutions, and SDG 17, Partnerships for the Goals.

The final section of the chapter investigates the range of international institutions and other actors that can affect access to decent work. These institutions include

[6] Stephanie Ware Barrientos, ''Labour Chains': Analysing the Role of Labour Contractors in Global Production Networks' (2013) 49(8) *Journal of Development Studies* 1058; Laura A. Carlson & Vera Bitsch, 'Social Sustainability in the Ready-made Garment Sector in Bangladesh: An Institutional Approach to Supply Chains' (2018) 21(2) *International Food and Agribusiness Management Review* 269.

[7] Thomas Pogge, 'Priorities of Global Justice' (2001) 32(1–2) *Metaphilosophy* 6. Regarding the process of SDG drafting, see also Thomas Pogge & Mitu Sengupta, 'The Sustainable Development Goals: A Plan for Building a Better World?' (2015) 11(1) *Journal of Global Ethics* 56.

[8] ILO, *Time to Act for SDG 8: Integrating Decent Work, Sustained Growth and Environmental Integrity* (ILO, 2019), Executive Summary, x, www.ilo.org/global/publications/books/WCMS_712685/lang–en/index.htm.

[9] *Cf.* Kenneth W. Abbott & Steven Bernstein, 'The High-level Political Forum on Sustainable Development: Orchestration by Default and Design' (2015) 6(3) *Global Policy* 222. But my focus here is on other international institutional actors.

various UN institutions and supervisory bodies, especially those relating to human rights at work, but my attention will be focused on the ILO institutions responsible for the adoption of standards and the mechanisms for their supervision. For example, the International Labour Office has reported on the scale of global compliance with SDG 8,[10] and the International Labour Conference has adopted the 2019 ILO Centenary Declaration for the Future of Work, which makes reference to sustainability objectives.[11]

This institutional activity in the ILO and elsewhere in the United Nations will be considered alongside the actions of international economic institutions, such as the World Trade Organization (WTO), the International Monetary Fund (IMF), and the World Bank Group. It is suggested that there may be scope to temper prevalent economic objectives and enhance the representation of 'developing countries' through such institutions as the UN Conference on Trade and Development (UNCTAD) and the UN Commission on International Trade Law (UNCITRAL). In addition, when considering the viability of global private, as well as public, partnerships for development, as envisaged in SDGs 16 and 17, the capacities of transnational worker organizations are likely to be important. The protection of freedom of association for all may be vital to securing representative and effective collective voice at work and in the international institutions that determine the parameters of decent work under international law.

8.2 THE CONTENT OF SDG 8 IN THE CONTEXT OF THE OTHER SDGS

This section considers the extent to which 'decent work' is protected, diluted, or enhanced by virtue of SDG 8 and the other SDGs. Further, the connections between SDG 8 and SDGs 16 and 17, which seek to operationalize other SDG objectives, are discussed with respect to the scope for collective voice on work-related issues.

8.2.1 *Internal Tensions within SDG 8*

SDG 8 is a complex goal since its very title is indicative of three itemized aims that can conflict: 'economic growth', 'full and productive employment', and 'decent work'. It might seem that economic aims are implicitly prioritized since they come first, both in the title to the goal and in target 8.1: 'Sustain per capita economic growth in accordance with national circumstances and, in particular, at least 7 per cent gross domestic product growth per annum in the least developed countries.' This objective and its prominence arguably reflect the dominance of business interests in the procedures established for drafting and adopting the

[10] See ILO, n. 8.

[11] 2019 ILO Centenary Declaration for the Future of Work, www.ilo.org/wcmsp5/groups/public/@ed_norm/@relconf/documents/meetingdocument/wcms_711674.pdf.

SDGs.[12] Economic growth is to be achieved under target 8.2 by achieving 'higher levels of economic productivity through diversification, technological upgrading and innovation, including through a focus on high-value added and labour-intensive sectors'. The accompanying indicator 8.2.1 requires measurement of the '[a]nnual growth rate of real GDP [gross domestic product] per employed person'. In this way, each worker is instrumentalized for economic growth, challenging the ILO's constitutionally endorsed assertion that 'labour is not a commodity'.[13]

Economic ambitions regarding growth in GDP reflect the undertaking in Agenda 2030 to build 'strong economic foundations for all our countries'.[14] The desirability of a concrete growth target, however, was called into question in the *UN Sustainable Development Outlook 2019*, which argued that there is a need for prioritizing other aspects of development.[15] Certainly, national and global circumstances in 2020 (following the coronavirus pandemic) have rendered the achievement of 7 per cent growth exceptionally unlikely in any country, at least within the medium term,[16] offering an opportunity to rethink both the viability and desirability of targets 8.1 and 8.2.

The 2019 ILO Centenary Declaration also mentions the promotion of youth employment and women's 'economic empowerment',[17] which can be linked to target 8.3, which seeks to support 'productive activities, decent job creation, entrepreneurship, creativity and innovation'. It is expected that the jobs created will be 'decent' and that there will be the 'formalization' of micro-, small- and medium-sized enterprises, which is a long-term objective of the ILO.[18] In target 8.5, it is emphasized that 'full and productive employment' is to be inclusive of women and men and young people as well as persons with disabilities, and it entails 'decent work' as well as 'equal pay for work of equal value'. The plan to boost youth employment under targets 8.6 is to be furthered under target 8.b by developing and operationalizing 'a global strategy' that involves implementing 'the Global Jobs

[12] Lou Pingeot, *Corporate Influence in the Post-2015 Process*, Working Paper Misereor–GPF–Brot fur die Welt, 2014, www.dawnnet.org/sites/default/files/articles/corporate_influence_in_the_post-2015_process_web.pdf; Regina Scheyvens, Glenn Banks, & Emma Hughes, 'The Private Sector and the SDGs: The Need to Move beyond 'Business as Usual'' (2016) 24(6) *Sustainable Development* 371.

[13] The first ILO Constitution to be found in Part XIII of the 1919 Treaty of Versailles stated in section II(a)(427) that 'labour should not be regarded merely as a commodity or article of commerce', and this was repeated in article I(a) of the 1944 ILO Declaration of Philadelphia.

[14] See *Transforming Our World*, n. 2, para. 27.

[15] UN Department of Economic and Social Affairs, *Sustainable Development Outlook 2019: Gathering Storms and Silver Linings* (United Nations, 2019) 2, 11, 16.

[16] Lora Jones, Daniele Palumbo, & David Brown, 'Coronavirus: A Visual Guide to the Economic Impact,',*BBC News*, 3 April 2020, www.bbc.co.uk/news/business-51706225.

[17] See *Transforming Our World*, n. 2, para. 27.

[18] Claire La Hovary & Jordi Agustí Panareda, 'What Is Work? A Malleable Notion in the ILO's Legal Pursuit of Social Justice,' in George P. Politakis, Tomi Kohiyama, & Thomas Lieby (eds.), *ILO 100: Law for Social Justice* (ILO, 2019), 893.

Pact of the International Labour Organization'. In this way, a broader social agenda embedded in respect for (and the inclusive application of) ILO labour standards seems to constrain the aim (and distribution) of growth and job promotion. The quality of jobs, as well as the number of jobs, will matter, as will the distribution of wealth derived from economic growth.

In target 8.4, the aim is to 'decouple' economic growth from environmental degradation. This goal is consistent with the approach taken in the promotion of jobs in tourism (in target 8.9), which is limited to what is 'sustainable'. Economic growth may still be regarded as 'good' under SDG 8, but despite its apparent primacy in the order of targets, its achievement depends on compliance with other social and environmental aims. Targets 8.7 and 8.8 elaborate on what is to be regarded as 'decent work'. At the ILO, decent work is usually understood as (1) promoting employment; (2) enhancing social protection; (3) promoting social dialogue and tripartism; and (4) respecting, promoting, and realizing the fundamental principles and rights at work.[19] Three out of the four 'fundamental principles and rights at work' (or 'core labour standards') recognized by the ILO are set out in the SDG 8 targets – namely, the eradication of forced labour, the elimination of child labour, and the elimination of discrimination.[20] 'Freedom of association and collective bargaining' appear in indicator 8.8.2, which was adopted in 2017.[21] There is reference to additional concerns such as trafficking and modern slavery (target 8.7) and the protection of migrant workers (target 8.8). In these ways, it may be said that SDG 8 offers more extensive protections than the ILO has so far attempted under the head of 'decent work' by addressing the concerns of the most vulnerable on the margins of the workforce.

Targets 8.10 and 8.a point to how these objectives may be achieved. Target 8.10 envisages strengthening 'the capacity of domestic financial institutions', while target 8.a envisages aid for trade and technical assistance for trade for developing (especially least developed) countries. This is not just about equity but also redistributive action, which we shall see chimes with other SDGs and the preamble's assertion that 'no one will be left behind'.

8.2.2 *Connections and Clashes with Other SDGs*

The reference to 'economic growth' in SDG 8 arguably has to be read as being moderated not only by specific SDG 8 targets and their wording but also by the other SDGs. For example, SDG 1, No Poverty, seeks to 'end poverty in all its forms everywhere' so that growth cannot be sought at the expense of others, especially

[19] See Declaration on Social Justice, n. 1, art. I(A).

[20] 1998 ILO Declaration on Fundamental Principles and Rights at Work, art. 2.

[21] International Institute for Sustainable Development, *Policy Brief: Getting to 2030: Tracking SDG Indicators for Evidence of Implementation Progress*, 2021, sdg.iisd.org/commentary/policy-briefs/getting-to-2030-tracking-sdg-indicators-for-evidence-of-implementation-progress/.

those living in developing and least developed states, as target 8.a provides. Previously, in relation to Millennium Development Goal 1 on poverty, the ILO had succeeded in lobbying for the adoption of a 'decent work' target that would 'achieve full and productive employment for all, including women and young people'.[22] The rationale was that work is a way of preventing poverty. It should be noted that the ILO is the custodian agency (or partner custodian) not just for SDG 8 but also for various other work-related indicators under other SDGs, including indicators 1.3.1 and 1.a.2.[23]

Further, SDG 10, Reduced Inequalities, aims to 'reduce inequality within and among countries', again constraining growth that creates global inequalities. Targets 10.2. and 10.3, in particular, offer an anti-discriminatory framework that can help to inform targets 8.5 and 8.8. concerning 'decent work' and 'labour rights' for 'all'. Additionally, targets 10.7 and 10.c make provision for the welfare of migrant workers in a way that is complementary to target 8.8. The objective of economic growth in SDG 8 must also be understood as being constrained by the environmental objectives set out in the other SDGs, including those relating to agriculture (SDG 2, Zero Hunger), water (SDG 6, Clean Water and Sanitation), climate change (SDG 13, Climate Action), oceans and seas (SDG 14, Life below Water) as well as ecosystems and biodiversity on land (SDG 15, Life on Land) and energy (SDG 7, Affordable and Clean Energy).[24]

The International Labour Office's 2019 report *Time to Act for SDG 8* endorsed an evolving approach to the protection of 'decent work' following a 'policy spiral', whereby the various targets in SDG 8 were also linked with, for example, SDG 1; SDG 3, Good Health and Well-being; SDG 4, Quality Education; SDG 5, Gender Equality; and SDG 10.[25] There is also arguably scope for connection with SDG 9, Industry, Innovation and Infrastructure, if we are to consider the role of industrial innovation and infrastructure in the future of work. However, in my view, it may well be SDGs 16 and 17 that are the key pivotal connections. SDG 16 is significant insofar as building 'effective, accountable and inclusive institutions at all levels', which is vital to the realization of SDG 8. Moreover, the idea of 'Global Partnership' sought through SDG 17 indicates how SDG 8 could be realized.

Beginning with SDG 16, of particular relevance appear to be targets 16.6 and 16.7. Target 16.6 seeks to '[d]evelop effective, accountable and transparent institutions at

[22] Diane F. Frey & Gillian MacNaughton, 'A Human Rights Lens on Full Employment and Decent Work in the 2030 Sustainable Development Agenda' (2016) 6(2) *Journal of Workplace Rights* 1, 6.

[23] *Id.*, 5.

[24] See Tonia Novitz & Margherita Pieraccini, 'Agenda 2030 and the Sustainable Development Goals: 'Responsive, Inclusive, Participatory and Representative Decision-making'?', in Margherita Pieraccini & Tonia Novitz (eds.), *Legal Perspectives on Sustainability* (University of Bristol Press, 2020), 46.

[25] See ILO, n. 8, 2.

all levels', presumably nationally and internationally. Target 16.7 aims to '[e]nsure responsive, inclusive, participatory and representative decision-making at all levels', which one would assume also includes the workplace as well as different levels of governance, locally, nationally, regionally, internationally, and transnationally. There is no express mention of trade unions in SDG 16, but the UN rapporteur on freedom of association was adamant that trade union rights, including a right to strike, must be taken to be implicit in the guarantee of 'fundamental rights' in target 16.10.[26] The International Labour Office in its report on *Time to Act for SDG 8* stressed that social dialogue and collective bargaining are vital to the achievement not only of SDG 8 but also of Agenda 2030 as a whole.[27] Collective bargaining is described as 'essential to provide coherence between real wage growth and shared productivity growth'.[28] Further, '[t]he full involvement of free, independent, strong and representative employers' and workers' organizations in policy-making and implementation is a powerful governance instrument for sustainable development, since it reinforces democratic ownership, inclusiveness and accountability'.[29] Collective voice is also recognized by the International Labour Office as a way to ensure the protection of the interests of migrant workers' interests alongside other precarious workers.[30] This seems consistent with indicator 8.8.2, which requires the compilation of statistics on compliance with labour rights, including freedom of association and collective bargaining, in line with ILO 'textual sources'.

SDG 17 aims to 'strengthen the means of implementation and revitalize the global partnership for sustainable development'. This SDG concerns diverse matters, including finance to assist developing countries, transfer of technologies, capacity building and trade as well as the ways in which to operationalize 'policy coherence' and 'partnership'. Trade, investment, and finance mechanisms have in the past obstructed attempts to promote sustainable development, including decent work,[31] which makes SDG 17 highly relevant to the potential realization of SDG 8. Additionally, both targets 17.16 and 17.17 recognize the multiplicity of 'stakeholders', including civil society (including presumably all forms of worker organizations) that could act as partners in this regulatory process. In this sense, the manifestation of freedom of association at multiple levels will be of importance to the realization of SDG 17.

[26] *Report of the Special Rapporteur on the Rights to Freedom of Peaceful Assembly and Association*, Doc. A/73/279, 7 August 2018, paras. 6, 58, 87–89.

[27] ILO, n. 8, 33–34, 70–75.

[28] *Id.*, 55, 60–61; *cf.* Florence Jaumotte & Carolina Osorio Buitron, *Inequality and Labor Market Institutions*, IMF Staff Discussion Note (IMF, 2015).

[29] ILO, n. 8, 74.

[30] *Id.*, 70–71.

[31] Discussed at length in Bob Hepple, *Labour Laws and Global Trade* (Hart, 2005); see also discussion later in this chapter.

8.3 POSITIONING SDG 8 IN INTERNATIONAL LAW

8.3.1 *The ILO's Notion of 'Decent Work' and Treatment of Labour Rights as Human Rights*

There is a vast range of legal principles embedded in ILO instruments that could be considered relevant to interpreting SDG 8. They include the signatory constitutional statement that 'labour is not a commodity', which should ideally enable resistance to the potential commodification of workers in respect of targets 8.2 and 8.7.[32] In addition, Article II(c) of the 1944 Declaration of Philadelphia requires that priority be given to social justice over economic aspirations, which is arguably indicative of where priority should lie in terms of the different economic and social objectives framed within SDG 8. Indeed, this is how the International Labour Office has advised that 'trade-offs' between SDGs should be addressed.[33]

What is notably absent from Agenda 2030 and the SDGs is the notion of 'just transitions'.[34] This principle stems from campaigns launched by trade unions in the 1970s, which sought to ensure that changes to working conditions and employment in response to environmental (and economic) concerns would take place gradually, enabling forms of compensation, training, and redeployment.[35] This could be a way to navigate the potential challenges directed at 'decent work' from SDG 8's economic targets or, indeed, those SDGs that are environmentally focused. It is curious that 'just transitions' receive attention in the preamble to the 2015 Paris Agreement[36] but not in the 2030 Agenda. Similarly, the 2015 ILO Guidelines on Just Transitions, which were signed prior to the adoption of Agenda 2030 and which refer to collective bargaining and agreements, do not receive any kind of mention, perhaps due to their non-binding recommendatory nature.[37] However, this will not much matter if, as the ILO suggests, social justice must ultimately prevail.

[32] See n. 13.

[33] ILO, n. 8, 27, 35, 79.

[34] See David Doorey, 'Just Transitions Law: Putting Labour Law to Work on Climate Change' (2017) 30(2) *Environmental Law and Practice* 201; see also discussion in Tonia Novitz, 'Engagement with Sustainability at the International Labour Organization and Wider Implications for Collective Worker Voice' (2020) 159(4) *ILR* 463, 467–68.

[35] Dimitris Stevis & Romain Felli, 'Global Labour Unions and Just Transition to a Green Economy' (2015) 15 *International Environmental Agreements* 29, 32.

[36] The 2015 Paris Agreement under the 1992 United Nations Framework Convention on Climate Change refers to 'the imperatives of a just transition of the workforce and the creation of decent work and quality jobs in accordance with nationally defined development priorities'. See further Navraj Singh Ghaleigh, 'Just Transitions for Workers: When Climate Change Met Labour Justice', Edinburgh School of Law Research Paper Series no. 219/30, 2019, 16–19.

[37] ILO, *Guidelines for a Just Transition towards Environmentally Sustainable Economies and Societies for All*, 2015, www.ilo.org/wcmsp5/groups/public/—ed_emp/—emp_ent/documents/publication/wcms_432859.pdf.

Most of the 'core labour standards' set out in article 2 of the 1998 Declaration of Fundamental Principles and Rights at Work are acknowledged in SDG 8 – namely, the prohibition of forced labour, child labour, and discrimination. Key aspects of 'decent work', as set out in the 2008 ILO Declaration on Social Justice for a Fair Globalization, are also recognized via the promotion of employment in targets 8.5, 8.6, and 8.b, while social protection is provided for in target 1.3. However, despite being described as an integral part of decent work in article IA of the 2008 Declaration on Social Justice, 'tripartism and social dialogue' and 'freedom of association and the right to effective collective bargaining' do not receive attention in SDG 8's targets. Notably, unlike the Declaration of Philadelphia, which was subsequently incorporated into the ILO Constitution, the 1998 and 2008 Declarations retain only declaratory effect, as does the 2019 ILO Centenary Declaration. That said, each declaration has come to be regarded as a 'constitutional moment' that is indicative of significant policy shifts at the ILO, such that their normative effects should not be underestimated.[38]

The fact that the right to strike is not mentioned in the SDGs may well be due to the resistance of the business lobby to the long-standing international protection of industrial action as an activity of workers under the 1948 ILO Convention no. 87 on Freedom of Association and Protection of the Right to Organise.[39] This omission may also be attributed to an ongoing challenge to established ILO supervisory mechanisms under the ILO Standards Review Mechanism established by virtue of the 2008 Declaration on Social Justice.[40] The influence of commercial interests and employers in the SDG drafting process may have ensured that there was minimal recognition of freedom of association or trade unions.[41] However, in its 2019 report, the International Labour Office was determined to assert the significance of collective bargaining for the promotion of SDG 8 and also other connected SDGs (while remaining silent on the subject of the right to strike).[42] The extent of their success is

[38] Tonia Novitz, 'Past and Future Work at the International Labour Organization: Labour as a Fictitious Commodity, Countermovement and Sustainability' (2020) 17(1) *International Organizations Law Review (IOLR)* 10, 17–27; see also Guy Standing 'The International Labour Organization' (2010) 15(2) *New Political Economy* 307; Brian Langille, 'Core Labour Standards: The True Story (Reply to Alston)' (2005) 16 *European Journal of International Law (EJIL)* 409, 410, 420.

[39] For the 2012 'walkout,' see Conference Committee on the Application of Standards, *ILO International Labour Conference Record of Proceedings* (ILO, 2012), part I/13, part I/19, discussed in Claire La Hovary, 'Employers' Group 2012 Challenge to the Right to Strike' (2013) 42 (4) *Industrial Law Journal (ILJ)* 338; Janice Bellace, 'The ILO and the Right to Strike' (2014) 153(1) *ILR* 29; Jeffrey Vogt et al., *The Right to Strike in International Law* (Hart, 2020).

[40] See Claire La Hovary, 'The ILO's Employers' Group and the Right to Strike' (2016) 22 (3) *Transfer: European Review of Labour and Research* 401, 404; Paul van der Heijden, 'The ILO Stumbling towards Its Centenary Anniversary' (2018) 15(1) *IOLR* 203, 219.

[41] See Pingeot, n. 12.

[42] See ILO, n. 8.

considered in the context of the activism of various international institutions discussed in the next section of this chapter.

A further interesting question is whether the ILO's constitutional and key declaratory instruments would be relevant to the interpretation of SDG 8 (and other connected SDGs), as well as the conventions and recommendations adopted by the ILO's International Labour Conference. The International Labour Conference is a tripartite body, consisting of one employer, one worker and two government representatives for each member state. Conventions are adopted by a two-thirds majority of the representatives and are binding on states when ratified. In addition, article 19(5) of the ILO Constitution requires those states that do not ratify a convention to report on the obstacles they have encountered and their progress towards ratification. Normally, an international instrument would not be regarded as entailing obligations for a non-ratifying party, which could limit their relevance for the interpretation of SDG 8 and other SDGs, but the peculiar status of the adopted conventions under the ILO Constitution may render them more pertinent as a reference point than is ordinarily the case.[43] Arguably, the reference in indicator 8.8.2 to the ILO's 'textual sources' suggests that ILO conventions and recommendations, as well as ILO constitutional documents, will be relevant.

Additionally, other key international human rights instruments also contain extensive coverage of rights at work. Important examples include the 1966 International Covenant on Civil and Political Rights (ICCPR) and the 1966 International Covenant on Economic, Social and Cultural Rights (ICESCR). Both defer to the ILO's expertise regarding international labour standards on the subject of freedom of association and the right to organize.[44]

Certain aspects of SDG 8 may go beyond the scope of the current ILO instruments, particularly regarding trafficking, modern slavery, and migrant workers' rights. Modern slavery is to some extent tackled through the 2014 Protocol to the 1930 ILO Convention no. 29 on Forced Labour. Other instruments that will be as relevant (if not more) to targets 8.7 and 8.8 are the 1926 Slavery Convention, the 2000 Palermo Protocol,[45] and the 1990 International Convention on the Protection of Migrant Workers and Their Families. The latter convention has had notoriously few ratifications to date,[46] so that another useful source of reference may be the 2018 UN Global Compact for Safe, Orderly and Regular Migration, which provides less extensive, and, therefore, potentially more readily acceptable, recommendations.

[43] See Frederic L. Kirgis, 'Specialized Law-making Processes,' in Oscar Schachter & Christopher C. Joyner (eds.), *United Nations Legal Order* (Cambridge University Press, 1995), 115.

[44] See ICCPR, art. 22(3); ICESCR, art. 8(3).

[45] 2000 Protocol to Prevent, Suppress and Punish Trafficking in Persons Especially Women and Children, supplementing the 2000 United Nations Convention against Transnational Organized Crime.

[46] With fifty-five state parties. See Office of the High Commissioner of Human Rights, *Ratification of Eighteen International Human Rights Treaties*, indicators.ohchr.org/.

Given that the ILO has not adopted conventions providing more effective protection for migrant workers' rights,[47] the SDGs and their potential linkage to these other international instruments may have the effect of enhancing decent work for this often vulnerable group. This possibility gives the SDGs potentially additional significance since Agenda 2030 may prompt further activity on these issues within the ILO, going beyond the accepted boundaries of a 'decent work' agenda. Additionally, existing ILO standards on racial discrimination, empowerment of women and girls, and disability may be enhanced by reference to the 1965 International Convention on the Elimination of All Forms of Racial Discrimination, the 1979 Convention on the Elimination of All Forms of Discrimination against Women, and the 2006 Convention on the Rights of Persons with Disabilities, alongside the findings of their supervisory bodies. These issues emerge by reason of the synergies between SDG 8 (especially targets 8.5. and 8.8) and SDGs 5 and 10, which relate respectively to gender equality and, more generally, to equality of opportunity and outcome not only between, but also within, states.

If we were only looking to ILO and other international human rights standards to inform the interpretation of SDG 8 and related SDGs, there seem to be opportunities for considerable enrichment of those objectives. However, the potentially problematic dilution of standards arises in the context of extant international norms relating to trade, investment, and finance. Economic law is notorious for being 'harder' and more influential than its soft social counterpart in the sphere of work.[48]

8.3.2 *The Significance of International Economic Law on Trade, Finance, and Investment for the Realization of SDG 8*

There are a number of international instruments arising under international economic law that are likely to have implications for the interpretation and application of SDG 8. These relate to trade, investment, and finance.

8.3.2.1 Trade Law

The WTO has determined that it will not as an institution impose conditions on trade relating to labour standards.[49] Rather, the instruments appended to the 1994 Agreement Establishing the World Trade Organization – namely, the General Agreement on Tariffs and Trade (GATT) and the General Agreement on

47 See 1949 ILO Convention no. 97 on Migration for Employment and 1975 ILO Convention no. 143 on Migrant Workers, which are discussed in Judy Fudge, 'Precarious Migrant Status and Precarious Employment: The Paradox of International Rights for Migrant Workers' (2012–13) 34 *Comparative Labor Law and Policy Journal* (*CLLPJ*) 95.

48 Eric Tucker, 'Labor's Many Constitutions (and Capital's Too)' (2011) 33 *CLLPJ* 355.

49 Singapore Ministerial WTO Declaration, Doc. WT/MIN96/DEC/W, 13 December 1996, para. 4.

Trade in Services (GATS) – contemplate ways in which member states may be able to take unilateral action to do so (which would otherwise be potentially in breach of overriding norms such as the most favoured nation principle or national treatment).

States can potentially restrict trade by reason of non-compliance with labour standards under the 'General Exceptions' provision in article XX of the GATT and article XIV of the GATS.[50] The application of this clause, however, is limited. From a 'decent work' perspective, the measures must be 'necessary' to protect public morals or to protect human life or health, or they must 'relate' to 'the products of prison labour'. Moreover, they must satisfy the requirements of the 'chapeau' such that they are neither 'a means of arbitrary or unjustifiable discrimination between countries' nor 'a disguised restriction on international trade'. Also, a proportionality requirement applies.[51] There has been little success for member states seeking to defend their conduct in WTO dispute settlement proceedings,[52] although, notably, Brazil successfully defended information technology subsidies before a panel with reference to the MDG target 8.f.[53] At the time of writing (in June 2021), we do not know whether the Appellate Body would have endorsed such a finding, due to it being rendered inoperable after the United States blocked the appointment of new members.[54] However, there remains some potential for jurisprudential development in the context of the stopgap, the 2020 Multiparty Interim Appeal Arbitration Arrangement, endorsed by the European Union (EU) and, initially, fifteen other states.[55]

We can see the SDGs as an attempt to address the vulnerability of developing countries under international trade law. Examples include the provision of 'Aid for Trade' support for developing countries in target 8.a. This is consistent with the recognition of the principle of special and differential treatment for developing countries under target 10.a. Those countries offering special preferences under the

50 Discussed in Clair Gammage & Tonia Novitz, 'Trade, Investment and Corporate Sustainability,' in Beate Sjafjell & Christopher M. Bruner (eds.), *The Cambridge Handbook of Corporate Law, Corporate Governance and Sustainability* (Cambridge University Press, 2020), 15.

51 See WTO, *European Communities – Measures Prohibiting the Importation and Marketing of Seal Products*, Appellate Body Report, WTO Doc. WT/DS400/AB/R & WT/DS401/AB/R, 22 May 2014, 174, which is discussed by Brendan P. McGivern, 'The WTO Seal Products Panel: The Public Morals Defense' (2014) 9(2) *Global Trade and Customs Journal* 73.

52 *Cf.* the one successful defence in WTO, *United States – Measures Affecting the Cross-Border Supply of Gambling and Betting Services*, Panel Report, Doc. WT/DS285/AB/R, 10 November 2004.

53 WTO, *Brazil – Certain Measures Concerning Taxation and Charges*, Panel Report, WTO Doc. WT/DS472, 30 August 2017, para. 7.563, which is discussed in Caroline E. Foster, 'The Problem with Public Morals' (2019) 10(4) *Journal of International Dispute Settlement* 622, 630–31.

54 See Bradly J. Condon, 'Captain America and the Tarnishing of the Crown: The Feud between the WTO Appellate Body and the USA' (2018) 52(4) *Journal of World Trade* 535; Joshua Paine, 'The WTO's Dispute Settlement Body as a Voice Mechanism' (2019) 20 *Journal of World Investment and Trade* 820.

55 See Ministerial Statement, 27 March 2020, trade.ec.europa.eu/doclib/docs/2020/march/tradoc_158684.pdf.

Generalised Systems of Preferences will still (it seems) be able to make these preferences conditional on compliance with labour standards and withdraw such preferences when deemed appropriate.[56] The WTO Appellate Body has set conditions on the conferment of preferences and their withdrawal – namely, that they must be non-discriminatory and transparent[57] – but the lack of recourse to the Appellate Body, starting in November 2020 and continuing at the time of writing, renders this finding less effective than it was previously. In reality, it may be primarily for more powerful trading entities, such as the EU, to interpret and apply trade conditionality on the basis of sustainability objectives.[58] In this context, it is helpful that target 17.10 seeks to 'promote a universal, rules-based, open, non-discriminatory and equitable multilateral trading system'.

Article XXIV of the GATT also enables the creation of 'customs unions' or 'free trade areas', with articles V and Vbis of the GATS also enabling agreements liberalizing trade in services. In this respect, the EU, in particular, has been proactive, creating what have been described as a 'new generation' of free trade agreements (FTAs) that contain a specific 'sustainability' chapter referencing 'decent work', including ILO core labour standards and referring to aspirations for ratification of ILO conventions.[59] For example, chapter 13 of the 2019 EU-Vietnam FTA specifically relies on both the ILO's decent work agenda (as set out in the 2008 Declaration on Social Justice) and Agenda 2030 as a basis for the parties' commitment to 'promote the development of international trade in such a way as to contribute to the objective of sustainable development, for the welfare of present and future generations'.[60] In 2021, an expert panel found that South Korea was in breach of article 13.4 of the 2010 EU-Korea FTA by virtue of non-compliance with the ILO's core labour standards relating to freedom of association and collective bargaining.[61] However, there is a danger that economic concerns regarding

[56] The enabling clause is entitled *Differential and More Favourable Treatment Reciprocity and Fuller Participation of Developing Countries*, Decision L/4903, 28 November 1979, www.wto.org/english/docs_e/legal_e/enabling1979_e.htm.

[57] See WTO, *European Communities – Conditions for the Granting of Tariff Preferences to Developing Countries*, Appellate Body Report, WTO Doc. WT/DS246/R, 1 December 2003.

[58] Robert Howse, 'India's WTO Challenge to Drug Enforcement Conditions in the European Community Generalized System of Preferences: A Little Known Case with Major Repercussions for 'Political' Conditionality in US Trade Policy' (2003) 4(2) *Chicago Journal of International Law* 385; Lorand Bartels, 'The WTO Legality of the EU's GSP+ Arrangement' (2007) 10 *Journal of International Economic Law* (*JIEL*) 869; Bruce Wardhaugh, 'GSP+ and Human Rights: Is the EU's Approach the Right One?' (2013) 16 *JIEL* 827.

[59] See, e.g., EU-Korea FTA, chap. 13; 2016 EU-Canada Comprehensive Economic Trade Agreement, chap. 23; 2019 EU-Singapore FTA, chap. 12.

[60] EU-Vietnam FTA, chap. 13, eur-lex.europa.eu/legal-content/EN/TXT/PDF/?uri=OJ:L:2020:186:FULL&from=EN#page=132.

[61] Panel of Experts, *Report of the Panel of Experts*, 20 January 2021, tradoc_159358.pdf (europa.eu). See Tonia Novitz, *Enforceable Social Clauses in Trade Agreements with 'Bite'? Implications of the EU–South Korea Panel of Experts Report of 20 January 2021* (European

trade may in this context outweigh the priority for social justice advocated in ILO instruments.[62]

8.3.2.2 International Investment Law and Finance

FTAs tend to cover more than merely trade in goods and services, and, as such, their influence often extends beyond the remit of the permissions given in the GATT and the GATS. In particular, they often include investment chapters. In addition, the protection of investors' interests may be regulated by the more conventional means of bilateral investment treaties (BITs) and multilateral investment agreements (MIAs). Investors have notoriously relied on the terms of these agreements to make claims (in investment arbitration) that seek to restrict state regulation of labour markets. In particular, the investor may claim that the introduction of improved labour standards has a negative effect on their investment, such that they should be compensated for indirect expropriation or a breach of fair and equitable treatment.

Both these claims were made in *Noble Ventures v Romania*, which concerned a claim for indirect expropriation and a breach of fair and equitable treatment following the alleged failure of the Romanian state to adequately prevent or police unlawful strikes. The award ultimately found against Noble Ventures in 2005, but the sums of money claimed against a vulnerable Eastern European state had been considerable.[63] The case of *Veolia v Egypt* concerned the government's decision to introduce a rise in the monthly minimum wage. The outcome of this claim was determined by an award issued in 2018, which has not been made public.[64] Investor-state dispute settlement (ISDS) has been known in this context to work in problematic ways from a rule-of-law perspective[65] and to the advantage of the larger multinational corporations that engage in investment as opposed to poorer and more vulnerable countries.[66]

Trade Union Institute, 2021), etui.org/sites/default/files/2021-05/Enforceable%20social%20clauses%20in%20trade%20agreements%20with%20%E2%80%98bite%E2%80%99_2021.pdf.

62 The US - Guatemala arbitration under the Dominican Republic - Central American FTA indicates that it is possible for severe violations of trade union freedoms to be regarded as irrelevant when they do not offer any trade advantage. See *Final Report of the Panel in the Matter of Guatemala: Issues Relating to the Obligations under Article 16.2.1(a) of the CAFTA-DR*, 2017.

63 ICSID, *Noble Ventures, Inc. v Romania*, ICSID Case no. ARB/01/11, 12 October 2005, icsid.worldbank.org/en/Pages/cases/casedetail.aspx?CaseNo=ARB/01/11.

64 ICSID, *Veolia Propreté v Arab Republic of Egypt*, ICSID Case no. ARB/12/15, 25 May 2018, icsid.worldbank.org/en/Pages/cases/casedetail.aspx?CaseNo=ARB/12/15.

65 Stephan W. Schill, 'Reforming Investor–State Dispute Settlement: A (Comparative and International) Constitutional Law Framework' (2017) 20(3) *JIEL* 649.

66 Thomas Schultz & Cédric Dupont, 'Investment Arbitration: Promoting the Rule of Law or Over-Empowering Investors? A Quantitative Empirical Study' (2014) 25(4) *EJIL* 1147.

Reinterpreting the terms of BITs, MIAs, and investment chapters in FTAs in accordance with the objectives established by the SDGs could bolster the case for host states to take regulatory action that coheres with SDG 8 – for example, improving health and safety or improving the treatment of migrant or other precarious workers in accordance with target 8.8. In that way, the Rana Plaza disaster might have been averted not only in Bangladesh (where the Bangladesh Sustainability Compact and Bangladesh Accord have gone some distance towards preventing further harm to workers in the garment sector)[67] but also more generally.

Once again, the development implications for the global South are recognized in target 10.a, which seeks to '[e]ncourage official development assistance and financial flows, including foreign direct investment, to States where the need is greatest, in particular least developed countries'. Moreover, just as the capacity of domestic financial institutions is to be expanded under target 8.10, in the same way (and arguably linked to this goal), targets 17.3 and 17.5 envisage enhancing investment promotion in developing countries.

Target 17.4 seems aimed at international financial institutions (IFIs) and their objective to '[a]ssist developing countries in attaining long-term debt sustainability through coordinated policies aimed at fostering debt financing, debt relief and debt restructuring'. This target seems to relate to the role of IFIs like the IMF and World Bank Group agencies (such as the International Finance Corporation) in providing loans to developing countries. However, the difficulty is that target 17.4 does not mention the use of conditionality in respect of such lending, which has been used to persuade states to diminish or downgrade labour protections.[68] This practice was notorious in the heyday of the so-called Washington Consensus, but it remains a basis of contemporary lending instruments.[69] Examples include the memoranda of understanding used when lending to European states during the financial crisis, with profound effects for workers.[70] So, while it is to be hoped that the targets in

[67] For relevant documents as updated, see European Commission, *Documents Archive on the Sustainability Compact*, trade.ec.europa.eu/doclib/cfm/doclib_section.cfm?sec=779; Accord on Fire and Building Safety in Bangladesh, May 2018, bangladeshaccord.org/ (Bangladesh Accord).

[68] Robin Broad & John Cavanagh, 'The Death of the Washington Consensus?' (1999) 16 *World Policy Journal* 79; *cf.* Alexander E. Kentikelenis, Thomas H. Stubbs, & Lawrence P. King, 'IMF Conditionality and Development Policy Space, 1985–2014' (2016) 23(4) *Review of International Political Economy (RIPE)* 543.

[69] See Franz Seitz & Thomas Jotz, 'The Role of the IMF in the European Debt Crisis,' Weidener Discussion Paper no. 32, 2012, www.econstor.eu/dspace/bitstream/10419/56452/1/689266685.pdf.

[70] For the ILO response to austerity measures taken in response to the financial crisis in Greece, see ILO, *Report on the High Level Mission to Greece*, 2011, www.ilo.org/wcmsp5/groups/public/—ed_norm/—normes/documents/missionreport/wcms_170433.pdf; see also Aristea Koukiadaki & Lefteris Kretsos, 'Opening Pandora's Box: The Sovereign Debt Crisis and Labour Market Regulation in Greece' (2012) 41(3) *ILJ* 276; *Report of the Independent Expert on the Effects of Foreign Debt and Other Related International Financial Obligations of States on the Full Enjoyment of All Human Rights, Particularly Economic, Social and Cultural Rights*, Doc. A/HRC/34/57, 27 December 2016, documents-dds-ny.un.org/doc/UNDOC/GEN/G16/

SDGs 10 and 17 will be read in conjunction with the decent work objectives included in SDG 8, and the other protections for those at work contained therein, there is precedent that suggests this may not be what happens in practice.

8.4 POSITIONING SDG 8 IN THE INTERNATIONAL INSTITUTIONAL CONTEXT

8.4.1 *An Intervention by Human Rights Supervisory Bodies in Support of ILO Standards*

In 2019, at a time when the ILO was struggling to protect a right to strike as a facet of freedom of association and collective bargaining (due to the employers' group rebellion), the supervisory bodies for the ICCPR and the ICESCR, the Human Rights Committee, and the Committee on Economic Social and Cultural Rights, issued a joint statement in support of that right consistent with the earlier findings of the ILO's supervisory bodies. They stated that the right to strike is a 'corollary to the effective exercise of the right to form and join trade unions', and both committees have sought to protect this entitlement on that basis.[71] This statement provides significant support for the established institutional workings of the ILO and is arguably consistent with the obligation to interpret the ICCPR and the ICESCR in accordance with ILO Convention no. 87. The statement should also have repercussions for the interpretation and application of SDGs 8 and 16 on the global stage.

8.4.2 *ILO Policy-Based Activity Relating to SDG 8 and Other SDGs*

Apart from these developments elsewhere in the UN system, the ILO has been very active on the topic of sustainability in the context of a larger project on 'the future of work' in the buildup to its centenary celebrations in 2019. In this context, the recommendations of the ILO Global Commission on the Future of Work (Global Commission) in its report *Work for a Brighter Future* indicated

4; *Report of the Independent Expert on the Effects of Foreign Debt and Other Related International Financial Obligations of States on the Full Enjoyment of All Human Rights, Particularly Economic, Social and Cultural Rights on His Mission to Institutions of the European Union*, Doc. A/HRC/34/57/Add.1, 28 December 2016, documents-dds-ny.un.org/doc/UNDOC/GEN/G16/442/13/PDF/G1644213.pdf?OpenElement.

71 'Freedom of association, including the right to form and join trade unions.' *Joint Statement by the Committee on Economic, Social and Cultural Rights and the Human Rights Committee*, Doc. E/C.12/2019/3-CCPR/C/2019/1, 23 October 2019, www.ohchr.org/Documents/HRBodies/CESCR_CCPR_Joint_STM.pdf.

appreciation of various connections between the decent work agenda in SDG 8 and the other SDGs.[72] An example is the relationship between SDG 8 and SDG 3, with the recommendation that 'safety and health at work … be recognized as a fundamental principle and right at work' alongside the four established core labour standards.[73] The Global Commission also took the view that these five labour standards, alongside an adequate living wage and maximum limits on hours at work (which many would see as intrinsic to health and safety),[74] be protected under a Universal Labour Guarantee, which would apply to 'all workers, regardless of their contractual arrangement or employment status'.[75] This view was reflected in article III(B) of the 2019 ILO Centenary Declaration, which affirmed the rights of 'all workers' to (1) 'their fundamental rights'; (2) 'an adequate minimum wage, statutory or negotiated'; (3) 'maximum limits on working time'; and (4) 'safety and health at work'. A supplementary resolution on the ILO Centenary Declaration requested the Governing Body 'to consider as soon as possible, proposals for including safe and healthy working conditions in the ILO's framework of fundamental principles and rights at work'.[76] Taking this step is arguably all the more significant today in the context of the COVID-19 pandemic, and further action on this issue is expected.[77] Further, the 2019 ILO Convention no. 190 on Violence and Harassment put the idea of a Universal Labour Guarantee into practice by ensuring the application of the convention (under article 2) for all those 'in the world of work … irrespective of their contractual status', and the ILO's pronouncements on the coronavirus pandemic also make reference to 'the world of work' in this inclusive way.

The Global Commission has further commented extensively on what it termed the conditions for 'sustainable work'.[78] In particular, it has made recommendations regarding the formalization of institutions of work (consistent with the ILO's past

[72] ILO Global Commission on the Future of Work (Global Commission), *Work for a Brighter Future* (ILO, 2019), Annex, 71–75, www.ilo.org/global/publications/books/WCMS_662410/lang–en/index.htm.

[73] *Id.*, 12, 39; see also Declaration on Social Justice, n. 1, art. I(A)(iv).

[74] See, e.g., the judgment of the Court of Justice of the European Union in *UK v Council*, [1996] ECR I-5755, para. 59, which found that 'the measures on the organization of working time … contributed directly to the improvement of health and safety protection of workers' and therefore the correct legal base had been applied for the adoption of Council Directive 93/104/EC concerning certain aspects of the organization of working time.'

[75] Global Commission, n. 72, 39.

[76] 2019 Resolution on the ILO Centenary Declaration for the Future of Work, 21 June 2019, www.ilo.org/wcmsp5/groups/public/—ed_norm/—relconf/documents/meetingdocument/wcms_711659.pdf.

[77] See the ILO's extensive policy coverage in ILO, *COVID-19 and the World of Work*, www.ilo.org/global/topics/coronavirus/lang–en/index.htm.

[78] Global Commission, n. 72, 10–13, 44–48.

efforts) that not only envisage the Universal Labour Guarantee but also other modes of reducing working poverty that can be regarded as a response to SDG 1.[79] The aim is to provide 'universal social protection from birth to old age', not just for those in a standard employment relationship but also for those precarious workers who are often excluded, such as migrant and digital workers.[80] This sensitivity to the needs of migrant workers can be linked to the specific acknowledgement of their vulnerability in SDGs 8 and 10 as well as other human rights developments within the wider UN human rights system.[81] Further, the Global Commission has advocated 'lifelong learning' from childhood onwards in line with SDG 4.[82] Its report additionally endorsed 'a transformative agenda for gender equality', which responds to recent technological developments, providing a plausible link with SDG 5.[83] Indeed, the commission's concern with a 'human-in-command' approach to technological development would also seem to temper the objectives in SDG 9.[84]

Notably, all these further facets of appreciation of an SDG-oriented agenda found their way into the 2019 ILO Centenary Declaration. Article I of the declaration references the significance of 'a fair, inclusive and secure future of work' for 'sustainable development'. 'A human-centred approach to the future of work' is to put 'workers' rights and the needs, aspirations and rights of all people at the heart of economic, social and environmental policies'. To this end, many of the Global Commission's recommendations (which pertain to different SDGs) found their way explicitly into article II(A), including 'universal access to comprehensive and sustainable social protection' (SDG 1), 'promoting the acquisition of skills, competencies and qualifications for all workers' (SDG 4), 'achieving gender equality at work through a transformative agenda' (SDG 5), 'harnessing the fullest potential of technological progress and productivity growth' (SDG 9), and 'promoting workers' rights as a key element for the attainment of inclusive and sustainable growth, with a focus on freedom of association and the effective recognition of the right to collective bargaining as enabling rights'. This development speaks to the concerns of the International Labour Office in *Time to Act for SDG 8*, indicator 8.8.2 and targets 16.7 and 16.10. If there is take-up of this normative frame and translation into action, the ILO will not only be broadening its sphere of concerns under SDG 8 but also responding positively to other related SDGs. The question is whether in the complex interactions of labour standards with trade, investment, and finance systems, ILO norms will indeed prevail.

79 *Id.*, 11, 18, 24.
80 *Id.*, 11, 35–36, 44.
81 See n. 45–47 and accompanying text.
82 Global Commission, n. 72, 30–32.
83 *Id.*, 34–35.
84 *Id.*, 43.

8.4.3 *Other Institutional Actors in the Realm of Trade, Investment, and Finance*

The ILO will not be the only member of a global partnership for development, nor will it necessarily lead the partnership. Other institutions are likely to exert significant sway over the application of the SDGs, including SDG 8. One such actor, which probably need not create any great alarm, is the World Health Organization, given the intersections and synergies between SDG 8 and SDG 3 discussed above.[85] The WTO could be another actor, but the damage to its credibility by the US blockage of appointments to the Appellate Body, starting in 2019, looks likely to diminish its influence, despite its potential scope to respond to sustainability objectives and adjudicate on SDG 8 and other SDGs.[86] It may be through the use of sustainability chapters (and clauses) in FTAs and in other instruments that set out trade preferences that we see the EU and other state actors implementing SDG targets relating to labour practices.[87]

ISDS, as it currently operates, raises the spectre that clauses in BITs, MIAs, and FTAs (for example, regarding indirect expropriation) will remain a threat to the practical application of decent work in developing countries reliant on foreign direct (or indirect) investment.[88] There are ongoing proposals for the reform and rationalization of this system for the settlement of investment disputes. For example, measures could be taken to enhance access of non-disputing parties, such as trade unions, to intervention in ISDS.[89] It is possible that UNCTAD[90] and the UNCITRAL[91] may yet play a role in the protection of workers' and developing countries' interests by pushing for a new multilateral framework, which is professionalized and defers to established human rights and even sustainability objectives. However, at the time of writing (in June 2021), UNCITRAL Working Group III is still seeking to achieve international consensus on a genuine shift of approach.[92] Moreover, there is no guarantee that, even if enabled to do so, developing countries would necessarily prioritize the elements of 'decent work' in SDG 8 in their domestic policies.

85 See n. 73–77 and accompanying text.
86 See n. 54.
87 See, for example, the EU-Korea dispute and expert panel report at n. 61.
88 See n. 63–66 and accompanying text.
89 See Beate Sjafjell et al., 'Securing the Future of European Business: SMART Reform Proposals', University of Oslo Faculty of Law Research Paper no. 2020-11, 2020, 52–54, papers.ssrn.com/sol3/papers.cfm?abstract_id=3595048&download=yes.
90 See UNCTAD, *Investment Policy Hub*, investmentpolicy.unctad.org/.
91 See United Nations Commission on International Trade Law (UNCITRAL), *Working Group III Investor-State Dispute Settlement Reform*, uncitral.un.org/en/working_groups/3/investor-state.
92 Cf. Alessandra Arcuri & Federica Violi, 'Human Rights and Investor-State Dispute Settlement: Changing (Almost) Everything, So That Everything Stays the Same?' (2019) 3 *Diritti umani e diritto internazionale* 579.

This may depend on whether they have the policy space to do so, which could be determined by the conditions for lending offered by the IFIs. Their enhanced lending, which was agreed to during the time of, and in response to, the COVID-19 crisis,[93] raises the spectre of a return to austerity policies in the years ahead, which were not kind to the protection of labour standards or a collective voice at work. Moreover, even when not engaged in lending conditionality, the mechanism for surveillance of macro-economic management by the IMF[94] and the precepts for 'Doing Business'[95] may be more conducive to economic objectives associated with employment and growth than the realization of 'decent work'.

8.4.4 *Transnational Private Actors: Employers, Corporations, Trade Unions*

The objective of 'responsive, inclusive, participatory and representative decision-making at all levels', set out in target 16.7, suggests that collective representation of management and labour may be significant for the 'multi-stakeholder partnerships' envisaged in target 17.16 and the 'civil society partnerships' mentioned in target 17.17. These objectives may take a variety of forms, one being a private-public partnership such as the Rana Plaza Arrangement, whereby the Bangladesh government has worked with domestic and transnational business representatives, trade unions, and other representatives of civil society to enable compensation for the victims.[96] Or they may take the form of international framework agreements or global framework agreements that seek to promote ILO norms, especially those relating to freedom of association, alongside sustainable development objectives.[97] Reingard Zimmer has also pointed to the emergence of hybrid models, such as the Bangladesh Accord for

93 IMF, *IMF Executive Board Approves Proposals to Enhance the Fund's Emergency Financing Toolkit to US$100 Billion*, 9 April 2020, www.imf.org/en/News/Articles/2020/04/09/pr20143-imf-executive-board-approves-proposals-enhance-emergency-financing-toolkit-us-billion; World Bank, *How the World Bank Group Is Helping Countries with COVID-19 (coronavirus)*, 26 May 2021, www.worldbank.org/en/news/factsheet/2020/02/11/how-the-world-bank-group-is-helping-countries-with-covid-19-coronavirus.

94 Franz Christian Ebert, 'International Financial Institutions' Approaches to Labour Law: The Case of the International Monetary Fund', in Adelle Blackett & Anne Trebilcock (eds.), *Research Handbook on Transnational Labour Law* (EE, 2015), 124.

95 For access to the World Bank's *Doing Business* reports, see www.doingbusiness.org/reports; for discussion, see Hannah Murphy, 'The World Bank and Core Labour Standards: Between Flexibility and Regulation' (2014) 22 *RIPE* 399.

96 *Understanding for a Practical Arrangement on Payments to the Victims of the Rana Plaza Accident and Their Families and Dependents for Their Losses*, 20 November 2013, ranaplaza-arrangement.org/MOU_Practical_Arrangement_FINAL-RanaPlaza-c34d165e591e40d43a603e95ac2b38e9.pdf. Discussed by Janelle M. Diller, 'The Role of the State in the Exercise of Transnational Public and Private Authority over Labour Standards' (2020) 17(1) *IOLR* 41.

97 See Tonia Novitz, 'Exploring Multi-Level Collective Bargaining: Transnational Legal Frameworks That Promote Worker Agency,' in Julia López López (ed.), *Collective Bargaining and Collective Action: Labour Agency and Governance in the 21st Century?* (Hart, 2019), 119.

Fire and Building Safety,[98] which involve not only global union federations and multinational corporations but also national-level trade union organizations and business associations.[99]

Ultimately, the success (or otherwise) of these international agreements and multilevel schemes seems likely to depend on genuine access to freedom of association, which, accordingly, as the special rapporteur suggests, must be regarded as implicit in target 16.10.[100] More importantly, the question arises of who will be entitled to exercise that freedom and how.[101] Ideally, this entitlement should also extend to the migrant and other precarious workers identified in targets 8.7 and 8.8. Thus, the recommendation by the Global Commission of a 'Universal Labour Guarantee'[102] is timely, as it would mean that everyone, regardless of their employment status, has rights not only to minimum pay, limited working time, and health and safety at work but also to freedom of association and collective bargaining.[103] It is therefore highly problematic that these core labour standards and human rights, which are recognized under international law, receive relatively little attention in SDGs 8, 16, and 17. It seems imperative that they be 'read in' to these goals and, more than this, that they be operationalized not only in the High Level Political Forum but also in the wider international institutional context.

8.5 CONCLUSIONS

This chapter has considered the ways in which SDG 8 serves both economic and social objectives, with particular reference to the principle of 'decent work' advocated by the ILO. It has highlighted the contradictions potentially arising in targets set out within the SDG and its connections and tensions with other SDGs. In so doing, it has suggested not only that certain SDG 8 targets and indicators, as well as other SDGs, may usefully supplement and enlarge the idea of 'decent work' but also

[98] Bangladesh Accord, n. 67.

[99] Reingard Zimmer, 'New Developments in the Area of International Framework Agreements: Better Implementation in the Bangladesh Accord and the Indonesian Freedom of Association Protocol' (2020) 17(1) *IOLR* 178; see also Beryl Ter Haar & Maarten Keune, 'One Step Forward or More Window-Dressing? A Legal Analysis of Recent CSR Initiatives in the Garment Industry in Bangladesh' (2014) 1 *International Journal of Comparative Labour Law and Industrial Relations* 14.

[100] See *Report of the Special Rapporteur*, n. 26.

[101] Valerio De Stefano, 'Non-standard Work and Limits on Freedom of Association: A Human Rights-based Approach' (2016) 46(2) *ILJ* 185.

[102] See Global Commission, n. 72.

[103] That view would also cohere with the views of the ILO's supervisory bodies. See Governing Body Committee on Freedom of Association, *Case 2888 (Poland)*, Report no. 363, March 2012, www.ilo.org/dyn/normlex/en/f?p=1000:50002:0::NO:50002:P50002_COMPLAINT_TEXT_ID:3057194; ILO Committee of Experts on the Application of Conventions and Recommendations, *Observation on Poland*, 2015, www.ilo.org/dyn/normlex/en/f?p=1000:13100:0::NO:13100:P13100_COMMENT_ID,P11110_COUNTRY_ID,P11110_COUNTRY_NAME,P11110_COMMENT_YEAR:3256747,102809,Poland,2015.

that there will still be scope for what the International Labour Office has described as 'trade-offs'. How these are to be navigated depends on the positioning of SDG 8 in international law and the international institutions that wield influence. If the ILO's notion of social justice and the findings of UN human rights institutions are to prevail, then an enhanced notion of 'decent work' could be realized, but other international economic norms and institutions pull in a potentially different direction. Of additional ongoing relevance will be the transnational representation of management and labour, which means that the protection of freedom of association and collective bargaining remain significant, despite their muted treatment in the SDGs. Moreover, extending the coverage of trade union freedoms to those in ever-increasing precarious work would seem to be consistent with the effective protection of decent work through SDG 8. It is the emphasis that SDG 8 places on inclusive protection of those engaged in all forms of work, including migrant and other precarious workers, that may have influence in the interpretation and application of existing international law and the policies pursued by international institutions. Access to collective voice for all these workers is vital to ensure that a sustainable rebalancing from the economic to the social operates in their interests.

9

SDG 9: Build Resilient Infrastructure, Promote Inclusive and Sustainable Industrialization and Foster Innovation

Andria Naudé Fourie

ABSTRACT

Sustainable Development Goal (SDG) 9, Industry, Innovation, and Infrastructure, aims to further economic advancement through investment in infrastructure, industrialization, and innovation. Implementing SDG 9, however, requires the realization of complex synergies and careful management of its potential disconnects. Positions about the role of international law in such matters differ significantly and depend on how SDG 9 and international law are conceptualized. Some, for instance, view international law's trade and investment treaties, complemented by the 'soft law' standards developed by international institutions, as instrumental in realizing SDG 9's synergies. Others view international law's environmental and human rights treaties, and the environmental, social, and governance (ESG) standards developed by international institutions, as paramount to manage the disconnects of SDG 9. The emergence of an 'ESG normative space' – involving state and non-state actors in norm creation, application, enforcement, and development – might provide an opportunity for unpacking and reconciling competing interests and conceptions.

KEYWORDS

SDG 9, infrastructure, industrialization, innovation, international law, environmental, social and governance (ESG) standards, multilateral development banks (MDBs), development finance operations, intellectual property protection, technology transfer, institutional standard setting, synergies, disconnects

9.1 INTRODUCTION

At first glance, Sustainable Development Goal (SDG) 9, Industry, Innovation, and Infrastructure, aims to solve an overarching problem – 'economic advancement', supporting 'human well-being'[1] – by tackling three intricately related issues: infrastructure, industrialization, and innovation. Building infrastructure facilitates industrialization and innovation, whereas innovation drives (further) investment in industrialization and infrastructure.[2] Infrastructure, industrialization and innovation, therefore, are instrumental in tackling problems addressed by other SDGs, including SDG 1, No Poverty; SDG 7, Affordable and Clean Energy; SDG 8, Decent Work and Economic Growth; and SDG 13, Climate Action. Upon closer scrutiny, focusing on the words preceding SDG 9's core areas – 'resilient', 'inclusive', 'sustainable', and 'foster' – SDG 9 illustrates a dual problem permeating the achievement of sustainable development in complex socio-environmental systems. That is, how to achieve

- the integration of economic, social, and environmental interests by realizing synergies or win-win outcomes – thus, involving positive or reinforcing feedback loops in which variables work with each other ('positive dynamics')[3] and
- the balance of economic, social, and environmental interests by managing disconnects, trade-offs, off-sets, mitigation, and remediation of adverse effects ('harm') – thus, involving negative or balancing feedback loops in which variables work against each other ('negative dynamics').[4]

The problem that SDG 9 seeks to address, in other words, is interwoven with the complex dynamics of entire systems of implementation.[5] Therefore, as this chapter suggests, SDG 9 and its relationship with international law need to be considered from this perspective.

[1] Target 9.1.

[2] Amar Bhattacharya, Jeremy Oppenheim, & Nicholas Stern, 'Driving Sustainable Development through Better Infrastructure: Key Elements of a Transformation Program', Brookings Global Working Paper no. 91, 2015, 1.

[3] That is, 'if the cause *increases*, the effect *increases above what it would otherwise have been*, and if the cause *decreases*, the effect *decreases below what it would otherwise have been*.' See J.D. Sterman, *Business Dynamics: Systems Thinking and Modeling for a Complex World* (Irwin McGraw-Hill, 2000), 138–39 (emphasis in original).

[4] That is, 'if the cause *increases*, the effect *decreases below what it would otherwise have been*, and if the cause *decreases*, the effect *increases above what it would otherwise have been*.' *Id.*

[5] Mark Stafford-Smith et al., 'Integration: The Key to Implementing the Sustainable Development Goals' (2017) 23 *Sustainable Science* 911, 917 (commenting that the 'first wave' of research emphasized 'integration among the substantive goals and targets'; however, we need intensified focus on 'obtaining a systems view and integrated approach to the means of implementation, scattered in an imbalanced way . . . through all the goals and specifically in Goal 17').

The implementation systems involved in realizing SDG 9 are typically transnational. They cut across local, national, and international (global) levels of governance and involve state and non-state actors. They intersect with domestic, regional, and international legal orders and engage with norms covering the entire spectrum – from 'legal' to 'non-legal' and everything 'in-between'.[6] Situating international law within dynamic transnational 'regulatory governance' systems has long been challenging.[7] The relationship between SDG 9 and international law provides another example of – and, perhaps, another opportunity for deepening insights into – how international law is changing and how it is changing our 'kaleidoscopic world'.[8]

This chapter aims to provide an overview of the wide range of issues covered by the three core areas of SDG 9, but certain limitations in scope are unavoidable. Concerning innovation, the chapter highlights intellectual property protection (IPP) and technology transfer (TT). Concerning infrastructure and industrialization, a particular implementation system is emphasized – namely, the development/investment project, which is defined here as a distinct initiative (or programme of initiatives) aimed at building infrastructure or effectuating industrialization. Such projects require capital investment, which might be sourced from private or public financiers. This chapter focuses on infrastructure/industrialization projects (co-)financed by multilateral development banks (MDBs),[9] involving public or private sector actors acting as MDB borrowers (clients)[10] and project sponsors.[11] The involvement of MDBs, which are recognized subjects of international law, provides a definite link with the international legal order, but there is another reason for this focus: MDB development financing operations[12] have amassed a significant body of knowledge about the project as implementation system, including its positive and

6 Matthias Goldmann, 'Inside Relative Normativity: From Sources to Standard Instruments for the Exercise of International Public Authority', in Armin von Bogdandy et al. (eds.), *The Exercise of Public Authority by International Institutions: Advancing International Institutional Law* (Springer, 2010), 661; Jutta Brunnée & Stephen J. Toope, *Legitimacy and Legality in International Law: An Interactional Account* (Cambridge University Press, 2010), 20–34.

7 See, e.g., Benedict Kingsbury, 'Global Administrative Law in the Institutional Practice of Global Regulatory Governance', in *The World Bank Legal Review*, vol. 3 (World Bank, 2012), 3; Nico Krisch, *Beyond Constitutionalism: The Pluralist Structure of Postnational Law* (Oxford University Press, 2010).

8 Edith Brown Weiss, 'On Being Accountable in a Kaleidoscopic World' (2010) 104 *American Society of International Law Proceedings* 477.

9 International organizations, founded by member states on the basis of a constitutive treaty – for example, International Development Association and International Bank for Reconstruction and Development (jointly, known as the World Bank), International Finance Corporation (IFC) IFC, Multilateral Investment Guarantee Agency (MIGA) and MDBs.

10 Entity with whom the MDB enters into a financing agreement.

11 Entity charged with designing and implementing projects. Note that project sponsors can also be co-financiers.

12 That is, MDB management and staff, policies, standards, procedures and mechanisms involved in project identification, design, appraisal, financing, implementation and closure. See, e.g., World Bank, *World Bank Project Cycle*, www.worldbank.org/en/projects-operations/products-and-services/brief/projectcycle.

negative dynamics.[13] This focus necessarily excludes projects financed solely through private sector (commercial) or state funds (for example, China's Belt and Road Initiative [BRI]). That said, projects are increasingly funded by multiple financiers, including MDBs, national development finance institutions (DFIs), and commercial banks. Indeed, the same can be said for many BRI projects.[14]

Section 9.2 of this chapter elaborates on the content of SDG 9 and explores its relationships with other SDGs. Section 9.3 analyzes the complex relationship of SDG 9 with specific areas of international law, notably international economic law, international human rights and labour law, international environmental law, and international institutional law. Section 4 considers the institutional context of SDG 9, emphasizing the role of institutional standard setting. Section 9.5 concludes.

9.2 THE CONTENT OF SDG 9 IN THE CONTEXT OF THE OTHER SDGS

The language of SDG 9, and Agenda 2030 in general, highlights positive dynamics.[15] Yet it neither reflects the complexities involved in triggering reinforcing feedback loops nor recognizes that core assumptions underlying SDG 9's professed synergies might be questionable. Aside from the inclusion of modifiers like 'resilient', 'inclusive', and 'sustainable', SDG 9 does not recognize the potential for any disconnects, although it obviously 'sits uneasily against' the environmental SDGs – including SDG 6, Clean Water and Sanitation; SDG 13, Climate Action; SDG 14, Life below Water; and SDG 15, Life on Land – as well as SDG 12, Responsible Consumption and Production.[16] Consequently, SDG 9 neither acknowledges the challenges involved in managing disconnects nor indicates how this ought to be achieved.[17] SDG 17, Partnerships for the Goals, is not much help either as it is

[13] E.g., Ibrahim Shihata, *The World Bank Inspection Panel: In Practice*, 2nd ed. (Oxford University Press, 2000), 1–7; Andria Naudé Fourie, *World Bank Accountability: In Theory and in Practice* (Eleven International, 2016); Daniel D. Bradlow & David B. Hunter (eds.), *International Financial Institutions and International Law* (Wolters Kluwer, 2010); Kinnari I. Bhatt, *Concessionaires, Financiers and Communities: Implementing Indigenous Peoples' Rights to Land in Transnational Development Projects* (Cambridge University Press, 2020). Note that much of this knowledge has been derived from the practice of institutional IAMs. See, e.g., Owen McIntyre & Suresh Nanwani (eds.), *The Practice of Independent Accountability Mechanisms (IAMs): Towards Good Governance in Development Finance* (Brill Nijhoff, 2020).

[14] Suresh Nanwani, 'The Belt and Road Initiative: An Interface with Multilateral Developments on International Cooperation and Global Governance', in Maria A. Carrai, Jean-Christophe Defraigne & Jan Wouters (eds.), *The Belt and Road Initiative and Global Governance* (EE, 2020), 96.

[15] *Transforming Our World: The 2030 Agenda for Sustainable Development*, UN Doc. A/Res/70/1, 25 September 2015, preamble, paras. 13, 55.

[16] Duncan French & Louis Kotzé, 'Introduction', in Duncan French & Louis Kotzé (eds.), *Sustainable Development Goals: Law, Theory and Implementation* (EE, 2018), 1, 2.

[17] *Id.*, 1.

essentially silent 'about interlinkages and interdependencies among goals'.[18] Like SDG 17, therefore, SDG 9 'leaves open the possibility of perverse outcomes'.[19]

9.2.1 *Foster Innovation*

There is growing recognition that innovation, broadly defined as the 'ability of actors to search, discover and apply technological knowhow into new products and processes,' is not limited to the 'activities of the firm' but, rather, depends on the complex 'interaction between economic and non-economic actors' as well as institutions and policies to 'facilitate these interactions'.[20] Yet how such 'interdependencies' are to be managed, in varying contexts, remains contentious.[21] For example, different research areas tend to emphasize the importance of different variables, such as the robustness of national innovation strategies and supporting policies;[22] national regulatory capability in key areas;[23] the availability of venture capital;[24] the design quality of 'systems of work' and 'production processes';[25] the degree of 'interoperability';[26] and participatory processes at 'grassroots' level.[27]

Furthermore, a wide range of 'outcomes' might be classified as 'innovations', including those related to 'products (goods and services), processes, marketing-methods, organizational arrangements, and management of external relations'.[28] Innovations also cover the full spectrum – from 'incremental' to 'highly novel'.[29] Some states might focus on 'incremental forms of innovation', whereas others might

[18] Stafford-Smith et al., n. 5, 912.

[19] *Id.*

[20] Padmashree Gehl Sampath & Pedro Roffe, 'Unpacking the International Technology Transfer Debate: Fifty Years and Beyond', International Centre for Trade and Sustainable Development (ICTSD) Programme on Innovation, Technology and Intellectual Property Working Paper no. 36, 2012, 19.

[21] *Id.*

[22] Nicholas A. Ashford & Ralph P. Hall, 'The Importance of Regulation-Induced Innovation for Sustainable Development' (2011) 3(1) *Sustainability* 270.

[23] Kassu Jilcha & Daniel Kitaw, 'Industrial Occupational Safety and Health Innovation for Sustainable Development' (2017) 20 *Engineering Science and Technology* 372.

[24] Ana Paula Faria & Natalia Barbosa, 'Does Venture Capital Really Foster Innovation?' (2014) 122 (2) *Economic Letters* 129.

[25] P. Béguin et al., 'Activity at Work, Innovation and Sustainable Development' (2012) 41(1) *Work* 89.

[26] Urs Gasser & John Palfrey, 'Fostering Innovation and Trade in the Global Information Society: The Different Facets and Roles of Interoperability', in Mira Burri & Thomas Cottier (eds.), *Trade Governance in the Digital Age* (Cambridge University Press, 2012), 123.

[27] Boru Douthwaite et al., 'Understanding How Participatory Approaches Foster Innovation' (2009) 7(1) *International Journal of Agricultural Sustainability* 42.

[28] David Ockwell & Rob Byrne, 'Improving Technology Transfer through National Systems of Innovation: Climate Relevant Innovation-System Builders (CRIBs)' (2016) 16(7) *Climate Policy* 836, 836–38.

[29] *Id.*, 838.

prioritize 'adaptive innovation'.[30] The innovation-related targets of SDG 9 make only limited reference to such matters, underscoring, instead, the importance of enhancing research and development (R&D) through investment.[31] Developing countries, moreover, are encouraged to 'ensur[e] a conducive policy environment', especially in areas related to 'industrial diversification and value addition to commodities'.[32] Finally, as in other SDGs, technology – including information and communications technology – is highlighted as a key driver of innovation and sustainability.[33]

Significantly, SDG 9 is silent on two issues featuring prominently in innovation discourse: IPP and TT.[34] Both issues, which are addressed by international law, are critical for an area such as biotechnology – which is, in turn, relevant for SDG 2, Zero Hunger; SDG 3, Good Health and Well-being; SDG 12, Responsible Consumption and Production; and SDG 15, Life on Land,[35] as well as for SDG 7, Affordable and Clean Energy; SDG 11, Sustainable Cities and Communities;[36] and SDG 13, Climate Action.[37] There are several contentions surrounding IPP and TT, including

- whether, or to which extent, IPP stimulates R&D and therefore fosters innovation, including questions about the validity of empirical evidence (used to support opposing positions) and the effectiveness and legitimacy of transplanting specific national IPP regulatory models to the international level[38]
- whether, or to what extent, IPP should be limited in specific areas or balanced against public interests (for example, in areas like public health, energy, and climate change) and how such balance should be achieved[39]

[30] *Id.*
[31] Target 9.5.
[32] Target 9.b.
[33] E.g., targets 8.2, 8.3, 17.6–8; see also targets 9.4, 9.5, 9.b, 9.c.
[34] Note that target 17.7 encourages 'development, transfer, dissemination and diffusion of environmentally sound technologies to developing countries' but only states that it should occur 'on favourable terms, including on concessional and preferential terms, as mutually agreed.'
[35] Yvonne Lokko et al., 'Biotechnology and the Bioeconomy: Towards Inclusive and Sustainable Industrial Development' (2018) 40 *New Biotechnology* 5.
[36] Ji Han et al., 'Innovation for Sustainability: Toward a Sustainable Urban Future in Industrialized Cities' (2017) 7(1) *Sustainable Science* 91.
[37] Ockwell & Byrne, n. 28.
[38] Claude Henry & Joseph E. Stiglitz, 'Intellectual Property, Dissemination of Innovation and Sustainable Development' (2010) 1(3) *Global Policy* 237; David G. Ockwell et al., 'Intellectual Property Rights and Low Carbon Technology Transfer: Conflicting Discourses of Diffusion and Development' (2010) 20(4) *Global Environmental Change* 729, 733.
[39] Ockwell et al., n. 38, 730.

- whether, or under which circumstances, IPP facilitates TT, including questions about the validity of empirical evidence (used to support opposing positions)[40]
- what TT entails and how it is to be achieved[41]
- whether 'international negotiations' involving TT accurately reflect 'country-level technological needs' and 'growing insights on how technological change takes place'[42] and
- whether (or to what extent) TT can be regulated, especially through international law.[43]

These are long-standing debates and positions are deeply entrenched, reflecting competing state interests. Since the 1970s, especially, matters involving TT and IPP have been positioned as differences between the 'developed North' and the 'developing (global) South'.[44] But positions are also influenced by competing conceptions about key concepts (for example, 'property' and 'property rights protection')[45] and key processes (for example, 'R&D investment' and 'technology diffusion').[46] Both factors adversely impact the effectiveness of international legal regimes regulating TT and IPP, including the multilateral negotiations surrounding them.[47]

9.2.2 *Build Infrastructure and Promote Industrialization*

SDG 9 emphasizes the need for constructing 'affordable' national, 'regional and transborder' infrastructure that provides 'equitable access for all'.[48] SDG 9 calls for the promotion of 'small-scale industrial and other enterprises', particularly in developing countries, by enhancing access to 'financial services, including affordable credit'.[49] Because SDG 9 positions infrastructure and industrialization as driving 'economic development', 'human well-being', and 'employment',[50] the realization of SDG 9 is expected to facilitate the realization of other SDGs,

40 Krishna Ravi Srinivas, 'Climate Change, Technology Transfer and Intellectual Property Rights: A Modest Exercise in Thinking Outside the Box', in Abbe E.L. Brown (ed.), *Environmental Technologies, Intellectual Property and Climate Change: Accessing, Obtaining and Protecting* (EE, 2013), 152; Chen Zhou, 'Can Intellectual Property Rights within Climate Technology Transfer Work for the UNFCCC and the Paris Agreement?' (2019) 9 *International Environmental Agreements: Politics, Law and Economics* 107.

41 Arnold Reisman, 'Transfer of Technologies: A Cross-Disciplinary Taxonomy' (2005) 33 *Omega* 189.

42 Gehl Sampath & Roffe, n. 20, 2.

43 *Id.*

44 Ockwell et al., n. 38.

45 *Id.*

46 *Id.*

47 *Id.*

48 Target 9.1.

49 Target 9.2.

50 Targets 9.1, 9.2.

including SDG 1, No Poverty; SDG 8, Decent Work and Economic Growth; and, because of the 'inclusivity' and 'equity' facets of SDG 9, also SDG 5, Gender Equality; SDG 10, Reduced Inequalities; and SDG 16, Peace, Justice, and Strong Institutions.

Yet pertinent questions remain about the assumptions underlying purported positive relationships and what it 'really takes' to realize these synergies, including

- whether, or the circumstances under which, enhanced infrastructure reduces poverty (as opposed to merely stimulating economic growth)[51] and
- whether, or the circumstances under which, foreign direct investment in infrastructure and industrialization projects translates to sustainable development, including local employment.[52]

A related matter concerns the degree to which citizens agree with their government's development model – as reflected, for instance, in the state's policies and investment treaties. Many communities reject arguments that certain economic activities can ever be done sustainably, the extractive industries providing a prominent example.[53] Many oppose (additional) investments because they are still dealing with the social and environmental fall-out of previous ones,[54] or they question the ability of investment treaties and contracts to achieve a fair balance between public and private (commercial) interests.[55] The degree of 'broad community support' for specific projects, furthermore, is influenced by local-level access to information, public participation in decision-making and access to justice, especially for Indigenous peoples and other vulnerable groups – issues, in other words, that are greatly dependent on the realization of SDGs 5, 10, and 16.[56]

51 Varun Chotia & N.V.M. Rao, 'Investigating the Interlinkages between Infrastructure Development, Poverty and Rural–Urban Income Inequality: Evidence from BRICS Nations' (2017) 34(4) *Studies in Economics and Finance* 466. On questions about correlations between poverty reduction and economic growth, see, e.g., John A. Donaldson, 'Growth Is Good for Whom, When, How? Economic Growth and Poverty Reduction in Exceptional Cases' (2008) 36(11) *World Development* 2127.

52 Viktoria Aust, Ana Isabel Morais, & Inês Pinto, 'How Does Foreign Direct Investment Contribute to Sustainable Development Goals? Evidence from African Countries' (2020) 245 (1) *Journal of Cleaner Production* 118823.

53 IFC/MIGA Compliance Advisor Ombudsman (CAO), *Extracting Sustainable Advantage? A Review of How Sustainability Issues Have been Dealt with in Recent IFC & MIGA Extractive Industries Projects*, 2003, 1, www.cao-ombudsman.org/howwework/advisor/index.html; Samantha Balaton-Chrimes & Fiona Haines, 'The Depoliticisation of Accountability Processes for Land-Based Grievances, and the IFC CAO' (2015) 6(4) *Global Policy* 446.

54 E.g., IFC/MIGA CAO, *Chile: Empresa Electrica Pangue S.A.-02/Upper Bio Bio Watershed*, 2002 (access CAO cases at www.cao-ombudsman.org/cases/).

55 Alessandra Arcuri & Francesco Montanaro, 'Justice for All? Protecting the Public Interest in Investment Treaties' (2018) 59(8) *Boston College Law Review* 2791.

56 Bhatt, n. 13. See, e.g., IFC, *Performance Standard 1 (Assessment and Management of Environmental and Social Risks and Impacts)*, www.ifc.org/ps1.

Furthermore, the infrastructure and industrialization ambitions of SDG 9 can potentially have a negative impact on the realization of other SDGs, including those goals that SDG 9 purportedly strengthens. For example, an infrastructure/industrialization project can aggravate poverty when some livelihoods are adversely affected but not restored.[57] Projects can trigger increased HIV-infection rates in surrounding communities due to an influx of construction workers;[58] result in human rights abuses perpetrated against communities living in the project area;[59] or cause physical and economic harm when occupational health and safety risks materialize and workers are not properly compensated.[60] Projects can adversely affect air quality, marine biodiversity[61] and the conservation of critical habitats,[62] or exacerbate coastal erosion, thereby intensifying climate change risks and affecting the livelihoods of coastal communities.[63]

Consequently, the due diligence with which infrastructure / industrialization projects are designed, appraised, financed, and implemented is paramount. Such due diligence emphatically includes the degree to which – and the effectiveness with which – projects, throughout the project cycle

- identify environmental, social, and governance (ESG) risks[64] and
- internalize those risks ('costs') by developing and executing plans to avoid, mitigate and remedy them (ESG risk management).[65]

Spearheaded by the World Bank, MDBs have been developing ESG risk management frameworks since the 1980s, aimed at providing guidance to their staff and

[57] E.g., World Bank Inspection Panel (WB IP), *India: Mumbai Road Transport Project*, 2004 (access WB IP cases at inspectionpanel.org/panel-cases).

[58] E.g., WB IP, *Chad-Cameroon: Petroleum Development & Pipeline*, 2001.

[59] E.g., WB IP, *Democratic Republic of Congo: High-Priority Roads Reopening and Maintenance Project*, 2017.

[60] IFC/MIGA CAO & African Development Bank Independent Review Mechanism (AfDB IRM), *Uganda: Bujagali Energy-04 & 06*, 2011 (access AfDB IRM cases at www.afdb.org/en/independent-review-mechanism-irm).

[61] IFC/MIGA CAO & Asian Development Bank Accountability Mechanism (ADB AM), *India: Tata Ultra Mega-01/Mundra and Anjar*, 2011 (access ADB AM cases at www.adb.org/who-we-are/accountability-mechanism/main).

[62] IFC/MIGA CAO, *Colombia: Eco Oro-01/Bucaramanga*, 2012; IFC/MIGA CAO, *Bolivia: Comsur V-01/Bosque Chiquitano*, 2003.

[63] IFC/MIGA CAO & Netherlands Entrepreneurial Development Bank (FMO) Independent Complaints Mechanism (ICM), *Togo: Togo LCT-01/Lomé*, 2015 (access FMO ICM cases at www.fmo.nl/independent-complaints-mechanism).

[64] 'Governance' is used here in a broad sense (for example, including matters of informed participation in decision-making) – thus, including but not limited to 'corporate governance', which is how ESG is typically understood in investment/sustainable finance communities. See, e.g., Karen Wendt (ed.), *Responsible Investment Banking: Risk Management Frameworks Sustainable Financial Innovation and Softlaw Standards* (Springer, 2015).

[65] See, e.g., IFC, n. 56; Diane Desierto, 'Due Diligence in World Bank Project Financing', in Heike Kriege, Anne Peters & Leonhard Kreuzer (eds.), *Due Diligence in the International Legal Order* (Oxford University Press, 2020), 331.

their public and private sector clients.[66] Moreover, MDBs' ESG risk management approach is progressively influencing the approach of national DFIs[67] and commercial financiers.[68] While the idea of ESG risk management remains a work in progress, it nevertheless represents our best attempts at balancing environmental, social, and economic interests and, therefore, addressing the disconnects of SDG 9. The silence of SDG 9 on these matters constitutes a missed opportunity. It is another matter altogether, however, to consider the role of international law in realizing the synergies of SDG 9 and managing its disconnects in a dynamically complex transnational regulatory governance system.

9.3 POSITIONING SDG 9 IN INTERNATIONAL LAW

SDG 9 does not have a clear relationship with a single area of international law, which is not only because of the wide range of issues that SDG 9 covers but also because of the transnational implementation systems involved in its realization. Viewed from the perspective of the implementation systems highlighted in this chapter, SDG 9 intersects with

- international economic law (international trade and investment law and international development law, referring to the 'rights and obligations of all actors involved in the development process')[69]
- international environmental law;
- international human rights and labour law (including the business and human rights field); and
- international institutional law (notably, institutional rule making and the international legal responsibility of international organizations).

[66] Laurence Boisson de Chazournes, 'Policy Guidance and Compliance: The World Bank Operational Standards', in Dinah Shelton (ed.), *Commitment and Compliance* (Oxford University Press, 2000), 281; David Freestone, *The World Bank and Sustainable Development* (Martinus Nijhoff, 2013), 9–62. See, e.g., IFC, *Sustainability Framework*, www.ifc.org/sustainabilityframework.

[67] See, e.g., Japan International Coordination Agency, *Environmental and Social Considerations*, www.jica.go.jp/english/our_work/social_environmental/index.html.

[68] Wendt, n. 64; see, e.g., Goldman Sachs, *Environment Policy Framework*, www.goldmansachs.com/s/environmental-policy-framework/index.html#environmentalSocialRiskManagement. It remains to be seen whether commercial financiers have fully grasped the implications of 'embracing ESG'; see Daniel D. Bradlow & Andria Naudé Fourie, 'Financing for Sustainable Development in 2019: Environmental, Social and Governance Considerations 'Go Mainstream' and Its Implications', in Lisa E. Sachs, Lise J. Johnson & Jesse Coleman (eds.), *Yearbook on International Investment Law & Policy (2019)* (Oxford University Press, 2021), 27.

[69] Daniel D. Bradlow, 'Differing Conceptions of Development and the Content of International Development Law' (2005) 21(47) *South African Journal of Human Rights* 1, 1.

9.3.1 *Dominance of Treaty Law*

In most of these areas, treaties constitute the bulk of 'hard' law. The dominance of treaty law creates different challenges for international law and its ability to help realize the synergies of SDG 9 and manage its disconnects. For innovation, which is discussed here in terms of TT and IPP arrangements in treaty regimes, the challenges lie with the adequacy of existing provisions and – given the centrality of state consent in these regimes – the difficulty of effectuating reforms.[70] For infrastructure and industrialization, which are discussed here in terms of ESG risk management in MDB-financed infrastructure/industrialization projects, the challenges lie with the prominent role played by non-state actors. For instance, it remains debatable if, or to what extent, international organizations such as MDBs have international legal obligations, especially in the areas of international human rights and environmental law.[71] And even if the primary rules pertaining to international organizations were clear, questions remain about the secondary rules, including the operational viability of the regime proposed in the Articles on the Responsibility of International Organizations, especially given MDBs' increasingly complex cooperation and co-financing arrangements, which trigger additional questions on 'shared responsibility'[72] and the normative content of international organizations' due diligence obligations under international law.[73]

Another problem concerns the status of MDBs' ESG risk management frameworks within international law. Various arguments have been made that at least some of the standards contained therein should be categorized as international law, but the status of international 'soft' or 'informal' law remains contentious.[74] Furthermore, problems arise when ESG risk management frameworks are applied and give rise to conflicting interpretations – by MDBs, their clients and project-affected people relying on the protection provided by these frameworks. Conflicts have arisen, for instance, on whether a project sufficiently considered alternative designs that would mitigate environmental and/or social impacts[75] if consultation

70 Ockwell et al., n. 38.

71 Daniel D. Bradlow & David B. Hunter, 'Introduction', in Daniel D. Bradlow & David B. Hunter (eds.), *International Financial Institutions & International Law* (Springer, 2010), 1.

72 International Law Commission, *Articles on the Responsibility of International Organizations, with Commentaries*, Doc. A/66/10, 2011; Antonella Angelini, 'A Trouble Shared Is a Trouble Halved: How the Structure of Cooperation Matters for the Engagement of Responsibility in the World Bank Partnership Programmes' (2016) 13 *International Organizations Law Review* 171; Olufemi Amao, 'Multinational Corporations', in André Nollkaemper & Ilias Plakokefalos (eds.), *The Practice of Shared Responsibility in International Law* (Cambridge University Press, 2017), 799.

73 International Law Association, *Study Group on Due Diligence in International Law (2012–16)*, www.ila-hq.org/index.php/study-groups; Desierto, n. 65.

74 Bradlow & Hunter, n. 13; Naudé Fourie, n. 13; Boisson de Chazournes, n. 66; see also Samantha Besson & Jean D'Aspremont, *The Oxford Handbook on the Sources of International Law* (Oxford University Press, 2017).

75 E.g., WB IP, *Nigeria/Ghana: West African Gas Pipeline*, 2006.

activities with Indigenous peoples constituted 'free, prior, informed consent';[76] or whether an MDB's supervision activities were 'commensurate to risk'.[77]

International law does not provide judicial fora in which such problems can be addressed. Exceptions notwithstanding, international organizations (and other non-state actors) do not have legal standing before international courts, whereas international organizations continue to enjoy immunity before domestic courts – even as some cracks in that armour seem to be appearing.[78] MDBs have attempted to address some of these problems by establishing 'citizen-driven', independent accountability mechanisms (IAMs) as part of their ESG risk management frameworks.[79] The efficacy of IAMs, however, has become another matter of long-standing debate, especially the extent to which IAM procedures result in remedial actions.[80]

9.3.2 *Fragmentation across Core Areas of SDG 9*

The familiar problem of international law's fragmentation also manifests here, although the core areas of SDG 9 highlight different facets thereof. Regarding innovation, the problem of fragmentation manifests itself in treaty regimes providing for TT and IPP as questions about the 'effect of overlapping mandates or competing legal regimes'[81] or the efficacy with which the regime incorporates (or balances) different interests, given its primary specialization.[82] The ability of the 1994 Agreement on Trade-Related Aspects of Intellectual Property Rights (TRIPS Agreement) to balance the IPP of pharmaceutical companies with public health interests of developing member states combatting diseases such as HIV-AIDS serves as a prominent example.[83] The World Trade Organization (WTO) has taken steps to strengthen flexibility measures aimed at balancing IPP with public interests, but

76 E.g., IFC/MIGA CAO, *Guatemala: Marlin-01/Sipacapa*, 2005.

77 E.g., IFC/MIGA CAO, *Mozambique: Mozal-01/Matola and Maputo*, 2010.

78 *Jam et al. v. International Finance Corp.*, 17 US 1001 (2019); see Diane Desierto, 'SCOTUS Decision in *Jam et al v. International Finance Corporation* (IFC) Denies Absolute Immunity to IFC … with Caveats', *EJIL: Talk!*, 28 February 2019, www.ejiltalk.org/scotus-decision-in-jam-et-al-v-international-finance-corporation-ifc-denies-absolute-immunity-to-ifc-with-caveats/.

79 McIntyre & Nanwani, n. 13.

80 SOMO (Centre for Research on Multinational Corporations), *Glass Half Full? The State of Accountability in Development Finance*, 2016, www.somo.nl/glass-half-full-2/.

81 Edward Kwawka, 'Some Comments on Rule-making at the World Intellectual Property Organization' (2002) 12 *Duke Journal of Comparative and International Law* 179, 184–87 (on competition between WIPO and the WTO).

82 Phillipe Cullet, 'Human Rights and Intellectual Property Protection in the TRIPS Era' (2007) 29(2) *Human Rights Quarterly* 403.

83 TRIPS Agreement, arts. 7, 8; Holger P. Hestermeyer, *Human Rights and the WTO: The Case of Patents and Access to Medicines* (Oxford University Press, 2007).

questions remain about their effectiveness[84] – questions, moreover, that have rapidly regained prominence in the context of equitable access to COVID-19 vaccines.[85]

Regarding infrastructure and industrialization, MDBs' ESG risk management frameworks seem to present an opportunity to reintegrate what has been fragmented. After all, these frameworks bring many areas of international law together,[86] even as criticisms remain about the extent to which they reference and reflect treaty law.[87] That said, the problem of fragmentation manifests itself here in distinctions drawn between different obligations (of MDBs, their clients, project sponsors, co-financiers, home/host states) and in the wide degree of 'managerial discretion' or 'professional leeway' provided for in ESG risk management frameworks.[88] While this might allow for reasonable differentiation among project contexts, it also results in fragmented application and enforcement.

The remainder of this section highlights two examples – TT provisions in treaty regimes and the international human rights obligations of MDBs and borrowers – that illustrate the problems presented in Sections 9.3.1 and 9.3.2.

9.3.3 *TT Provisions in Treaty Regimes*

Between 1970 and 1984, the United Nations Conference on Trade and Development (UNCTAD) spearheaded various initiatives aimed at placing TT on the international agenda. Notably, negotiations on 'an international code of conduct on transfer of technology' (TT Code) that would set 'universally acceptable norms and standards governing the exchange of technology among all countries' but especially between 'developed and developing countries'.[89] However, almost ten years of negotiations failed to culminate in a binding agreement.[90] Several reasons have been offered to explain this failure. Particularly, TT was positioned predominantly as a means of economic advancement for developing countries. Consequently, 'negotiations were

84 Duncan Matthews, 'TRIPS Flexibilities and Access to Medicines in Developing Countries: The Problem with Technical Assistance and Free Trade Agreements' (2005) 22 *European Intellectual Property Review* 420.

85 Lawrence O. Gostin, Safura Abdool Karim & Benjamin Mason Meier, 'Facilitating Access to a COVID-19 Vaccine through Global Health Law' (2020) *Journal of Law, Medicine and Ethics* 622.

86 E.g., environmental assessment, biodiversity, cultural heritage, Indigenous peoples, community health and safety, labour, and involuntary resettlement. See, e.g., *IFC Performance Standards*, www.ifc.org/performancestandards.

87 Daniel D. Bradlow & Andria Naudé Fourie, 'The Operational Policies of the World Bank, International Finance Corporation: Creating Law-Making and Law-Governed Institutions?' (2013) 10 *International Organizations Law Review* 3.

88 Bradlow & Naudé Fourie, n. 87; Asmita Kabra, 'Displacement, Resettlement, and Livelihood Restoration: Safeguard Standards in Practice' (2018) 28(2) *Development in Practice* 269; Naudé Fourie, n. 13, 192–203.

89 Surendra Patel, 'Technology in UNCTAD: 1970 to 1984' (1984) 15(3) *IDS Bulletin* 63.

90 Gehl Sampath & Roffe, n. 20, 17.

structured on a strict North-South divide with clear scepticism prevailing in major technology producing countries' about the 'consequences of such endeavour' and 'the usefulness of such an instrument'.[91] The TT Code also attempted to address core questions surrounding TT – notably, its meaning, means of implementation, and relationship with IPP. This, arguably, was a reasonable approach. But, because these questions were so central to the notion of TT, failure to reach consensus on them proved fatal for the negotiation process.[92]

The influence of UNCTAD's efforts continue – as reflected, for example, in the large number of treaties including TT provisions.[93] Nevertheless, 'the issues raised by the Code and the unresolved questions that led to its collapse' continue to echo throughout 'subsequent international negotiations' involving TT.[94] For example, some treaties provide a definition of technology but do not attempt to define TT.[95] Most treaties with TT provisions 'contain only "best efforts" commitments, rather than mandatory rules'.[96] And where they are phrased more clearly as 'mandatory rules', state parties are allowed considerable flexibility in determining the means of implementation.[97]

Likewise, the relationship between IPP and TT remains contentious. Article 16 of the 1992 Convention on Biological Diversity (CBD), for instance, recognizes that 'patents and other intellectual property rights may have an influence on the implementation of this Convention', and it aims to achieve a balance by obligating parties to 'cooperate in this regard' – albeit 'subject to national legislation and international law' – 'to ensure that such rights are supportive of and do not run counter to [the convention's] objectives'.[98] The inclusion of TT obligations in the TRIPS Agreement provide another example.[99] Yet questions remain whether this constitutes a feasible approach that would integrate the competing notions of TT with IPP or whether the inclusion of TT provisions was a mere by-product of negotiation between developed countries advocating for strengthening IPP and developing countries advocating for the inclusion of TT obligations. Indeed, the inclusion of

91 *Id.*, 15.
92 *Id.*, 17.
93 In 2004, more than '80 international instruments and numerous subregional and bilateral agreements' contained such provisions. UNCTAD, *Compendium of International Arrangements on Transfer of Technology*, Doc. UNCTAD/ITE/IPC/Misc.5, 2004, iii, unctad.org/en/Docs/psiteipcm5.en.pdf.
94 Gehl Sampath & Roffe, n. 20, 15.
95 *Id.*, vi–vii. E.g., CBD, art. 16(1); 2014 Nagoya Protocol on Access to Genetic Resources and the Fair and Equitable Sharing of Benefits Arising from Their Utilization, art. 23.
96 UNCTAD, n. 93, v. E.g., 2005 United Nations Scientific, Education, and Cultural Organization (UNESCO) Universal Declaration on Bioethics and Human Rights, arts. 14, 15, 24.
97 *UNCTAD*, n.93, viii. E.g., TRIPS Agreement, art. 66.2.
98 CBD, art. 16(5).
99 TRIPS Agreement, Annex, arts. 7, 66(2).

TT provisions guaranteed developing countries' support for adopting the TRIPS Agreement.[100]

Subsequent practice has left developing countries mostly disillusioned with how this 'grand bargain' has played out.[101] Although article 66(2) of the TRIPS Agreement is relatively specific in setting out 'the instrumentalities to be used to facilitate the transfer of technology' to least developed countries, implementation of this provision has proven to be problematic.[102] To date, moreover, the WTO's dispute resolution mechanism has played no role in enforcing TT-related provisions,[103] whereas a 'myriad of bilateral and regional trade agreements' contain provisions that further strengthen IPP ('TRIPS plus').[104]

In the 1992 United Nations Framework Convention on Climate Change (UNFCCC), TT is widely regarded as one of its 'pillars'.[105] Article 4(5), for example, obligates developed country parties to 'take all practicable steps to promote, facilitate and finance, as appropriate, the transfer of, or access to environmentally sound technologies and knowhow to other Parties', especially to 'developing country parties'. Indeed, article 4(7) stipulates that the 'effective implementation' of developed countries' commitments regarding climate finance and TT are prerequisites for developing countries meeting their obligations under the UNFCCC.

Significantly, the UNFCCC does not position TT as a means to economic advancement for developing countries but, rather, as an essential element in the attainment of a global common objective: climate change action. Furthermore, subsequent UNFCCC Conferences of the Parties (COPs) have highlighted an inherent tension: technology is both an essential cause of climate change and an essential component of addressing its effects.[106]

As for realizing TT and addressing the tension between TT and IPP, the UNFCCC regime's record is mixed. Although TT features prominently in the Clean Development Mechanism (CDM), set out in the 1997 Kyoto Protocol,[107]

[100] Gehl Sampath & Roffe, n. 20, 23.

[101] *Id.*, 24–26; Suerie Moon, 'Does TRIPS Art. 66.2 Encourage Technology Transfer to LDCs? An Analysis of Country Submissions to the TRIPS Council (1999–2007)', UNCTAD – ICTSD Project on IPRs and Sustainable Development Policy Brief no. 2, 2008.

[102] Gehl Sampath & Roffe, n. 20, 26.

[103] At point of writing, forty-two TRIPS-related disputes have been filed under the WTO's Dispute Settlement Understanding – none related to arts. 7 and 66(2), see www.wto.org/english/tratop_e/dispu_e/dispu_subjects_index_e.htm?id=G234. See also David M. Fox, 'Technology Transfer and the TRIPS Agreement: Are Developed Countries Meeting Their End of the Bargain?' (2019) 10(1) *Hastings Science and Technology Law Journal* 1, 33–37 (concluding that 'developing countries are not meeting the Article 66.2 mandate' and setting out a legal strategy how it might be enforced through WTO dispute resolution).

[104] Mark V. Shugurov, 'Perspectives of International Technology Transfer in the TRIPS-Plus Era: Problems and Solutions' (2015) 5(1) *European Journal of Social and Human Sciences* 49, 52.

[105] Gehl Sampath & Roffe, n. 20, 29.

[106] Zhou, n. 40, 120–21.

[107] Kyoto Protocol, arts. 3(14), 11.

there has been considerable criticism of the CDM's effectiveness in facilitating TT.[108] The 2010 Cancún COP yielded the establishment of a new body, the Technology Mechanism, which has been mandated to improve 'the transfer of climate-friendly technologies, particularly to developing countries'.[109] Some have hailed the Technology Mechanism's potential and commended its alignment with current TT research.[110] Others have highlighted ongoing challenges to operationalize the Technology Mechanism and attributed these to contestations that resurfaced during the 2015 Paris Agreement negotiations 'on the meaning of technological innovation and the resultant specific policy interventions by the UNFCCC to support developing countries'.[111]

The Technology Mechanism has been viewed as an important 'attempt to delink the discussion from the divisive issue' of IPP – 'at least in multilateral forums'.[112] Yet IPP is also positioned 'as the primary policy mechanism' of the UNFCCC to foster 'private investments in innovation' for producing 'mitigation and adaptation technologies as particularly advocated by industry'.[113] Subsequently, IPP consistently features in UNFCCC COP negotiations, with opposing positions invariably following the deep tracks of the 'North - South dichotomy',[114] even as the achievement of an acceptable balance between climate action, TT and IPP continues to present the reasonable way forward.[115]

The COVID-19 pandemic exposed brutal truths relevant for SDG 9 and international law. Amidst all the systemic weaknesses exposed by the pandemic, critical societal functions – including food production, global supply chains, service delivery and education – have proven to be resilient for many because these functions have become considerably automated (requiring no or limited human interaction) or could be 'moved online'.[116] For most, however, the pandemic only exacerbated the technological chasm and digital divide between the developed and developing

[108] Gary Cox, 'The Clean Development Mechanism as a Vehicle for Technology Transfer and Sustainable Development: Myth or Reality?' (2010) 6(2) *Law, Environment and Development Journal* 179; Ockwell et al., n. 38, 732.

[109] Gehl Sampath & Roffe, n. 20, 29–30.

[110] *Id.*, 30; Heleen de Coninck & Daniel Puig, 'Assessing Climate Change Mitigation Technology Interventions by International Institutions' (2015) 131 *Climatic Change* 417, 431.

[111] Chaewoon Oh, 'Discursive Contestation on Technological Innovation and the Institutional Design of the UNFCCC in the New Climate Change Regime' (2020) 25(4) *New Political Economy* 660; Karen M. Sullivan, 'Implementing the UNFCCC Technology Mechanism and the 5 Ps: Progress, Practicalities, Priorities, Pathways and the Public Sector' (2019) 15 *Law, Environment and Development Journal* 4.

[112] Gehl Sampath & Roffe, n. 20, 29.

[113] *Id.*

[114] *Id.*, 30; Zhou, n. 40, 120–21.

[115] Gehl Sampath & Roffe, n. 20, 35; Abbe Brown et al., 'Towards a Holistic Approach to Technology and Climate Change: What Would Form Part of an Answer?', University of Edinburgh School of Law Working Paper Series no. 2010/32, 2010, 2.

[116] Yuval Noah Harari, 'Lessons from a Year of Covid', *Financial Times*, 26 February 2021, www.ft.com/content/f1b30f2c-84aa-4595-84f2-7816796d6841.

world. The development and distribution of COVID-19 vaccines in record time have underscored the vital importance of innovation and the significant role of transnational scientific and industrial cooperation. Pfizer's mRNA vaccine, for instance, has been described as 'globalization in a needle'.[117] Yet, well into 2021, vastly inequitable access to these vaccines across the developing world belies such statements.[118] Despite indications that powerful actors like the United States might be inclined to support a waiver to the TRIPS Agreement, the harsh reality is that, without manufacturing capacity in developing countries – without technology transfer – such a waiver might not amount to much.[119]

Therefore, it seems that international law – notably, its 'hard', legally binding treaties – is quite effective in realizing synergies that benefit powerful actors but consistently fails to address disconnects that harm the less powerful and the vulnerable.

9.3.4 *International Human Rights Obligations: MDBs and Clients*

In earlier versions of MDBs' ESG risk management frameworks, distinctions between MDB and client obligations had not been drawn clearly and consistently.[120] This issue becomes problematic, for instance, in the context of IAM compliance review, where IAMs are explicitly limited to review MDBs' actions and omissions regarding MDBs' obligations, as set out in the institutions' ESG risk management frameworks.[121] The distinction is also important because ESG standards containing client obligations are incorporated into the financing agreement.[122] Non-compliance with these obligations, therefore, constitutes a scenario under which MDBs can exercise financial leverage to enforce 'conformity' with the financing agreement, 'notwithstanding the law of any state or political subdivision thereof or to the contrary'.[123] However, IAMs and MDB management differ about the obligatory nature of such actions. Management tends to view the exercise of financial leverage (for example, loan cancellation or suspending disbursements) as a tool of last resort, to be used at management's sole discretion. IAMs often consider

[117] Afshin Molavi, 'Globalization in a Needle', *Emerging World*, 30 April 2021, eworld.substack.com/p/globalization-in-a-needle.

[118] 'Inequity of COVID-19 Vaccines Grows "More Grotesque Every Day" – WHO Chief', *UN News*, 22 March 2021, news.un.org/en/story/2021/03/1087992.

[119] Erin Hannah et al., 'TRIPS Waiver: US Support Is a Major Step but No Guarantee of COVID-19 Vaccine Equity', *The Conversation*, 12 May 2021, theconversation.com/trips-waiver-us-support-is-a-major-step-but-no-guarantee-of-covid-19-vaccine-equity-160638; Shugurov, n. 104.

[120] Laurence Boisson de Chazournes, 'The World Bank Inspection Panel: About Public Participation and Dispute Settlement', in Tullio Treves et al. (eds.), *Civil Society, International Courts and Compliance Bodies* (T.M.C. Asser Press, 2005), 187, 193–94.

[121] E.g., IFC/MIGA CAO, *Operational Guidelines*, March 2013, 16, www.cao-ombudsman.org/howwework/documents/CAOOperationalGuidelines_2013.pdf.

[122] Boisson de Chazournes, n. 66, 289–90.

[123] Bradlow & Hunter, n. 71, 11.

management's refusal to exercise such leverage in the face of persistent or significant client non-compliance with ESG standards as indicative of management's non-compliance with its supervision obligations.[124]

The International Finance Corporation (IFC) made a notable attempt at clarifying the distinction between MDB and client obligations with the adoption of its 2006 Sustainability Framework,[125] an approach that has since been emulated by the World Bank.[126] In practice, however, the distinction remains problematic because MDB obligations are of a due diligence nature, which necessarily implies a relationship with client obligations.[127] Although they operate, in many respects, like commercial banks, MDBs have a public development mandate.[128] Unlike their commercial counterparts, therefore, MDBs are not only expected to provide financing but also, for instance, to help their clients build (ESG) capacity. And where such capacity is known to be deficient, MDBs are expected to 'step-in' and 'do more'; 'how much more', however, remains contested.[129]

These issues matter because many of the project scenarios under which harm materializes, including human rights violations,[130] involve an intricate mix of (host and home) state, MDB and (public or private sector) client obligations. For example, a project might trigger public protests, rooted in contestational differences between the state and parts of its society about the project's sustainability.[131] Protests can become violent, triggering measures undertaken by the state and/or the client (using state and/or private security personnel) aimed at suppressing violence and protecting property, which, in turn, can result in human rights abuses,[132] including 'reprisals' aimed at community or civil society leaders.[133] Attributing responsibility in such scenarios – not to mention, remedying harm – can be exceedingly difficult or, perhaps, create a situation where it is easier to avoid responsibility altogether.

To date, MDBs' ESG risk management frameworks typically do not contain specific human rights policies. They also vary in the degree to which they explicitly

[124] E.g., WB IP, *Argentina/Paraguay: Yacyretá Hydroelectric Project*, 1996; WB IP, *India: NTPC Power*, 1997; IFC/MIGA CAO, *Indonesia: Wilmar Group-03/Jambi*, 2011.

[125] Accessible at www.ifc.org/sustainabilityframework2006.

[126] World Bank, *Environmental and Social Framework*, 2018, www.worldbank.org/en/projects-operations/environmental-and-social-framework.

[127] Shihata, n. 13, 47–48; Boisson de Chazournes, n. 120, 193–95 (the 'project cycle' highlights the 'very close relationship, not to say dependency, between these actors in the conduct of operational activities').

[128] Bradlow & Hunter, n. 71, 1–3.

[129] Naudé Fourie, n. 13, 122–24.

[130] See Section 9.2.2.

[131] See n. 53 and accompanying text.

[132] E.g., IFC/MIGA CAO, *Guatemala: Marlin-01/Sipacapa*, 2005; IFC/MIGA CAO, *Democratic Republic of Congo: Anvil Mining Congo, SARL-01/World Bank President Request*, 2005.

[133] E.g., WB IP, *Statement of the Inspection Panel Regarding the Charges Filed against Pastor Omot Agwa in Ethiopia*, 25 September 2015, inspectionpanel.org/news/statement-inspection-panel-regarding-charges-filed-against-pastor-omot-agwa-ethiopia.

refer to human rights, but, for those frameworks that do, such references typically appear in the context of client obligations.[134] For MDBs' public sector clients, references to human rights should not be problematic – at least not insofar as they concern human rights treaty obligations accepted by the state. MDBs typically specify that they will not fund projects that will likely result in states breaching their international legal obligations, but IAM practice also demonstrates a reluctance to phrase such commitments explicitly with regard to international human rights (for example, as opposed to international environmental law).[135] Historically, MDBs have also been reluctant to deal with human rights issues arising from development financing operations explicitly in such terms, especially where civil and political rights are concerned, arguing it would impede their 'political neutrality'.[136] For private sector clients, MDBs have been noticeably more forthcoming in their commitments to ensure clients' compliance with human rights obligations, which are enshrined in national law (of the project's host state) and reflected in the UN Guiding Principles on Business and Human Rights (GPBHR).[137]

The reluctance of MDBs to address their own human rights obligations has been discussed at length elsewhere.[138] Arguably, MDBs, in practice, have been addressing human rights issues – albeit 'quietly' – since their adoption of ESG risk management frameworks.[139] However, the problem with this approach, aside from contestations about the legal nature of these frameworks,[140] remains that it essentially leaves it up to MDBs to determine the extent to which they accept human rights obligations and what those obligations entail.[141] That said, IAMs have made significant contributions to the progressive 'hardening' of MDBs' ESG risk management frameworks – largely, on the basis of procedural norms emanating from international environmental law (notably, access to information, participation, and justice) – through their authoritative (if not binding) interpretations and by

[134] E.g., World Bank, n. 126, 1–2.

[135] E.g., WB IP, *Honduras: Land Administration Project*, 2006; Naudé Fourie, n. 13, 152–54.

[136] WB IP, *Chad-Cameroon: Petroleum Development and Pipeline*, 2001. See, e.g., IBRD, *Articles of Agreement*, art. IV (Operations), section 10 (Political activity prohibited).

[137] GPBHR, *Implementing the United Nations 'Protect, Respect and Remedy' Framework, Doc. A/HRC/17/31*, 2011; see, e.g., Inter-American Development Bank (IDB) Invest, *Environmental and Social Sustainability Policy*, 2020, para. 17, www.idbinvest.org/en/consultation/environmental-and-social-sustainability.

[138] E.g., Mark Darrow, *Between Light and Shadow: The World Bank, the International Monetary Fund and International Human Rights Law* (Hart, 2006); Galit A. Sarfaty, *Values in Translation: Human Rights and the Culture of the World Bank* (Stanford University Press, 2012).

[139] Rachel Ball, 'Doing It Quietly: The World Bank's Engagement with Human Rights' (2008) 34 *Monash University Law Review* 331.

[140] See n. 74.

[141] Daniel D. Bradlow & David B. Hunter, 'Conclusion: The Future of International Law and International Financial Institutions', in Bradlow & Hunter, n. 13, 387.

reviewing the exercise of MDBs' 'managerial discretion'.[142] Moreover, public scrutiny surrounding cases filed at IAMs has encouraged MDBs to become more forthcoming about addressing human rights issues.[143]

International 'soft law' and the quasi-judicial grievance mechanisms established by MDBs have created opportunities for managing the disconnects of SDG 9 and for addressing some of the problems caused by fragmentation. ESG risk management frameworks, for instance, can facilitate integrated decision-making,[144] whereas IAMs can create avenues for recourse and redress.[145] However, the prolonged disconnect between 'conventional' conceptualizations of international law as being created by and for states and 'contemporary' reconceptualizations of international law as being created by and for states and non-state actors, including MDBs, weakens these opportunities.[146] Meanwhile, the need to clarify the international legal obligations of non-state actors, especially with regard to international human rights law and international environmental law, only intensifies as state and non-state actors cooperate to implement SDG 9 in progressively complex financial, contractual, and regulatory governance configurations.

9.4 POSITIONING SDG 9 IN THE INTERNATIONAL INSTITUTIONAL CONTEXT

This chapter approaches SDG 9 and its relationship with international law from an implementation systems perspective. An important component of such systems is the wide range of functions fulfilled by the international institutions[147] that operate across SDG 9's three core areas (infrastructure, industrialization, and innovation). These functions include providing policy advice, research, technical assistance, and capacity building;[148] tracking SDG progress;[149] providing knowledge management

[142] Daniel D. Bradlow & Andria Naudé Fourie, 'The Multilateral Development Banks and the Management of the Human Rights Impacts of their Operations', in Surya Deva & David Birchall (eds.), *Research Handbook on Human Rights and Business* (EE, 2020), 315, 326–31.

[143] E.g., WB IP, *Uganda: Transport Sector Development Project*, 2014.

[144] John C. Dernbach, 'Achieving Sustainable Development: The Centrality and Multiple Facets of Integrated Decisionmaking' (2003) 10(1) *Indiana Journal of Global Legal Studies* 247.

[145] Bradlow & Naudé Fourie, n. 142.

[146] See n. 74 and n. 202.

[147] 'International institutions' refers primarily to international (intergovernmental) organizations and treaty bodies but also includes 'hybrid' (involving state and non-state actors) and private sector–led governance structures.

[148] E.g., ITU, *Telecommunication Development Sector*, www.itu.int/en/ITU-D/Pages/default.aspx; OECD, *Innovation*, www.oecd.org/innovation/; ISO, *Capacity Building in Developing Countries*, capacity.iso.org/home.html.

[149] E.g., UNCTAD, *UNCTAD Takes the Pulse of the SDGs*, sdgpulse.unctad.org; OECD, *Measuring Distance to the SDG Targets*, www.oecd.org/sdd/measuring-distance-to-the-sdgs-targets.htm.

services;[150] and coordinating financing efforts and financing projects.[151] This section focuses on yet another such function: institutional rule making or standard setting and the processes involved in rule/standard creation, application, and enforcement.[152] The section also considers consequences of institutional standard setting – notably, normative proliferation, convergence, and development.[153] These matters are pertinent for SDG 9's implementation and for clarifying international law's role therein.

9.4.1 *Institutional Standard Setting*

The preceding sections have already introduced one example: MDBs' ESG risk management frameworks. However, there is a staggering – and growing – array of institutional standards in operation across the breadth of SDG 9-related topics. The International Organization for Standardization (ISO), for instance, notes that it has at least 1,521 standards contributing to the realization of SDG 9.[154] According to the Organisation for Economic Co-operation and Development (OECD), its 'recommendations' cover 'everything from consumer protection and chemical testing' to 'responsible business conduct' and environmental 'safeguarding'.[155] Moreover, mirroring the decided 'private turn' that development finance is undergoing, the ESG normative space is continuously expanding through private sector–led standard-setting initiatives (some involving international organizations).[156] Examples of these 'voluntary codes' include the Equator Principles;[157] the Principles of Responsible Investment;[158] the Principles for Positive Impact

[150] E.g., WIPO, *IPP Services*, www.wipo.int/services/en/; WIPO, *WIPO-Administered Treaties*, www.wipo.int/treaties/en/.

[151] E.g., World Bank, *Trust Funds and Programmes*, www.worldbank.org/en/about/unit/dfi/trust-funds-and-program.

[152] Anne Peters, Lucy Koechlin & Gretta Fenner Zinkernagel, 'Non-state Actors as Standard Setters: Framing the Issue in an Interdisciplinary Fashion', in Anne Peters et al. (eds.), *Non-State Actors as Standard Setters* (Cambridge University Press, 2009), 1, 12 (defining standard-setting as 'norm formulation or regulation', explaining their preference for 'standard' (over 'rule') because it is 'broader than the concept of law, and transcends analytical categories', which is useful since standards 'oscillate between facts and norms', including 'technical ones' that might be 'purely descriptive').

[153] Thus, 'institutional standards', as discussed here, are a form of 'international soft law', a term that enjoys mainstream recognition and usage, unfortunate (and inaccurate) as it arguably is.

[154] ISO, *Goal 9: Industry, Innovation and Infrastructure*, www.iso.org/sdg/SDG09.html.

[155] OECD, *How We Work*, www.oecd.org/about/how-we-work/.

[156] Celine Tan, 'Audit as Accountability: Technical Authority and Expertise in the Governance of Private Financing for Development', (2021) 20(10) *Social & Legal Studies* 1; Wendt, n. 64.

[157] Accessible at equator-principles.com.

[158] An 'investor initiative in partnership' with UN Environment Programme's Finance Initiative (UNEP FI) and the UN Global Compact. UNEP FI & UN Global Compact, *What Are the Principles of Responsible Investment*, www.unpri.org/pri/what-are-the-principles-for-responsible-investment.

Finance;[159] the Voluntary Principles on Security and Human Rights;[160] the Extractive Industries Transparency Initiative;[161] Social Accountability International's SA 8000";[162] and ISO's 2600 (Social Responsibility).[163]

The exception to this proliferation trend appears to be standard setting pertaining directly to TT. Institutions typically address TT through their research, policy advice, and capacity-building functions or, arguably, facilitate TT through standards adopted in other areas.[164] The UNFCCC's Technology Mechanism might evolve in this direction, but, right now, its 'recommendations' more closely resemble policy advice.[165]

Institutional standards involved in the implementation of SDG 9 share common characteristics. For instance, although non-legally binding, they can become legally binding when adopted as national legislation[166] or when incorporated into international agreements and contracts.[167] They are normative, moreover, as they aim to influence behaviour that would result in desired outcomes. However, their 'degree of normativity' varies – some standards occupy 'a grey zone of law, morals, economics and politics',[168] while others closely resemble the legal text.[169] Another characterization frequently employed is to distinguish between 'technical' and 'non-technical' standards.[170] Examples of technical standards relevant to SDG 9 would

159 A collaboration between UNEP FI and the 'global financial sector'. See UNEP FI, *Principles for Positive Impact Finance*, www.unepfi.org/about/.

160 Accessible at www.voluntaryprinciples.org.

161 Accessible at eiti.org.

162 Accessible at sa-intl.org.

163 Accessible at www.iso.org/iso-26000-social-responsibility.html.

164 E.g., UNCTAD, n. 93; ISO states its standards provide a 'platform for ensuring interoperability' that 'encourages investment and supports innovation', whereas standards like ISO 56002 (Innovation management systems) and ISO 56003 (Tools and methods for collaborative innovation partnership) purportedly help organizations to 'unleash their innovative potential'. See n. 154 and accompanying text.

165 E.g., UNFCCC, *Policies: TEC Recommendations for Climate Tech Action*, Doc. FCCC/SB/2012/2, unfccc.int/ttclear/policies (identifying IPP 'as an area for which more clarity would be needed on their role in the development and transfer of climate technologies based upon evidence' on an individual case basis).

166 As frequently happens with the technical standards of the International Electrotechnical Commission (IEC), the ITU and the ISO. See also Tim Büthe, 'The Power of Norms; the Norms of Power: Who Governs International Electrical and Electronic Technology?', in Deborah D. Avant, Martha Finnemore & Susan K. Sell (eds.), *Who Governs the Globe?* (Cambridge University Press, 2010), 294; Jason Morrison & Naomi Roth-Arriaza, 'Private and Quasi-Private Standard Setting', in Daniel Bodansky, Jutta Brunnée & Ellen Hey (eds.), *The Oxford Handbook of International Environmental Law* (Oxford University Press, 2007), 498, 502–3.

167 E.g., the incorporation of MDBs' ESG standards into financing agreements. See n. 122 and accompanying text.

168 Peters, Koechlin & Fenner Zinkernagel, n. 152, 13.

169 E.g., OECD, *Recommendation of the Council on the Governance of Infrastructure*, 2020, legalinstruments.oecd.org/en/instruments/OECD-LEGAL-0460; see also Goldmann, n. 6.

170 Peters, Koechlin & Fenner Zinkernagel, n. 152.

include 'criteria for optical cable installation with minimal existing infrastructure'[171] and standards covering the 'type and status of the soil' upon which buildings are constructed or the 'screw heads used on their roofs'.[172] Non-technical standards would cover issues like environmental assessment[173] and occupational health and safety.[174] In practice, however, this distinction is not as clear-cut. Technical standards might implicitly cover issues typically addressed by non-technical standards[175] and vice versa.[176] Technical standards are often positioned (especially by institutions) as 'value neutral', based on 'scientific fact' and created through expert (and, therefore, 'a-political') consensus-driven procedures.[177] Nevertheless, both categories contain 'explicit norms' and have become powerful instruments in the exercise of public power.[178] Consequently, there have been growing demands – grounded in growing expectations about transparency, legitimacy, and accountability – about the institutional procedures surrounding these standards.[179]

Hence, it matters how institutional standards are adopted and amended – how transparent these processes are, for instance, and to what extent they provide for participation in decision-making, especially of developing countries (and their experts) and civil society.[180] When it comes to applying and enforcing institutional standards, it matters whether they rely solely on the self-regulatory efforts of participants. Are there, at least, some forms of institutional compliance checking or auditing, third-party certification, or dispute resolution that also provides affected

[171] ITU, *Recommendations of the Council on the Governance of Infrastructure*, November 2018, www.itu.int/ITU-T/recommendations/rec.aspx?rec=13786&lang=en.

[172] ISO's description of its standards facilitating 'resilient infrastructure'. See n. 154 and accompanying text.

[173] E.g., the ITU's 'methodologies for the assessment of the environmental impact of the information and communication technology sector'. ITU, n. 171.

[174] E.g., ISO, *ISO 45001 (Occupational Health and Safety Management Systems)*, www.iso.org/standard/63787.html; IFC, *Performance Standard 2 (Labor and Working Conditions)*, www.ifc.org/ps2.

[175] E.g., ITU, *ITU-T Y.4000 Series (Smart Sustainable Cities)*, www.itu.int/rec/T-REC-Y.Sup34-202007-I ('set[s] the stage for stakeholders' engagement'); WIPO, *Handbook on Industrial Property Information and Documentation*, www.wipo.int/export/sites/www/standards/en/pdf/06-01-01.pdf (includes recommendations on 'minimum contents for intellectual property offices' websites' that facilitates transparency).

[176] E.g., World Bank, *OP/BP 4.37 (Safety of Dams)*, www.worldbank.org/en/projects-operations/environmental-and-social-policies.

[177] See, e.g., ISO, *Developing Standards: Who Develops Standards*, www.iso.org/who-develops-standards.html.

[178] Büthe, n. 166, 294, 315; Tan, n. 156.

[179] Peters, Koechlin & Fenner Zinkernagel, n. 152, 18–26.

[180] E.g., on ISO, see Morrison & Roth-Arriaza, n. 166, 502–3; on OECD, see Elisa Morgera, 'OECD Guidelines for Multinational Enterprises', in Thomas Hale & David Held (eds.), *Handbook of Transnational Governance: Institutions & Innovations* (Polity Press, 2011), 314, 315–18. On MDBs' ESG standards, see David Hunter, 'International Law and Public Participation in Policy-Making at the International Financial Institutions', in Bradlow & Hunter, n. 13, 199–238.

people with avenues to redress?[181] And, where such mechanisms exist, are they legitimate and effective?[182] Furthermore, concerns are mounting about the effect of private sector–led normative schemes that displace 'public oversight' and weaken regulatory and judicial systems in developing countries.[183] The plethora of 'private global' standards may well have become instrumental in implementing SDG 9, but they are not being applied in 'empty' normative 'spaces' – they compete with, and, in many instances, crowd out, both national and international law that arguably provide equivalent or stronger environmental, labour, and human rights safeguards.[184]

9.4.2 *Normative Convergence and Development*

As the proliferation of institutional standards continues, there are indications of normative convergence or harmonization. Yet the degree of convergence is uneven across the three core areas of SDG 9, and, here, the technical/non-technical categorization is of some use. Generally, technical standards such as those adopted by the International Electrotechnical Commission (IEC), the International Telecommunication Union (ITU), the World Intellectual Property Organization (WIPO), and the ISO reflect a higher degree of harmonization than non-technical standards – notably, those related to the ESG normative space. This is partly because institutions like the ITU, the IEC, and the ISO (founded, respectively, in 1865, 1906, and 1946) have been engaged in harmonization efforts much longer. Indeed, they describe themselves as 'sister organizations' cooperating 'to ensure that International Standards fit together seamlessly and complement each other'.[185] Importantly, the WTO's 1994 Agreement on Technical Barriers to Trade accelerated this

[181] E.g., on criticism about the continued absence of a citizen-driven accountability mechanism in the Equator Principles, see Christopher Wright, 'Global Banks, the Environment, and Human Rights: The Impact of the Equator Principles on Lending Policies and Practices' (2012) 12(1) *Global Environmental Politics* 56.

[182] E.g., on IAM effectiveness, see n. 80; on OECD, *National Contact Points for Responsible Business Conduct*, mneguidelines.oecd.org/ncps/, see Morgera, n. 180, 316; see also UN Office on the High Commissioner for Human Rights, *Enhancing Effectiveness of Non-State-based Grievance Mechanisms in Cases of Business-Related Human Rights Abuse*, Doc. A/HRC/44/32, 19 May 2020, www.ohchr.org/EN/Issues/Business/Pages/ARP_III.aspx.

[183] Tan, n. 156, 15–17.

[184] Tim Bartley, *Rules without Rights: Land, Labor, and Private Authority in the Global Economy* (Oxford University Press, 2018); Fiona Haines, Kate MacDonald & Samantha Balaton-Chrimes, 'Contextualizing the Business Responsibility to Respect: How Much Is Lost in Translation?', in Radu Mares (ed.), *The UN Guiding Principles on Business and Human Rights* (Brill/Nijhoff, 2012), 107.

[185] See IEC, *Vision and Mission*, www.iec.ch/about/?ref=menu. ITU, IEC, and ISO also issue mutual standards. See, e.g., ISO, ISO/IEC 20071-11:2019 – Guidance on Text Alternatives for Images, www.iso.org/standard/74345.html. On WIPO's harmonization efforts, see James Boyle, 'A Manifesto on WIPO and the Future of Intellectual Property' (2004) 9 *Duke Law and Technology Review* 1.

harmonization because the ISO, the IEC, and the ITU's standards are employed to ensure national and regional standards 'do not constitute barriers to trade'.[186]

The high degree of harmonization, combined with the fact that technical standards are frequently incorporated into national legislation and contracts (thereby enhancing their justiciability) place them in a strong position to help realize the synergies of SDG 9. The ESG normative space is young, by comparison, although there have been harmonization efforts that seem to be working, mostly spearheaded by the OECD and MDBs.[187] For instance, there is noticeable normative convergence among MDBs' ESG risk management frameworks.[188] There are also pronounced interfaces among these frameworks and institutional standards like the OECD Guidelines for Multinational Enterprises,[189] the United Nations GPBHR, and private sector standards like the Equator Principles.[190]

Convergence 'on paper', however, does not necessarily mean convergence 'in practice'.[191] Unlike technical standards, ESG standards allow for significant differentiation in their application and, as with all normative text, require interpretation.[192] The use of 'standardized screw heads' on infrastructure projects, therefore, is less likely to result in significant controversy than whether 'meaningful consultation' occurred with project-affected communities[193] or whether there was congruence between the 'intent spelled out in' ESG standards and their application.[194] Contestations on such matters, especially when involving MDBs, are less likely to be decided by courts or, as things stand at the time of writing in 2021, by quasi-judicial bodies that can make binding decisions. Furthermore, as noted, MDBs tend to avoid exercising contractual remedies to enforce compliance with ESG standards.[195] That said, there are indications that institutional standards like the

[186] IEC, *International Organizations*, www.iec.ch/about/globalreach/partners/wto/; Morrison & Roth-Arriaza, n. 166, 502.

[187] E.g., OECD, *Paris Declaration and Accra Agenda for Action*, www.oecd.org/dac/effectiveness/parisdeclarationandaccraagendaforaction.htm.

[188] *Cf.*, IFC, *2012 Sustainability Framework*, www.ifc.org/sustainabilityframework2012; World Bank, n. 126; IDB Invest, n. 137.

[189] Accessible at www.oecd.org/corporate/mne/.

[190] Elisa Morgera, 'From Corporate Social Responsibility to Accountability Mechanisms', in Pierre-Marie Dupuy & Jorge E. Viñuales (eds.), *Harnessing Foreign Investment to Promote Environmental Protection* (Cambridge University Press, 2013), 321; see also Wright, n. 181 (underscoring the IFC's influence in establishing the Equator Principles).

[191] Kabra, n. 88.

[192] Sanne Taekema, 'Relative Autonomy: A Characterisation of the Discipline of Law', in Bart van Klink & Sanne Taekema (eds.), *Law and Method: Interdisciplinary Research into Law* (Mohr Siebeck, 2011), 45; Bradlow & Naudé Fourie, n. 87.

[193] WB IP, *Chad/Cameroon: Petroleum Development & Pipeline*, 2001.

[194] IFC/MIGA CAO, *Uruguay/Argentina: Celulosas de M'Bopicua (CMB) & Orion-01*, 2005. Note that this case preceded *Argentina v Uruguay (Pulp Mills on the River Uruguay)*, [2010] ICJ Rep. 14. The ICJ case considered only state obligations, whereas the CAO case focused on MIGA and the IFC's obligations.

[195] See n. 124 and accompanying text.

United Nations GPBHR are 'hardening' through the adoption (and consideration) of national and regional human rights due diligence legislation and landmark rulings in host state courts.[196] Moreover, IAMs affiliated with MDBs – and, increasingly, with international treaty bodies and DFIs – continue to review the application of ESG standards.[197] Through their interpretations (contested as these may be by institutional management) and interactions in a vibrant community of practice ('IAMnet'),[198] IAMs continuously, if incrementally, add to the normative development of ESG standards, including the normative content of, at least, MDBs' international legal obligations.[199]

While non-technical standards like those in the ESG normative space may be in a weaker position, they hold significant potential to facilitate the implementation of SDG 9 by managing its disconnects – although, as noted, much of this potential remains unfulfilled because of the ambiguity surrounding the legal nature of many of these standards.

9.5 CONCLUSIONS

SDG 9 and international law invites widely different narratives – influenced both by how SDG 9 and international law are conceptualized. One narrative, for example, emphasizes that building resilient infrastructure promotes inclusive industrialization, which fosters innovation – thus, realizing synergies that support economic advancement and human well-being, which also support the realization of other SDGs. Here, international law's ('hard') treaties regulating trade, investment, and development finance are considered instrumental in achieving these objectives. The ('soft') standards developed by international law's institutions, also in cooperation with private sector actors, complement such efforts.

Another narrative underscores the importance of national law and policies in realizing the synergies of SDG 9 and the prominent role of private sector actors, acting as investors, financiers, project sponsors, and standard setters. International law, here, has a limited role to play. From the perspective of developing states, moreover, international 'hard' law has proven to be a weak instrument for advancing their interests – as vividly demonstrated in the IPP and TT areas. Institutional standards, moreover, are viewed as impeding state sovereignty, lacking legitimacy

[196] See Bart H. Meijer, 'Environmentalists, Farmers Win Dutch Court Case over Shell Nigeria Spills', *Reuters*, 29 January 2021, www.reuters.com/article/us-shell-nigeria-court-idUSKBN29Y1D2; Hanna Ziady, 'Court Orders Shell to Slash CO2 Emissions in Landmark Climate Ruling', *CNN*, 26 May 2021, edition.cnn.com/2021/05/26/business/shell-court-case-climate-change/index.html (note the prominence of the GPBHR given by the Dutch court).

[197] E.g., IFC/MIGA CAO & FMO ICM, n. 63; *Green Climate Fund's Independent Recourse Mechanism*, irm.greenclimate.fund.

[198] Accessible at independentaccountabilitymechanism.net.

[199] See n. 142 and accompanying text.

and weakening national regulatory governance systems and institutional capabilities required to realize SDG 9.

Yet another narrative stresses the potential of SDG 9 for triggering adverse economic, social, and environmental effects ('harm'). Such effects might also impede the realization of the synergies of SDG 9 (affecting 'development performance').[200] The predominant role of international law, here, is to address the disconnects of SDG 9 by curbing, for instance, the exercise of public authority, protecting the interests of less powerful and vulnerable actors, balancing economic, social, and environmental interests and facilitating accountability 'for performance and harm'.[201] Nevertheless, positions differ on what these aspects should entail. Importantly, they are often based on different conceptualizations of what international law is (what it 'is for'), how it is created, how it operates, and how we might strengthen its resilience.[202]

At a time when the distances between co-existing narratives appear ever-so-daunting – while the need to realize SDG 9 and Agenda 2030 intensifies – we need 'shared conceptual spaces' more than ever.[203] Spaces, in other words, where competing interests and conceptions can be unpacked so that we might construct 'shared understandings' about what needs to be done and how to do it.[204] The evolving ESG normative space, imperfect as it undeniably is, offers such an opportunity.

[200] Naudé Fourie, n. 13, 109–14.
[201] *Id.*
[202] Martti Koskenniemi, 'What Is International Law For?', in Malcolm D. Evans (ed.), *International Law*, 2nd ed. (Oxford University Press, 2006), 57; Jonas Ebbesson & Ellen Hey, 'Introduction: Where in Law Is Social-Ecological Resilience?' (2013) 18(3) *Ecology and Society* 25.
[203] See in general Brunnée & Toope, n. 6.
[204] *Id.*

10

SDG 10: Reduce Inequality within and among Countries

Philippe Cullet

ABSTRACT

Sustainable Development Goal (SDG) 10, Reduced Inequalities, addresses one of the fundamental building blocks for the realization of all SDGs in a very unequal world. It emphasizes both interstate and intrastate inequality and, in so doing, goes much beyond what the 2000 Millennium Development Goals offered. SDG 10 is a central goal because inequality conditions the realization of many other SDGs, some of which also directly address inequality. In the context of international law, SDG 10 reflects in part existing equity measures, such as preferential and differential treatment. It may be seen as strengthening the equity context in economic law but does not go beyond what sustainable development law already provides. Its main contribution is to link different types of inequalities and provide a framework for linking sustainable development law, economic law, and human rights.

KEYWORDS

SDG 10, inequality, differential treatment, equity, North-South, poverty

10.1 INTRODUCTION

Inequality is one of the most crucial constraints impeding the realization of human rights, environmental protection, and, more broadly, sustainable development. Regrettably, the world is marred by tremendous inequalities between countries and within countries. Worse, inequality has been rising over the past few decades and threatens to unravel sustainable development overall,[1] which is illustrated, for instance, by the fact that during a time of unprecedented expansion of the world economy, the share of least developed countries in world output has essentially stagnated since the 1970s.[2]

The idea that equality equates with equity is a structuring element at national and international levels. Two main conceptions of equity can be opposed in this regard. The first regards formal equality as the only measure against which equity is to be measured. In this way, the formal legal equality of states is the basis that is used to identify whether measures are fair. In terms of legal obligations, the consequence of formal equality is that each state takes on the same commitments as all other states that are parties to a given treaty. At the individual level, formal equality translates into universal rights and obligations of every person. Human rights are, for instance, universal insofar as they apply similarly for anyone recognized as a holder of rights.

Formal equality tends to lead to outcomes that may be optimal in aggregate terms, but such an observation may overlook the situation of the disadvantaged members of the community. At the international level, states have never been equal in economic, political, or military power. At the individual level, a universal framework does not provide the basis for considering systemic inequalities. In this context, the second concept of equity – that is, substantive equality – seeks to address some of the shortcomings of formal equality. It posits that what matters is not equality of rights or opportunities but, rather, equality of outcomes, which calls for treating like cases alike, while recognizing the dissimilarities between subjects of the law that warrant special attention or special treatment. At the international level, this special treatment has been called preferential or differential treatment. It has been applied mostly to recognize the different situation of developing and developed countries. At the national level, special treatment for specific groups of people have taken different names in different countries, such as affirmative action in the United States or reservation in India.

Inequalities have been acknowledged in international law for decades. Relevant examples, which will be further discussed below, include the following. First, in the context of international economic law, preferential treatment measures were adopted in recognition of the fact that developing countries could not compete as equal partners with developed countries. This idea has progressively faded, and, in the World Trade Organization (WTO), differentiation is seen as an exception to the rule of formal legal equality. Second, in international environmental law, differential treatment has been a structuring element of environmental regimes for decades. Third, differentiation has found its way into some other areas of international law. In intellectual property law, limited differential measures can be found in the

[1] United Nations, *The Sustainable Development Goals Report*, 2019, 2.

[2] Deepak Nayyar, 'Can Catch up Reduce Inequality?', in Peter A.G. van Bergeijk & Rolph van der Hoeven (eds.), *Sustainable Development Goals and Income Inequality* (EE, 2017), 169, 177.

1994 Agreement on Trade-Related Aspects of Intellectual Property Rights (TRIPS Agreement). In agricultural law, some of the specific concerns addressed, such as the recognition of farmers' rights, reflect priorities of the global South.

There are also deviations from formal equality that do not seek to foster substantive equality but, rather, reinforce existing inequalities. This is the case in the UN Security Council, where differentiation favours the more powerful states.[3] In the context of financing for development, the World Bank offers an example of an exception to the rule of one state, one vote since the voting share of each member state is linked to the amount of capital stock they hold. In international investment law, the long-standing rule that private entities are hierarchically inferior to states has been sidelined in treaties, allowing investors to sue host states. This policy is directly linked with issues of inequality in the context of the Sustainable Development Goals (SDGs) because it is relatively small countries of the global South that have been at the receiving end of these provisions.

In this broader context, the very existence of an SDG specifically concerned with inequality is a major step forward given that the 2000 Millennium Development Goals (MDGs) had remained largely silent on inequality. In fact, this was seen as one of the MDG's shortcomings that needed to be addressed.[4] The underlying context of increasing inequality in the wake of the economic crisis in the first decade of the 2000s is also relevant to understanding SDG 10, Reduced Inequalities, and it may well explain why SDG 10 focuses both on inequality between states and within states. The former is an obvious entry point for an international instrument. It is thus surprising that SDG 10 struggles to even confirm the frameworks that address inequality and that are already in place in international law. Instead, SDG 10 has more to say about inequality within countries than among states, which is apt to the extent that this aligns with the concerns of international human rights law. At the same time, the content of SDG 10 addresses issues that are largely seen as falling under the purview of sovereign states' internal policies, which limits its potential reach.

10.2 THE CONTENT OF SDG 10 IN THE CONTEXT OF THE OTHER SDGS

10.2.1 *Inequality in the SDG 10 Targets*

SDG 10 addresses three different types of inequality, including horizontal inequalities or inequalities between social, ethnic, linguistic, or other population groups; vertical inequalities or inequalities of wealth, income, or social outcome; and

[3] 1945 Charter of the United Nations, art. 27(3).

[4] See, e.g., Sakiko Fukuda-Parr, 'Reducing Inequality: The Missing MDG: A Content Review of PRSPs and Bilateral Donor Policy Statements' (2010) 41(1) *IDS Bulletin* 26, 34.

inequalities between countries.[5] Some of the targets of SDG 10 focus on vertical inequality within countries, with a particular focus on economic aspects, including income, tax, and social protection. The first target focuses on ensuring that income growth of the bottom 40 per cent of the population should be higher than the national average.[6] This approach is equivalent to seeking a reduction in income inequality, as measured by the share of the bottom 40 per cent of the population in national income.[7] It has been criticized as being insufficient because it fails to address overall income inequality and is framed in such a way that the target can be realized while income inequality increases overall and because it fails to address the fact that inequality increases are created mostly at the top end of the income scale.[8]

The next two targets address horizontal inequalities in a manner that is partly reminiscent of non-discrimination clauses in human rights. This approach goes beyond what the MDGs did, but neither of the two targets include clear measurable benchmarks against which their attainment is to be assessed.[9] Target 10.3, which promises to '[e]nsure equal opportunity and reduce inequalities of outcome', goes further than the long-standing understanding of equity by the World Bank, emphasizing the need for individuals to have equal opportunities and to 'be spared from *extreme* deprivation in outcomes'.[10] However, it neither addresses the fact that everyone is not in the same position to make use of existing opportunities nor refers to the role of the private sector in fostering and addressing inequality.

Other targets emphasize global and South - North dimensions – that is, inequalities between countries. Target 10.5 starts with a call for the regulation of global financial markets, a central issue affecting all countries but one that needs to be tackled mostly by the members of the Organisation for Economic Co-operation and Development. Target 10.6 again emphasizes economic and financial issues and focuses on the need to strengthen the position of developing countries in institutions where the one-state, one-vote rule does not apply, such as international financial institutions. This situation has been a contentious issue for decades, but it constitutes only one of the many inequalities that need to be addressed in the broader field of sustainable development. Target 10.7 focuses on migration, a central issue in North-South relations but one that reflects primarily the concerns of the North in terms of stemming the flow of migration rather than broader concerns about people

5 Gillian MacNaughton, 'Vertical Inequalities: Are the SDGs and Human Rights Up to the Challenges?' (2017) 21(8) *International Journal of Human Rights* 1050.

6 Target 10.1.

7 Edward Anderson, 'Equality as a Global Goal' (2016) 30(2) *Ethics and International Affairs* 189, 193.

8 *Id.*, 193; Rolph van der Hoeven, 'Can the SDGs Stem Rising Income Inequality in the World?', in van Bergeijk & van der Hoeven, n. 2, 208.

9 MacNaughton, n. 5, 1059.

10 World Bank, *World Development Report 2006: Equity and Development* (World Bank, 2005), 2 (emphasis added).

moving across borders. While refugees are technically migrants,[11] the absence of a reference to refugees is noteworthy because they are covered by a distinct international legal regime.[12] Furthermore, the lack of reference to displacement due to climate change points to a lack of synergy among the SDGs. While climate change is addressed in SDG 13, Climate Action, neither it nor SDG 10 addresses one of the main challenges the world is going to face in the coming decades.

The last three targets of SDG 10 also focus on inequality between countries. Target 10.a highlights the principle of special and differential treatment but emphasizes it only in the context of the WTO. Target 10.b focuses on encouraging official development assistance and foreign direct investment to the most vulnerable and marginalized countries. Target 10.c, which focuses on the high cost of migrant remittances, only highlights the symptoms of a much broader issue. Indeed, the question is not whether remittances reduce inequality, which they hopefully do. Rather, the issue is that remittances are so important today because they are comparatively much higher than official development assistance and foreign direct investment combined. Thus, the real issue is that the significance of remittances reflects states' abdication of their responsibilities to take the lead in tackling inequality.

Overall, the targets included in SDG 10 are weak, give insufficient weight to reducing income inequality,[13] and reflect a limited understanding of equity by focusing on economic and financial aspects. This approach is surprising given that equity has structured, in particular, international environmental law for decades. In addition, SDG 10 has nothing to contribute to intergenerational equity, a crucial dimension of equity for a policy framework that seeks to drive the world's development policy for fifteen years, and this is despite the fact that the first policy report on sustainable development emphasized, in particular, its intergenerational dimensions.[14]

SDG 10 breaks some new ground insofar as it recognizes the need to tackle inequality domestically and takes a step forward in calling for a reduction in inequalities of outcome.[15] This development could be the starting point for considering inequality as a common concern of humankind, which would then be addressed through cooperative action at the international level. At first sight, this goal looks very improbable, but two factors indicate that change may be forthcoming. First, inequality has reached such levels that governments around the globe are

[11] International Organization for Migration (IOM), *Migration and the 2030 Agenda* (IOM, 2018), 13.

[12] 1951 Convention Relating to the Status of Refugees.

[13] Van der Hoeven, n. 8, 210.

[14] World Commission on Environment and Development (WCED), *Our Common Future* (Oxford University Press, 1987).

[15] Malte Luebker, 'Poverty, Employment and Inequality in the SDGs: Heterodox Discourse, Orthodox Policies?', in van Bergeijk & van der Hoeven, n. 2, 141, 150.

finding it increasingly difficult not to address it, at least in limited ways.[16] Second, the potential long-lasting economic consequences of the COVID-19 pandemic could provide the basis for rethinking existing economic policies. However, real change will only be possible if policy-makers recognize the crucial role of private sector actors in tackling inequality given their dominant economic position. There is, however, no reference to private sector actors in SDG 10.

Limitations notwithstanding, SDG 10 has a crucial role to play in the broader framework of SDGs since it provides a link between the human and environmental dimensions of sustainable development and a basis for making the link between unequal development and environmental harm. This provision is crucial in a context where the SDGs do not give the kind of importance to the environment that would have been expected in the context of the shift from 'development' goals in the MDGs to 'sustainable development' goals. There are several goals that can be seen as adding up to an 'environment cluster', but there is no overarching environmental goal.[17] More fundamentally, the problem is that one would have expected the SDGs to be based on ecological sustainability, but they have remained welded to the development discourse.[18] SDG 10 thus calls into question not just the way in which inequalities are to be addressed but also the very process of development centred on economic growth. SDG 10, then, offers a reminder that addressing inequalities among states and within states is crucial to ensuring that 'development' does not threaten 'sustainability'.

10.2.2 *SDG 10 in the Context of the Other SDGs*

Inequality acts as a decisive constraint on the realization of most other SDGs, as confirmed by the UN High-Level Political Forum on Sustainable Development (HLPFSD) when it recognized that '[i]nequality between and within countries remains a major obstacle to the achievement of the Goals and inaction in this area risks derailing progress on the 2030 Agenda. Effective policies to reduce inequalities require partnerships and political will'.[19] Yet the SDGs are not organized in a hierarchical fashion, and no priority can be ascribed to SDG 10 over any other

[16] *World Social Report 2020: Inequality in a Rapidly Changing World*, UN Doc. ST/ESA/372, 2020.

[17] Werner Scholtz & Michelle Barnard, 'The Environment and the Sustainable Development Goals: "We Are on a Road to Nowhere"', in Duncan French & Louis J. Kotzé (eds.), *Sustainable Development Goals: Law, Theory and Implementation* (EE, 2018), 222, 231.

[18] Sam Adelman, 'The Sustainable Development Goals, Anthropocentrism and Neoliberalism', in French & Kotzé, n. 17, 20, 39.

[19] *Summary by the President of the Economic and Social Council of the High-level Political Forum on Sustainable Development*, UN Doc. E/HLPF/2019/8, 2019, para. 8(e).

goal.[20] The most immediately relevant SDG to SDG 10 is SDG 5, Gender Equality, which is the only other goal centred on issues of equity. The main difference between these two SDGs is that SDG 5 focuses specifically on gender equality and does not directly address the issue from an international perspective.

SDG 10 is also directly related to goals focusing on economic issues, such as SDG 1, No Poverty. Inequality and poverty are inseparable in that they contribute to each other.[21] Linking the two also helps to emphasize the non-economic dimensions of poverty that are not particularly prominent in SDG 1. SDG 8, Decent Work and Economic Growth, has direct links with inequality within and among countries. It (indirectly) suggests that the least developed countries need to grow faster than the rest of the world. SDG 12, Responsible Consumption and Production, recognizes in target 12.1 that the capabilities of developing and developed countries are different with regard to the implementation of policy goals on sustainable consumption and production patterns. It also focuses in target 12.a on the need to strengthen the scientific and technological capacity of developing countries. Attaining these aims would require technological innovation and technology transfer, but the latter is only addressed in generic terms in target 17.7, under SDG 17, Partnerships for the Goals, and crucially fails to include any reference to intellectual property rights. This is not to say that the negotiators did not understand the relevance of intellectual property rights in the SDG context, as is confirmed by a lone reference to access to medicines in target 3.b, under SDG 3, Good Health and Well-being.

There is also a strong link between inequality and the more social SDGs. SDG 2, Zero Hunger, is framed both around universality of access to sufficient and nutritious food and the need to focus on the needs of the poor and vulnerable. It also emphasizes the need to focus on agriculture to enhance farmers' livelihoods in a context of urban migration linked in part to rural neglect. SDG 3 includes, for instance, a focus on neglected tropical diseases and water-borne diseases. Similarly, SDG 6, Clean Water and Sanitation, focuses on people without access to sufficient water and sanitation, the majority of whom are found in developing countries. In other words, issues like access to food, health, and water are looked at largely in terms of the inbuilt inequalities that need to be addressed, both within and among countries. Another similarity among these goals is that they are all related to human rights. Yet none of the relevant SDGs refer to human rights or use human rights language.

Inequality is also present in the more environment-focused goals (SDG 13; SDG 14, Life below Water; and SDG 15, Life on Land). In each case, inequality aspects among countries are highlighted, though in much more limited ways than would be

[20] *Cf.* Rakhyun E. Kim, 'The Nexus between International Law and the Sustainable Development Goals' (2016) 25(1) *Review of European, Comparative and International Environmental Law (RECIEL)* 15.

[21] Felix Naschold, *Why Inequality Matters for Poverty* (Overseas Development Institute, 2002), 1.

expected. In the case of climate change, the central role of differential treatment is not mentioned, there is a striking lack of reference to developing countries when it comes to resilience (target 13.1), and there is a limited focus on the finance-related mitigation needs of developing countries (target 13.a). There is also nothing on the intrastate inequalities faced by people in terms of climate change adaptation, such as displacement. SDG 14 considers the special situation of certain categories of states, such as small island developing states (target 14.7) and emphasizes the unfavourable situation of small-scale artisanal fishers (target 14.b). SDG 15 includes some elements that have an inbuilt equity dimension, such as access and benefit sharing (target 15.6), and includes measures directly or indirectly targeting developing countries (targets 15 a–c). Overall, these environment-related goals recognize some of the relevant equity dimensions that arise, but they are less progressive than existing treaties in their treatment of inequality.

Various other SDGs include inequality-related targets. For example, SDG 7, Affordable and Clean Energy; SDG 9, Industry, Innovation, and Infrastructure; and SDG 11, Sustainable Cities and Communities refer to the special needs of developing countries or least developed countries. Thus, overall, inequality is present throughout the SDGs in a direct or indirect manner, which is unsurprising as equity has been a major concern since the notion of sustainable development gained widespread currency in the 1980s.[22] At the same time, from a legal perspective, the SDGs generally lag behind existing legal frameworks. International law, especially in human rights law and international environmental law, has reflected equity concerns in much more evolved ways than what is found in the SDGs.

10.3 POSITIONING SDG 10 IN INTERNATIONAL LAW

10.3.1 *The Fiction of Equality*

Inequality has been addressed in different ways in international law. The starting point is that the international legal framework is built around a fiction of equality structured around the principle of sovereign legal equality. This formal legal equality between sovereign states has been traditionally equated with equity.[23] It translates in practice into international norms that are reciprocal – in other words, norms in which each country takes on the same commitments.[24] Reciprocity started to be challenged after decolonization, which exposed the stark inequalities between

[22] WCED, n. 14.

[23] Georges Abi-Saab, 'Whither the International Community?' (1998) 9 *European Journal of International Law* 248.

[24] Bruno Simma, 'From Bilateralism to Community Interest in International Law' (1994) 250 *Recueil des Cours de l'Académie de Droit International* 217, 322.

states.[25] As a result, new states demanded preferential treatment in international economic law as a necessary step to overcome the disadvantages to which colonization had exposed them.[26] Until then, equity had been applied mostly at the level of the interpretation of reciprocal norms in the context of adjudication of disputes arising from the application of such norms.[27] Preferential treatment was supposed to break this model through the recognition that states are de facto not equal in various dimensions. Conceptually, this approach seeks to achieve substantive equality.

10.3.2 *Addressing Inequality between States in International Environmental Law and Beyond*

Since the 1980s, measures to foster substantive equality have focused on the introduction of differential treatment in international environmental law.[28] The new terminology reflects a different starting point from preferential treatment, which was grounded in large part in demands from developing countries for change. Differential treatment is based at least in part on shared values linked to the recognition that cooperative action is necessary to address common challenges – in particular, on global environmental issues. Conceptually, this has been relatively successful to the extent that environmental treaties over the past thirty years have included some form of differentiation. Yet strong forms of differentiation have come under severe pressure, as witnessed in the case of the climate change regime.[29] In addition, some issues that are crucial to tackle inequalities effectively have never been adequately addressed. The transfer of technology is a case in point. It has remained a partly unfulfilled agenda, something that target 17.7 indirectly acknowledges.

In international environmental law, national interests are overlaid with at least some level of recognition of the need to cooperate to address common and global challenges. As a result, different types of differential measures emerged progressively and have become a structuring element of modern treaties. To a large extent, the legitimacy of international environmental law is directly linked to differential treatment. International environmental law has been most successful in developing a framework for considering the different situation of the global South enshrined in

[25] See, e.g., Michael Byers, *Custom, Power, and the Power of Rules: International Relations and Customary International Law* (Cambridge University Press, 1999), 88.

[26] Wil Verwey, 'The Principle of Preferential Treatment for Developing Countries' (1983) 23 *Indian Journal of International Law* 343.

[27] Anastasios Gourgourinis, 'Delineating the Normativity of Equity in International Law' (2009) 11 (3) *International Community Law Review* 327.

[28] Philippe Cullet, *Differential Treatment in International Environmental Law* (Ashgate, 2003).

[29] Lavanya Rajamani, 'Ambition and Differentiation in the 2015 Paris Agreement: Interpretative Possibilities and Underlying Politics' (2016) 65(2) *International and Comparative Law Quarterly* 493.

the principle of common but differentiated responsibilities.[30] This development is reflected in commitments that are, on the whole, more balanced than those in trade or investment treaties, even if, in international environmental law, these commitments are not backed up by effective enforcement mechanisms. International environmental law, therefore, is weak in terms of enforcement options but strong in that it reflects a broader array of concerns and interests.

The development of preferential and subsequently differential treatment in international environmental contexts shows that international law can adapt to changing circumstances. The 1987 Montreal Protocol on Substances That Deplete the Ozone Layer illustrates this point. At the outset, developing countries were unwilling to contribute substantially to addressing an environmental crisis caused overwhelmingly by developed countries. The progressive realization that the ozone layer could only be effectively protected through universal cooperation led to the adoption of a regime that managed to effectively reflect the needs and capabilities of developing countries without compromising on the ultimate objective of addressing the environmental problems caused by ozone-depleting substances.[31] This accommodation was achieved through a combination of differential techniques, including delayed implementation, financial aid, and technology transfer.

The climate change regime has been much less successful than the ozone regime, illustrated by the fact that the measures taken since the early 1990s have been insufficient to tackle global warming. Yet, what has been achieved has only been possible because of an initial recognition that inequality was at the root of the climate issue. The structuring of the different legal instruments adopted in the climate change regime around the principle of common but differentiated responsibilities and respective capabilities (CBDR-RC) testifies to the importance of inequality in the climate change regime.[32] Attempts to sideline CBDR-RC in the run-up to the adoption of the 2015 Paris Agreement on Climate Change also confirm that it remains controversial. A compromise qualifying CBDR-RC by adding 'in light of different national circumstances' opened the way for the adoption of nationally determined contributions (NDCs).[33] This development has been seen as a positive sign that the world is moving beyond 'a bipolar, rigid and static type of differentiation'.[34] At the same time, NDCs do not just signal a retreat from internationally negotiated differentiation but also a move towards commitments determined by each individual state. This action has unsurprisingly led to a lack of

30 1992 Rio Declaration on Environment and Development, Principle 7.

31 See, e.g., David W. Fahey, 'The Montreal Protocol Protection of Ozone and Climate' (2013) 14 *Theoretical Inquiries in Law* 21.

32 *Cf.* Harald Winkler & Lavanya Rajamani, 'CBDR&RC in a Regime Applicable to All' (2014) 14 (1) *Climate Policy* 102.

33 *Lima Call for Climate Action*, Decision 1/CP.20, UN Doc. FCCC/CP/2014/10/Add.1, 14 December 2014, para. 3.

34 Sandrine Maljean-Dubois, 'The Paris Agreement: A New Step in the Gradual Evolution of Differential Treatment in the Climate Regime?' (2016) 25(2) *RECIEL* 151, 154.

collective ambition confirmed by the UN General Assembly noting 'with concern that the nationally determined contributions presented thus far by the parties to the Paris Agreement are not sufficient'.[35] In this context, SDG 10 fails to address this diminishing collective ambition to address inequality.[36]

Another example in the broader field of sustainable development is the regime covering plant genetic resources, which finds its origins in agriculture and environmental law. The main treaty addressing seeds – the 2001 International Treaty on Plant Genetic Resources for Food and Agriculture (ITPGRFA) – was born out of the need to address the inbuilt inequality in the regime at the time. That regime lacked recognition of farmers' rights in a context where breeders working in the formal sector benefited from a specific form of rights protection – namely, plant breeders' rights.[37] A non-binding and relatively vague recognition of farmers' rights in 1989 provided the basis for further developing this regime.[38] Developing countries argued for this even more strongly once it became clear that the global strengthening of intellectual property rights was planned in the context of the Uruguay Round of trade negotiations (1986–93), which would lead to a significant extension of life patenting that had the potential to collide with the interests of millions of farm-based livelihoods in the global South.

The ITPGRFA is the result of different equity-based compromises. First, it condones the sovereign rights of individual states over plant genetic resources, something that had become unavoidable following the assertion of sovereign rights over biodiversity in the 1992 Convention on Biological Diversity (CBD). Second, it enshrines farmers' rights in treaty form.[39] Third, it promotes 'facilitated' access to plant genetic resources while allowing intellectual property rights on plant genetic resources that have been changed after access.[40] These different compromises are linked to the development of life patenting in the context of the growth of the biotechnology industry. Overall, the treaty is strongly influenced by inequality between countries, but the final text is not particularly progressive, as exemplified in the case of the recognition of farmers' rights, where there is essentially no protection of the rights at the international level and substantive protection is left to the discretion of member states.[41]

[35] *Protection of Global Climate for Present and Future Generations of Humankind*, UN Doc. A/RES/75/217, 29 December 2020, para. 6.

[36] While the Paris Agreement was adopted after the SDGs, the changed understanding of common but differentiated responsibilities and respective capabilities was adopted in 2014. See *Lima Call for Climate Action*, n. 33.

[37] See, e.g., Graham Dutfield, *Food, Biological Diversity and Intellectual Property: The Role of the International Union for the Protection of New Varieties of Plants* (Quaker UN Office, 2011).

[38] Food and Agriculture Organization (FAO), *Farmers' Rights, Report of the Conference of FAO*, UN Doc. C 1989/REP, 1989.

[39] ITPGRFA, art. 9.

[40] *Id.*, art. 12.3.d.

[41] *Id.*, art. 9.2; Philippe Cullet, *Intellectual Property Protection and Sustainable Development* (Butterworths, 2005), 237.

Overall, in international environmental law, inequality has been addressed mostly through the lens of the dichotomy between developed and developing countries. It has, however, not made much progress either towards identifying more specific groups based on criteria directly linked to the subject matter of the treaty or towards the individualization of differentiation. Limited progress has been made to the extent that the climate change regime recognizes, for instance, vulnerability as an additional element that is to be considered.[42] Target 10.b also makes reference to 'least developed countries, African countries, small island developing States and landlocked developing countries', some of the special categories that are sometimes also recognized in international treaties.[43] Yet, the main grouping remains the simple division of the world in two broad categories, which is insufficient, in particular, to take into account the variety of situations within the vast group of 'developing' countries. In a context where the world only includes roughly two hundred countries, it would not be difficult to provide individualized differentiation, and this could easily be done in a structured manner, as in the case of member states' contributions to UN expenses that are apportioned by the UN General Assembly.[44]

The limitations of existing international environmental law notwithstanding, it goes much further than SDG 10. At best, SDG 10 reflects the general duty of solidarity among countries, a well-established principle of cooperation that can serve as the basis for various measures to fight inequality.[45] Solidarity is, however, only the foundation on which specific measures can be taken, such as differential treatment, financial aid, and technology transfer.[46] Seen from this perspective, SDG 10 confirms what is at the root of more progressive developments in law but does not build on them. In fact, it reflects the more conservative economic, trade, and investment law rather than the more open-minded and forward-looking environmental law.

10.3.3 *Addressing Inequality within Countries*

Regarding inequality within countries, it is human rights law that provides significant normative guidance for the implementation of SDG 10.[47] The focus of human

42 1992 UN Framework Convention on Climate Change, arts. 3.2, 4.4.

43 See, e.g., CBD, art. 20(6); 1994 Convention to Combat Desertification in Those Countries Experiencing Serious Drought and/or Desertification, Particularly in Africa, art. 3(c).

44 *Scale of Assessments for the Apportionment of the Expenses of the United Nations*, UN Doc. A/RES/73/271, 22 December 2018.

45 See, e.g., Ronald St. J. McDonald, 'The Principle of Solidarity in Public International Law', in Christian Dominicé et al. (eds.), *Études de droit international en l'honneur de Pierre Lalive* (Helbing, 1993), 275.

46 See, e.g., UN Human Rights Council, *Draft Convention on the Right to Development*, UN Doc. A/HRC/WG.2/21/2, 2020, art. 15.2.

47 Ignacio Saiz & Kate Donald, 'Tackling Inequality through the Sustainable Development Goals: Human Rights in Practice' (2017) 21(8) *International Journal of Human Rights* 1029.

rights law on individuals has provided the basis for giving importance to the fight against discrimination, which is something that SDG 10 also does in some respect, including the specific focus on gender equality taken up, for instance, through the 1979 Convention on the Elimination of All Forms of Discrimination against Women. In human rights law, the focus has been on non-discrimination provisions that mostly address inequalities at the individual level. At the same time, collective claims have been considered to an extent in general international law, particularly with the limited recognition of Indigenous peoples' rights.[48] At the regional level, there has been more progress in the recognition of collective rights – for instance, in the 1982 African Charter on Human and Peoples' Rights. The African Court on Human and Peoples' Rights also has applied the provision on the prohibition of non-discrimination between individuals to a group.[49] Human rights law can thus act as an excellent starting point for addressing inequalities at the individual and collective levels.

Human rights law provides another link to address inequality through the progressive development of debates around business and human rights.[50] These debates are imposing progressively – if slowly – the idea that conversations around human rights cannot exclude private sector actors that have increasingly significant impacts on the realization of human rights either through acts of commission or omission.[51] The realization that inequality also plays out in this context is not new and has been addressed in some respect in environmental law instruments through the development of civil liability regimes.[52] These regimes seek to reflect the growing contribution of private sector companies to environmental pollution and the disadvantaged position of individuals affected by their activities. Yet, this approach has not proven to be an effective template as several of the adopted regimes have not come into force many years after their adoption.[53] In this respect, the ongoing drafting of a treaty on human rights obligations of business is a welcome step as it emphasizes much more directly the inequality between private sector actors and individuals and groups in society.[54]

48 2007 Declaration on the Rights of Indigenous Peoples.

49 African Court on Human and Peoples' Rights, *African Commission on Human and Peoples' Rights v Republic of Kenya*, Application no. 006/2012, 26 May 2017, para. 146.

50 UN Human Rights Council, *Guiding Principles on Business and Human Rights: Implementing the United Nations 'Protect, Respect and Remedy' Framework*, UN Doc. A/HRC/17/31, 2011.

51 Denis G. Arnold, 'Corporations and Human Rights Obligations' (2016) 1 *Business and Human Rights Journal* 255.

52 See, e.g., 1997 Protocol to Amend the 1963 Vienna Convention on Civil Liability for Nuclear Damage.

53 See, e.g., 1999 Protocol on Liability and Compensation for Damage Resulting from Transboundary Movements of Hazardous Wastes and Their Disposal.

54 *Second Revised Draft: Legally Binding Instrument to Regulate, in International Human Rights Law, the Activities of Transnational Corporations and Other Business Enterprises*, 6 August 2020.

10.3.4 *Other Relevant Developments*

Different areas of international law have made different contributions to addressing inequality. In international trade law, special and differential treatment is now an exception to the principle of reciprocity, even if the WTO has maintained forms of special and differential treatment that were already enshrined in pre-existing trade treaties.[55] The idea that there was too much differentiation, rather than too little, in trade law is belied in the case of technology transfer. Developing countries accepted the TRIPS Agreement as part of the WTO package deal on the premise that stronger levels of intellectual property protection would lead to the desired technology transfer that had not happened until then.[56] The repeated extensions granted to the least developed countries for complying with their TRIPS obligations seem to confirm that stronger intellectual property rights protection is not the only factor explaining the lack of sufficient technology transfer. At the same time, developing countries are still being prodded today into acquiring, rather than developing, new technologies to help them 'cross the technological frontier'.[57] This would be an interesting proposition if all the relevant elements were aligned. However, many countries will either not be able to attract investors if they do not provide the level of intellectual property protection that is expected of them or may not be able to pay for the technology.

Inequality is also at the centre of the policies of international financial institutions. In the case of the World Bank, the basic dichotomy is between donor and borrowing countries. The World Bank has a wide-ranging regulatory framework structured around environmental and social policies, which applies to borrowers and not to donor countries.[58] These policies largely reflect international legal standards. However, while they are not international law, they dramatically influence the development of national laws and policies in borrowing countries. The result is a significant similarity, not to say uniformity, between legal frameworks in countries of the global South. At some level, this situation simply reflects the compliance with international standards to which sovereign states have willingly subscribed. At another level, it also reflects the often limited scope that countries of the global South – in particular, smaller ones – have to adopt distinct legal frameworks.[59]

55 See, e.g., Constantine Michalopoulos, *Role of Special and Differential Treatment for Developing Countries in GATT and the World Trade Organization* (World Bank, 2000).

56 See, e.g., Andreas Rahmatian, 'Neo-Colonial Aspects of Global Intellectual Property Protection' (2009) 12(1) *Journal of World Intellectual Property* 40.

57 Commission on Science and Technology for Development, *The Impact of Rapid Technological Change on Sustainable Development*, UN Doc. E/CN.16/2019/2, 2019, para. 34.

58 World Bank, *Environmental and Social Framework*, 2017.

59 See, e.g., Philippe Cullet, 'Environment and Development – The Missing Link', in Julio Faundez & Celine Tan (eds.), *International Economic Law, Globalization and Developing Countries* (EE, 2010), 354, 368.

Finally, inequality is also addressed in areas of regulation not covered by treaties, which is particularly true in the context of natural resources where there are vast gaps in the coverage that international law offers. The regulation of mining through treaties is one such example. These gaps have been filled progressively through private sector–led initiatives that tend to use the framework of mixed governance, in part to forestall the development of treaty law. Frameworks like the Extractive Industries Transparency Initiative where states are involved have the legitimacy that state participation brings but are firmly controlled by the private sector.[60] Similarly, the Kimberley Process, which ensures no 'blood diamonds' find their way to international markets, has been repeatedly referred to positively in UN General Assembly resolutions.[61] In addition, the WTO has framed a specific exception for the Kimberley Process to free trade rules.[62] These mixed governance frameworks focus on transparency measures, and, in that sense, they contribute to addressing equity concerns. At the same time, they are framed outside of the traditional international law framework and, to that extent, do not contribute to strengthening the democratic accountability of international law.

10.3.5 *Inequality in International Law and Beyond*

As identified above, inequality has been addressed in different ways and to a different extent in different branches of international law. There is, however, no consistent framing that applies to all areas of international law that is in keeping with its sectoral and non-hierarchical structure. Some of the measures that exist are directed more particularly at equity among states, which is what environmental treaties do. Some target mostly individuals and groups, which is the case with human rights treaties. It is also the case with human rights law, which straddles most effectively the national and international law divide. There is, however, no single framework that considers inequality per se in all its forms either at the national or international level, and this fact may be a strength to the extent that inequality is considered from various angles in various contexts. At the same time, it may also be a weakness, as identified in the context of trade and investment law, whose equity frameworks are much weaker than in some other branches of international law. In this context, SDG 10 offers a framework that reflects to some extent existing international law but, save in the case of international trade and investment law, is overall less progressive than existing international law.

60 Extractive Industries Transparency Initiative (EITI), *The Extractive Industries Transparency Initiative Standard* (EITI, 2019).

61 See, e.g., *The Role of Diamonds in Fuelling Conflict*, UN Doc. A/RES/75/261, 5 March 2021.

62 See, e.g., Joost Pauwelyn, 'WTO Compassion or Superiority Complex: What to Make of the WTO Waiver for Conflict Diamonds' (2003) 24 *Michigan Journal of International Law* 1177.

10.4 POSITIONING SDG 10 IN THE INTERNATIONAL INSTITUTIONAL CONTEXT

10.4.1 *Equality and International Institutions*

In the UN system, the fiction of legal equality rules throughout most UN bodies and specialized agencies. This is not to say that there have been no developments beyond the principle of sovereign legal equality. In several cases, the special situation of developing countries and least developed countries is recognized, including through the setting up of institutions specifically devoted to addressing their needs, as in the case of the UN Conference on Trade and Development. Further, inequality has been an important dimension in the development of various institutions that have a direct bearing on the implementation of SDG 10. These institutions have been established in environmental, human rights, and economic law. In addition, mixed governance institutions are increasingly important actors that have a strong bearing on equality at the international level. As in the case of international law, SDG 10 contributes to institutional debates to the extent that it reflects some of the debates around inequality in international institutions. At the same time, it does not really go beyond confirming matters that are already well covered and does not engage with new challenges, such as those related to mixed governance.

10.4.2 *Inequality and Institutional Context in International Environmental Law*

Debates over North - South inequality have been central in sustainable development institutions, as illustrated, for instance, in the case of the Global Environment Facility (GEF).[63] The GEF was established specifically to address North-South inequality through the provision of environment-specific financial aid.[64] Further, a specific attempt was made to ensure that the decision-making structure for disbursing funds would not replicate that of the World Bank. The attempt to better reflect donor and recipient countries in decision-making is thus noteworthy.[65] At the same time, the GEF has failed to address other types of inequalities. Thus, while the GEF has focused on addressing global environmental problems, something that falls squarely within the mandate of the UN Environment Programme (UNEP), it is neither physically located in Nairobi nor institutionally located within UNEP. In a context where UNEP is the only major UN body located in the global South, this

[63] See generally Laurence Boisson de Chazournes, 'The Global Environment Facility (GEF): A Unique and Crucial Institution' (2005) 14(3) *RECIEL* 193.

[64] 1994 Instrument for the Establishment of the Restructured Global Environment Facility (as updated).

[65] *Id.*, s. 25(c).

situation reflects a lack of willingness to trust UNEP to take an effective lead on environmental issues.[66] The same goes, to a lesser extent, for UN Development Programme (UNDP), which also finds itself as a junior partner to the World Bank in the GEF, something that reflects the broader inequality between the World Bank and UN bodies, despite the fact that the World Bank is itself a UN specialized agency.[67]

UNEP's weaker position is also confirmed by the way in which it was never given the lead on political discussions related to sustainable development, which became particularly visible in the context of the setting up of the Commission on Sustainable Development (CSD). The CSD was meant to take a lead on the development of sustainable development law and policy following the Rio summit in 1992.[68] In setting it up separately from UNEP, a message was given that sustainable development was something broader and politically more important than the environment. At the same time, in setting up a separate body located in New York rather than Nairobi, it did nothing to limit the marginalization from which UNEP was already suffering. The structural weakness of UNEP was addressed through measures taken at the 2010 UN Conference on Sustainable Development, such as by upgrading its Governing Council to universal membership.[69] At the same time, the HLPFSD, which was created to replace the CSD, remains separate from UNEP, both institutionally and geographically.[70]

10.4.3 *Inequality and Institutional Context in Human Rights Law*

Human rights institutions have also made a major contribution to the way in which SDG 10 is being implemented. They complement the framework on addressing inequality among states with two main contributions. The 1966 International Covenant on Economic, Social and Cultural Rights (ICESCR) offers a starting point with its recognition that states must take measures 'through international assistance and co-operation' to realize their rights.[71] This mandate gives a new meaning to the traditional understanding of human rights that has been limited to a vertical relationship between individuals and one state. Extraterritorial duties of states have been given increasing importance in recent years.[72] The importance of

[66] See, e.g., Joyeeta Gupta, 'The Global Environment Facility in its North-South Context' (1995) 4(1) *Environmental Politics* 19, 29.

[67] 1947 Agreement between the UN and the International Bank for Reconstruction and Development.

[68] *Institutional Arrangements to Follow up the United Nations Conference on Environment and Development*, UN Doc. A/RES/47/191, 22 December 1992.

[69] *The Future We Want*, UN Doc. A/RES/66/288, 2012, para. 88.

[70] *Id.*.

[71] ICESCR, art. 2.1.

[72] See, e.g., Takele Soboka Bulto, *The Extraterritorial Application of the Human Right to Water in Africa* (Cambridge University Press, 2014).

such diagonal human rights obligations stems in part from the fact that not all states are similarly placed to contribute to the realization of human rights. This notion reflects in a limited way the idea of solidarity rights structured around the idea that there are human rights that transcend a single state – the right to the environment at the centre of sustainable development law is a prime candidate.[73]

Human rights institutions also provide a different context to understand inequality by integrating individuals within international law regimes, something that remains an exception. This is crucial because it offers the only real link in international law between interstate and intrastate inequalities. The universality on which international human rights are premised is doubly relevant. It offers a mirror image to reciprocity of obligations, which traditionally has governed interstate relations and continues to do so in, for example, international trade law.[74] At the same time, developing countries have some leeway in the implementation of economic rights for non-nationals.[75] This situation confirms that universality is a principle and an ideal but that existing inequalities necessarily structure the way in which rights can be realized.

10.4.4 *Inequality and Institutional Context in International Economic Law*

Inequality has also been a central element in institutions overseeing international economic law. In the context of trade relations, the setting up of the WTO in the mid-1990s marked the formalization of a new understanding of equity in economic law. Where the 1994 General Agreement on Tariffs and Trade (GATT) had been at the centre of development of preferential treatment for the global South from the 1950s onwards, the WTO now became the torchbearer of a return to orthodoxy wherein the principle of sovereign legal equality was to regain its central mandate in framing international trade law. From the point of view of SDG 10, it is striking that this attempt to move the clocks back has only been partially successful. For instance, in the context of the TRIPS Agreement, some minor concessions were made for least developed countries,[76] which included, in particular, a longer delay for implementing norms that eventually were to be roughly the same for all countries. In the meantime, the irony of forcing these countries that only have a minuscule weight in international trade and very limited capacity to benefit from a strong regime of

[73] See, e.g., Krzysztof Drzewicki, 'The Rights of Solidarity: The Third Revolution of Human Rights' (1984) 53(3–4) *Nordisk Tidsskrift for International Ret* 26.

[74] Daniel Barstow Magraw, 'Legal Treatment of Developing Countries: Differential, Contextual and Absolute Norms' (1990) 1 *Colorado Journal of International Environmental Law and Policy* 69.

[75] ICESCR, arts. 2.1, 2.3.

[76] See, e.g., Andrew Michaels, 'International Technology Transfer and Trips Article 66.2: Can Global Administrative Law Help Least-Developed Countries Get What They Bargained For' (2009) 41(1) *Georgetown Journal of International Law* 223.

intellectual property rights has become increasingly apparent.[77] It has translated into a series of further extensions up to the point where this is now likely to be a permanent exception in all but name.[78]

The institutional context for international trade law also underlines some of the ways in which the lack of hierarchy between different branches of law and institutions at the international level does not reflect reality well. This situation is illustrated by the WTO's dispute settlement body and the way in which trade and environment disputes have ineluctably been brought to the WTO in the absence of any similar pull on the environmental side. As a result, a pattern has emerged in which environmental treaties addressing an issue arising in the trade dispute under consideration have been essentially sidelined. On several occasions, this has been because the United States was a party to the trade dispute and had not ratified the relevant environmental agreement, as in the case of the 'genetically modified organism' dispute with the European Union.[79] More generally, environmental treaties remain largely extraneous to the process of adjudication of trade disputes. As a result, it is essentially the equity framework applicable in the WTO that is applied, thus participating in a displacement of issues that have often been given more consideration in environmental treaties, as in the case of North - South equity.[80]

International investment law provides a different case study of an area of law that affects states and individuals directly but often acts from behind legal and institutional walls that make it appear innocuous. Over the past few decades, investment law has become particularly controversial from an equity point of view because of the way it often transcends the in-principle strict distinction between states and private sector actors at the international level.[81] In particular, the possibility offered in most treaties for private investors to sue states directly as equal partners raises fundamental questions about equality and equity. The principle of international law remains that there is a lack of hierarchy between sovereign states and a clear hierarchy between states and private actors that are subjected to the jurisdiction of the states in which they operate. The new reality thus goes against one of the most basic structuring elements of international law. It is particularly problematic because

[77] See, e.g., Omolo Joseph Agutu, 'Least Developed Countries and the TRIPS Agreement: Arguments for a Shift to Voluntary Compliance' (2012) 20(3) *African Journal of International and Comparative Law* 423.

[78] See, e.g., Council for TRIPS Agreement, *Extension of the Transition Period Under TRIPS Article 66.1 for Least Developed Country Members*, Doc. IP/C/W/668, 1 October 2020.

[79] WTO, *European Communities – Measures Affecting the Approval and Marketing of Biotech Products*, WTO Doc. WT/DS291/R, 292/R, 293/R, Panel Report, 21 November 2006.

[80] See, e.g., Amrita Narlikar, 'Fairness in International Trade Negotiations: Developing Countries in the GATT and WTO' (2006) 29(8) *World Economy* 1005.

[81] Mariel Dimsey, 'Arbitration and Natural Resource Protection', in Shawkat Alam, Jahid Hossain Bhuiyan, & Jona Razzaque (eds.), *International Natural Resources Law, Investment and Sustainability* (Routledge, 2017), 132.

it tends to pit economically and politically weaker states with large corporations. In addition, it displaces adjudication to forums that are outside of the state where the investment has taken place and where individuals may be affected by the investment. Further, arbitral tribunals generally fail to integrate human rights norms, even though limited progress may be seen, for instance, in the context of the International Centre for Settlement of Investment Disputes where the legitimacy of raising human rights claims has been upheld.[82]

10.4.5 *Inequality and Mixed Governance Institutions*

Inequality in the context of state-based institutions has been accentuated in recent years with the growth of mixed governance institutions. This situation is linked to the fact that the limited extent to which South - North differentiation has been built into state-based institutions tends to fade away where private sector actors lead institutional development.[83] The growth of mixed governance institutions over the past three decades is linked to the exponential rise of the influence of the private sector following the end of the Cold War and the tendency of state actors to withdraw from the provision of social goods. This development has left institutional gaps that have been filled by institutional structures where private sector actors are brought in to strengthen state-based institutions or where they lead the development of new structures.[84]

One example is that of the UN Compact, which brings together the United Nations and private sector actors, allowing the former to put some pressure on the latter to act as socially and environmentally conscious international actors and giving the latter access to the legitimacy that comes with being associated with the United Nations. The UN Compact, however, has not been devoid of criticism because many corporations do not seem to manage to meet what are generally understood as light reporting requirements.[85] A second example is the World Water Council (WWC). Formally, it is an association under French law whose membership includes a variety of public and private actors.[86] In a context where there is no effective institutional home for water in the UN system,[87] the WWC has carved out

[82] ICSID, *Aguas Bilbao Bizkaia v Argentina*, ICSID Case no. ARB/07/26, Award, 8 December 2016.

[83] See, e.g., Jennifer Clapp, 'The Privatization of Global Environmental Governance: ISO 14000 and the Developing World' (1998) 4(3) *Global Governance* 295.

[84] See, e.g., Robert Falkner, 'Private Environmental Governance and International Relations: Exploring the Links' (2003) 3(2) *Global Environmental Politics* 72.

[85] Andreas Rasche, 'The United Nations Global Compact and the Sustainable Development Goals', in Oliver Laasch et al. (eds.), *Research Handbook of Responsible Management* (EE, 2020), 228.

[86] The current list of members can be found at World Water Council, *List of Members*, www.worldwatercouncil.org/sites/default/files/Members/List_of_Members.pdf.

[87] UN Water is in essence a placeholder signalling to the outside world where water-related work takes place, within and beyond the UN system.

a leading space in framing international water policy-making. The most prominent event it organizes is the usually triennial World Water Forum (WWF), which has become the rallying point for international water policy-makers.[88] While the WWF does not have the legitimacy that a UN-sponsored international water conference would have, it is organized in such a way that it is projected as being the only relevant international forum on water policy. This projection is visible, for instance, in a 'ministerial declaration' adopted at the end of WWF sessions, which reflects the fact that each session includes a segment with state representatives.[89]

From an inequality perspective, mixed governance institutions like the WWC are awkward. In particular, they have no mandate to consider the special situation of the global South, which is particularly problematic in the case of water, which is not just a natural resource but also a human right and one of the basic building blocks of life on Earth. The problem is reflected in the promotion of the commodification of water, the privatization of water, and the lack of enthusiasm in recognizing the human right to water.[90] This is all the more significant since the United Nations is today unlikely to take a lead on the development of international water policy since it directly and indirectly contributes to processes organized under the auspices of the WWC.[91]

10.5 CONCLUSIONS

SDG 10 is undoubtedly pivotal because the realization of the other SDGs is conditioned by the extent to which inequality is addressed. This is true between states as the central role of differential treatment, particularly international environmental law, attests, and it is also true within countries as the importance of anti-discrimination provisions in human rights law attests. Inequality has played a central role in the development of environmental and human rights law. There have been, and there remain, many challenges in both areas of law. Concerning environmental law, the principle of common but differentiated responsibility has faced some level of opposition from the outset from developed countries. Since the principle has been understood as favouring developing countries, its restatement has also become a way for the South to assert itself on the international scene. Such assertions have been successful insofar as the principle has been repeatedly confirmed, including in the 2010s.[92] At the same time, the mechanisms through which differentiation is

88 World Water Forum, www.worldwatercouncil.org/en/world-water-forum.

89 World Water Forum, *Ministerial Declaration Seeking Decisive Action on Water*, 20 March 2018, 8, worldwaterforum.org/en/news/ministerial-declaration-seeking-decisive-action-water.

90 Sharmila L. Murthy, 'The Human Right(s) to Water and Sanitation: History, Meaning, and the Controversy Over-Privatization' (2013) 31(1) *Berkeley Journal of International Law* 98, 105.

91 The members of the WWC include intergovernmental organizations, such as the FAO, the UN Educational, Scientific and Cultural Organization, UN Habitat, and the World Bank.

92 *Transforming Our World: The 2030 Agenda for Sustainable Development*, UN Doc. A/Res/70/1, 25 September 2015, para. 12.

implemented have tended to weaken over time, as confirmed in the Paris Agreement, wherein North-South differentiation has given way to individual differentiation.[93] In human rights law, non-discrimination remains a strong basis for measures within countries, which needs to be pushed further towards the recognition of a right to economic and social equity to address more specifically vertical inequalities.[94]

SDG 10 does not challenge these areas of law to do more as it is more conservative than what has already been achieved. It fails in particular to offer a stronger basis for North-South differentiation in a world that remains extremely unequal. Put differently, it addresses inequality from the sidelines and fails to focus on some of the core issues that are arising, as illustrated by the very limited context within which target 10.a understands the relevance of differentiation in international law. International law has in fact already forged ahead of SDG 10, especially in the field of environmental law, which has developed differentiation to a significant extent. In other contexts, inequality has been given increasing visibility, as in the case of international human rights law where special rapporteurs on human rights and extreme poverty have been repeatedly appointed since 1998. Yet, here too, the vision is limited to addressing the same extreme poverty that defines the focus of SDG 1. Further, the vision for the mandate is in fact limited to a link with SDG 1 and makes no reference to SDG 10.[95] On the other hand, SDG 10 may be seen as challenging institutions like the WTO that frames its activities loosely around the sustainable development paradigm but mostly in terms of its own understanding of sustainability and equity, which remains much more conservative than environmental or human rights law.

Overall, SDG 10 essentially reflects the existing informal and formal power structure at the international level. This fact is unsurprising since the SDGs emerged out of a process of widespread consultation, hence reflecting a common minimum denominator. At the same time, it remains insufficient, and addressing inequalities in earnest must be a priority for policy-makers. International law cannot solve the problem of inequality by itself, but it can be a component of a broader solution, which will need to start with revisiting some of the building blocks of the neoliberal economy built around an unstated prohibition to tax more heavily corporations and the super-rich together with the need to rebuild the state, which remains the only organ of society that can effectively tackle inequalities. In other words, we need to move ahead from 'leave no one behind', which refers to an increasingly discredited development model. The current framework, centred on the belief that benefits of growth will eventually trickle down, has not been

93 Paris Agreement.

94 *Cf.*, UN Human Rights Council, *Report of the Special Rapporteur on Extreme Poverty and Human Rights, Philip Alston*, UN Doc. A/HRC/29/31, 2015, para. 54.

95 UN Human Rights Council, *Extreme Poverty and Human Rights*, UN Doc. A/HRC/RES/44/13, 16 July 2020.

effectively realized and is out of step with the amount of inequality that needs to be countered at present. This point is confirmed by the fact that the gap in human development between least developed countries and countries with high human development has remained essentially similar for decades.[96]

This situation is even truer about the inequality between people, which has increased tremendously over the past three decades. Drastic changes are necessary to ensure that inequalities are effectively tackled. SDG 10 contributes to linking the conversations happening largely in parallel at the interstate and intrastate level. Effectively addressing inequality at both levels will require taking much stronger steps. These steps cannot wait until 2030 in a context where the COVID-19 pandemic has set the clocks back in terms of poverty inequality for the 2020s.[97] Inequality needs to be addressed immediately much more vigorously than has been the case until now.

96 UNDP, *Human Development Report 2014* (UNDP, 2014), 167; UNDP, *Human Development Report 2020* (UNDP, 2020), 350.

97 World Bank, *Poverty and Shared Prosperity 2020: Reversals of Fortune* (World Bank, 2020).

11

SDG 11: Make Cities and Human Settlements Inclusive, Safe, Resilient and Sustainable

Anél du Plessis

ABSTRACT

This chapter considers Sustainable Development Goal (SDG) 11, Sustainable Cities and Communities, in the context of international law. The relevance of SDG 11, with its focus on urban sustainability, resilience, safety, and inclusiveness is considered from the perspective of cities as subnational authorities that are increasingly and in non-traditional ways involved in the making, implementation, and enforcement of international law. Traditional sources of international law do not deal with cities in any direct way. It is against this background that this chapter briefly engages the SDG negotiation process and the birth of SDG 11. Drawing on the possible normative meaning that the urban goal may have for how existing and future cities are designed and governed, the chapter also explains how SDG 11 intersects with other SDGs, what the latter intersection implies for the relationships and interactions between cities and different international structures as well as the future development of international law.

KEYWORDS

SDG 11, international law, sustainable urban development, sustainable cities, urban inclusivity, urban resilience, urban sustainability, urban safety, urban governance, urban law

11.1 INTRODUCTION

In 2013, the now oft-quoted statement was made that 'the battle for sustainable development will almost certainly be decided in cities'[1] and, soon after, that '[i]n all

[1] United Nations, *A New Global Partnership: Eradicate Poverty and Transform Economies through Sustainable Development: The Report of the High-Level Panel of Eminent Persons on the Post-2015 Development Agenda*, 2013, 17.

future scenarios of global society, cities play a crucial role'.[2] The idea of the internationalization of cities and the localization of sustainable development continues to gain traction in scholarship and international development policy as urbanization and accompanying injustices accelerate alarmingly fast in many world regions.[3] At the same time, as the attention has turned somewhat from the cumbersome complexity of sustainable development to the more pressing concern with finding a solution to climate change as a definitive feature of the Anthropocene, it is the world's cities that are said to be holding the proverbial torch of hope. This statement suggests a deviation from the status quo where traditional sources of international law do not deal with, or acknowledge, cities in any direct way. The manner in which cities govern has also been changing, and there is a clear 'reconstitution of urbanising landscapes'.[4] In the words of Neil Brenner and Christian Schmid, '[t]he terrain of the urban has been subjected to a high-intensity, high-impact earthquake through the worldwide social, economic, regulatory and environmental transformations of the post-1980 period'.[5] Planetary urbanization, postcolonial urbanism, and urban governance scholarship show how, over time, cities have generally obtained more power, more responsibilities, more functions but, in many instances, less financial support. These issues accompanied with geographic diversification, global value chains, mega world-level events such as the COVID-19 pandemic, population and labour mobility, and the need for global disease control all feed into an increasing focus on cities, localities, and subnational authorities in many subfields of international law. These fields include international migration law,[6] international trade law and economic diplomacy,[7] international sports law,[8]

2 Janne E. Nijman, 'Renaissance of the City as Global Actor: The Role of Foreign Policy and International Law Practices in the Construction of Cities as Global Actors', in Gunther Hellmann, Andreas Fahrmeir & Miloš Vec (eds.), *The Transformation of Foreign Policy: Drawing and Managing Boundaries from Antiquity to the Present* (Oxford University Press, 2016), 217.

3 See, e.g., Michele M. Betsill, 'Cities and the Multilevel Governance of Global Climate Change' (2006) 12(2) *Global Governance: A Review of Multilateralism and International Organizations* 141; Helmut Aust & Anél du Plessis (eds.), *The Globalisation of Urban Governance: Legal Perspectives on Sustainable Development Goal 11* (Routledge, 2019); Helmut Aust, 'Cities as International Legal Authorities: Remarks on Recent Developments and Possible Future Trends of Research' (2020) 4(1) *Journal of Comparative Urban Law and Policy* 82; Christopher J. Schell et al., 'The Ecological and Evolutionary Consequences of Systemic Racism in Urban Environments' (2020) 369 *Science* 369.

4 Neil Brenner & Christian Schmid, 'Towards a New Epistemology of the Urban' (2015) 19(2–3) *City* 151, 152.

5 *Id.*, 153.

6 See United Cities and Local Governments, *Migration*, www.uclg.org/en/issues/migration.

7 See Christine Cote, Saul Estrin, & Daniel Shapiro, 'Expanding the International Trade and Investment Policy Agenda: The Role of Cities and Services' (2020) 3 *Journal of International Business Policy* 199.

8 See Daniele Heerdt, 'Tapping the Potential of Human Rights Provisions in Mega-sporting Events' Bidding and Hosting Agreements' (2018) 17 *International Sports Law Journal* 170, 174.

international human rights law,[9] international anti-corruption law,[10] international health law,[11] international labour law,[12] and international climate change law.[13] Scholars and others explore the changing modalities of city governance from various angles as the impacts of globalism, the Anthropocene, and the urban question continue to intensify.

The inclusion of an urban goal in the Sustainable Development Goals (SDGs) may arguably be seen as the ultimate endorsement of the emergence of cities and transnational (global) associations of cities as a new type of actor on the international stage. Cities, as non-state actors, have managed to make it onto this platform because of their perceived contribution to unsustainable development as well as their potential to help effect positive change and critical transitions.[14] In the face of rapid urbanization and global change, SDG 11, Sustainable Cities and Communities, focuses on urban transformation and requires of countries – developed and developing and those in a global partnership – to make urban areas inclusive, safe, resilient, and sustainable. SDG 11 thus requires the translation of years of sustainable development and urban policy, and of scholarly claims, into practice. Bridging the divide between the 'think global, act local' rhetoric and practice, however, depends on various legally relevant factors as further elaborated in this chapter.

It is the symbolic meaning of a global goal focused on cities that triggers questions that may be of relevance to the legal discourse on the changing face of international law and global governance. From a strictly legal perspective, 'the city' and city-level authorities (municipalities) have been constructed traditionally from within a national legal order. Even before the adoption of SDG 11, Gerald Frug and David Barron described the two competing ideas of the city: first, the city as a creature of the state and, second, the city as a quasi-sovereign, a space of limited but real

9 Barbara Oomen & Moritz Baumgärtel, 'Frontier Cities: The Rise of Local Authorities as an Opportunity for International Human Rights Law' (2018) 29(2) *European Journal of International Law (EJIL)* 607.

10 See, e.g., 2014 African Charter on the Values and Principles of Decentralisation, Local Governance and Local Development, art. 14(3), which states that central governments and local governments or local authorities shall establish mechanisms to combat all forms of corruption.

11 See, e.g., Lawrence O. Gosten et al., 'The Legal Determinants of Health: Harnessing the Power of Law for Global Health and Sustainable Development' (2019) 393 *The Lancet* 1857, 1861.

12 See, e.g., Jonathan V. Beaverstock & Joanne Smith, 'Lending Jobs to Global Cities: Skilled International Labour Migration, Investment Banking and the City of London' (1996) 33(8) *Urban Studies* 1377.

13 Helmut P. Aust, 'The Shifting Role of Cities in the Global Climate Change Regime: From Paris to Pittsburgh and Back?' (2019) 28(1) *Review of European, Comparative and International Environmental Law* 57.

14 Of relevance is that, unlike other relatively new non-state actors such as private corporations and special interest groups, cities are still 'governmental'. See Swiney Chrystie, 'The Urbanization of International Law and International Relations: The Rising Soft Power of Cities in Global Governance' (2020) 41(2) *Michigan Journal of International Law* 227, 230.

autonomy with minimal state interference.[15] In short, the settling of the balance of powers and responsibilities between the city and the state has traditionally been considered a purely domestic matter and not a proper matter of concern to the international community. But things are changing as suggested by SDG 11 and other recent international developments, such as the explicit acknowledgement of the role of subnational authorities in the 2015 Paris Agreement on Climate Change and the particular local foci in the 2016 UN New Urban Agenda.[16] These changes also suggest that the city is becoming the sum of many tightly interwoven parts, including public authorities, civil society comprising of diverse communities, and the private sector. In addition to these developments, and as indicated above, the role of cities in matters of international migration, security, health governance, and human rights protection is also receiving increased attention.[17] It follows that the general consensus regarding the purely domestic character of the city-state relationship is being put into question by a series of developments that have collectively led to notions and expressions such as 'the internationalisation of cities', 'the international turn in urban history', and the 'global turn of the city'. This phenomenon is further fuelled by the proliferation of transnational alliances and global networks of cities that have an increasingly louder voice at the international table.[18]

SDG 11 has also come to underscore the understanding that 'cities have been particularly effective at presenting their cases in terms that reflect the dominant international development agenda. Among the values that unite the localist and internationalist agendas is an emphasis on human well-being and the virtues of community and its potential to drive democratisation through increased public participation in decision-making'. Participation is typically raised in discussions around the effective implementation of the SDGs and links with the substance of other goals such as SDG 16, Peace, Justice, and Strong Institutions.[19] But the international development agenda is also fixated on issues such as inclusivity, resilience, environmental degradation, the protection of cultural and natural heritage, sustainable human settlement planning, climate adaptation and mitigation, and access to adequate, safe, and affordable housing and basic services. All of these issues and more are featured in the ten targets of SDG 11. Yet, at the same time, these targets are quiet on the structural and financial dimensions of urban

[15] Gerald E. Frug & David J. Barron, 'International Local Government Law' (2006) 38(1) *The Urban Lawyer* 1, 1.

[16] UN Habitat III, *New Urban Agenda*, 2016, uploads.habitat3.org/hb3/NUA-English.pdf.

[17] See also Aust, n. 3, 84.

[18] See Sofie Bouteligier, *Cities, Networks and Global Environmental Governance: Spaces of Innovation, Places of Leadership* (Routledge, 2013); Jolene Lin, *Governing Climate Change: Global Cities and Transnational Lawmaking* (Cambridge University Press, 2018); Aust, n. 13, 57.

[19] See, e.g., Lisa-Maria Glass & Jens Newig, 'Governance for Achieving the Sustainable Development Goals: How Important Are Participation, Policy Coherence, Reflexivity, Adaptation and Democratic Institutions?' (2019) 2 *Earth System Governance* 1.

governance and accountable local government – three iron beams that remain critical to keep cities everywhere standing and in a position to deliver.

Canvassed against this background, this chapter consists of the following parts: first, a discussion of SDG 11, the process that led to its adoption, and how the urban goal intersects with the content and implementation of a number of other SDGs. Second, a critical evaluation of the symbolic and tangible meaning of SDG 11 considered from the perspective of international law and the more traditional understanding of its creators and subjects. Third, the international institutional context of relevance to cities and the implementation of the goal. The chapter concludes with some views on the future research required to be able to make more meaningful sense of the implications of SDG 11 and the international mobilization of cities as non-state actors for the development of international law, on the one hand, and of domestic urban law, on the other.

11.2 THE CONTENT OF SDG 11 IN THE CONTEXT OF THE OTHER SDGS

11.2.1 A *Clear Subnational Component*

Despite ongoing recognition of the critical role of cities for delivering development outcomes and achieving the objectives of subject-specific international laws and policies, the adoption of the SDGs marked the first time that a UN statistical reporting mechanism includes a clear subnational component.[20] The fact that urban systems have received this level of attention in the SDG process is telling, considering that the 2000 Millennium Development Goals (MDGs) did not have a corresponding goal. Much can be said about the symbolic and tangible meaning of this historical development, but the fact that cities in the global North and South are disproportionate contributors to global ecological dysfunction and the sites of a significant proportion of economically productive activity is not in dispute. As Ileana Porras claims, 'cities – with their economies of scale, relative concentration of wealth, people, businesses, and educational institutions – have much to contribute to the pursuit of sustainable development and to the response to climate change. Less clear is whether cities can deliver'.[21] It follows that, as laudable as its objectives may be, SDG 11 speaks to a complex context that cannot be separated from (geo) politics, the so-called erosion of the sovereign nation state, the constitution of the nation state, formal and informal economies, the state of the natural

[20] Zarina Patel et al., 'Local Responses to Global Sustainability Agendas: Learning from Experimenting with the Urban Sustainabe Development in Cape Town' (2017) 12(5) *Sustainability Science* 785, 788.

[21] Ileana M. Porras, 'The City and International Law: In Pursuit of Sustainable Development' (2009) 36(3) *Fordham Urban Law Journal* 537, 542–43.

environment, or the rich mixture of people and cultures that inhabit and govern cities across the globe.

11.2.2 *The Historical Build-Up to the Drafting and Inclusion of an Urban Goal in the SDGs*

As the period for attaining the MDGs drew to a close, 2012 saw the introduction of the process to produce a set of universal goals that would meet the urgent environmental, political, and economic challenges facing the world. Like the MDGs, the SDGs are not legally binding, and states are expected to take ownership and establish national frameworks to achieve the seventeen goals. States must follow up and review their progress in implementing the goals, for example. This process is heavily dependent on quality, accessible, and timely data collection, while world regions should follow up and review progress based on national-level analyses.

The architecture of the SDGs is interesting from the perspective of the city as a delineated geographical space and as a subnational authority ('governor') operating within the physical boundaries of the state. It is interesting because many of the threats to sustainable development (for example, inefficient use of land and natural resources; inequality; water, air, and soil pollution; waste; and the absence of long-term integrated planning) have their origins in urban areas, while the majority of society affected by, and contributing to, unsustainable development have their livelihoods rooted in cities. Yet the MDGs never addressed the role of cities as subjects in the development discourse. It only concentrated on slums. This narrow way of situating systemic urban problems in the sustainable development discourse has been flagged as a serious shortcoming of the MDGs.[22] The (new) goal pronounced in SDG 11 is to make cities inclusive, safe, resilient, and sustainable. Ten targets underpin this goal and speak to what is deemed necessary for its implementation.

The question arises about how the urban goal and the targets came about. The UN Conference on Sustainable Development's (Rio + 20) outcome document in 2012, *The Future We Want*, recognized systematic urban development as an important driver for sustainability and outlined its sub-themes, which formed the basis for the subsequent negotiation of SDG 11.[23] It emphasized the importance of well-planned and developed cities through integrated planning and management approaches and a holistic approach to urban development and human settlements. Further, it highlighted access to basic services, housing, and mobility in combination with conservation, protection of natural and cultural heritage, and

[22] Noora Arajärvi, 'Including Cities in the 2030 Agenda: A Review of the Post-2015 Process', in Aust & du Plessis, n. 3, 18.

[23] *The Future We Want: Outcome Document of the United Nations Conference on Sustainable Development*, Doc. A/RES/66/288, 11 September 2012, para 134; Arajärvi, n. 22, 17.

participation in decisions around urban development.[24] Significant urban issues such as inclusive housing and social services; affordable and sustainable transport and energy; protection and representation of vulnerable groups; decent jobs; access to sanitation; the implementation of the waste hierarchy, and disaster and climate risk reduction also received attention.[25] *The Future We Want* made reference to the importance of information and (sex-disaggregated) data, including demographic trends, income distribution, and informal settlements as well as the role of municipal governments in setting a vision for sustainable cities.[26] The matter of cooperation and partnerships for sustainable urban development also featured prominently.[27] Notably, despite the flagging of the urban context and its relevance for global sustainable development in the Rio + 20 outcome document, 'it was by no means certain that there would be sufficient support of states for a stand-alone goal for urban sustainable development' because, to date, 'it has not been a typical goal for development'.[28]

Authors such as Noora Arajärvi, Jacqueline Klopp, and Danielle Petretta extensively explain the transition from the MDGs to the SDGs and the eventual inclusion of an urban goal.[29] The Open Working Group (OWG) on Sustainable Development Goals, which consists of seventy-seven member states, with the support of the UN Technical Support Team (TST), facilitated the government-led SDG negotiation process. The UN Human Settlements Programme (UN-Habitat) and the United Nations Environment Programme (UNEP) led the drafting of the *TST Issues Brief: Sustainable Cities and Human Settlements*, with twelve other UN entities contributing.[30] During this time, various other institutions were vocal about the role of sustainable cities and human settlements for the post-2015 agenda. Some of these included the Group of Friends of Sustainable Cities, the Sustainable Development Solutions Network, the Global Task Force for Sustainable Cities and Regions, and the Institute for Advanced Sustainability Studies.[31]

As anticipated, the SDG negotiation process generated varying views on the viability of a stand-alone goal on cities. Arajärvi explains that while it received unequivocal support from the beginning from countries such as Saudi Arabia, China, Indonesia, Kazakhstan, Belarus, France, Germany, Switzerland, and the Caribbean community, countries such as India, Argentina, Canada, Israel, and the

[24] *Id.*, paras. 134, 135.
[25] *Id.*, para. 135.
[26] *Id.*, para. 136.
[27] *Id.*, paras. 136, 137.
[28] Arajärvi, n. 22, 18.
[29] *Id.*, 18–27; Jacqueline M. Klopp & Danielle L. Petretta, 'The Urban Sustainable Development Goal: Indicators, Complexity and the Politics of Measuring Cities' (2017) 63 *Cities* 92, 93–94.
[30] *TST Issues Brief: Sustainable Cities and Human Settlements*, n.d., 1–6, sustainabledevelopment.un.org/content/documents/2306TST%20Issues%20Brief%20Cities_FINAL.pdf; Arajärvi, n. 22, 19.
[31] See Arajärvi, n. 22, 19.

United States flagged concerns with a stand-alone goal on cities, such as the distinction that the goal would draw between rural and urban landscapes, livelihoods, and issues as well as the benefits of mainstreaming or integrating cities into the other goal areas.[32] However, as Arajärvi states, 'SDG 11 was at no point the cause for a heated debate. Rather, it was generally accepted that cities must be represented in the agenda, and while some states were hesitant to question the value of having a stand-alone urban goal, they were eventually persuaded by the majority in the OWG'.[33] At the final session of the OWG, it became clear that states were generally content with the language and objectives of SDG 11, with no objections raised about its substance or the envisioned implementation strategies. The uncontested passing of SDG 11 may be ascribed to a combination of a strong global commitment to make cities safe, inclusive, resilient, and sustainable and the approval of the SDG's vague, non-committal, and 'nebulous language'.[34]

11.2.3 *SDG 11 in a Web of Interrelated Global Goals*

Many agree that cities are governance actors: simultaneously part of the problems that are characteristic of the urban age and of the solutions to such problems.[35] A prominent feature of SDG 11 is that it is one of only a few actor-oriented goals among the SDGs, which otherwise focus on concrete outcomes such as SDG 1, No Poverty; SDG 5, Gender Equality; and SDG 13, Climate Action. SDG 11 also speaks to a particular level of governance and, as such, serves as a bridge between global and local (subnational) levels of governance. While the SDGs were adopted by UN member states and are also directed at states for their implementation, SDG 11 emphasizes (1) the city as a governance actor and (2) the fact that many local sustainable development issues have a cascading effect as they escalate beyond mere local concerns and trigger a need to respond both within and beyond the city's administrative boundaries.[36]

As stated, the issues captured in SDG 11 centre on urban safety, inclusiveness, sustainability, and resilience; all four of these 'city matters' are very elastic and, therefore, hard to confine in terms of their meaning and scope. However, we know that each of these issues forms the centre of its own discourse in the fields of law and development, urban geography, environmental governance, economics, politics, security studies, anthropology, climate change, international relations, sociology,

[32] *Id.*, 24–25.
[33] *Id.*, 24–25.
[34] *Id.*, 26–27.
[35] See David Satterthwaite, 'Successful, Safe and Sustainable Cities: Towards a New Urban Agenda' (2017) 19 *Commonwealth Journal of Local Governance* 3, 3–4.
[36] Helmut Philip Aust & Anél du Plessis, 'Good Urban Governance as a Global Aspiration: On the Potential Limits of SDG 11', in Duncan French & Louis Kotzé (eds.), *Sustainable Development Goals: Law, Theory and Implementation* (EE, 2018), 208.

history, and human rights, among others. It is perhaps for this reason that in-depth and useful scholarly analyses of the scope and meaning of SDG 11's wording are hard to come by. In fact, the statement has been made that '[t]he goal is broadly framed, relates to various other SDGs, and speaks to all of the dimensions of sustainable development' and, further, that the 'main targets, the inclusiveness, resilience, safety and sustainability of cities come across as desirable maxims, and they seem to be in tune with general trends of global governance'.[37]

From the available literature, it would seem that urban safety generally denotes physical safety and security of the person, including a safe and healthy work and living environment. Inclusiveness in cities refers to matters of social justice, cohesion, and inclusionary participation in urban governance. Urban sustainability points at environmental, economic, and social sustainability in cities. Resilience refers to the ability of people, governance systems, and infrastructure to bounce back to a state of safety and sustainability. SDG 11's targets develop these issues in more detail and give a slightly clearer view of the city that the world envisions by 2030. The clarity of the targets, however, is diluted by the potential for conflict between the things that the SDG 11 seeks to achieve. As previously explained,

> attempts to make a city safe might be in conflict with notions of inclusiveness. Inclusiveness might call for a maximization of participation opportunities of all individuals present in a given city, regardless of their citizenship and formal voting rights at the national level. Also, security concerns can lead to a dissolution of informal settlements whose inhabitants are then pushed further out towards the margins of a given city, or even beyond. Particularly in megacities of the Global South, there is an ongoing struggle to define city limits. Informal settlements are often found not only within administrative city boundaries, but also on the margins of the city. The decision whether or not to extend city limits is often an emotionally charged political process. Legalizing informal settlements within the administrative boundaries of a given city might mean a considerable improvement in the quality of the lives of the inhabitants of these informal settlements, yet existing social and political problems in the informal settlements *extra muros* might prove to be an obstacle to the legalization of property titles and settlement structures. The image of an existing city as safe and sustainable might be tarnished if the existing governance problems no longer just pertain to an illegal settlement, but need to be addressed by formal administrative avenues.[38]

These inevitable tensions may be read to suggest a need for prioritization. Every state and every city should be expected to prioritize safety, inclusivity, resilience, and sustainability along the lines of what is posing their own biggest short- and long-term threat(s) to sustainable urban development.

[37] *Id.*, 213, 216.

[38] *Id.*, 217. On the inherent contradictions and challenges of such processes of legalization, see Luis Eslava, *Local Space, Global Life: The Everyday Operation of International Law and Development* (Cambridge University Press, 2015), 190 *et seq.*

Some cities will be more prone to crime and bodily insecurity or be more vulnerable to climate risks than others, for example. The priority setting obviously will have to be done with the entire SDG framework and overarching national development plans in mind. As this volume shows, the SDGs create an intricate web of intersecting goals and targets. SDG 11 is inseparable from a number of other SDGs by virtue of the fact that cities are industrial hubs, homes to billions of people, the creators of inequality and waste, and the heartbeat of economic growth and local economic development. Most directly, SDG 11 intersects with SDG 1; SDG 3, Good Health and Well-being; SDG 6, Clean Water and Sanitation; SDG 7, Affordable and Clean Energy; SDG 8, Decent Work and Economic Growth; SDG 9, Industry, Innovation, and Infrastructure; SDG 10, Reduced Inequalities; SDG 12, Responsible Consumption and Production; SDG 13; SDG 15, Life on Land; SDG 16, Peace, Justice, and Strong Institutions; and SDG 17, Partnerships for the Goals. Considering these thematic groupings, it follows that SDG 11 also intersects with a number of the subfields of international law wherein cities and subnational authorities are increasingly found.

11.2.4 *The Ambiguity around 'Cities', Universality, and Other Concerns Emanating from SDG 11*

Lawyers in different legal disciplines and other researchers have highlighted concerns and problems with the SDG architecture.[39] These problems will not be elaborated here. For present purposes, however, it is necessary to highlight at least four of the most prominent concerns about SDG 11 that specifically may impact its implementation and, ultimately, its success. First, SDG 11 speaks in rather universal language to 'cities', while it is not clear which areas exactly it includes and excludes. Does SDG 11 include all 'urban' areas or only large towns, mega cities, and metropolitan areas with thousands and millions of inhabitants? Can a medium-sized or so-called secondary city claim to be included? Does SDG 11 speak to existing, as well as future, cities? What exactly is SDG 11's stance towards the water-food-energy nexus and other nexuses that exist between the infrastructures, resources, and ecosystems of cities (however defined) and their adjacent as well as more remote rural areas? These questions are important since they affect not only the national progress reporting but also the actual success with pursuing the urban goal.

Second, as suggested earlier, failing local governance, deficient municipal structures, absent governance principles, norms, and standards towards good local governance, insufficient investment as well as poor financial management, public

[39] See, e.g., Thomas Pogge & Mitu Sengupta, 'The Sustainable Development Goals (SDGs) as Drafted: Nice Idea, Poor Execution' (2015) 24(3) *Washington International Law Journal* 571; Farhana Sultana, 'An(Other) Geographical Critique of Development and SDGs' (2018) 8(2) *Dialogues in Human Geography* 186.

sector corruption, and insufficient revenue are some of the most pronounced threats to sustainable urban development in the global North and South. Yet these issues do not receive attention in SDG 11 or its targets. The reason may be that these issues are deemed to be the prerogative of states, but, ironically, it is this basket of ground-level 'city' issues that may be critical for the realization of several other SDGs, including, for example, SDG 5, SDG 6, and SDG 16. Third, city-level data generation and capturing poses a challenge – one that highlights the difference between cities in the global North and South and even between cities in the same world region. Klopp and Petretta explain this challenge with reference to informality and the poor availability of urban data in African and Asian cities where 90 per cent of urbanization is expected to happen by 2050.[40]

Fourth, cities and their local authorities will not be able to deliver on SDG 11 and its ambitious targets on their own. Some of the reasons, in addition to the scale(s) of sustainable development, include the fact that some cities are becoming increasingly privatized, which erodes the exclusivity of their public function; that politics, the community, and public participation is a force to reckon with at the city level; and that cities are creatures of states, subservient to, and dependent on, the state while often exercising only delegated powers.[41] Despite the benefits of these advances, such as local economic development through entrepreneurship and innovative forms of accountability, the privatization of municipal services (for example, water, waste, and electricity services) and infrastructure provision such as public transport is a cause of concern.[42] As a result of privatization, many of the operations of cities are de facto not in the hands of the states who have previously sat around the SDG negotiation table. Instead, the private sector, market forces, profits, investments, and primary interests other than urban sustainability have become the potential drivers of change and the shapers of urban form. This situation remains in need of further research.

11.3 POSITIONING SDG 11 IN INTERNATIONAL LAW

11.3.1 *Mounting City Participation in International Law*

As indicated earlier, traditional sources of international law do not deal with cities in an upfront way.[43] SDG 11 also establishes no enforceable legal rule, mandate, or

[40] Klopp & Petretta, n. 29, 96.

[41] See Sara Hughes & Jacqueline Peterson, 'Transforming Municipal Services to Transform Cities: Understanding the Role and Influence of the Private Sector' (2018) 10(1) *Sustainability* 1.

[42] See Nico Steytler, 'Socio-economic Rights and the Process of Privatising Basic Municipal Services' (2004) 8(2) *Law, Democracy and Development* 157; Sharon A. Jones et al., 'Privatization of Municipal Services: Sustainability Issues of Production and Provision' (2004) 10(4) *Journal of Infrastructure Systems* 139.

[43] Chrystie, n. 14, 233.

procedure. Instead, SDG 11 is 'the latest emanation of the thickening layer of international normative guidance on questions of "good urban governance"'.[44] SDG 11 may thus be deemed a normative compass indicating a relative direction for how cities should be governed, which points towards specific (development) objectives. With the publication of the 1987 Brundtland report and its conceptualization of sustainable development, the 'remit of cities in addressing environmental issues was recast as central to the new [sustainable development] agenda'.[45] The report's chapter 9 on 'The Urban Challenge' was premised on the understanding that, since most members of the world's future population will live in urban areas, cities should be central to the pursuit of sustainable development.[46] Today, it is widely agreed that the impact of urbanization will continue to bring about major multi-scale changes, especially with many countries in the developing world now entering the high-growth and rapid-transition features of an era of booming urbanization. This growing attention on the city level resonates with the theoretical work of Saskia Sassen, who has long argued that contemporary cities are sites of the global regulatory realm, 'where policy design and implementation [are] more feasible than at the national level'.[47] It follows that, while cities cannot be deemed formal subjects of international law as of today, developments such as the adoption of SDG 11 through the involvement of cities and networks of cities cannot be ignored by the international law community.

There is a growing body of scholarship, spanning different disciplines, trying to pin down the status and standing of cities in international law. Sometime before the adoption of the SDGs, Janne Nijman stated that

> [c]ities start to understand international law and global policies as meaningful to their behavior. . . . The constitution of the city's global actorhood is fully established when it finds recognition in foreign policy and international law practices. In turn, the city as a new global actor brings about change in the global system. Its participation in foreign policy and international law practices transforms the meaning of these practices and of the ideas, beliefs, expectations, and identities on which it is dependent. . . . [T]he constitution of the city as a global actor takes place in the social practices and processes wherein the global ideational structure exists. . . . An important part of the city's socialisation as a global actor is the recognition and

44 Aust & du Plessis, n. 36, 201.

45 Harriet Bulkeley & Michele M Betsill, 'Rethinking Sustainable Cities: Multilevel Governance and the 'Urban' Politics of Climate Change' (2005) 14(3) *Environmental Politics* 42, 44; World Commission on Environment and Development (WCED), *Our Common Future* (1987).

46 Critical towards proclamations of a so-called urban age and the underlying statistics, see Neil Brenner & Christian Schmid, 'The 'Urban Age' in Question' (2014) 38(3) *International Journal of Urban and Regional Research* 731.

47 Saskia Sassen, 'A Focus on Cities Takes Us Beyond Existing Governançe Frameworks', in Joseph E. Stiglitz & Mary Kaldor (eds.), *The Quest for Security: Protection without Protectionism and the Challenge of Global Governance* (Columbia University Press, 2013), 243.

respect with which the city's new role as an independent global actor is met by the global community.[48]

The question arises as to the extent to which cities (and the explosion of global city networks) have been helping to transform international law, if at all. Helmut Philipp Aust indirectly responds to this question by arguing for the 'observation of processes by which cities (and other actors) assert themselves as internationally relevant actors, together with an analysis of how the established structures of international law respond to these processes'.[49] I agree with the author who further states that the 'assessment of the evolution of the international legal system is thereby never frozen in time, but can only provide snapshots of its development at a respective point in time'.[50] In other words, what we observe now in relation to mounting city participation in international law and the role of the city in the quest for global sustainable development may very well look entirely different a hundred odd years from now. It is close to impossible to predict whether the role of the city in the transformation of international law will intensify or diminish in real terms.

11.3.2 *Cities as Non-state Actors and Their Growing Recognition in Some Sectors of International Law*

Michael Riegner makes the point that, 'despite their increasing significance, relations between international institutions and cities are still an unusual topic for legal research. While international lawyers have accepted international organisations as legal subjects and significant actors, cities are still treated primarily as sub-national entities mediated by their nation states.'[51] He further shows that it is not only international lawyers who stand to be blamed for this situation since local government lawyers have also traditionally paid little attention to cities' international relations.[52] Relevant for the present purpose is Riegner's further explanation that, in recent years,

> this dualist framework has been challenged by legal scholars who argue that an 'international local government law' or a 'law of the global city' is emerging. … [I]nternational institutions have discovered local governments as allies in the fulfillment of their global mandates. Aid institutions promote decentralisation as a development strategy, and the UN forges global city networks to combat climate

48 Nijman, n. 2, 226–27.

49 Helmut Philipp Aust, 'Shining Cities on the Hill? The Global City, Climate Change, and International Law' (2015) 26(1) *EJIL* 255, 273.

50 *Id.*, 273.

51 Michael Riegner, 'International Institutions and the City: Towards a Comparative Law of Glocal Governance', in Aust & du Plessis, n. 3, 38–39.

52 *Id.*, 38–39.

change. These two dynamics, one bottom-up and one top-down, have added another dimension to multilevel global governance: the 'glocal' city.[53]

It is in this context that cities feature prominently in some sectors or subfields of international law. As mentioned earlier, these fields range from international trade law and international migration law to international health law and international climate change law. Given the strong link that it has with sustainable development and, thus, the crux of the SDGs, this section focuses primarily on international climate change law as an example of how cities are gaining prominence as international actors.

While cities will probably never be deemed the chief agents in environmental governance, they are central in the global response to climate change since the envisaged climate change law and policy at the global, regional, national, and local levels are fast moving closer to each other. From the 2015 Paris Agreement,[54] the 2015 Sendai Framework for Disaster Risk Reduction,[55] and SDGs 11, 13, and 15[56] to the 2016 New Urban Agenda, the underlying message is clear: cities are needed for an effective, long-term response to the causes and effects of climate change. At the same time, global city agglomerations such as the C40 Climate Change Leadership Group (C40)[57] and the International Council for Local Environmental Initiatives (ICLEI) – Local Governments for Sustainability[58] continue to release reports and to develop projects that convey a very strong message of cities needing to be recognized as an 'accelerant for transitions in energy and industrial systems, land, and ecosystems'[59] and that limiting global warming to 1.5 degrees Celsius depends, at least in part, on urban actions and policies. This message follows on the understanding of these institutions that an effective response to climate change depends on the transition of systems as well as on 'rapid advancements in how societies develop and navigate transitions in four systems: energy, land and ecosystems, urban and infrastructure, and industry'.[60] The urban system is deemed to be a factor in each of these systems everywhere, given the fact that the world is now predominantly urban. But, as Susan Parnell and Jennifer Robinson warn, 'there is a real danger that despite the greater prominence of cities ... some cities may in fact now slip further behind

53 *Id.*

54 See also Aust, n. 13.

55 United Nations, *United Nations Sendai Framework for Disaster Risk Reduction 2015–2030*, 2015.

56 *Transforming Our World: The 2030 Agenda for Sustainable Development*, Doc. A/Res/70/1, 25 September 2015.

57 See C40, *C40 Cities*, 2020.

58 See ICLEI – Local Governments for Sustainability, *ICLEI: Local Governments for Sustainability*, 2020.

59 International Panel on Climate Change, *Summary for Urban Policy Makers: What the IPCC Special Report on Global Warming of 1.5°C Means for Cities*, 2018, 17.

60 *Id.*, 9.

in the framing of urban opportunities and dilemmas – not least because of the influence of scientific modes of research that do not do enough to make visible unconventional, unrecorded and under-measured cities'.[61]

In the most ordinary sense, the link between climate change, cities, and the changing global governance landscape that lies within urbanization is deeply rooted in everyday life (and its processes contribute to climate change) as well as in the quality of urban space that involves a complex constellation of material, social, institutional, environmental, and everyday transformations.[62] Sassen explains that 'cities are the terrain where some of the global conditions marking the twenty-first century hit the ground'.[63] We know that the quality of urban space is increasingly being affected by global climate change as well as by the mitigative and adaptive measures required to address it. The reciprocal relationship between cities and climate change speaks to the way in which cities and urban processes contribute to climate change as well as to the present and future impacts that climate change will have on the health and well-being of urban dwellers, city infrastructures and services, the built environment, and the ability to predictively plan urban development. Scientific reports indicate that urban areas are a major source of carbon dioxide emissions, contributing to greenhouse gas–induced climate change, and that associated waste heat released into the environment in cities is a driver of urban micro-climates.[64] Cities thus have a meaningful part to play in climate mitigation efforts. At the same time, as the COVID-19 pandemic serves to show, cities are dense areas of people, economic activity, and infrastructures that are heavily impacted when risks such as disaster, health, or environmental risks materialize in their areas. For this reason, cities and the socio-ecological systems that they support have to be resilient and part of the global process of transformation towards climate change adaptation and resilience more broadly.[65]

Michelle Betsill remarked in as early as 2006 that the need to address environmental problems at the local level has been a 'long-standing tenet of green political thought',[66] voiced initially in the 1987 Brundtland report[67] and subsequently in chapter 28 of the 1992 Agenda 21, which called for a Local Agenda 21.[68] In the years

61 Susan Parnell & Jennifer Robinson, 'The Global Urban: Difference and Complexity in Urban Studies and the Science of Cities', in Suzanne Hall & Ricky Burdett (eds.), *The Sage Handbook of the Twenty-first Century City* (Sage Publications, 2018), 17.

62 See 1992 United Nations Framework Convention on Climate Change (UNFCCC); UNFCCC, *Fifth Assessment Report of the IPCC*, 2014, 90–93; Neil Brenner & Christian Schmid, 'Elements for a New Epistemology of the Urban', in Hall & Burdett, n. 61, 57.

63 Saskia Sassen, 'Global Cities: Places for Researching the Translocal', in Hall & Burdett, n. 61, 144.

64 See, e.g., World Meteorological Organization, *Climate and Urban Development*, 1996; UNFCCC, 90.

65 See UNFCCC, chap. 12.

66 Betsill, n. 3, 142.

67 WCED, n. 45, chap. 9.

68 *Agenda 21*, UN Doc A/CONF. 151/26, 13 June 1992.

to follow, commentators argued that cities, rather than nation states, 'may be the most appropriate arena in which to pursue policies to address specific global environmental problems'.[69] As the research of Christophe Sohn and Bernard Reitel has shown, however, there is a danger in devaluing the role of the nation state in regard to any problem or initiative spanning national borders.[70] This is an issue that is not further explored here. However, de facto, a large number of cities actively participate in global climate governance – that is, in a sphere of power that is remote from, yet relevant to, local communities. There has been keen interest in understanding this phenomenon for reasons that range from cities seemingly side-stepping the state to shifting power dynamics in the international arena, where states previously governed alone.

The body of knowledge on cities and global climate governance has steadily developed over the past two decades. Some of the key understandings include, first, that cities are sites of high energy consumption, industrial pollution, and waste production and, in general, local authorities have control over these processes with functional powers in relation to land use planning, urban transport, energy supply, and management and building regulations. Many municipalities thus have a handle on processes that are critical for emissions reduction towards climate mitigation.[71] Second, cities are home to vulnerability – of human beings and socio-ecological systems – and may be best placed to facilitate the inclusive articulation and formulation of short- and longer-term adaptation and transformation needs. Here, the emphasis is on inclusiveness, responsiveness, and accountability as key features of democratic local governance.[72] Third, as public administrations, many cities are democratic institutions that can foster partnerships, engage stakeholders, facilitate public participation, and lobby national or federal authorities in efforts to respond to climate change.[73] Fourth, many cities have joined one or more global or transnational city networks. This 'ecosystem of city networks' creates a global forum for information sharing that is meaningful for individual municipalities devoted to environmental sustainability and for innovative climate change response

[69] Betsill, n. 3, 143.

[70] The authors' research into the role of national states in the construction of cross-border metropolitan regions in Europe revealed that politics of scale matter and that the '(s)ymbolic and *a fortiori* territorial recognition of an initiative or scale of governance by a state contributes to strengthening its legitimacy, in the first instance in the eyes of those actors that are part of that state'. Christophe Sohn & Bernard Reitel, 'The Role of National States in the Construction of Cross-Border Metropolitan Regions in Europe: A Scalar Approach' (2013) 23 (3) *European Urban and Regional Studies* 306, 316.

[71] See UNFCCC, chap. 12.

[72] See Alex De Sherbinin, Andrew Schiller & Alex Pulsipher, 'The Vulnerability of Global Cities to Climate Hazards' (2007) 19(1) *Environment and Urbanisation* 39.

[73] See Benjamin Barber, *Democracy and Climate Change: How Cities Can Do What States Can't* (Center for Humans and Nature, 2013). However, it is also true that in a number of cities much of the power is in criminal networks, mafias, and gangs with a significant degree of corruption.

action.[74] As already indicated, cities further play a nuanced, yet increasingly visible, role in transnational climate change law and policy-making,[75] and, while international agreement and consensus on climate response action often get stuck as a result of nationalistic sentiments, fears, and the protection of domestic interests, cities have been bold in making commitments on emission reduction targets, which is just one example.[76]

There are, however, also critiques of the statement that cities are global climate change actors. The critics warn, and justifiably so, that there are localities that have been 'left behind' and that representativity in the global arena leans towards the major, well-resourced, and well-capacitated cities mostly situated in the global North.[77] They further warn, as alluded to earlier, that a focus on cities and urban localities in making sense of the 'local' in 'global' climate governance signals a level of ignorance about critical rural-urban linkages and the interdependence of life-supporting systems embedded in ecosystems, water systems, and micro-climates within as well as beyond city borders.[78] Of further concern should be the kind of role played by cities in countries where democratic processes are undermined. These concerns serve to caution against broad-sweeping generalizations as well as romanticizing an absolute role for cities in global climate change governance. It is true, though, that those responsible for urban governance have no choice but to question if and how global climate change demands that things be done differently, bearing in mind the impact of climate change on the present and future generations and the ways in which it affects the core functions of local authorities such as the delivery of basic services.[79]

11.3.3 *Boundaries Created by Domestic Constitutional Law and the Rural - Urban Nexus*

It is argued that how the actual role of cities in the making and implementation of international law continue to unfold will depend on at least two factors: (1) the authority (and autonomy) of cities in terms of domestic legal infrastructures and

74 See Michele Acuto, 'Understanding the Global Ecosystem of City Networks' (2020) *Urban Studies* 1; Aust, n. 13, 57–66.

75 See Lin, n. 18.

76 See, e.g., C40, *Global Aggregation of City Climate Commitments: Methodological Review*, c40-production-images.s3.amazonaws.com/researches/images/24_Working_Together_Global_Aggregation.original.pdf?1411483385.

77 See Jennifer S. Bansard, Philipp H. Pattberg & Oscar Widerberg, 'Cities to the Rescue? Assessing the Performance of Transnational Municipal Networks in Global Climate Governance' (2017) 17(2) *International Environmental Agreements: Politics, Law and Economics* 229, 242.

78 See UNFCCC, chap. 9.

79 Hayley Leck & Debra Roberts, 'What Lies Beneath: Understanding the Invisible Aspects of Municipal Climate Change Governance' (2015) 13 *Current Opinion in Environmental Sustainability* 61.

(2) the degree to which the rural-urban nexus is leveraged for development. The first of these factors actually points towards the elephant in the room: what about the relative autonomy of cities and the limitation of their governing powers by states and domestic legal infrastructures, the risk of resistance by domestic legal systems, and the critical role of local politics in how municipalities govern? In this regard, Helmut Aust and I hold that,

> [d]espite the noble ideas of inclusive global governance that sees a role for cities, the challenges of effective and connected governance are real. The search for more sustainable forms of urbanization and for inclusive, safe, sustainable and resilient cities depends on political and institutional (governance) structures and decisions promoting cooperation among different governance actors operating on different scales. In particular, the nation-state will remain central to any role cities can play, locally as well as globally. Despite all the talk about its demise, the nation-state remains the key player in international relations and international law.[80]

It follows that cities do not have free rein in the global governance arena. Cities are governed by people with power that has been granted from below – people that have the foremost task of being responsive to local needs and being accountable to local communities (not foreign states). City authorities have governing powers firmly situated in, and shaped by, national and sometimes even regional legal architectures that can create barriers to the way in which cities participate in the international law arena – for example, in reference to formally committing to carbon dioxide emission reduction targets or attracting cross-border investment and labour for urban transport or electricity infrastructure development. Breaking free from the dictates of the state and domestic law may threaten the legitimacy and sustainability of the work of cities at the international level. While this outcome may result for the individual city that hails from a specific country, an altogether different result may occur when the dynamics are between individual cities and global city networks and where it is actually the latter that acts as the representative agent at the international level. However, this question is not explored further in this chapter.

The city has been labelled an ecosystem of its own kind.[81] However, this metaphorical ecosystem is alive because of the processes and resources that exist beyond urban boundaries. The fact that cities cannot survive on their own (that is, without the life-support services and products provided by agricultural, conservation, energy, water, mineral, and biodiversity systems) will have to become mainstreamed in the planning and priority setting for sustainable urban development. There is a real danger in framing urban development (in international law and policy discourse) with a predominant focus on, and preoccupation with, the safety, resilience, sustainability, and inclusiveness of the city as a geographically delineated space. It is

80 Aust & du Plessis, n. 3, 205.

81 Antonio Bodini, Cristina Bondavalli, & Stefano Allesina, 'Cities as Ecosystems: Growth, Development and Implications for Sustainability' (2012) 245 *Ecological Modelling* 185.

argued that, for cities to sustainably contribute to the development and implementation of international law and policy around development questions, meaningful relationships and channels of communication will have to be established to cross the bridge between the city and its rural hinterlands. Divestment in one city could have an impact on another city, which suggests that the flow of resources, capital, and people between cities inter se should also be considered. In other words, optimal understanding of spatial interactions as well as proper representation is necessary for cities (in the collective) to stake out a claim in the ongoing processes of making and implementing international law and policy.

11.4 POSITIONING SDG 11 IN THE INTERNATIONAL INSTITUTIONAL CONTEXT

As this chapter has alluded to earlier, the successful implementation of SDG 11 with its ambitious targets heavily depends on multi-stakeholder and multi-level involvement because of the complex powers at play in how cities are designed and how they operate. SDG 11 is not a passive goal. It requires positive action via resource allocation, investment, planning, budgeting, innovation and technological advancement, engineering, monitoring, construction, decisions, programmes, projects, standard setting, experimentation and strategic roadmaps, to name but a few. This mixture of actions involves international, regional, and domestic actors, the public and private sector, and local communities. But what is the international institutional context within which SDG 11 should be implemented?

Global city networks and the international structures responsible for the United Nations' human settlements and environmental agenda, together with institutions such as the World Bank and non-governmental organizations such as the World Economic Forum, are critical for the support necessary to see states and cities rising to places of sustainability, safety, inclusiveness, and resilience. It is these institutions that may be necessary for legitimizing the positive action(s) above and for scaling these up. The World Bank and the World Economic Forum specifically do this by way of extensive research in, with, and for cities from across the globe. The research and skills development initiatives of these institutions focus on policy levers such as institutions and regulations, infrastructure, and land, skills, and innovation as well as enterprise support and finance. In addition to the research dimension of the work that aims at improving cities as investment hubs for economic development, as sites of labour productivity, and as fertile geographies for growth coalitions of public and private stakeholders for poverty alleviation and economic development, the World Bank typically also develops support tools and initiates activities tailored to the specific needs of cities and their levels of progress.[82] It further mobilizes investment

[82] World Bank, *Planning and Financing Low Carbon, Liveable Cities*, www.worldbank.org/en/news/feature/2013/09/25/planning-financing-low-carbon-cities.

in urban infrastructure.[83] For example, the World Bank in recent years developed greenhouse gas inventories and assessments for low-carbon investment planning and financing solutions for cities in developing countries.[84] These initiatives are critical to assist countries in reaching their international climate change obligations.

A fair amount of work has been done on understanding global city networks as institutions and as global governance actors. In a nutshell, these networks have done an incredible amount in terms of local experimental governance (especially in the climate change response sector) and, at the same time, have blurred the established boundary between public and private actors in international law and global governance.[85] The C40 Climate Change Leadership Group (C40), for example, has developed a framework to help cities monitor, evaluate, and report on the impacts of climate adaptation initiatives. This framework includes a focus on equity and inclusivity, providing cities with a very necessary means to assess the equitable distribution of the impact of climate programmes, actions, and policies.[86]

Within the UN system, it is UN-Habitat that is primarily charged with the normative and operational issues of cities and human settlements. In 2001, it replaced the Commission on Human Settlements, which comprised fifty-eight member countries and was serviced by the Centre for Human Settlements, which served as the focal point for human settlement actions and the coordination of activities within the UN system.[87] UN-Habitat is a UN programme governed by a Governing Council that reports directly to the UN General Assembly. It aims to support the work of national statistical offices to improve the formulation of evidence-based policies, strategies, and programmes, for example. As the international focal point for sustainable urbanization and human settlements, UN-Habitat has been designated as the custodian agency for nine of the fifteen indicators under SDG 11, and it supports the monitoring and reporting of four indicators in other goals.[88] As such, UN-Habitat is leading the methodological development of guides and tools for the urban-related SDG indicators and targets as well as working with other UN agencies and various stakeholders to strengthen the capacity of

[83] ESI Africa, *World Bank Invests in Maputo's Critical Urban Infrastructure*, www.esi-africa.com/industry-sectors/finance-and-policy/world-bank-invests-in-maputos-critical-urban-infrastructure/.

[84] See Sustainable Development Goals Knowledge Platform, *The State of City Climate Finance 2015*, https://sustainabledevelopment.un.org/index.php?page=view&type=400&nr=2201&menu=35.

[85] For an extensive discussion of examples of interventions, initiatives, and collaborations, see Bouteligier, n. 18; Lin, n. 18; Aust, n. 13, 57–66.

[86] See C40, *Measuring Progress in Urban Climate Change Adaptation: A Monitoring, Evaluating and Reporting Framework*, www.c40knowledgehub.org/s/article/Measuring-Progress-in-Urban-Climate-Change-Adaptation-A-monitoring-evaluating-and-reporting-framework?language=en_US.

[87] See Hannah Birkenkötter, 'Ensuring Access to Public Space as a Dimension of 'Safe Cities': The Role of UN Entities in Shaping the Global Urban Governance Agenda', in Aust & du Plessis, n. 3, 132.

[88] See United Nations Department of Economic and Social Affairs, *UN-Habitat*, sdgs.un.org/un-system-sdg-implementation/united-nations-human-settlements-programme-un-habitat-24511.

countries and cities to efficiently monitor and report on these indicators.[89] UN-Habitat also enters into agreements with city partners on some of its initiatives such as its integrated urban planning and management model to help cities build resilience against disasters such as the Hurricane Sandy, which crashed through coastlines from the Caribbean to North America's Atlantic seaboard in 2012.[90] However, Hannah Birkenkötter shows that there is significant uncertainty as to the legal personality and legal status of partnerships concluded between entities such as UN-Habitat and a group of mayors or a single mayor.[91] This uncertainty concerns the traditional and emerging subjects of international law and the fact that international legal personality depends on whether an entity (such as a global city) or an individual (such as a mayor or councillor responsible for a city's climate change response portfolio) bears rights or obligations under international law.

It is anticipated that, in addition to existing partnerships and agreements between cities, city alliances, and UN-Habitat, the implementation of SDG 11 may generate significantly more in the period between 2020 and 2030. It is relevant in this context to take note of Riegner's reminder that a prerequisite for cities to establish relationships with international institutions (whether it is the World Bank or UN-Habitat) is that national law allows them to do so[92] as well as of his argument based on case examples from Italy, South Africa, and Brazil, that the 'local' competences of cities 'are increasingly interpreted to encompass relationships with international institutions'.[93] Riegner, however, is sceptical about the cooperation between international institutions and cities:

> International cooperation mobilises resources for local investment, enables mutual learning and the exchange of experience across countries, and it incentivises local actors to consider problems and externalities that transcend city boundaries. International institutions can be and often have been advocates of more equitable city development. At the same time, such cooperation faces criticisms of a lack of effectiveness, legitimacy, and distributive justice. Cities may not be the right level for effective cooperation on issues with mobile causes and spill-over effects. Local climate change coalitions may simply displace emissions to the next city, or not include cities with emission-heavy industry [sic]. Upgrading informal neighborhoods within the bounds of a city leads to the physical or economic displacement of poor populations to the periphery beyond the municipal boundaries. In these situations, the risks of bypassing higher levels of government become particularly apparent.[94]

89 *Id.*

90 See UN-Habitat, *A New UN-Habitat City Resilience Profiling Programme*, mirror.unhabitat.org/content.asp?cid=11638&catid=145&typeid=6.

91 Birkenkötter, n. 87, 142.

92 Riegner, n. 51, 53.

93 *Id.*, 54.

94 *Id.*, 57–58.

Be that as it may, with scant international law scholarship on this matter, it would appear that the jury is still out on the legal status and legal implications of the relationship between international organizations and cities and that the international institutional context for the implementation of SDG 11 is all but clear.

11.5 CONCLUSIONS

Over time, cities have found in sustainable development a strong and increasingly relevant anchor for making themselves indispensable partners in global governance and in the development and implementation of international law and policy. While much attention has thus far been paid to cities operating in global environmental governance and in international climate change law and policy, these areas should not be seen as the only ones where cities add value. Boris Vormann actually claims that 'many now see sustainable and smart cities as a panacea for the challenges of globalisation. Proponents of this view suggest that the success of the post-industrial city can be replicated globally, thereby fostering social progress even in the most remote corners of the world. In the tradition of liberalism, cities are assigned a special role in this 'civilising' process'.[95] SDG 11 certainly endorses this view. The urban SDG suggests that, by now, cities are globally viewed as partners in the complex web of stakeholders, decision-makers, and implementers of global sustainable development policy in the quest for social progress in every nation state. SDG 11 further suggests that more traditional actors in the international arena are eager to partner with cities as subnational authorities in the pursuit of global sustainable development and that, slowly but surely, city authorities are obtaining a voice in the hallways and meeting rooms where international law and policy are conceptualized.

Having a voice, however, is not to say that 'cities can deliver'.[96] The symbolism of SDG 11, as far as it concerns the city as an active participant in global governance and international law and policy-making, should not be overstretched. It is an uncontested fact that cities are crucial vehicles for assisting from the bottom up with the pursuit of urban sustainability and shaping urban space and activity (such as communication, travel, and international trade) to advance, and not to impede, global sustainable development as embodied in the SDGs. Bridging the divide between the 'think global, act local' rhetoric and practice, however, depends on various legally relevant factors – many of which are trapped in domestic, regional, and international politics, international relations, and economic power. Whereas global city networks and transnational alliances are influential internationally and do a lot to foster transnational collaboration, peer learning, and solidarity among some cities, these networks cannot deliver on the most local of sustainable

95 Boris Vormann, 'City Limits: Sustainable Urban Governance in Planetary Infrastructural Regime', in Aust & du Plessis, n. 3, 65.

96 Porras, n. 21, 542–43.

development needs in every single nation state. An organization such as ICLEI or C40 cannot ensure or be answerable for safety or inclusivity in the cities of Dhaka, Kigali, Moscow, San Jose, Johannesburg, Osaka, or Jakarta, for example, which means that the role of transnational and global city networks in the eventual implementation of international law and policy should equally not be overstretched. These networks are not legally accountable or responsible to perform or deliver. Their active participation in global sustainable development initiatives and in climate change law and policy development remains at this point very much an international relations exercise – albeit a very relevant one at that.

The argument set out here is in agreement with Eric Biber who holds that the Anthropocene 'will erode fundamental distinctions between what is global and local' and, further, that the consequences of human impairment of global systems will inevitably force the adaptation and development of legal systems.[97] All legal systems are affected by the unsustainable development that is accompanying the Anthropocene. It is yet to be seen how international law, on the one hand, and domestic urban law, on the other hand, will be required to adapt and to develop. It is anticipated that the subjects, objects, and stakeholders of international law will continue to expand and that we will see subnational authorities and 'local' issues such as inclusive and non-discriminatory urban development, public and private investment in (smart) urban infrastructure, the local protection and realization of human rights and social justice as well as the local protection of ecosystems feature ever more prominently in the international law and policy agenda. At the same time, we can expect to see international law working for urban dwellers much more visibly in matters of daily life.

Future research in this field will have to look, inter alia, into understanding conflicting legal systems and regimes; the co-existence of multi-level legal regimes and legal pluralism in the city space; local and democratic representativity in international law and policy-making; the nexus between locally generated data and the benchmarking of international law and policy success; the merger of the public and private sectors within the city's boundaries as well as beyond; and the possible unintended and unexpected (positive or negative) consequences of conceptually tinkering with the international law architecture that has yielded significant success since the Second World War.

97 Eric Biber, 'Law in the Anthropocene Epoch' (2017) 106(1) *Georgetown Law Journal* 1, 41, 49.

12

SDG 12: Ensure Sustainable Consumption and Production Patterns

Alessandra Arcuri and Enrico Partiti

ABSTRACT

Sustainable Development Goal (SDG) 12, Responsible Consumption and Production, operates in a context shaped by contrasts between thriving consumers and exploited workers and rampant unsustainable practices. This contribution critically discusses the areas of international law that are relevant for SDG 12, with a focus on international trade and investment regimes. It argues that the environmental and human rights agreements currently in force are much weaker than the powerful regimes of international economic law, whose main preoccupation is the liberalization of trade and investment and not the material footprints and redistributive consequences of sustainable production and consumption. With its focus on voluntarism and the lack of reference to key human rights instruments, SDG 12 is likely to reproduce the structural conditions that have generated enormous social and environmental damages rather than providing orientation for much needed transformative change.

KEYWORDS

SDG 12, sustainable production and consumption, WTO law, investment law, private regulation, sustainability, regional trade agreements, bilateral investment treaties, business and human rights, dispute settlement

12.1 INTRODUCTION

The concept of sustainable consumption and production (SCP) is hard to capture in a single definition. The UN Environmental Programme's (UNEP) 2015 text

Sustainable Consumption and Production: A Handbook for Policymakers identifies common features of various characterizations of SCP.[1] According to UNEP, SCP refers to '[i]mproving the quality of life without increasing environmental degradation and without compromising the resource needs of future generations' and to '[d]ecoupling economic growth from environmental degradation'.[2] Despite the recognition of the importance of SCP, consumption and production continue to grow unsustainably under the current Sustainable Development Goal (SDG) framework. As reported by the UN Secretary-General in one of the progress reports on the SDGs, '[i]n 2017, worldwide material consumption reached 92.1 billion tons, up from 87 billion in 2015 and a 254 per cent increase from 27 billion in 1970, with the rate of extraction accelerating every year since 2000'.[3] The global material footprint has been exponentially increasing in the past decades, with high-income countries contributing the most to this unsustainable use of resources.[4]

On the one hand, SDG 12, Responsible Consumption and Production, could be seen as a welcome development for raising the question of production and consumption patterns to the level of a sustainable development goal. Discursively, SDG 12 enables global politics to garner attention and support towards achieving SCP and to break with unsustainable patterns. The collection of data on SDG 12 helps to expose the contribution of global patterns of production and consumption to unsustainability. On the other hand, SDG 12 can be seen as dodging key issues for sustainable patterns of production and consumption because it orients action in some areas but remains elusive on the central problem – that is, the existing socioeconomic system, which is arguably the major cause of the unsustainable patterns of consumption and production. This system is shaped and enabled by a cobweb of international laws, regulations, and governance schemes and, in some policy areas, by a lack of laws, regulations, and governance. In such a system, consumers often thrive at the expense of the material producers of their wealth, those invisible precarious workers who are rarely lifted up from poverty. Communities are displaced and oppressed in the course of such production processes, and the environment is squandered.

This chapter relates SDG 12 to areas of international law that are directly or indirectly relevant to SCP, particularly to the body of international economic law and to instances of private regulation, which are allegedly enacted to make consumption and production sustainable. Our main argument is that the environmental

1 UNEP, *Sustainable Consumption and Production: A Handbook for Policymakers* (UNEP, 2015).

2 *Id.*, 10.

3 United Nations, *Report of the Secretary-General on SDG Progress 2019 Special Edition* (United Nations, 2019), 22.

4 The Statistics Division of the UN Department of Economic and Social Affairs in a dedicated webpage defines the material footprint as 'the total amount of raw materials extracted to meet final consumption demands'. UN Department of Economic and Social Affairs, *Ensure Sustainable Consumption and Production Patterns*, unstats.un.org/sdgs/report/2019/goal-12/.

and human rights agreements currently in force are dismal when compared to the powerful regime of international economic law. The international legal system is built around strong institutions to protect capital, while offering weak enforcement mechanisms for environment and human rights and remaining relatively disengaged with the material footprints and the redistributive consequences of production and consumption processes. Such an asymmetric legal order cannot be conducive to SCP because it rests on an extractivist ethos that furthers the liberalization of trade and investment. While a major overhaul of the system seems necessary, our analysis also discusses openings in the legal system, hinting at the interstitial space where there is hope for making consumption and production sustainable.

12.2 THE CONTENT OF SDG 12 IN THE CONTEXT OF THE OTHER SDGS

For its emphasis on the necessity of reducing environmental degradation, SDG 12 is naturally related to the other SDGs, particularly SDG 7, Affordable and Clean Energy; SDG 13, Climate Action; SDG 14, Life below Water; and SDG 15, Life on Land. Several SDG 12 targets and indicators in fact directly relate to these SDGs. Target 12.c, for example, aims to diminish harmful subsidies to fossil fuels, which is clearly linked to both SDGs 7 and 13. In addition, target 12.4, on minimizing the chemical contamination of air, water, and soil, is clearly related to SDGs 14 and 15.

The emphasis on the impacts of production and consumption on the environment is crucial, especially in light of critiques that the environment is a 'secondary concern ... for the international community'.[5] Yet the lack of attention to the inequalities within which current patterns of production and consumption are embedded is problematic at best. For example, labour rights are mentioned in the targets and indicators of SDG 8, Decent Work and Economic Growth, but not in those of SDG 12. Is the implication that a certain production process can be considered sustainable when even a living wage is not being paid to its material producers?[6]

The history of how the concept of SCP has penetrated UN discourse and reached the status of a standalone goal illustrates the tensions between different visions of development and different ideas on how to share responsibilities and costs between developed and developing countries for more sustainable consumption and production policies. For instance, states have been divided as to whether SCP should have been a cross-cutting theme or a standalone goal, with developing countries wanting

[5] Paolo Galizzi, 'From Stockholm to New York, via Rio and Johannesburg: Has the Environment Lost Its Way on the Global Agenda?' (2005) 29(5) *Fordham International Law Journal* 952, 1002.

[6] Genevieve LeBaron, *Researching Forced Labour in the Global Economy: Methodological Challenges and Advances* (Oxford University Press, 2018).

it to be a standalone goal.[7] Despite having obtained this status, the targets to achieve SCP have been criticized for being vaguely framed, often lacking clarity, with elusive indicators that are hard to quantify. For example, proposals to include a specific percentage reduction in per capita/overall waste were dismissed in the negotiations. In this sense, the eleven targets and thirteen indicators of SDG 12 are a fairly limited achievement.

In line with the desiderata of transnational capital, the emphasis of SDG 12 is on voluntarism – for example, on merely 'encouraging' companies to adopt sustainable practices. According to some authors, the main problem underpinning SDG 12 is its focus on efficient production methods (efficiency approach), which diverts attention from considerations of 'overall volumes of consumption, distributional issues, and related social and institutional changes' (systemic approach).[8] This problem arguably has its roots in an obsession with economic growth, discernible also in other SDGs, which prioritize human-focused economic development at the expense of approaches centred on planetary boundaries and Earth-system integrity.[9] According to Sam Adelman the 'SDGs reproduce growth fetishism' and an overwhelmingly rich scholarship has argued that unlimited growth is incompatible with sustainability.[10] We echo this scholarship in maintaining that, if we want to achieve SCP, we need to focus on economies that make 'us thrive, whether or not they grow'.[11] Making economies more equitable and sustainable also requires a fundamental reassessment of the notion of value creation, which should be disassociated from marginalist approaches identifying economic value only on the basis of market exchange and prices.[12]

In short, SDG 12 is shrouded in a serious ambiguity underpinning the whole SDG agenda. On the one hand, it aspires to avert incoming ecological breakdowns and revert dramatic forms of social injustice. On the other hand, it remains anchored to the epistemic foundations that are arguably at the basis of a socio-economic system that has enabled environmental degradation and widespread inequalities and are reflected in the international legal regime, as discussed in the next sections.

7 Des Gasper, Amod Shah, & Sunil Tankha, 'The Framing of Sustainable Consumption and Production in SDG 12' (2019) 10 *Global Policy* 83, 87, 88.

8 Magnus Bengtsson et al., 'Transforming Systems of Consumption and Production for Achieving the Sustainable Development Goals: Moving beyond Efficiency' (2018) 13 *Sustainability Science* 1533, 1536.

9 Louis J. Kotzé, 'The Sustainable Development Goals: An Existential Critique alongside Three New-Millennial Analytical Paradigms', in Duncan French & Louis J. Kotzé (eds.), *Sustainable Development Goals Law, Theory and Implementation* (EE, 2018), 41–65.

10 For a literature overview, see Sam Adelman, 'The Sustainable Development Goals, Anthropocentrism and Neoliberalism', in French & Kotzé, n. 9, 15, 34.

11 Kate Raworth, *Doughnut Economics, Seven Ways to Think Like a Twenty-first Century Economist* (Penguin, 2017), 245.

12 Mariana Mazzucato, *The Value of Everything: Making and Taking in the Global Economy* (Penguin, 2018).

12.3 POSITIONING SDG 12 IN INTERNATIONAL LAW

A multitude of environmental and human rights treaties indirectly facilitate sustainable production processes. Yet focusing on these treaties diverts the attention from the lack of genuine engagement of the international legal system with SCP. In this system, environmental and human rights norms are weak when compared to the international economic law regime. At its core, the legal system is geared towards the protection of a capitalist society thriving on extractivism and inequalities, and this system is arguably antithetical with SCP. We develop this argument in four steps. In Section 12.3.1, we first touch upon the root causes of the problem – namely, the colonial origin of contemporary international law. In Section 12.3.2, we zoom in on the regime of environmental and human rights law by focusing on the legal regimes specifically mentioned in SDG 12 and reflect on the lack of reference in SDG 12 to the business and human rights regime. In Section 12.3.3, we analyze how international trade and investment law is implicated in unsustainable consumption and production patterns. Finally, in Section 12.3.4, we critically discuss transnational private regulation.

12.3.1 *The Incongruous Core of International Law for SCP*

The unsustainability of production and consumption patterns is entangled with colonialism and its exploitation of both resources and people.[13] Scholars in the Third World Approaches to International Law movement have exposed how modern international law is the offspring of colonial relations.[14] Against this background, it is pertinent to note that the negotiations on SCP were fraught with a lack of consensus on who should take chief responsibility towards SCP. Many developing countries have argued that the principle of common but differentiated responsibilities (CBDR) in Principle 7 of the 1992 Rio Declaration on Environment and Development should have been central in SCP.[15] Developed countries contrasted this view by arguing that CBDR pertains to multilateral environmental agreements and not to the SDGs.[16] Eventually, a compromise was found, whereby developed countries have taken leadership in some areas (for example, in target 12.1). The dispute on how and whether to use a legal principle to guide the work on SDG 12 reflects the dense and tense relationship not only between developing and

[13] Joseph McQuade, 'Earth Day: Colonialism's Role in the Overexploitation of Natural Resources', *The Conversation*, 18 April 2019, theconversation.com/earth-day-colonialisms-role-in-the-overexploitation-of-natural-resources-113995.

[14] Antony Anghie, *Imperialism, Sovereignty and the Making of International Law* (Cambridge University Press, 2012).

[15] Gasper, Shah & Tankha, n. 7, 88.

[16] See Statements by Australia-Netherlands-UK, Poland-Romania, Japan, and Portugal, in the 2014 report of the UN Open Working Group, as cited by Gasper, Shah, & Tankha, n. 7, 88.

developed countries but also between a managerial and rights-based ethos to guide action on achieving SCP.

The argument that CBDR pertains to environmental law and not to the SDGs echoes another fundamental problem underpinning the international legal system. With its various regimes – international environmental, human rights, or economic law – the system is founded on a schism, pitting the 'economic' against the 'non-economic'. This dichotomy is questionable and counterproductive in light of the multidimensionality inherent to the concept of sustainability that transcends an economic/non-economic divide. The labelling of certain activities as economic issues (for example, trade and investments) and their separation from their wider socioeconomic effects obfuscates the ways in which sustainability can be attained. This dichotomy enables the marginalization of allegedly non-economic goals within the system of international law.[17]

12.3.2 *International Environmental Law and Human Rights as the Weak Links to the Promotion of SCP*

The only reference to binding obligations in SDG 12 is to existing international legal frameworks on chemicals and hazardous waste (indicator 12.4.1). However, these frameworks are rather weak. For example, the list of banned chemicals under the 1998 Rotterdam Convention on the Prior Informed Consent Procedure for Certain Hazardous Chemicals and Pesticides in International Trade (Rotterdam Convention) requires the agreement of all parties for toxic substances to be listed as banned. Chrysotile asbestos is a case in point: despite overwhelming scientific consensus about its carcinogenicity, it has not been listed because of Russian opposition.[18] The Rotterdam Convention, as a system oriented towards the containment of hazardous substances, is structurally under-equipped to live up to its objectives partly because it rests on a consensus-based decision-making process. Rather paradoxically, states that have prohibited the marketing of asbestos products had to defend such measures before the World Trade Organization's (WTO) adjudicatory bodies.[19]

The example mentioned above is no exception to a general picture, where environmental conventions remain of marginal significance in tackling SCP. Think of waste, for example, which has become an egregious threat to the environment to the extent that some refer to the current era as 'the Molysmocene' – that is

[17] Alessandra Arcuri, 'International Economic Law and Disintegration: Beware the Schmittean Moment' (2020) 23(2) *Journal of International Economic Law (JIEL)* 323, 340–41.

[18] Oman George & Laurie Kazan-Allen, *The Rotterdam Convention* 2019, 10 May 2019, www.ibasecretariat.org/og-lka-the-rotterdam-convention-2019.php.

[19] WTO, *European Communities – Measures Affecting Asbestos and Asbestos-Containing Products*, WTO Doc. WT/DS135/AB/R, 5 April 2001.

'a geological era shaped by human waste and its management'.[20] Waste, which is the direct result of production and consumption processes, contributes to climate change and to the pollution of land, oceans, and freshwater. It should be straightforward then that SCP can only be attained if waste is addressed seriously. The 1989 Basel Convention on the Control of Transboundary Movements of Hazardous Wastes and Their Disposal (Basel Convention), which is referred to in SDG 12, is arguably the most powerful international legal instrument to address this problem. In its preamble, the Basel Convention acknowledges 'that that the most effective way of protecting human health and the environment from the dangers posed by such wastes is the *reduction* of their generation to a minimum in terms of quantity and/or hazard potential'.[21] Yet, since the entry into force of the Basel Convention, the amount of hazardous waste generated globally has increased steadily, and it is projected to continue to increase.[22] While much attention is paid to waste management, little has been done to contain the production of waste. In this context, it has been argued that '[t]hroughout the production, management, and distribution processes, the law acts as a lustration tool: the law purifies and expiates waste's corrupted nature by transforming it into a valuable commodity. In such a world, environmental protection thus becomes marginal or, at best, a mere collateral effect of international environmental law'.[23]

The examples above are meant to draw attention to a broader problem of international environmental law. As with waste, in several other international legal regimes, environmental problems are framed as 'externalities' that can be turned into valuable commodities (for example, emission-trading schemes). This framing, often coupled with a decentralized approach, whereby countries decide about key definitions (for example, what is hazardous under the Basel Convention) or how much they contribute to diminish their environmental impacts (for example, nationally determined contributions to the 2015 Paris Agreement on Climate Change), is doomed to miss the mark.

Given the link between economic activity underpinning SCP and human rights, it is also remarkable that SDG 12 fails to make any reference to business and human rights. The widely accepted and praised UN Guiding Principles on Business and Human Rights (GPBHR) have set the coordinates of firms' responsibility to seek to identify, prevent, and use leverage to mitigate human rights violations connected to

20 Michael Hennessy Picard, Olivier Barsalou & Tina Beigi, 'Welcome to the Molysmocene', *Critical Legal Thinking*, 21 November 2017, criticallegalthinking.com/2017/11/21/welcome-to-the-molysmocene/.

21 Basel Convention, 4, third preambular paragraph (emphasis added).

22 Olivier Barsalou & Michael Hennessy Picard, 'International Environmental Law in an Era of Globalized Waste' (2018) 17(3) *Chinese Journal of International Law* 887, 898.

23 *Id.*, 889.

their activities.[24] If a company has caused or contributed to a human rights impact, it should cease such an impact and offer remediation. If a firm is directly linked to a human rights impact by means of commercial relations – for example, through a supplier – it should leverage that supplier to cease such an impact.[25]

Human rights due diligence identifies practices to achieve SCP and includes clear responsibilities for remediation in case of breach and procedural mechanisms to involve affected stakeholders in corporate decision-making.[26] A reference to the GPBHR in SDG 12 would have cemented its position as a leading instrument for responsible business conduct. Failure to fully refer to the GPBHR framework is even more surprising as it contains reporting requirements aimed at supply chain transparency that are expressly mentioned in target 12.6. Further testifying to the imbalance between regimes aiming at social and environmental objectives and those pursuing economic liberalization, both the GPBHR and the SDG framework suffer from voluntarism, which stands in stark contrast with the binding and enforceable rights and obligations established under international trade and investment law.

12.3.3 *The Elephant in the Room: International Economic Law and SDG 12*

12.3.3.1 International Trade Law and the Regulation of SCP

The opening up of markets spurred by the 1994 WTO Agreements, and the consequent trade increase, established a narrative that trade and sustainability are mutually supportive. This claim is difficult to demonstrate empirically as there is evidence that many production externalities in domains such as agriculture, which were actively liberalized with the 1994 WTO Agreement on Agriculture, are caused and enabled by trade liberalization.[27] Strikingly, the WTO's own webpage recognizes the links with many SGDs but not with SDG 12.[28]

Implementing SCP action plans as per target 12.1 and the agreements referred to in SDG 12 requires market regulation. States can regulate SCP features of products produced in their territory with limited risk of breaching WTO obligations. This approach, however, cannot tackle the impact of internal demand for unsustainable

[24] UN Human Rights Council, *Guiding Principles on Business and Human Rights: Implementing the United Nations 'Protect, Respect and Remedy' Framework*, UN Doc. A/HRC/17/31, 21 March 2011, Principle 17.

[25] *Id.*, Principle 13.

[26] Enrico Partiti, 'Trust in Global Governance: Ensuring Trustworthiness of Transnational Private Regulators' (2020) 52(2) *New York University Journal of International Law and Politics* 415, 475; Chiara Macchi, 'The Climate Change Dimension of Business and Human Rights: The Gradual Consolidation of a Concept of "Climate Due Diligence"', *Business and Human Rights Journal* (forthcoming).

[27] Jennifer Clapp, 'The Trade-ification of the Food Sustainability Agenda' (2016) 44(2) *Journal of Peasant Studies* 335.

[28] WTO, *The WTO and the Sustainable Development Goals*, n.d., www.wto.org/english/thewto_e/coher_e/sdgs_e/sdgs_e.htm.

products originating abroad. States thus decide to regulate marketing or importing of products, but, as trade and competitive relations are affected, WTO scrutiny is triggered. Under WTO law, a rigid treaty structure that distinguishes between obligations aimed at trade liberalization and exceptions allowing other legitimate objectives hinders the regulation of social and environmental aspects at the heart of SCP. WTO law does not allow members to demonstrate that their trade restrictive measures are not protectionist.[29] A finding of disparate impact between the group of imported and like domestic products results in prima facie discrimination and leaves the matter to the exceptions under Article XX of the 1948/1994 General Agreement on Tariffs and Trade (GATT).

This dichotomy between economic and non-economic goals is unduly narrow and at odds even with non-interventionist approaches to market regulation, which, nonetheless, recognize a need for state intervention to correct market failures and externalities such as pollution.[30] Under WTO law, instead, such legitimate interventions are dealt with under the exceptions and their requirements of necessity and lack of arbitrary or unnecessary trade restrictiveness. It is unlikely that SDG 12 could affect this divide, although it may have an expansive effect on how certain exceptions are interpreted and applied by WTO adjudicatory bodies.

A crucial aspect of WTO law that complicates implementation of SDG 12 is the notion of likeness. Measures enacted by WTO members must not generate disparate impacts on the competitive conditions between groups of 'like products'. In the presence of like products, discriminatory measures must be justified. Responsibly produced goods are likely to be considered as 'like', 'regular', or 'irresponsible' products.[31] If production should be sustainable as per SDG 12, it would seem logical that sustainable products are 'unlike' non-sustainable products and that regulators can regulate them differently. However, as a key WTO goal concerns the protection of competitive relations between products, there seems to be little margin in play for SDG 12 to affect how likeness is assessed.

The relevance of SDG 12 is thus relegated to the exceptions. The outcome under Article XX of the GATT is not only relatively permissive but also unpredictable, which may deter WTO members from regulating SCP. Relevant exceptions for SCP-related measures include Article XX(b) (protection of human, animal or plant life or health) and Article XX(g) (protection of exhaustible natural resources). Article XX(a) (protection of public morals) has been interpreted to justify measures pursuing animal welfare goals and can be used to justify human rights–related

[29] Lothar Ehring, '*De Facto* Discrimination in World Trade Law: National and Most-Favoured-Nation Treatment – or Equal Treatment?' (2002) 36(5) *Journal of World Trade* (*JWT*) 921.

[30] Following Paul A. Samuelson, 'The Pure Theory of Public Expenditure' (1954) 36(4) *Review of Economics and Statistics* 387.

[31] WTO, *Philippines – Taxes on Distilled Spirits*, UN Doc. WT/DS403/AB/R, 21 December 2011, paras. 220–21.

restrictions.[32] WTO law incorporates a preference for multilateralism in disciplining sustainability, and it is accepted that international obligations entered into by the parties to a dispute are the baseline on which to determine whether discrimination is justifiable.[33] This notion is reflected in the requirement to seek multilateral solutions before establishing unilateral trade-restrictive measures in the social and environmental domain. Failure to reach an agreement would make unilateral action permissible.[34]

Noting that sustainable development is one of the objectives of the 1994 WTO Agreements, the Appellate Body has emphasized the need to interpret the notion in light of evolving concerns about environmental protection and conservation. Animal species susceptible to depletion and extinction because of human activity are considered 'exhaustible natural resources' under Article XX(g).[35] SDG 12 is arguably part of that normative material that can be mobilized in interpreting WTO provisions.[36] SDG 12 could inform the interpretation of the boundaries of the justificatory grounds in Article XX of the GATT. At the same time, it is doubtful that the weak language of SDG 12 can make substantial difference in interpreting provisions that already grant some margins to members, especially as it does not clarify the hierarchy between SCP and trade liberalization. Nonetheless, it could support expansive interpretation of GATT Article XX(a), (b), and (g) and create additional normative backing to unilateral action.

Specific WTO Agreements are relevant for individual targets of SDG 12. Target 12.7 on promoting sustainable public procurement touches upon the 1994 WTO Agreement on Governmental Procurement. Different from the GATT, this agreement does not refer to like products. Arguably, it provides contracting authorities with greater flexibility in requesting the compliance of a contracted good with various requirements.[37] Target 12.c requires removing and rationalizing harmful subsidies such as those for fossil fuels. The 1994 Agreement on Subsidies and Countervailing Measures (SCM Agreement) generally prohibits subsidies. However, fossil fuel subsidies are not in clear violation of WTO rules as they normally subsidize consumption rather than production, with WTO rules being more concerned with

32 Lorand Bartels, 'Article XX of GATT and the Problem of Extraterritorial Jurisdiction: *The Case of Trade Measures for the Protection of Human Rights*' (2002) 36(2) *JWT* 353.

33 Robert Howse, 'The Appellate Body Rulings in the *Shrimp/Turtle* Case: A New Legal Baseline for the Trade and Environment Debate' (2002) 27(2) *Columbia Journal of Environmental Law* 491, 506.

34 WTO, *United States – Import Prohibitions on Certain Shrimp and Shrimp Products*, WTO Doc. WT/DS58/AB/R, 12 October 1998, para. 166.

35 *Id.*, paras. 128–31.

36 WTO, *United States – Standards for Reformulated and Converted Gasoline*, WTO Doc. WT/DS02/AB/R, 29 April 1996, para. 17.

37 Maria Anna Corvaglia, 'Public Procurement and Private Standards: Ensuring Sustainability under the WTO Agreement on Government Procurement' (2016) 19(3) *JIEL* 607.

the latter.[38] Instead, it is renewable energy subsidies that face larger WTO hurdles (and have been the subject of several disputes). These subsidies have to be directed towards producers and subsidize production as there is not yet a sufficient supply of green energy. Renewable energy subsidies are also often contingent on export targets and the employment of domestic inputs, which are strictly sanctioned under the SCM Agreement.[39]

The dichotomy between economic and non-economic concerns is reproduced and reinforced through the network of regional trade agreements (RTAs) entered into bilaterally by WTO members. RTAs entered into by the European Union (EU) contain 'trade and sustainability' chapters that create a closer link with international social and environmental obligations affecting production, trade, and investment.[40] However, these chapters remain disconnected from, and less enforceable than, those providing for trade liberalization. They are subject to separate dispute settlement mechanisms that do not result in withdrawing trade concessions if a party breaches sustainability-related obligations.[41] A perception persists of WTO law as an 'obstacle' in the way of regulation aiming at non-economic objectives.[42] This perception could deter countries from adopting unilateral SCP measures. State inaction and WTO constraints arguably have contributed to spur private actors not covered by WTO rules to engage in regulatory activities in the domain of SCP.

12.3.3.2 International Investment Law: A Stumbling Block on the Road to SCP?

Foreign direct investments (FDIs) are often mentioned as key drivers for sustainable development.[43] At the same time, FDIs are often implicated in unsustainable patterns of production and consumption. Most particularly, research has shown that in less-developed countries in relation to the secondary sector (that is, manufacturing) and the primary sector (that is, agriculture, forestry, mining), FDIs tend to stimulate 'highly polluting and environmentally unfriendly processes and facilities,

38 Cleo Verkuijl et al., *Tackling Fossil Fuel Subsidies through International Trade Agreements* (Climate Strategies, 2017), 30.

39 *Id.*

40 2016 European Union - Canada Comprehensive Economic and Trade Agreement (not yet in force).

41 Lorand Bartels, 'Human Rights and Sustainable Development Obligations in EU Free Trade Agreements' (2013) 40 *Legal Issues of Economic Integration* 297.

42 Ken Conca, 'The WTO and the Undermining of Global Environmental Governance' (2000) 7 (3) *Review of International Political Economy* 484.

43 See UN Economic and Social Commission for Asia and the Pacific, *Foreign Direct Investment and Sustainable Development in International Investment Governance*, Studies in Trade, Investment and Innovation no. 90, 2019, 1.

much of which are outsourced from developed countries'.[44] The theory of 'ecologically unequal exchange' provides a lucid explanation for these findings, whereby the natural resources and labour in developing countries are over-exploited to the benefit of rich countries and multinational corporations.[45] Today, FDIs are protected by more than three thousand bilateral and sectoral investment treaties. Such treaties offer protection without demanding that investments are sustainable and do not establish accountability mechanisms for unsustainable investors. In this respect, the SDG framework suffers from the same blunders. For example, targets 17.3 and 17.5, which strive to enhance FDIs, include no qualifier vis-à-vis the nature and impacts of FDIs.

The central provisions of investment treaties establish several rights for foreign investors. These include broadly framed provisions on fair and equitable treatment (FET) and indirect expropriation. If, on their face, such provisions may sound legitimate, in practice, they impede the realization of a more sustainable economy. A concrete example may clarify how in practice international investment agreements hinder SCP. Take the case of waste, briefly discussed in Section 12.3.1. Externalizing waste by exporting it far away from the site of production became a common modus operandi in developed countries, which led to the phenomenon variously labelled as 'garbage imperialism'[46] or 'toxic waste colonialism',[47] which was rampant in the 1980s. The system of international investment law has been a useful tool to stifle resistance to garbage imperialism.

Think of one of the landmark cases – *Tecmed v Mexico* – in which a Spanish company transporting and managing toxic waste engaged in persistent violations of Mexican law relating to the treatment of hazardous waste.[48] In light of these violations, the Mexican government decided not to renew a permit to operate a landfill. Instead of supporting the Mexican state in implementing its environmental laws, the investment arbitration tribunal granted damages to the company because the lack of a permit renewal was considered to amount to expropriation and violation of the FET standard. This case is illustrative of a general problem, by which international economic law rewards the status quo and punishes legal action to transition towards sustainable production process. By making the status quo legal,

44 Andrew K. Jorgenson, 'The Sociology of Ecologically Unequal Exchange, Foreign Investment Dependence and Environmental Load Displacement: Summary of the Literature and Implications for Sustainability' (2016) 23(1) *Journal of Political Ecology* 334.

45 Jorge E. Viñuales, 'Law and the Anthropocene' (2016) 4 *Cambridge Centre for Environment, Energy and Natural Resource Governance Working Papers* 30.

46 Kenyon R. Stebbins, 'Garbage Imperialism: Health Implications of Dumping Hazardous Wastes in Third World Countries' (2010) 15(1) *Medical Anthropology* 81, 82.

47 Laura A. Pratt, 'Decreasing Dirty Dumping? A Reevaluation of Toxic Waste Colonialism and the Global Management of Transboundary Hazardous Waste' (2011) 35 *William & Mary Environmental Law and Policy Review* 581.

48 ICSID, *Tecnicas Medioambientales Tecmed S.A. v United Mexican States*, Award, ICSID Case no. ARB(AF)/00/2, 29 May 2003.

and change towards sustainability most often illegal, international investment law can be seen as antithetical to the achievement of SCP.[49] Fearing to have to pay damages, governments refrain from adopting environmental and/or socioeconomic regulation necessary for realizing SCP, a phenomenon also referred to as 'regulatory chill'.[50]

Tecmed is not an isolated instance. Cases where international investment law has been used to curb resistance to a variety of unsustainable production processes abound, ranging from the extractive industries, such as gold mining (for example, *Bear Creek v Perù* and *Copper Mesa v Ecuador*),[51] the extraction of basalt (for example, *Clayton/Bilcon v Canada*),[52] and oil extraction (for example, *Chevron v Ecuador*),[53] to agriculture (for example, *Bernhard von Pezold v Zimbabwe*)[54] and climate change (*RWE v The Netherlands* and *Uniper v The Netherlands*).[55]

More generally, investment treaties create significant barriers for local government to adopt environmental regulation as these could be framed as breach of the investors' rights.[56] A major pitfall of the international investment law system is that it entrusts foreign investors with strong rights, without establishing obligations for investors and rights for host states and/or local communities.[57] The historical pedigree of international investment law, tainted by its colonial origin,[58] may explain why rules have been designed in the interest of capital-exporting countries, while the communities of the host territory have been in many ways ignored. As will

[49] Julia Dehm, 'Law and the 'Value' of Future Expectations: Climate Change, Stranded Assets and Capitalist Dynamics', *Verfassungsblog*, 6 March 2020, verfassungsblog.de/law-and-the-value-of-future-expectations-climate-change-stranded-assets-and-capitalist-dynamics/.

[50] Kyla Tienhaara, 'Regulatory Chill in a Warming World: The Threat to Climate Policy Posed by Investor-State Dispute Settlement' (2017) 7 *Transnational Environmental Law* 229, 232; see also David Chriki 'Strapping Down Regulatory Space with Investment Arbitration: A New Breed of International SLAPPs' (2020) 51 *Georgetown Journal of International Law* 415.

[51] ICSID, *Bear Creek Mining Corporation v Republic of Perú*, ICSID Case no. ARB/14/21, 30 November 2017, partial dissenting opinion of Philippe Sands; PCA, *Copper Mesa Mining Corporation v Republic of Ecuador*, PCA Case no. 2012-2, 15 March 2016.

[52] PCA, *Bilcon of Delaware et al v Government of Canada*, Award on Jurisdiction and Liability, PCA Case no. 2009-04, 17 March 2015.

[53] PCA, *Chevron Corporation and Texaco Petroleum Corporation v Ecuador*, First Partial Award on Track I, PCA Case no. 2009-23, 17 September 2013.

[54] ICSID, *Bernhard von Pezold and Others v. Zimbabwe*, Award, ICSID Case no. ARB/10/15, 28 July 2015; Jesse Coleman, Thierry Berger & Sarah Brewin, 'Agricultural Investments under International Investment Law', *Social Sciences Research Network*, 2018, ssrn.com/abstract=3335193.

[55] ICSID, *RWE AG and* RWE *Eemshaven Holding II BV v Kingdom of the* Netherlands, ICSID Case no. ARB/21/4, 2 February 2021; ICSID, *Uniper SE, Uniper Benelux Holding B.V. and* Uniper *Benelux N.V. v Kingdom of the Netherlands*, ICSID Case no. ARB/21/22, 30 April 2021

[56] Kyla Tienhaara, *The Expropriation of Environmental Governance Protecting Foreign Investors at the Expense of Public Policy* (Cambridge University Press, 2009).

[57] Andrew Paul Newcombe, 'Sustainable Development and Investment Treaty Law' (2007) 8(3) *Journal World Investment and Trade* 357.

[58] Kate Miles, 'International Investment Law: Origins, Imperialism and Conceptualizing the Environment' (2010) 21 *Colorado Journal of International Environmental Law and Policy* 1.

be discussed in the next subsection, this asymmetry echoes the imbalance of the international legal system, characterized by strong institutions in the field of international economic law and much weaker ones in the field of international environmental and human rights law. The challenge is to reconcile these disconnected systems.[59]

Recent treaty reforms partly address this issue.[60] New (model) treaties, particularly from developing countries, include various provisions establishing investors' obligations[61] and home state liability for investors that cause 'significant damage', personal injury, and loss of life in the host state.[62] Overall, these agreements represent an important step towards making investment law more compatible with the goal of sustainability. However, none of these treaties has yet entered into force, and most of the provisions on investors' obligations lack enforcement mechanisms. Without credible enforcement mechanisms, such obligations will preserve the subordination of sustainability to the interests of capital. In the ongoing multilateral negotiations of the UN Commission on International Trade Law's Working Group III, the question of investor obligations or any other questions pertaining to substantive rules of sustainability have been sidelined.[63] Efforts to integrate the business and human rights agenda with international investment law have also been made in the context of the negotiations for a dedicated treaty.[64] In this context, the general lack of participation by developed countries is regrettable. If international investment law is to become compatible with goals set by SDG 12, reforms establishing clear and enforceable obligations on investors and limiting protection to sustainable investments only are needed.[65]

59 Alessandra Arcuri, 'Boundary-Work and Dynamics of Exclusion by Law: International Investment Law as a Case Study', in Marija Bartl, Pola Cebulak & Jessica Lawrence (eds.), *The Politics of European Legal Research: Behind the Method* (EE, forthcoming)

60 Gudrun Zagel, 'Achieving Sustainable Development Objectives in International Investment Law', in Julien Chaisse, Leila Choukroune & Jusoh Sufian (eds.), *Handbook of International Investment Law and Policy* (Springer, 2020), 1.

61 2015 Model Text for the Indian Bilateral Investment Treaty, art. 12; 2012 South African Development Community Model Bilateral Treaty Template, art. 15.

62 2016 Reciprocal Investment Promotion and Protection Agreement, Morocco-Nigeria, art. 24 (requiring investors and host states to assess the potential impact of an investment on the local community).

63 Alessandra Arcuri & Federica Violi, 'Human Rights and Investor-State Dispute Settlement: Changing (Almost) Everything, So That Everything Stays the Same' (2019) 3 *Diritti umani e diritto internazionale, Rivista quadrimestrale* 579.

64 See Human Rights Council, *Elaboration of an International Legally Binding Instrument on Transnational Corporations and Other Business Enterprises with Respect to Human Rights*, UN Doc. A/HRC/RES/26/9, 2014, para 1.

65 Surya Deva, 'International Investment Agreements and Human Rights: Assessing the Role of the UN's Business and Human Rights Regulatory Initiatives', in Chaisse, Choukroune, & Sufian, n. 60.

12.3.4 *Private Regulation*

By '*encouraging* companies to adopt sustainable practices', target 12.6 legitimizes voluntary approaches to SCP.[66] The question is whether these solutions have so far delivered on their promises. Transnational private regulation has offered several voluntary global governance tools in the area of sustainability. These schemes often encompass a human rights dimension in combination with environmental goals – for example, ensuring environmentally sustainable forest management that also respects Indigenous peoples' rights. Since the mid-1990s, voluntary sustainability standards have emerged as popular instruments disciplining social and environmental aspects of global production.[67] The lack of multilateral agreements and the jurisdictional limits of unilateral state action has created the ideal conditions for private 'rule entrepreneurs' to operate. Sustainability standards, where they rely on labels visible to consumers, have established a direct link between sustainable production and consumption. Sustainability regimes demand producers' compliance with international provisions in the environmental, human rights, and social domains. Some standards also have sophisticated institutional features ensuring formal participation of a wide range of interests. These regimes have been considered as a normatively desirable global governance tool to mobilize.[68] The diffusion of private standards, however, should not lead us to conclude that these solutions supplant the need for public intervention and international law in defining and enforcing criteria for SCP. Quite the opposite, standards foster the impression that adequate rules are in place, possibly deterring additional (mandatory and more profound) forms of public intervention that remain indispensable in defining the features and goals of SCP.[69]

Far from being the output of enlightened transnational constituencies, private regulation is also the product of powerful business interests even in multi-stakeholder organizations that bring together different groups and deliberate over how to ensure sustainable production.[70] Business communities arguably remain the key constituencies of sustainability standards since the success of private standard setters depends ultimately on corporate uptake.[71] This situation can only be ensured if a standard guarantees market premiums and market growth – goals that are hardly

66 Emphasis added.

67 Jan Wouters & Axel Marx, 'Competition and Cooperation in the Market of Voluntary Sustainability Standards', in Panagiotis Delimatsis (ed.), *The Law, Economics and Politics of International Standardisation* (Cambridge University Press, 2015), 215.

68 Kenneth W. Abbott & Duncan Snidal, 'Strengthening International Regulation through Transnational New Governance: Overcoming the Orchestration Deficit' (2009) 42(2) *Vanderbilt Journal of Transnational Law* 501.

69 Neil Malhotra, Benoît Monin & Michael Tomz, 'Does Private Regulation Pre-empt Public Regulation?' (2019) 113(1) *American Political Science Review* 19.

70 Phillip Paiement, *Transnational Sustainability Laws* (Cambridge University Press, 2017).

71 Aseem Prakash & Matthew Potoski, 'Collective Action through Voluntary Environmental Programs: A Club Theory Perspective' (2007) 35(4) *Policy Studies Journal* 773.

reconcilable with the more profound understandings of SCP and that potentially hinge on reducing production. Private standards may fail to include affected communities, other non-business affected groups, and especially the producers (often in developing countries) that ultimately have to comply with the requirements.[72]

Instead of fostering alternative models for SCP, some transnational private regimes have empowered Northern producers to exploit the profitable possibilities of 'green capitalism'. Managing and exploiting sustainability claims in value chains becomes a crucial feature for firms' success, which creates economic value from which the firms directly benefit at the expense of global South producers that end up carrying most of the implementation costs.[73] Such schemes have empowered retailers and supply chain leaders with powerful tools to monitor suppliers' performance and to impose comprehensive sustainability-related requirements.[74] Private standards permit the generation of information and transparency that is exploited by downstream economic firms to 'squeeze' the margin of producers and simultaneously extract profits while marketing products as 'green'. The need for solidarity in meeting SCP, which is recognized in SDG 12, is often disregarded and subverted in private initiatives.

Voluntary notions of SCP also affect consumption. The question becomes whether relying on consumer preferences as a driver for SCP without direct public intervention is feasible. Sustainable consumption that is enabled by private regimes remains limited for large brands, especially in some sectors. Relying on voluntary choices in fostering SCP is hindered by the fact that consumers' stated preferences for ethical or sustainable products may not be matched by their purchasing practices.[75] Consumers will never be in the position to evaluate effectiveness of private standards since the product features at hand are credence goods that remain unobservable. This factor can undermine consumer trust in labels, which can be exploited by schemes that in fact are mere 'greenwashing'. Relying on voluntary sustainable consumption is unlikely to curtail social and environmental harms.[76] Sustainable consumerism may even prevent the emergence of more efficient pathways of social change, such as consumption taxes.[77]

In line with other recent initiatives from international organizations, the SDGs attempt to 'orchestrate' various global governance components and, in particular,

[72] Elizabeth A. Bennett, 'Who Governs Socially-Oriented Voluntary Sustainability Standards? Not the Producers of Certified Products' (2017) 91(1) *World Development* 53.

[73] Stefano Ponte, 'Green Capital Accumulation: Business and Sustainability Management in a World of Global Value Chains' (2020) 25(1) *New Political Economy* 72.

[74] Fabrizio Cafaggi, 'Regulation through Contracts: Supply-Chain Contracting and Sustainability Standards' (2016) 12(3) *European Review of Contract Law* 218.

[75] Eleni Papaoikonomou, Gerard Ryan & Matias Ginieis, 'Towards a Holistic Approach of the Attitude-Behavior Gap in Ethical Consumer Behaviors: Empirical Evidence from Spain' (2011) 17 *International Advances in Economic Research* 77.

[76] Tim Bartley, 'Transnational Private Regulation in Practice: The Limits of Forest and Labor Standards Certification in Indonesia' (2010) 12(3) *Business and Politics* 1.

[77] Andrew Szasz, *Shopping Our Way to Safety: How We Changed from Protecting the Environment to Protecting Ourselves* (University of Minnesota Press, 2007).

those in the regime complex of SCP under SDG 12.[78] While this action is valuable, attempting to align public and especially private regimes in the domain of SCP by goal setting is difficult. Lacking a final 'arbiter' that clarifies what is SCP risks resulting in a cacophony of claims of sustainable production, a proliferation of conflicting and overlapping approaches, and attempts at diluting SCP in line with business interests.[79] Given the lack of a definition of SCP, basically every private regulator and firm can claim to be contributing to SDG 12. By not solving the tensions inherent to private governance, the SDGs become just another channel for greenwashing.

The SDGs, and SDG 12 in particular, have missed the opportunity to clarify two key issues. What are the institutional forms that transnational tools should take for designing and implementing SCP? What are the substance and the boundaries of public and private responsibilities in defining and enforcing SCP? Section 12.4.2 illustrates successful institutional forms that deploy private authority in achieving sustainable production. Concerning the second issue of private responsibility, which is also addressed in Section 12.3.1, SDG 12 omits important international instruments in the domain of corporate responsibility. International soft law tools for responsible business conduct, such as the Organisation for Economic Co-operation and Development's (OECD) Due Diligence Guidance for Responsible Business Conduct, have recognized that certain business models are just unsustainable in light of their structural negative implications for human rights. Transnational corporations in the global North are responsible for enabling systemic labour rights violations through unsustainable business models based on low supplier margin, tight delivery times, and cut-throat upstream competition.[80] In this context, the possibility that labour rights will be violated in order to continue to operate and trade with Western brands is heightened dramatically. Any legitimate claim of SCP made by private actors should therefore include a profound reflection about the extent to which current business models structurally create the conditions for unsustainable production and whether these are tackled by private regulation.

12.4 POSITIONING SDG 12 IN THE INTERNATIONAL INSTITUTIONAL CONTEXT

12.4.1 *Neoliberal Legality*

Generally, the institutions of the international legal order reflect a model of neoliberal legality problematic for the realization of SDG 12. As historian Quinn

[78] Kenneth W. Abbott et al., *International Organisations as Orchestrators* (Cambridge University Press, 2015).

[79] Enrico Partiti, 'Polycentricity and Polyphony in International Law: Interpreting the Corporate Responsibility to Respect Human Rights' (2021) 70(1) *International and Comparative Law Quarterly (ICLQ)* 133.

[80] OECD, *Due Diligence Guidance for Responsible Business Conduct* (OECD Publishing, 2018), 24.

Slobodian has shown, neoliberals and ordoliberals have always been aware of the importance of legal institutions. In his recollection, '[a] 2006 article clarified that the founders of the neoliberal movement added the syllable "neo" because they recognized the need to establish "the role of the state both more clearly and differently", including increased attention to the "legal-institutional framework"'.[81] Such a framework is constituted, on the one hand, to protect property rights and, on the other, to tame democracy.[82] As illustrated in the previous section, the system of international economic law is a paradigmatic example of how legal institutions have been shaped for the protection of markets at the expense of other systems of rights, which are the more natural offspring of democracy, such as labour rights. In the following subsection, we focus on dispute settlement mechanism to further illustrate how legal institutions have put the rights of capital on 'legal steroids'.[83]

12.4.2 A *Great Institutional Disparity and Some Reasons for Hope*

The significant institutional disparity between dispute settlement mechanisms (DSM) under international economic law and other international legal regimes reveals that, while the interests of transnational capital can be effectively protected through legal adjudication, other public interests (for example, interest in a healthy environment, in decent working conditions, and so on) can only be defended before a court (or a quasi-judicial body) in rather weak ways. Such disparity is highly problematic for realizing SCP. To illustrate this disparity, we offer a succinct comparison of the main features of the DSM in the WTO and international investment law with the DSM under international law. We also discuss recent developments and the regime of business and human rights to identify possible departures from, and openings for, alleviating this disparity.

In 2012, in an interview, John Jackson characterized the WTO's dispute settlement system as 'the most powerful dispute settlement system at the international level that exists'.[84] This statement was no hyperbole at the time. The introduction of a DSM with compulsory jurisdiction, which came about with the establishment of the WTO in 1995, was a remarkable departure from the GATT practice where disputes were resolved in quasi-diplomatic ways. Under WTO law, when a panel or the WTO Appellate Body (AB) issues a report, the Dispute Settlement Body (DSB) adopts it by negative consensus, and members are authorized to adopt suspensions of concessions, also known as 'retaliatory measures' in case of non-compliance with Panel/AB reports. This system has arguably led to a high level of compliance with

[81] Quinn Slobodian, *Globalists: The End of an Empire and the Birth of Neoliberalism* (Harvard University Press, 2018), 6.

[82] *Id.*

[83] Katharina Pistor, *The Code of Capital: How the Law Creates Wealth and Inequality* (Princeton University Press, 2019), 11.

[84] 'Interview with John Jackson', *Youtube*, 3 July 2012, www.youtube.com/watch?v=Efoe6bbRRSs.

the DSB's reports. Other international courts, such as the International Court of Justice and the various human rights courts, lack this level of access and enforceability. As seen, WTO law does not pre-empt members to adopt measures ensuring SCP.[85] Yet the prospects of a WTO dispute are often used by domestic regulators as a pretext to not enact sustainable policies.

The system of international investor-state dispute settlement (ISDS) is even more powerful than the WTO's DSM. Under investor-state arbitration, foreign investors have the right to initiate a dispute against the host state. If the host state is condemned, it may have to pay a significant amount of money.[86] This system is fairly unique in international law for granting private actors the possibility to sue states. Under human rights law, for example, it is also possible to initiate a dispute against a state, but only after having exhausted domestic legal remedies. By contrast, there are typically no rules requiring foreign investors to exhaust domestic legal remedies in investment treaties. Moreover, the degree of enforceability of ISDS awards is relatively high.

In the past years, new bilateral trade and investment agreements have been negotiated that include trade and sustainable development (TSD), trade and environment, and trade and labour chapters. These chapters have brought about interesting institutional developments, such as the establishment of special committees, which could promote cooperation in the area of sustainable development and hence contribute to the promotion of SCP. However, the TSD chapters are also characterized by a lack of 'credible enforcement mechanisms'.[87] Even when considering these new chapters, the strength and enforceability of the dispute settlement provisions of both trade and investment regimes stands in stark contrast to the voluntary and hortatory nature that characterizes other regimes intersecting with SCP, such as the business and human rights regime.

In this context, the OECD's Guidelines on Multinational Enterprises contain complex substantive and procedural guidance about responsible business conduct, but their enforcement is almost entirely left to the firms that implement them.[88] The OECD's guidelines establish a system of national contact points (NCPs) for disputes concerning firms' implementation of the guidelines and their sector-specific

[85] A deeper critique is that the international trade law system is at odds with sustainability because it rests on flawed analytical apparatus. For an analysis of comparative advantage as constituted by social inequality, see Donatella Alessandrini, 'Value-capture, Development and Social Reproduction in International Trade Law', *Verfassunsgblog*, 4 March 2020, verfassungsblog.de/value-capture-development-and-social-reproduction-in-international-trade-law/.

[86] Toni Marzal, 'We Need to Talk About Valuation in ISDS', *Verfassungsblog*, 5 March 2020, verfassungsblog.de/we-need-to-talk-about-valuation-in-isds/.

[87] James Harrison & Sophia Paulini, 'The Trade and Sustainable Development Chapter in the EU Mercosur Association Agreement: Is It Fit for Purpose?', *Client Earth*, July 2020, 7, www.documents.clientearth.org/wp-content/uploads/library/2020-07-15-the-trade-and-sustainable-development-chapter-in-the-eu-mercosur-association-agreement-ext-en.pdf.

[88] OECD, *OECD Guidelines for Multinational Enterprises* (OECD Publishing, 2011)

guidance documents. However, the NCPs are a forum for discussion and mediation between the corporation involved and other parties (often non-governmental organizations [NGOs]) concerning alleged breaches. The NCPs cannot declare that the OECD Guidelines on Multinational Enterprises have been breached, but they can offer their good offices to help the parties to resolve the dispute. Only if there is a lack of cooperation by the responding party can the NCP, after an assessment, release a non-binding statement with recommendations about compliance with the guidelines.[89] The NCPs have contributed to advancing important aspects of responsible business conduct and SCP. Recent proceedings include two cases against multi-stakeholder certifications for alleged violations of land rights from business entities that nonetheless received certification, further testifying to the contested nature of private initiatives for SCP.[90]

In the context of non-financial due diligence, however, the voluntary framework established by the GPBHR is being made mandatory in several jurisdictions. Mandatory regulation, inclusive of public monitoring, enforcement, and a liability regime is indispensable to establish proper incentives and expectations for firms to operationalize SDG 12. Mandatory human rights due diligence has been established in France;[91] in the Netherlands, however, it has been limited to child labour[92] and to requiring companies to state whether due diligence processes are in place; in the United Kingdom, it has been limited to forced labour.[93] In the EU, the 2017 Regulation of Minerals in Conflict Areas was the first instrument establishing mandatory due diligence in line with the OECD's Guidelines on Multinational Enterprises in the supply chains of minerals associated with armed conflict.[94] The EU is also discussing an across-the-board mandatory human rights due diligence measure.[95] These initiatives establish degrees of liability for firms, building on recent legal developments on corporate civil liability concerning parent company and supply chain liability for human rights violations.[96]

89 OECD, *Procedural Guidance* (OECD Publishing, 2011), 72–77, 85.

90 Before the Swiss NCP: *TuK Indonesia v Roundtable on Sustainable Palm Oil (RSPO)*, 23 January 2018; before the UK NCP: *IDI, EC, and LICADHO v Bonsucro*, 11 March 2019.

91 Loi no 2017-399 relative au devoir de vigilance des sociétés mères et des entreprises donneuses d'ordre, 27 March 2017.

92 Wet zorgplicht kinderarbeid, Stb. 2019, 401.

93 2015 Modern Slavery Act, c. 30, s. 54.

94 Council Regulation (EU) 2017/821 Laying Down Supply Chain Due Diligence Obligations for Union Importers of Tin, Tantalum and Tungsten, Their Ores, and Gold Originating from Conflict-Affected and High-Risk Areas, [2017] OJ L130/1.

95 *European Parliament Resolution with Recommendations to the Commission on Corporate Due Diligence and Corporate Accountability*, Doc. 2020/2129(INL), 10 March 2021.

96 Nicolas Bueno & Claire Bright, 'Implementing Human Rights Due Diligence through Corporate Civil Liability' (2020) 69(4) *ICLQ* 789.

12.4.3 *The Public-Private Interface*

As discussed in Section 12.3.4, the open-ended character of the SDGs and their limited institutional underpinnings allow private regulators to jump on the global bandwagon and further their claim to contributing to global goals expressed in SDG 12 and the others SDGs.[97] This process legitimizes private governance initiatives that escape public regulation and may advance economic goals and interests. Testifying to their successful exploitation of the narrative offered by the SDGs,[98] private standards are increasingly employed as a complement in public measures – for example, in public procurement.[99] These interactions between the public and private sphere constitute channels through which influence is exercised between public and private authority.[100] They could be used to influence requirements of private regulation and to step up their criteria and impact.

The proliferation of private SCP schemes and their interplays with public authority has also contributed to the diffusion of regulatory tools and instruments that are typical of business actors to the public domain and its institutions and rules.[101] Auditing and certification are now found in public instruments, bringing into public measures a conflict of interest and the difficulty of uncovering non-compliance when it occurs. Public initiatives in the human rights domain aim to make human rights due diligence mandatory, which is basically a form of firm-level management-based regulation transposed away from its original economic goals. Incidentally, the 'goal setting' of the SDGs itself constitutes yet another 'new governance' technique that draws its origin from private management[102] and, in being transposed to the international stage, aims at steering different areas of international law and global governance.[103] SDG 12 has done little to affect a context where both definition and implementation of SCP lie in the hands of economic interests, and it could actually further exacerbate these trends.

The interaction between public and private authority can also take institutionalized and mutually reinforcing forms. In the domain of deforestation connected to

[97] ISEAL, *Sustainability Standards and the SDGs*, www.isealalliance.org/get-involved/resources/sustainability-standards-and-sdgs.

[98] The link between private standards and the SDGs has also been drawn in UN-sponsored publications. United Nations Forum on Sustainability Standards (UNFSS), *Voluntary Sustainability Standards, Trade and Sustainable Development* (UNFSS, 2018).

[99] Enrico Partiti, 'Orchestration as a Form of Public Action: The EU Engagement with Voluntary Sustainability Standards' (2019) 25(1) *European Law Journal* 94.

[100] Burkard Eberlein et al., 'Transnational Business Governance Interactions: Conceptualisation and Framework for Analysis' (2014) 8(1) *Regulation and Governance* 1.

[101] Fabrizio Cafaggi, 'New Foundations of Transnational Private Regulation' (2011) 38(1) *Journal of Law and Society* 20.

[102] Gary P. Latham & Edwin A. Locke, 'A Theory of Goal Setting and Task Performance' (1991) 50 *Academy of Management Review* 212.

[103] Rakhyun E. Kim, 'The Nexus between International Law and the Sustainable Development Goals' (2016) 25(1) *Review of European Community and International Environmental Law* 19.

agricultural production, multi-actor pledges establishing zero-deforestation commitments in global value chains recently have emerged.[104] Among the few of these that have successfully affected practices on the ground, the 2006 Brazilian Soy Moratorium is a widely recognized success story.[105] In aiming to eradicate the deforestation in the Amazon that is driven by soy production, a coalition of NGOs, central and local Brazilian authorities, and the main agribusiness firms are committed to sourcing from soy producers that are not generating deforestation.[106] The moratorium implements a monitoring system through satellite imagery where NGOs locate non-complying producers and share this information with enforcement authorities and the traders party to the agreement that are contributing to its implementation at the first point of sale. Here, the presence of public authority is essential not just in giving clarity about, and offering support to, the substantive requirements of SCP but also in assisting private enforcement enabled by NGO monitoring and private contracting through public enforcement.

In the domain of garment manufacturing, the 2013 Accord on Fire and Building Safety in Bangladesh (Bangladesh Accord), and its multiple stakeholders, is a remarkable example of a private regime strengthening the human rights and labour rights components of SCP in combination not so much with public authority but, rather, with mandatory enforcement through arbitration. In the aftermath of the Rana Plaza tragedy, where 1,134 workers died in the collapse of a garment factory in Dhaka, Western brands committed to require their Bangladeshi suppliers to undergo a system of safety audits, the disclosure of information in auditors' reports, the implementation of necessary factory remediations, and the payment to suppliers of an amount sufficient to operate safely.[107] A distinctive feature of the Bangladesh Accord is that it allows trade unions party to the agreement to trigger arbitration before the Permanent Court of Arbitration if the brands fail to implement their commitments. The mechanism has been successfully used to obtain million-dollar settlements to improve worker safety.[108] The Bangladesh Accord is widely considered to be effective in light of the cooperation it has fostered between suppliers and retailers. In spite of a more marginal role of public authority, if compared to the 2006 Brazilian Soy Moratorium, the involvement of international trade unions has resulted in clear requirements not only for producers (as under most voluntary

[104] Eric F. Lambin et al., 'The Role of Supply-Chain Initiatives in Reducing Deforestation' (2018) 8 *Nature Climate Change* 109; see also 2015 UN New York Declaration on Forests.

[105] Holy Gibbs et al., 'Brazil's Soy Moratorium: Supply-Chain Governance Is Needed to Avoid Deforestation' (2015) 247(6220) *Science* 377.

[106] *Id.*

[107] Bangladesh Accord, arts. 9, 11–12, 22.

[108] Isabelle Glimcher, 'Arbitration of Human and Labour Rights: The Bangladesh Experience' (2019) 52(1) *New Journal of International Law and Politics* 232.

standards) but also for corporate buyers and Western brands, which are readily enforceable through the agreement's binding form.[109]

12.5 CONCLUSIONS

Does the SDG system provide an opportunity to challenge the current deficiencies of the international legal system related to SCP patterns? According to some, the answer is negative: '[T]here is nothing in the SDGs that deviates from international economic law and policy as practised and the very same strategies that have created the immiseration we know today; and there is nothing there that opens up space for real alternatives.'[110] SDG 12 evades pressing issues for the transformation of production such as responsibility for the economic actors that bear the blame for making production unsustainable. Furthermore, the notable omission of human rights considerations and of key international instruments for SCP perpetuates the ill-fated strategy that has generated fragmentation between the various domains of international law. This approach does not reverse the dichotomy between economic and non-economic systems that is well grounded within international law, and this factor has almost structurally constrained public regulatory intervention.

At a more fundamental level, this dichotomy prevents us from imagining a more humanized economy.[111] It rests on a faulty premise, according to which the economy is a self-contained system, whose purpose has collapsed with its measuring rod – growth. The dichotomy is reinforced by strong institutional arrangements, especially concerning dispute resolution. Not only are emerging regimes on business and human rights and responsible corporate conduct notoriously weaker than regimes protecting the liberalization of international trade and investment, but the possibilities for actors pursuing non-economic interests to initiate arbitration, or just to formally complain about non-trade concerns in a trade agreement, are also much more limited if compared to those available to corporations. Finally, SDG 12 is silent about the larger role that public institutions should exercise in the transnational private regulation of SCP. To merely encourage companies (as in target 12.6) to adopt sustainable production methods, and to adopt practices such as sustainability reporting that can only be effective in countries with stronger enforcement mechanisms,[112] is not enough in light of the pressing challenges and the deterritorialization of production.

[109] Philip James et al., 'Regulating Factory Safety in the Bangladeshi Garment Industry' (2019) 13 (4) *Regulation and Governance* 431.

[110] John Linarelli, Margot Salomon & Muthucumaraswamy Sornarajah, *The Misery of International Law: Confrontations with Injustice in the Global Economy* (Oxford University Press, 2018), 266–67.

[111] See Arcuri, n. 59.

[112] Ioannis Ioannou & George Serafeim, 'The Consequence of Mandatory Corporate Sustainability Reporting', Harvard Business School Research Working Paper 11-100, 2011.

Promising institutional settings have emerged that contemplate a more prominent function for public institutions or that are equipped with stronger mandatory aspects and dispute settlement. Making mandatory due diligence in the social and environmental domain is a promising venue to establish adequate incentives through legal sanctions and civil remedies for SCP. In this way, state action contributes to the emergence of duties for corporations and not just rights of market access, investments, and assets protection. The notion that firms bear responsibilities for SCP should be extended to regional and bilateral trade agreements with the design of institutions that do not only sanction states for breach of their obligations but that also contain mechanisms to sanction corporations' social and environmental violations. In this respect, the elaboration of procedural rules for human rights arbitration is a welcome step in the right direction; however, it still depends on the agreement of firms to accept the fact that disputes will be initiated against them.[113]

Sustainable conduct by corporations and consumers is still generally framed as an exceptional virtue. The normality is vice. For the international legal system to grapple with the aims of SDG 12, a radical change is needed. To normalize virtue, it is necessary to dignify and hear the voices of the periphery, those who suffer the most from environmental degradation and exploitation. This transformation can partly occur by cementing existing rights and creating new institutions, which will enable the marginalized to enforce their rights domestically and transnationally.

[113] 2019 Hague Rules on Business and Human Rights Arbitration.

13

SDG 13: Take Urgent Action to Combat Climate Change and Its Impacts

Daniel Bodansky

ABSTRACT

Sustainable Development Goal (SDG) 13, Climate Action, is an anomaly among the SDGs. Although combating climate change is critical to achieving the SDGs and vice versa, SDG 13 itself is of relatively little consequence. When the SDGs were developed, it had to be included, given the importance of the climate change issue. But it needed to be a placeholder in order to ensure that it did not interfere with the Paris Agreement on Climate Change negotiations, which were underway concurrently. As a result, the importance of the interlinkages between climate and the SDGs is reflected less in SDG 13 than in non-climate SDGs, including those addressing energy, industry, infrastructure, consumption and production, and cities.

KEYWORDS

SDG 13, climate change, global warming, adaptation, mitigation, international law

13.1 INTRODUCTION

Climate change is integrally related to sustainable development in all its dimensions – economic, social, and environmental. On the one hand, climate change threatens to exacerbate poverty, inequality, lack of access to clean drinking water and sanitation, the spread of tropical diseases, the degradation of terrestrial and marine ecosystems, and conflict.[1] Some scientists already link climate change to the

[1] As one commentator says, "[i]t is difficult to overstate the threat that climate change poses to sustainable development, equality, and the enjoyment of human rights." Tessa Khan, "Climate Justice: How Climate Change Battles Are Increasingly Being Fought, and Won, in Court," in

2003 European heat wave that killed more than thirty thousand people[2] and to extreme weather events such as Typhoon Haiyan,[3] which killed more than six thousand people and damaged or destroyed more than a million homes. On the other hand, addressing climate change will require making energy, transportation, agriculture, industry, infrastructure, and cities more sustainable. Sustainable Development Goal (SDG) 13, Climate Action, and the other SDGs are thus codependent: achieving SDG 13 will make it easier to achieve the other SDGs and vice versa.

Both climate change and sustainable development first emerged as issues internationally in the 1980s, and both played a central role at the 1992 Rio Conference on Environment and Development. But, from the start, the two agendas developed along separate, only loosely coordinated, institutional tracks: the climate change agenda under the 1992 UN Framework Convention on Climate Change (UNFCCC) and its associated instruments; the sustainable development agenda under the Commission on Sustainable Development and now the High-Level Political Forum (HLPF).

The concurrent negotiations of the 2015 Paris Agreement on Climate Change and the 2030 Agenda for Sustainable Development reflected this division of labor. The 2011 Durban Platform, which launched the Paris process, had required delicate compromises on several overarching issues that had long bedeviled the climate negotiations – in particular, legal form and differentiation.[4] Addressing climate change in the SDG process risked undermining the Paris negotiations by providing states unhappy with the Durban Platform an alternative forum in which to pursue their objectives. To avoid the potential for competition and even conflict between the two processes, states agreed, in effect, that climate change would be negotiated in the Paris process and that SDG 13 would play a dependent role. This understanding is made explicit in a footnote to SDG 13, which acknowledges that the UNFCCC is "the primary forum for negotiating the global response to climate change." Although the footnote does not preclude addressing climate change through targeted initiatives – for example, at the regional level or on a sectoral basis – it reaffirms and entrenches the priority of the UN climate regime over the HLPF in the development of global climate change policy.

The subsidiary status of SDG 13 makes it a bit of an anomaly among the SDGs. SDG 13 does not fill a gap in international policy since climate change

Barbara Adams et al. (eds.), *Exploring New Policy Pathways: How to Overcome Obstacles and Contradictions in the Implementation of the 2030 Agenda* (Civil Society Reflection Group, 2018), 147.

[2] Daniel Mitchell et al., "Attributing Human Mortality during Extreme Heat Waves to Anthropogenic Climate Change" (2016) 11(7) *Environmental Research Letters* 074006.

[3] Kevin E. Trenberth, John T. Fasullo & Theodore G. Shepherd, "Attribution of Climate Extreme Events" (2015) 5 *Nature Climate Change* 725.

[4] *Establishment of an Ad Hoc Working Group on the Durban Platform for Enhanced Action*, Decision 1/CP.17, UN Doc. FCCC/CP/2011/9/Add.1, 11 December 2011.

was already the subject of several international instruments when the SDGs were adopted, with another on the way. It could hardly raise the political profile of the climate change issue, which has much more salience than the SDGs and was already receiving attention at the highest possible level – that is, heads of state. And it did not set ambitious new targets to reduce emissions or to adapt to climate change but, instead, simply reiterated well-established goals of the UN climate change regime.

However, SDG 13 represents only the tip of the iceberg of the SDG's potential contribution to the goal of "taking urgent action to address climate change and its impacts." Ironically, other SDGs contribute much more to international climate change policy than SDG 13 itself. The Paris Agreement addresses climate change at a macro level, through nationally determined contributions (NDCs) to limit emissions and through national adaptation plans (NAPs), rather than by addressing the substance of climate change mitigation and adaptation policy through sectoral policies relating to energy, transportation, urban planning, coastal zone management, and so forth.[5] As a result, the SDGs on energy, industry, infrastructure, cities, consumption and production, hunger, water and sanitation, and life below water and on land did not raise concerns about possible competition with the Paris Agreement negotiations, unlike SDG 13. Rather, they potentially complement the Paris Agreement by addressing what states might include in their NDCs and NAPs.

By the same token, the Paris Agreement represents only the tip of the iceberg of the climate change regime's engagement with the SDGs. Although it focuses on national emissions of greenhouse gases rather than specific sectors, work under the UN climate change regime is relevant to many of the SDGs, including initiatives relating to renewable energy and energy efficiency, responsible consumption and production, gender equality, and the climate-ocean nexus. Because of the subordinate role of SDG 13 in the international effort to address climate change, this chapter will not focus exclusively on SDG 13. Instead, it will examine the problem of climate change more generally in the context of the SDGs. Section 13.2 provides a brief overview of SDG 13 and its relationships with the other SDGs and then examines the interrelationships of climate change and the SDGs more generally. Section 13.3 reviews how international law addresses climate change and then examines the interlinkages between the UN climate change regime, the sustainable development agenda, and other areas of international law. Section 13.4 analyzes the complex institutional arrangements relevant to climate change. Section 13.5 presents brief concluding thoughts.

5 The one exception is forestry, which is addressed in the Paris Agreement, art. 5.

13.2 THE CONTENT OF SDG 13 IN THE CONTEXT OF THE OTHER SDGS

The interconnections between SDG 13 and the other SDGs can be considered in terms of the specific and quite limited content of SDG 13 or in terms of the more general goal articulated in SDG 13 – namely, to "take urgent action to combat climate change."

13.2.1 *SDG 13*

In comparison to other SDGs, the five targets articulated in SDG 13 are modest. Other SDGs set specific targets regarding substantive outcomes, often in specific, quantitative terms – for example, to "end hunger" (target 2.1); to "double agricultural productivity" (target 2.3); to "reduce child mortality to less than 70 per 100,000 live births" (target 3.1); to achieve "universal access" to clean drinking water (target 6.1); or to "double the global rate of improvement in energy efficiency" (target 7.3). By contrast, the targets of SDG 13 are all stated in general, qualitative terms – to "strengthen" resilience and adaptive capacity; to "integrate" climate change measures into national policies; to "improve" education. The only target with any specificity – namely, to implement the commitment of developed countries to mobilize US$100 billion per year by 2020 from all sources (target 13.a) – merely reiterates an existing target (established in the 2009 Copenhagen Accord) rather than setting a new one. Moreover, although three of SDG 13's five targets (13.1, 13.2, and 13.3) are designated as "outcome" targets as opposed to "means-of-implementation" targets, even these relate largely to the development of national strategies, plans, and programs, not actual climate outcomes (for example, levels of temperature increase or emissions) since those were the province of the Paris Agreement negotiations.

13.2.2 *Climate Change and the SDGs*

In contrast to the specific content of SDG 13, which is quite limited and has relatively few implications for the other SDGs, SDG 13's overarching goal of combating climate change is interlinked with virtually every SDG in one way or another, since climate change is not simply an environmental issue but a social, economic, and security issue as well.[6] The causal connections between SDG 13 and the other SDGs run in both directions. On the one hand, climate change undermines our ability to achieve many of the SDGs, so action to mitigate and adapt to climate change is essential to the success of the sustainable development agenda.

6 See generally International Council of Scientific Unions (ICSU), *Review of Targets for the Sustainable Development Goals: The Science Perspective* (ICSU, 2015).

On the other hand, a number of SDGs address key drivers and impacts of climate change, including energy production, urban development, poverty, gender inequality, and agriculture, so the achievement of these SDGs can help countries mitigate and adapt to climate change.

Most of the interactions between SDG 13 and the other SDGs are positive; progress in achieving SDG 13 will help achieve other SDGs and vice versa. But there can be trade-offs as well as synergies, in which progress in achieving one goal may impede progress in achieving another.[7] Consider, for example, the relationship of SDG 13 and SDG 1, No Poverty. On the one hand, the two goals have clear synergies: lifting people out of poverty will give them greater capacity to address climate change, and addressing climate change will limit the droughts, flooding, and extreme weather events that tend to exacerbate poverty. On the other hand, there are also potential trade-offs. Increasing people's standard of living typically entails greater energy use, potentially leading to higher greenhouse gas emissions, so we need to pursue poverty alleviation in a climate-friendly way. Conversely, technologies to lower emissions can be expensive and divert resources away from poverty alleviation efforts, so we need to address climate change in a way that relieves the financial burden on poor countries and people. For this reason, we need to pursue the climate change and sustainable development agendas in an integrated manner, capitalizing on the synergies and avoiding the trade-offs.[8]

13.2.2.1 Impacts of Climate Change on the Achievement of the SDGs

It is "universally accepted that climate change will have dramatic impacts on our ability to achieve the [SDGs]."[9] One study found that climate change could undermine the ability to achieve seventy-two targets across sixteen SDGs.[10] Negative impacts include the following:

7 Christian Kroll, Anne Warchold. & Prajal Pradhan, "Sustainable Development Goals (SDGs): Are We Successful in Turning Trade-offs into Synergies?" (2019) 5 *Palgrave Communications* 140, doi.org/10.1057/s41599–019-0335-5.

8 Luis Gomez-Echeverri, "Climate and Development: Enhancing Impact through Stronger Linkages in the Implementation of the Paris Agreement and the Sustainable Development Goals (SDGs)" (2018) 376(2119) *Philosophical Transactions of the Royal Society* 1, doi.org/10.1098/rsta.2016.0444.

9 Daniel Chong, "The Sustainable Development Goals and Climate Change" (2018) 37(1) *Social Alternatives* 43, 43.

10 Francesco Fuso Nerini et al., "Connecting Climate Action with Other Sustainable Development Goals" (2019) 2 *Nature Sustainability* 674, 675. Although climate change may also have some positive effects for other Sustainable Development Goals (SDGs) (for example, by increasing agricultural productivity in some regions), these are likely to be limited. Also, it is worth noting that the IPCC concluded that "the literature on climate-SDG interactions is still an emergent field of research and hence there is *low to medium confidence* in the precise magnitude of the majority of these interactions." IPCC, *Global Warming of 1.5°C: An IPCC Special Report* (Cambridge University Press, 2018), 157 (emphasis added).

- Increased poverty (SDG 1): Droughts, sea-level rise, hurricanes, and other impacts of climate change will destroy people's livelihoods, thereby exacerbating poverty and inequality. A World Bank study in 2016 estimated that climate change could drive 100 million people into extreme poverty by 2030.[11]
- Lower agricultural productivity and malnutrition (SDG 2, Zero Hunger): Although the interactions between climate change and agriculture are complex, the net global impact of climate change on agriculture is expected to be negative, due to higher temperatures, droughts, wildfires, and flooding. In its Fifth Assessment Report, the Intergovernmental Panel on Climate Change (IPCC) concluded with high confidence that climate change will potentially affect "[a]ll aspects of food security, … including food access, utilization, and price stability."[12]
- Harms to human health (SDG 3, Good Health and Well-being): The heat stress, extreme weather events, poor sanitation, and lower agricultural production resulting from climate change will harm human health in various ways. For example, a warmer climate will increase the spread of vector-borne diseases such as dengue fever and malaria. Additionally, climate change will make it more difficult to reduce maternal mortality and preventable deaths of children under five years old since pregnant woman and young children are particularly vulnerable to heat exposure, insufficient food and water, and poor sanitation.[13]
- Reduced access to clean drinking water and sanitation (SDG 6, Clean Water and Sanitation): A 2016 literature review concluded that climate change will make it harder to achieve the goals relating to clean water and sanitation set forth in SDG 6, including universal and equitable access, adequate sanitation, improved water quality, improved water-use efficiency, and the restoration of water ecosystems.[14]
- Increased stresses on the marine environment and terrestrial ecosystems (SDG 14, Life below Water, and SDG 15, Life on Land): Special reports by the IPCC explore in great detail the negative impacts of climate change on marine and terrestrial ecosystems.[15] These impacts run

[11] Stephane Hallegatte et al., *Shock Waves: Managing the Impacts of Climate Change on Poverty* (World Bank, 2016).

[12] IPCC, *Climate Change 2014: Impacts, Adaptation, and Vulnerability* (Cambridge University Press, 2014), Part A, 18.

[13] Charlotta Rylander et al., "Climate Change and the Potential Effects on Maternal and Pregnancy Outcomes" (2013) 6(1) *Global Health Action* 19538.

[14] Guy Howard et al., "Climate Change and Water and Sanitation: Likely Impacts and Emerging Trends for Action" (2016) 41 *Annual Review of Environment and Resources* 253.

[15] IPCC, *Special Report on the Ocean and Cryosphere in a Changing Climate* (Cambridge University Press, 2019); IPCC, *Special Report on Climate Change and Land: Summary for Policymakers* (IPCC, 2019).

directly counter to many of the targets articulated in SDGs 14 and 15, including minimizing ocean acidification (target 14.3), combating desertification (target 15.3), and ensuring the conservation of mountain ecosystems (target 15.4).

- Exacerbation of conflict (SDG 16, Peace, Justice, and Strong Institutions): Changes in precipitation and temperature associated with climate change create stresses on access to food, water, and other resources. These stresses, in turn, tend to exacerbate conflict and undermine social justice.[16]

Given the negative impacts of climate change, reducing climate change will be critical to achieving the SDGs.[17] The IPCC found that a 2 degree Celsius or higher warming would produce "high risks of failure to meet SDGs such as eradicating poverty and hunger, providing safe water, reducing inequality and protecting ecosystems, and these risks are projected to become severe and widespread if warming increases further to about 3°C."[18] By contrast, achieving the SDGs would be "markedly easier" if we were able to limit warming to 1.5 degrees Celsius.[19]

13.2.2.2 Impacts of Climate Change Measures on Achieving the SDGs

Policies to combat climate change can also affect the achievement of the SDGs either positively or negatively. In general, the effects are positive since mitigating and adapting to climate change will reduce the negative impacts described above. One study found that 134 of the SDG targets have positive synergies with climate change and that only 34 involve trade-offs.[20] But trade-offs are a real concern. For example, taking climate action can be costly, diverting scarce resources away from poverty alleviation programs; without policies to ensure a "just transition," moving away from fossil fuels can adversely affect communities relying on fossil fuel production; policies to raise energy costs can limit access to energy and exacerbate inequality; and creating monoculture tree plantations to produce biofuels or sequester carbon can reduce food production, cause biodiversity loss, and displace local and Indigenous communities.

Given the potential for trade-offs as well as synergies between climate change action and other SDGs, how we address climate change matters. There are many different 1.5 or 2 degree Celsius emission pathways, some better for achieving the SDGs and others worse. One study of alternative pathways concluded that "the way that the climate problem is addressed strongly affects the prospects of meeting

16 Solomon M. Hsiang, Marshall Burke, & Edward Miguel, "Quantifying the Influence of Climate on Human Conflict" (2013) 341(6151) *Science* 1235367, doi.org/10.1126/science.1235367.
17 Christiana Figueres, "Goal 13: Taking Urgent Action to Combat Climate Change: SDGs and the Paris Climate Agreement" (2014) 51(4) *UN Chronicle* 30.
18 IPCC, n. 10, 253.
19 *Id.* 453.
20 Nerini et al., n. 10, 675–76.

numerous other SDGs and vice versa."[21] Similarly, the IPCC concluded with "very high confidence" that the design of mitigation portfolios and policy instruments to limit warming will "largely determine the overall synergies and trade-offs between mitigation and sustainable development."[22]

13.2.2.3 Implications for Climate Change of Achieving the Non-Climate SDGs

Just as limiting climate change would make it easier to achieve the non-climate SDGs, achieving the non-climate SDGs would help address climate change. For example, substantially increasing the share of renewable energy in the global energy mix (target 7.2) and doubling the global rate of improvement in energy efficiency (target 7.3) would decrease greenhouse gas emissions from the energy sector. Similarly, halting deforestation (target 15.2) would decrease emissions from land-use change, and resilient infrastructure (target 9.1) would foster climate resilience, one of the goals of the Paris Agreement. Cities are major contributors to greenhouse gas emissions, so achieving SDG 11, Sustainable Cities and Communities, would help make it easier to limit temperature increase to 1.5 degrees Celsius.[23] SDG 5, Gender Equality, could also play an important role in mitigating and adapting to climate change, since women's participation in climate policy-making helps improve outcomes.[24]

Achieving the non-climate SDGs, however, could also involve trade-offs with the goal of combating climate change. For example, universal access to affordable energy services (target 7.1) would tend to increase greenhouse gas emissions, unless the energy were produced from nonfossil fuel sources. The same is true of the goal of halving the proportion of people living in poverty (target 1.2) and its corollary of achieving sustained income growth (target 10.1), both of which generally involve greater energy use. Thus, just as it is important to address climate change in a manner that is attentive to the non-climate SDGs, the non-climate SDGs need to be pursued in a manner that does not cause greenhouse gas emissions to increase.

13.3 POSITIONING SDG 13 IN INTERNATIONAL LAW

International law could potentially play a variety of roles in relation to the climate change issue generally and to SDG 13 in particular. It could require action to mitigate and/or adapt to climate change; facilitate action through the provision of

[21] Christoph von Stechow et al., "2°C and SDGs: United They Stand, Divided They Fall?" (2016) 11 *Environmental Research Letters* 1, 1, doi.org/10.1088/1748-9326/11/3/034022.

[22] IPCC, n. 10, 45.

[23] *Id.*, 318.

[24] UN Women, *Turning Promises into Action: Gender Equality in the 2030 Agenda for Sustainable Development* (UN Women, 2018).

financial and technical support; coordinate action – for example, through joint programs; or limit climate action in order to protect other values such as human rights or free trade. This section begins by describing the different roles that the UN climate change regime has played with respect to mitigation and adaptation. Then, it analyzes the regime's relationships to the SDGs. Finally, it explores the interconnections between the climate change problem and other areas of international law, including trade law, human rights law, migration law, and investment law.

13.3.1 *The UN Climate Change Regime*

Since its inception in the early 1990s, the UN climate change regime has served as the focal point for international action to address climate change.[25] It consists of

- three international agreements: the UNFCCC, the 1997 Kyoto Protocol, and the Paris Agreement;
- a Conference of the Parties (COP) that meets annually, subsidiary bodies on science and implementation, a Secretariat, and a multitude of institutions addressing particular issues such as adaptation, technology transfer, capacity building, finance, and transparency;
- numerous decisions of the parties, including the 2001 Marrakesh Accords,[26] which operationalized the Kyoto Protocol; the 2010 Cancun Agreements,[27] which built on the 2009 Copenhagen Accord[28] and laid the groundwork for the Paris Agreement; and the 2018 Katowice Rulebook,[29] which elaborated the Paris Agreement.

Although mitigation of climate change (by reducing net emissions) and adaptation to its impacts are, in theory, coequal pillars of the UN climate change regime, the regime, in practice, has focused more on mitigation. This emphasis reflects the very different nature of the two problems. On the one hand, mitigation is a quintessential collective action problem: no one country can solve the climate change problem on its own, and individual countries have an incentive to act only if there is sufficient action by others. An important role of international law, in this context, is to provide an assurance of collective action by committing states to contribute to the global effort. Both the Kyoto Protocol and the Paris Agreement

[25] See generally Daniel Bodansky, Jutta Brunnée, & Lavanya Rajamani, *International Climate Change Law* (Oxford University Press, 2017).

[26] *Marrakesh Accords*, Decisions 2-19/CP.7, UN Doc. FCCC/CP/2002/13/Add.1-Add.2, 10 November 2001.

[27] *Cancun Agreements*, Decision 1/CP.16, UN Doc FCCC/CP/2010/7/Add.1, 10–11 December 2010.

[28] *Copenhagen Accord*, Decision 2/CP.15, UN Doc. FCCC/CP/2009/11/Add.1, 19 December 2009.

[29] *Matters Relating to the Implementation of the Paris Agreement*, Decisions 3 - 20/CMA.1, UN Doc. FCCC/PA/CMA/2018/3/Add.1, 15 December 2018.

seek to provide this assurance of collective action, albeit in different ways. The Kyoto Protocol took a legalistic approach, involving legally binding emission targets for Annex I parties and a compliance procedure that included an enforcement branch with authority to impose consequences for noncompliance. By contrast, the Paris Agreement, although a binding agreement under international law, takes a more flexible approach. It encourages collective action by requiring all parties to formulate and report on an NDC to mitigate climate change, but it allows each country to define its own NDC and relies on transparency, rather than legal bindingness, to promote implementation and compliance.

In contrast, adaptation produces largely local, rather than global, benefits. As a result, individual states have an incentive to adapt regardless of what others do, and international law does not need to require adaptation action. The Kyoto Protocol does not address adaptation at all, focusing exclusively on mitigation. The Paris Agreement recognizes that adaptation is a "global challenge" but addresses it quite differently than mitigation. Rather than impose legal commitments on parties to take adaptation measures,[30] it seeks to promote international cooperation to facilitate adaptation, including through information sharing, capacity building, and financial assistance.

13.3.1.1 SDG 13 and the UN Climate Change Regime

As noted earlier, SDG 13 was formulated in the shadow of the Paris Agreement negotiations and plays a subordinate role. Each of its five specific targets simply tracks existing elements of the UN climate change regime and thus neither advances nor detracts from existing international climate change law. Target 13.1 calls for strengthening resilience and adaptive capacity to climate-related hazards and natural disasters in all countries, consistent with the goals set forth in article 7 of the Paris Agreement. Various elements of the UN climate change regime seek to achieve these goals, including the Nairobi work program on impacts, vulnerability, and adaptation to climate change[31] and the 2010 Cancun Adaptation Framework.[32]

Target 13.2 calls for the integration of climate change measures into national policies, strategies, and planning, one of the key goals of the UN climate change regime from the start. This goal is reflected in article 4.1(h) of the UNFCCC, which requires parties to "take climate change considerations into account in their relevant social, economic and environmental policies and actions"; article 4.19 of the Paris Agreement, which encourages parties to formulate long-term low greenhouse gas

[30] The only obligation of parties is to engage in adaptation planning, and this obligation is qualified by the phrase "as appropriate." Paris Agreement, art. 7.9

[31] The Nairobi Work Program was established in 2005 at the eleventh Conference of the Parties (COP-11), Decision 2/CP.11, UN Doc. FCCC/CP/2005/5/Add.1, 9–10 December 2005, and renamed the Nairobi Work Program the following year at COP-12.

[32] Cancun Agreements, n. 27, paras. 11–35.

emission development strategies; and article 7.9, which requires parties to engage in adaptation planning processes, including through the formulation of national adaptation plans and the assessment of climate change impacts and vulnerability.

Target 13.3 focuses on improving education, public awareness, and human and institutional capacity. This target echoes article 6 of the UNFCCC, the 2014 Lima Ministerial Declaration on Education and Public Awareness,[33] and article 12 of the Paris Agreement, which all aim to enhance climate change education, public awareness, public participation, and public access to information.

Target 13.a calls on states to implement the finance goal already adopted under the Copenhagen Accord and Cancun Agreements – namely, that developed country parties mobilize jointly US$100 billion per year in climate finance from all sources, a goal extended to 2025 by the COP decision adopting the Paris Agreement.[34] Determining what should count toward meeting this US$100 billion goal has been controversial – for example, whether to include export credit insurance and non-concessional loans.[35] A 2020 report of the Organisation for Economic Co-operation and Development (OECD), which comprises developed states, included both of these categories and concluded that developed countries mobilized US$71 billion in 2017 and US$79 billion in 2018 for climate action in developing countries, a trajectory likely to come close to the US$100 billion goal in 2020. Of the US$79 billion in 2019, public finance accounted for more than US$62 billion, and private finance mobilized by developed countries amounted to US$15.7 billion.[36] Finally, target SDG 13.b aims to raise capacity for effective action in least developed countries and small island developing states, a goal addressed in article 11 of the Paris Agreement.

13.3.1.2 The UN Climate Change Regime and the SDGs

In contrast to SDG 13, which has few implications for the UN climate change regime, the UN climate change regime could have significant implications for the SDGs, either positive or negative. To align the two agendas, the UN climate change regime reflects the general goal of sustainable development in a number of ways:

- The UNFCCC includes, as a guiding principle, the principle that states "have a right to, and should, promote sustainable development."[37]

[33] Decision 19/CP.20, UN Doc FCCC/CP/2014/10/Add.3, 13 December 2014, 37.

[34] Adoption of the Paris Agreement, Decision 1/CP.21, UN Doc. FCCC/CP/2015/10/Add.1, 12 December 2015, para. 52.

[35] Mariama Williams, *The State of Play of Climate Finance: UNFCCC Funds and the $100 Billion Question* (South Centre, 2019), 5.

[36] OECD, *Climate Finance Provided and Mobilized by Developed Countries in 2013–2018* (OECD, 2020).

[37] UNFCCC, art. 3.4.

- The UNFCCC affirms in its preamble that "responses to climate change should be coordinated with social and economic development in an integrated manner with a view to avoiding adverse impacts on the latter, taking into full account the legitimate priority needs of developing countries for the achievement of sustained economic growth and the eradication of poverty."[38]
- The COP decision adopting the Paris Agreement welcomed the adoption of the 2030 Agenda for Sustainable Development and, in particular, SDG 13.[39]
- The Paris Agreement's preamble emphasized the "intrinsic relationship" that climate change actions have with "equitable access to sustainable development."[40]
- Article 2 of the Paris Agreement provides that the agreement's aim is to strengthen the global response to the threat of climate change "in the context of sustainable development and efforts to eradicate poverty."
- Article 6 of the Paris Agreement provides that cooperative approaches between countries must promote sustainable development. Indeed, the new mechanism established under article 6.4 is often referred to as the "sustainable development mechanism" because one of its core purposes is to "support sustainable development."

Although none of these provisions establishes any legal commitment to achieve either the SDGs generally or any particular SDG, they provide hooks that states, international institutions, and civil society organizations could use to argue for implementation of the Paris Agreement in a manner consistent with the SDGs.[41]

From the outset of the UN climate negotiations, developing countries sought to ensure that the climate regime would not limit their ability to develop. The Paris Agreement contains several provisions aimed at limiting trade-offs – and, to a lesser degree, promoting synergies – with particular SDGs:

- The preamble recognizes the "fundamental priority of safeguarding food security and ending hunger" (SDG 2).
- It encourages parties, in taking action to address climate change, to respect their obligations on the right to health (SDG 3) as well as gender equality (SDG 5).

[38] *Id.*, preamble, para. 21.
[39] Paris Agreement, preamble, para. 4.
[40] *Id.*, preamble, para. 8.
[41] On the compatibility of the NDCs put forward in Paris and the SDGs, see Eliza Northrop et al., *Examining the Alignment between Intended Nationally Determined Contributions and Sustainable Development Goals* (World Resources Institute, 2016).

- It recognizes the importance of education (SDG 4, Quality Education) and of sustainable patterns of consumption and production (SDG 12, Responsible Consumption and Production).
- Articles 2.1 explicitly acknowledges that the Paris Agreement's goals should be undertaken "in the context of . . . efforts to eradicate poverty," and Article 4.1 repeats this language with respect to the agreement's emissions goals (SDG 1).[42]
- Article 2.1(b) further provides that adaptation should be done in a manner that does not threaten food security (SDG 2).[43]

The UN climate regime does not do more to promote synergies between climate change action and specific SDGs because it addresses mitigation and adaptation in general terms rather than in terms of specific types of mitigation and adaptation measures. With respect to mitigation, both the UNFCCC and the Paris Agreement focus on national, economy-wide greenhouse gas emissions and say next to nothing about particular sectors such as energy, transportation, or agriculture.[44] Instead, they allow each individual country to decide how to limit emissions – whether by promoting renewables, energy efficiency, public transport, or sustainable industrial policies – and they do not expressly promote, much less require, the achievement of the SDGs on these subjects (targets 7.2, 7.3, 11.2, 12.6 respectively). Similarly, although the Paris Agreement seeks to foster climate resilience, it articulates this goal at a general level[45] and does not say anything about particular goals such as enhancing the resilience of the poor, reducing their vulnerability to climate-related extreme events (target 1.5), or building resilient infrastructure (target 9.1).

However, although neither the UNFCCC nor the Paris Agreement themselves address specific sectors, work under the two agreements often has a sectoral orientation and facilitates synergies with the SDGs, including by considering the SDGs in the design of the NDCs. For example, the UN climate change regime's technology transfer framework has supported projects on energy efficiency, renewable energy,

[42] Paris Agreement, art. 2.1.

[43] Interestingly, *id.*, art. 2.1(a) establishing the Paris Agreement's mitigation goal does not include parallel language.

[44] The only sector specifically addressed in the Paris Agreement is forestry. The UNFCCC, likewise does not mention specific sectors, except in a preambular reference to the possibility of achieving greater energy efficiency (preambular recital 22) and in the technology transfer provision (art. 4.1(c)), which calls for the transfer of technologies to limit emissions in all relevant sectors, including energy, transport, industry, agriculture, forestry, and waste management (art. 4.1(c)). In contrast, the Kyoto Protocol identified possible policies and measures in a number of specific sectors, including energy, agriculture, transport, and waste management (art. 2.1(a)).

[45] Paris Agreement, art. 7.1 (establishing the goal of "enhancing adaptive capacity, strengthening resilience and reducing vulnerability to climate change"), art. 8.4(h) (providing that areas of cooperation and facilitation under the 2013 Warsaw International Mechanism for Loss and Damage may include "resilience of communities, livelihoods and ecosystems").

green transport, and groundwater recharge. Similarly, the thematic technical expert meetings convened under "workstream 2" of the 2011 Durban Platform aimed to identify policies and practices in particular sectors that have high mitigation potential.[46] The UN climate change regime has also undertaken a work program on gender in order to advance gender balance and integrate gender considerations into its work,[47] consistent with SDG 5, and has initiated a dialogue on climate-ocean linkages, consistent with SDG 14.[48] More generally, the UN climate change regime's financial mechanism, including its Green Climate Fund, is a potential source of funding for initiatives relating to specific SDGs such as ensuring access to affordable and clean energy (SDG 7, Affordable and Clean Energy); building resilient infrastructure and promoting sustainable industrialization (SDG 9, Industry, Innovation, and Infrastructure); making cities resilient and sustainable (SDG 11); and ensuring sustainable consumption and production patterns (SDG 12).

13.3.2 *Climate Change Mitigation beyond the UN Climate Change Regime*

Complementing the UN climate change regime, states have addressed particular types of emissions using other areas of international law – in particular, through international transport law and the regime to protect the stratospheric ozone layer.[49]

13.3.2.1 Transport Law

Emissions from international transport are difficult to address on a national basis through the UN climate change regime since they often take place in areas beyond national jurisdiction and, in any event, are difficult to allocate to particular countries, given the international character of the maritime shipping and civil aviation industries. Regulating these emissions through sectoral measures avoids this difficulty and ensures common global standards rather than a patchwork of national standards.

States have addressed emissions from maritime transport by developing energy efficiency standards for ships in a 2011 amendment to Annex VI of the 1973/1978 International Convention for the Prevention of Pollution from Ships.[50] In 2018, acting through the International Maritime Organization (IMO), they adopted global

[46] Thematic areas included renewable energy, energy efficiency, land use, and urban environment.

[47] *Enhanced Lima Work Programme on Gender and Its Gender Action Plan*, Decision 3/CP.25, UN Doc. FCCC/CP/2019/13/Add.1, 15 December 2019.

[48] *Chile Madrid Time for Action*, Decision 1/CP.25, UN Doc. FCCC/CP/2019/3/Add.1, 15 December 2019, para. 31.

[49] See Bodansky, Brunnée & Rajamani, n. 25, chap. 8.

[50] *Amendments to MARPOL Annex VI on Regulations for the Prevention of Air Pollution from Ships by Inclusion of New Regulations on Energy Efficiency for Ships*, Resolution MEPC.203 (62), IMO Doc. MEPC/62/14/Add.1, 15 July 2011.

emissions goals for maritime shipping[51] and are currently developing design and operational measures to implement these goals. Meanwhile, in 2016, the International Civil Aviation Organization (ICAO) adopted the Carbon Offset and Reduction Scheme for International Aviation,[52] which aims to ensure carbon neutral growth from 2020 onwards by requiring airlines to offset emissions above 2020 levels through purchases of emission credits from outside the civil aviation sector.

13.3.2.2 Montreal Protocol on Substances That Deplete the Ozone Layer

Although the 1987 Montreal Protocol on Substances That Deplete the Ozone Layer is aimed at protecting the stratospheric ozone layer, states have increasingly used it to address the climate change effects of ozone-depleting substances (ODS) and their substitutes, many of which are also greenhouse gases (GHGs). In 2007, the Montreal Protocol parties adopted an amendment accelerating the phase-out schedule of hydrochlorofluorocarbons, primarily due to their potency as GHGs rather than ODS. The 2016 Kigali Amendment goes even further, establishing a phase-down schedule for hydrofluorocarbons (HFCs), which do not harm the ozone layer but are very potent GHGs.[53] In doing so, the Kigali Amendment resolves a tension between the ozone regime, which had previously encouraged the use of HFCs as a substitute for ODS, and the climate change regime, which had attempted to discourage the use of HFCs because of their contribution to global warming.

13.3.3 *Other Fields of International Law and SDG 13*

Because of the multidimensional character of the climate change issue, many other areas of international law – although not specifically about climate change – are also relevant to climate change action.[54] General principles of international environmental law are referenced by the UNFCCC[55] and are arguably relevant in interpreting its provisions. Conversely, climate change will affect many specific topics of international environmental law, including the protection of biodiversity, habitats, and world heritage sites.

Looking beyond the ambit of international environmental law, both human rights law and trade law involve synergies as well as trade-offs with climate change policy.

[51] *Initial IMO Strategy on Reduction of GHG Emissions from Ships*, Resolution MEPC.304(72), IMO Doc. MEPC/72/17/Add.1, 13 April 2018.

[52] ICAO Resolution A39–3, 2016.

[53] 2016 Amendment to the Montreal Protocol on Substances That Deplete the Ozone Layer, reprinted in (2017) 56(1) *International Legal Materials* 193.

[54] See Bodansky, Brunnée & Rajamani, n. 25, chap. 9.

[55] UNFCCC, preambular para. 8 (duty to prevent), art. 3.3 (precautionary principle).

Human rights law has increasingly been invoked to drive climate change action, on the ground that climate change threatens human rights. But it could also limit climate change policies that adversely impact the rights of particular individuals or groups. Similarly, trade law could promote the more efficient use of resources, but it could also be used to challenge climate change policies that distinguish between products based on the carbon emitted to produce them.

Apart from human rights and trade law, other areas of international law could complement the UN climate change regime by addressing particular impacts of climate change or particular mitigation issues. For example, the law of the sea could address the impact of climate change on maritime baselines and fisheries, and international migration law could address the problem of climate "refugees." Intellectual property law is relevant to the transfer of technology. Finally, international investment law raises concerns as a potential basis to challenge climate policies, but it could also be used to help make private capital flows consistent with the goals of the Paris Agreement.

13.3.3.1 International Environmental Law

Several general principles of international environmental law are relevant to the climate change problem, including the duty to prevent significant transboundary pollution, the precautionary principle, and the principle of intergenerational equity. Some scholars argue that these principles may be used in interpreting parties' obligations under the various climate change instruments, including the Paris Agreement.[56] In addition, climate change is interconnected with a variety of specific areas of international environmental law, including the regimes addressing biodiversity, desertification, and world heritage sites. For example, climate change is expected to exacerbate biodiversity loss; conversely, the conservation of biodiversity could help address the climate change problem through the provision of ecosystem services. Thus, there are many potential synergies between the climate change regime and the 1992 Convention on Biological Diversity.[57] Similarly, climate change is one of the biggest threats to world heritage sites,[58] so the 1972 World Heritage Convention has an important role to play in enhancing the resilience of these sites, consistent with target 13.1.[59]

56 Benoit Mayer, *The International Law on Climate Change* (Cambridge University Press, 2018), chap. 5.

57 Frédéric Jacquemont & Alejandro Caparrós, "The Convention on Biological Diversity and the Climate Change Convention Ten Years after Rio: Towards a Synergy of the Two Regimes?" (2002) 11(2) *Review of European Community and International Environmental Law* 169.

58 Elena Osipova et al., *IUCN World Heritage Outlook 3* (International Union for Conservation of Nature, 2020) (concluding that climate change is a high or very high threat to a third of natural world heritage sites).

59 1972 Convention for the Protection of the World Cultural and Natural Heritage.

13.3.3.2 Human Rights Law

Global warming has been called "the greatest threat to human rights in the twenty-first century," potentially undermining the rights to health, food, and housing, among others.[60] Responses to climate change can also raise human rights concerns, as the Paris Agreement acknowledges.[61] For example, using corn to produce ethanol can raise food prices and produce shortages, undermining the right to food and driving people into poverty. Similarly, hydroelectric projects can displace local communities.[62] The increasing focus on the interconnections between human rights and climate change highlights these synergies and trade-offs. It makes available to climate change activists additional legal arguments to employ in national courts as well as additional forums to make these arguments, including human rights treaty bodies, UN Charter-based institutions such as the Human Rights Council and its special procedures, and regional human rights institutions.[63]

Between 2015 and 2020, thirty-six cases in twenty-three national jurisdictions and five international tribunals were brought, arguing for stronger action to combat climate change on the basis of human rights law.[64] Prominent among these cases is a national court decision, *Urgenda v State of The Netherlands*, in which the Dutch Supreme Court found that articles 2 and 8 of the 1950 European Convention on Human Rights (protecting the right to life and the right to respect for private and family life) impose a positive obligation on the state to take suitable measures to respond to the risk of climate change and affirmed an order directing the government to increase the stringency of its emission reduction target.[65] At the international level, in *Sacchi et al. v Argentina*, sixteen children from twelve countries filed a petition to the UN Committee on the Rights of the Child, claiming that five countries had violated the petitioners' rights under the 1989 Convention on the

[60] Quoted in *Report of the Special Rapporteur on the Issue of Human Rights Obligations Relating to the Enjoyment of a Safe, Clean, Healthy and Sustainable Environment*, UN Doc. A/HRC/31/52, 1 February 2016, 7.

[61] Paris Agreement, preamble, para. 11.

[62] UNEP, *Climate Change and Human Rights* (UNEP, 2015).

[63] Franciscans International, A *Toolbox: Human Rights, Sustainable Development and Climate Policies: Connecting the Dots* (Franciscans International, 2018).

[64] Joana Setzer & Rebecca Byrnes, *Global Trends in Climate Change Litigation: 2020 Snapshot* (Grantham Research Institute on Climate Change, 2020), 14; see also Sam Varvastian, "The Human Right to a Clean and Healthy Environment in Climate Change Litigation," Max Planck Institute for Comparative Public Law and International Law Research Paper no. 2019-09, 10 April 2019.

[65] *State of the Netherlands v Urgenda Foundation*, Case no. 19/00135, Judgment of the Supreme Court of the Netherlands, 12 December 2019, uitspraken.rechtspraak.nl/inziendocument?id=ECLI:NL:HR:2019:2006. A more recent French decision by the Administrative Court of Paris found that the French government is responsible for "non-respect of its engagements" to reduce emissions and could be liable for "ecological damage." *Notre Affaire à Tous and Others v France*, Case nos. 1904967, 1904968, 1904972, 1904976, Tribunal Administratif de Paris, 3 February 2021.

Rights of the Child by insufficiently reducing their GHG emissions.[66] In *Duarte Agostinho and Others v Portugal and 32 Other States*, four Portuguese children and two adults brought a case in September 2020 arguing that failure by thirty-three European countries to take stronger action against climate change violated their rights under the European Convention on Human Rights.[67]

13.3.3.3 Trade Law

Trade law is also highly relevant to SDG 13, both in positive and potentially negative ways.[68] On the one hand, it could be used to address domestic policies that exacerbate the climate change problem, such as fossil fuel subsidies. But it could also potentially be invoked to challenge national climate change policies on the ground that they disadvantage imported goods. For example, renewable energy subsidies could be challenged in the World Trade Organization's (WTO) dispute settlement mechanism as a violation of multilateral subsidy rules,[69] and carbon-pricing mechanisms based on the carbon emitted in the production process may raise issues under the national treatment principle if they differentially impact domestic and imported goods.

In addition to the general interrelationships between the climate change and trade regimes, particular elements of each regime are interrelated. For example, the 1994 Agreement on Trade-Related Aspects of Intellectual Property Rights (TRIPS Agreement) is relevant to the issue of technology transfer in the climate change regime. As with other climate-trade issues, the TRIPS Agreement could have both positive and negative implications. On the one hand, its strict patent protections arguably are an impediment to the transfer of climate-friendly technologies. On the other hand, it gives parties some flexibility to override its restrictions in order to promote environmental goals.[70]

Efforts to address the tensions between international trade law and climate change law through multilateral negotiations have generally not been successful thus far. Beginning in 2014, a group of WTO members attempted to negotiate a plurilateral agreement to eliminate tariffs on certain environmental goods. But these negotiations stalled, and the group has not met since 2016. As a result, trade and environment issues, in practice, have been addressed primarily through non-WTO

66 Committee on the Rights of the Child, *Sacchi et al. v Argentina et al.*, Case nos. 104-108/2019, 23 September 2019.

67 ECtHR, *Duarte Agostinho and Others v Portugal and 32 Other States*, Application no. 39371/20, 13 November 2020.

68 See generally Andrew Prag, "Trade and SDG 13: Action on Climate Change," Asian Development Bank Institute Working Paper no. 735, 2017.

69 Henok Birhanu Asmelash, "Energy Subsidies and WTO Dispute Settlement: Why Only Renewable Subsidies Are Challenged" (2015) 18 *Journal of International Economic Law* 261.

70 Wei Zhuang, *Intellectual Property Rights and Climate Change: Interpreting the TRIPS Agreement for Environmentally Sound Technologies* (Cambridge University Press, 2017).

trade agreements and adjudication.[71] In most cases, domestic climate change measures would likely survive a WTO challenge under the 1994 General Agreement on Tariffs and Trade (GATT) exception permitting nondiscriminatory, non-protectionist measures related to the conservation of an exhaustible natural resource.[72] But trade law might pose a problem for measures adopted to discourage free riders, such as border tax adjustments on imported goods from countries lacking strong climate policies.[73]

13.3.3.4 Law of the Sea

Climate change will have profound effects on the ocean.[74] In principle, the 1982 UN Convention on the Law of the Sea (UNCLOS) could be used as a basis to limit emissions, on the ground that GHG emissions are a source of marine pollution either directly (for example, by acidifying the ocean) or indirectly (by causing global warming and thereby introducing energy into the ocean). The law of the sea more generally might also address the ocean impacts of climate change – for example, through fisheries or marine pollution agreements.[75] Traditionally, there has been a disconnect between climate change and ocean law, so these potential linkages were not explored. But, in the last decade, this situation has begun to change,[76] with Ocean Action Days held at the annual climate COPs from 2009 on, Chile's "Because the Ocean" initiative in 2015, Fiji's launch of the Ocean Pathways initiative under the UNFCCC in 2017, and the adoption of a COP decision in 2019 calling for a dialogue on ocean-climate issues.[77]

One of the few ocean-climate issues that has received significant attention – the legal effect of sea-level rise on maritime baselines and the outer limit of maritime zones – is now the subject of study by the International Law Commission (ILC).[78] Traditionally, UNCLOS has been interpreted to provide for "ambulatory" baselines – that is, baselines that move as the coastline shifts. But some states argue for fixed baselines and maritime zones in the context of sea-level rise in order to provide legal stability and certainty, and the International Law Association supported this

[71] Kasturi Das et al., "Making the International Trade System Work for the Paris Agreement: Assessing the Options" (2019) 49(6) *Environmental Law Reporter* 10553.

[72] GATT, art. XX(g).

[73] Michael A. Mehling et al., "Designing Border Tax Adjustments for Enhanced Climate Action" (2019) 113 *American Journal of International Law* 433.

[74] IPCC, n. 15.

[75] Millicent McCreath & Amber Rose Maggio (eds.), "Special Issue: Climate Change and the Law of the Sea Convention" (2019) 34(3) *International Journal of Marine and Coastal Law* 387.

[76] Daniel Bodansky, "The Ocean and Climate Change Law: Exploring the Relationships," in Ronan Long & Richard Barnes (eds.), *Frontiers in International Law: Oceans and Climate Challenges* (Brill, 2021), 317.

[77] See n. 48.

[78] ILC, *Sea-Level Rise in Relation to International Law*, Report of the International Law Commission at Its Seventy-Second Session, UN Doc. A/CN.4/740, 2020.

view in 2018 at the recommendation of its Committee on International Law and Sea-Level Rise.[79] A preliminary survey of state practice by the ILC concluded in 2020 that it was "too early" to draw a "definitive conclusion" on the issues.[80]

13.3.3.5 Migration Law

Climate change is likely to displace large numbers of people as a result of sea-level rise, drought, and extreme weather events, both within countries and across borders,[81] raising significant issues of migration law.[82] Internal displacement is addressed by the 1998 Guiding Principles on Internal Displacement, which articulate the rights of displaced persons and call for the provision of humanitarian assistance.[83] Although the Guiding Principles are not legally binding, they were endorsed by the 2005 World Summit Outcome as "an important international framework for the protection of internally displaced persons"[84] and have been incorporated into a number of regional legal agreements.[85] Their definition of internationally displaced persons as those "who have been forced or obliged to flee or to leave their homes ... as a result of ... natural or human-made disasters" could include climate refugees, although it might be limited to those displaced by immediate disasters rather than slow onset changes such as sea-level rise.[86]

With respect to cross-border displacement, victims of climate change who take refuge in another country are not considered "refugees" within the meaning of international refugee law.[87] Instead, cross-border displacement is addressed through various soft law initiatives, including

- the 2015 Nansen Initiative on Disaster-Induced Cross Border Displacement and its 2016 agenda for the protection of cross-border displaced persons

79 International Law Association, *Report of the Seventy-Eighth Conference of the International Law Association*, Resolution 5/2018, 19–24 August 2018.

80 ILC, n. 78, 42, para. 104(i).

81 Estimates range from 25 million to 2 billion. Bodansky, Brunnée, & Rajamani, n. 25, 313.

82 Jane McAdam, *Climate Change, Forced Migration and International Law* (Oxford University Press, 2012).

83 *Guiding Principles of Internal Displacement*, UN Doc. E/CN.4/1998/53/Add.2, 1998.

84 2005 *World Summit Outcome*, UN Doc. A/RES/60/1, 24 October 2005, para. 132.

85 For example, 2009 African Union Convention for the Protection and Assistance of Internally Displaced Persons in Africa; 2006 Great Lakes Protocol on the Protection and Assistance to Internationally Placed Persons.

86 2009 African Union Convention for the Protection and Assistance of Internally Displaced Persons in Africa, art. 1(k).

87 Under the 1951 Convention Relating to the Status of Refugees and the 1967 Protocol Relating to the Status of Refugees, the definition of "refugees" is limited to those who are unable to return to their country due to a well-founded fear of racial, religious, political, or ethnic persecution. In the *Teitiota* case, the Human Rights Committee found that New Zealand's rejection of refugee status by a Kiribati national did not violate his rights under the 1966 International Covenant on Civil and Political Rights. *Views Adopted by the Committee Concerning Communication no.* 2728/2016, UN Doc. CCPR/C/127/D/2728/2016, 24 October 2019.

in the context of disasters and climate change, which has been endorsed by more than one hundred states, and[88]

- the 2015 Sendai Framework for Disaster Risk Reduction, which calls for enhanced action to prevent and mitigate displacement.[89]

Both the Nansen Initiative and the Sendai Framework seek to reduce vulnerability and build resilience to disaster displacement risk and thus dovetail with target 13.1, which also focuses on building resilience.

13.3.3.6 Investment Law

International investment law can support or inhibit climate change action. On the one hand, it can support climate change action by encouraging investments in low-emitting technologies and discouraging investments in high-emitting ones. On the other hand, it can limit climate change action by serving as a basis to challenge domestic climate change measures that affect foreign investments – for example, on the ground that they indirectly expropriate a foreign investment by reducing its profitability.[90]

As noted earlier,[91] developed country parties agreed under the UNFCCC to mobilize US$100 billion in climate finance for mitigation and adaptation in developing countries. In addition, the Paris Agreement establishes the more general goal of "[m]aking finance flows consistent with a pathway towards low greenhouse gas emissions and climate-resilient development."[92] Both of these goals have implications for private foreign investment. The US$100 billion mobilization goal includes not only public finance but also foreign direct investment in climate-friendly energy and infrastructure that government policies stimulate. Similarly, the Paris Agreement finance goal encompasses not only encouraging green finance flows but also limiting brown flows – for example, investments in new coal-fired power plants or infrastructure developments that encourage higher emissions.

Harmonizing international investment law with climate change policy is already "well underway" and has two dimensions.[93] First, international investment law could play a positive role in encouraging green finance and discouraging brown finance. Some international investment agreements have begun to do this by extending protection only to investments that satisfy climate-related performance standards. Governments could also incentivize green versus brown finance by

[88] *Nansen Initiative on Disaster-Induced Cross-Border Displacement*, nanseninitiative.org.
[89] UN Doc. A/CONF.224/CRP.1, 18 March 2015.
[90] See generally Daniel M. Firger & Michael B. Gerrard, "Harmonizing Climate Change Policy and International Investment Law: Threats, Challenges and Opportunities," in Karl P. Sauvant (ed.), *Yearbook on International Investment Law and Policy 2010–2011* (Oxford University Press, 2010), 517.
[91] See n. 34 and accompanying text.
[92] Paris Agreement, art. 2.1(c).
[93] Firger & Gerrard, n. 90.

providing political risk insurance and debt financing only to green finance. These policies would further not only SDG 13 but also SDGs 7, 9, 11, and 12. Second, international investment law could seek to eliminate its negative effect on domestic climate policy by giving host countries greater flexibility in adopting mitigation and adaptation measures. For example, international investment agreements could narrow the definition of indirect expropriations or include climate-specific exemptions.[94]

13.4 POSITIONING SDG 13 IN THE INTERNATIONAL INSTITUTIONAL CONTEXT

Many institutions address the climate change issue, operating at all levels of governance (global, regional, national, and local) and involving both public and private actors as well as various combinations of the two. A 2016 study identified eighty-nine institutions focusing on international climate change governance,[95] and this number is undoubtedly now much higher. In addition to climate-specific institutions, many international organizations also have competence to address aspects of the climate change issue, including

- the IMO and the ICAO, which address emissions from international maritime transport and civil aviation respectively;
- the Montreal Protocol, which has addressed the contribution to climate change of ODS and their substitutes;
- the Food and Agriculture Organization, which provides assistance to developing countries on mitigation and adaptation in the agriculture sectors; and
- the UN Security Council, which has devoted a number of sessions to the security implications of climate change.

This "Cambrian explosion" of climate-related institutions has both benefits and costs.[96] On the positive side, it brings the resources of many institutions to bear on the climate change problem: international organizations, national and subnational governments, civil society organizations, the financial sector, industry, and so forth. It also allows experimentation with different approaches, which is particularly valuable for policy areas that we do not understand well – for example, how to mobilize climate finance or engage in capacity building effectively. Finally, it avoids putting all of our eggs in one basket. If one governance approach is not working,

[94] *Id.*

[95] Oscar Widerberg, Philipp Pattberg, & Kristian Kristensen, *Mapping the Institutional Architecture of Global Climate Change Governance*, vol. 2 (Institute for Environmental Studies, 2016).

[96] Robert O. Keohane & David G. Victor, "The Regime Complex for Climate Change" (2011) 9 (1) *Perspectives on Politics* 7, 12.

others can be tried. For example, if actions at the international and/or national level fall short, actions by provinces and cities can help fill the gap. If governmental action is lacking, action by nongovernmental organizations and business assume greater importance.

But institutional abundance also comes with potential costs – in particular, fragmentation, duplication of effort, and conflict. So coordination among the multiplicity of climate-related actors is crucial. Within the climate change domain, coordination has taken place along several dimensions, in many forms, and for many purposes. The UN climate change regime has recognized the competence of the IMO and the ICAO to address emissions from international transport.[97] Subnational actors such as cities, for example, have coordinated horizontally to set common standards through transnational institutions such as the C40 Cities Climate Leadership Group and the Global Covenant of Mayors. Business actors have established coordinating mechanisms such as the International Investors Group on Climate Change and the Cement Sustainability Initiative in order to share information and develop common approaches.

Even if we focus only on SDG 13, each of its targets has its own complex institutional ecosystem, within which coordination is challenging. Target 13.1, on strengthening resilience and adaptive capacity to climate-related hazards and natural disasters, is addressed within the UN climate change regime by multiple institutions, including the Cancun Adaptation Committee, the Warsaw International Mechanism on Loss and Damage, and the Adaptation Fund. These must coordinate not only among themselves but also with the UN Office for Disaster Risk Reduction, which oversees implementation of the Sendai Framework, the principal international initiative addressing target 13.1.

Integrating climate change measures into national policies, strategies, and planning, the subject of target 13.2, has long been pursued through country study programs by national development agencies as well as by international institutions such as the UN Development Program (UNDP). In 2016, a coalition of governments and international institutions launched the NDC Partnership, which works with developing countries to identify priorities, coordinate climate policies across government, and mobilize support. Currently, the NDC Partnership includes more than one hundred countries and more than sixty international institutions and nongovernmental organizations.

Target 13.a, on implementing the commitment undertaken by developed country parties to mobilize US$100 billion in climate finance, involves national aid agencies, multilateral development banks such as the World Bank, the Global Environment Facility (GEF), the Green Climate Fund, and private banks and

[97] Kyoto Protocol, art. 2.2 (stating the intent of the parties to address emissions from aviation and maritime shipping through the ICAO and the International Maritime Organization respectively).

investors. Target 13.b, on raising capacity in least developed countries and small island developing states, is addressed in the UN climate change regime by the Adaptation Committee, the Consultative Group of Experts, the Climate Technology Centre and Network, the Least Developed Country Expert Group, the Paris Committee on Capacity Building, the Adaptation Fund, and the Least Developed Country Fund, as well as by the GEF, the UNDP, and the UN Environment Programme (UNEP), among others.

The proliferation of institutions within the UN climate change regime has prompted calls for consolidation. The costs of institutional proliferation and congestion affect all countries to some degree. But they are particularly acute for developing countries, which lack the resources and staff to engage effectively in the myriad institutions and processes. In theory, the COP and Secretariat could provide overall coordination, and more specialized bodies such as the Cancun Adaptation Committee, the Standing Committee on Finance, and the Paris Committee on Capacity Building could coordinate particular issues. In practice, however, each component part of the regime tends to develop its own constituency and power base, making efforts to streamline the regime difficult.

The problem is more acute for coordination between the climate change and sustainable development regimes since they have continued to operate on separate tracks, with no overarching body that could serve to integrate the two agendas. The HLPF was intended to play a key role in integrating the economic, social, and environmental dimensions of sustainable development and has SDG 13 within its purview. But states continue to view the UN climate change regime as the primary forum to address the issue, as they agreed in SDG 13. As a result, it is unclear how big a role the HLPF's periodic reviews of SDG 13 will play in the development of international climate change policy.

Finally, although states have preferred to develop international climate change law through negotiations rather than adjudication, courts and tribunals have recently begun to play a greater role in addressing the climate change problem, in significant part due to efforts by advocacy groups, and litigation is now seen by some as a distinct climate change governance tool in its own right.[98] At the national level, more than 1,500 climate change cases were initiated between 1986 and July 2020, 1,213 in the United States and 374 in other countries, including 37 in the global South.[99] Of the non-US cases, climate change figured centrally in 41 percent of the cases. Fewer cases have been brought internationally, but many courts and tribunals could potentially consider climate change cases, including

[98] Setzer & Byrnes, n. 64, 2–3; see also Jacqueline Peel & Hari Osofsky, "Climate Change Litigation" (2020) 16 *Annual Review of Law and Social Science* 21; Bodansky, Brunnée & Rajamani, n. 25, 283–90.

[99] Setzer & Byrnes, n. 64, 4.

- human rights tribunals, which have already considered a number of cases addressing climate change, as discussed above;
- the WTO's dispute settlement system, which could hear cases concerning potential conflicts between national climate policies and international trade law;
- the International Tribunal for the Law of the Sea, which some suggest could hear cases involving the impact of climate change on the ocean;[100] and
- the International Court of Justice, which island states have considered using to request an advisory opinion about the customary international law duties of states to reduce their GHG emissions.[101]

13.5 CONCLUSIONS

To a significant degree, achieving the SDGs and combating climate change are codependent. On the one hand, combating climate change will require making energy production, transportation, agriculture, industry, and cities more sustainable. On the other, eliminating poverty and hunger, promoting well-being, and protecting life below water and on land will require limiting climate change. But the climate change and sustainable development agendas could also compete for scarce political and economic resources or work at cross-purposes. Sustainable development could be pursued in a manner that increases GHG emissions or be used as an excuse not to take action to combat climate change. Conversely, climate change policies could undermine food security by incentivizing biofuels or make energy less affordable by raising costs.

To maximize the synergies and minimize the trade-offs, the climate change and sustainable development agendas need to be pursued in an integrated manner. In this regard, SDG 13 is important not so much for what it says – which is derivative of the UN climate change regime – as for incorporating the climate change issue into the SDG process. It needs to be complemented by efforts to consider the SDGs within all of the different international processes addressing the climate change issue as well as within national governments. Several developments suggest that the climate change and sustainable development agendas are beginning to work together, despite their separate institutional homes. In its 2018 *1.5 Degree Report*, the IPCC included an extensive discussion of the relationship between limiting temperature increase to 1.5 degrees Celsius and achieving the SDGs. Increasing efforts have also been made to model "shared socio-economic pathways" rather than

[100] Meinhard Doelle, "Climate Change and the Use of the Dispute Settlement Regime of the Law of the Sea Convention" (2005) 37(3–4) *Ocean Development and International Law* 319.

[101] Philippe Sands, "Climate Change and the Rule of Law: Adjudicating the Future in International Law" (2016) 28 *Journal of Environmental Law* 19.

only emission scenarios.[102] In 2019, the UN Department of Economic and Social Affairs and the UNFCCC Secretariat partnered to organize a global conference on SDG-climate synergies and established a global knowledge platform on these synergies. Moreover, the UN climate change regime has increasingly incorporated the work of non-state actors, including through the Marrakesh Partnership for Global Climate Action and the Non-State Actor Zone for Climate Action portal. Finally, judicial decisions have focused on the socioeconomic impacts of climate change and climate change policies on human rights. If we are to succeed in achieving both the SDGs' and the Paris Agreement's goals, closer integration along these lines will be essential.

[102] Gomez-Echeverri, n. 8, 7.

14

SDG 14: Conserve and Sustainably Use the Oceans, Seas and Marine Resources for Sustainable Development

Karen N. Scott

ABSTRACT

This chapter explores the complex and challenging relationship between Sustainable Development Goal (SDG) 14, Life below Water, and the relevant international legal frameworks. It shows that the effective implementation of SDG 14 may be compromised by the structural limitations of international law in general as well as by the idiosyncrasies of the law of the sea. Yet the SDG 14 targets may serve to strengthen existing regimes, operate as interstitial norms connecting distinct regimes, or identify gaps in ocean governance and inspire new regulation. However, where the SDG 14 target is expressed in weaker or more general terms than existing obligations or goals, SDG 14 may undermine existing instruments. In the absence of an overarching 'Ocean Council', the regime complex that is in place provides as many opportunities for duplication of, or contradictory, efforts as it does for the development of mutually supportive measures. It is also posited that SDG 14 fails to provide the necessary conceptual framework for the law of the sea in the Anthropocene.

KEYWORDS

SDG 14, law of the sea, ocean governance, regime complex, marine resources

14.1 INTRODUCTION

Sustainable Development Goal (SDG) 14, Life below Water, seeks to conserve and sustainably use the oceans, seas, and marine resources for sustainable development. The ocean covers 70 per cent of the earth's surface and is fundamental to all life on the earth. It generates half of the oxygen we breathe[1] and currently absorbs around 26 per cent of all anthropogenic carbon dioxide.[2] The oceans are integral to processes of nutrient recycling and filtration, and coastal ecosystems play a key role in flood defences. In total, 40 per cent of the global population lives within two hundred kilometres of the oceans, and twelve of the world's fifteen mega cities are situated on the coast.[3] Fish comprise 17 per cent of the animal protein intake for the global population,[4] and the oceans provide the primary source of protein for over a billion people.[5] It is (conservatively) estimated that ocean economic sectors contribute US$1.5 trillion to the global gross domestic product, and this figure is expected to double by 2030.[6] The blue economy supports more than 350 million jobs associated with fishing, tourism, and research,[7] and it is estimated that areas within one hundred kilometres of the oceans generate 61 per cent of gross national product.[8] In total, 80 per cent of world trade (by volume) travels by sea,[9] and 99 per cent of all transoceanic communications are transported on undersea cables.[10]

However, the ocean is also at risk from threats such as pollution, climate change, invasive species, habitat degradation, and overfishing. The upper ocean has increased in temperature by between 0.65 and 1.06 Celsius between 1880 and 2012,[11] and a study in 2018 suggests that the temperature increase is in fact at the

[1] Peter Harris et al., 'Chapter 1. Introduction – Planet, Oceans and Life', in *The First Global Integrated Marine Assessment (World Ocean Assessment I) by the Group of Experts of the Regular Process under the auspices of the United Nations General Assembly and its Regular Process for Global Reporting and Assessment of the State of the Marine Environment, including Socioeconomic Aspects* (UN, 2016), 1, www.un.org/Depts/los/global_reporting/WOA_RegProcess.htm.

[2] *Id.*, 2.

[3] Martin Visbeck, 'Ocean Science Research Is Key for a Sustainable Future' (2018) 9(690) *Nature Communications* 1.

[4] FAO, *The State of World Fisheries and Aquaculture 2018: Meeting the Sustainable Development Goals* (FAO, 2018), 2.

[5] Laura Recuero Virto, 'A Preliminary Assessment of the Indicators for Sustainable Development Goal (SDG) 14 "Conserve and Sustainably Use the Oceans, Seas and Marine Resources for Sustainable Development"' (2018) 98 *Maine Policy* 47, 48.

[6] Andrés M. Cisneros-Montemayor et al., 'Social Equity and Benefits as the Nexus of a Transformative Blue Economy: A Sectoral Review of Implications' (2019) 109 *Marine Policy* 103702-1, 103702-2.

[7] Virto, n. 5, 48.

[8] *Id.*, 48.

[9] UN Conference on Trade and Development, *Review of Maritime Transport 2018*, unctad.org/webflyer/review-maritime-transport-2018.

[10] Douglas Main, *Undersea Cables Transport 99 Percent of International Data*, 4 February 2015, www.newsweek.com/undersea-cables-transport-99-percent-international-communications-319072.

[11] D.L Hartmann et al., 'Observations: Atmosphere', in T.F. Stocker et al., *Climate Change 2013: The Physical Science Basis. Contribution of Working Group I to the Fifth Assessment Report of the Intergovernmental Panel on Climate Change* (Cambridge University Press, 2013), 161 (*IPCC Fifth Assessment Report*).

high end of previous estimates.[12] Temperature increases impact both the biology and the chemistry of the oceans. The thermal expansion of the oceans, combined with melting sea ice and glaciers, is predicted to lead to a rise in sea levels, and it is estimated that global sea levels have already risen by 0.19 of a metre between 1901 and 2010.[13] Research suggests that sea levels could rise by more than 2 metres by 2100.[14] It is estimated that 93 per cent of the world fisheries are fully exploited, overexploited, or depleted,[15] although the percentage of maximally sustainable fish stocks has increased since 1989, owing to the implementation of global management measures.[16] Land-based source pollution continues to be a major threat to the oceans, and there is an increasing focus on marine plastics. It is estimated that during just one year (2010) between 4.8 and 12.7 million tonnes of plastic entered the ocean,[17] and plastic is so ubiquitous that it has been proposed as a key geological indicator for the Anthropocene.[18]

The international regulatory context for SDG 14 comprises primarily the law of the sea, international environmental law, international trade and investment law, and, to a lesser extent, human rights law. These bodies of law, like the targets within SDG 14 itself, are simultaneously mutually supportive and in potential conflict, depending on their diverse values and priorities. The law of the sea is substantially codified with the 1982 United Nations Convention on the Law of the Sea (UNCLOS), which comprises the 'constitution' for the oceans and provides an overarching framework for all activities taking place on, in, or under the oceans. The law of the sea allocates rights and duties on the basis of the zone (within and beyond the national jurisdiction of states) and the activity (navigation, fishing, environmental protection, and so on). It embraces rights and resources allocated on the basis of sovereignty (such as fish and minerals within a state's exclusive economic zone [EEZ]), res communis (with respect to the high seas), and the common heritage of humankind (in relation to minerals on or under the deep seabed known as the 'Area'). It provides the framework within which to navigate the relationship and tensions between traditional high seas freedoms (such as navigation, fishing, marine scientific research, and so on) and other principles, including, but not limited to, environmental protection, security, and equity. The law of the sea

12 L. Resplandy et al., 'Quantification of Ocean Heat Uptake from Changes in Atmospheric O_2 and CO_2 Composition' (2018) 563 *Nature* 105.

13 *IPCC Fifth Assessment Report*, n. 11, 258.

14 M. Oppenheimer & R.B. Alley, 'How High Will the Seas Rise?' (2016) 354(6318) *Science* 1375, 1375.

15 FAO, *The State of World Fisheries and Aquaculture 2018: Meeting the Sustainable Development Goals* (FAO, 2018), 6.

16 *Id.*

17 Patricia Villarrubia-Gómez, Sarah E. Cornell, & Joan Fabres, 'Marine Plastic Pollution as a Planetary Boundary Threat: The Drifting Piece in the Sustainability Puzzle' (2018) 96 *Marine Policy* 213, 213.

18 Jan Zalasiewica et al., 'The Geological Cycle of Plastics and Their Use as a Stratigraphic Indicator of the Anthropocene' (2016) 13 *Anthropocene* 4.

comprises treaties, customary international law, and general principles as well as informal or soft law.

This chapter will explore the relationship between SDG 14 and the law of the sea and examine the various functions it performs in the context of ocean governance. These include strengthening existing commitments within established regimes, performing a linking or interstitial role between regimes in respect of issues that have traditionally fallen between those regimes, and highlighting and addressing regulatory gaps within regimes. The SDG 14 targets are generally drafted in aspirational terms and therefore complement, rather than substantively contribute to, existing regulation. Nevertheless, their broad articulation can potentially undermine existing, more detailed goals, and the emphasis on non-binding targets can reduce incentives to negotiate binding commitments. In some respects, SDG 14 challenges the law of the sea – for example, while its targets are applicable to a wide range of actors, the law of the sea remains traditionally state focused. In other respects, SDG 14 relies on outmoded concepts such as maximum sustainable yield in the context of fisheries. The ten targets associated with SDG 14 undoubtedly contribute to the conservation and sustainable use of the oceans and its resources, but they comprise a very partial list of ocean-focused priorities and are emphatically Anthropocentric in focus.[19] Nevertheless, in the absence of an 'Oceans Council' or any body with overarching authority for the oceans, SDG 14 provides a useful mechanism of identifying goals and targets that can be taken up and implemented through the multitude of institutions and regimes that have responsibility for parts of, or activities taking place within, the oceans.

14.2 THE CONTENT OF SDG 14 IN THE CONTEXT OF THE OTHER SDGS

14.2.1 *The Content of SDG 14*

SDG 14 comprises ten targets that address the three dimensions of sustainable development as set out in UN General Assembly (UNGA) Resolution 70/1: economic, social, and environmental.[20] Each target is accompanied by a global indicator, agreed to by the UNGA in 2017.[21] The global indicators are designed only to be a proxy for measurement,[22] and it is intended that states will develop more detailed

[19] See Sam Adelman, 'The Sustainable Development Goals, Anthropocentrism and Neoliberalism', in Duncan French & Louis J. Kotzé (eds.), *Sustainable Development Goals, Law, Theory and Implementation* (EE, 2018), 15.

[20] *Transforming Our World: The 2030 Agenda for Sustainable Development*, UN Doc. A/Res/70/1, 25 September 2015.

[21] *Work of the Statistical Commission Pertaining to the 2030 Agenda for Sustainable Development*, UNGA Resolution 71/313, 6 July 2017.

[22] Virto, n. 5, 49.

indicators.[23] The inclusion of a designated SDG on ocean issues reflects the emergence of a 'global oceans conservation agenda' over the last decade[24] and represents a significant departure from the 2000 Millennium Development Goals, where the oceans were largely ignored and which included only brief reference to the protection of coastal ecosystems.[25]

The SDG 14 targets can be broadly divided between the categories of environmental protection, sustainable resource management, and capacity building. The ten targets are generally (although not always) characterized by a relative absence of detail and, in some cases, a failure to specify a temporal deadline. For example, target 14.1 neither specifies which sources of pollution (other than nutrients and marine debris) are included within its remit nor the reduction objectives. Target 14.2 fails to define key terms such as 'significant adverse impacts', 'resilience', and 'restoration'. Target 14.3 on ocean acidification does not specify a temporal target, in addition to being expressed in very general terms. Targets 14.a, 14.b, and 14.c all fail to specify temporal goals, which makes measuring success (or otherwise) against these and other targets challenging. Even where a target is clear and measurable, its sparse expression may lead to ambiguity or inappropriate implementation. For example, target 14.5 clearly states that 10 per cent of marine and coastal areas must be protected by 2020. However, no detail is provided relating to what ecosystems should be protected or the nature of that protection, and concern has been expressed that it creates an incentive to designate very large protected areas that are little more than 'paper parks'.[26]

Even where a target is precisely defined in both scope and temporal terms, its achievement may be unrealistic in the specified time scale. For example, target 14.4 is clear in aim – to 'effectively regulate harvesting and end' illegal, unreported, and unregulated (IUU) fishing and overfishing – but the target date of 2020 seems over ambitious at best. Most targets are not in fact new and reiterate (in varying degrees of detail) existing commitments. For example, the 2010 Aichi Biodiversity Targets[27] address area-based protection,[28] ocean acidification,[29] and sustainable fishing.[30] The World Trade Organization (WTO) made a commitment to address fishing subsidies

[23] *Id.*, 49.

[24] Lisa M. Campbell & Noella Gray, 'Area Expansion versus Effective and Equitable Management in International Marine Protected Areas Goals and Targets' (2019) 100 *Marine Policy* 192, 192.

[25] 2000 Millennium Development Goals, Goal 7.B. See Martin Visbeck et al., 'Securing Blue Wealth: The Need for a Special Sustainable Development Goal for the Ocean and Coasts' (2014) 48 *Marine Policy* 184.

[26] Bárbara Horta e Costa et al., 'A Regulation-based Classification System for Marine Protected Area (MPAs)' (2016) 72 *Marine Policy* 192, 192

[27] *The Strategic Plan for Biodiversity 2011 – 2020 and the Aichi Biodiversity Targets*, CBD Decision X/2, 2010.

[28] 2010 Aichi Biodiversity Targets, target 11.

[29] *Id.*, target 10.

[30] *Id.*, target 6.

in 2001,[31] although negotiations that were due to end in 2019 were still ongoing in 2021.[32] Target 14.1 reflects customary international law as reflected in article 194 of UNCLOS and in numerous global and regional instruments that address land-based and other sources of marine pollution.

The indicators, which were added in 2017, provide a basic proxy by which to measure implementation and, in some cases, add some helpful clarification to the target.[33] In general, however, the extent to which the indicators provide a useful measure of the implementation of a target is questionable. Most indicators highlight a very narrow aspect of their respective target and therefore provide a minimal indication as to whether, and to what extent, any individual target is achieved. For example, indicator 14.1.1 merely requires the creation of an index of coastal eutrophication and floating plastic density. It does not measure action taken to address these sources of pollution and does not cover land-based sources of pollution more generally. Indicator 14.3.1 is similarly research focused and is confined to measuring marine acidity at an agreed set of sampling stations rather than assessing the extent to which measures 'minimize and address the impacts of ocean acidification'. The indicators for targets 14.4 and 14.5, however, do appear to provide a reasonable basis of measuring the extent to which the target is achieved through measuring the proportion of fish stocks within biologically sustainable levels and the coverage of protected areas respectively.

For the most part, the relationship between the SDG 14 targets is mutually supportive. For example, reducing pollution (target 14.1) will support the sustainable management and protection of marine and coastal ecosystems (target 14.2). Target 14.2 is also supported by the objectives of target 14.3 (to minimize and address ocean acidification), particularly with respect to coastal coral reef ecosystems. The introduction of area-based protection may also support objectives to reduce pollution (target 14.1), to effectively regulate fishing (target 14.4), and to more generally manage the coast sustainably (target 14.2). Effective regulation of fishing (target 14.4) is also clearly supported by ending fishing subsidies that contribute to overcapacity and to IUU fishing (target 14.6). However, there are possible tensions between some of these targets. Area-based protection (target 14.5) has the potential to either enhance or restrict small-scale artisanal fishing (target 14.b), aquaculture, and tourism (target 14.7). Similarly, providing access to markets and resources for artisanal fishers may require subsidies, contrary to target 4.6, although it should be noted that target 4.6 does not necessarily seek to end all subsidies.

[31] WTO, *Negotiations on Fisheries Subsidies*, n.d., www.wto.org/english/tratop_e/rulesneg_e/fish_e/fish_e.htm.

[32] International Institute for Sustainable Development, *WTO Members Delay Agreement on Fisheries Subsidies to 2021*, 16 December 2020, sdg.iisd.org/news/wto-members-delay-agreement-on-fisheries-subsidies-to-2021/.

[33] For a detailed assessment of the indicators, see Virto, n. 5.

SDG 14 'for the first time groups key ocean issues into a cohesive package, increasing their visibility and role in the sustainable development agenda'.[34] Nevertheless, SDG 14 represents only a selection of ocean issues and has been criticized as failing to articulate 'a compelling narrative of change'.[35] From an environmental perspective, there are perhaps some surprising omissions from SDG 14, such as action associated with invasive species, the protection of endangered species, and habitat degradation. Some have argued that SDG 14 is focused on environmental considerations and does not sufficiently address issues of development or equity.[36] This is perhaps a little unfair and overlooks the role that SDG 14 can play in supporting other SDGs, a point emphasized by the 2017 call for action, which is discussed below.[37] SDG 14 is undoubtedly aspirational in nature, and the targets were developed in order to provide 'necessary flexibility for national governments to set their own targets and incorporate these into their national planning processes, policies and strategies'.[38] In contrast to other sectors, there is no one regime with oversight of all oceans issues, and institutional oversight has been described as 'weak',[39] although a more accurate description would be 'diffuse': there are bodies with oversight functions, but these are fragmented according to region or activity.

Some of the shortcomings identified above have been addressed in the UNGA resolution *Our Ocean, Our Future: Call for Action*. The call for action was adopted at the 2017 high-level and multi-stakeholder United Nations Conference to Support the Implementation of Sustainable Development Goal 14 and was subsequently endorsed by the UNGA.[40] The call for action, among other things, adds 'conceptual clarity to the interpretation of SDG 14 and its targets by including reference to terms and instruments not previously incorporated into SDG 14'.[41] For example, it specifies additional sources of pollution in the context of target 14.1 (including plastics, microplastics, untreated waste water and solid waste discharges, hazardous substances,

[34] G. Wright et al., *Partnering for a Sustainable Ocean: The Role of Regional Ocean Governance in Implementing SDG 14* (IDDRI, IASS, TMG & UN Environment, 2017), 9.

[35] Mara Ntona & Elisa Morgera, 'Connecting SDG 14 with the Other Sustainable Development Goals through Marine Spatial Planning' (2018) 93 *Marine Policy* 214, 215.

[36] *Id.*

[37] *Our Ocean, Our Future: Call for Action*, UN Doc. A/Res/71/312, 6 July 2017, paras. 13, 13(a), 13 (b), 13(c).

[38] Roland Cormier & Michael Elliott, 'SMART Marine Goals, Targets and Management: Is SDG 14 Operational or Aspirational, Is "*Life Below Water*" Sinking or Swimming?' (2017) 123 *Marine Policy* 28, 29.

[39] Frank Biermann, Norichika Kaine, & Rakhyun E. Kim, 'Global Governance by Goal-setting: The Novel Approach of the UN Sustainable Development Goals' (2017) 26 *Current Opinion in Environmental Sustainability* 26, 27.

[40] *Our Ocean, Our Future*, n. 37.

[41] Daniela Diz, Elisa Morgera, & Meriwether Wilson, 'Marine Policy Special Issue: SDG Synergies for Sustainable Fisheries and Poverty Alleviation' (2019) 110 *Marine Policy* 102860-1, 102860-2.

pollution from ships, and abandoned or otherwise discarded fishing gear), specifies action relating to plastics and waste prevention and minimization, and also identifies other threats including underwater noise, invasive species, and ship strikes.[42] Another example is the helpful expansion of targets 14.4 and 14.5 to expressly incorporate both precautionary and ecosystem-based approaches.[43]

Furthermore, the call for action expressly connects the health of coastal ecosystems (target 14.2) with the threat of climate change and recognizes the function of the coast as a potential sink for carbon dioxide through mangrove and seagrass ecosystems as well as contributing to coastal resilience.[44] It also calls upon states to actively engage in the negotiations for an internationally legally binding instrument under UNCLOS on the conservation and sustainable use of biodiversity beyond national jurisdiction (BBNJ),[45] supporting the objectives in target 14.c.[46] Finally, the call for action emphasizes that SDG 14 must be implemented 'in an integrated way taking into account the critical interlinkages among the targets and between SDG 14 and other goals and other processes that support SDG targets'.[47]

14.2.2 *Support and Tension: SDG 14 and Other SDGs*

As the 2017 call for action emphasizes, SDG 14 must be implemented 'in an integrated way taking into account the critical interlinkages ... between SDG 14 and other goals'.[48] In most cases, these interlinkages are mutually supporting, but, in some instances, there are tensions or potential contradictions between SDG 14 and other goals. In a 2017 study on the interactions between the SDGs,[49] the authors found that SDG 14 intersects with SDGs 1, 2, 8, 11, 12, and 13 with ninety-seven target-level interactions, sixty-one of which are positive (mutually supportive), one is neutral, and thirty-five are negative (creating tension or conflict).[50] In fact, SDG 14 arguably interacts with every other SDG at some point.

Perhaps the strongest interaction is between SDG 14 and the goals relating to SDG 1, No Poverty; SDG 2, Zero Hunger; and SDG 3, Good Health and Well-

42 *Our Ocean, Our Future*, n. 37, para. 13(g), 13(h), 13 (i).
43 *Id.*, para. 13(j), 13(l).
44 *Id.*, para. 13(k).
45 *International Legally Binding Instrument under the United Nations Convention on the Law of the Sea on the Conservation and Sustainable Use of Marine Biological Diversity of Areas Beyond National Jurisdiction*, UN Doc. A/Res/72/249, 24 December 2017.
46 *Our Ocean, Our Future*, n. 37, para. 13(s).
47 *Id.*, para. 13(a).
48 *Id.*
49 International Council for Science, *A Guide to SDG Interactions: From Science to Implementation*, 2017, council.science/publications/a-guide-to-sdg-interactions-from-science-to-implementation/.
50 *Id.*, 16; see also Gerald G. Singh et al., 'A Rapid Assessment of Co-benefits and Trade-offs among Sustainable Development Goals' (2018) 93 *Marine Policy* 223.

being.[51] However, the inherent tension between the 'environment' and the 'economy' within the concept of sustainable development also creates the potential for conflict between these goals, notably between area-based management (target 14.5) and fishing and development, which may have negative implications for SDGs 1, 2, and 3. A reduction in fishing subsidies (target 14.6) could also have negative implications for poverty alleviation. SDG 13, Climate Action, directly intersects with target 14.3 on ocean acidification as well as target 14.2 on the sustainable management of coastal ecosystems, which have the potential to mitigate (through the drawdown of carbon dioxide) and contribute to adaptation to climate change.[52] Creating climate refugia is an increasingly significant component of area-based management,[53] and, thus, SDG 13 also intersects with target 14.5. SDG 7, Affordable and Clean Energy, is a crucial component of any climate change mitigation strategy and thus intersects with both SDG 13 and SDG 14. However, there may be tensions arising from the placement of offshore renewable energy structures in sensitive coastal locations (target 14.2) or areas subject to special protection (target 14.5).

The integrated implementation of the SDGs is fundamental in order to overcome the 'siloed list of thematic, equally significant global priorities',[54] and this goal is illustrated in the context of the linkages between SDG 14; SDG 15, Life on Land; and SDG 6, Clean Water and Sanitation. SDG 15 clearly supports the SDG 14 targets in relation to combating land-based pollution (target 14.1) and sustainable management of coastal environments (target 14.2) and supporting small-island developing states in relation to activities such as tourism and aquaculture (target 14.7). More specifically, target 6.3 requires stakeholders to 'improve water quality by reducing pollution, eliminating dumping and minimising release of hazardous chemicals and materials, halving the proportion of untreated wastewater and substantially increasing recycling and safe refuse globally' by 2030. This target directly supports targets 14.1 and 14.2 as most land-based pollution reaches the ocean through terrestrial waterways.

In conclusion, the interactions between SDG 14 and the other SDGs are numerous and complex. While Agenda 2030 describes the three dimensions of sustainable development – economic, social, and environmental – as integrated and indivisible, they are not equally represented within each of the SDGs,[55] which therefore creates tensions between (and sometimes within) the goals. SDG 14 has a strong and

[51] See Diz, Morgera & Wilson, n. 41.

[52] For a discussion between the SDGs, including SDG 14 and the climate and biodiversity regimes, see A. Meriwether, W. Wilson, & Catherine Forsyth, 'Restoring Near-Shore Marine Ecosystems to Enhance Climate Security for Island Ocean States: Aligning International Processes and Local Practices' (2018) 93 *Marine Policy* 284.

[53] See, e.g., David Edward Johnson & Ellen Lorraine Kenchington, 'Should Potential for Climate Change Refugia Be Mainstreamed into the Criteria for Describing Ebsas?' (2019) 12 *Conservation Letters* 312634.

[54] Ntona & Morgera, n. 35, 214.

[55] *Transforming Our World*, n. 20.

universal environmental focus whereas its targets relating to the blue economy are aimed primarily at developing states. Nevertheless, on balance, the interlinkages between SDG 14 and the other SDGs are more supportive of one another than otherwise. How they are actually implemented in mutual support or managed in order to minimize conflict between them depends, in part, on the overarching international legal and institutional framework within which they sit, and it is this framework to which this chapter now turns.

14.3 POSITIONING SDG 14 IN INTERNATIONAL LAW

14.3.1 *UNCLOS as a Constitutional Framework in a Complex Legal Setting*

The SDGs have been described as 'a novel type of global governance where goal-setting features as a key governance strategy ... [are] largely detached from the international legal system'.[56] The SDGs are not binding in international law in and of themselves, but they are clearly intended to have normative effect in that they are designed to influence and change the behaviour of states and other stakeholders. As Mara Ntona and Elisa Morgera assert, '[i]nternationally agreed goals and targets are increasingly accepted as having a significant political and instrumental value, insofar as they provide a "globally shared normative framework" that complements international conventions and other tools of international law by catalyzing action, mobilizing stakeholders and fostering collaboration between members of the international community'.[57] This approach to international governance – whereby overarching goals are set with maximum flexibility, allowing states to decide how to meet those goals and the widespread use of voluntary commitments – is arguably being developed as an alternative to traditional international environmental law. It is this approach that underpins the 2015 Paris Agreement, which allows states to choose how to meet the target to hold global average temperature increase to well below two degrees Celsius above industrial levels through a set of voluntary commitments amalgamated in a nationally determined contribution (NDC).[58] Nevertheless, while the SDGs, as a collective, may be 'largely detached from the international legal system', to use Frank Biermann, Norichika Kaine, and Rakhyun E. Kim's phrase,[59] SDG 14 and, more particularly, its individual targets, are, to varying degrees, embedded within, or supported by, international legal frameworks. Indeed, the role of international law in implementing SDG 14 is specifically recognized in target 14.c, which calls upon stakeholders to 'enhance the conservation and sustainable use of oceans and their resources by implementing international law as reflected in

[56] Biermann, Kaine, & Kim, n. 39, 26.
[57] Ntona & Morgera, n. 35, 214.
[58] Paris Agreement, arts. 2(a), 4.
[59] Biermann, Kaine, & Kim, n. 39.

UNCLOS, which is the legal framework for the conservation and sustainable use of the oceans and their resources, as recalled in paragraph 158 of *The Future We Want*'.

Nevertheless, the relationship between SDG 14 and the relevant international legal frameworks is complex and, at times, challenging. The effective implementation of SDG 14 is arguably compromised by the structural limitations of international law, in general, as well as by the idiosyncrasies of the law of the sea, in particular. For example, notwithstanding the increased emphasis on an ecosystem-based approach (target 14.2) that has developed over the last couple of decades,[60] regulation and management of the land-sea interface remains weak, particularly at the global level, and this is most clearly demonstrated by the fact that the international rules relating to land-based source pollution are significantly weaker than pollution from ships, dumping, and offshore activities. This situation creates a challenge for the implementation of targets 14.1 and 14.2 as well as for the integration of SDG 14 with SDG 13.

Despite these limitations, however, it is clear that existing international law and ocean governance frameworks are crucial to the implementation of SDG 14. UNCLOS provides the constitutional framework for all ocean law, including SDG 14, as acknowledged in target 14.c, which contains an explicit reference to the convention. Part XII of UNCLOS establishes a general obligation to prevent, reduce, and control pollution from any source (targets 14.1 and 14.3)[61] and to protect and preserve rare and fragile ecosystems (targets 14.2, 14.5),[62] to fish sustainably (targets 14.4 and 14.6)[63] and to support scientific research and technology transfer (target 14.c).[64] Beyond UNCLOS, however, there is a multiplicity of treaties and regimes that have a mandate to support one or more of the SDG 14 targets. These range from instruments regulating marine pollution and fisheries, to those with a mandate to protect marine biodiversity and ecosystems, and to those that operate in the fields of trade and human rights. Moreover, the legally binding instrument for managing activities affecting biodiversity beyond national jurisdiction, currently being negotiated under the auspices of the United Nations, will provide an important framework for implementing SDG 14 in areas beyond national jurisdiction (ABNJ), particularly targets 14.1, 14.2, 14.3, and 14.5.

At both the global and the regional levels, there are also instruments, which might be described as informal or unconventional, that nevertheless are lawmaking or, at the very least, normative and that have legal effect and contribute to ocean

60 Anastasia Telesetsky & Rebecca Bratspies, 'Marine Environmental Law: UNCLOS, Ocean Governance and Fisheries', in Erika Techera et al. (eds.), *Routledge Handbook of International Environmental Law*, 2nd ed. (Routledge, 2021) 157, 170–71.

61 UNCLOS, art. 194(1).

62 *Id.*, art. 194(5).

63 *Id.*, arts. 118, 119.

64 *Id.*, Parts XIII, XIV.

governance and the implementation of SDG 14.[65] These instruments include, but are by no means limited to, the 2010 Aichi Biodiversity Targets, the International Maritime Organization's (IMO) measures such as the Polar Code[66] and particularly sensitive seas areas (PSSAs),[67] as well as the numerous guidelines and policy action frameworks issued by the UN Food and Agriculture Organization (FAO) in relation to sustainable fisheries.[68]

Just as importantly, the various principles that span across, and, in some cases, underpin, treaty regimes support, enhance, and provide a framework for the implementation of SDG 14. Moreover, these principles may also play a significant role in integrating the economic, environmental, and social elements of sustainability across the SDG 14 targets and between SDG 14 and the other SDGs noted above. These principles include the ecosystem approach,[69] the precautionary approach, environmental impact assessment, and strategic environmental assessment. Principles or environmental 'tools' developed in the 2010s, such as marine spatial planning (MSP) and integrated coastal zone management (ICZM) have a particularly important role in mediating multiple ocean and coastal interests in the context of developing a sustainable blue economy sensitive to environmental concerns.

One way of exploring the relationship between SDG 14 and the ocean governance regime complex is to ask what function the SDGs play within that complex and the extent to which SDG 14 enhances or undermines ocean governance. For the purposes of this chapter, three principal functions are identified. First, the SDG 14 targets may serve to strengthen existing regimes and motivate states and institutions to address target areas within those regimes. Second, the SDG 14 targets may operate as interstitial norms in-between and connecting distinct regimes. Third, the

65 See Natalie Klein (ed.), *Unconventional Lawmaking in the Law of the Sea: Current Practice and Future Prospects* (Oxford University Press, 2021).

66 *International Code for Ships Operating in Polar Waters*, IMO Resolution MSC.385(94), 21 November 2014 and IMO Resolution MEPC.264, 15 May 2015. While much of this code has been made binding through amendments to the 1973/78 International Convention for the Prevention of Pollution from Ships (MARPOL Convention), the 1974 International Convention for the Safety of Life at Sea and the 1988 Sofia Protocol, and the 1995 International Convention on Standards of Training, Certification and Watchkeeping for Seafarers, many of the environmental provisions remain recommendatory at this stage.

67 *Guidelines for the Designation of Special Areas and the Identification of Particularly Sensitive Sea Area*, IMO Resolution A. 720(17), 6 November 1991, which was consolidated and revised by the *Revised Guidelines for the Identification and Designation of Particularly Sensitive Sea Area*, IMO Resolution A. 982(24), 1 December 2005, and the *Guidelines for the Designation of Particularly Sensitive Sea Areas*, IMO Resolution 927(22), 29 November 2001; see also *Procedures for the Identification of Particularly Sensitive Sea Areas and the Adoption of Associated Protective Measures and Amendments to the Guidelines Contained in Resolution* A.720(17), IMO Resolution A. 885(21), 25 November 1999.

68 See generally FAO, *Fisheries*, www.fao.org/fisheries/en/.

69 See, e.g., Daniela Diz, 'The Ecosystem Approach as a Frame for SDG 14 Implementation' (2019) 33 *Ocean Yearbook* 187.

SDG 14 targets may identify gaps in ocean governance where issues are unregulated and where new initiatives are required.

14.3.2 *Using SDG 14 to Strengthen Existing Regimes*

Several SDG 14 targets serve to strengthen existing regimes and act as a catalyst for action to address target areas within those regimes. This function is demonstrated by the continued (and arguably strengthened) focus on IUU fishing within the regional fisheries management organizations (RFMOs) and the reinvigorated negotiations on the issue of fisheries subsidies within the WTO. Perhaps the clearest example of this function is performed by target 14.5 that encourages the conservation of at least 10 per cent of coastal and marine areas by 2020, consistent with national and international law. This target, which reinforces Aichi Biodiversity Target 11, has provided an important catalyst for the designation of marine protected areas (MPAs) at the global and, more particularly, regional levels.[70] Organizations that are actively developing MPA networks include (but are by no means limited to) the IMO,[71] the International Seabed Authority (ISA),[72] the OSPAR Commission for the North East Atlantic,[73] and the Commission for the Conservation of Antarctic Marine Living Resources (CCAMLR).[74] Moreover, the parties to the 1992 Convention of Biological

[70] See generally Karen N. Scott, 'Unconventional Law-making in the Law of the Sea and Area-based Conservation Measures', in Klein, n. 65.

[71] The IMO, in particular, contributes to area-based management through the designation of particularly sensitive seas areas. See the resolutions in n. 68.

[72] The ISA has begun to develop a network of MPAs through the adoption of regional environmental management plans – the first (and, thus far, only) has been adopted in respect of the Clarion-Clipperton Zone. See the *Environmental Management Plan for the Clarion-Clipperton Zone*, Doc. IBSA 17/LTC/7, 13 July 2011, para. 21, formally endorsed by *Decision of the Council Relating to an Environmental Management Plan for the Clarion-Clipperton Zone (adopted at the Eighteenth Session of the ISBA*, Doc. IBSA/18/C/22, 16–27 July 2012. See generally Michael Lodge et al., 'Seabed Mining: International Seabed Authority Environmental Management Plan for the Clarion-Clipperton Zone: A Partnership Approach' (2014) 49 *Marine Policy* 66.

[73] See OSPAR Recommendation 2003/3 (amended in 2010) that defines a MPA for the purposes of OSPAR and aims to develop an ecologically coherent network of MPAs by 2012 that is well managed by 2016. See also the *Guidelines for the Identification and Selection of Marine Protected Areas in the OSPAR Maritime Area*, OSPAR Agreement Doc. 2003-17 (as amended by the Biodiversity Committee [BDC] in 2007 [BDC Summary Record Doc. 07/12/1, 2007, para. 3.43b] and in 2016 [BDC Summary Doc. 16/9/1, 2016, paras. 5, 27, and Annex 13]).

[74] See CCAMLR, *General Framework for the Establishment of CCAMLR Marine Protected Areas*, Conservation Measure no. 91-04, 2011. See, in particular, CCAMLR, *Protection of the South Orkney Islands Southern Shelf*, Conservation Measure no. 91-03, 2009; *Ross Sea Region Marine Protected Area*, Conservation Measure no. 91-05, 2016. See generally Karen N. Scott, 'MPAs in the Southern Ocean under CCAMLR: Implementing SDG 14.5' (2021) 9 *Korean Journal of International and Comparative Law* 84.

Diversity (CBD),[75] the FAO,[76] and the International Union for the Conservation for Nature (IUCN)[77] have all developed criteria and processes for identifying areas suitable for protection or other forms of area-based management.

The contribution of target 14.5 to the international legal framework for area-based protection lies in its motivational function and as a catalyst for action at the global and local levels. The target itself, as noted above, does not define 'conserve' and sets out no criteria or distinction between the various forms of area-based protection. To a limited extent, this distinction has been addressed in the 2017 call for action, which expanded its scope to include integrated and cross-sectoral approaches to area-based conservation, including MSP and ICZM, as well as expressly referring to ecosystem and precautionary approaches to management. Nevertheless, defining the target in crude area-based terms – as exemplified by the indicator for target 14.5 – risks favouring size over effectiveness and thus undermining existing and evolving area-based protection regimes. The designations of very large MPAs over the last decade have been critiqued for doing just that.[78] This criticism notwithstanding, however, target 14.5 has engaged state and non-state actors at all levels in area-based protection, including beyond national jurisdiction in the context of the BBNJ negotiations.

14.3.3 *Using SDG 14 to Connect Existing Regimes*

Other SDG 14 targets operate as interstitial norms between and connecting distinct regimes. This bridge-building or integrative function is perhaps best illustrated by target 14.3 on ocean acidification. Although ocean acidification is a consequence of excess amounts of carbon dioxide in the ocean and can be classified as 'pollution' for the purposes of UNCLOS, it is not directly regulated by either the climate change regime or the law of the sea, although both regimes have a clear mandate

75 The CBD has developed criteria for identifying ecologically or biologically significant marine areas. See *Marine and Coastal Biodiversity*, CBD Decision XI/20, 2008, Annex I. See further D.C. Dunn et al., 'The Convention on Biological Diversity's Ecologically or Biologically Significant Areas: Origins, Development and Current Status' (2014) 49 *Marine Policy* 137; Daniela Diz et al., 'Mainstreaming Marine Biodiversity into the SDGs: The Role of Other Effective Area-Based Conservation Measures (SDG 14.5)' (2018) 93 *Marine Policy* 251.

76 The FAO has developed the concept of the vulnerable marine ecosystem. See the *International Guidelines for the Management of Deep-Sea Fisheries*, 2009, www.fao.org/fishery/topic/166308/en.

77 The IUCN had adopted guidelines for applying protected area management categories generally and in the marine environment. See Nigel Dudley (ed.), *Guidelines for Applying Protected Area Management Categories*, 2008, portals.iucn.org/library/sites/library/files/documents/2008-106.pdf; Jon Day, Nigel Dudley, & Marc Hockings (eds.), *Guidelines for Applying the IUCN Protected Area Management Categories to Marine Protected Areas*, 2nd ed. (IUCN, 2019), www.iucn.org/content/guidelines-applying-iucn-protected-area-management-categories-marine-protected-areas-0.

78 See Horta e Costa et al., n. 26, 192.

to address it.[79] Target 14.3 has arguably not only provided a catalyst for action – particularly in the climate change regime – but, more importantly, has played an important interstitial role in connecting regimes. For example, since 2016, a number of initiatives have been developed with the climate change regime that are designed to increase focus on the oceans, in general, and ocean acidification, in particular. These initiatives include the establishment of the Global Ocean Acidification Observing Network, a collaborative network of institutions undertaking research on ocean acidification processes in order to inform policy development,[80] as well as the adoption of a strategic roadmap on oceans and climate (in 2016)[81] and an oceans partnership pathway (in 2017).[82]

More than 70 per cent of the 161 states that have submitted NDCs pursuant to article 4(2) of the 2015 Paris Agreement on Climate Change refer specifically to marine issues.[83] Fifty NDCs address the ocean mitigation of climate change, in addition to adaptation,[84] and actions taken to mitigate climate change – in particular, the reduction of carbon dioxide emissions – will directly or indirectly address ocean acidification. Ocean acidification, to a greater or lesser extent, is on the agendas of a wide range of global and regional ocean regimes, including the Arctic Council, the CCAMLR, the IMO, and the CBD.[85] The 2017 call for action further embeds the connection between SDG 14 and SDG 13, highlighting (as part of target 14.3) the other impacts of climate change on the oceans, such as sea level rise.

Target 14.3 therefore makes an important contribution to ocean governance through connecting and integrating regimes and initiatives around an issue that falls between regulatory regimes. It operates at all levels of governance since, while ocean acidification is an issue that largely requires a global response, its associated indicator is regional or national in nature, requiring the measurement of marine acidity at a suite of representative sampling stations. Like target 14.5,

[79] See generally Karen N. Scott, 'Ocean Acidification and Sustainable Development Goal 14: A Goal but No Target?', in Myron H. Nordquist, John Norton Moore, & Ronan Long (eds.), *The Marine Environment and United Nations Sustainable Development Goal 14: Life below Water* (Koninklijke Brill, 2018), 323.

[80] See *Global Climate Action Event: Oceans*, 12 November 2016, climateaction.unfccc.int/media/1055/gca-oceans-programme.pdf.

[81] B. Cicin-Sain et al., *Toward a Strategic Action Roadmap on Oceans and Climate: 2016–2021* (Global Ocean Forum, 2016), globaloceanforumdotcom.files.wordpress.com/2013/03/strategic-action-roadmap-on-oceans-and-climate-november-2016.pdf.

[82] *The Ocean Pathway: Towards an Ocean Inclusive UNFCCC Process*, n.d., cop23.com.fj/the-ocean-pathway.

[83] N.D. Gallo, D.G. Victor & L.A. Levin, 'Ocean Commitments under the Paris Agreement' (2017) 7 *Nature Climate Change* 833833.

[84] *Id.*, 834.

[85] For an overview of the ocean acidification regime complex, see Karen N. Scott, 'Ocean Acidification: A Due Diligence Obligation under the LOSC?' (2020) 35 *International Journal of Marine and Coastal Law* 382.

however, target 14.3 adds little to the ocean governance framework in terms of what states and other actors are required to do in order to minimize and address the impacts of ocean acidification. The target is expressed in aspirational terms with no guidance as to the definition of 'impact' and no temporal deadline. The focus is on scientific cooperation, as expressed in the target itself and the indicator. Its importance therefore lies in target 14.3 operating as a catalyst for action within existing regimes and as an interstitial norm that functions between, across, and linking regimes.

14.3.4 *Using SDG 14 to Fill Gaps in Existing Regimes*

The third function of SDG 14 is the identification of, and action in relation to, regulatory gaps in ocean governance. The most high-profile example of this function is arguably target 14.1, which ambitiously seeks to prevent and significantly reduce marine pollution of all kinds, including marine debris and land-based pollution by 2025. A major focus of target 14.1, as demonstrated by indicator 14.1.1 and the 2017 call for action, is oceans plastics, and although there is a relatively comprehensive global and regional framework for marine pollution, the regulation of land-based pollution is notoriously weak, and there is no overarching instrument addressing ocean plastics.[86] Part XII of UNCLOS requires states to address all forms of marine pollution,[87] including land-based marine pollution,[88] but, with the exception of shipping[89] and dumping,[90] the global regime is dominated by soft law instruments.[91] At the regional level, regimes such as OSPAR and a number of UN Environment Programme regional seas conventions, as well as states at the domestic level,[92] have taken limited action to respond to target 14.1.[93]

While target 14.1 does not fill the regulatory gap with measurable standards and targets, it has nevertheless motivated international regimes to develop rules to address plastics pollution. For example, the parties to the 1989 Convention on the Control of Transboundary Movements of Hazardous Wastes and Their Disposal adopted amendments in 2019 to specifically regulate the export, import, and transit

[86] See generally Anastasia Telesetsky & Rebecca Bratspies, 'Global Plastic Pollution: Curbing Single-use Plastic Production', in Techera et al., n. 60, 457.

[87] UNCLOS, art. 194(1).

[88] *Id.*, art. 207.

[89] The MARPOL Convention addresses plastics in Annex V.

[90] The dumping of plastics from vessels is governed by the dumping regime under the 1972 Convention on the Prevention of Marine Pollution by Dumping of Wastes and Other Matter (London Convention) and the 1996 Protocol to the London Convention.

[91] See, e.g., the Global Programme of Action, adopted in 1995, identified litter as a priority action in 2012. See UNEP, *Addressing Land-Based Pollution*, n.d., www.unep.org/explore-topics/oceans-seas/what-we-do/addressing-land-based-pollution.

[92] Telesetsky & Bratspies, n. 86, 462–63, Appendix 1.

[93] *Id.*, 461.

of plastics, including for recycling.[94] The UN Environment Assembly adopted a resolution on marine litter in 2018[95] and on single-use plastic pollution in 2019.[96] Nevertheless, with respect to ocean plastics, target 14.1 operates in something of a regulatory black hole, and there is a developing consensus that this gap needs to be addressed through either adapting existing instruments[97] or adopting a new instrument, perhaps based on the model of the highly successful 1987 Montreal Protocol on Substances That Deplete the Ozone Layer.[98]

14.3.5 *SDG 14 as a Catalyst for Action*

These examples illustrate how SDG 14 supports and enhances ocean governance through international legal frameworks by strengthening, linking, or gap filling existing regimes. Its primary function is providing a catalyst for action at all levels of governance. However, the impact of SDG 14 on international law is not inevitably positive. For example, where the SDG 14 targets are expressed in weaker or more general terms than existing obligations or goals, SDG 14 may serve to undermine existing instruments or initiatives. This criticism has been made in relation to target 14.5, which is expressed in much cruder terms than Aichi Biodiversity Target 11 and could incentivize states to prioritize basic area coverage over ecological and other criteria. The focus on the SDG 14 targets may lead states to neglect other areas of environmental concern such as invasive or endangered species. Similarly, a narrow articulation of developing state interests in the blue economy (target 14.7) could prejudice the interests of those states in other resources, such as marine genetic resources or deep-sea minerals within other forums such as the ISA or the BBNJ negotiations. Finally, the adoption of non-binding targets may reduce incentives to negotiate and develop binding targets, a criticism not limited to SDG 14 or, indeed, the SDGs more generally.

14.4 POSITIONING SDG 14 IN THE INTERNATIONAL INSTITUTIONAL CONTEXT

14.4.1 *The Institutional Ocean Regime Complex*

Within the field of ocean governance, there is no international body or regime of global reach with overarching responsibility for the oceans. Rather, there is a

94 1989 Convention on the Control of Transboundary Movements of Hazardous Wastes and Their Disposal, Annexes II, VIII, IX were amended (and entered into force in January 2021). See *Amendments to Annexes II, VIII and IX to the Basel Convention*, Doc. BC-14/12, 2019.

95 *Marine Litter and Microplastics*, Doc. UNEP EA.3/Res.7, 30 January 2018.

96 *Addressing Single-use Plastic Products Pollution*, Doc. UNEP/EA.4/Res.9, 28 March 2019.

97 See, e.g., Karen Raubenheimer & Alistair McIlgorm, 'Can the Basel and Stockholm Conventions Provide a Global Framework to Reduce the Impact of Marine Litter?' (2018) 96 *Marine Policy* 285.

98 See, e.g., Karen Raubenheimer & Alistair McIlgorm, 'Is the Montreal Protocol a Model That Can Help Solve the Global Marine Plastic Debris Problem?' (2017) 91 *Marine Policy* 322.

multiplicity of global and regional organizations and institutions with mandates to regulate activities on the basis of sector (such as shipping, fishing, and mining) or area (for example, beyond national jurisdiction or in a particular region). For example, at the regional level, regional seas conventions play an important role in implementing target 14.1 relating to marine pollution, target 14.2 on coastal resilience, and target 14.5 on area-based management. Similarly, RFMOs and arrangements will lead initiatives related to IUU fishing (target 14.4). Yet area-based management measures adopted by regional seas bodies may have implications for fishing activities, and fishing activities will impact the state of marine ecosystems. Although some RFMOs are beginning to work with regional seas bodies, particularly in the context of area-based protection, this remains the exception rather than the rule.[99] Likewise, at the global level, measures adopted by the IMO, the ISA, and a possible new body with competences regarding access to marine genetic resources in ABNJ are likely to impact each other as well as initiatives adopted by regional seas bodies or RFMOs. This situation inhibits the adoption of an integrated and holistic approach to ocean governance.[100]

Ocean governance, then, is characterized as a 'regime complex' – functionally overlapping parallel regimes and institutions that are non-hierarchical but that nevertheless affect one another's sphere of operation.[101] This regime complex provides as many opportunities for duplication of, or contradictory, effort as it does for the development of mutually supportive measures. The absence of any one body such as an 'Oceans Council' with an overarching mandate for the oceans means that SDG 14, in practice, has functioned to set, or at least to significantly influence, the agenda of most of the relevant institutions.

Post-2015, two important institutional initiatives designed to support the implementation of SDG 14 and, in a very limited way, to address the absence of an overarching body are worth noting. First, in 2017, the first special envoy for the oceans (or 'oceans ambassador') was appointed by the UN Secretary-General in order to follow up on the outcomes of the 2017 Oceans Conference, including the voluntary commitments, and to work with, and connect, the various stakeholders

[99] The most advanced example of this is the collaboration between the OSPAR Commission and the North-East Atlantic Fisheries Commission in the North-East Atlantic, which has resulted in the establishment of mutually managed protected areas under both instruments. There has also been more limited collaboration between the CCAMLR Commission and the parties to the 1959 Antarctic Treaty in relation to Southern Ocean fisheries, in general, and the Ross Sea MPA, in particular.

[100] See Karen N. Scott, 'Integrated Oceans Management: A New Frontier in Marine Environmental Protection', in Donald R. Rothwell et al. (eds.), *Oxford Handbook on the Law of the Sea* (Oxford University Press, 2015), 463.

[101] See further K.J. Atler & S. Meunier, 'The Politics of International Regime Complexity' (2009) 7 *Perspectives on Politics* 13; T. Gehring & B. Faude, 'The Dynamics of Regime Complexes: Microfoundations and Systemic Effects' (2013) 19 *Global Governance* 119; K. Raustiala & D.G. Victor, 'The Regime Complex for Plant Genetic Resources' (2004) 58 *International Organisation* 277.

associated with SDG 14.[102] Second, also in 2017, the United Nations proclaimed a 'Decade of Ocean Science for Sustainable Development'.[103] This initiative is supported by the Intergovernmental Oceanographic Commission of the UN Educational, Scientific and Cultural Organization and is intended to 'provide a unifying framework across the UN system to enable countries to achieve all of their ocean-related Agenda 2030 priorities ... [and] contribute to the UN processes protecting the ocean and its resources'.[104]

Thus, SDG 14 plays an important coordinating role among organizations and regimes and supports a level of institutional integration with minimal overarching institutional infrastructure. This is undoubtedly a positive role, and it goes some way to addressing the absence of a formal overarching global oceans body. However, this function is inherently limited from a broader law of the sea perspective in that the SDG targets embody some, but not all, ocean priorities and are clearly not intended to implement a holistic or comprehensive approach to ocean governance.

14.4.2 *SDG 14 and the Private Sector*

One of the salient characteristics of SDG 14, as with the other SDGs, is that its targets apply to a wide range of stakeholders and are not limited to states. This is most visibly demonstrated in the 1,642 voluntary commitments made by stakeholders at the 2017 Oceans Conference, of which only 634 commitments were made by states. Moreover, the UN Decade of Ocean Science for Sustainable Development was adopted in part to mobilize the scientific community, policy-makers, business, and civil society 'around a program of joint research and technical innovation', in addition to supporting coordination within the United Nations.[105] In an attempt to expand and formalize the private sector's implementation of SDG 14, the UN Global Compact[106] launched the Sustainable Ocean Principles in September 2019, which are intended to provide a framework for responsible business practices across sectors with respect to ocean health and productivity, ocean governance and engagement, and data and transparency.[107]

[102] See United Nations, *Peter Thomson: UN Secretary-General's Special Envoy for the Ocean*, n.d., oceanconference.un.org/SpecialEnvoy. Ambassador Peter Thompson of Fiji was appointed special envoy for the ocean.

[103] *Oceans and the Law of the Sea*, UN Doc. A/Res/72/73, 5 December 2017, paras. 292–95.

[104] UN Decade of Ocean Science for Sustainable Development, *About*, www.oceandecade.org/about?tab=our-story; see also *Oceans and the Law of the Sea*, n. 103, paras. 292–95.

[105] Martin Visbeck, 'Ocean Science Research Is Key for a Sustainable Future' (2018) 9 *Nature Communications* 690.

[106] The UN Global Compact was launched as a special initiative of the UN Secretary-General in 2000 and is intended to support and guide the global business community in advancing UN goals and values in relation to human rights, labour, the environment, and anti-corruption. See UN Global Compact, *Our Mission*, www.unglobalcompact.org/what-is-gc/mission.

[107] *Sustainable Ocean Principles*, September 2019, d306pr3pise04h.cloudfront.net/docs/publications%2FSustainable+Ocean+Principles.pdf.

The nine principles have been endorsed by over seventy-five companies to date[108] and encourage companies to consider the impact of their activities on the oceans (Principle 1); plan activities to ensure long-term sustainability (Principle 4) and consider business opportunities that protect or restore ocean health (Principle 2); take action to reduce greenhouse gas emissions to prevent ocean warming and ocean acidification (Principle 3); engage responsibly with regulatory frameworks and respect human, labour, and Indigenous peoples rights (Principles 5, 6, and 7); and share data and other information (Principles 8 and 9). In 2020, the UN Global Compact issued the Ocean Stewardship 2030 report,[109] which sets out ten ambitions and recommendations for growing sustainable ocean business relating to sustainable seafood, decarbonized shipping, ocean electricity, an end to plastic waste and excessive nutrients from entering the ocean, and the collection, management, and sharing of ocean data.

The incorporation of the private sector into SDG 14, as particularly developed by the 2017 Oceans Conference and the UN Global Compact, is an important development in the law of the sea. It has even been asserted that this constitutes 'a new conception of oceans commons governance', comprising a rebalancing of interests between the public and private sectors.[110] Currently however, any rebalance is taking place at the margins of international law, and ocean 'governance' is still largely state based. Nevertheless, non-state actors, including private sector organizations are undoubtedly playing an increasingly important role in implementing SDG 14, and this effort, together with the growing significance of soft or non-traditional sources of law – such as SDG 14 itself – is inevitably expanding what constitutes 'the law of the sea'.

14.4.3 *SDG 14 and the Role of Courts and Tribunals*

Institutions that interpret the law of the sea, such as the International Court of Justice and the International Tribunal for the Law of the Sea, could make a significant contribution to embedding and incorporating SDG 14 into the ocean governance framework through the interpretation of the law of the sea in light of SDG 14. An important development in the law of the sea over the last decade has been the explicit adoption and clarification of the standard of due diligence in the context of Part XII of UNCLOS and other obligations relating to marine environmental protection and fisheries management. This has largely been driven by key decisions of law of the sea courts and tribunals with respect to the responsibility of

108 UN Global Compact, *Signatories to the Sustainable Ocean Principles*, n.d., www.unglobalcompact.org/take-action/ocean/signatories.

109 UN Global Compact, *Ocean Stewardship 2030*, 2020, unglobalcompact.org/library/5742.

110 Nadia Sánchez Castillo-Winckels, 'How the Sustainable Development Goals Promote a New Conception of Ocean Commons Governance', in French & Kotzé, n. 19, 117.

states for environmental harm in the Area,[111] for vessels engaged in IUU fishing within the EEZ of coastal states,[112] and for fishing and damaging the environment in contested areas.[113] Due diligence is a 'variable concept'[114] that may change over time in response to scientific or technological knowledge and in relation to the risks involved in the activity.[115] Arguably, however, the targets developed by, or in association with, SDG 14 may be relevant in determining whether a state has met its due diligence obligation in respect of areas such as ocean acidification,[116] area-based protection, or ecosystem conservation, for example.

14.5 CONCLUSIONS

SDG 14 has undoubtedly influenced the global ocean governance agenda and has served as a catalyst for new initiatives around specific issues such as plastics, ocean acidification, and the designation of MPAs within existing regimes and institutions at all levels of governance. It has inspired and directly led to processes such as the 2017 Oceans Conference and the High Level Panel for Sustainable Ocean Economy, established in 2018. The latter initiative comprises fourteen heads of states and governments representing 30 per cent of the EEZs,[117] and is committed 'to bold transformations towards a sustainable ocean economy where environmental protection and conservation, and economic production and prosperity, go hand in hand'.[118] Both initiatives are notable for having deliberately expanded ocean governance to encompass a wider range of actors, including private and civil society organizations.

SDG 14 has also influenced the parameters of the BBNJ negotiations, and this instrument will be important not only in addressing some of the substantive goals in relation to environmental protection (such as area-based protection) but also in respect of target 14.a relating to research and knowledge transfer and target 14.c that calls for the enhancement of the global legal framework for ocean governance. SDG 14 has also contributed to the expansion of the sources we regard as being relevant to ocean governance and an increasing reliance on informal sources of

[111] ITLOS, *Responsibilities and Obligations of States with Respect to Activities in the Area*, Advisory Opinion, ITLOS Case no. 17, 1 February 2011, 10, para. 110.

[112] ITLOS, *Request for Advisory Opinion Submitted by the Sub-Regional Fisheries Commission*, Advisory Opinion, ITLOS Case no. 21, 2 April 2015, 4, para. 129.

[113] UNCLOS Annex VII Tribunal, *In the Matter of the South China Sea Arbitration (Republic of the Philippines v People's Republic of China)*, Award, PCA Case no. 2013-19, 12 July 2016, para. 757.

[114] ITLOS, n. 112, para. 117.

[115] *Id.*

[116] See, e.g., Scott, n. 85.

[117] High Level Panel for a Sustainable Ocean Economy, *About the Ocean Panel*, n.d., www.oceanpanel.org/about#panel.

[118] See Ocean Panel, *Transformations for a Sustainable Ocean Economy: A Vision for Protection, Production and Prosperity*, December 2020, www.oceanpanel.org/about#panel.

law – instruments that are normative but not lawmaking. These efforts notwithstanding, SDG 14 does not fundamentally challenge the law of the sea in terms of its scope or foundations and does not represent or require a transformational change in its principles and values. SDG 14 is profoundly Anthropocentric in focus and relies on principles and concepts that reinforce, rather than challenge, existing law and institutions. This is evident in its endorsement of maximum sustainable yield in target 14.4, for example, and in its focus on static area coverage with regard to target 14.5. Moreover, SDG 14 is not, in and of itself, binding and, thus far, has had limited success in each of its targets, notwithstanding the fact that a number of them were intended to be achieved by 2020. Most importantly, however, SDG 14 is a product of thinking based on assumptions and approaches characterizing the Holocene: relative environmental stability and progress through perpetual economic growth. We have moved into the age of the Anthropocene,[119] where these assumptions are challenged and where our relationship with – and separation from – nature is fundamentally different.[120] The greatest challenge for future ocean governance is developing a law of the sea fit for the Anthropocene.[121] While SDG 14 has contributed to the beginning of that process – particularly with respect to the sources or actors within the law of the sea – it fundamentally fails to provide the necessary conceptual framework for the law of the sea in the Anthropocene.

[119] See Will Steffen, Paul J. Crutzen & John R. McNeil, 'The Anthropocene: Are Humans Now Overwhelming the Great Forces of Nature?' (2007) 36 *Ambio* 614; Davor Vidas et al., 'What Is the Anthropocene – and Why Is It Relevant for International Law?' (2015) 25 *Yearbook of International Environmental Law* 3.

[120] See Tim Stephens, 'What Is the Point of International Environmental Law Scholarship in the Anthropocene?', University of Sydney Law School, Legal Studies Research Paper Series no. 19/25, May 2019.

[121] See Davor Vidas, 'The Anthropocene and the International Law of the sea' (2011) 369 *Philosophical Transactions of the Royal Society* A 909.

15

SDG 15: Protect, Restore and Promote Sustainable Use of Terrestrial Ecosystems, Sustainably Manage Forests, Combat Desertification, and Halt and Reverse Land Degradation and Halt Biodiversity Loss

Elisa Morgera

ABSTRACT

This chapter illuminates the extent to which the targets of SDG 15, Life on Land, reflect the international obligations of, and guidance adopted under, the 1992 Convention on Biological Diversity as an umbrella convention with overarching legal principles and concepts. In doing so, it demonstrates the extent to which international human rights law can support joined-up implementation of the convention and other international environmental agreements with a view to realizing SDG 15 through policy coherence, notably in the context of land-based investments.

KEYWORDS

SDG 15, terrestrial biodiversity, land, sustainable use, conservation, human rights, investment, forest, desertification, wetlands, Indigenous peoples, international law

15.1 INTRODUCTION

The 2019 *Global Assessment of Biodiversity and Ecosystems Services* report (*Global Assessment* report) underscored that the rate of global biodiversity degradation during the past fifty years is unprecedented in human history.[1] For instance, the average abundance of native species in most major terrestrial biomes has fallen by at least 20 per cent. As a result, current negative trends in biodiversity will undermine

[1] Sandra Díaz et al., *Summary for Policymakers of the Global Assessment Report on Biodiversity and Ecosystem Services of the Intergovernmental Science-Policy Platform on Biodiversity and Ecosystem Services* (IPBES Secretariat, 2019), 11, doi.org/10.5281/zenodo.3553579.

progress towards 80 per cent of targets (thirty-five out of forty-four) assessed within the Sustainable Development Goals (SDGs) related to poverty, hunger, health, water, cities, climate, and oceans (SDG 1, No Poverty; SDG 2, Zero Hunger; SDG 3, Good Health and Well-being; SDG 6, Clean Water and Sanitation; SDG 11, Sustainable Cities and Communities; SDG 13, Climate Action; and SDG 14, Life below Water).[2] The direct drivers of biodiversity loss have been identified as changes in land use (such as unsustainable agriculture), direct exploitation of organisms (such as overgrazing), climate change, pollution, and invasion of alien species, with climate change also increasingly exacerbating the impact of other drivers.[3]

The *Global Assessment* report also noted that biodiversity is generally declining more rapidly elsewhere than in Indigenous peoples' lands, which cover at least a quarter of the global land area. At the same time, areas of the world projected to experience significant negative effects from global changes in climate and biodiversity are also home to large concentrations of Indigenous peoples and many of the world's poorest communities.[4] For that reason, the *Global Assessment* report has underscored the need for transformative processes to address biodiversity loss as well as inequalities, especially regarding income and gender. These inequalities undermine: the capacity for sustainability; inclusive decision-making; the fair and equitable sharing of benefits arising from the use of biodiversity and its conservation; and the respectful inclusion of the knowledge and innovations of Indigenous peoples and local communities in environmental governance.[5]

SDG 15, Life on Land, and its targets mainly confirm existing international environmental law objectives on terrestrial biodiversity that focus specifically on forests, wetlands, drylands, and mountains ecosystems as well as, more generally, on endangered species and genetic resources.[6] They are all addressed under the 1992 Convention on Biological Diversity (CBD) and other biodiversity-related treaties of global scope,[7] the 1994 UN Convention to Combat Desertification in

[2] *Id.*, 15.

[3] *Id.*, 12.

[4] *Id.*, 15.

[5] *Id.*, 16.

[6] See Alessandro Fodella, 'Mountain Biodiversity', in Elisa Morgera & Jona Razzaque (eds.), *Encyclopedia of Environmental Law: Biodiversity and Nature Protection Law* (EE, 2017), 161; Analisa Savaresi, 'Forest Biodiversity', in Morgera & Razzaque, *id.*, 203; Feja Lesniewska, 'Forests: Learning Lessons from Our Interventions', in Elisa Morgera & Kati Kulovesi (eds.), *International Law and Natural Resources* (EE, 2016), 155; Elsa Tsioumani, 'Dryland Biodiversity: Ecosystems, People and the Law', in Morgera & Razzaque, *id.*, 215; Erika J. Techera, 'Species-based Conservation', in Morgera and Razzaque, *id.*, 97; Riccardo Pavoni & Dario Piselli, 'Access to Genetic Resources and Benefit-sharing', in Morgera & Razzaque, *id.*, 237.

[7] Other international biodiversity treaties include CITES; the CMS; the 1951 International Plant Protection Convention; the 2001 International Treaty on Plant Genetic Resources for Food and Agriculture; the Ramsar Convention; and the 1972 Convention Concerning the Protection of the World Cultural and Natural Heritage.

Countries Experiencing Serious Drought and/or Desertification, Particularly in Africa (UNCCD) as well as in regional biodiversity-related and mountain conventions.[8] In addition, these objectives have been addressed indirectly under other international environmental treaties (such as on climate change and international freshwater agreements).[9] Given the vast array of international legal instruments related to SDG 15,[10] this chapter will focus mainly on the CBD as the umbrella convention that has provided overarching legal concepts and approaches for the more specific objectives of other biodiversity-related conventions and other environmental treaties. In effect, the SDG 15 targets are largely based on an earlier global goal-setting process under the CBD that encompassed other biodiversity-related conventions. In that respect, SDG 15 does not add to the coordination of existing legal frameworks already attempted under the CBD's Aichi Biodiversity Targets.[11]

SDG 15 also interacts (positively and negatively) with international economic law. International trade in endangered species, for instance, is the specific object of the 1973 Convention on International Trade in Endangered Species of Wild Fauna and Flora (CITES), whereas trade in timber or trade in goods that may contribute to the spread of invasive alien species are regulated in non-environmental regimes.[12] Although repeated concerns have been voiced over tensions and conflicts with the international regulation of trade, investment, and intellectual property and the realization of international environmental objectives to conserve and use sustainably terrestrial biodiversity,[13] these issues appear to have been left out of the framing of the SDG 15 targets. In this chapter, attention will be focused in particular on the tensions between land-based investment and biodiversity protection as an illustration of a wider range of tensions between international biodiversity and economic objectives. This focus is in line with the finding contained in the 2019 *Global Sustainable Development Report* that the negative long-term trend for SDG 15 should be addressed through 'a reduction in the total amount of land appropriated

8 1991 Convention for the Protection of the Alps; 2003 Framework Convention on the Protection and Sustainable Development of the Carpathians.

9 Ruby Moynihan, 'Inland Water Biodiversity: International Law on Protection of Transboundary Freshwater Ecosystems and Biodiversity', in Morgera & Razzaque, n. 6, 189.

10 For an earlier discussion, see Werner Scholtz & Michelle Barnard, 'The Environment and the Sustainable Development Goals: "We Are on a Road to Nowhere"', in Duncan French & Louis J. Kotzé (eds.), *Sustainable Development Goals: Law, Theory and Implementation* (EE, 2018), 222; Rakhyun E. Kim, 'The Nexus between International Law and the Sustainable Development Goals' (2016) 25(1) *Review of European, Comparative and International Environmental Law* (*RECIEL*) 15.

11 *The Strategic Plan for Biodiversity 2011–2020 and the Aichi Biodiversity Targets: CBD*, Decision X/2, 2010.

12 2006 International Tropical Timber Agreement. Stanley W. Burgiel, 'Invasive Alien Species', in Morgera & Razzaque, n. 6, 145.

13 See, e.g., Shawkat Alam, 'Trade, Investment and Biodiversity Conservation', in Morgera & Razzaque, n. 6, 320.

for food production'.[14] Instead, supporting the use of terrestrial biodiversity for a broader notion of bio-economy[15] should rely on the 'scientific understanding of complex social-ecological dynamics' revealing trade-offs necessary to achieve SDG 15, including 'who will be impacted and how and who holds the key to transformative pathways'.[16]

Conflicts with the objectives promoted under international economic law are often raised, but not directly addressed, under the CBD.[17] The challenges that SDG 15 gives rise to for international law are therefore the same challenges that the implementation of international biodiversity law has been facing for a while. These challenges do not only concern conservation efforts but also the sustainable use of living organisms, which remains an elusive objective in international law. The CBD defines it as 'the use of components of biological diversity in a way and at a rate that does not lead to the long-term decline of biological diversity, thereby maintaining its potential to meet the needs and aspirations of present and future generations'.[18] Even if sustainable use can be considered a customary international rule in as far as living natural resources are concerned, however, it is 'highly contextualized and has no single fixed meaning' in different sectors (sustainable forest management, sustainable land management, and the wise use of wetlands).[19] As such, this objective is particularly dependent on the valuation and mainstreaming of biodiversity in different sectors that directly or indirectly affect the use of forests, wetlands, and freshwater (such as mining and infrastructure development, for instance). Thus, in its decisions under the CBD, the Conference of the Parties (COP) has focused on biodiversity mainstreaming in various sectors as a contribution to the implementation of Agenda 2030, which is also captured in target 15.9.[20]

The notion of trade-offs chimes with the balancing exercises that characterize international human rights law and its monitoring and enforcement mechanisms, which may become increasingly relevant for supporting the realization of SDG 15. They can complement the international biodiversity compliance structures, which remain unevenly developed (as will be discussed below). In addition, several

[14] Independent Group of Scientists Appointed by the Secretary-General, *Global Sustainable Development Report 2019: The Future Is Now – Science for Achieving Sustainable Development* (United Nations, 2019), 70.

[15] *Id.*

[16] *Id.*, 114.

[17] On the missed opportunity to address intellectual property and other aspects of World Trade Organization (WTO) law under the Nagoya Protocol, see Riccardo Pavoni, 'The Nagoya Protocol and WTO Law', in Elisa Morgera, Matthias Buck & Elsa Tsioumani (eds.), *The 2010 Nagoya Protocol on Access and Benefit-Sharing in Perspective: Implications for International Law and National Implementation* (Brill & Martinus Nijhoff, 2013), 185.

[18] CBD, art. 2.

[19] Catherine Redgwell, 'Sustainable Use of Natural Resources', in Ludwig Krämer & Emmanuela Orlando (eds.), *Principles of Environmental Law* (EE, 2018), 103, 115.

[20] CBD Decision XIV/3, 2018; CBD Decision XIII/3, 2016; *Transforming Our World: The 2030 Agenda for Sustainable Development*, UN Doc. A/Res/70/1, 25 September 2015.

land-based interventions that threaten biodiversity are also intertwined with human rights violations: agribusiness has become the sector that is 'most often implicated in killings of land and environmental defenders' due to land tenure-related conflicts[21] as well as raising human rights concerns because of the use of pesticides.[22] Equally, the realization of SDG 15 can contribute to the realization of economic, social, and cultural rights.[23]

In this connection, the legal concept of fair and equitable benefit sharing is relevant at the intersection of international biodiversity, human rights, and economic goals dependent on terrestrial ecosystems. Such benefit sharing is particularly important in relation to the human rights of Indigenous peoples,[24] the lack of reference to whom under the SDGs has been considered 'the most shocking weakness in the 2030 Agenda in the area of equality and non-discrimination'.[25] Regrettably, SDG 15 limits itself to address fair and equitable benefit sharing only in relation to access to genetic resources[26] for bioprospecting purposes – that is, transnational bio-based research and development. This focus reflects the prominent role of benefit sharing as the third objective of the CBD, which has received more political priority in this process. But benefit sharing has also emerged under the CBD as a component of the ecosystem approach, in conjunction with the need to protect and reward the conservation and sustainable use of Indigenous peoples' and local communities' lands and their traditional knowledge.[27]

This approach is in recognition of the relationship between the stewardship of lands, natural resources, and ecosystems that are traditionally used by Indigenous peoples (even where their formal property is not recognized). It equally applies to the production and inter-generational transmission of traditional knowledge, which

[21] Karol Boudreaux & Scott Schang, 'Threats of, and Responses to, Agribusiness Land Acquisitions' (2019) 4(2) *Business and Human Rights Journal* 365, 366.

[22] Concerning impacts of pesticides on human rights, see David C. Strouss, 'Bringing Pesticide Injury Cases to US Courts: The Challenges of Transnational Litigation' (2019) 4(2) *Business and Human Rights Journal* 337; Hilal Elver, *Report of the Special Rapporteur on the Right to Food*, UN Doc. A/HRC/34/48, 2017.

[23] Lynda M. Collins, 'Sustainable Development Goals and Human Rights: Challenges and Opportunities', in French & Kotzé, n. 10, 66.

[24] See Principle 15 in *Report of the UN Special Rapporteur on Human Rights and the Environment: Framework Principles on Human Rights and the Environment*, UN Doc. A/HRC/37/59, 2018 (*UN Framework Principles*). For a discussion, see Elisa Morgera, 'Under the Radar: Fair and Equitable Benefit-Sharing and the Human Rights of Indigenous Peoples and Local Communities Connected to Natural Resources' (2019) 23(7) *International Journal of Human Rights* 1098.

[25] Collins, n. 23, 87.

[26] Nagoya Protocol. See Morgera, Buck, & Tsioumani, n. 17.

[27] *Principles of the Ecosystem Approach*, CBD Decision V/6, 2000, para. 9; *Bonn Guidelines on Access and Benefit-Sharing*, CBD Decision VI/24, 2002, Annex, para. 48; *Tkarihwaié:ri Code of Ethical Conduct on Respect for the Cultural and Intellectual Heritage of Indigenous and Local Communities*, CBD Decision X/42, 2010, Annex, para. 14; *Refinement and Elaboration of the Ecosystem Approach*, CBD Decision VII/11, 2004, Annex, rationale to Principle 4.

embodies traditional lifestyles (a communal way of life) based on the link between communities' shared cultural identity, the biological resources that they use, and their customary rules about natural resource management.[28] Along similar lines, but based on different premises (human rights to property, development, and culture), benefit sharing has been increasingly recognized by international human rights judicial and quasi-judicial bodies[29] as an implicit component of Indigenous peoples' rights to their territories and natural resources.[30] In the human rights context, however, benefit sharing is mainly conceived as a tool to protect communities against third parties' natural resource development (mining and logging) or conservation measures that can negatively affect these communities' way of life.[31] These international developments remain outside the explicit scope of SDG 15, perhaps as a reflection of the fact that the engagement of the CBD parties with the international human rights of Indigenous peoples remains a matter of contention.[32]

The main reason for this reluctance is that terrestrial biodiversity is still perceived as a matter close to the core of national sovereignty.[33] States have accepted that certain parameters are set at the international level to address matters of shared concern (such as migratory species or species subject to international trade). States, however, have otherwise been very cautious in allowing other interferences of international law on the exercise of their sovereignty on the basis of a common concern in the health of the global biosphere.[34] For this reason, states have accepted broadly formulated treaty obligations on biodiversity and have resisted the application of international human rights law that can more clearly determine the limit of their margin of manoeuvre under the CBD and other biodiversity-related conventions.[35] Nevertheless, states have prolifically engaged in the development of soft law

[28] On the basis of the wording of the CBD, art. 8(j). See generally Brendan Tobin, *Indigenous Peoples, Customary Law and Human Rights: Why Living Law Matters* (Routledge, 2014).

[29] African Commission on Human and Peoples' Rights, Centre for Minority Rights Development (Kenya), and Minority Rights Group International, *Endorois Welfare Council v Kenya*, Communication 276/2003, 25 November 2009; IACtHR, *Case of the Kaliña and Lokono Peoples v Suriname*, Judgment (Merits, Reparations and Costs), 25 November 2015 (*Kaliña and Lokono*).

[30] Namely, *UN Declaration on the Rights of Indigenous Peoples*, UN Doc. A/RES/61/295, 13 September 2007, arts. 25–26; *Report of the UN Special Rapporteur on Indigenous Peoples Rights*, UN Doc. A/HRC/15/37, 2010, paras. 76–77; *UN Framework Principles*, n. 24, where benefit sharing is included under Principle 15.

[31] Morgera, n. 24.

[32] Elisa Morgera, 'Dawn of a New Day? The Evolving Relationship between the Convention on Biological Diversity and International Human Rights Law' (2018) 53(4) *Wake Forest Law Review* 101.

[33] Lorenzo Cotula, 'Land', in Morgera & Kulovesi, n. 6, 137.

[34] Duncan French, 'Common Concern, Common Heritage and Other Global(-ising) Concepts: Rhetorical Devices, Legal Principles or a Fundamental Challenge?', in Michael Bowman, Peter Davies & Edward Goodwin (eds.), *Research Handbook on Biodiversity and the Law* (EE, 2016), 334.

[35] See generally Morgera, n. 24.

guidance under the CBD in order to further specify good practices (if not the legal interpretations of their obligations).[36] They have also developed regional agreements for transboundary cooperation of different legal status.[37]

Against this background, this chapter will focus on the extent to which the targets of SDG 15 reflect the international obligations of, and guidance adopted under, the CBD. It will also consider to what extent international human rights law can support coordinated implementation of the CBD and other international agreements with a view to realizing SDG 15 through policy coherence, notably in the context of land-based investments.

15.2 THE CONTENT OF SDG 15 IN THE CONTEXT OF THE OTHER SDGS

SDG 15 is strongly connected to all other SDGs, notably poverty, hunger, health, gender, freshwater, energy, climate change, and oceans (SDGs 1–3; SDG 5, Gender Equality; SDG 6; SDG 7, Affordable and Clean Energy; SDGs 13–14). These SDGs, in effect, find correspondence with the CBD areas of work/programmes.[38] Several of these connections can be best explored through the lens of the interdependency of biodiversity and international human rights. For instance, factual and legal correlations between biodiversity and the right to food have been clear for a while,[39] so the connection between SDG 15 and SDG 2 finds resonance in a series of international legal instruments addressing the responsible tenure of land and responsible agribusiness.[40] Similarly, SDG 15 connects to the human right to water,[41] although there are complex trade-offs to be addressed in the interplay

[36] *Id.*

[37] There are numerous regional regimes for the protection of nature, mountain, and freshwater ecosystems that complement the global regimes by developing more specific institutional structures to apply the global-level rules. See, e.g., CMS agreements, www.cms.int/en/cms-instruments/agreements.

[38] The CBD's Conference of the Parties (COP) has established seven thematic work programmes – namely, on agricultural biodiversity, dry and sub-humid lands biodiversity, forest biodiversity, inland waters biodiversity, island biodiversity, marine and coastal biodiversity, and mountain biodiversity – and five cross-cutting work programmes on incentive measures – namely, the Global Taxonomy Initiative, protected areas, Article 8(j) (traditional knowledge), and technology transfer and cooperation. Work has also been undertaken on a series of other cross-cutting issues, including climate change and biodiversity, the ecosystem approach, and sustainable use of biodiversity. See Convention on Biological Diversity, *Thematic Programmes and Cross-cutting Issues*, www.cbd.int/programmes/.

[39] Hilal Elver, *Critical Perspective on Food Systems, Food Crises and the Future of the Right to Food, UN Special Rapporteur on the Right to Food*, UN Doc. A/HRC/43/44, 2020; Tsioumani, n. 6, 224–25; Claudio Chiarolla, 'Agriculture and Biodiversity Conservation', in Morgera & Razzaque, n. 6, 251, 261.

[40] See OECD & FAO, *Guidance for Responsible Agricultural Supply Chains*, 2016, doi.org/10.1787/9789264251052-en.

[41] See generally Owen McIntiyre, 'International Water Law and SDG 6: Mutually Reinforcing Paradigms', in French & Kotzé, n. 10, 173.

between the human right to water, the human right to food, non-discrimination, and environmental sustainability.[42]

Clarity on the factual relationship between biodiversity and the human right to health is a more recent international development. For instance, reduced human contact with biodiversity may lead to reduced diversity in the human microbiota, weakening human immune-regulatory systems and favouring the onset of non-communicable diseases.[43] In addition, human-caused changes in ecosystems, such as modified landscapes, intensive agriculture, and antimicrobial use, are increasing the risk and impact of infectious disease transmission.[44] The linkages between SDG 3 and SDG 15 are thus crucial from a human rights perspective but still little understood. For that reason, the CBD parties and the Assembly of the World Health Organization (WHO) have recommended addressing the unintended negative impacts of health interventions on biodiversity and incorporating ecosystem concerns into public health policies, considering relevant health-biodiversity linkages in developing and updating national health policies, and adopting preventive measures for human health based on strengthening the resilience of socio-ecological systems.[45]

The linkages between SDG 15 and SDG 5 can be explained also in human rights terms.[46] Women's human rights in the ownership, acquisition, management, administration, enjoyment, and disposition of land, non-discrimination in rural areas, as well as participation in rural development[47] (which is understood to comprise agricultural and water policies, forestry, livestock, fisheries, and aquaculture) can be affected by decisions on the conservation and sustainable use of terrestrial biodiversity.[48] Accordingly, the Committee of the 1979 Convention on the Elimination of Discrimination against Women (CEDAW) has recommended ensuring that rural development projects are implemented only after participatory gender and environmental impact assessments are conducted with the full participation of rural women, obtaining their free, prior-informed consent and ensuring fair and equitable benefit sharing (for instance, in revenues generated by large-scale

42 Elisa Morgera et al., *The Human Right to Water for Food and Agriculture* (FAO, 2020).

43 WHO, *Report by the Director-General: Health, Environment and Climate Change – Human Health and Biodiversity*, Doc. A71/11, 2018.

44 *Id.*

45 *Id.*; CBD Decision XIII/6, 2016; CBD Decision XIV/4, 2018.

46 Karen Morrow, 'Gender and the Sustainable Development Goals', in French & Kotzé, n. 10, 149.

47 CEDAW, arts. 16(1)(h), 14(2).

48 Naomi Kenney & Mika Schröder, 'Gender Equality and Benefit Sharing: Exploring the Linkages in Relation to Land and Genetic Resources', *BENELEX Blog Post*, 5 December 2016, benelexblog.wordpress.com/2016/12/05/gender-equality-and-benefit-sharing-exploring-the-linkages-in-relation-to-land-and-genetic-resources/.

development projects).[49] While the CBD's 2015–20 Gender Plan of Action merely refers to a list of 'possible actions for State Parties',[50] states that are both party to CEDAW and the CBD should consider their legally binding human rights obligations in their implementation of CBD guidance.[51]

A human rights lens, furthermore, is critical to understand the interface between SDG 15 and SDG 16, Peace, Justice and Strong Institutions.[52] Matters that are generally labelled as 'good governance' under international biodiversity law should be understood in legally binding terms when considered as procedural environmental rights.[53] According to their general human rights treaty obligations, once applied to the interdependence of human rights and biodiversity, states must ensure affordable, effective, and timely public access to information on biodiversity, in a language that is understandable to those affected; public participation in decision-making on biodiversity and taking the views of the public, including children's views, into account; and access to effective remedies for violations of human rights and biodiversity laws by private and public actors.[54] In addition, states must develop laws and institutions that effectively 'regulate harm to biodiversity from private actors as well as government entities in a way that is non-retrogressive and non-discriminatory',[55] including additional measures to protect the human rights of the most vulnerable (children and communities that have a close relationship with lands and resources on which they depend for their material needs and cultural life).[56] Furthermore, states authorizing any activity – either conservation or sustainable use of biodiversity – must ensure that no unjustified, foreseeable infringements of human rights may arise from their decisions by conducting prior assessments of

49 CEDAW Committee, General Recommendation no. 34 on the Rights of Rural Women, Doc. CEDAW/C/GC/34, 2016; CEDAW Committee, *Concluding Observations on the Seventh Periodic Report of Argentina*, Doc. CEDAW/C/ARG/CO/7, 2016.

50 CBD Decision XII/7, 2014; see Victoria Jenkins, 'Gender and the Convention on Biological Diversity', in Morgera & Razzaque, n. 6, 331.

51 Elisa Morgera, *Biodiversity as a Human Right and Its Implications for the EU's External Action: Report to the European Parliament*, 2020, www.europarl.europa.eu/RegData/etudes/STUD/2020/603491/EXPO_STU(2020)603491_EN.pdf.

52 Collins, n. 23, 78–83; see generally Niko Soininen, 'Torn by (Un)certainty: Can There Be Peace between the Rule of Law and Other Sustainable Development Goals?', in French and Kotzé, n. 10, 222.

53 John Knox, 'Human Rights, Environmental Protection and the Sustainable Development Goals' (2015) 24 *Washington International Law Journal* 517; Marcos Orellana, 'Governance and the Sustainable Development Goals: The Increasing Relevance of Access Rights in Principle 10 of the Rio Declaration' (2016) 25 *RECIEL* 50.

54 John Knox, *Report of the Special Rapporteur on the Issue of Human Rights Obligations Relating to the Enjoyment of a Safe, Clean, Healthy and Sustainable Environment*, UN Doc. A/HRC/34/49, 2017, paras. 27–32. Reiterated, in general terms, in the *UN Framework Principles*, n. 24, Principles 4–5, 7–10, 12; see also discussion in Lalanath de Silva, 'Public Participation in Biodiversity Conservation', in Morgera & Razzaque, n. 6, 217.

55 Knox, n. 54, para. 69.

56 As reflected in more general environmental terms in the *UN Framework Principles*, n. 24, Principles 11, 14–15.

possible socio-cultural and environmental impacts of projects or policies that may affect biodiversity.[57] States' obligations also extend to preventing business entities from violating human rights as well as in the context of land-based extractives, agriculture, the creation of protected areas, climate change response measures, or renewables development.[58] Finally, states must protect biodiversity defenders as human rights defenders, including activists that 'protect components of ecosystems whose benefits to humans may be less obvious, such as endangered species'.[59]

Based on the interconnectedness of marine, terrestrial, and freshwater ecosystems, SDG 15 is also related to SDG 14. Certain targets under SDG 15 (such as those related to halting biodiversity loss, preventing species extinction, sharing benefits from access to genetic resources, addressing invasive alien species, and integrating biodiversity values into planning and accounts) are also relevant for the conservation and sustainable use of marine biodiversity. In turn, certain targets under SDG 14 are clearly intertwined with the conservation and sustainable use of terrestrial and freshwater biodiversity, such as reducing land-based marine pollution, protecting coastal ecosystems, and sustainably managing tourism. In addition, target 14.b on ensuring access to resources and markets for small-scale fisheries raises questions related to the human rights of small-scale fishing individuals and communities, who also rely on the conservation and sustainable use of terrestrial ecosystems.[60] While states may be already alerted to the need to address in integrated ways terrestrial and marine ecosystems within their national jurisdiction, as well as of the opportunities to apply relevant human rights standards across terrestrial and marine ecosystems,[61] current implementation levels leave much to be desired. In addition, states have conflicting views on whether and to what extent to apply the CBD to marine areas beyond national jurisdiction.[62] On this basis, the CBD remains an underutilized international instrument in the ongoing UN negotiations on areas of marine

57 Knox, n. 54, para. 69; as reflected in more general environmental terms in the *UN Framework Principles*, n. 24, Principle 8.

58 Knox, n. 54, paras. 33–34.

59 *Id.*, paras. 31–32, 68; see also 1999 Declaration on the Rights and Responsibility of Individuals, Groups and Organs of Society to Promote and Protect Universally Recognized Human Rights and Fundamental Freedoms.

60 *United Nations Declaration on the Rights of Peasants*, UN Doc. A/HRC/RES/39/12, 28 September 2018; *Voluntary Guidelines for Securing Sustainable Small-scale Fisheries in the Context of Food Security and Poverty Eradication* (FAO, 2018); Elisa Morgera & Julia Nakamura, 'Shedding a Light on the Human Rights of Small-scale Fisherfolk: Complementarities and Contrasts between the UN Declaration on Peasants' Rights and the Small-Scale Fisheries Guidelines', in Mariagrazia Alabrese et al (eds), Commentary on the Declaration on the Rights of Peasants (Routledge, 2022) 62.

61 For instance, in relation to the creation and management of marine protected areas, see David R. Boyd, *Report of the Special Rapporteur on the Issue of Human Rights Obligations Relating to the Enjoyment of a Safe, Clean, Healthy and Sustainable Environment*, UN Doc. A/75/161, 2020.

62 Elisa Morgera, 'Competence or Confidence? The Most Appropriate Forum to Address Multi-Purpose High Seas Protected Areas' (2007) 16(1) *RECIEL* 1.

biodiversity beyond national jurisdiction (BBNJ).[63] More generally, several questions remain as to the relevance of the various SDGs in the BBNJ negotiations as well as their relevance from an international human rights perspective.[64]

The links between SDG 15 and SDG 13 (and their relevance for SDG 14) have been extensively explored under the CBD.[65] The CBD parties have systematically identified potential and actual threats that climate change and climate change response measures pose to the conservation and sustainable use of biodiversity, along with ways to assess and prevent negative impacts on biodiversity through mutually supportive interpretation and application of international climate and biodiversity law.[66] These contributions have been based on the CBD's ecosystem approach and have (often implicitly) contributed to defining a rights-based approach to climate change adaptation and mitigation, mainly with regard to the human rights of Indigenous peoples and local communities.[67] At a high level, the CBD parties have committed to integrating ecosystem-based approaches when updating their nationally determined contributions, taking into account the importance of ensuring the integrity and functionality of all ecosystems, including oceans; recognizing that ecosystems can be managed to limit climate change impacts on biodiversity and support people's resilience, taking into account multiple social, economic, and cultural co-benefits for local communities; and recognizing the role of Indigenous and community conserved areas and biodiversity-based livelihoods in the face of climate change.[68]

In addition, the CBD parties have adopted more specific guidance on the ecosystem-based approach to mitigation on geo-engineering,[69] biofuels production,[70]

[63] Elisa Morgera & Mara Ntona, 'Linking Small-Scale Fisheries to International Obligations on Marine Technology Transfer' (2018) 93 *Marine Policy* 214.

[64] As UN Special Rapporteur on Human Rights and the Environment, David Boyd recommended in 2020 that states need to '[e]nsure that the proposed agreement on the conservation and sustainable use of marine biodiversity beyond areas of national jurisdiction includes appropriate consideration of human rights'. Boyd, n. 61, para. 90(j). For an exploration, see Elisa Morgera, 'Fair and Equitable Benefit-Sharing in a New International Instrument on Marine Biodiversity: A Principled Approach towards Partnership Building?' (2018–19) 5 *Maritime Safety and Security Law Journal* 48; Nadia Sánchez Castillo-Winckels, 'How the Sustainable Development Goals Promote a New Conception of Ocean Common Governance', in French & Kotzé, n. 10, 117.

[65] See, e.g., Sandrine Maljean-Dubois & M. Wemaëre, 'Biodiversity and Climate Change', in Morgera & Razzaque, n. 6, 295; Harro van Asselt, 'REDD+ and Biodiversity', in Morgera & Razzaque, *id.*, 309; Seita Romppanen, 'Biofuels', in Morgera & Razzaque, *id.*, 346.

[66] Elisa Morgera, 'No Need to Reinvent the Wheel for a Human Rights-Based Approach to Tackling Climate Change: The Contribution of International Biodiversity Law', in Erkki Hollo, Kati Kulovesi & Michael Mehling (eds.), *Climate Change and the Law* (Springer, 2013), 350.

[67] *Id.*

[68] CBD Decision XIV/5, 2018.

[69] CBD Decision X/33, 2010; CBD Decision XI/20, 2012, paras. 6–7; CBD Decision XIII/14, 2016, para. 4.

[70] CBD Decision IX/2, 2008.

and reducing emissions from deforestation and forest degradation,[71] which can affect the mountain, wetland, and forest ecosystems addressed under SDG 15. However, despite these contributions to policy coherence and gap filling by the CBD's COP,[72] there is still limited impact from the CBD's guidance on implementation practices under the international climate change regime.[73] The CBD parties have further adopted voluntary guidelines for the design and effective implementation of ecosystem-based approaches to adaptation and disaster risk reduction[74] and voluntary guidelines on socio-ecological resilience in relation to coral reefs and closely associated ecosystems (such as mangroves and sea grasses),[75] which can support coherent action across SDGs 13, 14, and 15.

The main implication for international law is that guidance intergovernmentally adopted under the CBD can contribute to ensure mutually supportive interpretation of international law in the areas of the sea, climate change, and human rights with a view to supporting synergies among SDG 15 and many other SDGs, thereby contributing to policy coherence (target 17.14).

15.3 POSITIONING SDG 15 IN INTERNATIONAL LAW

15.3.1 *The CBD as a 'Catch-All Regime'*

This section takes a deeper look at the nature and significance of the international biodiversity law objectives covered by SDG 15. Terrestrial biodiversity is addressed in international law through a series of independent treaties that differ in terms of membership, approaches, and compliance mechanisms, due to the diverse history and scope of each instrument's application.[76] Despite this multiplicity of international legal instruments, all of the treaties have as their objective the conservation and sustainable use of biological resources, thus being aligned substantively with the overarching normative framework provided by the CBD. Because of its broad coverage and openness to inputs from non-state actors (including Indigenous peoples' and local communities' representatives), the CBD has functioned as a

[71] *Id.*

[72] Harro van Asselt, 'Managing the Fragmentation of International Environmental Law: Forests at the Intersection of the Climate and Biodiversity Regimes' (2010) 44(4) *New York University of International Law and Politics* 1205, 1258.

[73] The lack of cross-reference in decisions taken in the context of the international climate change regime to relevant decisions taken in the context of the CBD has been emphasized by van Asselt. *Id.*, 1258–59 (referring specifically to decisions on forests); Jamie Pittock, 'A Pale Reflection of Political Reality: Integration of Global Climate, Wetland and Biodiversity Agreements' (2010) 1(3) *Climate Law* 343, 355.

[74] CBD Decision XIV/5, 2018.

[75] CBD Decision XII/23, 2014.

[76] Antonio Cardesa-Salzmann, 'Monitoring and Compliance Mechanisms', in Morgera & Razzaque, n. 6, 55.

'catch-all regime' that has addressed, far beyond the expectation of its drafters, new threats to biodiversity and the livelihoods of Indigenous peoples and local communities.[77] It has influenced how other international biodiversity treaties have been interpreted.[78] It has also been relied upon by international human rights bodies, notably with respect to Indigenous peoples' rights in the context of land-based extractives, agriculture, renewables, and conservation.[79]

The CBD has developed a multitude of sub-processes for the further refinement of its provisions, which have led to the intergovernmental development of guidelines for national implementation, often recommending reforms of national laws, policies, and administrative practices. In addition, guidance developed under the CBD provides indications to intergovernmental organizations, business enterprises, and civil society in the context of complex biodiversity governance processes. In terms of the legal status of these international guidelines, the CBD parties often emphasize their voluntary nature; however, this does not exclude the value of CBD decisions as interpretative tools of the convention obligations as they can be considered the expression of subsequent agreement or subsequent practice related to the convention. In the few exceptional cases in which parties have excluded their value as treaty interpretation tools,[80] in order to pre-empt limitations to states' discretion in developing national legislation,[81] the CBD's guidelines can be considered 'best practices' that serve to 'facilitate the implementation' of existing international obligations.[82] This means that it becomes increasingly difficult for a state to defend any substandard approach, particularly when the state has joined the consensus in accepting these guidelines after its participation in intergovernmental negotiations.[83]

77 Elisa Morgera & Elsa Tsioumani, 'Yesterday, Today and Tomorrow: Looking Afresh at the Convention on Biological Diversity' (2011) 21(1) *Yearbook of International Environmental Law* 3.

78 For instance, the CBD Addis Ababa Principles and Guidelines on Sustainable Use of Biological Resources have also been adopted under the Ramsar Convention: *Ramsar Convention COP-9*, Doc. 23, 2005, para. 41. See, however, the controversy on this under the CMS, n. 7. *Sustainable Use*, Resolution 08.01, 2005.

79 Morgera, n. 24, 1100.

80 CBD Decision VII/12, 2004, para. 2(c), with reference to the 1969 Vienna Convention on the Law of Treaties, art. 31(3)(a), (b) or special meaning as provided for in art. 31(4). This is without prejudice to the interpretation or application of the convention in accordance with art. 31(3)(c).

81 The *Mo'otz Kuxtal Voluntary Guidelines*, CBD Decision XIII/18, 2016, for the development of mechanisms, legislation, or other appropriate initiatives to ensure the 'prior and informed consent', 'free, prior and informed consent', or 'approval and involvement', depending on national circumstances, of Indigenous peoples and local communities for accessing their knowledge, innovations, and practices, for fair and equitable sharing of benefits arising from the use of their knowledge, innovations, and practices relevant for the conservation and sustainable use of biological diversity, and for reporting and preventing unlawful appropriation of traditional knowledge.

82 Morgera et al., n. 42, 15. This applies by analogy the reasoning in *UN Framework Principles*, n. 24, para. 9.

83 See Alan Boyle & Christine Chinkin, *The Making of International Law* (Oxford University Press, 2007).

15.3.2 *Human Rights Law*

For his part, the UN Special Rapporteur on human rights and the environment assessed the CBD's obligations in 2017 as a matter of international human rights law, based on the unequivocal understanding that the full enjoyment of everyone's human rights to life, health, food, and water depend on healthy ecosystems and their benefits to people.[84] These clarifications are critical to guide individual states' endeavours to contribute to the realization of SDG 15. Furthermore, international obligations about interstate cooperation at the nexus of biodiversity and human rights[85] should guide states' bilateral and multilateral efforts to support the realization of SDG 15. As donors, for instance, states should ensure integrating certain human rights considerations into biodiversity finance,[86] technology transfer, capacity building, information sharing, and scientific cooperation.[87] Furthermore, states are expected to consider the linkages between international biodiversity law and human rights in the context of international trade and investment agreements.[88]

15.3.3 *International Economic Law*

As anticipated above, the relationship between international biodiversity law as reflected in SDG 15 and international economic law is one fraught with actual and potential tensions. It has been widely documented that international trade and foreign investment can increase pressures on biodiversity as well as lead to violations of biodiversity-dependent human rights. International trade law, international investment law, and intellectual property law can also place limitations on the capacity of states to conserve or ensure the sustainable use of biodiversity. However, biodiversity conservation can both provide opportunities for foreign investment and justify interference with foreign investments that may damage biodiversity. Thus, in the international investment arbitration *David Aven v Costa Rica*, the tribunal found that Costa Rica's actions to protect wetlands in an investment area was in line with the 1971 Convention on Wetlands of International Importance Especially as Waterfowl Habitat (Ramsar Convention) and the CBD and therefore did not breach the relevant investment agreement and the international obligations to ensure fair and equitable treatment.[89]

84 Knox, n. 54, para. 5.
85 *Id.*, paras. 36–48
86 CBD Decision XII/3, 2014.
87 Elisa Morgera, 'Fair and Equitable Benefit-sharing at the Crossroads of the Human Right to Science and International Biodiversity Law' (2015) 4(4) *Laws* 803; Morgera & Ntona, n. 63.
88 Knox, n. 54, paras. 36–39.
89 ICSID, *David Aven et al. v Republic of Costa Rica*, ICSID Case no. UNCT/15/3, Award, 18 September 2018, paras. 390, 394, 418, 419, 423, 708, www.italaw.com/sites/default/files/case-documents/italaw9955_0.pdf.

Furthermore, bilateral investment treaties have been increasingly used to make a positive impact on biodiversity conservation and sustainable use. Introducing incentives based on access to international markets has proven to be beneficial to generate political will to engage with bilateral biodiversity cooperation. For instance, European Union (EU) bilateral trade agreements refer in their trade and sustainable development chapters to the CBD and CITES,[90] including detailed provisions related to climate change[91] and forestry[92] that are of relevance for SDG 15. Occasionally, these provisions make reference to human rights implications,[93] such as ensuring the protection of traditional knowledge,[94] promoting the inclusion of forest-based local communities and Indigenous peoples in sustainable supply chains of timber and non-timber forest products,[95] and providing benefits to stakeholders in the value-chain of CITES-listed species.[96] Another notable example is provided by the EU's Forest Law Enforcement, Governance and Trade Action Plan,[97] which has explicitly drawn on global soft law commitments[98] and sought compatibility with ongoing, albeit partial, multilateral efforts to address deforestation by exporter and importer countries.[99] Relying on potential bilateral trade sanctions to enhance compliance with the CBD,[100] however, has proven to have had negative impacts on the rights of Indigenous peoples, as it has been documented in the context of the United States' bilateral agreements.[101] These results appear consistent with Gracia Marín Durán's argument that bilateral trade sanctions are not suitable to support sustainable development objectives because of 'scant and mixed' empirical evidence on their presumed compliance-inducing effect and because of the 'risk of

[90] See, e.g., 2012 Trade Agreement between the European Union and Its Member States, of the One Part, and Colombia and Peru, of the Other Part (EU-Colombia and Peru FTA), arts. 267 (2)(b), 270(2).

[91] In particular, the 2000 Partnership Agreement between the Members of the African, Caribbean and Pacific Group of States of the One Part and the European Community and Its Member States of the Other; *Second Revision of the Cotonou Partnership Agreement*, 11 March 2010, arts. 1, 8, 11, 32bis, www.ec.europa.eu/development/icenter/repository/second_revision_cotonou_agreement_20100311.pdf.

[92] See, e.g., 2019 EU - Mercosur Association Agreement, Trade and Sustainable Development Chapter (EU - Mercosur Association Agreement), art. 8.

[93] Morgera, n. 64.

[94] E.g., EU - Colombia and Peru FTA, n. 90, art. 272.

[95] EU - Mercosur Association Agreement, n. 92, Trade and Sustainable Development Chapter, art. 8.2.b.

[96] 2018 EU - Mexico Agreement, Trade and Sustainable Development Chapter, art. 6.3.c.

[97] European Commission, *Forest Law Enforcement, Governance and Trade Action Plan: Conclusions – Forest Law Enforcement, Governance and Trade (FLEGT)*, [2003] OJ C268/1.

[98] World Summit on Sustainable Development, *Johannesburg Plan of Implementation*, UN Doc. A/CONF.199/20, 2002, Resolution 2, 5.

[99] Namely, timber species listed under CITES. European Commission, n. 97, 109, 20.

[100] Sikina Jinnah & Elisa Morgera, 'Environmental Provisions in American and EU Free Trade Agreements: A Preliminary Comparison and Research Agenda' (2013) 22(3) *RECIEL* 324.

[101] *Id.*

compromising the current value-based purpose and comprehensive scope of [bilateral agreements]'.[102]

Another key aspect to consider is the extent to which international law has addressed the role of the private sector in contributing to efforts towards realizing SDG 15. The CBD expressly calls for private sector involvement in ensuring the sustainable use of biodiversity components and has developed a series of guidelines that can be directly applied to private actors.[103] As a result, several self-regulation initiatives have contributed to addressing the concerns enshrined in SDG 15 on the basis of the CBD and its guidelines.[104] The Organisation for Economic Co-operation and Development (OECD) and the Food and Agriculture Organization's (FAO) joint Guidance for Responsible Agricultural Supply Chains, in addition, calls upon agribusiness to control and minimize the spread of invasive alien species and spells out sustainable use standards in terms of 'good agricultural practices', such as maintaining or improving soil fertility, avoiding soil erosion, and supporting habitats and related livelihoods against the effects of climate change through adaptation measures.[105] The relevance of the CBD's guidance for the private sector has also been recognized by international human rights bodies.[106] Whether the CBD's guidance is fully upheld in multi-stakeholder standard-making exercises and leads to positive impacts on the ground, however, remains a matter for sustained empirical investigation.[107] On the whole, SDG 15 captures some, but not all, of the dimensions of the protection and sustainable use of terrestrial biodiversity as they are addressed under the CBD.

15.4 POSITIONING SDG 15 IN THE INTERNATIONAL INSTITUTIONAL CONTEXT

This section focuses on the institutional dimensions of policy coherence in pursuing SDG 15, focusing, in turn, on inter-institutional coordination mechanisms, compliance mechanisms, and funding across different international treaties and organizations.

[102] Gracia Marín Durán, 'Sustainable Development Chapters in EU Free Trade Agreements: Emerging Compliance Issues' (2020) 57(4) *Common Market Law Review* 1031, 1062.

[103] CBD, art. 10(e) reads as follows: 'Encourage cooperation between its governmental authorities and its private sector in developing methods for sustainable use of biological resources.' See discussion in Elisa Morgera, *Corporate Environmental Accountability in International Law*, 2nd ed. (Oxford University Press, 2020).

[104] See, e.g., Roundtable on Sustainable Palm Oil (RSPO), *Principles and Criteria for Sustainable Palm Oil Production* (RSPO, 2007), www.rspo.org/file/RSPO%20Principles%20&%20Criteria%20Document.pdf.

[105] OECD & FAO, n. 40.

[106] See, e.g., Special Rapporteur James Anaya, *Extractive Industries Operating within or near Indigenous Territories*, UN Doc. A/HRC/18/35, 2011, para. 63; UN Expert Mechanism, *Advice no. 4: Follow-up Report on Indigenous Peoples and the Right to Participate in Decision-making, with a Focus on Extractive Industries*, UN Doc. A/HRC/21/55, 2012, para. 8.

[107] Morgera, n. 103, 263.

15.4.1 *Inter-Institutional Coordination Mechanisms*

While the CBD, the other biodiversity-relevant treaties, and the other two Rio Conventions –that is, the 1992 UN Framework Convention on Climate Change (UNFCCC) and the UNCCD – are independent international processes, they have been connected institutionally to some extent. The Liaison Group of Biodiversity-related Conventions, for instance, 'explores opportunities for synergistic activities and increased coordination, and to exchange information', which could support coordinated implementation of SDGs 14 and 15.[108] In addition, the Joint Liaison Group between the three Rio Conventions was established as an informal forum for exchanging information and exploring opportunities for synergistic activities among the officers of the conventions' scientific subsidiary bodies, the executive secretaries, and members of the secretariats.[109] A further example is the Inter-agency Liaison Group on Invasive Alien Species,[110] which is an initiative of the CBD's Secretariat with membership extending to ten secretariats from intergovernmental organizations including the FAO, the International Maritime Organization, the International Civil Aviation Organization, and the World Trade Organization. The regular opportunity for dialogue provided for by this group is intended to 'address the gaps and inconsistencies in the international regulatory frameworks for the prevention, control and eradication of invasive alien species' and aims to facilitate the development of norms and standards as well as promote information sharing and capacity building.[111]

In addition, the UN Environment Programme and the FAO are both leading the international exchanges of lessons learned and good practices on the implementation of SDG 15 as well as providing advisory services to specific governments on the implementation of the international law that underpins SDG 15. Both bodies have made strides in integrating human rights into their work in this connection. The CBD's decisions on biodiversity mainstreaming recognized these and other institutional connections, such as the Platform on Biodiversity and Agricultural Sectors launched by the FAO for governments and communities of practice to identify synergies and develop integrated cross-sectoral approaches to mainstreaming biodiversity in the agriculture and forestry sectors. The CBD's parties also have underscored the Collaborative Partnership on Forests, which is an informal, voluntary arrangement among fifteen international organizations and secretariats with substantial programmes on forests (such as the secretariats of CITES, the FAO, the

[108] See, e.g., CBD, *Liaison Group of Biodiversity-related Conventions*, www.cbd.int/blg/; CBD Decision VII/26, 2004; CBD Decision IX/27, 2008.

[109] See, e.g., CBD, *Joint Liaison Group*, www.cbd.int/cooperation/liaison.shtml.

[110] See, e.g., CBD, *Inter-agency Liaison Group on Invasive Alien Species*, www.cbd.int/invasive/lg/.

[111] *Id.*

UNFCCC, and the UNCCD) to collaborate to streamline their work towards improving forest management and conservation and the production and trade of forest products.[112]

15.4.2 *Compliance Mechanisms*

On compliance, the CBD has yet to develop a systematic or credible system for monitoring implementation by states. The CBD's COP does not review individual national reports but, rather, offers conclusions on the basis of the CBD Secretariat's syntheses of these reports.[113] This examination tends to focus only on the submission of the report and on a quantitative analysis of legislative developments (for instance, the percentage of parties with biodiversity-related legislation in place) rather than on a qualitative analysis of the content of the national reports, including the quality and comprehensiveness of national legislation and impacts of state measures on biodiversity and achievement of the CBD's objectives. To complement these practices, since 2016, the CBD's Body on Implementation has engaged in a voluntary peer-review mechanism[114] aimed at assessing the development and implementation of national biodiversity strategies and action plans (NBSAPs), providing opportunities for peer learning for parties directly involved and other parties and creating greater transparency and accountability for the development and implementation of NBSAPs to the public and other parties.[115]

A potential avenue for assessing compliance at the interface of international biodiversity law and human rights law could be the compliance mechanism under the CBD's 2014 Nagoya Protocol on Access to Genetic Resources and the Fair and Equitable Sharing of Benefits Arising from Their Utilization, albeit this would have limited subject-matter application focused on bio-based innovation (research and development based on genetic resources). The Nagoya Protocol's Compliance Committee can receive information from Indigenous peoples and local communities on alleged non-compliance by parties, although the Secretariat will decide whether or not to trigger the compliance procedures after attempting to solve the issue among the Indigenous people/local community in question and the state

[112] CBD Decision XIII/3, 2016.

[113] Yibin Xiang & Sandra Meehan, 'Financial Cooperation, Rio Conventions and Common Concerns' (2005) 14(3) *RECIEL* 212, 218.

[114] CBD, *Voluntary Peer-Review Mechanism for National Biodiversity Strategies and Action Plans*, UN Doc. UNEP/CBD/SBI/1/10/ADD1, 2016; see also CBD, *Report of the Informal Working Group on the Development of a Methodology for Voluntary Peer-Review of the Implementation of the Convention on Biological Diversity*, UN Doc. UNEP/CBD/SBI/1/INF/27, 2015; CBD Decision XII/29, 2012, para. 3.

[115] CBD, A *Methodology for Voluntary Peer Review of the Revision and Implementation of National Biodiversity Strategies and Action Plans*, UN Doc. UNEP/CBD/SBI/1/INF/30, 2016, Appendix 1.

concerned. Furthermore, in examining the cases brought to its attention, the Compliance Committee may seek information from affected communities and advice from community experts and undertake, upon invitation of the party concerned, information gathering in the territory of that party.[116]

Another interesting example is the review mechanism under the 1979 Convention on Migratory Species of Wild Animals (CMS), which allows for a trigger by any agency technically qualified in protection, conservation, and management of migratory species, which is either an international non-governmental agency or body or an accredited national non-governmental agency or body.[117] One of the most sophisticated compliance regimes among biodiversity-related agreements is that of CITES. It initially focused on national-level implementation (the control of individual shipments by national authorities of member countries), and, more recently, it has relied on international monitoring and support.[118] As a result, the compliance regime under CITES currently counts on a multiplicity of processes, with the possibility to impose trade sanctions on parties,[119] and it has allowed, in practice, significant input from the international civil society.[120] Another innovative instance is the joint site inspection among the regional 1979 Berne Convention on the Conservation of European Wildlife and Natural Habitats, the Ramsar Convention, and the CMS to develop cross-treaty supportive compliance measures.[121]

In addition, international human rights monitoring systems are increasingly taking the opportunity to assess compliance with the CBD and other international biodiversity agreements. For instance, the Committee on the Elimination of Racial Discrimination has underscored state obligations to ensure adequate socio-cultural and environmental impact assessments in accordance with relevant CBD guidance as part of the obligations to respect Indigenous and tribal peoples' human rights.[122] In 2015, in the *Kaliña and Lokono* decision, the Inter-American Court of Human Rights underscored states' obligations to protect, in a manner compatible with their international biodiversity obligations, Indigenous peoples' rights to a dignified life and to cultural identity connected with natural resources on their traditional

[116] CBD, *Cooperative Procedures and Institutional Mechanisms to Promote Compliance with the Nagoya Protocol and to Address Cases of Non-Compliance*, UN Doc. UNEP/CBD/NP/COP-MOP/DEC/1/4, 2014.

[117] See CMS Resolution 12.9, 2017; CMS Decisions 12.6–12.9, www.cms.int/sites/default/files/document/cms_cop12_decisions_e_0.pdf and www.cms.int/en/activities/review-mechanism.

[118] See Cardesa-Salzmann, n. 76.

[119] Based on CITES, art. XI, coupled with majority-voting decision-making. See CITES, *Countries Currently Subject to a Recommendation to Suspend Trade*, cites.org/eng/resources/ref/suspend.php.

[120] Karen Scott, 'Non-Compliance Procedures and the Implementation of Commitments under Wildlife Law', in Bowman, Davies & Goodwin, n. 34, 414, 424.

[121] Ibid, 414, 426–27.

[122] Committee on the Elimination of Racial Discrimination, *Concluding Observations on the Combined Thirteenth to Fifteenth Periodic Reports of Suriname*, UN Doc. CERD/C/SUR/CO/13-15, 2015, para. 26.

territories,[123] including those obligations that are in line with the consensus guidance adopted under the CBD.[124]

Furthermore, international economic law can support compliance with international biodiversity law. For instance, an international investor running a nature sanctuary in Barbados lodged a complaint against the government of Barbados for failing to implement its international obligations under the Ramsar Convention and the CBD, which had negatively affected the value of the investment in the sanctuary.[125] And the EU's bilateral trade agreements include a cooperative institutional apparatus to support the implementation of their sustainable development and biodiversity commitments, with civil society and expert participation.[126]

15.4.3 *Funding across Different International Treaties and Organizations*

The Global Environment Facility (GEF) contributes to biodiversity financing to support the implementation of targets 15.a and b. The GEF Council is obliged to 'act in conformity' with the policies, priorities, and eligibility criteria decided by the CBD's COP when acting as its financial mechanism.[127] Consequently, the CBD's COP is empowered to review the effectiveness of the GEF serving as the convention's financial mechanism.[128] Policy alignment between the GEF and the CBD's COP, however, has been a matter of contention.[129] For instance, before the entry into force of the Nagoya Protocol, the CBD parties raised concerns about the use of a GEF-run fund to support the private sector's engagement in transactions on genetic resources. This system seemed to run counter to the CBD parties' prioritization of support to governments in implementing the Nagoya Protocol through the

[123] *Kaliña and Lokono*, n. 29, paras. 181, 193.

[124] CBD, arts. 8(j), 10, 14: *Kaliña and Lokono*, n. 29, paras. 173–74, 177–78, 181, 214, 247 (making reference to the Addis Ababa Principles and Guidelines for the Sustainable Use of Biodiversity); CBD Decision VII/12, 2004, Annex II; for information on the CBD's work programme on protected areas, see n. 38.

[125] PCA, *Peter Allard v Barbados*, PCA Case no. 2012-06, Final Award, 27 June 2016, paras. 178, 190, 198, 230, 238, 244, www.italaw.com/sites/default/files/case-documents/italaw7594.pdf.

[126] 2012 Agreement Establishing and Association between the European Union and Its Member States, on the One Hand, and Central America on the Other, art. 296(2); 2011 Free Trade Agreement between the European Union and Its Member States, of the One Part, and the Republic of Korea, on the Other Part, art. 13.14(2); Rok Žvelk, 'Environmental Integration in EU Trade Policy: The Generalised System of Preferences, Trade Sustainability Impact Assessments and Free Trade Agreements', in Elisa Morgera (ed.), *The External Environmental Policy of the European Union: EU and International Law Perspectives* (Cambridge University Press, 2012), 174.

[127] 2010 Instrument for the Establishment of the Restructured Global Environment Facility as amended by Fourth Assembly of the GEF, paras. 15, 26. See Jacob Werksman, 'Consolidating Governance of the Global Commons: Insights from the Global Environment Facility' (1996) 6(1) *Yearbook of International Environmental Law* 27, 60; Patricia Birnie, Alan Boyle & Catherine Redgwell, *International Law and the Environment*, 3rd ed. (Oxford University Press, 2009), 94.

[128] CBD, art. 21(3).

[129] CBD Decision III/8, 1997, para. 2.

development of national legislation and consultations with national stakeholders.[130] Consultations with national stakeholders were also necessary to ensure respect for the human rights of Indigenous peoples. Other issues identified with the GEF's support of the conservation and sustainable use of terrestrial biodiversity are the difficulty in tracking biodiversity finance and shifts in finance from protected areas to sustainable use activities.[131] In addition, the CBD's COP has already adopted safeguards against negative impacts on human rights of biodiversity financing.[132]

An often underestimated international institution that contributes to the realization of SDG 15 through private sector efforts is the International Finance Corporation (IFC),[133] which has translated international biodiversity and human rights obligations into standards for corporate behaviour as part of its Performance Standards for private sector clients.[134] On the basis of the Performance Standards, the IFC's compliance advisor/ombudsman (CAO) investigates specific instances as well as systemic problems and provides recommendations to the IFC.[135] For instance, in a 2019 compliance investigation, it underscored the IFC's shortcomings in ensuring the integration of biodiversity concerns in impact assessments, the consideration of high biodiversity value and nationally protected areas, as well as ecosystem services in the context of an ecotourism project.[136] Nevertheless, the CAO found that the IFC requested the retention of a biodiversity expert to design and manage the implementation of a biodiversity monitoring programme.[137] This discovery led to biodiversity concerns being addressed during project implementation on the basis of additional biodiversity studies that the client was expected to analyse in the context of the project's areas of influence and in consultation with the affected stakeholders.[138]

While the CAO itself has not yet addressed human rights in explicit terms in its mandate, it often addresses instances that involve both human rights and biodiversity issues and is seen as 'an opportunity for the implementation of practical human

[130] Intergovernmental Committee for the Nagoya Protocol, Recommendation 2/1, 2012, Annex II, para. 3, which is integrated in CBD Decision XI/5, 2012 (financial mechanism); 'Summary of the Second Meeting of the Intergovernmental Committee for the Nagoya Protocol' (2012) 9 (579) *Earth Negotiations Bulletin* 15, enb.iisd.org/events/2nd-meeting-intergovernmental-committee-nagoya-protocol-access-and-benefit-sharing-cbd-5.

[131] Soledad Aguilar, 'The International Finance for Biodiversity and the Global Environment Facility', in Morgera & Razzaque, n. 6, 477.

[132] CBD Decision XII/3, 2014.

[133] See Priscilla Schwartz, 'International Financial Institutions and Biodiversity Conservation', in Morgera & Razzaque, n. 6, 399; Morgera, n. 126, 129–34.

[134] IFC, 2012 *Performance Standards*, www.ifc.org/wps/wcm/connect/Topics_Ext_Content/IFC_External_Corporate_Site/Sustainability-At-IFC/Policies-Standards/Performance-Standards.

[135] *Id.*, 1297.

[136] CAO, *Annual Report* (CAO, 2019), 18, cao-ar19.org/.

[137] CAO, *Compliance Investigation Report (IFC Investment in Enso Albania, Complaint 01)*, 25 June 2018, 15.

[138] *Id.*, 22–23.

rights outcomes' as a result of its mediation.[139] In effect, it may provide a distinctive approach compared to other international compliance mechanisms, as it focuses on creating the conditions for more collaborative interactions between companies and human rights holders, setting out steps for establishing or strengthening dialogue.[140] This process has arguably allowed consideration of the connections between conflicts around projects and the broader historical issues within a certain country. It has also supported trust-building processes through scientific assessments that respond to questions co-identified by concerned communities and addressed by independent experts co-selected by communities through a competitive process, with a view to changing the 'dynamics of long-term conflicts'.[141] Once again, SDG 15 does not add to the institutional connections pursued under or in relation to the CBD.

15.5 CONCLUSIONS

The main challenge that SDG 15 poses for international law and international institutions is the effective and urgent implementation of existing obligations under international biodiversity law in the face of competing economic pressures. The complexity of the trade-offs in part lies in the misrepresentation/misunderstanding of competing socioeconomic issues. Nature protection is traditionally seen as an alternative or an obstacle to economic and social development in the short term. But the growing understanding of the interdependencies of biodiversity and human rights reveals that decisions favouring nature protection bring about socioeconomic and cultural benefits for everybody's long-term well-being (notably in relation to the human right to healthy, food, and water) as well as short-term impacts on specific groups (notably, Indigenous peoples, women, and children).[142] Even when biodiversity is seen as an engine for a green economy, the complexity of the trade-offs lies in the mainstream neoliberal approach to sustainable development that assumes compatibility between economic growth and environmental constraints.[143] This situation has indeed been a frequent critique of SDG 15 in the academic literature as a missed opportunity to prioritize the respect of planetary boundaries for the realization of all the other SDGs.[144] That said, hegemonic strategies in the fragmentation of

[139] Adam McBeth, *International Economic Actors and Human Rights* (Routledge, 2010), 231.

[140] See, e.g., CAO, *Assessment Report of the Complaint Regarding the Electron Investment S.A. Pando-Monte Lirio Hydroelectric Project, Ciriqui Province, Panama*, July 2010, 20–21, www.cao-ombudsman.org/cases/document-links/documents/Panama_AssessmentReport_ENG.pdf.

[141] *Id.*, 29, 31; Morgera, n. 126, 260.

[142] Morgera, n. 62.

[143] Sam Adelman, 'The Sustainable Development Goals, Anthropocentrism and Neoliberalism', in French & Kotzé, n. 10, 15.

[144] Louis J. Kotzé, 'The Sustainable Development Goals: An Existential Critique alongside Three New-Millennial Analytical Paradigms', in French & Kotzé, n. 10, 41.

international law,[145] and the resulting power imbalances embedded in international economic law,[146] represent a much more concrete obstacle to the respect of planetary boundaries and human rights than the framing of SDG 15 in and of itself.

A possible way forward is harnessing international human rights to systematically underpin the urgency of, and limits to, the exercise of state sovereignty in implementing relevant international biodiversity law, including in the context of climate, ocean, renewables, gender, and other SDG-related areas.[147] Human rights emphasize the need for the transparency, inclusivity, and justiciability[148] of national biodiversity efforts and of international cooperation.[149] At best, SDG 15 can add to international biodiversity law when read in the light of Agenda 2030's overarching approach to 'leaving no-one behind', which arguably requires everyone concerned 'to prioritize the most marginalized'.[150] In other words, SDG 15 can serve to call attention to instances in which conservation measures or 'the expansion of extractivist models' in the use of terrestrial biodiversity result in human rights violations.[151]

145 Eyal Benvenisti & George Downs, *Between Fragmentation and Democracy: The Role of National and International Courts* (Cambridge University Press, 2017).

146 See, e.g., Lorenzo Cotula, *Human Rights, Natural Resource and Investment Law in a Globalized World: Shades of Grey in the Shadow of the Law* (Routledge, 2012).

147 Francesco Francioni, 'Human Rights', in Morgera & Kulovesi, n. 6, 66.

148 Morgera, n. 24.

149 On the latter, see *UN Framework Principles*, n. 24, Principle 13 ('States should cooperate with each other to establish, maintain and enforce effective international legal frameworks in order to prevent, reduce and remedy transboundary and global environmental harm that interferes with the full enjoyment of human rights'); Principle 16 ('States should respect, protect and fulfil human rights in the actions they take to address environmental challenges and pursue sustainable development').

150 Graham Long, 'Underpinning Commitments of the Sustainable Development Goals: Indivisibility, Universality, Leaving No One Behind', in French & Kotzé, n. 10, 91, 103.

151 Lorenzo Cotula, 'Between Hope and Critique: Human Rights, Social Justice and Re-Imagining International Law from the Bottom Up' (2020) 48 *Georgia Journal of International and Comparative Law* 473, 484, 521.

16

SDG 16: Promote Peaceful and Inclusive Societies for Sustainable Development, Provide Access to Justice for All and Build Effective, Accountable and Inclusive Institutions at All Levels

Pål Wrange[*]

ABSTRACT

Sustainable Development Goal (SDG) 16, Peace, Justice, and Strong Institutions, is both the most legal and the most political sustainable development goal. Not only does it underpin all the other SDGs, it concerns the makeup of the whole international system. For reformers, SDG 16 looks promising by putting governance, justice, and accountability at the centre of development. Disappointingly, however, the targets and indicators often reduce the goal, sometimes beyond recognition. By and large, SDG 16 leaves the fragmented international political and legal order as it is. Nevertheless, SDG 16 has a rhetorical potential beyond its nitty-gritty content, and its malleability enables interpretations that go beyond those intended by states.

KEYWORDS

SDG 16, access to justice, rule of law, good governance, governing by indicators, inclusion, fragmentation

16.1 INTRODUCTION

Sustainable Development Goal (SDG) 16, Peace, Justice, and Strong Institutions, is clearly the most legal goal. It concerns all SDGs and, thereby, those areas of international law that are implicated by them, like international economic law, international environmental law, and the law of the sea. Since it also concerns

[*] I would like to thank Per Bergling and Anna Wrange for helpful comments. Warm thanks are also due to Jonas Ebbesson and Ellen Hey as well as to the participants in the online workshop on this handbook in June 2020.

governance in general, all areas of international law are touched, not least those that are constitutional in some sense, like the law of the 1945 Charter of the United Nations and human rights law. For the same reasons, SDG 16 is also the most political goal. It deals not only with the implementation of the other goals but also with the political organization of both national societies and the international order. Several of the concepts in this goal are politically charged; in fact, they are 'essentially contested' concepts about how a society should be governed. The political nature of these issues is manifest also in the conscious omission of concepts like 'good governance' and 'human rights'.

There are many ways to understand SDG 16. The banner version – peace, justice, and strong (or inclusive) institutions – could be called progressive, promising to promote these important goods.[1] However, although all of the targets and indicators can easily be associated with international obligations, SDG 16 does not add much in terms of explicit normative content, and the actual elaboration of the goal in targets and indicators is conservative – by and large, leaving international law and politics as they are and sometimes even reducing the agreed obligations. Nevertheless, SDG 16 is not meaningless. Even if there will never be a universally accepted understanding of 'peaceful', 'justice', or 'inclusive', SDG 16 draws attention to the need to consider such issues in development discourse. A generous interpretation can be used to push the envelope. Hence, the goal can serve different legal and political purposes, depending on what one chooses to emphasize.

This chapter briefly discusses the content of SDG 16 in the context of the other SDGs (Section 16.2), positions SDG 16 in international law (Section 16.3), critically situates it in the international institutional framework (Section 16.4), and ends with a few reflections. Since SDG 16 to a large extent covers issues already addressed by international law, the focus will be on how these regulations should be thought of in the development context. The analysis will proceed from the dual character of SDG 16 as eminently legal and political, exploring the gap between the potential of the banner version and the problematic and sometimes reductive features of the targets and indicators – or between the promise and the disappointment, if you will.

16.2 THE CONTENT OF SDG 16 IN THE CONTEXT OF THE OTHER SDGS

16.2.1 *Sub-Goals and 'Big Concepts' in SDG 16*

At face value, SDG 16 is incredibly broad. It addresses the societal and institutional preconditions for the SDGs and thus enables and 'underpins the other sixteen

[1] See, e.g., *Sixteen: Promote Peaceful and Inclusive Societies for Sustainable Development, Provide Access to Justice for All and Build Effective, Accountable and Inclusive Institutions at All Levels*, sdgs.un.org/goals/goal16.

SDGs'[2] as the 'powerhouse from which all other SDGs flow'.[3] It has a multitude of relationships to the targets of the other SDGs. However, its presence as an independent goal indicates that it also has intrinsic value.[4] SDG 16 expresses three sub-goals: 'peaceful and inclusive societies'; 'access to justice for all'; and 'inclusive institutions at all levels'. The interrelationship between them is far from clear, as is the relationship between them and the targets (which will all be further discussed in Section 16.3).[5] Four big concepts were consciously left out of SDG 16: 'peace', 'good governance', 'rule of law', and 'human rights'. The first three can each be linked to a sub-goal (Sections 16.2.2–16.2.4), but human rights require separate consideration (Section 16.2.5).

16.2.2 *Promote Peaceful and Inclusive Societies for Sustainable Development*

The first sub-goal has three components: 'peaceful', 'inclusive', and 'sustainable development'. While 'peaceful' is an intrinsic value, it is also a precondition for the successful outcome of the other goals, as reiterated in many solemn UN declarations, including *Transforming Our World*.[6] 'Peaceful' here seems to mean 'non-violent' in general, as suggested by target 16.2 (end abuse of children) and target 16.4 (combat illicit flows and organized crime), while target 16.1 (reduce violent deaths) could also relate to armed conflicts. Although peacefulness is a precondition for the other SDGs, there are not many explicit links. Target 16.2 overlaps with target 5.2 on violence, trafficking, and sexual exploitation of girls (and women) as well as with target 8.7 on child labour, including the recruitment and use of child soldiers. Target 4.7 provides that 'all learners' should get education for the 'promotion of a culture of peace and non-violence'.

2 Charmaine Rodrigues, 'Goal 16 Advocacy Toolkit: A Practical Guide for Stakeholders for National-Level Advocacy around Peaceful, Just and Inclusive Societies, Transparency, Accountability and Participation for 2030 Agenda', *TAP Network*, 8, sustainabledevelopment.un.org/content/documents/9935TAP%20Network%20Goal%2016%20Advocacy%20Toolkit.pdf; Ronald Hope Kempe, 'Peace, Justice and Inclusive Institutions: Overcoming Challenges to the Implementation of Sustainable Development Goal 16' (2020) 32 *Global Change, Peace and Security* 57, 59.

3 Peride Blind, 'A Post-SDG Summit Governance Primer: Interlinking the Institutional, Peace and Justice Dimensions of SDG16' (United Nations, 2020), 16, 165, www.un.org/development/desa/publications/working-paper/wp165.

4 A *New Global Partnership: Eradicate Poverty and Transform Economies through Sustainable Development: The Report of the High-Level Panel of Eminent Persons on the Post-2015 Development Agenda, United Nations*, 2013, 4, 52; see also Per Bergling & Sophie Jin, 'The New Black on the Development Catwalk: Incorporating Rule of Law into the Sustainable Development Goals' (2015) 24 *Washington International Law Journal (WILJ)* 435, 438.

5 As Arajärvi notes, the goal 'lacks internal logic'. Noora Arajärvi, 'The Rule of Law in the 2030 Agenda' (2018) 10 *Hague Journal on the Rule of Law* 187, 209.

6 *Transforming Our World: The 2030 Agenda for Sustainable Development*, UN Doc. A/Res/70/1, 25 September 2015.

The term 'inclusive' also has both an extrinsic and intrinsic value. Without inclusivity, development potential is left untapped. However, inclusion also gives sense to peoples' lives. 'Inclusive' can have ambitious or more restricted meanings: affirmative engagement with underprivileged groups or just 'non-discriminatory' as a negative obligation. The latter interpretation is supported by target 16.b. Inclusivity is also reflected in the other two sub-goals ('justice for all' and 'inclusive' institutions) and is featured in SDG 4, Quality Education; SDG 8, Decent Work and Economic Growth; SDG 9, Industry, Innovation, and Infrastructure; SDG 10, Reduced Inequalities; and SDG 11, Sustainable Cities and Communities, or in their targets, and a number of other targets are relevant for inclusivity without using that word, such as target 1.4 about equal rights to basic services and control over land, as well as target 10.3 on equal opportunity and inequalities of outcome and so on.[7] In fact, inclusivity, as a shorthand for 'leave no one behind' could be said to be a leitmotif for Agenda 2030.[8]

The third element of this sub-goal is perhaps conceptually the most interesting one. 'For sustainable development' means that the society in question must be organized in such a way that sustainable development can be achieved (see Section 16.3.2).

16.2.3 *Provide Access to Justice for All*

For many observers, the second sub-goal constitutes an unfortunate retreat from the broader 'rule of law', as will be further discussed in Section 16.3.[9] 'Justice' could be interpreted to refer to justice in a broad sense, including distributive justice. However, 'access to justice' is an established term of art in international law, with a more restricted meaning related to the availability of legal remedies. Many targets can be associated with this sub-goal (see Section 16.3); in fact, access to justice is directly or indirectly related to several, if not most, of the other goals. Targets may require legislation, and enforcement thereof will be more effective if those affected can claim their rights before courts. To take an arbitrary example: target 1.4 is to 'ensure that ... the poor and the vulnerable, have equal rights to ... ownership and control over land'. This goal seems difficult to ensure without access to justice.[10]

16.2.4 *Build Effective, Accountable, and Inclusive Institutions at All Levels*

'Effective, accountable and inclusive institutions' are necessary to implement Agenda 2030. This sub-goal could clearly be associated with 'good governance',

7 See also target 10.2 on 'the social, economic and political inclusion of all'; target 1.3 on social protection systems; and target 5.1 on discrimination against women and girls.

8 *Transforming Our World*, n. 6.

9 Frauke Lachenmann, 'Sustainable Development Goal 16 at a Cross-Roads' (2019) 22 *Max Planck Yearbook of United Nations Law Online* 171, 17.

10 See also target 10.2, target 1.3, and target 5.1.

which was, however, too controversial to feature explicitly in any of the targets. Nevertheless, target 16.4 (on corruption), target 16.5 (on illicit arms and financial flows), target 16.6 (on institutions), target 16.7 (on decision-making), and target 16.8 (participation of developing countries) all relate to this concept. A large number of targets linked to other SDGs imply the need to develop domestic institutions, by using words or phrases like 'capacity' (targets 3.d, 6.a), 'planning' (targets 11.a, 13.b, 15.9), 'policies' (targets 8.3 11.b, 13.2), 'programmes' (target 12.1), and 'management plans' (target 14.4). Target 17.1 on capacity building 'for tax and other revenue collection' and target 17.9 on 'capacity-building . . . to support national plans' also assume the existence of institutions. As mentioned, it is difficult to imagine any target being reached without effective institutions. For example, target 11.1 is to 'ensure access for all to adequate, safe and affordable housing'. Markets can satisfy the housing needs of many people, but that has not sufficed in any country, so action by public institutions is required.

The expression 'at all levels' means that the goal applies also at the international level. International institutions are implicated in a large number of targets, such as targets 2.b, 3.b 16.8, 10.5, 10.6, 10.a, 17.10–14, and 17.16, but, disappointingly, this is not well developed in SDG 16, with the minor exception of target 16.8, and I will return to this in Sections 16.3 and 16.4.

16.2.5 *Human Rights*

During the last few decades, the role of human rights in development discourse has changed from being external to being not only instrumental but also integral to development, as in the 'rights-based approach to development'.[11] While economic and social rights were addressed in the 2000 Millennium Development Goals (MDGs) – albeit not as rights – civil and political rights were not. By contrast, in the outcome document of the 2005 World Summit, human rights was one of the three pillars, along with development and international peace and security,[12] and at the 2010 UN Conference on Sustainable Development (Rio + 20), states agreed that sustainable development should be supportive of international human rights standards.[13] The UN inter-agency technical support team that prepared drafts for

[11] See David Kennedy, 'The 'Rule of Law,' Political Choices, and Development Common Sense', in Alvaro Santos & David M. Trubek (eds.), *The New Law and Economic Development: A Critical Appraisal* (Cambridge University Press, 2006), 156–58.

[12] *World Summit Outcome*, UN Doc. A/Res/60/1, 16 September 2005. This was confirmed in *Strengthening and Coordinating United Nations Rule of Law Activities: Report of the Secretary-General*, UN Doc. A/68/213/Add.1, 11 July 2014.

[13] *Technical Support Team Issues Brief: A Compendium of Issues Briefs Prepared by the United Nations Inter-Agency Technical Support Team for the United Nations General Assembly Open Working Group on Sustainable Development Goals – Sustainable Development Knowledge Platform* (UN Department for Economic and Social Affairs, 2014), 144, sustainabledevelopment.un.org/, quoting *The Future We Want: Outcome Document of the United Nations Conference on Sustainable Development*, UN Doc. A/RES/66/288, 11 September 2012, para. 58.

the SDGs stated that human rights can 'identify our priorities and set the standards with which to align goals, targets and indicators and monitoring mechanisms'.[14] The chairpersons of the ten UN human rights treaty bodies 'urge[d]' member states to . . . incorporate explicit references to human rights'.[15] Still, even though the term appears fourteen times in *Transforming Our World*, human rights are directly referenced in none of the actual goals and in only one target peripherally.[16]

Nevertheless, as several commentators have found, human rights are reflected throughout the SDGs, with linkages to human rights and labour standards in 156 of the 169 targets, according to one count.[17] It is therefore no surprise that eighteen out of the twenty-three indicators of SDG 16 are directly relevant to human rights.[18] And, in target 16.10, there is a potentially promising reference to 'fundamental freedoms'. Given these linkages, some observers think that a self-standing 'human rights' goal would be superfluous.[19] However, as John Knox points out, goals are not 'concrete and focused enough to effectively promote human rights',[20] and Thomas Pogge and Mitu Sengupta emphasize that, while '[t]he development goals discourse invites an incremental approach', the human rights discourse 'suggests that deprivations must be ended right away'.[21]

16.3 POSITIONING SDG 16 IN INTERNATIONAL LAW

16.3.1 *International Law, Targets, and Indicators*

SDG 16 puts the relation between the SDGs and international law in a particularly strong spotlight. The goal itself, its targets, indicators, and 'metadata'[22] implicate or

[14] *Technical Support Team Issues Brief*, n. 13, 144.

[15] *Joint Statement of the Chairpersons of the United Nations Human Rights Treaty Bodies on the Post-2015 Development Agenda*, 18 January 2015, www.ohchr.org/EN/NewsEvents/Pages/DisplayNews.aspx?NewsID=15505.

[16] Target 4.7; *Transforming Our World*, n. 6.

[17] See Birgitte Feiring, Francesca Thornberry, & Adrian Hassler, 'Building a Pluralistic Ecosystem of Data to Leave No One Behind: A Human Rights Perspective on Monitoring the Sustainable Development Goals' (2017) 33 *Statistical Journal of the IAOS* 919; see also John H. Knox, 'Human Rights, Environmental Protection, and the Sustainable Development Goals' (2015) 24 *WILJ* 517, 525.

[18] Blind, n. 3, 4.

[19] Knox, n. 17, 518.

[20] *Id.*, 518. For a more positive view, see Lynda M. Collins, 'Sustainable Development Goals and Human Rights: Challenges and Opportunities', in Duncan French & Louis Kotzé, *Sustainable Development Goals* (EE, 2018), 66.

[21] Thomas Pogge & Mitu Sengupta, 'Assessing the Sustainable Development Goals from a Human Rights Perspective' (2016) 32 *Journal of International and Comparative Social Policy* 83, 84.

[22] See Sustainable Development Goals, *SDG Indicators: Metadata Repository*, 18 November 2018, unstats.un.org/sdgs/metadata/.

even paraphrase existing core international law obligations directly.[23] As is explained in the introductory chapter to this volume, the SDGs certainly do not constitute law,[24] but they may affect legal thinking. For instance, do the SDGs constitute the purpose of a putative global constitution?[25] Will the SDG's clustering of issues affect how we conceptualize legal norms? For instance, could target 16.1 on violence in both peace and armed conflict make us rethink the distinction between the international rules on organized crime and armed conflict? Or will SDG 16 change how we think about the relative salience of different norms since any selection of targets X, Y, and Z (say, access to justice, birth registration, the protection of journalists) means that issues T, U, and V (privacy, nationality, and freedom of movement) are deprioritized?[26]

Goal setting seeks to steer behaviour, inter alia, by establishing priorities, identifying targets, and providing yardsticks.[27] While compliance with rules is assessed with words, goals are largely assessed with numbers.[28] Numbers are problematic for legal concepts; one cannot have a target of say, a 50 per cent reduction in torture, when all states are bound to not torture at all.[29] While there is supposedly a causal relation between indicator and target, an indicator always has 'an attenuated relationship to the legal norm at issue'[30] since numbers can never catch legal and factual complexities.[31] Therefore, indicators and statistical data can have a reductive effect.[32] For SDG 16, the indicators are particularly significant since they were developed to a large extent in parallel to the formulation of the targets.[33] It was surely no

[23] Lachenmann, n. 9, 177.

[24] See also Duncan French, 'The Global Goals: Formalism Foregone, Contested Legality and "Re-Imaginings" of International Law' (2017) *Ethiopian Yearbook of International Law* 151, 165.

[25] Anne Peters, 'Global Constitutionalism: The Social Dimension', Max Planck Institute for Comparative Public Law and International Law Research Paper no. 2017-25, 2017.

[26] *Cf.* Norichika Kanie et al., 'Introduction: Global Governance through Goal Setting', in Norichika Kanie & Frank Biermann (eds.), *Governing through Goals: Sustainable Development Goals as Governance Innovation* (MIT Press, 2017), 24.

[27] Oran R. Young, 'Conceptualization: Goal Setting as a Strategy for Earth System Governance', in Kanie & Biermann, n. 26, 32.

[28] *Cf.* Young, n. 27.

[29] Most of the indicators actually adopted appear to have avoided this particular problem, but not completely. See, e.g., target 16.9.

[30] Ann Janette Rosga & Margaret L. Satterthwaite, 'Measuring Human Rights: UN Indicators in Critical Perspective', in Kevin E. Davis et al. (eds.), *Governance by Indicators: Global Power through Quantification and Rankings* (Oxford University Press, 2012), 314.

[31] See Kevin E. Davis, Benedict Kingsbury & Sally Engle Merry, 'Introduction: Global Governance by Indicators', in Kevin E. Davis et al., *Governance by Indicators* (Oxford University Press, 2012), 8.

[32] Feiring, Thornberry, & Hassler, n. 17, 923.

[33] Michael Jandl, *Towards the Monitoring of Goal 16 of the United Nations' Sustainable Development Goals (SDGs): A Study of the Selection, Rationale and Validity of Indicators with Suggestions for Further Improvements*, UN Sabbatical Leave Research Report, Research Officer Data Development and Dissemination Unit Division for Policy Analysis and Public Affairs, United Nations Office on Drugs and Crime, January 2017, 39.

coincidence that ambition not only declined 'significantly' from the goals to the targets but also dropped from the targets to the indicators.[34] Once in place, there is a tendency for indicators to become targets,[35] by being at the centre of the follow-up since 'what gets measured gets done'.[36] The follow-up process of the SDGs in the annual High-Level Political Forum (HLPF) and elsewhere is built on the indicators and other figures in the SDG reports by the UN Secretary-General as well as in the voluntary national reviews.[37]

Having explained why indicators are particularly relevant for SDG 16, I will now discuss the three sub-goals in turn.

16.3.2 *Promote Peaceful and Inclusive Societies for Sustainable Development*

The aspiration of 'peacefulness' is both important and complex. As will be explained, not only is the reductive elaboration of the goal into indicators and targets problematic but so too is the goal itself. The banner version – which is simply 'peace' – means the absence of violent conflict. Reports by the UN Office of the High Commissioner for Human Rights, the World Bank, and others suggest that development contributes to the prevention of conflict.[38] Conversely, of course, development is very difficult in war.[39] While both observations are correct, the political consequences are controversial. The understanding of 'peaceful' as the 'absence of armed conflict' suggests preventive diplomacy or even military action and, thus, securitizes justice and governance issues and suggests the involvement of international security bodies.[40] Many states were opposed to any explicit inclusion of peace issues in the SDGs because of the fear that it would invite interference.[41] Further, concerns have been raised that SDG targets on conflict and violence could be used to condition aid[42] and/or that official development assistance could include

[34] Gaia Tascioni, 'SDGs and Human Rights: How to Measure States' Compliance?' (2016) 6 *European Journal of Sustainable Development* 140, 146.

[35] Rosga & Satterthwaite, n. 30, 304–5.

[36] *Cf.* Office of the High Commissioner for Human Rights, *Human Rights Indicators: A Guide to Measurement and Implementation*, UN Doc. HR/PUB/12/5, 2012, 1; Davis, Kingsbury, & Merry, n. 31, 16; Bertrand Ramcharan & Robin Ramcharan, *Conflict Prevention in the UN's Agenda 2030: Development, Peace, Justice and Human Rights* (Springer International, 2020), 28–29.

[37] *Transforming Our World*, n. 6, paras. 83–84.

[38] Ramcharan & Ramcharan, n. 36, 18; *Technical Support Team Issues Brief*, n. 13, 227; Kempe, n. 2, 58.

[39] See *Technical Support Team Issues Brief*, n. 13, 226.

[40] Liora Lazarus, 'Doing Violence to the Rule of Law', *Social Sciences Research Network*, 2018, papers.ssrn.com/sol3/papers.cfm?abstract_id=3170649; Ole Waever, 'Securitization and Desecuritization', in Ronnie D. Lipschutz (ed.), *On Security* (Columbia University Press, 1995).

[41] Arajärvi, n. 5.

[42] Jandl, n. 33, 38.

military costs.[43] Consequently, the self-standing term 'peace' appears nowhere in the SDGs or the targets.

At any rate, the elaborated version means the general absence of violence rather than the specific absence of violent conflict.[44] All of the targets implicated by this sub-goal (targets 16.1, 16.2, 16.4, 16.5, 16.a, 16.b) are instrumental, while in particular targets 16.1 and 16.2 also have an intrinsic value.[45] Target 16.1 aims to '[s]ignificantly reduce all forms of violence and related death rates everywhere', and the indicators cover both criminal and belligerent violence. The rate of intentional homicide (indicator 16.1.1) refers to violations of criminal law, while conflict-related deaths (indicator 16.1.2) may be the result of violations of international humanitarian law, and the indicators on subjection to violence (indicator 16.1.3) and feeling of safety (indicator 16.1.4) could relate to both peace and war. Target 16.2 on abuse and exploitation of children is relevant also in war, but, as developed in the indicators, it is generally not connected to warfare as such.[46]

Under international law, these different forms of violence and abuse are regulated by quite different regimes. The right to life in article 6(1) of the 1966 International Covenant on Civil and Political Rights (ICCPR) and other relevant human rights provisions, including in the 1989 UN Convention on the Rights of the Child (UNCRC), means obligations to both respect and protect, while international humanitarian law protects civilians but not combatants, and international criminal law enjoins states to prosecute atrocities.[47] Although the borders between international humanitarian law and international human rights law are less entrenched than just a couple of decades ago, they still exist. Nevertheless, target 16.1 may help us see that violence and insecurity take many forms – from large and small wars to gang wars or sexual violence.[48] At the ground level, violence from different sources may seem to be on a sliding scale of severity or even be indistinguishable rather than be qualitatively different phenomena under different regimes.

43 Ziad Abdel Samad, 'Implementation of SDG 16 Vital for the Middle East and North Africa', in *Spotlights on the SDGs: Report by the Reflection Group on the 2030 Agenda for Sustainable Development*, 2016, 116, www.2030spotlight.org/en/book/605/chapter/spotlight-sustainable-development-2016.

44 As the targets and indicators reveal, the meaning of peaceful is a limited one: 'negative peace'. However, the SDGs as a whole contribute to the broader conception of positive peace.

45 Target 16.5 and target 16.a also contribute to the sub-goal to promote accountable institutions.

46 The indicators 16.2.1–16.2.3 cover some, but not all, forms of abuse, exploitation, or violence: physical punishment and/or psychological aggression by caregivers; victims of human trafficking by sex, age, and form of exploitation; women and men who experienced sexual violence by the age of eighteen. It is covered by various provisions in the UNCRC as well as the 2000 Convention against Transnational Organised Crime (including the 2000 Protocol to Prevent, Suppress and Punish Trafficking in Persons, especially Women and Children, and 2001 Protocol against the Illicit Manufacturing of and Trafficking in Firearms).

47 Target 8.7 lumps together the recruitment and use of child soldiers with other 'worst forms of child labour'. This target clearly bridges the divide between the laws of peace and armed conflict. It is a reference to the ILO's 1999 Convention no. 182 on the Worst Forms of Child Labour.

48 *Technical Support Team Issues Brief*, n. 13, 226.

However, SDG 16 may also be reductive, if not dangerous. First, the targets do not explicitly cover internal state violence.[49] Often, the security sector is a major cause of violent deaths,[50] but a proposed target on accountability for security and justice institutions did not survive the negotiations.[51] Further, target 16.a, on the strengthening of national institutions to prevent violence and combat terrorism and crime,[52] may even be invoked to legitimate such violence since the otherwise common caveat for respect for human rights is not included.[53] (However, perhaps the curiously placed indicator can count as such a caveat: the existence of independent national human rights institutions (NHRIs) in compliance with the 1993 Paris Principles.)[54]

Target 16.4 is also problematic: '[To] significantly reduce illicit financial and arms flows, strengthen the recovery and return of stolen assets and combat all forms of organized crime.' For sure, to reduce arms flows[55] contributes to curbing organized crime,[56] terrorism,[57] and other forms of violence.[58] However, the target also, e contrario, seems to legitimate 'licit' arms flow.[59] The same goes for the target on financial flows, which does not explicitly address the huge net 'licit' flows of capital

[49] The closest one is indicator 16.3.2 on unsentenced detainees.

[50] See Robert Zuber, 'There Can Be No Sustainable Development without Peace and No Peace without Sustainable Development', in *Spotlights on the SDGs: Report by the Reflection Group on the 2030 Agenda for Sustainable Development*, 2016, 120, www.2030spotlight.org/en/book/605/chapter/spotlight-sustainable-development-2016.

[51] There were various arguments for this outcome. See Jandl, n. 33, 31.

[52] Action against terrorism is covered by international agreements as well as international processes to provide technical assistance. See the documents published by the UNSC's Counter-Terrorism Committee, *Legal Issues*, www.un.org/securitycouncil/ctc/content/legal-issues, as well as the global international agreements published by the UN Office of Counter-Terrorism at www.un.org/counterterrorism/international-legal-instruments. On international cooperation against crime including multilateral treaties, see the documents published by the UN Office on Drugs and Terrorism, www.unodc.org/unodc/.

[53] For such routine mementos, see UNSC Resolution 1456, 20 January 2003, Annex, para. 6.

[54] The 1993 Paris Principles are the international minimum standards for effective, credible national human rights institutions. See *Paris Principles*, UN Doc. A/Res/48/134, 20 December 1993.

[55] The two indicators address illicit flows in general and are thus relevant for both crime and armed conflict. The second indicator – indicator 16.4.2 – is the proportion of seized, found, or surrendered arms whose illicit origin or context has been traced or established by a competent authority in line with international instruments. The metadata do not define the international instruments. See Sustainable Development Goals, n. 22. The term could plausibly cover the UN 2013 Arms Trade Treaty and various UNSC arms embargoes.

[56] This is addressed under international law, inter alia, by the 2000 Convention against Transnational Organized Crime. See also Paris Principles, n. 54.

[57] Addressed under international law, inter alia, by the 2000 Convention against Terrorist Financing and a number of UNSC resolutions, most famously UNSC Resolution 1373, 28 September 2001. Paris Principles, n. 54.

[58] The target significantly reduces the ambitions of international law by using the term 'reduce' and by postponing the attainment of the goal until 2030.

[59] *Cf.* Zuber, n. 50, 120. The 2013 Arms Trade Treaty limits such trade.

that travel from the developing to the developed world.[60] This target is the remainder of an earlier draft target to reduce international tax dodging.[61] However, the indicator on the total value of inward and outward illicit financial flows (indicator 16.4.1) may broaden the interpretation of target 16.4 since the metadata[62] includes references to both tax evasion and trade misinvoicing[63] (to the concern of the International Chamber of Commerce).[64]

As mentioned, the second aspect of the first sub-goal – that societies should be inclusive – is linked to all three sub-goals. It could encompass active measures to empower vulnerable groups, but it could also be limited to non-discrimination in a formal sense. Disappointingly, perhaps, target 16.b clarifies that it is the latter sense that prevails: 'Promote and enforce non-discriminatory laws and policies for sustainable development', with its indicator on 'discrimination prohibited under international human rights law'.[65] While this is a great improvement to the silence of the MDGs, it is a passive understanding of inclusion. To some extent, this reductive effect is offset by some other goals and targets, such as SDG 10, Reduced Inequalities.[66] Having said this, target 16.9, which aims to provide legal identity for all, including birth registration,[67] is not only well covered by human rights law[68] but also urgent. In order to access justice or public services or participate in the political process, legal identity is essential.[69] This problem is particularly acute in sub-Saharan Africa, where the births of more than half of all children are not being

[60] UNCTAD, 'Topsy-Turvy World: Net Transfer of Resources from Poor to Rich Countries', Policy Brief no. 78, May 2020. SDG 10, Reduced Inequalities, and SDG 17, Partnerships for the Goals, try to increase inward financial flows to developing countries but do not address the outward flows. Obviously, this is a complex issue.

[61] Thomas Pogge & Mitu Sengupta, 'The Sustainable Development Goals (SDGs) as Drafted: Nice Idea, Poor Execution' (2015) 24 *WILJ* 571, 575.

[62] Indicators are developed in metadata documents, which define the relevant terms, the methodology, and the data sources as well as the responsible agency.

[63] Sustainable Development Goals, n. 22. *Cf.* Global Financial Integrity, *Illicit Financial Flows*, gfintegrity.org/issue/illicit-financial-flows/.

[64] See *ICC Position Paper: Tax and the United Nations Sustainable Development Goals*, iccwbo.org/publication/tax-united-nations-sustainable-development-goals/.

[65] Under this interpretation, the target is well covered by existing prohibitions of discrimination in human rights conventions (see also target 16.7). It is rather curious that the target proscribes discrimination only for sustainable development policies.

[66] See Collins, n. 20. However, target 10.3, to '[e]nsure equal opportunity and reduce inequalities of outcome' is elaborated in the single, reductive indicator: 'Proportion of population reporting having personally felt discriminated against or harassed in the previous 12 months on the basis of a ground of discrimination prohibited under international human rights law.'

[67] It is well reflected in the indicator: '16.9.1: Proportion of children under 5 years of age whose births have been registered with a civil authority, by age.'

[68] The target is covered by international human rights law (UNCRC, art. 7). It is relevant also for other human rights issues, like the right to be recognized as a person. UDHR, art. 6, 10.

[69] *Technical Support Team Issues Brief*, n. 13, 232; *Report of the Special Rapporteur on Extreme Poverty and Human Rights, Philip Alston, Submitted in Accordance with Human Rights Council Resolution* 35/19, Doc. A/74/493, 11 October 2019, 6.

registered.[70] In many cases, lack of legal identity is the result of poverty, but it may also relate politically to citizenship, as is the case for the Rohingya in Myanmar.[71]

The third aspect of the first sub-goal is that societies shall be organized 'for sustainable development', which is partly reflected in target 16.b but in none of the indicators. This fundamental, but vague, aspect of SDG 16 brings to mind article 28 of the 1948 Universal Declaration of Human Rights (UDHR)[72] as well as the controversial 1986 Declaration on the Right to Development.[73]

16.3.3 *Provide Access to Justice for All*

After the deliberations in the UN open-ended working group, 'access to justice' came to replace the 'rule of law', which was demoted to a target.[74] Some states found that the 'rule of law' went beyond the agreed three-tiered definition of sustainable development – economic, social, and environmental[75] – and some feared that it would justify interventions in internal affairs.[76] The sub-goal is reflected in several targets,[77] of which target 16.3 is the most significant one since it contains the rule-of-law formula: '16.3 Promote the rule of law at the national and international levels and ensure equal access to justice.' This ambitious target can be divided into three: national and international rule of law and access to justice. While all three hold promise, the indicators are disappointing. Rule of law at the international level is important for many states. In a thin sense, it means respect for international law, as indicated in the 2012 UN General Assembly's (UNGA) Declaration on the Rule of Law at the National and International Levels (Rule-of-Law Declaration).[78]

70 *Special Edition: Progress towards the Sustainable Development Goals, Report of the Secretary-General*, Doc. E/2019/68, 8 May 2019, para. 37.

71 *Report of the Independent International Fact-finding Mission on Myanmar*, Doc. A/HRC/39/64, 12 September 2018, 6.

72 It calls for a 'social and international order' in which human rights can be realized. UDHR, 71.

73 1986 Declaration on the Right to Development, art. 2(3), which reads: 'States have the right and the duty to formulate appropriate national development policies that aim at the constant improvement of the well-being of the entire population and of all individuals, on the basis of their active, free and meaningful participation in development and in the fair distribution of the benefits resulting therefrom.'

74 Nevertheless, SDG 16 is widely held to be a rule-of-law target. See, e.g., Niko Soininen, 'Torn by (Un)Certainty: Can There Be Peace between Rule of Law and Other Sustainable Development Goals?', in Duncan French & Louis Kotzé, *Sustainable Development Goals* (EE, 2018), 250.

75 Julinda Beqiraj & Lawrence McNamara, 'The Rule of Law and Access to Justice in the Post-2015 Development Agenda: Moving Forward but Stepping Back', Bingham Centre Working Paper no. 2014/04, August 2014, 4.

76 Jandl, n. 33, 38.

77 Target 16.5 (on corruption), target 16.9 (legal identity), target 16.10 (access to information), target 16.b (promote and enforce non-discriminatory laws).

78 *Cf. Declaration on the Rule of Law at the National and International Levels*, UN Doc. A/RES/67/1, 24 September 2012, para. 3 (*Rule-of-Law Declaration*), which paraphrases arts. 1 and 2 of the 1945 Charter of the United Nations.

In a thicker sense, it could mean constitutionalization and judicialization in the international sphere. However, it is addressed by none of the indicators, which confirms the impression that the international order is by and large unaffected by the SDGs (see Section 16.3.4 and Section 16.4).

It is a widespread view that rule of law at the domestic level is critical to sustainable development, as stated in the outcome documents of the 2005 World Summit and 2010 Rio + 20 as well as, of course, in the Rule-of-Law Declaration, which concluded that 'the advancement of the rule of law ... is essential for ... sustainable development'.[79] However, it is also very difficult to attain. There are different conceptions of the rule of law.[80] Arguably, the most authoritative formula is that of the Rule-of-Law Declaration, which is a principle of governance whereby 'all persons, institutions and entities, public and private, including the State itself, are accountable to just, fair and equitable laws and are entitled without any discrimination to equal protection of the law'.[81] The UN Secretary-General's 2004 report on the rule of law and transitional justice has a thicker definition, which includes international human rights norms, supremacy of law, separation of powers, participation in decision-making, and procedural and legal transparency.[82] Different conceptions of the rule of law can serve different political purposes and thus have different connotations. For some, it is necessary for the empowerment of the poor,[83] and, for others, it is a means to an improved market economy.[84] Hence, calls for the rule of law invite different conversations about constitutions, human rights, markets, and the poor.[85]

Rule-of-law obligations may flow not only from human rights law but also from a number of sectorial obligations of states – for instance, to combat transnational crime or to ensure 'fair and equitable treatment' for investors. However, while access-to-justice aspects are represented by indicators 16.3.1–16.3.3, no indicator addresses constitutional aspects like the supremacy of the law.[86] Access to justice

[79] *Technical Support Team Issues Brief*, n. 13, 229; see also *World Summit Outcome*, n. 12, paras. 119, 134; *Keeping the Promise: United to Achieve the Millennium Development Goals*, UN Doc. A/RES/65/1, 19 October, 2010, para. 11; *Future We Want*, n. 13, paras. 8, 10; *Rule-of-Law Declaration*, n. 78, para. 7.

[80] Beqiraj & McNamara, n. 75, 5.

[81] *Rule-of-Law Declaration*, n. 78, para 2.

[82] *The Rule of Law and Transitional Justice in Conflict and Post-conflict Societies*, UN Doc. S/2004/616, 23 August 2004.

[83] Rosie Wagner, *The Rule of Law and the Post-2015 Development Agenda*, 26 March 2013, 9; Alvaro Santos, 'The World Bank's Uses of the "Rule of Law" Promise in Economic Development', in David M Trubek & Alvaro Santos (eds.), *The New Law and Economic Development* (Cambridge University Press, 2006).

[84] Terry Miller & Brett Schaefer, 'UN Repeating Past Mistakes in New Sustainable Development Goals', *Heritage Foundation*, 23 July 2014, www.heritage.org/report/un-repeating-past-mistakes-new-sustainable-development-goals.

[85] *Cf.* Kennedy, n. 11, 158–63.

[86] See, e.g., European Commission for Democracy through Law, *Rule of Law Checklist*, Council of Europe Doc. CDL-AD(2016)007, 11–12 March 2016, 11.

is guaranteed in global and regional human rights conventions[87] and, for environmental issues, in the 1998 Aarhus Convention on Access to Information, Public Participation in Decision-Making and Access to Justice in Environmental Matters (Aarhus Convention) and in the 2018 Regional Agreement on Access to Information, Public Participation and Justice in Environmental Matters in Latin America and the Caribbean (Escazú Agreement). However, many justice gaps are not ensured by international human rights guarantees and mechanisms: it is often difficult practically for private subjects to hold their own or foreign states to account in domestic or international procedures,[88] with the partial exception of investors that can frequently resort to arbitration (investor-state dispute settlement [ISDS]).[89] Further, it is often difficult to hold foreign corporations accountable,[90] although some businesses have introduced corporate 'grievance mechanisms'.

The first two indicators of target 16.3 cover criminal procedure aspects of access to justice: indicator 16.3.1 reflects the population's confidence in effective access to criminal justice.[91] Indicator 16.3.2 refers to the prohibition of arbitrary detention, addressing the situation when an individual needs access to justice against public authorities.[92] Lastly, indicator 16.3.3 addresses access to justice for civil (private) law matters and could be interpreted to address some of the gaps outlined above.[93]

The placement of the call to protect 'fundamental freedoms' in target 16.10 is curious, but its potential nevertheless warrants a brief discussion. The term appears in the title of the 1950 European Convention on Human Rights and Fundamental

87 See, e.g., UDHR, art. 10; ICCPR, art. 14(1).

88 Under international law, the better view is that civil rights obligations apply extraterritorially. See, e.g., Human Rights Committee, *General Comment 31: Nature of the General Legal Obligation on States Parties to the Covenant*, UN Doc. CCPR/C/21/Rev.1/Add.13, 2004, paras. 3, 6, 10. It is more controversial whether this applies also to economic, social, and cultural rights. Olivier de Schutter, *Interim Report of the Special Rapporteur on the Right to Food*, Doc. A /68/ 288, 2013, 9.

89 The practice of concluding investment treaties, which is implicitly supported by target 17.5, may conflict with other goals, depending on the content of the treaty.

90 Two common problems are *forum non-conveniens* and the corporate veil. Part III of the 2011 UN Guiding Principles on Business and Human Rights mention (in a neutral tone) the option of extraterritorial protection against abuses by businesses, and also recommends that businesses provide 'grievance mechanisms'. The principles are annexed to the final report to the Human Rights Council by the Special Representative of the Secretary-General. *Final Report on the Issue of Human Rights and Transnational Corporations and Other Business Enterprises*, Doc. A/HRC/17/31, 16 June 2011 (and referenced in *Transforming Our World*, n. 6, para. 67).

91 Proportion of victims of violence who reported their victimization. This also relates to the state's obligation to protect the right to life and so on. See also 1985 Declaration of Basic Principles of Justice for Victims of Crime and Abuse of Power.

92 Addressed in ICCPR, art. 10.

93 Proportion of those who experienced a legal problem in the last two years who could access appropriate information or expert help and were able to resolve the problem. This indicator was apparently added only in 2019. *Report of the Inter-Agency and Expert Group on Sustainable Development Goal Indicators*, UN Doc. E/CN.3/2020/2, 20 December 2019.

Freedoms, in the preamble of the UDHR, and in the constitutions of some countries.[94] In some conceptions, it refers to freedom from interference, such as freedom of speech and freedom of assembly. But the term has also been interpreted broadly to include the freedoms from want and fear, as proclaimed in President Franklin D. Roosevelt's famous 1941 State of the Union address and invoked by the UN Secretary-General.[95] This interpretation points towards the maintenance of international peace and security as well as economic, social, and cultural rights, and it suggests an undertaking, for instance, to protect against land grabs. As pointed out below, however, the indicator (on journalists and advocates) significantly narrows down the scope of this target.

16.3.4 *Build Effective, Accountable, and Inclusive Institutions at All Levels*

As already indicated, institutions have a necessary role for all SDGs – not least, to coordinate and prioritize the many synergies and trade-offs between different goals and targets,[96] as will be discussed in Section 16.4. Many commentators take SDG 16 – in particular, the part on institutions – to be a governance goal.[97] The term 'good governance' was introduced into development policy by the World Bank in 1989. Governance has been defined by the World Bank as 'the way power is exercised in the management of a country's economic and social resources for development'.[98] Broader definitions cover 'the purposeful and authoritative steering of societal processes by political actors',[99] which under some views extends into the private sphere.[100]

In policy circles, it is a widely held truism that good governance is key to sustainable development.[101] For the World Bank, 'good governance' comprises 'public services that are efficient, a judicial system that is reliable, and an

[94] *Rights of Individuals: Civil and Political, Human and Constitutional Rights Resource Page*, www.hrcr.org/chart/civil+political/freedoms.html.

[95] *Strengthening and Coordinating United Nations Rule of Law Activities*, n. 12.

[96] Independent Group of Scientists appointed by the Secretary-General, *Global Sustainable Development Report 2019: The Future Is Now – Science for Achieving Sustainable Development* (United Nations, 2019), 28; Viktoria Spaiser et al., 'The Sustainable Development Oxymoron: Quantifying and Modelling the Incompatibility of Sustainable Development Goals' (2017) 24 *International Journal of Sustainable Development and World Ecology* 1.

[97] Frank Biermann et al., 'Global Goal Setting for Improving National Governance and Policy', in Kanie & Biermann, n. 26, 79.

[98] World Bank, *Managing Development: The Governance Dimension A Discussion Paper*, 29 August 1991, i, documents1.worldbank.org/curated/en/884111468134710535/pdf/34899.pdf.

[99] Biermann et al., n. 97, 75.

[100] Blind, n. 3, 3.

[101] Niheer Dasandi, David Hudson & Tom Pegram, 'Report of the Inter-Agency and Expert Group on Sustainable Development Goal Indicators', in Jeff Waage & Chris Yap, *Thinking beyond Sectors for Sustainable Development* (Ubiquity Press, 2015), 67; Biermann et al., n. 97, 77.

administration that is accountable to the public'.[102] Hence, it is related to the rule of law but is wider. As pointed out by Frank Biermann and others, however, there has been less focus on equitableness, including distribution,[103] and little focus on its democratic (or not) forms. Good governance has been a basis for conditionality by the international financial institutions (IFIs).[104] Thus, good governance is controversial both because of the outcomes it has rendered and because of its potentially interventionist effects. Like the rule of law, it can mean different things to different people – from cost-cutting to human rights–based rule of law.[105] While the content of 'good' may be suggested in other SDGs, SDG 16 refers to the less charged and perhaps more precise and formal concept of institutions.

The adjectives 'effective, accountable and inclusive' provide some hope. Effectiveness is necessary; accountability can be interpreted to have constitutional and democratic implications; and inclusivity can be a call for participation. Likewise, there is potential for SDG 16 to contribute to an opening up also of global governance institutions. Nevertheless, as a closer look will bear out, those who hold such hopes will be disappointed by the targets and indicators, particularly by targets 16.5, 16.6, 16.7, 16.10, and 16.b.[106]

The target to substantially reduce corruption and bribery in all their forms (target 16.5) affects people's everyday lives, but it is also instrumental since corruption corrodes institutions. Corruption is addressed by the 2003 UN Convention against Corruption and a number of regional conventions. The indicators for corruption (indicators 16.5.1–16.5.2) are rather restrictive, however, and suggest that the problems can be found in the public sector rather than at the political level or in the private sector.[107]

Target 16.6 enjoins states to '[d]evelop effective, accountable and transparent institutions at all levels'. The indicators measure mainly effectiveness (reliability of government budgets [indicator 16.6.1] and the satisfaction with public service [indicator 16.6.2]), while neither accountability nor transparency is measured. However,

[102] Blind, n. 3, 3.
[103] Biermann et al., n. 97, 76. Equity is mentioned in SDG 4, Quality Education, and in eight targets, however.
[104] *Id.*, 76.
[105] Blind, n. 3, 3–4; Jolle Demmers, *Good Governance in the Era of Global Neoliberalism: Conflict and Depolitization in Latin America, Eastern Europe, Asia and Africa* (Routledge, 2004). For a broad conception, see Rumu Sarkar, *International Development Law: Rule of Law, Human Rights and Global Finance*, 2nd ed. (Springer International, 2020), 176–88.
[106] Blind, n. 3, 4.
[107] Indicators 16.5.1 and 16.5.2 are the proportion of persons or businesses who paid or were asked to pay a bribe to a public official, which will be measured through surveys of firms. This metadata clearly assumes that corruption is driven by members of the public sector rather than the private sector. The 2005 UN Convention against Corruption, arts. 15–27, in contrast, applies in both the private and the public sector and at all levels.

transparency[108] is also promoted by target 16.10: 'Ensure public access to information ... in accordance with national legislation and international agreements.'[109] Public access to information is protected by international law in fairly general terms, through article 19 of the UDHR and the ICCPR as well as in international environmental law under the Aarhus Convention, the Escazú Agreement, and the 1991 Convention on Environmental Impact Assessment in a Transboundary Context.[110] Indicator 16.10.2 on 'constitutional, statutory and/or policy guarantees for public access to information' is adequate, although it is not clear if it applies to private entities with public functions. Indicator 16.10.1 has a more limited scope but highlights the importance of media and advocates.[111]

Target 16.6 can also be supported by the promising target 16.7: 'Ensure responsive, inclusive, participatory and representative decision-making at all levels.' Article 21 of the UDHR and article 25 of the ICCPR recognize the right 'to take part in the conduct of public affairs, directly or through freely chosen representatives'. Disappointingly, this is not measured in any of the indicators, which only focus on the distribution of positions in institutions between certain categories of people (indicator 16.7.1) and the population's perception of inclusiveness (indicator 16.7.2).[112]

In addition to the domestic level, this sub-goal, like target 16.6 and target 16.7, also addresses the international level: as in the rule of law, the debate was about whether the efforts should focus on the domestic or the international level or on both, which partly reflects the difference of opinion regarding the main causes of underdevelopment. If underdevelopment is caused, to a significant degree, by external factors – like exploitation, structural inequalities, the way in which the commodity markets work, or the lending policies of IFIs – then the remedies must obviously target international institutions.[113]

[108] On the importance of transparency, see Independent Group of Scientists, n. 96, 34; *Special Edition: Progress towards the Sustainable Development Goals*, n. 70, para. 84.

[109] I have already discussed fundamental freedom, which is the other part of target 16.10. The better interpretation of the proviso 'in accordance with national legislation and international agreements' is that state organs should live up to both international law and national legislation, which is an aspect the rule of law. See also Knox, n. 17, 527.

[110] See also 1992 Rio Declaration on Environment and Development, Principle 10, annexed to UN Doc. A/CONF.151/26, 12 August 1992.

[111] 'Number of killings and other attacks on media personnel, trade unionists and human rights advocates.' This relates, inter alia, to freedom of speech and to the state's obligation to protect the right to life and the freedom from torture. See ICCPR, arts. 6, 7, 19.

[112] Target 16.7.1 (proportions of positions in national and local institutions, including (1) the legislatures; (2) the public service; and (3) the judiciary, compared to national distributions, by sex, age, persons with disabilities, and population groups); target 16.7.2 (proportion of population who believe decision-making is inclusive and responsive, by sex, age, disability, and population group). This closed list does not include, for instance, sexual orientation or social group.

[113] Peters, n. 25, 45 (and sources referred therein); Jason Hickel, *The Divide: A Brief Guide to Global Inequality and Its Solutions* (William Heinemann, 2017).

Decision-making in international organizations is regulated by their charters, which are all different. As for accountability, formal international organizations are legal subjects and, hence, responsible in principle, but it is often not clear which rules they are bound by, and there is usually no legal forum with jurisdiction.[114] Further, they are generally immune under domestic law.[115] Hence, it is very difficult for states, individuals, private entities, and communities to hold international organizations legally accountable.

The only target that addresses the international level with any precision is target 16.8: 'Broaden and strengthen the participation of developing countries in the institutions of global governance.' This is pertinent; even though no country is bound by agreements to which it has not consented, in reality, a state that wants to participate in the global economy will have to accept a number of norms that have been established without its effective participation – for instance, in the Group of Twenty (G20). However, the sole indicator limits the scope: 'Proportion of members and voting rights of developing countries in international organizations.' Though relevant as such, this target is both unrealistic and insufficient. It is very unlikely that standard-setting bodies like the Basel Committee on Banking Supervision or the Organisation for Economic Co-operation and Development (OECD) would open their doors to many developing countries and equally unlikely that the voting rules of the World Bank or the International Monetary Fund (IMF) would change dramatically. In any event, developing countries often lack both the capacity and the clout to pursue their interests in such organizations.

As argued by Livingstone Sewanyana, the right for individuals to participate in decision-making may extend to international institutions.[116] Participation can take place through national governments or through civil society organization (CSOs). In formal international organizations, like the World Bank and the IMF, CSOs often have good access, though it is often 'tokenistic'.[117] By contrast, in the proliferating 'global governance spaces' outside the UN system, access is often problematic. The G20 and the informal group made up of Brazil, Russia, India, China, and South Africa, known as BRICS, for instance, favour the business sector over CSOs. Lastly, one must note that none of the targets or indicators suggests that 'institution' includes private corporations. To summarize, with the exception of the cautious

[114] Jan Klabbers, *An Introduction to International Institutional Law*, 2nd ed. (Cambridge University Press, 2009), 131–52.

[115] *Id.*, 292. A rare exception is constituted by *Jam et al. v International Finance Corporation*, which was brought by a group of Indian farmers and fishermen adversely affected by an investment by the International Finance Corporation. *Jam et al v International Finance Corporation*, 586 U.S. ___ (2019), www.supremecourt.gov/opinions/18pdf/17-1011_mkhn.pdf.

[116] Livingstone Sewanyana, *Report of the Independent Expert on the Promotion of a Democratic and Equitable International Order*, Doc. A/HRC/42/48, 30 July 2019, para. 27. See also the Human Rights Committee, *General Comment 25: The Right to Participate in Public Affairs, Voting Rights and the Right of Equal Access to Public Service Adopted*, Doc. 2 CCPR/C/21/Rev.1/Add.7, 1996, para. 5.

[117] Sewanyana, n. 116, paras. 39, 42, 44, 75–76.

target 16.8, the indicators for targets 16.6, 16.7, 16.10, and 16.a only address domestic public institutions, which strongly suggests the view that development shall be primarily enabled by changes in domestic, public institutions.

16.4 POSITIONING SDG 16 IN THE INTERNATIONAL INSTITUTIONAL CONTEXT

16.4.1 *A Fragmented Structure Favours the Powerful*

This section will discuss the fairly fragmented institutional setting of SDG 16, which is related to the international side of the third sub-goal – 'to build effective, accountable and inclusive institutions at all levels'. I will focus on some of those institutions that are most relevant for the SDGs. Since the different sub-goals and targets of SDG 16 are handled to a large extent by the same institutions (within and outside the UN system), I will not follow the outline of the preceding two sections and, instead, first present the fragmented system and thereafter discuss the weak institutions for coordination.

The 2019 *Global Sustainable Development Report* emphasized synergies, trade-offs, and unintended consequences,[118] while target 17.14 called for enhanced policy coherence. This is a matter not only of effectiveness but also of values and equity. Needless to say, whether coherence is good or not depends on whether the policies are good or bad (and for whom) – that is, how values and interests are balanced and integrated.[119] In his special SDG report in 2019, the UN Secretary-General called for 'fair globalization' and pointed out the 'need to promote an equitable distribution of development opportunities and income at the international level'.[120]

At the ground level, it is the responsibility of each state to coordinate and implement the SDGs. Target 17.15 rightly provides for respect for each country's policy space. How that policy space will be exercised depends of course on its own governance as well as on how it is affected by international norms and institutions.[121]

At the international level, the picture is fragmented: for the goal of promoting peaceful societies, all bodies that deal with peace and conflict are relevant, including the UN Security Council (UNSC) and numerous regional bodies, such as the Organization for Security and Co-operation in Europe and the African Union. The many human rights implications of the SDGs are anchored in the global and

[118] Independent Group of Scientists, n. 96, 4ff. Kim offers the following example: the goal of feeding everyone (Goal 2) may call for greater use of fertilizers, which jeopardizes SDG 14, Life below Water, and SDG 15, Life on Land. Rakhyun E. Kim, 'The Nexus between International Law and the Sustainable Development Goals' (2016) 25 *Review of European, Comparative and International Environmental Law* 15, 17.

[119] *Cf.* Kanie et al., n. 26, 13

[120] *Special Edition: Progress towards the Sustainable Development Goals*, n. 70, para. 97.

[121] *Cf.* Anne Orford, 'Food Security, Free Trade, and the Battle for the State' (2015) 11 *Journal of International Law and International Relations* 1.

regional human rights bodies (the UN Human Rights Council, the human rights treaty bodies, and the European, inter-American, and African courts of human rights). Some of the other international organizations involved in the SDGs have human rights among their tasks, including the International Labour Organization (ILO) and the World Health Organization, while others, such as the World Bank, deal with human rights only very reluctantly[122] and yet others, like the World Trade Organization (WTO), have no noticeable human rights perspective.[123] Environmental bodies are also essential, from the UN Environmental Programme (UNEP) to the many secretariats of multilateral environmental agreements, some of them managed by UNEP or by regional bodies.

Given the fundamental importance of the economy, the WTO, the IFIs, and UN organs like the UN Development Programme and the UN Conference on Trade and Development are crucial. As mentioned, many states are greatly affected by bodies of which they are not even members, like the OECD, the European Union (EU), the Basel Committee on Banking Supervision, the Paris Club for debt restructuring, the Group of Seven/Group of Eight, the G20, and so on.[124] Further, today, much regulation takes place in ambitious regional free-trade agreements and other arrangements, which are open by invitation only and with limited influence from small states.[125]

While targets 16.6–16.8 address international institutions in general (though timidly), a number of targets of other goals explicitly point to concerns in the economic and financial institutions. Five targets directly address the WTO,[126] while target 10.6 speaks about 'enhanced representation and voice . . . in global international economic and financial institutions' and target 17.13 is looking for 'policy coordination and policy coherence'. While these targets can be interpreted to address the above-mentioned concerns, their indicators do not.[127] Perhaps even more importantly, multinational enterprises (MNEs), empowered by globalization, can exercise the power of 'exit' in a way that often marginalizes the citizenry's power of vote, and states have still not agreed to enforce human rights standards on corporations. Many MNEs can avoid taxes or play out states and suppliers against each other in a race to the bottom. A number of UN special procedures mandate holders have highlighted

[122] As the Special Rapporteur on Extreme Poverty and Human Rights, Philip Alston, noted in a 2015 report: 'For most purposes, the World Bank is a human rights-free zone.' *Report of the Special Rapporteur*, n. 69, 20.

[123] All international organizations are in principle obliged to respect at least most human rights, which constitute customary law, but, for the most part, their statutes do not include human rights among the purposes of the organizations, and they are not parties to human rights conventions.

[124] The G20 often discusses Agenda 2030. Sewanyana, n. 116, para. 17.

[125] *Cf.* Bernd G. Janzen & Emily S. Fuller, 'Assessing the UN Sustainable Development Goals through the Lens of International Trade Law' (2015) 44(1) *International Law News* 23, 23.

[126] See targets 2.b, 3.b, 10.a, 17.10, 17.12

[127] Indicator 10.6.1 is an exception.

the risks that investment agreements and ISDS pose to the regulatory space that states need for human rights and the SDGs.[128] Yet the power of MNEs is addressed in none of the SDGs.[129]

16.4.2 *Arbiters and Coordinators Are Weak*

Different legal orders and different organs favour different actors and interests. When rules and policies contradict one another – as is inevitable – an arbiter and a coordinator is needed. As for legal obligations, different bodies guard different regimes (and interests); existing international courts and supervisory bodies generally have jurisdiction only over certain issues or regions but not over the whole. Therefore, when different considerations go against each other – such as investment protection and social rights – the strongest process wins. For investments, there are often strong investor-state mechanisms, and, in the WTO's dispute settlement system, the large economies (but not the small ones) can effectively use sanctions against violators.[130] The IFIs can, through their loan and assistance conditions, ensure that their recommendations (conditionality) are complied with. By contrast, for international environmental law, international humanitarian law, and international human rights law (including international labour law), the existing dispute resolution and monitoring mechanisms are significantly weaker, if not toothless.[131] The most global legal body – the International Court of Justice – has jurisdiction only over states and only by consent.

As for policy, the UN Secretary-General hopes that '[t]he fragmented nature of today's multilateralism must evolve into a networked multilateralism, with the United Nations at the core'.[132] The UNGA has tasked the HLPF to '[e]nhance integration of the three dimensions of sustainable development in a holistic and cross-sectoral manner at all levels'.[133] Kenneth W. Abbott and Steven Bernstein

[128] *Letter from Mandates of the Working Group on the Issue of Human Rights and Transnational Corporations and Other Business Enterprises; the Special Rapporteur on the Right to Development; the Special Rapporteur on the Issue of Human Rights Obligations Relating to the Enjoyment of a Safe, Clean, Healthy, and Sustainable Environment; the Independent Expert on the Effects of Foreign Debt and Other Related International Financial Obligations of States on the Full Enjoyment of all Human Rights, Particularly Economic, Social, and Cultural Rights; the Special Rapporteur on the Rights of Indigenous Peoples; The Independent Expert on the Promotion of a Democratic and Equitable International Order; and the Special Rapporteur on the Human Rights to Safe Drinking Water and Sanitation*, Doc. OL ARM 1/2019, 7 March 2019, 2, www.ohchr.org/Documents/Issues/Development/IEDebt/OL_ARM_07.03.19_1.2019.pdf.

[129] *Technical Support Team Issues Brief*, n. 13, 144

[130] Only the winning party in a dispute can impose sanctions. When Antigua and Barbuda won a case against the United States, it was impossible to make the United States abide by the ruling.

[131] With the exception of the European Court of Human Rights, the existing human rights institutions are weak.

[132] *Special Edition: Progress towards the Sustainable Development Goals*, n. 70, para. 97.

[133] *Future We Want*, n. 13, para. 84.

think of the HLPF as an 'orchestrator' in 'indirect, soft governance',[134] which enlists intermediary actors to govern 'in line with the orchestrator's goals'.[135] Whether the HLPF will be successful depends on the extent to which it can make others act 'altruistically and cooperatively towards the mutually beneficial goal of sustainable development'.[136]

For sure, the SDG process 'multilateralizes' and broadens previously bilateral donor-recipient discussions.[137] However, while the HLPF has become a 'go-to forum' regarding the SDGs, it is a weak forum, and the same goes for the UNGA. The economic fora have been insulated from the United Nations,[138] and strong states do not allow discussions in the HLPF about the global economic order. For example, the United States holds that discussions in the HLPF should not affect negotiations in the WTO,[139] and the EU has adopted the common position that debt restructuring should not be debated at the UNGA.[140] When some of the most important economic issues cannot be discussed effectively in the HLPF or even in its 'mother institution', the UNGA, it is difficult to see the HLPF becoming an effective orchestrator. Hence, the global political and legal structure remains fragmented, dysfunctional, and unbalanced. There is no international body with the power to weigh human rights, development, environment, and so on, and there is little that SDG 16, with its tepid targets, can do about that.

16.5 CONCLUSIONS

SDG 16 is the most legal goal, potentially implicating basic features of international law like sovereignty, human rights, and the regulation of the global economy. For the same reasons, it is also the most political goal. For those who want to reform international society, SDG 16 looks promising. The clustering of issues may incentivize us to rethink conceptual borders, like domestic/international or peace/war. Further, those worthwhile rights that are covered may benefit from the added

[134] Kenneth W. Abbott & Steven Bernstein, 'The High-Level Political Forum on Sustainable Development: Orchestration by Default and Design' (2015) 6 *Global Policy* 222, 223.

[135] *Id.*, 224.

[136] Kim, n. 118, 19.

[137] Barbara Adams, 'Democratic Global Governance: If It Doesn't Challenge Power It Isn't Democratic', in Barbara Adams et al. (eds.), *Spotlight on Sustainable Development 2019: Reshaping Governance for Sustainability: Global Civil Society Report on the 2030 Agenda and the SDGs* (Social Watch et al, 2019), 35, 35.

[138] *Id.*, 42.

[139] United States Mission to the United Nations, *Explanation of Vote on a High-Level Statement at the High-Level Political Forum on Sustainable Development, Jason Lawrence Adviser for Economic and Social Affairs U.S. Mission to the United Nations New York City*, 19 July 2018.

[140] *Draft EU Common Position on the UN Draft Resolution A/69/L.84 on Basic Principles on Sovereign Debt Restructuring Processes*, Doc. ECOFIN 688 UEM 342 ONU, 7 September 2015, 106. The European Union will cease participation in these discussions unless they reflect work undertaken by the International Monetary Fund and the Paris Club.

attention and resources of the development sector. Disappointingly, however, the operational targets and indicators often reduce the goal itself, sometimes beyond recognition, and there are some risks that existing obligations will be watered down in the follow-up actions.

On the whole, SDG 16 leaves the fragmented and inequitable global political and legal order as it is. There is some, but not strong, support for civil and political rights, no provision for access to justice beyond the domestic sphere, and the kind of participation in governance envisioned by SDG 16 is not even a thin, formal version of democracy. SDG 16 (very expectedly) also accepts the institutions of the sovereign state as they are and does not really challenge the power of governments. Like the other SDGs, SDG 16 intends to soften economic globalization and take advantage of its positive effects, but it takes the basic features of the global economy, including the power of gigantic global corporations, as a given. Further, even though the SDGs call for some change in the WTO and the IFIs, SDG 16, by and large, accepts the role and setup of existing international institutions. Nevertheless, SDG 16 – like the other SDGs – has a rhetorical potential beyond its nitty-gritty content. While the SDGs are not a blueprint and even less a ready-made vehicle for a new world order of equitable sustainable development, their malleability makes it possible to give them meaning beyond what the states intended. Legal documents will be interpreted in accordance with established canons, but a political text is in the hands of its reader.

17

SDG 17: Strengthen the Means of Implementation and Revitalize the Global Partnership for Sustainable Development

Duncan French and Louis J. Kotzé

ABSTRACT

There are two elements to Sustainable Development Goal (SDG) 17, Partnerships for the Goals: (1) efforts to improve the implementation of Agenda 2030 and (2) efforts to improve collective action globally in pursuit of sustainable development as envisaged by the SDGs. If taken as distinct components, the first phrase might suggest itself as relating to the implementation of the other sixteen SDGs – or perhaps sustainable development as a more generic objective (as broadly expressed by Agenda 2030) – whereas the latter phrase might indicate the re-energizing of a more substantive, and perhaps overarching, architecture of global collaboration. As this chapter will explore, SDG 17 is paradoxical in several important respects and, to the extent that it underpins the SDG agenda more broadly, is emblematic of the tensions at the heart of the SDGs, especially with respect to the normative context in which the SDGs are situated. For SDG 17, that context – and its situation therein – is particularly contested and contestable. Moreover, a focus on trade, investment, and voluntarism excludes and omits other important building blocks of human rights, rule of law, and civil society engagement.

KEYWORDS

SDG 17, means of implementation, global partnership, international cooperation, solidarity, international trade, governance through goals, international law

17.1 INTRODUCTION

The purpose of this chapter is to analyze Sustainable Development Goal (SDG) 17, Partnerships for the Goals – the final SDG – which concerns itself with the 'means of implementation' and 'revitaliz[ing] the global partnership for sustainable development'. As the last of the seventeen SDGs, and unlike the others, SDG 17 is generally considered to be an 'overarching goal' of a generic nature,[1] which sets out the general means towards specific ends – namely, to mobilize collective global actions to implement and revitalize the global partnership for sustainable development[2] or, alternatively phrased, to promote partnerships and collaborative governance with the view to achieving all other sixteen SDGs within the context of sustainable development.[3] Practically speaking, this approach implies that realizing SDG 17 would possibly require linking it back to the other sixteen SDGs, their objectives, and their targets. Therefore, while SDG 17 is a stand-alone goal, more than any other SDG, it is central to the success of the entire Agenda 2030.[4] To this end, SDG 17 is clear that 'without a serious partnership made up of a continuous dialogue and thorough negotiations, the SDGs will largely remain on paper. A global partnership is the only possible and realistic road ahead for the SDG agenda'.[5] Supporters of SDG 17 would thus seek to argue that it brings to life the necessity of the broader framework that is vital to allow the other SDGs to succeed. Some might go further and note that SDG 17 is also a rather stark reminder that, within the highly politicized global context of the SDGs, 'means are more important than ends'.[6]

Following this line of argumentation, SDG 17, perhaps even more so than any of the other SDGs, embodies the essence of 'global governance by goal-setting'.[7] This is a novel type of governance approach that is grounded in, yet detached from, international law; it is achieved through weak, as opposed to complex, top-down institutional arrangements operating at the intergovernmental level that seek to facilitate 'bottom-up, non-confrontational, country-driven, and stakeholder-oriented aspects of governance'; it is an approach that more fully embraces 'global inclusion and comprehensiveness' to improve representation, legitimacy, and democracy; and, ultimately, it leaves considerable leeway and freedom for stakeholders

1 Jeff Waage et al., 'The Millennium Development Goals: A Cross-sectoral Analysis and Principles for Goal Setting after 2015' (2010) 376 *Lancet* 991.

2 Nathan Cooper & Duncan French, 'SDG 17: Partnerships for the Goals: Cooperation within the Context of a Voluntarist Framework', in Duncan French & Louis J. Kotzé (eds.), *Sustainable Development Goals: Law, Theory and Implementation* (EE, 2018), 271.

3 See, e.g., Adriane MacDonald et al., 'Multi-stakeholder Partnerships (SDG #17) as a Means of Achieving Sustainable Communities and Cities (SDG #11)', in Walter Filho (ed.), *Handbook of Sustainability Science and Research* (Springer, 2018), 193.

4 *Transforming Our World: The 2030 Agenda for Sustainable Development*, UN Doc. A/Res/70/1, 25 September 2015.

5 Gianni Vaggi, *Development: The Re-balancing of Economic Powers* (Palgrave Macmillan, 2018), 129.

6 *Id.*

7 Frank Biermann, Norichika Kanie, & Rakhyun Kim, 'Global Governance by Goal-setting: The Novel Approach of the UN Sustainable Development Goals' (2017) 26–27 *Current Opinion in Environmental Sustainability* 26.

'to determine their own ambition and pathways to implement the goals'.[8] The unique nature and purpose of a 'governing-through-goals' approach is therefore very much compatible with, receptive of, and responsive to innovative global partnerships that are primarily embedded in interstate partnerships. Such an approach opens up the possibility of going well beyond the traditional interstate architecture and its international law paradigm to more fully embrace, and to benefit from, polycentric global governance and the multitude of stakeholders that such a plural constellation would imply.[9]

Before progressing on to the content of SDG 17, and to help reflect on its likely achievements, purpose, and broader context, this chapter finds the metaphor of archaeology – if not the method – discussed by Hilary Charlesworth and Christine Chinkin in their seminal work *The Boundaries of International Law: A Feminist Perspective* to be informative.[10] To quote Charlesworth and Chinkin, 'like archaeologists digging down into an ancient site',[11] the layers of SDG 17 need to be carefully stripped away.[12] At the most superficial level, one might query the text of SDG 17, why the specific targets (and indicators) have been selected and framed as they have. At the next level, one might ask what is missing and omitted. A third layer might be to seek to understand how SDG 17 relates to the other SDGs, while a fourth considers the links between SDG 17 and international law (both soft and hard) in this area: trade, investment, environment, development, and human rights. Similarly, and almost in a parallel track, one might consider the contribution of SDG 17 to global objectives and national priorities. For example, how will SDG 17 contribute to the achievement of the SDGs overall or to sustainable development more generally at a city, national, regional, and international level? At a deeper level, one might question whether SDG 17 will support – or frustrate – the objectives of the other SDGs (without querying the value of these other goals). At a deeper

[8] *Id.*, 26–27.

[9] For a general overview of polycentric governance, see Paul Aligica & Vlad Tarko 'Polycentricity: From Polanyi to Ostrom, and Beyond' (2012) 25(2) *Governance: An International Journal of Policy, Administration, and Institutions* 237.

[10] Hilary Charlesworth & Christine Chinkin, *The Boundaries of International Law: A Feminist Analysis* (Manchester University Press, 2000).

[11] *Id.*, 18. This is not to suggest that feminist analysis is the only lens by which to critically unpick the SDGs or, in the alternative, that feminist analysis has the least to say on the subject – in fact, there are very strong grounds for utilizing feminist insights into analyzing the SDGs – but, rather, that the metaphor of archaeology seems highly apt on an issue as contestable and multilayered as SDG 17. See, e.g., Jane Briant Carant, 'Unheard Voices: A Critical Discourse Analysis of the Millennium Development Goals' Evolution into the Sustainable Development Goals' (2017) 38(1) *Third World Quarterly* 16; Christiane Struckmann, 'A Postcolonial Feminist Critique of the 2030 Agenda for Sustainable Development: A South African Application' (2018) 32(1) *Agenda* 12.

[12] Several studies are underway to determine the achievements of the SDGs to date, including, for example, Frank Biermann, Thomas Hickmann & Carole-Anne Sénit (eds.), The Political Impact of the Sustainable Development Goals: Transforming Governance Through Global Goals? (Cambridge University Press, 2022).

level still, one might question the focus, purpose, and drive of the entire SDG endeavour. And, of particular interest and at its deepest level perhaps, whether the paradox at the heart of the SDGs – that humans and the more-than-human world can co-exist harmoniously – is truly achievable in light of the imperatives of human development as we seem to understand it at present and as these imperatives seem to be embodied in the SDGs. As we note, we find this metaphor appealing because we recognize that SDG 17 does require a slightly distinctive approach – which is different from the analysis in other chapters in this collection on the other SDGs – whereby we look at the deeper archaeology, first, of the nature of global partnership (in Section 17.2) and, then, to the more textual (including omissions) aspects of the SDG as we progress through the chapter. We do not seek to slavishly employ it throughout the chapter, as to do so would be constraining and artificial, but we invite the readers to use it themselves when reflecting on SDG 17 and, indeed, on all the other SDGs.

17.2 THE CONTENT OF SDG 17 IN THE CONTEXT OF THE OTHER SDGS

17.2.1 *SDG 17 and the Contested Nature of Global Partnership*

There are two clear, basic elements to SDG 17: (1) efforts to improve the implementation of Agenda 2030 and (2) efforts to improve collective action globally in pursuit of sustainable development as envisaged by the SDGs. If taken as distinct components, the first phrase might suggest itself as relating to the implementation of the other sixteen SDGs – or perhaps sustainable development as a more generic objective (as broadly expressed by Agenda 2030) – whereas the latter phrase might indicate the re-energizing of a more substantive, and perhaps overarching, architecture of global collaboration. As is often the case with other aspects of the SDGs, it is not at all clear, however, whether these components were indeed intended to be read in this way or if they hold separate meanings. Indeed, they are not unrelated, especially to the extent that cooperation by the many actors in global governance will have a demonstrably tangible impact on the extent to which implementation occurs and vice versa, but, equally, nor are they necessarily synonymous with each other. As this chapter will explore, SDG 17 is paradoxical in several important respects and, to the extent that it underpins the SDG agenda more broadly, is emblematic of the tensions at the heart of the SDGs more generally. This is especially the case in regard to the normative context in which the SDGs are situated. For SDG 17, that context – and its situation therein – is particularly contested and contestable.

What is apparent, and is notably more so when looking at the targets set in relation to SDG 17 (as we do below), is that it entrenches a largely traditional understanding of the role of trade, finance, and international institutions, inter alia, in achieving development, even though it is now clothed – and, arguably, has been since 1987 with the publication of the Brundtland report – as sustainable development.[13] What is thus presented in SDG 17 in terms of 'strengthening' and 'revitalizing' is a series of measures that has, almost by definition, not yet been achieved over the numerous decades of development cooperation; is non-radical in nature;[14] and has formed the basis for previous sustainable development consensuses. This old-wine-in-new-bottles approach is increasingly subjected to mounting criticism and rightly so, we believe. As Sam Adelman points out:

> Within five years of the publication of *Our Common Future*, more than 70 definitions of sustainable development had been proposed, demonstrating the chameleon-like capacity of the concept to mean all things to all people, but it is this vague capaciousness that enables states and transnational corporations to greenwash unsustainable activities by misleading the public about the environmental impacts of their products or services. Most of these definitions perpetuate instrumental rationality, progress and economic growth and they conceive nature as capital.[15]

Whether strengthening and revitalizing past and new consensuses will alone be sufficient to achieve the SDGs, or the global partnership, raises a further set of complex questions around adequacy (of resource and capability), ownership, inclusivity, equity,[16] and, indeed, purpose. What is the objective, nature, and content of the global partnership being sought? This last question may seem either faintly ridiculous – do the SDGs themselves not set out the purpose(s) to be achieved? – or straining towards the utopian. Both, and neither, might in fact be true. But without a clear sense of what is the purpose of such a global partnership, or at least a limited consensus around that idea, the implementation of targets (however effective) will invariably be diminished against the attainment of the substantive objectives.

Of course, international cooperation, including multilateralism, in its truest sense is an essential element, if not one of the most basic existential conditions, of the post–Second World War order (despite worrying recent trends suggesting a preference for unilateralism, isolation, and self-preservation, exemplified, among others, by the maxim 'America First' during the Trump presidency). International cooperation is firmly entrenched as a central objective in the 1945 Charter of the United

[13] *Report of the World Commission on Environment and Development: Our Common Future*, 1987, sustainabledevelopment.un.org/content/documents/5987our-common-future.pdf.

[14] This must importantly include consideration of omissions – those proposals that failed to find favour in the diplomatic consensus. For a critique on the SDGs' lack of regulatory ambition, see also Louis J. Kotzé, 'The Sustainable Development Goals: An Existential Critique alongside Three New-millennial Analytical Paradigms', in French & Kotzé, n. 2, 41.

[15] Sam Adelman, 'The Sustainable Development Goals, Anthropocentrism and Neoliberalism', in French & Kotzé, n. 2, 22–23.

[16] This is not to neglect sustainability; rather, the terms refer to the quality of the partnership between stakeholders.

Nations (UN Charter) and runs through virtually all the provisions of, what some consider to be, the international community's only 'global constitution'.[17] In such a global constitutional sense, 'international cooperation', and the associated notions such as solidarity and multilateralism, might even be considered a central guiding principle of the international constitutional order, in the same way as human rights standards are often considered[18] The UN Charter determines one of the key objectives of the United Nations: '[T]o achieve international co-operation in solving international problems of an economic, social, cultural, or humanitarian character, and in promoting and encouraging respect for human rights and for fundamental freedoms for all without distinction as to race, sex, language, or religion.'[19] Chapter 9 of the UN Charter provides in detail for measures to facilitate 'international economic and social cooperation', with a view to creating 'conditions of stability and well-being which are necessary for peaceful and friendly relations among nations'.[20] Such a framing suggests that international cooperation is an important means to an end – namely, the achievement of the many, often complexly intertwined, objectives of the United Nations and its burgeoning global governance machinery. Whether a legal duty of cooperation between states exists, either generally or specifically in the field of development, is a matter of continuing debate.[21] Notwithstanding such legal uncertainty, it is generally accepted that, while the objectives of the United Nations are spelled out in the UN Charter, these objectives have been, and continue to be, reaffirmed, repackaged, and/or re-prioritized through the process of further global goal-setting.[22]

Thus, international cooperation has always been central to the post–Second World War order and was unsurprisingly explicitly expressed as a global goal in the 2000 Millennium Development Goals (MDGs) as MDG 8: 'to develop a global partnership for development'. It has again found a central place in the successor to the MDGs as SDG 17. As noted above, by a pure textual reading, the word

[17] Bardo Fassbender, *The United Nations Charter as the Constitution of the International Community* (Martinus Nijhoff, 2009).

[18] Erika de Wet, 'The International Constitutional Order' (2006) 55 *International and Comparative Law Quarterly* 51.

[19] Art. 1.

[20] Art. 55.

[21] Even most recently within the context of the global pandemic, there is no agreed position on a legal duty to cooperate. Rana Moustafa Fouad, 'The Legal Duty to Cooperate amid COVID-19: A Missed Opportunity?', *EJIL: Talk!* 22 April 2020, www.ejiltalk.org/the-legal-duty-to-cooperate-amid-covid-19-a-missed-opportunity/?utm_source=mailpoet&utm_medium=email&utm_campaign=ejil-talk-newsletter-post-title_2 ('despite the necessity of cooperation for the realization of human rights, it would be a weak argument to rely solely on the general comments of the Committee to justify the legal existence of a general duty to cooperate among States in realizing their economic and social rights').

[22] Biermann Kanie & Kim, n. 7.

'revitalize' would suggest that there has always been some degree of international cooperation but that this has since dwindled, despite previous visions and almost always high rhetoric of global governance and multilateralism.[23] SDG 17, therefore, even on a limited reading, recognizes that the international community must now pursue international cooperation with some measure of renewed energy. What needs to be examined is how far this will be sufficiently galvanized by the targets set out in SDG 17 in order to achieve this goal or whether, in light of the prevailing, politically more acceptable and accommodative terms of a mutually beneficial and amicable 'global partnership',[24] its primary goal of a revitalized global partnership 'for sustainable development' is simply more rhetorical language at the expense of real change.[25]

It is thus important to place SDG 17 within the context of the politics, diplomatic nuances, and (there is no way to ignore the sheer) institutional wrangles of development cooperation. This chapter seeks to pull out a number of key themes from texts before 2015 by which to locate, and to measure, SDG 17. There were a number of important documents between the 2000 UN Millennium Declaration (setting out the MDGs) and the 2015 report *Transforming Our World*,[26] which highlighted the importance of a development partnership, including the 2002 Monterrey Consensus on Financing for Development, the 2005 World Summit Outcome, and the 2008 Doha Declaration on Financing for Development. Separately, specific agendas were progressed within the remits of such global institutional settings such as the World Bank, the World Trade Organization (WTO), as well as other institutions and networks, such as the Group of Eight/Group of Seven, Group of Twenty, Club of Paris, and so forth. Some of these texts are themselves consensus-based documents between North and South; others predominantly articulate the needs and/or positions of developed or developing countries or of civil society. In short, they highlight three key messages: first, the lack of 'newness' in SDG 17; second, building on that, the lack of radical innovation offered by SDG 17; and, third, the continued absence of meaningful (and critical) engagement with sustainability in the development cooperation discourse.

Of perhaps most interest to SDG 17 is the outcome document of the 2013 Ethiopia Symposium of the Development Cooperation Forum, notably at a

[23] See, e.g., W. Andy Knight, *A Changing United Nations: Multilateral Evolution and the Quest for Global Governance* (Palgrave Macmillan, 2000).

[24] For some context, see Pavel Nováček & Peter Mederly, *Global Partnership for Development* (Palacky University, 2002).

[25] Of course, some argue that the SDGs 'provide nothing new or radical in terms of the type of development they seek to achieve; the developmental paradigm they pursue remains a weak, anthropocentric one where socio-economic interests of (certain privileged) human beings reign supreme'. Kotzé, n. 14, 49; see also Michelle Lim, Peter Jørgensen, & Carina Wyborn, 'Reframing the Sustainable Development Goals to Achieve Sustainable Development in the Anthropocene: A Systems Approach' (2018) 23(3) *Ecology and Society* 1.

[26] *Transforming Our World*, n. 4.

time when negotiations on the SDGs were progressing. The focus of this symposium – which was not exclusively a Southern perspective but certainly pro-development – in '[s]haping a renewed global partnership for development' is of particular interest for its ambition, its understanding on what such a partnership might entail, and how very different SDG 17 looks in comparison.[27] Four themes are especially noted: first, an emphasis on tackling the systemic and structural causes of weak development (the need to address the 'big picture' issues); second, equal attention to sharing knowledge and capabilities as much as resources; third, the requirement to make more explicit (to 'codify') the principles on which development cooperation occurs; and, fourth, an emphasis on development that moves away from self- or mutual interest towards a deeper level of partnership. As its 'Closing Remarks' point out, '[s]till other fundamental principles in international cooperation should guide our policy making. These range from solidarity and non-interference, to common but differentiated responsibilities and capabilities, and the right to development and greater distributive justice'.[28] On each of these points, SDG 17 is arguably lacking and, in some respects, notably so. Moreover, as the preparatory sessions before the final 2015 UN General Assembly session revealed, numerous substantive proposals put forward (at varying levels of detail) – ranging from suggestions for a technology facilitation mechanism and sovereign debt restructuring through to innovative financial tools – are also not evident in the final SDG text, not even as placeholders for further consideration. There is instead reference to ideas already extant – or in train – but more as a continuation of long-running efforts than anything particularly new, innovative, or ambitious.

The selected means of implementation for SDG 17 are broadly centred on its five categories of nineteen targets – namely, finance, technology, capacity building, trade, and systemic issues. The finance target focuses on domestic resource mobilization, development aid, long-term debt sustainability, and investment promotion, especially for least developed countries. The technology target revolves around the means to improve access to science, technology, and innovation and efforts to promote knowledge sharing. The North–South transfer of environmentally friendly technologies as well as technology sharing and development in least developed countries are also part of this target. The capacity-building target specifically focuses on developing countries to support national plans for the implementation of the SDGs as well as 'North-South, South-South and triangular cooperation'.[29] The trade target is very much related to the finance target above and essentially focuses on efforts to liberate trade globally and to create systems of free trade, while at once

[27] See Ethiopia Symposium of the Development Cooperation Forum, 5–7 June 2013, www.iri.edu.ar/publicaciones_iri/anuario/cd_anuario_2014/cooperacion/53.pdf.

[28] UN Department of Economic and Social Affairs, *A Renewed Global Partnership for Development for a Post-2015 Era*, 7 June 2013, www.un.org/en/desa/renewed-global-partnership-development-post-2015-era.

[29] Target 17.9.

seeking to increase the exports of developing countries. It is notable that it explicitly mentions the completion of the trade negotiations under the Doha Development Agenda, which broke down later in 2008, signalling a wider malaise in the WTO system. Finally, the systemic issues focus specifically on policy and institutional coherence and embrace concerns revolving on global macroeconomic stability; fostering respect for national development policies; increasing multi-stakeholder partnerships; and promoting data aggregation and overall capacity for monitoring and accountability. One particular area of note in relation to the systemic issues is the concept of host ownership and sovereign control. Although one has to '[r]espect each country's policy space and leadership', nevertheless 'to establish and implement policies for poverty eradication and sustainable development' has often seemed a secondary consideration when developing countries are confronted by the operational and policy imperatives of both international institutions and the aid agendas of many developed countries, as practice continues to suggest.[30]

SDG 17 is thus both broad in its scope and reach and narrow in its focus. Human rights concerns are lacking, the role of civil society is largely ignored, and the responsibility of businesses, and especially transnational corporations as potentially influential drivers of innovation and positive stakeholders, is at best partial. Moreover, as noted above, other (arguably more innovative and ambitious) principles and initiatives, such as those offered by the 2013 Ethiopia Symposium of the Development Cooperation Forum, did not find their way into the final version. SDG 17 thus reflects much of the traditional compromise of development cooperation between commitments (often still to be secured) and (untested and untestable) ambition, often unilaterally given and capable of unilaterally being withdrawn. In other words, '[r]evisiting traditional strategies is a non-contentious way of international diplomacy. … Moreover … the individual forms of cooperation and the idea of a global partnership are noticeable in their disjointed characterisation. The instrumentality of the targets of SDG 17 gives little sense of how a more comprehensive and coordinated approach to global development will take shape'.[31]

Moreover, though much has been said about the SDGs providing challenges to both North and South alike, there is little in SDG 17 that suggests it is truly inclusive of the responsibility of developed states, as we believe it should be. Reference is obviously made to aid and investment, but beyond these traditional strategies, nothing is particularly new, innovative, or challenging. In fact, as Sam Adelman points out, SDG 17 makes no mention whatsoever of 'tax avoidance and evasion or debt service, which drain developing countries of vast amounts of income that could be spent on poverty reduction. The SDGs call for "debt financing, debt relief, and debt restructuring, as appropriate" but not *cancellation*. Parts of the Agenda clearly read as if they were written by groups that had not been introduced to each

[30] Target 17.15.
[31] Cooper & French, n. 2, 302.

other',[32] notably across the North-South divide it would seem. Any significant achievement of 'inclusive economic sustainability' through SDG 17's vision of global partnerships and implementation would therefore seem to be, at least for now, a pipe dream.[33]

17.2.2 *Positioning the Content of SDG 17 in the Context of the Other SDGs*

Premised upon what has already been said, SDG 17 is perhaps the most integrated of all the SDGs and relates most obviously across Agenda 2030 as a whole. The 'means of implementation' is, by its very nature, cross-cutting. However, this is somewhat of a superficial response and masks both the deeper linkages between SDG 17 and other specific SDGs (and, especially, the specific targets therein) as well as ignores – critically, some might substitute this for 'undermining' – broader disconnects between SDG 17, the underlying policy objectives of Agenda 2030, and perhaps even the ultimate goal of sustainable development itself.

But, in terms of synergies and linkages, there are some very notable links between SDG 17 and the other SDGs. Specific mention may be made, for instance, of SDG 10, Reduced Inequalities, with particular attention on institutional fairness within international economic institutions; SDG 5, Gender Equality; and SDG 16, Peace, Justice and Strong Institutions. In relation to SDG 5, one might draw attention, for instance, to target 5.5, which seeks to ensure women's 'full and effective participation and equal opportunities for leadership at all levels of decision-making in political, economic and public life'. We would also identify targets 5.a and 5.b, both relating to meaningful autonomy as empowerment – namely, to '[u]ndertake reforms to give women equal rights to economic resources, as well as access to ownership and control over land and other forms of property, financial services, inheritance and natural resources, in accordance with national laws'[34] and '[e]nhance the use of enabling technology, in particular information and communications technology, to promote the empowerment of women'.[35] What one selects – and focuses upon – and how one links the SDGs is itself a political act and could have progressive or regressive outcomes. For example, by focusing purely on the rather worthy and formalistic target 5.5, one might miss the economic potential of target 5.a. But, as noted below, SDG 17 in its focus on the macro largely eschews – we would argue purposely eschews – structural inequalities.

Similarly with SDG 16, one might naturally – and rightly – identify target 16.8 as a key link with SDG 17 – namely, to '[b]roaden and strengthen the participation of developing countries in the institutions of global governance'. But to do so again ignores the broader challenges that other targets in SDG 16 hint at in relation to the

[32] Adelman, n. 15, 36–37.
[33] Arno van Niekerk, 'Inclusive Economic Sustainability: SDGs and Global Inequality' (2020) 12 *Sustainability* 1.
[34] Target 5.a.
[35] Target 5.b.

global 'means of implementation', including target 16.6 (to '[d]evelop effective, accountable and transparent institutions at all levels') and target 16.10 (to '[e]nsure public access to information and protect fundamental freedoms, in accordance with national legislation and international agreements').

If it is not a truism to say that our focus determines our reality, it is certainly true to say that the SDGs encourage us to view the achievement of sustainable development in a particular way and from a particular perspective. In addition to the questions that the targets above raise for us as to what 'means of implementation' might entail if alternatively construed, SDG 17 itself – even in and on its own terms – raises difficult questions for how SDG 17 should be contextualized in regard to the other SDGs. In particular, SDG 17 envisions progress on finance, technology, trade, and capacity building as if they were some of the essential 'building blocks' of the SDGs – why else would they be included? But one might genuinely ask how this connects with the relatively weak targets in SDG 17, on the one hand, and the policy-oriented focus of many of the SDGs (certainly in comparison to some of the quantitative based MDGs), on the other. And what of those aspects conspicuous by their omission: human rights, ecological sustainability, civil society engagement, the rule of law, and so on? Are they any less relevant to the attainment of holistic and integrated means of implementation?

Of course, for some, the very notion of global trade and ecological sustainability are mutually incompatible, and it seems likely that the promotion of free trade through the SDGs (and particularly through SDG 17) might very well undermine sustainability. There is the convincing view that

> in recent years a wish list of allegedly desirable socio-economic goals have come to dominate sustainability discussions at the expense of even shallow environmental factors. This is unfortunate because it diminishes the role of the most fundamental dimension of the sustainability conundrum – a stable productive ecosphere remains prerequisite to everything else. … The fact is that all major national governments and most mainstream international agencies remain fixated on a mythic vision of global development and poverty alleviation centered on unlimited economic expansion and fuelled by economic integration, open markets and more liberalized trade. Indeed, 'sustainability' has been subsumed under this wider agenda via the glib assumption that through the machinations of the marketplace, increased factor productivity and the efficiency gains of trade will be sufficient means to achieve sustainability's end.[36]

We do not seek to undermine such positions. However, we make a more modest – perhaps textual – point, querying how the focus of SDG 17 primarily (though not exclusively) on global targets and indicators, but certainly on the economic means, can achieve either the social and outcome-orientated nature of many of the other

[36] William Rees, 'Globalization, Trade and Migration: Undermining Sustainability' (2006) 59 *Ecological Economics* 220, 220–22.

SDGs or, indeed, the balanced integration envisaged within the sustainable development policy rhetoric. There are three principal arguments one might seek to make in this regard that we feel pervade the paradoxes at the heart of SDG 17 and thus can also be felt in the next two sections on how SDG 17 is located within international law and within its institutional context.

First, there is the idea that SDG 17 reflects the dominant paradigm of neoliberalism since the 1980s, the belief that a sound economic base is essential for any social good, aptly expressed through the Malthusian conundrum that 'resources unused are resources wasted'.[37] This emphasis on economic growth and consumption – in some form – has been at the heart of the sustainable development debate ever since the Brundtland report, *Our Common Future*, and is most notably present in Agenda 2030 in both the focus on economic growth in SDG 8, Decent Work and Economic Growth (notably target 8.1), and on the selectivity of the themes of SDG 17: finance, technology, capacity building, and trade. And if we think these are not selective, why does a section on 'implementation' not have more to say on training and education, human rights, ecological sustainability, good governance, rule of law, and support for particularly vulnerable segments of society? What is omitted is as important as what is included in our focus on what counts.

Second, one might suggest that it is actually not surprising that a goal on international cooperation reflects the principal economic tools at the international community's disposal and that there is much that can be achieved within the confines of the current economic order. We know that the WTO is not operating as fairly as it might.[38] Development assistance – whatever its challenges – should be significantly enhanced and redirected, as should the focus on technology transfer, capacity building, and financial instruments, such as taxation, investment promotion, and matters of debt. In other words, SDG 17 is an important part of a sustainable development strategy, even if its links with the other SDGs are less about 'implementation' and more about relating to the necessity of parallel change elsewhere in the broader system. If so, and certainly there is a strong case for suggesting that this is a more honest interpretation of the role of SDG 17, it can be critiqued for its choice of targets and its failure to address some notable gaps. To give just one example, its provision on debt sustainability is noticeably weaker than many in civil society would have liked. One might ask: what of the perennial talk of a sovereign debt restructuring mechanism? Was SDG 17 about what is necessary to achieve the SDGs or simply the art of the possible?

The previous two propositions flow from the basis that the targets of SDG 17 will either support or not support the attainment of the other SDGs. Both positions are quite binary in nature. Either they are – or they are not – conducive to the

[37] *Id.*, 221.

[38] See, e.g., Claude Barfield, 'Free Trade, Sovereignty, Democracy: Future of the World Trade Organization' (2001) 2(2) *Chicago Journal of International Law* 403.

achievement of sustainable development, which is the central building block of all the SDGs – indeed, of the entire Agenda 2030. And this brings us to the third point: while the pursuit of sustainable development through SDG 17 might very well be a false assumption, we suggest alternatively that SDG 17 at least reflects a more pluralistic understanding of sustainable development –namely, that sustainable development has always had many different meanings, and, as a matter of empiricism, this plurality needs to be recognized and not ignored. As just one way of conceiving this notion, 'it is arguable that sustainable development can be divided into four core elements: environment, economy, equity and empowerment ... as well as being different elements of sustainable development, these four issues are different angles from which sustainable development can be perceived'.[39] And, in this light, SDG 17 is a meaningful – within its own narrative – understanding of sustainable development. Yet, as a normative statement, this understanding can (and we would suggest must) always be questioned and contested.

17.3 POSITIONING SDG 17 IN INTERNATIONAL LAW

Of course, the SDGs themselves do not constitute binding international law, although they often relate to issues that are deeply entwined with either international law norms, such as trade and investment rules, human rights protection or environmental obligations, and/or the policies and operation of relevant international institutions, such as the World Bank and the International Monetary Fund (IMF). As a general truism, many of the SDGs can be said to be 'grounded in international law and made consistent with existing commitments expressed in various [binding] international agreements and other soft law instruments',[40] though it must be noted that, in relation to SDG17, this relationship is even more complex and nuanced as international development law is itself a much more opaque body of law, process, and principles.[41] SDG 17 thus captures, and fails to capture, this complex relationship between law, economics, and policy (and politics) in this area.

SDG 17 is both grounded in international law and eschews it, in a not dissimilar way to how international development practice has related to law for decades. This is neither criticism – per se – nor praise. And as with many of the other SDGs, its relationship to many different parts of international law is nuanced and varying in normative proximity to what is included. In relation to SDG 17, one can – and must – make mention of the 'hard' regimes of trade and investment, the

[39] Duncan French, *International Law and Policy of Sustainable Development* (Manchester University Press, 2005), 24.

[40] Rakhyun E. Kim, 'The Nexus between International Law and the Sustainable Development Goals' (2016) 25(1) *Review of European, Comparative and International Environmental Law* 15, 15.

[41] See, e.g., Rumu Sarkar, *International Development Law: Rule of Law, Human Rights and Global Finance*, 2nd ed. (Springer, 2009).

politico-normative dominance of international financial institutions, as well as the 'softer' regimes of development aid and the inchoate rules on technology transfer.[42] It is also important to recognize that SDG 17 raises issues that span other public and private obligations, most notably debt accrual and debt relief.

There are also omissions, both obvious and often remarked upon (such as human rights), and perhaps those that we have been schooled not to consider as relevant. And these are as evident in SDG 17 as they are in other areas of international law. As Hilary Charlesworth and Christine Chinkin very astutely note, selectivity is often not considered as relevant as it should be: '[W]hy are highly migratory species of sea life regulated by treaty while the use of breast milk substitutes remains subject to voluntary codes?'[43] One might indicate the obvious gaps – mention has already been made of human rights – but one could also mention SDG 17's and international law's silence on the (international) legal responsibility of transnational corporations as well as their collective failure to offer clear linkages with multilateral environmental agreements and development partnerships. But what of other, less obvious (or even more difficult) linkages? International law, for instance, still insufficiently provides for extraterritorial obligations of economic assistance, a duty of solidarity is vague and politicized, and sea-level rise has yet to create duties of territorial cession for historically polluting states.[44] And one might go on; identifying and positioning SDG 17 within international law is itself a selective exercise, involving judgements as to what is important, what is relevant, and what is impossible. It is with this caveat that this chapter now seeks to better understand the normative situation of this particular SDG.

Just as with MDG 8, SDG 17 is implicit on the normative context in which it is situated, and it is 'captured by ongoing debates as to the normative divide between obligation and voluntarism, between legally binding solidarity and weaker, optional, variations'.[45] Of course, one can point to the multilateral trade regime within the context of the WTO – stronger in effect in 2015 than it is presently – as well as the broad array of preferential and regional trade and investment regimes and many hundred more bilateral investment treaties. Together, these legally binding rules constitute, along with the legally binding commitments made under the global and regional financial institutions, the core features of the international economic system. Whether, and how far, these can be made parallel to (and set alongside) development objectives, as articulated in Agenda 2030, is a contestable proposition. For instance, SDG 17 in target 17.5 talks of '[a]dopt[ing] and implement[ing] investment promotion regimes for least developed countries'. Is one to suppose that these regimes are a good in and of themselves? Does not the quality and content of

[42] See also Chapter 9 in this volume.
[43] Charlesworth & Chinkin, n. 10, 18–19.
[44] On extraterritorial duties, see also Chapter 1 in this volume.
[45] Cooper & French, n. 2, 302.

such treaties (if one assumes that a regime should be legally binding) matter? Are we to assume integration between this target and others, both within and without SDG 17, for instance, on gender, sustainability, and poverty eradication? Or, as suggested in the section above, is the existence of such a regime assumed to also meet the ever-present neoliberal expectations of development?

Similarly, in regard to those targets within SDG 17 that would seem to connect it to soft(er) law provisions and inchoate regimes (not to mention the international institutions discussed below), the international law context remains purposely vague, or expansive, as it has always done and will probably continue to do. One example is target 17.4 on debt sustainability, which mentions 'coordinated policies . . . debt relief and debt restructuring'. As noted above, debt relief brings together private (contractual) law and international activity. The international legal content is thus both presently secondary and speculative (when one considers the continued absence of a legally binding sovereign debt restructuring mechanism). Similarly, targets 17.6–17.8 on technology and technology transfer are suggestive of soft and hard international law – recognizing, for example, previous attempts at codes of conduct in this area as well as treaty-specific instances of technology transfer – but law is neither explicitly mentioned nor predicated as a necessity. Nor does it highlight those instances where (hard) international law does exist but may well prove an impediment to developmental goals (for instance, intellectual property limitations). Much of this ambiguity is symptomatic of a wider neglect in international lawmaking in this field as well as the result of hegemonic pressures and political manoeuvring.

Of course, there are some positive sentences – in the sense of hyperbole, if not binding normativity – contained in Agenda 2030 that relate its grand development vision to international law: '[W]e will foster a dynamic and well-functioning business sector, while protecting labour rights and environmental and health standards in accordance with relevant international standards and agreements and other ongoing initiatives.'[46] But there is little in the way of substantive detail, never mind substantive follow through. More generally, the Agenda 2030 text is notable for its use of language, for which one can insert one's own interpretation. For instance, it talks of 'an enabling international economic environment, including coherent and mutually supporting world trade, monetary and financial systems, and strengthened and enhanced global economic governance'.[47] Lawyers see terms such as 'enabling', 'system', and 'governance' and either seek or critique the absence of legal form – but this is invariably not the case. Setting to one side the limitations of the significance of textual references alone in such a document, international law – at least in the form of treaty law – is but one part of the complex structure. For some individuals, this is indicative of the secondary role that law has to play in this area. For others, it is more troubling as it is indicative of a broader lack of urgency or political will.

46 *Transforming Our World*, n. 4, para. 63.

47 *Id.*, para. 63.

In thus thinking through the specific and general normative context in which SDG 17 is positioned, one cannot neglect the rhetoric of the 2015 text – notably, its narrative around a global partnership. As with previous declarations and documents of such a nature, the language is inspiring. More so in SDG 17, as the duality of the goal is both strengthening the means of implementation and revitalizing the global partnership; unless these two things are formally and distinctly separate, one must consider them as integrally connected. What is being implemented but a stronger global partnership? Or, at least, it should be a consequence of strengthening that implementation. But, again, one looks generally in vain to discern the presence of legal validation. There are, of course, implicit references to standards and even some explicit mention of binding treaties (such as the 1989 Convention on the Rights of the Child), but these are as selective as they are fleeting. There is no overarching legal commitment to any form or duty of international cooperation or solidarity. Even when mention is made to the Guiding Principles on Business and Human Rights (themselves not even binding), they are mentioned as exemplars of what might be followed rather than viewed as prescription.[48] In other words, Agenda 2030 merely sketches out a weak suggestion to follow an equally weak and non-binding guideline on corporations and their relationship with human rights.

The lack of mention of general international law, however, should not be surprising. Agenda 2030, and the SDGs which it includes, is representative of the siloed nature of the international political (and legal) discourse where distinctive subject matters jostle for attention but where development promises (as they are rarely in binding form) are always secondary to trade and investment rules. Moreover, there is a lack of systemic integration. Development agendas rarely link to peace, human rights, or environmental processes (and when they do, it is invariably under the green-washed ideological palliative of 'sustainable development').[49] To the extent that they do, the linkages are usually ambiguous and uncertain, with little attempt to clarify the overarching structure. There is little appetite – almost none at the diplomatic level – to ascertain and cement what a duty of solidarity might look like; even less to develop such a duty that would challenge the status quo ante. Notably, to this end, the work of the independent expert on human rights and international solidarity seems to be in vain.[50]

[48] UN Human Rights Council, *Guiding Principles on Business and Human Rights: Implementing the United Nations 'Protect, Respect and Remedy' Framework*, UN Doc. A/HRC/17/31, 21 March 2011.

[49] Benjamin Richardson, 'A Damp Squib: Environmental Law from a Human Evolutionary Perspective' Osgoode Hall Law School Comparative Research in Law and Political Economy Research Paper Series no. 08/2011, 2011, papers.ssrn.com/sol3/papers.cfm?abstract_id=1760043.

[50] UN Office of the High Commissioner on Human Rights, 'Independent Expert on Human Rights and International Solidarity', www.ohchr.org/EN/Issues/Solidarity/Pages/IESolidarityIndex.aspx.

To the extent that a global partnership is empirically descriptive of what the SDGs are looking like in progress, there may be some value in its nomenclature. But, as a means to describe either the international law that sits over SDG 17 or the normative end goal, it is much less convincing. As the next section will indicate, though there is much activity in the implementation of SDG 17 – often by means of the operational autonomy of international institutions, the bestowal (and withdrawal of) unilateral preferences of developed states, and private finance – such activity also reveals the weakness of any normative basis for a global partnership. The continued absence of customary norms in this field, never mind the selectivity of treaty provisions on those topics that developed states largely consider important, reaffirms the political, but not the legal, nature of a global partnership. And this might prove to be the persistent problematic thorn in the flesh when it comes to truly implementing all the SDGs by means of a global partnership that is based on even a shallow sense of solidarity.

17.4 POSITIONING SDG 17 IN THE INTERNATIONAL INSTITUTIONAL CONTEXT

Though there is likely to be no direct correlation between the effective implementation of an SDG and the strength of the (international) legal framework in which it operates, as many distinct policy drivers will contribute to determine its success or otherwise, it must at least be arguable that, where the overall context of an SDG is uncertain, its implementation must be questionable. This would seem particularly true for SDG 17 where the juxtaposition of formalized (international) institutional oversight, the discretion inherent within broad policy space, networks of partnerships, and the existence of private action all push and pull to varying degrees to make effective implementation both difficult to plan and measure, if not entirely impossible. Cooperation, both as an end in itself and as a means of achieving 'policy coherence' in the language of the 2015 text, is thus pivotal to the achievement of SDG 17. How to achieve such cooperation remains at the heart of the dilemma in development law and practice, and the implementation of SDG 17 is as much about guiding the policy space given over to states to implement these specific development objectives – whether that of developing states working on their own development within their own territories or of developed states in their external strategies and actions – as it is the organizational frameworks and regimes that exist around trade, finance, development, and investment and, to a much lesser extent, those weaker processes that relate to debt, sustainability, and (even weaker) technology transfer.

Thus, the call for much needed policy coherence within Agenda 2030 is as much about how to coordinate the inherent discretion in much of the implementation left to states as it is about improving synchronism between international organizations.[51] Of course, this statement oversimplifies the notion of partnerships greatly as there is

[51] *Transforming Our World*, n. 4, para. 65.

a broader panoply of actors, which together will be required to promote a more comprehensive implementation of SDG 17 – perhaps best reflected in the conceptualization of 'multi-stakeholder partnerships'.[52] In the words of Agenda 2030, it will take 'effective public, public-private and civil society partnerships, building on the experience and resourcing strategies of partnerships'.[53] Of course, while such voluntary partnerships are an important and credible part of the implementation of SDG 17, attempts to create, and then to maintain, such voluntary partnerships have proved frustratingly elusive in development practice over several decades. And for many countries – especially least developed countries – it is the actions of the World Bank, the IMF, and agencies such as the UN Development Programme that are pivotal to the meaningful implementation (or otherwise) of the SDGs for the world's poorest people. Not only in terms of the resource and capacities that they themselves hold but also for the levers, influence, and signals that they possess and that galvanize the private and charity sector, as well as encouraging further preferential action from developed states, it is these organizations that are key to the effective implementation of the SDGs. And as with the MDGs, these organizations have proactively affirmed and endorsed the SDGs as key to contemporize their mandates, while remaining true to their constituent instruments. Of course, many other international organizations have a stated interest in achieving one or many of the SDGs – across the broad spectrum of global and regional organizations, be they generalized and specific (for example, health, labour, food, and agriculture) – but because of both the complex patchwork of institutional mandates and (we would argue as significant) the state and institutional desire to protect (and delimit) these mandates, fundamental action and radical reform is inhibited.

Nevertheless, to the extent that the SDGs provide a common language – a common terminology – for all to discuss development objectives, the SDGs (and the MDGs before them) have undoubtedly been politically successful. But this success is limited; as noted above, institutional silo-ism still exists, and, in their essential functions and work, the institutions remain largely the same. It is therefore unsurprising that developing countries have always sought to include tackling the governance challenges within these institutions as core development objectives, and, again, these can be found within the SDG targets. Even here, however, the wording is opaque and sufficiently general to protect the institutional autonomy of the Bretton Woods institutions, in particular, and, arguably, therefore, the interests of the developed states that these institutions are ultimately seen to serve. It is a matter of ongoing, and ever growing, concern that

> [p]erpetuating global inequalities associated with globalization, the International Monetary Fund (IMF), the World Bank and the World Trade Organization (WTO) remain plagued with criticism: the structural underrepresentation of the

[52] Target 17.16.
[53] Target 17.17.

> global South; undermining of democratic ownership; biased and inconsistent decision making; effective impunity regarding harms caused; and a largely unfair international trading system. It is well recognized that the neoliberal structural adjustment policies that were required by the World Bank and the IMF in the 1980s and 1990s from developing countries did much damage to their economies. The ensuing social costs, slowdown in economic growth, and rising inequality eventually put them at a grave disadvantage. In the same vein, the WTO is criticized for enabling exploitation by multinational companies (MNCs) of local industries and firms, thus reducing cultural diversity and economic inclusivity.[54]

So, there is much left for these institutions to operationalize – and not just with SDG 17 but throughout the SDGs – at their discretion. As Agenda 2030 notes, the targets in SDG 17 are by no means unique in this regard: 'The means of implementation targets under each Sustainable Development Goal and Goal 17 . . . are *key to realizing* our Agenda and are of equal importance with the other Goals and targets'.[55] How such institutions approach these targets is pivotal and in many ways determinative of their on-the-ground success, especially, as we have said, for least developed countries. If this is true for all SDGs, then it is particularly relevant for SDG 17 as it is this SDG that, above all others, seeks to promote the systemic conditions necessary for broader, and more conducive, conditions for wider implementation of other development objectives. Critics, of course, might rightly question whether this focus, which is largely on the macro-level of development, is truly the most relevant or applicable to ensuring meaningful partnerships, especially when many of the SDGs are policy orientated and seek domestic change. Others would counter with recognizing the interconnections between North and South, economic development, and social change and the need not to separate development from the key global drivers of growth.

For those who worry that the SDGs do not sufficiently recognize the environmental constraints in which the SDGs must be achieved, the focus on economic implementation highlights a tried-and-tested (and failed) anachronism at the heart of the SDGs.[56] For sure, the SDGs are 'greener' than the MDGs in many important respects, but in terms of the cross-fertilization between SDGs, it would have been reassuring to see something more on the principle and process of integration as espoused most prominently in the 1992 Rio Declaration on Environment and Development within the SDGs. Nevertheless, even if a macro perspective is important, SDG 17 is Janus-faced when it comes to partnerships. It makes mention of the need for breadth and diversity in such relationships, but it focuses in detail almost exclusively on the state level, with limited focus given to the role of civil society and

[54] Van Niekerk, n. 33.

[55] *Transforming Our World*, n. 4, para. 40 (emphasis added).

[56] See, e.g., Yiwen Zeng et al., 'Environmental Destruction Not Avoided with the Sustainable Development Goals' (2020) 3 *Nature Sustainability* 1.

only partial recognition of the role of business and the private sector. Challenges around transparency and accountability are glossed over too lightly, and though there is much included on technology facilitation, it merely serves to highlight the opposing positions on the issue.

Seeking to outline the implementation of SDG 17 simply highlights the very structural weaknesses of SDG 17. Voluntary action, deference to organizational mandate, and weak references to non-state actors characterize implementation in this area. Progress is to be measured, of course, but as with many of the other targets in the other SDGs, measurement is itself a policy choice and a political endeavour. It is, for instance, extremely noticeable that the targets on data, monitoring, and accountability are focused upon improving statistical capacity in developing countries (itself a good thing, for sure) rather than a means by which all states are held to account for their attempts to meet the targets.[57] With no recognition in the targets of the need for greater transparency in the collection, dissemination, and assessment of the data itself (which is limited elsewhere in the 2015 text) or the specific leadership role of developed countries in this regard, the data challenge becomes representative of a broader theme. Improved data, like so many of the other issues in the SDGs, becomes seen as something that needs to be bequeathed to (or improved in) developing countries rather than a common endeavour between North and South.

17.5 CONCLUSIONS

Where does this leave us? As with all archaeology, we are left to decipher differing layers of evidence. Our analysis above has tried to show, we hope, that the goals that SDG 17 overtly seeks to achieve – its core motivation and its internationalist orientation – are at many levels all desirable, good, and critically necessary, especially in the current world that seems to be ripping itself apart at its seams from COVID-19 pressures, growing support for (racist) nationalism movements, anti-rationalist anxieties, post-truth politics, and populist agendas. We are, however, far more sceptical about the ability of SDG 17 to confront the magnitude of the challenges created by such forces and its potential to meaningfully provide the means of implementation for its own targets and those of the other sixteen SDGs. And our scepticism seems to be shared with another comprehensive recent assessment of the steering effects and transformative power of the SDGs.[58]

Moreover, it seems highly unlikely that SDG 17 will succeed in revitalizing the global partnership for sustainable development, simply because of the magnitude of such a challenge and because it seems merely to reinforce the path dependency of the previous approach and to reiterate and build on past unsuccessful approaches. And even if it does succeed, we are not entirely convinced that there will be any

[57] Targets 17.18, 17.19.
[58] Biermann, Hickmann & Sénit, n. 12.

significant, truly sustainable, improvement over the long term for 'everyone', simply because SDG 17, like the rest of Agenda 2030, remains captured by a decades old green-washed vision of neoliberal development, whose greatest achievement has been to continue benefiting those privileged few who have always benefited from 'sustainable' development at the cost of a vulnerable living order.

Index